Contents

Contents vii

Preface

This book, comprising original papers and previously published materials, is designed primarily as a collateral text for undergraduate courses dealing with the development of American film. My goal in bringing together these readings is to present a systematic survey of the history of the industry, allowing the individual materials to suggest to the reader ways in which the realities of economics, changing legal restraints, technological advances, studio organization and procedures, financing, distribution trade practices, and exhibitor preferences have influenced the form and content of the movies. No other American art form, including theater, dance, music, and fine arts, has been subjected to so many constraints, nor has any other art been influenced so heavily by the predilections of the business world.

The organization of the book delineates the development of the industry in terms of its economic structure. It is divided into four parts, each of which is preceded by an introduction presenting an overview of the period as an aid to the reader in placing the readings in context.

Part I (1894–1908) describes the period when motion pictures changed from a novelty into a business enterprise of national dimensions. As the industry developed, three branches became distinct and functioned separately. Exhibition was the fastest growing branch because of its small investment requirements. Distribution, still in its embryonic stage, was slow in forming due to the unpredictability of the film supply. Producers were locked in internecine warfare based on patent rights, with the goal of capturing control of the market. Meanwhile, foreign suppliers, particularly, the French, capitalized on conditions by meeting the demand.

The period covered by Part II (1908–1930) is characterized by the growth of the industry into a mature oligopoly. Struggles for control of the business began with the establishment of the Motion Picture Patents Company, a monopoly based on patent rights, and continued with the attempts of other companies to gain dominant economic power in the marketplace through various means—the exploitation of the star system, the supplanting of one- and two-reelers by feature films, and the vigorous acquisition of motion picture theaters. During this struggle, the strong survived and grew. More and more power fell into the hands of fewer and fewer companies, as they merged production, distribution, and exhibition efforts. The advent of sound, which might be expected to have revolutionized the industry's structure, merely served to hasten this vertical integration.

Part III (1930–1948) describes the behavior and organizations of the oligopoly. The period of struggle was essentially over, and the industry, then dominated by five giant companies, entered an era of cooperation as a means of preserving the structure, protecting itself from governmental and civic regulation, and maximizing profits. Earnings plunged during the Depression, but the major companies capitalized on an opportunity granted them by the National Industrial Relations Act to tighten their grip on the marketplace. The industry emerged from the Depression unscathed, soared to new heights during World War II, and enjoyed unbridled prosperity until 1948, when television and an important Supreme Court antitrust decision brought this rosy era to a close.

Part IV (1948 to the present) describes the profound effects of the Supreme Court's *Paramount* decision on the industry. The Court's decrees forced the integrated companies to divorce their exhibition branches from their production and distribution operations and outlawed several trade practices upon which the industry had depended to preserve the status quo. In adjusting to the forced reorganization of its entire business structure, the industry also had to confront the competition of television, increasing resistance to the export of its product by foreign governments, and the witch hunts of the House Committee on Un-American Activities. The industry adjusted surprisingly well to these major tremors, and today a relatively small number of firms, some of which are part of huge multinational conglomerates, still control the bulk of the business.

For this revised edition, I am pleased to include original chapters written by Robert C. Allen, Robert Anderson, Janet Staiger, Douglas Gomery, Cathy Klaprat, and Robert Gustafson. Their research has greatly enlarged our understanding of the industry by re-evaluating such subjects as the chaser theory pertaining to film in vaudeville, the Patents Company, modes of production, exhibition strategies, and conglomerates. I have revised my chapter on United Artists to focus on the career of Mary Pickford. This case study of the early star system is designed to complement Klaprat's study of Bette Davis' career during the studio era. Original chapters retained from the first edition are by Russell Merritt, Thomas Guback, and Richard S. Randall. The chapters by Ruth A. Inglis and David C. Londoner have been specially adapted with their cooperation for inclusion in this collection. The other new chapters from previously published materials are chapter 20, Michael Conant's update of the *Paramount* case, and the supplement to chapter 21, an essay from a Warner Communications Inc. annual report.

All illustrations appearing in the book have been especially gathered from the following sources: the British Film Institute; the Bruce Torrence Historical Collection, c/o First Federal of Hollywood; the Museum of Modern Art; Warner Communications Inc.; and the Wisconsin Center for Film and Theater Research.

Although scholars have been drawn to the field of film industry studies, making this revised edition possible, our knowledge is still rudimentary. It is my hope that this edition will further stimulate new research not only on Hollywood but on foreign film industries as well.

TINO BALIO

Madison, Wisconsin
June 1984

The American Film Industry

Part I

A Novelty Spawns Small Businesses, 1894–1908

On April 14, 1894, the world's first Kinetoscope parlor opened its doors at 1155 Broadway in New York City (ch. 2). No one knows who the customers were on that day, or exactly how many of them parted with some change to satisfy their curiosity about the new picture machine—but we can be sure that they had no idea of their place in history as they gazed into the peepholes in amazement. They were the motion pictures' first paying customers, a handful of unwitting pioneers destined to be followed by countless millions in America's long and exciting romance with the movies. That day and that place marked the commercial beginnings of the motion picture industry in the United States.

The Kinetoscope which amused Broadway strollers was a peephole machine which showed a short filmstrip. This machine and the camera that supplied it with films, called the Kinetograph, were perfected at the Edison laboratories in nearby West Orange, New Jersey, by William Kennedy Laurie Dickson. A syndicate consisting of A. O. Tate, Thomas R. Lombard, and Erastus A. Benson was the first to see the moneymaking possibilities of the machine, and acquired a concession from Edison to market it. The resulting Kinetoscope Company was soon installing Kinetoscopes in department stores, hotels, saloons, and public phonograph parlors in major cities throughout the country. Another firm, headed by Frank Z. Maguire and Joseph D. Baucus, acquired the foreign rights and marketed America's new plaything abroad.

Kinetoscope parlor, 1896

Public interest was short-lived, however, and Kinetoscope business faced the doldrums within a year. Nonetheless, the Kinetoscope far exceeded in importance the many optical wonders that came before it. As Jacques Deslandes has said, "The essential act, the point of departure which finally led to the practical realization of animated projections, was the nickel which the American viewer dropped in the slot of the Edison Kinetoscope, the 25 centimes which the Parisian stroller paid in September 1894 to glue his eyes to the viewer of the Kinetoscope. ... This is what explains the birth of the cinema show in France, in England, in Germany, in the United States. ... Moving pictures were no longer just a laboratory experiment, a scientific curiosity, from now on they could be considered a commercially viable public spectacle.[1]

Debut of the Projector

The major limitation of the Kinetoscope peepshow was that it could be viewed by only one person at a time. What if the picture image could be projected onto a screen, so that the small change of a large audience could be collected all at one time? No sooner had entrepreneurs dreamed of such an advance than technicians turned the dream into a reality. Through the work of the Lumière brothers in France, Robert W. Paul in England, and Otway and Gray Latham, C. Francis Jenkins, Herman Casler, and Dickson in America, the motion picture projector became a commercial reality two years after the unveiling of the first Kinetoscope.

Norman C. Raff and Frank R. Gammon introduced the Vitascope projector on April 23, 1896, at Koster & Bial's Music Hall, Herald Square, New York City. Although it was touted as Edison's "Latest Marvel," the projector was actually the handiwork of C. Francis Jenkins and Thomas Armat of Washington, D.C. The rights to this machine had been hurriedly acquired by Raff and Gammon, the two surviving members of the Kinetoscope Company, in January of that year after news reached them that Louis and Auguste Lumière had patented and publicly exhibited a camera/projector in Lyons, France, and were negotiating with several vaudeville managers in New York to debut the machine in the United States. Raff and Gammon had turned to Edison for help to no avail; after the Kinetoscope fiasco, Edison had lost all interest in motion pictures. He did agree to manufacture the Vitascope and supply Raff and Gammon with films, however.

The Vitascope did not have the field to itself for long. On June 29, 1896, the Lumière Cinématographe made its New York debut at Keith's Union Square Theatre. Despite a sweltering heat wave, the Cinématographe doubled box

1. Jacques Deslandes, *Histoire comparée du cinéma*, 2 vols. (Paris, 1966–68), pp. 213–14. Quoted in Michael Chanan, *The Dream That Kicks: The Prehistory and Early Years of Cinema in Great Britain* (London: Routledge & Kegan Paul, 1980), p. 105.

office gross for weeks on end. This debut was an event of
major importance to motion picture business. Since J.
Austin Fynes, manager of the Keith theater, was highly
respected by vaudeville managers, his acceptance of motion
pictures and of the Lumière projector was a clear signal to
other vaudeville houses.

Also appearing on the scene was the Biograph projector,
which was capable of showing pictures significantly larger
than its precursors, and much clearer and sharper, too.
It was the invention of Dickson, then a partner in the
American Mutoscope Company (soon to be called the
American Mutoscope and Biograph Company). Dickson's
Biograph made its New York debut on October 12, 1896,
at Hammerstein's Opera House. It was an instant success.
The Biograph moved to the Union Square Theater on
January 18, 1897, and, with only a four-month hiatus,
closed on July 15, 1905, after eight and a half years—"an
incomparably long run in the history of the American the-
atre to that date," in the words of Gordon Hendricks.[2]

The Movies and Vaudeville

"Vaudeville served as the primary exhibition outlet for
American films for roughly the first ten years of commercial screen exhibition," says Robert Allen (ch. 3). Vaudeville underwent great commercial expansion during this
period to become the preeminent American popular entertainment. Competition between theaters was keen, leading
managers to search out the latest novelty acts. And since
the biggest audience pleasers were visual spectacles—puppetry, living pictures, and magic lantern shows—it was only
natural for movies to be included on the programs.

The presentational format of vaudeville easily accommodated the new novelty. Vaudeville consisted of a variety
of acts lasting from ten to twenty minutes each, performed
sequentially with no thematic connection between one act
and another. In other words, vaudeville was modular in
form—a dog act might be followed by a lyric tenor, and
then by a slapstick comic. Since early films were around

2. Gordon Hendricks, *Beginnings of the Biograph* (New York: Beginnings of American Film, 1964), p. 51.

fifty feet in length, it was necessary merely to present around ten subjects to fill a time slot. At Koster & Bial's, for example, the Vitascope program consisted of twelve subjects and was one of eight acts given before the first intermission. The films were probably accompanied by music—in the large houses by the versatile pit orchestras, and in the smaller ones by a piano. The movies proved to be the most successful single act ever to appear in vaudeville.

Motion picture producers were attracted to vaudeville, in turn, because vaudeville provided easy access to a receptive audience. Hundreds of theaters coast to coast entertained more than a million people each week. In turning to vaudeville, producers were spared having to invest their own capital in exhibition outlets. Moreover, the large theater circuits offered special advantages. Consisting of the most profitable and best-appointed houses, they were organized to take advantage of economies of scale. They had centralized managements that scheduled bookings, formulated advertising and promotion campaigns, and attended to the myriads of business details. In playing a circuit, a new act would open in the flagship theater and then move to the other houses in sequence. This so-called peripatetic form of entertainment distribution ideally suited the infant film business with its limited number of film subjects, equipment, and trained personnel.

The company best adapted to servicing the American vaudeville market was Lumière. All the business of the firm was handled by a representative in New York who was responsible for arranging exhibitions, scheduling tours, and providing a supply of films. He put together packages, each containing a Cinématographe, projectionist, and films. These self-contained units traveled the circuits as easily as an acrobat or trained dog act. The Cinématographe, moreover, had unique features that gave it a competitive edge over other projectors. Weighing a little over sixteen pounds and hand cranked, it could play any town regardless of the current and voltage of its electrical system (a national standard for municipal electricity did not exist at the time). In addition, because it was designed to operate also as a camera and printer, it could be easily taken out into the streets by day to shoot local scenes that could be incorporated into the evening's performance—to the delight of audiences. Within months of the Cinématographe New York debut, twenty-one packages had been sent out on tour.

Biograph, Vitagraph, Lubin, and other companies that were to come, followed the Lumière marketing approach, but not Raff and Gammon. After the Koster & Bial debut, which was arranged to beat the Cinématographe into the field and to capitalize on the use of Edison's name, the Vitascope was marketed on a franchise basis, like the Kinetoscope before it. Raff and Gammon were interested in selling rights, not exhibiting films. In selling a franchise for a state or group of states, they offered the agent rights to lease projectors on a monthly basis and to purchase Edison films. He could then arrange for exhibition wherever and whenever he wished. This scheme militated against the interstate arrangement of vaudeville circuits and was one of several factors that stifled the projector business of Raff and Gammon. Now that motion pictures were proving commercially viable, Edison's interest perked up. He brought out a projector of his own devising in late 1896, which he dubbed the "Edison Projecting Kinetoscope," and bypassed Raff and Gammon by selling the machine on the open market with no geographical strings attached. This bold move killed the Vitascope venture and signaled the return of a more aggressive Edison, as will be explained shortly.

Robert Allen has described the Lumière marketing plan as "pre-industrial." Providing a service to vaudeville "temporarily obviated the need for the American cinema to develop its own exhibition outlets, but it also prevented film from achieving industrial autonomy. The industrial structure of vaudeville did not call for a division of labor in the usual sense. Rather, the division came within the vaudeville presentation itself: each act was merely one of eight or more functional units, one cog in the vaudeville machine. . . . Neither did the use of films in vaudeville require a division of the industry into distinct production, distribution, and exhibition units. In fact, it favored the collapsing of these functions into the operator, who, with his projector, became the self-contained vaudeville act. It was not until the American cinema achieved industrial autonomy with the advent of store-front movie theaters that a clear separation of functions becomes the dominant mode of industrial organization, and film enters its industrial phase."[3]

Motion Picture Exhibitions on the Road

While films were finding a ready place in metropolitan vaudeville houses, they had also taken to the road. Lumière's showmen began the first of their long tours in the summer of 1896. One of the first Vitascope franchises went to William T. Rock, who purchased the rights for Louisiana. Rock opened a motion picture "store" in New Orleans on June 28, 1896. After three months, his meager supply of films exhausted the market, forcing him to take the show into smaller cities.

Soon after, in August 1896, Thomas L. Tally opened a "Phonograph and Vitascope Parlor" in Los Angeles. Although he, too, was plagued by a scarcity of films, he survived by making the broadest possible use of the various machines on the market: he offered customers not only the Kinetoscope, but also the Vitascope, the phonograph, and the Mutoscope, a peephole machine which flipped printed cards before the viewer's eyes, giving the illusion of motion.

Other traveling showmen brought the movies to small-town America, wherever there were enough people in one place with money in their pockets and adventure in their hearts. In New England, audiences packed amusement parks, club halls, and vacant storefronts on Sundays when legitimate theaters were closed. Harry and Herbert Miles lugged a projector all the way to Juneau, Alaska, where they played the gold camps on the outskirts of town. All of these showmen traversed rural America for reasons of their own: the promise of financial reward, the lure of the open road, the excitement of "show business." But together they performed an invaluable service for the entire industry, for they helped to create a public taste for motion pictures on a national level.

3. Robert C. Allen, "Vitascope/Cinematographe: Initial Patterns of American Film Industrial Practice," *Journal of the University Film Association* 31 (Spring 1979): 17–18.

Motion Picture Production, 1896–1907

Although the technical novelty of moving pictures was enough to thrill the first audiences, producers soon realized that if business was to continue, a steady supply of fresh films was required. The Edison Manufacturing Company supplied the films for Vitascope exhibitions. The Kinetograph camera remained in the custody of Edison, who kept a watchful eye on it to prevent piracy. Because it was an awkward device, electrically driven and weighing hundreds of pounds, it was not easily transportable in any case. A studio situation best served it, the result being the "Black Maria," an irregularly shaped frame structure, tar papered, and mounted on a pivot to capture the sun. Inside this structure, vaudeville turns, circus acts, and minute extracts from plays were performed before the Kinetograph. For technical reasons associated with the camera, film subjects were around fifty feet in length and had a playing time of around fifteen seconds.

As was pointed out earlier, the Cinématographe was camera, projector, and printer all in one. It was portable and required no electricity to operate. The Lumières, as a result, developed a production policy quite different from Edison's. Their cameramen were sent all over the world and could offer patrons scenes of the czar's coronation, Venice as viewed from a moving gondola, and Trafalgar Square. These travel films were extremely popular, enabling the Cinématographe to outcompete the Vitascope.

Edison, now thoroughly convinced of the commercial viability of motion pictures, sought to cement the market for himself. He instituted a series of patent infringement suits in December 1897 against nearly every organization and individual of consequence that had entered the business. In pressing the cases, his lawyers insisted that all inventors and manufacturers of motion picture equipment, and all producers in the United States, were operating in violation of the patent rights that Edison had secured on his Kinetoscope. Lumière departed the American market shortly thereafter, but Edison's biggest competitor—the American Mutoscope and Biograph Company—stood and fought by entering counterclaims.

The Biograph Company was founded in 1895 by Herman Casler, Harry Marvin, Elias Koopman, and Edison's former employee W. K. L. Dickson. It originally intended to manufacture and distribute a peephole machine called the Mutoscope to compete with the Kinetoscope, but after the advent of projected pictures, the company changed direction. The result was the famous Biograph projector. This machine and the camera that supplied it were designed with Dickson's assistance, so as not to infringe on Edison's patents.

With a $200,000 loan from the New York Security and Trust Company, the first such loan to a pioneer film company by a major financial institution, Biograph established its headquarters at 841 Broadway in January 1896. On the roof, Dickson constructed an open-air studio. A stage was mounted on wheels and revolved on tracks. The camera, also mounted on wheels, could be tracked back and forth at right angles to the stage.

The rooftop stage was used primarily to shoot scenes from celebrated plays or individual performances. The fame of the company rested on its documentary productions, however. In 1900, five cameramen were employed, one to film entertainment subjects on the roof, while the others worked in the Philippines and Hawaii and covered events at home.

The method of production that characterized operations until 1907 was the "cameraman" system. Cameramen were responsible for all aspects of the craft. With camera in hand and a knowledge of photography, they would select the subject matter, stage it, photograph the scene, and develop and edit the finished product. Since the number of cameras and skilled craftsmen was limited, this system could not be used to supply films in mass production.

It is a commonly held notion that projected motion pictures by 1898 had lost much of their novelty, just like peep shows before them. The simple film subjects lost their appeal, prompting vaudeville managers to relegate them to the position of "chasers," signals that the show was over and it was time to clear the house for the next performance. This "chaser theory" ignores the great variety of film subjects produced during the first decade of motion picture business and overstates the case, argues Robert Allen. Producers were constantly searching for ways to keep in tune with their patrons. In addition to vaudeville turns and

The Mutograph photographing the Pennsylvania Limited running sixty miles an hour

An Open-Air Studio: The American Mutoscope Company

The American Mutoscope Company, founded on December 27, 1895, by Herman Casler, Harry Marvin, W. K. L. Dickson, and Elias Koopman, rested on the invention of the Mutoscope, a peephole device that flipped printed cards before the viewer's eye, riffle fashion, creating an illusion of motion. It differed in this way from the Kinetoscope, which used a continuous band of film. The Mutoscope was conceived by Dickson but brought to fruition by Casler, who applied for the patent—wisely so, since Dickson's contribution to the machine was made while he was an employee of Edison (he left on April 2, 1895).

American Mutoscope's headquarters were established at 841 Broadway, New York, in January 1896. Dickson again put his considerable talents to work in designing the roof stage and laboratory facilities, which were described fully in the *Scientific American* of April 17, 1897. These facilities are full testament

Drying and retouching room, Mutoscope shown in the foreground

to Dickson's ingenuity. The open-air stage was mounted on wheels and re-volved on tracks. The camera, also mounted on wheels, could be tracked back and forth at right angles from the stage. The film processing rooms were large, well equipped, and designed for efficiency of operation.

The novelty of Edison's Kinetoscope began to wear off after the autumn of 1895, especially as screen projection became more common. American Mu-toscope, reacting to the winds of change, postponed any further development and promotion of its peephole machine and concentrated its efforts on per-fecting a projector. The result was Muotoscope's greatest triumph—the famous Biograph, which showed pictures larger than and photographically superior to those of any other projector. Again, Dickson and Mutoscope had out-Edisoned Edison himself. As this projector outstripped the competition in popularity, cameramen turned out subjects weekly to satisfy the eager and growing public demand. By this time, "Biograph" had proudly been added to the American Mutoscope name.

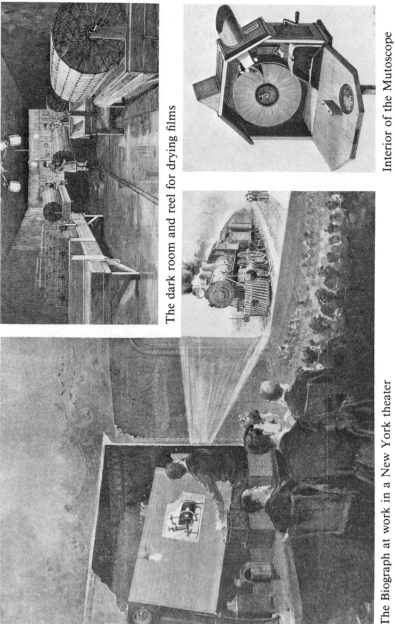

Interior of the Mutoscope

The dark room and reel for drying films

The Biograph at work in a New York theater

Movable stage for photographing scenes with the Mutograph

comic vignettes, local actualities, kinesthetic films (e.g., rushing locomotives), visual newspapers (e.g., news about the Spanish-American War), disaster films, and sporting subjects all had their special appeal to different segments of the vaudeville audience.

The Organization of Exchanges

If there was an inhibiting factor in the growth of film business, it was distribution. A ready supply of films was not generally available before 1903. Companies such as Lumière, Biograph, Vitagraph, and Lubin were engaged in providing a complete motion picture service to vaudeville—they sent out packages consisting of projector, operator, and films. Whatever films they produced were used by their own people exclusively. Besides, film gauges and equipment had yet to become standardized.

In the beginning, only Raff and Gammon sold films on the open market to Vitascope customers, but they were mainly interested in selling rights, not motion pictures, as was pointed out earlier. One assumes that when Edison brought out his projector, he picked up the pace of production. In 1900, the Edison Manufacturing Company constructed a rooftop studio in New York City. It was not until 1903 that Biograph began selling films. This was probably the result of a favorable court decision that disallowed Edison's claim of patent infringement. In that year, Biograph moved its operations to a converted brownstone at 11 East Fourteenth Street in Manhattan.

A larger film supply solved only part of the problem. Films were offered for sale outright by the foot. Subjects were ordered by mail from a catalogue. A showman might pay fifty dollars or more for a picture which he exhibited until he saturated the market or the film literally fell apart. After which, he had the choice of moving his act to another region or purchasing additional titles. This method of distribution, obviously, did little to encourage expansion of the industry, since the costs of films remained relatively high in comparison to their potential for producing income. Many exhibitors began to appear after 1903, and these small operators could scarcely afford to keep buying films, laying each aside after a short run. Moreover, as demand increased around 1907, exhibitors realized that they had to change their programs frequently, perhaps even several times a week.

A temporary solution was to trade films among fellow exhibitors, but not until motion picture exchanges came into existence did conditions permanently improve. Harry and Herbert Miles of San Francisco have been credited with organizing the first such exchange in 1903. They reputedly purchased a supply of films and rented them to exhibitors for one-fifth of the list price. The idea worked to everyone's satisfaction and created the nickelodeon boom. By 1907, between 125 and 150 such exchanges were in operation, serving all areas of the country.

The evolution of this method of distribution pleased exhibitors because it cut their costs and enabled them to change their programs more frequently to stimulate movie attendance. It was a boon to exchange operators who could continue to rent out films long after their purchase costs had been recovered. Manufacturers benefited the least. Although they could now deal with a few large exchanges instead of thousands of small exhibitors, selling pictures outright prevented them from participating fully in the profits of a burgeoning market. The situation would soon change, however.

This distribution system would rapidly undergo refinements. For the moment, only two need be mentioned—the release date and the standing order. At the start, producers put out their pictures as they were made, which meant any time of the year. They soon discovered that exhibitors were willing to pay more for new releases because fresh subjects had a greater drawing power than older ones. Production schedules were instituted, as a result, and exchanges were charged more for new releases, a cost they naturally passed on to theaters for the privilege of playing a picture on a first-run basis. A differential in pricing based upon a temporal factor had been created. The release date gave rise to the standing order. Producers required exchanges to purchase at least one print of every picture made—block booking of a sort. This practice buttressed production schedules and guaranteed that new releases were immediately marketed.

The Nickelodeon Theater

Beginning in 1905, exhibition expanded prodigiously. Thousands of theaters were springing up all over the country, but were concentrated for the most part in large urban areas. New York, for example, supported 123 theaters in 1908. This unprecedented growth was the result of developments in distribution and, in part, of the industry's conversion to mass production of motion pictures.

The exhibition boom did not entail the construction of special theaters—this would take place in the 1920s. For a while, rented storefronts, restaurants, or amusement parlors sufficed. Investment requirements were minimal; all one needed was a projector and a supply of films, chairs, piano, and perhaps a gaudy sign outside. The name given to these early theaters, "nickelodeon," was probably coined by Harry Davis and John P. Harris, who operated a successful theater in Pittsburgh, where they charged five-cent admissions.

Although scholars have long contended that the nickelodeon theater revolutionized mass entertainment in America, only a few studies have tested traditional accounts. In these, nickelodeon theaters are described as dingy, dimly lighted, and smelly, concentrated in working-class neighborhoods in industrial cities with large immigrant populations, and offering programs of film lasting fifteen to twenty minutes. Now it might be true that initially the blue-collar worker and his family were the mainstays of the audience; Garth Jowett has shown that immigrants and rural Americans were flocking into urban areas during this period, and because the workweek for industrial workers was declining, albeit slowly, they had some leisure time for entertainment. The circus, burlesque, theater, vaudeville, billiard parlors, and saloons prospered as well as the movies, but the low cost of the movies, five or ten cents maybe, provided a special inducement and contributed greatly to the success of the nickelodeon.[4] But nickelodeons were the primary form of exhibition until 1912, and as Russell Merritt demonstrates in his case study of Boston nickelodeon theaters, the movies did not remain the province of the working class for long (ch. 4). Exhibitors were more inter-

4. Garth Jowett, "The First Motion Picture Audiences," *Journal of Popular Film* 3 (Winter 1974): 39–54.

ested in attracting the affluent middle class. They located
in the main business districts, rather than in working class
residential areas, and developed schemes to make motion
pictures a respectable (i.e., middle-class) entertainment.

Robert Allen, in his study of exhibition patterns in Manhattan, has observed a similar situation. Most theaters
there were hardly dingy. William Fox, for example, converted the Dewey Theatre, a former legitimate house that
had a seating capacity of a thousand. Twelve uniformed
ushers greeted patrons who were presented shows lasting
almost two hours and consisting of a mixed program of
films and vaudeville acts. This form of exhibition became
known as small-time vaudeville and "radically altered the
nature of moviegoing in New York City, if not the entire
country," as early as 1907.[5]

Motion picture entrepreneurs had to build an audience.
They had to compete with existing forms of dramatic and
live entertainment; they had to assuage fears of local politi-
cians regarding the fire hazard of flammable nitrate film;
and they had to prove to the establishment, the guardians
of public morality, that theaters and motion pictures were
suitable for the family. David O. Thomas in his study of
early motion picture exhibition in Winona, Minnesota,
shows that the successful nickelodeons established themselves as an organic part of the community. Public relations
was important. The Orpheum on the eve of an election in
1908 announced "Complete Election Returns at the Orpheum Theater All Night Tonight." Admission was charged
until 10:00 P.M., after which the doors were thrown open
to the public. Films were shown free the night long, and,
during the reel changes, returns from city hall and the wire
services were announced.[6]

This single public relations gimmick is not particularly
impressive by itself but seen together with the schemes,
experiments, and hunches of myriad other entrepreneurs
might provide the causality lacking in Benjamin Hampton's
classic explanation of the nickelodeon phenomenon:

5. Robert C. Allen, "Motion Picture Exhibition in Manhattan, 1906-
1912: Beyond the Nickelodeon," *Cinema Journal* 18 (Spring 1979): 2–15.
6. David O. Thomas, "From Page to Screen in Smalltown America:
Early Motion Picture Exhibition in Winona, Minnesota," *Journal of the
University Film Association* 33 (Summer 1981): 3–13.

[Within a decade,] ten million—maybe twenty million . . . new entertainment buyers had suddenly appeared in all parts of America, and were pouring their nickels into the ticket-windows. The small coins of the masses had created . . . a business larger in volume than that of all spoken-drama theaters, dime museums, variety houses, lecture bureaus, concert halls, circuses, and street carnivals combined. Experienced purveyors of entertainment and amusement were dazed. There were no precedents by which such an extensive public movement could be appraised. Not only were movies new to the world, but this surge of millions of people to ticket-windows was something incomprehensible, incredible, fantastic."[7]

Mass Production of Motion Pictures, 1907–1909

Simultaneously with the growth of the nickelodeons and motion picture exchanges, the industry accommodated itself to mass production. The increased demand for motion pictures had a tremendous effect on subject matter and the mode of production. As pointed out earlier, audiences had enjoyed a wide range of motion picture types. Documentaries of all sorts were popular, more so, perhaps than comic and dramatic narratives. The records of the Biograph Company reveal that in the period 1900-1906, the studio produced more nontheatrical subjects than dramatic films, 1,035 and 774, respectively.[8] By 1908, however, the industry concentrated its production efforts on narratives almost exclusively. This shift was the result not of a sudden decline in demand for documentaries, but rather of the logistics, costs, and uncertainties surrounding documentary production. Newsworthy events happened anywhere; it was expensive to transport cameraman and equipment halfway across the continent or the world and back again. Also, disasters, assassinations, and wars were random in their occurrence and could not ensure a steady supply of product.

Narratives, on the other hand, offered the advantage of regularizing and stabilizing production. Fictional events could be gleaned from the classics and popular literature,

7. Benjamin B. Hampton, *A History of the Movies* (New York: Covici, Friede, 1931), p. 57.

8. Paul Spehr, "Filmmaking at the American Mutoscope and Biograph Company, 1900–1906," *Quarterly Journal of the Library of Congress* 37 (Summer-Fall 1980): 421.

or fabricated by the fecund imaginations of studio writers. Stories could be made to conform to the limitations of the studio and the surrounding locale. Production could be scheduled to utilize personnel efficiently and to operate at capacity.

It should be emphasized that the shift to narratives occurred after the nickelodeon boom. Standard accounts of the history of the cinema state that the business was stymied until the motion picture grew out of its "primitive" stage to attain a certain length, around one thousand feet, fifteen minutes of screen time. This length allowed filmmakers to tell an effective story with a beginning, middle, and an end. *The Great Train Robbery*, directed by Edwin S. Porter in 1903, paved the way. Its extraordinary length (1,100 feet) and the method in which the picture was edited to tell a compelling story with a daring train holdup, a brave and desperate pursuit, and a thrilling last-minute capture stimulated the industry as nothing had ever done before. This "narrative structure" theory can be found in the histories of Terry Ramsaye, Benjamin Hampton, Lewis

Edwin S. Porter's *The Great Train Robbery* (Edison, 1903)

Jacobs, and others, but in light of recent research by young scholars such as Robert Allen, Janet Staiger, and Charles Musser, a revision of our understanding of this entire early period is in order.

The years 1907 to 1909 marked the first attempt by the industry to mass-produce narratives. Janet Staiger describes the mode of production as the "director" system. The staging of the narrative and its photography were divided between two individuals—the director and the cameraman. Providing the financing was the task of the production company. The director had overall responsibility for the product. Using a scenario of his own devising, or one available from the company, he would plot the action, decide on locations and stage settings, give instructions to carpenters, painters, and property men, and choose a cast. During the shooting he coached the actors and supervised camera setups. Finally, the director edited the finished film, bringing it down to the desired length. The cameraman handled the lighting, shot the film, and processed the negative.

Professional actors were in great demand. Vitagraph and other producers hired actors from the legitimate stage and formed stock companies as pools for acting talent. They offered top wages—and steady work. For a day's labor, a leading player might be paid ten dollars; the rank and file got five dollars; and extras two or three dollars. Stories were also greatly needed. Plots were appropriated from short stories, novels, and stage plays. And since copyright laws had not anticipated motion pictures, compensation was not paid to the authors of the original works. Writing for the movies attracted newspapermen and free-lancers who wanted to supplement their incomes with the five to fifteen dollars producers paid per scenario.

There were about six well-established companies in 1907—Edison, Biograph, Vitagraph, Kalem, Essanay, and Lubin, and a host of smaller producers. Others, notably George Kleine, supplied pictures by importing them from Europe. Production was centered mainly in New York, Chicago, and Philadelphia. The migration to Hollywood was a few years away, but because sunshine was at a premium in the East during the winter months, producers began to explore Florida, Cuba, and Southern California.

Corporate Struggle for Industry Control

The seemingly insatiable demand for motion pictures after 1905 had the overall effect of transforming the structure of the industry. The profit motive naturally led each company to carve out for itself the largest possible piece of the business. As pointed out earlier, Edison wanted the entire pie for himself. Soon after he received his original camera patent on August 31, 1897, he brought suit against his competitors in an attempt to drive them out of business. Edison's strategy was to harass and annoy producers and exhibitors. If one suit might accomplish his ends, seven were filed. Edison fought his case in the press, trade journals, and in circulars. With good reason, these legal actions have come to be described as the "patent wars." Mae Huettig provides the best perspective on the subject:

Each principal producing company [in this period] was, in fact, a manufacturer of equipment, holding patents on various devices which modified or improved the basic machinery designed by Edison. Each contended that its patents gave it the right to continue in business without the consent of Edison. In addition to fighting against Edison, they fought bitterly among themselves, and still more bitterly against the group which was then still on the outside trying to break into the industry by means not strictly legitimate.[9]

After driving Lumière from the field, Edison concentrated on his major competitor, the American Mutoscope and Biograph Co. In July 1901, it appeared that Edison had achieved his goal. After a federal court upheld his patents in an important test case, the Edison Manufacturing Company announced: "*We Have Won.* Decision handed down by Judge Wheeler of the United States Circuit Court Sustains Thomas A. Edison's Patent on the Art of Producing Animated Pictures and grants Mr. Edison the only right to Manufacturing Motion Picture Machines and Films."[10] Although Biograph quickly appealed, pending the appeal the company was enjoined to deposit its weekly proceeds

9. Mae Huettig, *Economic Control of the Motion Picture Industry* (Philadelphia: University of Pennsylvania Press, 1944), p. 13.

10. *New York Clipper*, July 27, 1901, p. 480. Quoted in Charles Musser, "The Early Cinema of Edwin Porter," *Cinema Journal* 19 (Fall 1979): 12–13.

with a trustee. Vitagraph was reduced to the role of exhibitor, and the Lubin firm relocated to Germany. For the time being, Edison had a virtual monopoly in film production and distribution.

Edison's victory was short-lived, however, for in March 1902 the appeals court reversed the decision:

> It is obvious that Mr. Edison was not a pioneer, in the large sense of the term, or in the more limited sense in which he would have been if he had also invented the film. . . . The predecessors of Edison invented apparatus, during a period of transition from plates to flexible paper film, and from paper film to celluloid film, which was capable of producing negatives suitable for reproduction in exhibiting machines. No new principle was to be discovered, or essentially new form of machine invented, in order to make the improved photographic material available for that purpose. . . . Undoubtedly Mr. Edison, by utilizing this film and perfecting the first apparatus for using it, met all the conditions necessary for commercial success. This, however, did not entitle him, under the patent laws, to a monopoly of all camera apparatus capable of utilizing the film. Nor did it entitle him to a monopoly of all apparatus employing a single camera.[11]

It was now Biograph's turn to announce victory to the trades. But Edison was tenacious. He applied for patent reissues that were specifically defined to cover the camera and motion picture film, and when he received them he again went after Biograph and the others.

The details of the lawsuits need not concern us here. The point to be made, however, is that the patent wars seriously hampered expansion of the industry. Established producers were making money, but no one could tell when profits might cease. Stated another way, companies were unwilling to invest surplus into plant and equipment and thus improve their operations. Smaller firms without a large amount of capital to purchase foreign-made equipment or to fight lawsuits simply closed their doors. Thus the patent wars curtailed competition by creating barriers of entry.

The situation changed dramatically in 1908. There had yet to be a final adjudication in the courts concerning Edison's patent claims. But the growth of nickelodeons made

11. *Edison v. American Mutoscope Co.*, 114 F. 934 (C.C.A. 2, 1902).

it imperative to establish peace if the industry was to prosper. Tired and financially depleted by the interminable legal wrangling, manufacturers approached Edison regarding the feasibility of creating some sort of licensing system. Realizing that his company did not have the resources to produce enough films to meet the growing demand, Edison acceded to their offer. He would cease and desist his litigation against the major producers and distributors and create a licensing association. In return for the protection of a license that would allow producers the right to use his equipment, all Edison required was that producers pay him a royalty of one half-cent for every foot of film they produced. Although the price was stiff, it would be cheaper than fighting Edison in the courts. Vitagraph, Pathé, Kalem, Essanay, Méliès, Lubin, and Selig signed up in February 1908. The exchanges that signed up were organized into the Film Service Association. They agreed to distribute licensed films to exhibitors who, in turn, agreed to show licensed films exclusively. The Eastman Company joined forces with Edison by limiting to licensed producers the sale of raw stock. Thus did Edison attempt to add considerable revenues to his coffers and take control of the industry.

Once again, Biograph proved to be an obstacle. Edison excluded Biograph from the licensing scheme in an attempt to drive the company out of business. Biograph fought back instead and teamed up with the Kleine Optical Company, an importer of films, to capture a share of the market. Thus there were two distinct factions in the industry, and competition remained keen. Biograph offered to defend in court free of charge anyone using Biograph products, among other inducements to increase its sphere of business. Within a few short months, however, both factions recognized the absurdity of continued warfare. Edison and Biograph declared a truce in summer 1908, and formed the Motion Picture Patents Company. By joining forces they could now control the industry without a doubt.

1

A. R. FULTON

The Machine

Although the attempt to represent the illusion of motion by pictures is older than civilization, the art of the motion pictures was not created until the twentieth century. From that prehistoric day when an artist drew a many-legged boar on the wall of a cave in Altamira, Spain, down through the ages, during which time various other devices were originated to depict motion, man had to wait until modern times before the motion pictures could be born. This waiting was necessary because the motion pictures depend, to a greater extent than any other art, upon machinery. The motion pictures, the newest of the arts, the only art to originate in the twentieth century, are a product of the Machine Age.

The motion pictures did not originate as art but as a machine. They were invented. That is, the machinery that makes the pictures, and that makes them motion pictures, was invented. Thus the term *motion pictures* means the device as well as the art.

If one were to hold a piece of motion picture film up to the light, he would see that it is a series of little pictures arranged crosswise to the length of the film. Each picture, or frame, is approximately four-fifths of an inch wide and three-fifths of an inch high. Examining the frames in relation to one another, one notices that, although each frame may be a picture of the same scene, the position of the objects in each frame is slightly different. When the film, which contains sixteen frames

From *Motion Pictures: The Development of an Art*, rev. ed. (Norman: University of Oklahoma Press, 1980), pp. 3–13.

to each foot of film, is run through the motion picture projector at the rate of twenty-four frames per second, enlarged images of the frames are cast in corresponding succession onto the screen.

The projector operates on the principle of that old toy the magic lantern (and of its modern counterpart, the slide projector). When a glass slide was inserted in the lantern, an image of the slide was cast upon the screen by means of a light directed through the slide and, to enlarge the image, through a magnifying lens. The frames in the film are comparable to the slides in the magic lantern. The images of the frames as they are cast upon the screen do not move any more than the images of the magic lantern slides moved. The term *motion pictures* is therefore misleading. The pictures do not move but only seem to.

The illusion of motion is caused partly by what has been called persistence of vision, that is, the fact that the eye retains an observed image a fraction of a second after the image has disappeared. Accordingly the motion picture projector includes a mechanism which draws the film between the light and the lens in a stop-and-go motion, the film pausing a fraction of a second at each frame for the eye to take in the image; then a shutter closes and remains closed, also for a fraction of a second, while the eye retains the image and the mechanism propels the film ahead to the next frame.[1]

The perforations along the edge of the film enable the teeth of the driving mechanism to engage the film and not only to move it along from one frame to the next but also to hold it steady. The stop-and-go motion gives the illusion of a continuous picture. If the film did not pause at each frame, the impression that the eye receives would be blurred.

The illusion that motion pictures move depends also on the imagination of the spectator. Watching a succession of pictures, each one representing a change in the position of the image from that of the preceding one, the spectator imagines that the image is moving because he associates it with a corresponding object that he has seen actually moving. Furthermore, he imagines that he sees more than the camera has photographed. The film moves through the camera at the rate of twenty-four frames a second. Every second, then, the camera takes

---

1. Michael Chanan contends that persistence of vision does not account for the perceived motion in a film, that the gaps caused by the closed shutter do not impinge on attention because of the brevity of their duration. His contention does not alter the fact that motion pictures seem to move because of a mechanism of the machine. As Chanan himself declares, "Theories can be wrong, but the inventions based on them can still work." *The Dream That Kicks: The Prehistory and Early Years of Cinema in Britain,* (London: Routledge & Kegan Paul, 1980), pp. 54–69.

twenty-four individual snapshots, each of which, in a standard motion picture camera, is exposed in 1/60 second. Like the projector, the camera operates with a stop-and-go motion, the shutter opening for 1/60 second to allow the exposure and then closing for the film to move ahead to the next frame. Because the shutter is closed more than half the time, the camera photographs less than half of what happens. But when the film is projected onto the screen, persistence of vision compensates for the missing action. Accordingly, the spectator has the illusion not only that the pictures are moving but that he is seeing more than twice as much as he actually sees. What he would see, for example, in a two-hour film would be only forty-eight minutes of pictures.

Some of the principles of motion picture machinery were understood long before the motion picture machine was invented and rudimentary variations of it were devised. Apart from such early devices as Leonardo da Vinci's *camera obscura,* its origin is the magic lantern, the first known version of which was invented by the Dutch scientist Christian Huygens about 1655.[2] Samuel Pepys records in his diary for August 19, 1666, that a Mr. Reeves, a London perspective glass maker, brought him "a lanthorn with pictures in glasse, to make strange things appear on a wall, very pretty." In 1828 Joseph Plateau, a Belgian physicist, devised a machine he called a Phenakistiscope ("deceitful view"), whereby the illusion of motion was effected by pictures on a revolving disc viewed through notches on a second revolving disc. Six years later Simon Ritter von Stampfer, a professor of geometry at the Vienna Polytechnical Institute, constructed a similar device, the Stroboscope ("whirling view"). One of the popular early versions of the motion picture projector was the Zoetrope, or wheel of life. Devised in 1833 by the British mathematician William George Horner as the Daedaleum (after Daedalus), it consisted of a shallow cylinder about a foot in diameter with vertical slots in the edge and, on the inside, a series of pictures that, seen through the slots, seemed to move when the cylinder was turned. By 1853 Franz von Uchatius, an Austrian artillery officer, had constructed a projector incorporating the principle of the Phenakistiscope with that of the magic lantern. By means of a revolving light passing through a series of twelve pictures arranged in a circle on glass, his machine projected images of the drawings onto

2. Athanasius Kircher is said to have invented the magic lantern in 1646 because he makes that claim in his book *Ars Magna Lucis et Umbrae,* first published in that year. Kenneth Macgowan in *Behind the Screen* (New York: Delacorte, 1965), p. 27, points out that Kircher mentions the magic lantern only in the second edition of his book, in 1671, contending that he had described and pictured it in the first edition.

a wall so that they appeared to move. Another kind of wheel machine, patented in 1861 by Coleman Sellers, a Philadelphia machinist, was an arrangement whereby photographs were mounted on paddles. Sellers called it the Kinematoscope. Of such were the gropings toward the motion picture machine. They were, however, gropings in the direction of motion picture projection. The motion picture camera had to wait for the invention not only of photography but of photographic film.

Photography originated in 1837 when the Frenchman Louis Daguerre invented a process whereby a photograph could be exposed on a chemically coated plate. Although the sitter for a daguerreotype had to remain motionless for the several minutes required to expose the plate, refinements in the process decreased the time. The next step consisted of negatives on glass, after which came the wet plate process.

Thus it was that in 1872 Eadweard Muybridge, a San Francisco photographer, in order to determine whether a trotting horse simultaneously lifts all four feet off the ground, was able to take some photographs at Sacramento. In May of that year, according to his own account, he "made several negatives of a celebrated horse named Occident, while trotting, laterally, in front of his camera . . . ," and the resulting photographs "were sufficiently sharp to give a recognizable silhouette portrait of the driver, and some of them exhibited the horse with all four of his feet clearly lifted, at the same time, above the surface of the ground."[3] With the cooperation of Leland Stanford, a former governor of California and the owner of race horses, Muybridge continued his investigation at Stanford's stock farm at Palo Alto. (The story is that Stanford was trying to win a bet of $25,000 that a trotting horse takes all his feet off the ground simultaneously.) By means of a row of electrically controlled cameras set up parallel to a track and triggered by the wheels of the sulky, Muybridge obtained a series of photographs representing a trotting horse. He experimented further by photographing with two-lensed cameras, thereby producing stereoscopic pictures. By placing the appropriate halves of the pictures in a pair of Zoetropes, which were revolved at the same speed, the halves being made simultaneously visible by means of mirrors, he obtained "a very satisfactory reproduction of an apparently solid miniature horse trotting, and of another galloping.[4] Improving on his use of the Zoetropes, he devised an instrument he called a Zoopraxiscope, which he demonstrated in a lecture in San Francisco in 1880 and in the Paris laboratory of the French physiologist Etienne Marey in 1881.

3. Edweard Muybridge, *Animals in Motion*, ed. Lewis S. Brown (New York: Dover, 1957), p. 13.
4. Ibid., p. 14.

Like Muybridge, Marey studied the movement of animals and, to facilitate his study, invented some photographic devices. In 1882 he constructed what he called a photographic gun. An instrument for photographing birds in flight, the gun operated on the principle of the revolver, the chambers containing photographic plates which recorded pictures when the trigger was released. In 1888 Marey explained to the French Academy of Science an apparatus that he had devised for recording a series of impressions at the rate of twenty a second. "If by means of a special device, based on the employment of an electromagnet," he told the Academy, "the paper is arrested during the period of exposure, 1/5,000 second, the impression will possess all the clearness that is desirable."[5]

In 1887, if not before, Ottomar Anschutz, in Germany, invented his electrical Tachyscope. This was a viewing machine on which photographs, which Anschutz had taken with twenty-four cameras, were mounted on the periphery of an iron wheel. As the wheel turned, the photographs, lighted by an intermittent electrical flash, were viewed directly, that is, not projected. In 1894, however, Anschutz obtained a French patent for "a process of projection of images in stroboscopic movement."

Meantime Emile Reynaud, a French inventor, by improving on the Zoetrope, developed a viewing machine called the Praxinoscope, which in 1882 he combined with a projector for showing animated drawings. At first he put the drawings on paper rolls, but in 1888 he put them on celluloid ribbon perforated between the frames. Then in 1892 he opened his performances of "living pictures" at the Musée Given in Paris, inaugurating the enterprise with a presentation of some of Muybridge's animal photographs, and successfully continued the performances for several years after cinematography had become a reality.

Thomas Edison has been given credit for inventing motion pictures. It would be more nearly accurate to say that Edison, coordinating the ideas of other inventors, promoted in his laboratory the building of both a motion picture camera and a motion picture projector. Edison was an inventor aware of the importance of patents on devices that could be manufactured for profit. Since he saw no commercial value in motion pictures, it is remarkable that he concerned himself with them at all. But he was trying to perfect his phonograph, and he said that in 1887 the idea occurred to him that "it was possible to devise

5. Quoted by Gordon Hendricks, *The Edison Motion Picture Myth*, (Berkeley and Los Angeles: University of California Press, 1961), p. 170, from *Wilson's Photographic Magazine*, January 5, 1889. Hendricks, however, questions the 1/5,000 second as seeming short.

an instrument which should do for the eye what the phonograph does for the ear, and that by a combination of the two, all motion and sound could be recorded and reproduced simultaneously."[6] He investigated the idea so desultorily, however, that nine years elapsed before the projection of motion pictures onto a screen became a practical reality. He assigned one of his assistants, twenty-eight year old William Kennedy Laurie Dickson, to the project.

Edison said years later that he had only one fact to guide him, "the principle of optics technically called the persistence of vision."[7] But he and Dickson were also familiar with the Zoetrope, and they knew about Muybridge's horse pictures and Marey's photographic gun. In fact, Edison said that the germ of his idea came from the Zoetrope and the work of Muybridge, Marey, and others. Dickson started with the Zoetrope. Since Edison had already invented a phonograph record and since the purpose was to give eyes to the phonograph, Dickson built a device that seemed to incorporate both Zoetrope and record. It was a cylinder somewhat larger than the phonograph cylinder and containing microscopic photographs. Dickson placed it and a phonograph cylinder side by side on a shaft and recorded sound on the phonograph cylinder as synchronously as possible with the photographs. But the pictures were less satisfactory than the sound, and Dickson tried something different.

Incorporating in his camera a stop-motion device, he took pictures on sheets of sensitized celluloid—pictures so small that he recorded about two hundred of them in a spiral arrangement around a single cylinder. After developing and fixing the celluloid, he placed it on a transparent drum. When the drum was turned, a device lighted up each image from the inside. Here, gropingly but unerringly, he had established an important principle—that motion pictures depend on light passing through the frame, whether the frame is projected onto a screen or viewed directly. But the curvature of the cylinder brought only the center of each picture into focus. Dickson took another step.

Abandoning the idea of a cylinder, he obtained some celluloid-based film recently developed by John Carbutt of Philadelphia.[8] Perforations

---

6. Foreword to article by Antonia and William Kennedy Laurie Dickson, "Edison's Invention of the Kinetophonograph," *Century Magazine* 48 (June 1894): 208.

7. Thomas Alva Edison, *The Diary and Sundry Observations of Thomas Alva Edison*, ed. Dagobert D. Runes (New York: Philosophical Library, 1948), p. 71.

8. Hendricks contends (*Edison Motion Picture Myth*, p. 40) that although film historians credit the Eastman Company with the invention of celluloid-based film, the invention was Carbutt's, a year or two earlier, and that "Eastman's contribution was improvement of manufacturing methods and not inventive novelty."

along the edge enabled the teeth of a locking device to hold the film steady as a mechanism moved it, in a stop-and-go motion, through the camera. The year was 1891. Dickson had discovered motion picture film and recorded a motion picture on it.

From the negative he made a positive print. So that the pictures could be viewed, he placed the printed film in a boxlike structure about four feet high and two feet square. Propelled by a battery-powered motor, the film ran on a loop between an electric lamp and a shutter. The pictures were viewed by flashes under a magnifying lens as the viewer looked through a slit in the top of the box. The little viewing machine was called a Kinetoscope, the name representing a combination of the Greek *kinetos* (movable) and *scope* (viewing). The camera was called the Kinetograph (*graphein,* to write).

Like the original phonograph—an apparatus equipped with earphones—the Kinetoscope was a device for an individual viewer, not for a group, although there is evidence that in 1889, while experimenting with the Kinetoscope, Dickson succeeded in projecting a moving picture onto a screen by means of a converted Tachyscope. The evidence has been controverted, but it has been established that the next year, at the Edison Paris Exposition in New York, a moving picture was indeed projected. Quoting a report in the *Western Electrician* of April 12, 1890—"A magic lantern of almost unimaginable power casts upon the ceiling from the top of the tower such pictures as seem to be the actual performances of living persons"—Gordon Hendricks declares. "Here we have what was surely a Tachyscope projection by Dickson."[9]

In 1891, Edison applied for patents on his camera and on "an apparatus for exhibiting photographs of moving objects." The patents were granted in the spring of 1893, and Edison contracted to manufacture Kinetoscopes for the Kinetoscope Company, which had been organized expressly to sell them. Thus on April 14, 1894, a Kinetoscope parlor was opened in a converted shoe shop at 1155 Broadway in New York. In it had been set up ten Kinetoscopes, each containing a fifty-foot film made with the Kinetograph at the Edison plant in West Orange, New Jersey. Within the year Kinetoscope parlors, as well as single Kinetoscopes, were in operation in cities and towns throughout the country.

The year before, a building for the taking of motion pictures had been put up at the Edison plant. Designed by Dickson, it was forty-eight feet long by fourteen feet wide—narrowing to ten feet in width

9. Ibid., p. 92.

Cripple Creek Barroom (Edison, 1898), shot in the Black Maria studio

for the twenty feet at the end where the camera was housed—and so constructed that a fifteen-by-fourteen-foot section of the roof, about midway, could be opened to admit light. Any desired angle of the rays of the sun could be obtained, for the whole building was swung on a graphited center in the manner of a swinging bridge and turned on a circular track. Dickson called it the "Kinetograph Theatre." Because it was covered with tar paper on the outside and painted black on the inside—to bring the actors into sharp relief—it was familiarly known as the Black Maria. In it Dickson filmed bits of current variety show acts—dancers, acrobats, contortionists, trained animals—each abridged to be photographed on not more than fifty feet of film. Sandow the Strong Man appeared before the Kinetograph, as did Annie Oakley, Buffalo Bill, and Ruth St. Denis. One film represented part of a scene from a popular farce of the day, Charles Hoyt's *A Milk White Flag.* The repertoire included reenacted scenes such as *The Execution of Mary Queen of Scots,* which, however, was not filmed in the Black Maria but outdoors. This little film was one of the first to incorporate trick photography; in it the beheading of the unfortunate lady leaves nothing to the imagination.

Keeping in mind Edison's having declared it possible to record and reproduce sound and motion simultaneously, Dickson had experimented accordingly, but the experiments were not successful. The nearest he seems to have come to synchronization was to record pictures and music separately and then to accompany the pictures with the sound. In the spring of 1895 some of the Kinetoscopes were equipped with phonographs so that, by means of earphones, the viewer could hear music while looking at the pictures. Kinetoscopes so equipped were called Kinetophones.

Not long after the Kinetoscope parlor opened, it attracted the attention of Otway and Gray Latham, two young southerners visiting in New York. It occurred to the Latham brothers that this new toy might be a means of making money if it were used to present pictures of prizefights. Accordingly, with Samuel J. Tilden, Jr., and Enoch Rector they formed the Kinetoscope Exhibition Company, and in August of 1894, they opened a parlor at 83 Nassau Street, in New York. The films they offered the public for the occasion were of a six-round fight between Michael Leonard and Jack Cushing, photographed in a ten-foot ring in the Black Maria. The capacity of the Kinetoscope had been increased for the occasion from 50 to 150 feet of film, and each of the six enlarged Kinetoscopes presented a short round of the fight. About 950 feet in length, this was the longest motion picture that had yet been made. Shortly thereafter, when Colonel Woodville Latham, the father of Otway and Gray, visited the parlor, Otway asked him whether the films they were showing in the Kinetoscopes could be projected onto a screen. The answer was yes.

The Lathams set about devising a projection machine as well as a motion picture camera. Because their projector—for which, incidentally, they received suggestions from William Kennedy Dickson—only copied the principle of the Kinetoscope, it was of less significance than their camera. In the Kinetograph, the film was wound and unwound directly from one reel to another. Since the resulting strain of more than forty or fifty feet of film would break the film, the Kinetograph could not take a continuous picture of more than about fifteen seconds in length. Enoch Rector devised a sprocket which slackened off enough film in a loop to prevent the stop-and-go motion from tugging at the unwinding reel. Allowing the camera to take as long a film as a reel would hold, this little device—called the Latham loop—was an important contribution to the motion picture machine.[10]

At the time Edison applied for a United States patent on the Kinetoscope, he was asked whether he wished to take out foreign patents

10. Hendricks, *Edison Motion Picture Myth*, pp. 169–70. Hendricks finds evidence, however, that the apparatus which Marey described to the French Academy of Sciences in 1888 contained such a loop—"a continuously moving feed roller with a loop to avoid jerking."

on it as well. When told that foreign patents would cost $150 more, Edison is said to have replied, "It isn't worth it."[11] Thus when Robert W. Paul, a London manufacturer of scientific instruments, was asked, in 1894, to duplicate the Kinetoscope, he not only did so but—finding to his amazement that it was not patented in England—manufactured and sold, within the next two years, about sixty of the machines. Then, to supply his customers with films, he built a camera which not only incorporated a stop-motion device similar to that originated by Edison and Dickson but was portable. He also built a projector—the Bio-scope—which took into account the all-important principle of persistence of vision and thus effected the necessary intermittent motion. As the film passed through the projector, it was made to pause longer at each frame than between frames and thereby allowed the eye time to "take in" each picture. He demonstrated this machine, for the first time, at Finsbury Technical College, in February of 1896.

Meanwhile, in Germany, Max Skladanowski had built and patented a motion picture machine which he modeled, like Paul's, after the Kinetoscope and which he also called the Bioscope. In November of 1895, Skladanowski demonstrated it as the concluding entertainment on a variety bill at the Wintergarten in Berlin. The showing consisted of two films of about forty-eight frames each.

In France the Lumière brothers—Auguste and Louis—manufacturers of photographic equipment, had also been experimenting with motion pictures. Beginning, as Paul did, with the Kinetoscope, which was shown in France for the first time in 1894—only a few months after it had been introduced in the United States—they found that the continuous motion in the Kinetoscope would not do for a projection machine. Accordingly they built a stop-motion device. They also built a camera which differed from Edison's Kinetograph in the speed at which the film was fed through it; that is, in the number of pictures, or frames, it recorded each second. Whereas the Kinetograph took forty-eight frames a second, the Lumières decided on sixteen as the proper rate. (The standard rate has since been established as twenty-four.) By early 1895, they had completed both projector and camera and had taken some pictures, and on March 22, at their factory in Lyons, they demonstrated their accomplishment. They called their projector the Cinématographe, a name reminiscent of Sellers' paddle-wheel machine, as well as of the Kinetoscope and the Kinetograph,

11. Birt Acres, in a letter to the *British Journal of Photography* in 1896, suggests another reason why Edison did not take out foreign patents: that the Edison Company, relying on the difficulty of making films, stipulated with the sale of films that they were to be used only in their machines. (Quoted in Chanan, *Dream That Kicks*, p. 224).

and anticipating the universal word for motion pictures—*cinema* (Gr. *kinema,* motion).

After several other demonstrations, including one at the Sorbonne, the Lumières opened an establishment in Paris to show their machine to the public and charge admission. They rented the Salon Indien in the basement of the Grand Café on the Boulevard des Capucines, putting the enterprise under the direction of their father, Antoine Lumière, and there on the afternoon of December 28, 1895, the premiere took place. Each film, like Edison's, was fifty feet long, and there were about ten films. Included were *Lunch Hour at the Lumière Factory,* which shows workers leaving the plant at Lyons; *Arrival of a Train at a Station,* in which the oncoming locomotive is said to have terrified the spectators; *A Game of Cards,* in which the players are Antoine Lumière, the conjurer Trewey, who sits opposite him and is the dealer, and Louis Lumière's father-in-law, Winckler, the Lyons brewer, who pours out some beer; *Baby's Lunch,* a picture that Louis Lumière had taken of Auguste and Mme Lumière with their infant daughter on the walk beside the Lumière house; *Blacksmiths, The Rue de la République,* a Lyons traffic scene: and *Bathing Beach,* in which the waves break on the shore. Admission was one franc, and the receipts on that opening day were thirty-five francs. The essential principles of motion

Pastime in the Family Circle (Lumière, 1896), with Auguste and Louis Lumière and family

picture photography and projection having at last been applied in a commercial enterprise, motion pictures were born.

The idea that Edison had begun investigating eight years before had thus become a reality. Edison originated the idea which, by the ingenious work of Dickson, took the form of the Kinetoscope; but the Kinetoscope became the motion picture independently of Edison, in a way that he had not originally intended and over a course that he could not have foreseen. Even the Kinetoscope was not Edison's invention. First, there was Dickson; and besides Dickson, other inventors contributed to the process which led deviously from the laboratory in West Orange, New Jersey, to the Grand Café in Paris, from the peep-show box to motion pictures.

Then there were those who, although they were off the path of this progress, were experimenting with motion pictures at the time. There was, for example, William Friese-Greene, a photographer of Bath, England. Friese-Greene's epitaph describes him as "The Inventor of Cinematography," and attempts have been made to support this claim. Together with John Rudge, an optician, and Mortimer Evans, a civil engineer, Friese-Greene built a motion picture camera and applied for a patent on it in 1889; but it has not been established that he effected the successful projection of motion pictures onto a screen. Although Friese-Greene apparently wrote to Edison suggesting that moving pictures might be made a part of the phonograph—after Edison already had this idea—he neither completed a machine for this purpose nor directly contributed to the course leading from the Kinetoscope to motion pictures as perfected by the Lumières.

The tendency to simplify has given Edison credit as the inventor of motion pictures. To point out that he was not, that in fact no one individual may be said to have been the sole inventor, is not to minimize the importance of his idea or even of the Kinetoscope. That it was the Lumières who first built a machine incorporating the progress made by other inventors, who improved the rate of speed at which a film should pass through a camera, and who first demonstrated the completed machine as a commercial reality is a fact that those who would simplify cannot disregard. Ironically, however, if the premiere at the Grand Café late in 1895 had been delayed only four months, Edison would have had the distinction not only of originating the idea that led to motion pictures but also of introducing the motion picture machine to the world. As it was, on April 23, 1896, he introduced it to the United States.

Even though, at the time he was working on the Kinetoscope, Dickson had effected the projection of a motion picture onto a screen,

Edison had refused to put projection machines on the market. When Norman Raff proposed that they do so, Edison is reported to have replied that the company was selling Kinetoscopes for $300 to $350 apiece and making money and that if they sold machines which would enable a large group of people to see the films simultaneously, there would be use for only about ten of them in all the United States. But now the Lathams had a projector, which, as the Pantopticon, they demonstrated publicly on May 20, 1895, in New York City. The Pantopticon operated on the principle of the Kinetoscope—that is, in its continuous motion—but it projected a four-minute film of a boxing match which Otway Latham had directed on the roof of Madison Square Garden. Here was competition. Edison assigned one of his assistants, Charles H. Kayser, to the project of building a machine that would be better than the Lathams'. Meanwhile, however, Francis Jenkins had constructed a stop-motion mechanism for a projector. According to Gordon Hendricks, Thomas Armat, a Washington real estate operator, having obtained an interest in Jenkins' invention, represented it as his own.[12] Edison was informed of the invention, and, early in 1896, an agreement was reached whereby the Edison Company could manufacture the projector under the Edison name but label it "Armat designed." The name chosen for the new machine was Vitascope.

April 14, 1896, under the ambiguous headline "Edison's Latest Triumph," the *New York Times* reported:

Raff & Gammon advertisement

12. Gordon Hendricks, *The Kinetoscope: America's First Commercially Successful Motion Picture Exhibition* (New York: Beginnings of American Film, 1966), p. 143.

Thomas A. Edison and Albert Bial have perfected arrangements by which Edison's latest invention, the vitascope, will be exhibited for the first time anywhere at Koster & Bial's Music Hall. Edison has been at work on the vitascope for several years.

The vitascope projects upon a large area of canvas groups that appear to stand forth from the canvas, and move with great facility and agility, as though actuated by separate impulses. In this way the bare canvas before the audience becomes instantly a stage upon which living beings move about.

Mr. Bial said yesterday: "I propose to reproduce in this way at Koster & Bial's scenes from various successful plays and operas of the season, and well-known statesmen and celebrities will be represented as, for instance, making a speech or performing some important act or series of acts with which their names are identified. No other manager in this city will have the right to exhibit the vitascope."

Five days later, the first newspaper advertisement of a moving picture appeared in the *Times*. At the foot of Koster & Bial's theater announcement of their current attraction—the monologuist Albert Chevalier "together with all the other Great Foreign Stars"—could be read: "Extra—Due notice will be given of the first public exhibition of Edison's latest marvel, THE VITASCOPE." The "due notice," appearing two days later, gave the date of the premiere—April 23—and on that morning the Koster & Bial advertisement gave the Vitascope top billing, Chevalier and the "Great Foreign Stars" being summarily relegated to second place.

The premiere of the Vitascope was more auspicious than that of the Cinématographe on that winter afternoon four months before in the basement room on the Boulevard des Capucines. Koster & Bial's, in Herald Square, was one of New York City's popular music halls. Edison himself came over from New Jersey for the occasion and occupied a box seat. Armat was there, too, taking charge in the projection booth set up in the second balcony.

The next morning the *Times* reported as follows:

The new thing at Koster & Bial's last night was Edison's vitascope, exhibited for the first time. The ingenious inventor's latest toy is a projection of his kinetoscope figures in stereopticon fashion, upon a white screen in a darkened hall. In the center of the balcony of the big music hall is a curious object, which looks from below like the double turret of a big monitor. In the front of each half of it are two big oblong holes. The turret is neatly covered with the blue velvet brocade which is the favorite decorative material in this house. The white screen used on the stage is framed like a picture. The moving figures are about half life size.

When the hall was darkened last night a buzzing and roaring were heard in the turret, and an unusually bright light fell upon the screen. Then came into

view two precious blond young persons of the variety stage, in pink and blue
dresses, doing the umbrella dance with commendable celerity. Their motions
were all clearly defined. When they vanished, a view of an angry surf breaking
on a sandy beach near a stone pier amazed the spectators. The waves tumbled
in furiously and the foam of the breakers flew high in the air. A burlesque
boxing match between a tall, thin comedian and a short, fat one, a comic
allegory called "The Monroe Doctrine," an instant of motion in Hoyt's farce,
"A Milk White Flag," repeated over and over again, and a skirt dance by a
tall blonde completed the views, which were all wonderfully real and singularly
exhilarating. For the spectator's imagination filled the atmosphere with electricity, as sparks crackled around the moving lifelike figures.

So enthusiastic was the appreciation of the crowd long before the extraordinary exhibition was finished that vociferous cheering was heard. There were
loud calls for Mr. Edison, but he made no response.

Of the films included in that first showing of the Vitascope, it was,
the *Times* reported in its Sunday edition two days later:

the waves tumbling in on a beach and about a stone pier that caused the
spectators to cheer and marvel most of all. Big rollers broke on the beach,
foam flew high, and weakened waters poured far up on the beach. Then great
combers arose and pushed each other shoreward, one mounting above the
other, and they seemed to fall with mighty force and all together on the shifty
sand, whose yellow receding motion could be plainly seen.

Edison apparently realized, however, that the use of motion pictures
to provide entertainment by the sheer novelty of the device itself could
not be exploited for long. The *Times* announced:

Mr. Edison is working hard for the absolute perfection of his machine, and
at the same time is arranging for the securing of pictures the like of which, in
other than inertness, the public has never seen.

He has bought, for about $5000, two ancient, but still serviceable locomo-
tives and several dozen flat cars. He has built about a quarter of a mile of
railroad track in a secluded spot, not far from his laboratory. In a few weeks
he will start a train from each end of the track, and will run them to a crash.
The engines and cars will be manned, just as trains are in active service, and
all the incidents of a train wreck will be caught by machines stationed at short
intervals near the track.

Machines have been sent to Rome, and in a short while the entire stage at
Koster & Bial's will be occupied by a realistic representation of Pope Leo XIII,
saying mass in the Sistine Chapel.[13]

This kind of use of motion pictures had, in fact, been predicted a
year before. After the Lathams had publicly projected their boxing
match picture, Howard B. Hackett wrote in the *New York World:*

13. *New York Times*, April 26, 1896, p. 10.

You will sit comfortably and see fighters hammering each other, circuses, suicides, hangings, electrocutions, shipwrecks, scenes on the exchanges, street scenes, horse races, football games—almost anything in fact in which there is action, as if you were on the spot during the actual event.[14]

Hackett's prediction was coming true. In 1896, when motion pictures had become a practical reality, when they had evolved into the device essentially as it was to remain, their future lay, it seemed, in providing entertainment by presenting scenes of actuality.

Charles Frohman, the theatrical producer, saw how this use might be extended to the theater. After attending that first showing of the Vitascope, he declared:

That settles scenery. Painted trees that do not move, waves that get up a few feet and stay there, everything in scenery we simulate on our stages will have to go. When art can make us believe that we see actual living nature, the dead things of the stage must go.

And think what can be done with this invention? For instance, Chevalier comes on the screen. The audience would get all the pantomime of his coster songs. The singing, words fitted to gestures and movements, could be done from the wings or behind the curtain. And so we could have on the stage at any time any artist, dead or alive, who ever faced Mr. Edison's invention.[15]

Whether the invention may be called "Mr. Edison's" is—as the records show—open to question. But there is no question about motion pictures' having originated, not as an art, but as a machine. The ingenuity and effort, not of artists, but of inventors, mechanics, photographers, engineers, and manufacturers made the machine possible. The purpose of these men—from Muybridge with his pictures of Leland Stanford's horses to Edison with his Vitascope—was not artistic, but utilitarian: to perfect a machine that would have a use. The machine is still being perfected, but in Edison's Armat-designed Vitascope, or in the Lumières' Cinématographe, the invention culminated. Appropriately, the first motion picture shows were billed as machines: at the Grand Café, "LE CINÉMATOGRAPHE" (*"Cet appareil,"* the announcement began) and at Koster & Bial's, "Edison's latest marvel, the VITASCOPE."

14. Quoted by Terry Ramsaye. *A Million and One Nights: A History of the Motion Picture*, 2 vols. (New York: Simon and Schuster, 1926), 1: 134.
15. *New York Times*, April 26, 1896, p. 10.

2

GORDON HENDRICKS

The History of the Kinetoscope

Early in 1894 there appeared in the American marketplace a peep-hole picture machine known as the Kinetoscope. It stood on the floor to a height of four feet. Through an eyepiece on the top a customer could, upon application of the coin of the realm, cause the machine to whirr briskly and show motion pictures of dancing girls, performing animals, etc. The vast majority of these customers were enormously excited by the exhibition, came back again and again to see it, and told their friends about the new wonder. Some were impelled to build machines of their own; others, more significantly, devoted themselves to the task of projecting the pictures on a screen, so that many more than one viewer at a time could see the show. From the work of these latter came America's first projectors and the subsequent rich burgeoning of the industry in 1896 and afterward.

The Kinetoscope was the source of their inspiration, and at the same time supplied them, by stimulating public interest, with a market. It must therefore be given more than a small share of credit for the beginnings of the American motion picture industry. By 1895, the Kinetoscope was losing its lustre, however, and the camera was beginning to furnish motion picture subjects for the screen.

To West Orange, New Jersey, in 1887 came a young Scotsman, named W. K. L. Dickson, whose contribution to this work has been overshadowed by the illustriousness and aggressiveness of his em-

Adapted by the editor from *The Kinetoscope: America's First Commercially Successful Motion Picture Exhibition* (New York: Beginnings of American Film, 1966).

ployer, Thomas Alva Edison. Dickson was much interested in photography, and brought this interest—and the excellent facilities of the Edison laboratory—to bear upon the problem of a camera and the Kinetoscope. By the end of 1892 he had produced both.[1]

The Kinetograph Camera

The camera (named the Kinetograph) was the fountainhead from which flowed all West Orange motion pictures. Every subject known to us up to May 1896 was shot by this instrument—and many of those

Shooting an Annabelle Serpentine dance in the Black Maria studio. From *Frank Leslie's Popular Monthly,* February 1895. The figure at the left is apparently meant to be Dickson. Note the "MB" in monogram at stage left (indicating a Maguire and Baucus production), the door at the left, the power line to the outside, the track for the camera, the counter on the camera, and the handle for starting and stopping the phonograph.

1. For an account of the development of the camera and Kinetoscope, see Gordon Hendricks, *The Edison Motion Picture Myth* (Berkeley and Los Angeles: University of California Press, 1961).

afterward. It was probably with this camera that Edison reentered the motion-picture-taking business in the fall of 1896, and with its patent specifications tied up the whole industry for years. It is thus as important as any other camera in the history of the business.

For all this significance, however, the details of its construction are not clear. Patent specifications are frequently ambiguous and conflicting claims profuse. Its average rate of taking pictures was thirty-eight to forty frames a second. [The sketch from *Frank Leslie's Popular Monthly* (February 1895), which is here reproduced and was first brought to public attention in *The Kinetoscope*, gives a good idea of at least the external appearance of the camera.—Ed.]

The Kinetoscope

The Kinetoscope's overall dimensions were 18″ x 27″ x 48″, including the base and the eyepiece. A clear and authoritative description of the Kinetoscope's operation has been provided by Herman Casler in a lecture delivered around 1909 in Syracuse, New York:

A ribbon of transparent film carrying the pictures is laced up and down over idle spools at the lower part of the case. The ends of the film are joined, forming an endless band passing over two guide drums near the top of the case. One of these drums is driven by motor and feeds the film along by means of sprocket teeth which engage with perforations along the edges of the film. Just above the film is a shutter wheel having five spokes and a very small rectangular opening in the rim directly over the film. An incandescent lamp . . . is placed below the film between the two guide drums, and the light passes up through the film, shutter opening, and magnifying lens . . . to the eye of the observer placed at the opening in the top of the case.

The film had a continuous motion, and, I believe, showed the pictures at the rate of forty per second. The shutter was probably about 10″ in diameter and, judging from the photograph, the opening must be about 3/4″ wide. As the shutter made one revolution for each picture, the length of exposure would be between 1/1600 and 1/1700 part of one second.[2]

The length of the film used varied from twenty-five to thirty feet in the earliest Kinetoscope to forty-two to forty-eight feet in the later ones.

The Black Maria

Granting the existence of an effective camera and an effective device for the exhibition of the product of that camera, the first substantial step in the establishment of the American motion picture industry was

2. Original transcript in the collection of Gordon Hendricks, New York.

a proposal to Edison on October 31, 1892. [. . .] This proposal was for the exploitation of the Kinetoscope at the World's Columbian Exposition in Chicago and was made by a syndicate consisting of the following: A. O. Tate, Edison's private secretary; Thomas R. Lombard, a partner in a firm that marketed the Edison phonograph as a dictating machine; and Erastus A. Benson, an Omaha banker and president of the Chicago Central Phonograph Company, which distributed the Edison phonograph in Chicago. The deal called for Edison to sell the syndicate 150 Kinetoscopes for use at the exposition. The first proceeds were to go to Edison in payment for the machines, after which he was to split the profits with the three others.

"The Black Maria" was felt to be necessary as soon as motion picture plans for the fair began to outgrow the 1889 photograph building. The stage area of that building was small and the skylight lighting insufficient. So Dickson set about designing a larger, lighter, more flexible stage. Many new subjects would have to be taken to supply the fair Kinetoscopes, and they would have to be taken quickly. A new studio was needed.

The Black Maria was presumably 48′ x 10′ by 14′ x 18′; certain contemporary records are vague. It was lined at least partially with black tar paper, although it was said more than once to have been painted black inside. The lining was not entire. It covered, so far as I have been able to determine, that part of the Maria surrounding the

The Black Maria studio

shooting area or stage. This area, the outer confines of which were somewhat altered to conform with the late-1894 alterations, was delineated at first by a raised platform and later by chalk marks, wooden barriers, or otherwise limned space.

The Black Maria swung suspended on a central vertical axis over a graphite pivot to accommodate the need for sunshine, even though as a matter of practice nearly all Maria subjects seem to have been shot close to noon, which would have made the pivoting less important.

The Maria was further supported by rollers, used less and less as time went on. The rollers were necessary, along with the iron trusses, to support the Maria's considerable end weight.

The Black Maria camera was mounted on steel tracks. It was drawn in and out of the small room facing the stage for loading and reloading.

This "revolving photograph building" was under construction from December 1892 to January 1893, and cost $637.67. It has often been called the world's first motion picture studio, but this is incorrect; the 1889 photograph building at the West Orange laboratory, if no other, predated it considerably. If we were to call the Black Maria the world's first studio specifically built for motion picture production, we would be on firm ground; I have found no earlier.

Building the First Model

The Black Maria was no more than fairly completed when Dickson had a nervous breakdown and went south for ten weeks' rest. Delays in manufacture, largely brought about by Edison's continuing preoccupation with ore milling and his lack of interest in nearly anything which was not money making, prevented its introduction to the general public until April 1894. Plans to have Kinetoscopes ready for the exposition opening had to be abandoned in April 1893, and the syndicate surrendered the Kinetoscope concession. Nonetheless, it had hopes of installing at least a few Kinetoscopes before the fair closed in November and placed an order for twenty-five machines.

The manufacturer's model of the Kinetoscope was given its first "official" demonstration on May 9, 1893, at the annual meeting of the department of physics of the Brooklyn Institute of Arts and Sciences. This meeting was said by the institute to be "the first time that a Kinetograph [that is, a Kinetoscope] had been exhibited outside of the Edison laboratory . . . where it was invented and manufactured."

In spite of persistent, poignant cries, Tate and his associates never got their World's Fair Kinetoscopes. Nevertheless, one machine apparently made its way to the fair, and before the season closed, was installed in the second floor of the Electricity Building for all and sundry to see.

The First Kinetoscope Parlors

The Tate-Lombard-Benson order for twenty-five Kinetoscopes was not filled until April 1894. The syndicate now had three more names associated with it: Andrew M. Holland, Norman C. Raff, and Frank R. Gammon. It hoped to acquire the exclusive marketing rights to the Kinetoscope, but Edison's plan at the time was to sell the machine on the open market. As a result, the syndicate contented itself with operating parlors to exhibit the Kinetoscope.

On April 6, 1894, ten of the twenty-five Kinetoscopes then in existence were shipped to Andrew M. Holland at 1155 Broadway, New York. The machines cost $250 apiece. Sometime between April 6 and April 14 Dickson personally delivered the ten films for the debut, one film for each of ten machines: *Sandow, Horse Shoeing, Barber Shop, Bertholdi (Mouth Support), Wrestling, Bertholdi (Table Contortion), Blacksmiths, Highland Dance, Trapeze,* and *Roosters.* They were charged at $10 each and were paid for on the day of the opening.[3]

Tate offers an eyewitness account of the commercial debut of the Kinetoscope:

We then decided to install ten of these [the original 25] in New York. . . . in preparation for this I leased a small store, formerly a shoe shop, No. 1155 Broadway, on the west side near Twenty-seventh Street. . . . Here the ten machines were placed in the center of the room in two rows of five each, enclosed by a metal railing for the spectators to lean against when viewing the animated picture. One ticket, at the price of twenty-five cents, entitled the holder to view one row of five machines. If he wanted to see both rows he bought two tickets. On the right of the entrance door a ticket booth was erected. At the back of the exhibition room was a smaller room for use as an office and for repairing the films. In the window there was a printed announcement or advertisement whose legend I cannot now recall, and a plaster bust of Edison painted to simulate bronze. It was an excellent portrait but a few weeks later I received a message from Edison asking me to remove it. He thought its display undignified.

By noon on Saturday, the 14th day of April, 1894, everything was ready for the opening of the exhibit to the public on the following Monday. My brother, the late Bertram M. Tate, was to act as manager, and a mechanic to supervise the machines and an attractive young woman to preside over the ticket booth were to report for duty at nine o'clock in the morning of that day. At one o'clock on this notable Saturday afternoon, after locking the street door, Lom-

3. According to Terry Ramsaye, *A Million and One Nights* (New York: Simon and Schuster, 1926), 1: 88, Edison spent "a total of precisely $24,118.04 in the motion picture business, between 1887 and April 1, 1894."

bard, my brother and I went to lunch. Returning at two o'clock, I locked the door on the inside and we all retired to the office in the rear to smoke and engage in general conversation. We had planned to have an especially elaborate dinner at Delmonico's, then flourishing on the south east corner of Broadway and Twenty-sixth Street, to celebrate the initiation of the Kinetoscope enterprise. From where I sat I could see the display window and the groups who stopped to gaze at the bust of Edison. And a brilliant idea occurred to me.

"Look here," I said, pointing towards the window, "Why shouldn't we make that crowd out there pay for our dinner tonight?"

They both looked and observed the group before the window as it dissolved and renewed itself.

"What's your scheme?" asked Lombard with a grin.

"Bert," I said to my brother, "you take charge of the machines. I'll sell the tickets and," turning to Lombard, "you stand near the door and act as a reception committee. We can run till six o'clock and by that time we ought to have dinner money."

We all thought it a good joke. Lombard stationed himself at the head of the row of machines, my brother stood ready to supervise them, and I unlocked and opened the door and then entered the ticket booth where printed tickets like those now in use were ready to be passed out. And then the procession started.

Drawing of the parlor at 1155 Broadway, New York. From William Kennedy Laurie Dickson and Antonia Dickson, *History of the Kinetograph, Kinetoscope and Kinetophonograph* (1895). The Dicksons wanted to give the effect of elegance and added palms, carpets, and waxed floors, none of which may have been there. It is also difficult to credit the genteel patronage shown here. Note the incandescent dragons at right and left and the bronzed bust of Edison in the foreground.

I wish now that I had recorded the name of the person to whom I sold the first ticket. I cannot recall even a face. I was kept too busy passing out tickets and taking in money. It was a good joke all right, but the joke was on us. If we had wanted to close the place at six o'clock it would have been necessary to engage a squad of policemen. We got no dinner. At one o'clock in the morning I locked the door and we went to an all-night restaurant to regale ourselves on broiled lobsters, enriched by the sum of about one hundred and twenty dollars.[4]

Since tickets to the Kinetoscope parlor cost twenty-five cents each, it would be fair to estimate that about 480 people saw the Kinetoscope during the debut. Tate's picture of congestion is thus, to put it mildly, somewhat overdrawn, and his "squad of police," hyperbole. By the end of May, though, the parlor was staying open on Sunday to accommodate the crowds.

In May, the syndicate opened a second parlor, in Chicago, at 148 State Street. Ten machines were installed at that address. In June, it installed the remaining five machines at a third parlor, at 946 Market Street in San Francisco, under the management of Peter Bacigalupi.

As additional Kinetoscopes were manufactured, the syndicate, in association with the Columbia Phonograph Company, opened a parlor in Atlantic City on the boardwalk and began to wholesale the machines to other concerns.

Within four months of its public debut, the Kinetoscope had thus captured the vaudeville public, whose taste had been catered to from the first by the Kinetoscope subjects comprising almost exclusively vaudeville turns.

Before the American motion picture had ended its first months of exhibition, it had also had its first brushes with the law. The earliest of these was with Senator James A. Bradley, the well known founder of Asbury Park, New Jersey. The *Newark Evening News* (July 17, 1894) printed the following account:

Senator Bradley has been shocked again, this time by the display of Carmencita's ankles in one of the series of pictures shown by the aid of "Wizard" Edison's latest invention, the kinetoscope. . . . Founder Bradley said he would have to have a look at the pictures to see if they were the proper views for the people sojourning in the twin cities by the sea to witness without causing blushes to mount to their cheeks. . . . on the night of the first day Founder Bradley and Mayor Ten Broeck went to the pavilion and proceeded to pass judgement on the pictures that Inventor Edison had so carefully prepared. The

4. Alfred O. Tate, *Edison's Open Door* (New York: E. P. Dutton, 1938), pp. 285–87.

first picture shown the Senator and Mayor was that of the barroom and fight, and it was decided that the supremacy of the law over the rougher element had a good moral tone. . . .

Then the exhibitor, pleased with his success as pleasing the powers that be [*sic*], thought that he would spring a great surprise upon the founder and the Mayor. He took a little tin can from a grip that he carried and placed a celluloid roll of pictures in the machine, at the same time remarking to the Senator, who had his eyes glued to the peep-hole: "Now you will be surprised, Senator. This is one of the best pictures in the collection."

And the Senator was surprised, but not in the way . . . intended. . . . The view was that of Carmencita in her famous butterfly dance, and the Senator watched the graceful gyrations of the lovely Spanish dancer with interest that was ill-concealed. But near the end of the series of pictures the Spanish beauty gives the least little bit of a kick, which raises her silken draperies so that her well-turned ankles peep out and there is a background of white lace.

That kick settled it. The Senator left the peep-hole with a stern look on his face. . . . While he was trying to collect his scattered thoughts sufficiently to give full swing to his wrath Mayor Ten Broeck applied his eye to the peephole. . . . The Mayor also was greatly shocked and agreed with the Founder that the picture was not fitted for the entertainment of the average summer boarder, and the exhibitor was told he would have to send for some new views or shut up shop.

The Latham Kinetoscope Parlor

After seeing the Kinetoscope machines in operation in the 1155 Broadway parlor and at the West Orange laboratory, Otway and Gray Latham made their first important contribution to Kinetoscope history. They proposed the exhibition of prizefight films in an enlarged machine. Such films would enforce a considerably longer period of action than the customary ten- or twenty-second films in the regulation Kinetoscope. And the perfectly obvious recourse—to enlarge the capacity of the camera and the Kinetoscope—was an important step forward in Kinetoscope fortunes.

The enlargement of the Kinetoscope appears to have involved little more than the addition of spools to the spool bank. If the motor was thought to have needed additional strength, perhaps the Kinetoscope motor ordered on June 1 was the answer. But whatever was needed was supplied, and on June 14, the first prizefight (between Jack Cushing and Mike Leonard) for the new 150-foot machine was filmed.

With Enoch Rector and Samuel J. Tilden, Jr., the Latham brothers formed the Kinetoscope Exhibition Company for the express purpose of exploiting special peepshows with prizefight pictures. In August 1894 they opened a parlor at 83 Nassau Street in downtown New York.

Each of the six special Kinetoscopes contained a round of the fight. A sign in the window and a barker at the door proclaimed the wonders of "the living pictures of the great prize fight."

Then on September 8, 1894, the anniversary of Corbett's fight with Sullivan (as a result of which he had become heavyweight champion of the world), Corbett met Pete Courtney, a Trenton heavyweight who was said to have "stood up against" Fitzsimmons for some rounds. They met in the Black Maria for six rounds of 1.16, 1.24, 1.12, 1.29, 1.23, and 50 seconds, appropriate lengths for the Latham enlarged Kinetoscope. This fight served to focus national attention on the Kinetoscope and the motion picture as no other event had yet done.

The Kinetoscope Company

By the summer of 1894, the commercial potential of the Kinetoscope had made an impression on Edison. He signed a contract on August 18, effective on September 1, assigning the exclusive domestic marketing rights to the Kinetoscope Company, formed by Norman C. Raff and Frank R. Gammon and having as stockholders the members of the syndicate earlier alluded to. The Kinetoscope Company thereupon went into business selling the territorial rights on the business of the Kinetoscopes, following the same merchandising pattern of the Edison phonograph. According to a Kinetoscope Company financial statement dated March 15, 1895, reprinted in Ramsaye,[5] stockholders invested $17,940 to capitalize the company, $10,000 of which may have been paid to Edison as a cash bonus in consideration of his signing the contract. One can surmise that the Kinetoscope Company assumed the production costs for Kinetoscope films and that it paid Edison a royalty for the use of the camera.

As far as production costs were concerned, a subject like the "oriental dance" of October 1, costing $25, was relatively expensive. The money paid for it was two and a half times the amount paid the lady fencers and equal to the amount paid a prominent vaudeville act like Walton and Slavin.

The first Raff and Gammon film catalog, dated 1895, listed over fifty titles, most of which sold for from $10 to $15 each.[6]

Some of the titles and accompanying advertising are:

5. *Million and One Nights*, 2: 835–37.
6. Ramsaye, *Million and One Nights*, 1: 837, dates the catalogue 1894, although *Professor Attila* was not produced until spring 1895. The list that follows comes from the Raff and Gammon catalogue reprinted in Ramsaye.

1. *Bertholdi*, The Marvellous Lady Contortionist
2. *Annie Oakley*, The "Little Sure Shot" of the "Wild West," Exhibition of Rifle Shooting at Glass Balls, etc.
3. *Finale of 1st Act Hoyt's "Milk White Flag."* Showing 34 Persons in Costume. The largest number ever shown as one subject in the Kinetoscope
4. *Robetta and Doretto.* Chinese Opium Den
5. *Professor Attilla.* The World Famous Athlete and Strong Man Trainer

The Kinetoscope Company by the end of 1894 had installed machines in over sixty parlors, department stores, drugstores, hotels, barrooms, and phonograph parlors in major cities throughout the country. A typical response to the machine was printed in the *Port Jervis Union* on December 14. The story sang the praises of the machine, its inventor, and the enterprising local citizen who had brought "the greatest marvel of the age" to town:

The Kinetoscope at the Clarendon Hotel
The greatest of modern inventions is on exhibition at the Clarendon Hotel in this village. We refer to Edison's far-famed and marvelous kinetoscope. This wonderful mechanism is worth going a thousand miles to see, but the enterprise of Mr. James Joyce, the proprietor of the Clarendon, has made that sacrifice of time and money unnecessary by purchasing one of the machines and placing it on exhibit at his hotel where it may be seen by everybody for the small price of ten cents. The scene which is displayed in Mr. Joyce's kinetoscope is that of three blacksmiths working at an anvil. It is perfectly natural and life-like in every respect. Mr. Joyce has another series representing two boxers in a four round contest which will be placed on exhibition in due time. Two years ago the pictorial representation of motion would have been scouted as the wildest of impossibilities, the crazy emanation of a disordered brain.

This seeming impossibility has been converted into a reality by the wizard genius of Edison. As we remarked before the greatest marvel of the age is now on exhibition at the Clarendon Hotel.

Net profits of the Kinetoscope Company's first month of operation (September 1 to October 1) came to $8,377.13. An interesting abstract of the company's September 1 to October 16, 1894, finances is in Harvard University's Baker Library collection. It lists office expenses, cash transactions, purchases from Edison, all film expenses in which the Hollands were involved, etc., and contains the following essential facts: (1) as of October 16, 1894, the Kinetoscope Company had paid Edison $7,940 for Kinetoscopes and $369.35 for film subjects; and (2) as of October 16, 1894, the Kinetoscope Company had received $15,878.56 from customers.

With the close of 1894 the Kinetoscope business was not working out in the way Raff and Gammon had expected. Business was good for the first six months after public exhibition began, but they did not enter the field until September, and although the fall sustained itself, the end of the year brought difficulties.

Maguire and Baucus

To market the Kinetoscope abroad, Edison contracted with a firm headed by Frank Z. Maguire and Joseph D. Baucus.

By September 10, 1894, according to corporation records in the New York City Hall of Records, Maguire and Baucus set up the Continental Commerce Company at their 44 Pine Street office, and laid plans for Kinetoscope parlor openings in London and in Paris.

A November 9 letter from Maguire at the London office of the Continental Commerce Company at 70 Oxford Street (which was also a Kinetoscope parlor) gives a first ominous sound of the foreign competition that Edison failed to inhibit.

George Georgiades and George Trajedes, having bought Kinetoscopes from the Holland brothers and having taken them to England, entered into an arrangement with Robert W. Paul to copy the Edison-manufactured Kinetoscope for European sale, free of Edison restriction.

So far as I have found, nothing was done to help Edison's European agents in their efforts to stop "the pirate who is infringing and making bogus Kinetoscopes in Europe." Edison may have felt that such attempts would have been useless, since there was no patent protection in England for the Kinetoscope.

I have found no documentary evidence that Edison's reason for not taking out foreign patents was a disinclination to waste money, though Ramsaye, with his ease at quoting conversation after the lapse of years, has remarked that this exchange took place: "How much will it cost?" Edison asked casually. "Oh, about $150." . . . "It isn't worth it!" . . .

Maguire and Baucus, long eager to become associated with Edison, had succeeded in doing so, and remained some months stormily connected. But when Kinetoscope sales fell off in the spring of 1895 their business fell off, too. For much of the crucial early period of the motion picture business in America, however, they worked hard to gain a foreign market for the Kinetoscope and its film. They gained this market, and have thus earned a place in this record.

The Kinetophone

For years Edison thought of many new products of his laboratory as being only "improvements" on his phonograph. The motion picture camera was no exception. The Edison encounter with the motion picture problem was only an urge to improve his beloved phonograph:

I am experimenting upon an instrument which does for the Eye what the phonograph does for the Ear, which is the recording and reproduction of things in motion, and in such a form as to be both Cheap practical and convenient.[7]

On June 16 the *Electrical World* stated the situation as of June 1894 neatly:

While the kineto-phonograph has not been brought to a sufficiently practical form for public exhibition, as has the kinetoscope, the experiments in the inventor's laboratory have been so successful that it is regarded only as a question of time, by those engaged in the work, when the apparatus will be perfected.

But such simultaneous talking and recording experiments were abandoned as fruitless, and it was decided to insert a slightly altered model of the phonograph in the Kinetoscope case, and use sound as nonsynchronized accompaniment to, rather than illustration of, action. This consisted in playing dance or band records while a performer was seen in the film, and attaching ear tubes for listening. Synchronization was abandoned. So far as speech or other nonmusical sounds were concerned they were never seriously considered.

Only forty-five Kinetophones were made and sold, and, like Kinetoscopes, are correspondingly rare.

The Kinetophone's claim to distinction was its compactness: the picture and the accompaniment were in the same box. The Kinetophone was thus an esthetic as well as a technical advance in the history of the motion picture.

Business Falls Off

By the close of 1894, it was evident that Kinetoscope business was not as successful as had been hoped. For one thing, there was competition between Raff and Gammon's business and the Latham group. For another, public enthusiasm had waned. At the close of business on March 15, 1895, the assets of the Kinetoscope Company totalled

7. From Edison's Motion Picture Caveat I, dated October 8, 1888, reproduced in Hendricks, *Edison Motion Picture Myth*, pp. 158–61.

$31,379.37. Against this there was balanced a "Dividend #1" for $5,000, a $25,794.31 gross profit on Kinetoscopes, $2,870.91 on films, and $602.40 on batteries. Operating expenses to date had been $7,283.37 and bills payable $6,305.87. Stock on hand—Kinetoscopes, batteries, etc.—was valued at $8,089.25. The stockholders were told on March 20: "Our business at this time is rather quiet, but we have considerable confidence in the Spring and Summer trade."

By fall 1895, business had deteriorated to the point where only seventeen Kinetoscopes were made in September, two in October, nine in November, and two in December. Raff and Gammon had been thinking about going into another business for some time, and now they were giving it additional thought. They were also trying to sell the Kinetoscope business, and were guilty of the usual colossal exaggerations in the process: "[The Kinetoscope business] has earned in the neighborhood of $50,000.00 . . . of net profits in but little over 1½ years . . ."

Then shortly before December 8, 1895, a momentous event occurred. A Washingtonian named Thomas Armat announced that he had a new projector. Raff and Gammon saw it and it worked.

C. Francis Jenkins had developed a workable projector, and Armat, a Washington real estate operator, had gotten an interest in the new machine and was now representing to Raff and Gammon and sundry that it was his own. Before the season was out, the Vitascope (as the new projector was to be called) had a sensational opening in New York, and the Kinetoscope, America's first commercially successful motion picture exhibitor, was delivered its death blow.

In the next few years fewer and fewer Kinetoscopes were manufactured. Laboratory records show that as of the time of the Vitascope debut on April 23, 1896, there had been 905 manufactured. As of December 8, 1899, there had been 973 Kinetoscopes manufactured. By the end of the century, after only six years of business, Kinetoscopes had all but passed from the American scene.

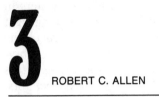

ROBERT C. ALLEN

The Movies in Vaudeville: Historical Context of the Movies as Popular Entertainment

Film historians tend to emphasize the "newness" of the cinema when dealing with its early history in America—the uniqueness of its power of visual representation, the curiosity early exhibitions provoked even among jaded New York reporters, the wonderment experienced by those first audiences at watching the Coney Island surf seeming to break in their laps. The early inventors and entrepreneurs themselves capitalized on the public's idolatry of scientific innovation and faith in technological progress by stressing the novelty of moving pictures. A new era of cultural and artistic history *does* begin with the innovation of the movies in the 1890s, but the "newness" of the movies should not obscure the fact that the initial uses of motion picture technology do not stand outside of history but are part of it. One important aspect of the historical context of the origins and development of the cinema in America is its relationship with other popular entertainment forms of the nineteenth and early twentieth centuries. It is only by examining the movies as one element in a historically specific show business system that we can understand what the cinema "meant" as a cultural phenomenon to its first audiences and that we can explain the early history of the motion picture industry. The most important show business institution in 1896 and the one crucial to the movies' early development was vaudeville.

57

The Historical Development of Vaudeville

The first movie audiences in America were vaudeville audiences. The Edison/Armat Vitascope, Lumière Cinématographe, Biograph, and Vitagraph all made their debuts in New York vaudeville theaters in the 1896–97 season as one twelve- to fifteen-minute "act" among eight or nine others on the vaudeville program. Until the advent of the nickelodeon around 1906, American vaudeville provided the embryonic motion picture industry with hundreds of exhibition outlets across the country and an audience of millions of middle-class spectators. Vaudeville ceased to be an important element of the American popular entertainment industry in the 1930s, and today most people know it only as a vague relic of show business's past. In 1896, however, it was the American entertainment form without equal in industrial power and popular appeal. By this time, says vaudeville historian Albert McLean, vaudeville "had outdistanced by many lengths its closest rival—the circus, minstrel shows, musical comedy—and was ready to bask in two decades of glory and wealth."[1]

American vaudeville has its immediate origins in the fragmentation of the American theater audience that occurred in the mid 1800s. In the early nineteenth century, theatrical performances appealed to a large and socioeconomically diverse audience. Consequently, stage entertainments often included not only a drama, but comic opera, farce, and/or an assortment of *entr'acte* "acts" as well: singers, dancers, jugglers, and even circus performers. As theater historian David Grimsted puts it, "The early nineteenth-century theatre had managed to present tragedy, comedy, opera, dance, farce, melodrama, and miscellany in proportions that, if they did not satisfy, at least attracted all classes."[2] Hence, what were later to become vaudeville "acts" were performed in "legitimate" theaters in the early 1800s.

By the 1850s, however, this heterogeneous theater audience began to break apart under pressure of increasing class consciousness brought about by industrialization. Theatergoers at the upper end of the socioeconomic scale became less and less tolerant of what they saw as the demonstrative and "uncivilized" behavior of the working-class occupants of the gallery seats.[3] Thus, as more and more working-class

---

1. Albert McLean, *American Vaudeville as Ritual* (Lexington: University of Kentucky Press, 1965), p. 21.

2. David Grimsted, *Melodrama Unveiled: American Theater and Culture, 1800–1850* (Chicago: University of Chicago Press, 1968), p. 74.

3. Ibid; Foster Rhea Dulles, *A History of Recreation* (New York: Appleton-Century-Crofts, 1965), p. 114.

people were added to the popular entertainment audience, theater managers devised entertainments to appeal primarily to them, while the "legitimate" theater increasingly became the domain of the upper crust.

Variety acts, which had once been a regular part of theatrical performance, were in the latter half of the century performed as part of these new popular entertainment forms. Both the blackface minstrel show, which arose in the 1840s, and burlesque, which became an autonomous form in the 1870s, used variety performers.

One of the most important new homes for "variety," as the sum of these peripatetic performers was then called, was the concert saloon. While they varied widely in elaborateness and quality from city to city and oftentimes within cities, the concert saloon was essentially a large barroom where customers were kept in a drinking mood by the antics of singers, dancers, jugglers, comics and circus performers. Particularly in New York, the concert saloons quickly acquired a reputation for sexual license both onstage and off. The humor of the comics was often salacious, and the barmaids, encouraged to drink with patrons, prompted one critic to call New York's Canterbury Music Hall "a truly diabolic form of shameless and avowed Bacchus and Phallus worship . . . a portico to the brothel."[4]

Some concert saloon managers realized that while erotic titillation might attract working-class male patrons, it discouraged the attendance of "respectable" (read: middle-class) men and women. Tony Pastor, a popular variety singer turned entrepreneur, removed drinking and smoking from his variety theater in New York in 1881. He also forbade suggestive humor onstage. Pastor was successful in attracting a more middle-class audience and in removing much of the taint of immorality from variety in New York.

Vaudeville also emerged from quite another context—one that did not include liquor or connotations of immorality. In Boston, where municipal ordinances prohibited the performance of theatrical entertainments where liquor was served, variety was performed primarily in dime museums. The dime museum emerged as a distinctive American entertainment form in the 1860s and 1870s, following a pattern set down by P. T. Barnum some years before. The museums, located in retail shopping and entertainment districts of large cities, contained at least two entertainment areas: a curio hall, where various curiosities and oddities (bearded ladies, dwarfs, two-headed chickens, etc.) were presented, and a theater for variety performances. George Odell, de-

4. *New York Evening Post*, January 2, 1862, in Harvard Theatre Collection.

scribing the dime museums of the New York Bowery in the 1880s, speaks of "the gaudy pictures of 'freaks' that lurked from the entrance, and the 'barkers' who invoked pedestrians to invest their dimes. . . . One passed from these congregated museum-pieces to a 'theatre' on the stage of which a wild, half-amateurish 'variety' aggregation entertained auditors who may never have heard of Edwin Booth or Miss Cushman."[5] As Odell suggests, the audience for these dime museums shows was predominantly working class; the admission charge for both curio hall and variety show was rarely more than ten cents. Unlike the concert saloon, however, the dime museum appealed to both men and women, and was entirely "respectable," if somewhat plebian in its offerings.

The transformation of variety from a supplementary entertainment presented in the context of burlesque, minstrel shows, concert saloons, and dime museums into vaudeville, an autonomous entertainment form, is illustrated by the early career of Boston showman Benjamin Franklin Keith.

Keith opened a dime museum on Boston's busy Washington Street in January 1883 with a single attraction, "Little Alice, the smallest baby ever born live."[6] In May, Keith separated the curio exhibition room from the performance area of the converted hatters store by adding a second-floor "Theatre Room," equipped with 123 chairs, a small elevated stage, and a hired organ. The first variety performance presented there included Professor Thomas Pryor, "the man with the talking hands"; Professor Angelo and his performing birds; and an Irish tenor.[7]

For the first two years of the museum's operation Keith did not fare especially well. He drew enough working-class passersby and day-tripping farm folk to keep his doors open, but by December 1884, Keith's partner threatened to pull out his financial backing in hopes of finding a more lucrative show business venture. What dissuaded him from doing so, and what marked the turning point in Keith's career, was the decision (probably not Keith's but his business manager's, Fred Kyle) to emphasize stage performance over freaks and to broaden the audience base of the enterprise to include more middle-class patrons. Around Christmas the museum began offering Sunday variety performances, which they called "sacred concerts" to get around municipal blue laws. As most other theatrical entertainments were suspended on Sundays, these concerts attracted what the *Boston Herald's* theatrical

5. George C. D. Odell, *Annals of the New York Stage*, (New York: Columbia University Press, 1949), 10:484
6. *Boston Herald*, January 14, 1883, p. 3.
7. *Boston Herald*, May 20, 1883, p. 11

correspondent called "a good class of people," many of whom would not have ventured in during the week to see a two-headed calf.[8] In the spring of 1885, the stage performance element of the museum was doubled when a dramatic company was added to the bill. The company's first vehicle was a parody of Gilbert and Sullivan's hugely successful operetta *H.M.S. Pinafore.*

Over the next decade (1885–95) Keith took a number of steps to broaden the audience base for his business. Cashing in on the tremendous vogue for light opera in the early 1880s, Keith offered popular works by Gilbert and Sullivan, Audran, and others for a quarter of the cost of the "high-class" Boston theaters. The freak show origins of Keith's theater were pushed into the background. In 1886, Keith moved his operation into a nearby theater, one of the most elegantly appointed in New England. Its debut under Keith's management was attended by the mayor and other civic dignitaries.[9]

Many middle-class patrons who were drawn to the Bijou for its "bargain" opera stayed for the variety performance as well. Keith took great pains to assure the variety portion of the program was of high quality and had nothing in it to offend the most delicate sensibilities. By the early 1890s, variety had overtaken opera as the primary attraction at Keith's, and the name "Keith's" had become synonymous with "high-class," "family" vaudeville.

Through years of trial-and-error experiments in attracting the largest show business audience, Keith and other show business entrepreneurs had discovered that, in the words of historian Ray Ginger, "in most American cities from 1877 to 1893, the entire social structure was moving upward rapidly."[10] Vaudeville managers like Keith in Boston, E. F. Proctor and Oscar Hammerstein, Jr., in New York, and Martin Beck in San Francisco were among the first show-business-men to base the appeal of their enterprises on the tastes and values of the ascendant American middle class. This class expanded eightfold between 1870 and 1910, and was "to form the basis of the mass consumer market."[11]

But while vaudeville's success was based on the support of the "white-collar" class, its ticket prices, presentational format, and physical environment enabled it to extend its appeal to both the more affluent above and the nearly middle class below. Ticket prices for vaudeville in the mid-1890s ranged from as little as fifteen cents for a matinee gallery seat to $1.25 for a box seat on Saturday night.

As variety became vaudeville in the 1880s, its presentational format

8. *Boston Herald*, December 28, 1884, p. 10.
9. *New York Clipper*, September 4, 1886, p. 388
10. Ray Ginger, *The Age of Excess* (New York: Macmillan, 1965), p. 93.
11. McLean, *American Vaudeville as Ritual*, p. 41.

came to be a series of ten- to twenty-minute "acts," sequentially performed, and contentually unrelated. In other words, there was no narrative or thematic connection between one act and another in vaudeville. The bill was chosen and arranged with an eye toward both balance and diversity among the acts—something for everyone. A typical vaudeville bill in 1895 might include a trained animal act, a slapstick comedy routine, a recitation of "inspirational" poetry, an Irish tenor, magic lantern slides of the wilds of Africa, a team of European acrobats, and a twenty-minute dramatic "playlet" performed by a Broadway star and his/her company. The department store clerk, bookkeeper, and doctor in the audience might not like the same things on the bill, but they almost certainly liked something. In 1896, the *Dramatic Mirror*, a respected theatrical trade paper, noted that vaudeville was "popular not only with the masses, but also with the well-to-do classes, who seem to prefer [it] to performance of a higher and more serious character. [Vaudeville houses] are frequented by well-dressed crowds, while many of the theatres devoted to dramatic work of a meritorious kind are neglected."[12]

One reason those "well-dressed crowds" felt so at home in a vaudeville theater was that the architectural and interior environments in which vaudeville was presented rivaled if not exceeded those of legitimate houses in comfort and ornateness. When E. F. Proctor's "Pleasure Palace" opened on Labor Day 1895, in New York, for example, it was quite unlike anything New York audiences had ever seen. Designed by the prestigious theatrical architectural firm McElfatrick and Sons, its Romanesque facade extended for two hundred feet along Fifty-eighth Street between Third and Lexington in Manhattan's Upper East Side shopping district. Inside there was not only a main auditorium, but also a roof garden, German café (in keeping with the neighborhood's German, middle-class character), and a smaller auditorium, the "Garden of Palms." In the basement was a library, barbershop, Turkish bath, and stands for the sale of flowers, books, and Turkish coffee. Once patrons had paid their admission fee, they could enjoy the continuous vaudeville in the main auditorium (shows ran nonstop from ten in the morning until midnight) or roof garden, take refreshments below in the German café, where still more vaudeville was presented, or use any of the Pleasure Palace's other facilities.[13] Hence, environmentally as well as presentationally, vaudeville offered something for everyone.

12. *Dramatic Mirror*, March 21, 1896, p. 14.
13. William H. Burkmire, *The Planning and Construction of American Theatres* (New York: John Wiley and Sons, 1896), pp. 34–37.

In short, what the vaudeville managers of the 1880s and 1890s endeavored to achieve was the reintegration of the American theatergoing audience—an audience that had been broken apart by the transformation of America from an agrarian to an industrial economy. Granted, this reintegrated audience did not include as much of the economic spectrum as did the theatrical audience of the 1820s—vaudeville was not a common pastime of the industrial aristocracy or the urban proletariat—but vaudeville's appeal did include a broad middle range of American entertainment seekers, and its audience was larger and more socioeconomically diverse than that of any other entertainment form during the industrial era—until, of course, the movies came along.

The Movies Enter Vaudeville

As has been pointed out, vaudeville served as the primary exhibition outlet for American films for roughly the first ten years of commercial screen exhibition (1896–1906). Two basic questions need to be asked if we are to understand the meaning of this film-historical fact. First, what prompted vaudeville managers to use motion pictures on their programs? And, conversely, what attracted early motion picture producers to vaudeville?

One of the hallmarks of vaudeville as an American popular entertainment form was its adoption of what were at the time modern business principles. Keith, for example, was not content, as his show business predecessors of a generation before might have been, to operate only his theater in Boston. Rather, he moved quickly to expand his brand of "family vaudeville" into other urban areas. In 1887, he opened a theater in Providence, and two years later built a huge new theater in Philadelphia. In 1893 he took over and completely remodeled the Union Square Theatre in New York. The establishment of circuits of theaters had several economic advantages: economies of scale came into play, certain management functions could be centralized, and acts could be booked simultaneously to play at several theaters in sequence, rather than at just one.

Keith was not the only vaudeville magnate to engage in circuit building in the late 1880s and 1890s, and by the 1890s intense competition had developed, particularly in the populous urban areas of the Northeast, for a share of the lucrative middle-class popular entertainment market. It was in New York, the theatrical capital of the United States, that competition among vaudeville interests was sharpest.

Keith's Union Square Theatre was one of several offering vaudeville in the fall of 1893. E. F. Proctor, while building a circuit of theaters

Keith's Union Square Theatre

in New England, also presented vaudeville at his Twenty-third Street Theatre. Pioneer vaudeville performer/manager Tony Pastor operated a theater just a few doors down from Keith's on Union Square. Koster and Bial's was offering "truly amazing aggregations" of vaudeville, as one chronicler has put it, at their Music Hall on Thirty-fourth Street.[14] Among these theaters and others soon to open there developed such competition for patronage and prestige that the theatrical trade press was soon speaking of a "vaudeville craze."

The touchstone in this vaudeville war was "novelty": which theater could outdo all the others in presenting the most "spectacular," "unusual," "expensive" acts. Proctor featured popular musical stars of concert stage and opera, and succeeded in attracting a "high-class" audience and considerable press attention. To counter, Keith drew the stars of the legitimate stage to his theater by offering them large salaries for performing vaudeville "playlets," condensed one-act dramas or comedies placed in the middle of the vaudeville bill. In April 1894, Tony Pastor orchestrated what New York theater historian George Odell has called "the greatest event for vaudeville for that season, or perhaps, for any season preceding" by importing the famous English music hall performer Vesta Tilley.[15]

The vaudeville boom in Manhattan continued unabated during the following theatrical season (1895–96), and competition intensified with

14. Odell, *Annals of the New York Stage*, 15: 681.
15. Ibid., p. 689.

the opening of two gigantic vaudeville houses, Proctor's Pleasure Palace and Oscar Hammerstein's Olympia. Among the novelties desperately sought by vaudeville managers to enhance their competitive positions were visual spectacles of one sort or another. The use of visual novelties in vaudeville was nothing new; vaudeville already had absorbed puppetry, shadowgraphy (the making of shadow pictures with the hands), magical illusions, and magic lantern presentations (what we would call slide shows). The previous season (1894–95), vaudeville patrons had made a "craze" of living pictures acts. Living pictures consisted of a proscenium-size picture frame enclosing a dark curtain. The curtain was drawn aside to reveal "actors" frozen in poses depicting a famous painting, piece of statuary, or mythical event. The backdrop would be either painted or projected by a magic lantern. After a minute or so for the audience to take in the spectacle, the curtain would be closed, allowing the actors to arrange themselves in another pose. While living pictures had been a part of American show business on and off since 1847, it was not until Oscar Hammerstein staged a program at Koster and Bial's in the spring of 1894 that they became a vaudeville "fad."[16] Keith soon added the Glass Brothers in "Roman statue impersonations," and at Proctor's living pictures proved to be one of the most popular attractions during the summer of 1894.[17]

By the beginning of the 1895–96 season, however, the vaudeville audience had tired of living pictures, and vaudeville managers scrambled for a visual novelty to top the living statuary in appeal. Feeling that he had exhausted the spectacular attractions in the United States, Keith departed in April 1896 for Europe to sign up performers and novelties that had not yet been seen in America. Hence he was not in New York for the debut of the most successful novelty—visual or otherwise—ever to appear in vaudeville: the moving pictures.

At the same time that vaudeville was expanding across the United States and rapidly becoming the preeminent American popular entertainment (1885–95), the motion picture camera and projector were being invented. The circumstances surrounding the invention of the Kinetograph camera and Kinetoscope peep-show viewer have been detailed elsewhere. Several points, however, deserve reiteration. The device Edison developed to exhibit motion picture films was not a screen projector, but a peep-show viewer. The Kinetoscope, as it was called, was placed in penny arcades, hotel lobbies, and other public places beginning in April 1894. In the fall of that year, two Ohio busi-

16. *New York Clipper*, May 19, 1894, p. 166.
17. *New York Clipper*, June 16, 1894, p. 230; June 20, p. 262.

nessmen, Frank R. Gammon and Norman C. Raff, were granted exclusive domestic rights to the Kinetoscope. Within a few months, however, it became apparent that the Kinetoscope would not realize huge profits. In May 1895, in fact, Raff wrote a business acquaintance, "The demand for Kinetoscopes [during 1895] had not been enough to even pay expenses of our company. . . . In fact our candid opinion is that the Kinetoscope business . . . will be a 'dead duck' after this season."[18]

Adding to Raff's and Gammon's woes was the news (which reached them in May 1895) that a workable camera-projector had been developed in France by Louis and Auguste Lumière, and that in America Woodville Latham and his sons Gray and Otway, former Kinetoscope exhibitors, were making films and had plans to project them. These plans were executed in August 1895 when the Latham projector, the Eidoloscope, headed the vaudeville bill at Chicago's Olympia Theatre. Advertised as the "Wonder of the Age," the Eidoloscope produced disappointing results and lasted but a week at the Olympia. The failure of the Eidoloscope can be attributed to an indistinct screen image caused by a technical imperfection in the projector. The Latham experiment was successful, however, in demonstrating the possibility of commercial screen projection and in suggesting the suitability of the movies as a vaudeville act.[19]

Raff and Gammon saw that screen projection was the only possible salvation for their rapidly failing business and urged Edison to bring out a projector before others could enter the American market. Edison, busy with myriad other projects, refused their entreaties, and Raff and Gammon offered what was left of their Kinetoscope business for sale. In December 1895, they learned of a projector that had been demonstrated at an exposition in Atlanta in September and which represented a considerable technical advance over the Eidoloscope. Raff and Gammon immediately entered into negotiations with the machine's inventors, Francis Jenkins and Thomas Armat, and in January 1896 purchased exclusive marketing rights to the projector. Raff and Gammon also arranged for the Edison Manufacturing Works to build the projector, called the Vitascope, and to supply them with films.[20]

Raff and Gammon bought the rights to the Vitascope not so they could exhibit films themselves, but so they could sell the right to do so to others. They devised a plan for selling Vitascope franchises in

18. Raff to Thomas R. Lombard, May 31, 1895, Raff and Gammon Collection, Baker Library, Harvard University. Hereafter referred to as Raff and Gammon Collection.

19. Raff to T. Lombard, May 31, 1895, Raff and Gammon Collection; *Chicago Tribune*, August 27, 1895, p. 5; September 1, p. 36.

20. Raff to Mssrs. Daniel and Armat, January 17, 1896, Raff and Gammon Collection.

the United States and Canada in large territorial blocks (mostly state by state). An entrepreneur could buy the rights to the Vitascope for a state or group of states, and then lease projectors (for $25–$50 per month) and buy Edison films to show on them. The exhibition format was left entirely up to the rights purchasers. They also had the right, as Raff and Gammon repeatedly pointed out in their promotional materials, to subdivide and subfranchise the territory.[21]

It is clear from their correspondence and business papers that Raff and Gammon were interested in selling rights, not exhibiting films. It is also clear that they did not see vaudeville as the primary market for the Vitascope—in fact their territorial franchise scheme militated against the use of the Vitascope as a vaudeville act. As we have seen, in 1896 vaudeville was in the midst of a period of interstate circuit building—the circuits ignoring the political boundaries the Raff and Gammon marketing plan was based upon. Most vaudeville acts were booked from New York along a route of theaters for a dozen or more weeks at a time, covering as many states. For the Vitascope to be booked in a similar manner would require a dozen separate agreements with the rights holders for each state. In addition, the films for the Vitascope were to be sold, not rented. With a stock of only fifteen to twenty films at the beginning of the marketing campaign, Raff and Gammon were not in a position to supply vaudeville managers with the regular change of program their audiences had come to expect.

Why then was the premiere of the Vitascope held at a vaudeville theater, New York's Koster and Bial's Music Hall? In the early spring, while organizing their franchise marketing scheme, Raff and Gammon learned that several vaudeville managers were attempting to secure the Lumière Cinématographe for their theaters. Realizing the adverse publicity value of having another machine open in New York ahead of the Vitascope and the potential economic advantages of a combination between vaudeville and foreign motion picture interests, Raff wrote to Abraham Bial on April 7 offering him the use of the Vitascope "at a largely reduced compensation," out of a consideration for "a certain benefit to us from your advertising, etc."[22]

The success of the Vitascope debut at Koster and Bial's on April 23, 1896, has been well documented; what is less well understood is that the very success of the machine in vaudeville proved to be the beginning of the end for Raff and Gammon. The Koster and Bial

21. Raff and Gammon to M. Hendersholt, April 4, 1896, Raff and Gammon Collection.
22. Raff and Gammon to Thomas Armat, March 21, 1896; Raff and Gammon to A. Bial, April 7, 1896, Raff and Gammon Collection.

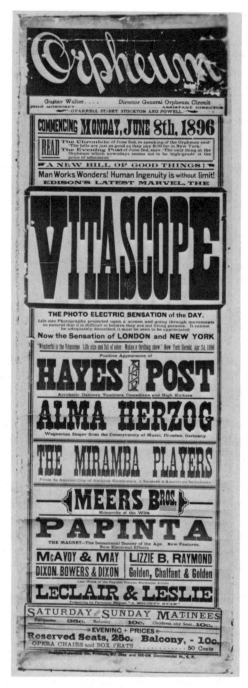

The Vitascope receives top billing at San Francisco's Orpheum

engagement of the Vitascope and its attendant publicity were a signal
to vaudeville managers in New York and across the country that here
was the greatest vaudeville novelty of all times. The "latest invention"
of the hero of the age, Thomas Edison (Edison had nothing to do with
the invention of the Vitascope, yet it was marketed as if he alone had
developed screen projection), could easily be adapted to form a
vaudeville act. Because of the marketing scheme of Raff and Gammon
and their general unpreparedness for full-scale exploitation of the Vitascope, however, they were not only unable to satisfy the demands
of vaudeville managers spawned by the Koster and Bial exhibition,
but they also left the American vaudeville market open to competitors
who could service them.

The first company to do so was that of the Lumières. The Cinématographe made its American debut at Keith's Union Square Theatre
in June to great public and press acclaim. Despite a sweltering heat
wave in New York, the Cinématographe produced a doubling of ticket
sales at Keith's over previous weeks.[23] Soon after the Cinématographe's
premiere, Keith contracted with the Lumières for movie service in all
four of his theaters, dropping the Vitascope at his Boston theaters,
where it had been running since May 18.

Keith's decision was for Raff and Gammon, but as the competitive
advantages of the Cinématographe over the Vitascope as a vaudeville
attraction became more apparent over the summer and fall of 1896,
more and more vaudeville managers engaged the Lumière machine.
In addition to the unsuitability of the marketing plan for the Vitascope,
Raff and Gammon had several other problems. First, since the Edison
Company manufactured both projectors and films, Raff and Gammon
had no direct control over production schedules for either, and the
April 23 marketing "kickoff" for the Vitascope campaign soon proved
to be premature. Delivery dates of Vitascopes to the territorial agents
had to be postponed.[24] The Cinématographe, on the other hand, was
marketed in the United States by employees of the Lumières. From
an office in New York, a Lumière representative made arrangements
for an "operator" (a Lumière employee) to provide a vaudeville theater
with projector, technician, and films. Some twenty-one of these operators were touring vaudeville theaters within the first six months of
the Cinématographe's New York opening. The New York representative was not a rights speculator but an agent for the Cinématographe;
he provided vaudeville managers with a self-contained act that could
travel an interstate circuit as easily as an acrobat or juggler.

23. *Dramatic Mirror*, July 4, 1896, p. 17; July 11, p. 17; July 18, p. 17.
24. A. F. Rieser to Raff and Gammon, May 8, 1896, Raff and Gammon Collection.

Another key difference between the Vitascope and Cinématographe was their respective sources of power. The Vitascope was driven by an electric motor designed to be run off the theater's electrical system. All the early Vitascopes contained direct current motors. Unfortunately, as the Vitascope rights holders quickly discovered, the current and voltage of the Vitascope were frequently incompatible with the municipal power grid in a particular city. One Vitascope showman wrote Raff and Gammon in September, "If the small towns of the continent are to be worked, a radical change will have to be made in the construction of the machines so that exhibitions can be utterly independent of electric power companies."[25] The Cinématographe was hand cranked, and hence needed no external power supply to run the projector. Illumination could be supplied by limelight or another non-electrical means.[26]

The Edison camera, the Kinetograph, was also powered by electricity. Thus, most early Edison Vitascope subjects were shot at the "Black Maria" studio outside the Edison works in West Orange, New Jersey. Few of the early Edison subjects were different from the vaudeville turn Kinetoscope films of 1894–95. The portability of the Lumière camera, on the other hand, enabled them to extend the contents of their films in two important directions. First, they would offer their patrons scenes of exotic locales and important personages from around the world. Lumière cameramen were sent to film the coronation of the czar, Venice as seen from a moving gondola, and Trafalgar Square. These travel films were so popular that in August 1896, Raff and Gammon resorted to having the English agents for the Vitascope surreptitiously purchase Lumière films shot in Russia, Italy, and France for use with the Vitascope in the United States.[27] Also, with camera/projector and printer in one, the Lumière operators could take, develop, and show films at vaudeville theaters while on tour. These "local actualities," as the Lumières called them, gave that company a decided competitive edge. A Vitascope licensee wrote Raff and Gammon in late September 1896, "We have been to Chicago and seen the Cinématographe and if you people don't get a move on you and get some new films we are going to be left in the hole. They have a far better selection of film and have a man in Chicago making new films of places of interest in Chicago."[28]

25. A. Holland to Raff, September 9, 1896, Raff and Gammon Collection.

26. Georges Sadoul, *Louis Lumière* (Paris: Editions Seghers, 1964), p. 67.

27. Raff and Gammon to Maguire and Baucus, August 26, 1896, Raff and Gammon Collection.

28. Hixom and Wollam to Raff and Gammon, September 28, 1896, Raff and Gammon Collection.

The Raff and Gammon Vitascope business was hopelessly handicapped as a provider of vaudeville attractions. Its demise was hastened, however, not only by the Lumières but by Edison himself. In the fall of 1896, the Edison laboratories finally developed its own projector, the Projecting Kinetoscope. Rather than marketing it through Raff and Gammon, however, Edison offered it for outright sale with no territorial restrictions for $350—one-tenth of what some rights holders had paid for the privilege of leasing the Vitascope for $25–$35 per week. Oddly enough, the Lumières left the American market not much later (May 1897), apparently out of fear of patent litigation from Edison.[29] But by the end of the 1896–97 vaudeville season a pattern of commercial exhibition for the motion picture in America had been established that would last for the next decade.

The attraction of the movies to vaudeville and vice versa should now be clear. To American vaudeville managers, the movies provided the latest visual novelty, a possible trump card in the very serious game of intracity vaudeville rivalry. Indeed, the movies proved to be the most successful single act ever to appear in vaudeville. For the early motion picture companies, vaudeville provided a weekly audience of a million or more entertainment seekers and a tradition of visual novelties. The format of vaudeville with its brief, autonomous, "modular" acts was well suited to the presentation of a program of short films. With hundreds of elaborately appointed vaudeville theaters from coast to coast available as exhibition outlets, early movie producers did not have to invest precious capital of their own in theater building—a major consideration at a time when a successful patent litigation could put a production company out of business overnight. It is, then, no wonder that the movies were primarily known as vaudeville acts in the years between 1896 and the advent of the nickelodeon movie theater around 1906.

The "Chaser" Issue

Some film historians have seen the decade 1896–1906 as the low point of early American cinema history. Early film producers, they argue, did not keep pace with the vaudeville audience's taste for novelty and innovation, and within a year or two after their introduction into vaudeville, the movies sank to the level of "chaser" on the vaudeville program—an act so unpopular that managers used it to clear the

29. Sadoul, *Louis Lumière*, pp. 135–36.

house when another group of patrons were waiting to take their seats.[30] Much of the blame for the use of films as "chasers" in vaudeville is placed on the lack of appeal of "simple" nonnarrative filmic subjects. In Jowett's words, vaudeville audiences "soon tired of having to watch the same type over and over again."[31]

A closer examination of the use of films in vaudeville between 1897 and 1903 reveals much more public support for the movies than the above accounts would suggest and casts considerable doubt on the "chaser theory." While it is true that the first American filmmakers were more business-minded showmen than self-conscious artists, their work was much more popular and diverse than is usually given credit. Films of the 1896–1903 era were not all simple reproductions of some object in motion; many were carefully planned and executed to speak to a particular interest of the vaudeville audience.

The Biograph Company continued for several years the practice begun by the Lumières of making local actualities. In 1897, for example, Biograph cameras recorded the Atlantic City fire department answering a mock call; a huge steam shovel in Philadelphia digging the Reading subway; and the Yale football team at practice, among other local phenomena. It is not difficult to explain public fascination with these seemingly simple images—we experience it today every time we view home movies. When local actualities were presented in vaudeville theaters they were often the featured attraction.[32]

The cinema has the power to make us both view the familiar afresh and become familiar with places and people we've never seen off the screen. The latter use of the cinema was exploited by early filmmakers through travel films. Building on a vaudeville tradition of using magic lantern slides to show faraway places, early filmmakers showed vaudeville audiences motion pictures of life in exotic locales. The travelogue was one of the most frequently made types of film between 1896 and 1903.[33]

30. Joseph North, *The Early Development of the Motion Picture, 1887–1909* (New York: Arno, 1973), pp. 184–85; Lewis Jacobs, *The Rise of the American Film* (New York: Teachers College Press, 1939), p. 5; Gerald Mast, *A Short History of the Movies* (New York: Pegasus Books, 1971), p. 44; Garth Jowett, *Film: The Democratic Art* (Boston: Little, Brown, 1975), p. 29.

31. Jowett, *Film*, p. 29.

32. *Atlantic City Press*, August 16, 1897; *Philadelphia North American*, September 9, 1897; *New Haven News*, December 8, 1897; *New York Clipper*, September 11, 1897, p. 456; all quoted in Kemp R. Niver, ed., *Biograph Bulletins, 1896–1908* (Los Angeles: Locare Research Group, 1971).

33. Richard Arlo Sanderson, "A Historical Study of the Development of American Motion Picture Content and Technique prior to 1904," Ph.D. diss., University of Southern California, 1961, p. 111.

A different sort of travel film also provoked considerable excitement among vaudeville audiences. This type of film was designed to produce an almost physiological thrill in audiences by giving the illusion either of being in the path of a moving object or of actually moving through space. A contemporary reviewer describes Biograph's *Haverstraw Tunnel*, a film made in the summer of 1897 at a railroad tunnel in upstate New York:

The scene was the passage of the famed Haverstraw tunnel, and a panoramic effect was gained by placing the photographic apparatus on the front of a flat car, which in turn was run in front of the engine. All the curves of the road were shown as the rails slip by the beautiful scenery on each side, and the tunnel entrance is shown up to the very instant that the train plunged into its dark recess. There is a moment of darkness, and then a faint ray of light is seen glimmering ahead, which gradually enlargens [*sic*], and the picture again shows the roadbed and surrounding scenery on the other side with a mountain in the distance.[34]

It is easy to underestimate the appeal of such a film. What would seem to us an incredibly pedestrian viewing experience prompted notice in at least thirty-seven newspaper articles in the United States and England during the fall of 1897.[35]

The most enduring and popular use of the movies prior to 1903 was the news film—brief glimpses of current events that prefigure both the later movie newsreels and television news coverage of today. The clearest indication of the success of the movie's news-gathering function came during the Spanish-American War of 1898. During the winter of 1898, Americans were subjected to a constant barrage of public invective, especially from the Hearst newspapers, against supposed Spanish repression in Cuba. On February 15, the American battleship *Maine* was sunk in Havana harbor, and the outcry for retribution grew even more shrill. By the time war against Spain was declared on April 25, American foreign policy was the focus of tremendous public debate. War fever continued even after the nation's ten-week military adventure in Cuba, as the theater of war shifted from the Caribbean to the Pacific where by 1899, 75,000 American troops were fighting both Spanish troops and Philippine nationalists for control of the islands.[36] Filmmakers capitalized on the war hysteria by providing vaudeville audiences with images of American troops leaving for the front, camp life in Cuba, the triumphal return of the war's heroes, Admiral Dewey and Teddy Roosevelt.

34. *Boston Journal*, September 21, 1897, quoted in Niver, *Biograph Bulletins*, p. 28.
35. Niver, *Biograph Bulletins*, pp. 27–36.
36. Barbara Tuchman, *The Proud Tower*, (New York: Macmillan, 1962), p. 163.

Among the first of the films to exploit the war was one of the *Maine* prior to its sinking, which was shown the first week of March 1898 at Proctor's Pleasure Palace in New York. The theater's patrons stood and cheered as the brief shot flickered by.[37] By the end of April, the movies were, in the words of the theatrical trade paper, the *Dramatic Mirror*, "the biggest sensation in the program" at vaudeville theaters.[38] The movies became so identified with war news that Edison renamed his Projecting Kinetoscope the "Wargraph" for the duration of the hostilities. While the Biograph Company sent a cameraman to Cuba for footage, other filmmakers found less expensive ways to "cover" the war. Albert Smith and J. Stuart Blackton, founders of the newly formed Vitagraph Film Company, staged a patriotic tableau on a Manhattan rooftop.

Blackton and I rigged up a miniature flagpole and attached a Spanish flag at the top, and the Stars and Stripes at the base. The camera took in the full length of the flagstaff as Blackton's bare arm reached in from the underside of the picture, seized the Spanish flag, and ripped it off. Then pulling on a cord, he raised the Stars and Stripes to the top of the staff.

After Admiral Dewey's defeat of the Spanish fleet at Manila Bay, Blackton "recreated" the event using cutout photographs of warships floating on a tabletop sea, with his wife providing special effects with cigarette smoke.[39] By mid June, military subjects were being shown in vaudeville theaters across the country, and the proportion of American motion picture output devoted to news had increased from 2.2 percent the year before to 35.2 percent.[40]

As with the travelogue, the use of the motion picture as visual newspaper was not without precedent in vaudeville. The hallmark of vaudeville was novelty, and managers like Oscar Hammerstein made a specialty of turning famous and notorious public figures into vaudeville attractions. As vaudeville historian Frederick Snyder puts it, "the times of the day found a literal voice in vaudeville in the appearance of contemporary celebrities and political commentators on the stage."[41] Sports figures, explorers, murderers, and even a miner who had survived a cave-in translated newspaper headlines into vaudeville acts.

Although American military involvement in the Philippines contin-

37. *Dramatic Mirror*, March 5, 1898, p. 18.

38. *Dramatic Mirror*, April 23, 1898, p. 18.

39. Albert E. Smith and Phil Koury, *Two Reels and a Crank* (Garden City, N.Y.: Doubleday, 1952), pp. 54–67.

40. Sanderson, "Historical Study," p. 111.

41. Frederick E. Snyder, "American Vaudeville: Theatre in a Package," Ph.D. diss. Yale University, 1970, p. 118.

ued until 1901, public interest in the Spanish-American War waned by 1900. But the motion picture continued to have a news function in vaudeville. Whenever cameramen could capture scenes of war, natural catastrophe, or the activities of notable world figures, the motion picture "act" was prominently featured on vaudeville programs. Obviously, however, filmmakers could not rely upon matters of topical interest for motion picture subjects if movies were to be a regular vaudeville attraction. If the popularity of the movies was tied directly to public interest in the events, places, or people represented on the screen, then filmmakers would be at the mercy of exigencies beyond their control or prediction. As Thomas Armat wrote to Thomas Edison in November 1901,

The problem with the motion picture business is that as things are now business runs by spurts. If there happens to be a yacht race or the assassination of a president there is a good run on films for a few months. Then it drops down to a demand that keeps the large force busy for about one-fourth of the time while much money is wasted on experimenting with costly subjects that the public will not buy.[42]

As we have seen, the popularity of the movies in vaudeville in the years after 1897 did not sink to the scandalously low level that the term "chaser" suggests. However, heavy reliance by producers on the topical or news film was sure to produce huge vacillation in public interest in these films.

Dramatic and Comic Narrative Films

In the early 1900s two new types of film were shown in vaudeville; both were big hits with the public. Narrative films, particularly comic narratives, had become staples in the vaudeville movie act by the 1902–3 vaudeville season. In 1903 comedies comprised nearly 30 percent of total American film output. Dramatic narrative films began to appear on vaudeville programs in 1903, but the growth of this genre was considerably slower than that of the comedy.[43] Some dramatic films, however, proved to be extremely popular. When first shown at Keith's in Boston on July 13, 1903, Edwin S. Porter's *Life of an American Fireman* "went as big as anything on the bill." At the same theater

42. Armat to Edison, November 15, 1901, Edison Archives, Edison National Historic Site, West Orange, New Jersey.
43. According to copyright records, in 1902 the dramatic film comprised only 4 percent of total American output, 6 percent in 1903, 7 percent in 1904, and 15 percent in 1905.

Porter's *The Great Train Robbery* was "applauded as much as any act of the show."[44]

Even more popular with vaudeville audiences were the magical trick films of French magician-filmmaker Georges Méliès, which began to appear in American vaudeville in the fall of 1902. Méliès' films such as *A Trip to the Moon, Cinderella, Little Red Riding Hood,* and *Fairyland,* replete with magical transformations, spectres, and spectacular stage effects, were so popular at Keith vaudeville theaters that they were often held over for several weeks. The manager of Chase's Theatre in Washington reported to Keith that *A Trip to the Moon* was "one of the features of the bill and the best film what has ever been produced."[45]

Unfortunately for Méliès, his films were so popular and yet so difficult to imitate (because of the scrupulous planning they required) that some American producers simply duplicated copies of his works and exhibited them as their own. Comic and dramatic narrative films were much easier to make, and they helped to solve the problem Armat alluded to in the use of films in vaudeville. By substituting the fictional events of the narrative film for the actual events of the topical subject, producers regained some of the control over motion picture subject matter and production situation they did not have with the topical film. The comedy and drama obviated the need to rely entirely upon news events or exotic locales for motion picture subject matter. Scenic requirements of these films could be made to conform to the limitations of the movie studio and its environs. With a few canvas drops and some furniture, the Biograph studio on Fourteenth Street in Manhattan could become a middle-class parlor in the morning and a Chinese opium den in the afternoon. Production schedules were dependent upon the speed with which new comic or dramatic situations could be thought up and shot, and not, as with the topical film, on the speed with which a cameraman could be transported halfway across the continent and back again. This is not to say, however, that narrative films replaced travelogues and news films on vaudeville programs. Between 1904 and 1906, documentary films accounted for nearly half (42 percent) of total American film production.

The Nickelodeon

The relationship between vaudeville and film, and, indeed, the nature and scope of the film industry as a whole were changed dramat-

44. Managers' Reports, Keith Theatre, Boston, July 12, January 4, 1903, Keith-Albee Collection, University of Iowa Library, Iowa City.

45. Keith Report Books, 1902–3, Keith-Albee Collection, University of Iowa.

ically by the rise of the nickelodeon during the period 1905–8. Vaudeville was not the only exhibition outlet for motion pictures in the late 1890s and early 1900s. Some traveling showmen bought projectors and films and displayed them in tents, at fairs, and in rented halls. Other entrepreneurs rented storefronts and showed movies there, as had several of the Raff and Gammon licensees, or partitioned off the back of penny arcades for screen projection. These "nickelodeons," as the small, converted storefront movie theaters were called, offered a brief program of pictures for a small admission fee—usually no more than five cents. The number of nickelodeons across the United States in the early 1900s is difficult, if not impossible, to determine, but from the business papers of early film companies and theatrical trade papers, it does not appear that as motion picture outlets they were nearly so important as vaudeville theaters until around 1906. Within a very short time, however, nickelodeons began springing up in urban areas all over the United States. By October 1906, *Variety*'s Chicago correspondent reported that there were one hundred nickelodeons in that city alone. In early 1907, *Variety* estimated the total number of five-cent movie theaters in the United States at 2,500, but warned "they are increasing so rapidly that positive figures are unobtainable." In May 1907, the new motion picture trade paper, *Moving Picture World*, claimed there were 2,500–3,500 nickelodeons in the country.[46]

What caused this nickelodeon "explosion"—a period during which the number of motion picture exhibition outlets increased from 300–400 (mostly vaudeville theaters) to 3,500 or more? Much more research is needed before we can satisfactorally answer this important question, but we can identify several possible causal factors. First, the nickelodeon explosion was part of a more general expansion in popularly priced entertainment forms between 1905 and 1908. The number of vaudeville theaters increased during this period. Burlesque reached its apex around 1906 when more than seventy burlesque companies were employed. Immediately preceeding the rise of the nickelodeon was the equally rapid development of a cheaper form of vaudeville show, variously called "ten-cent," "nickel," or "family" vaudeville.[47]

This more general theatrical expansion, aimed at working and lower-middle-class Americans, was spurred by an almost unbroken spurt of economic prosperity in the United States between 1894 and 1907. As

46. "Will Close Five-Cent Theatres," *Variety*, October 6, 1906, p. 5; "Film Notes," *Variety*, January 26, 1907, p. 140; "The Nickelodeon," *Moving Picture World*, May 4, 1907, p. 140.

47. "Vaudeville, 1906–07," *Variety*, March 10, 1906, p. 4; May 12, 1906, p. 5; "Ten Cent Theatres in the West," *Dramatic Mirror*, June 3, 1905, p. 16.

this prosperity, in the form of shorter working hours and real wage increases, filtered down through the economy the bottom layer of potential popular entertainment patrons expanded greatly.

By 1908, the vaudeville theater was no longer the primary exhibition outlet for motion pictures. Vaudeville theaters continued to use one or two reels of film (12–24 minutes) in their programs as one act, but the nickelodeons were providing producers a market for more than ten times the amount of film being used in vaudeville.

One of the effects of the nickelodeon explosion seems to have been the rapid ascendancy of the narrative film and the consequent eclipsing of the documentary. As I have noted, the dramatic and comic film enabled producers to obviate the logistical and scheduling problems caused by their reliance upon topical subjects. With the burgeoning market for films caused by the growth of the nickelodeon (many of which changed programs three or more times weekly), producers felt an even greater need to regularize production. Copyright records suggest that the narrative film enabled producers to turn out large numbers of films on a regular, predictable basis. In 1907, comedy and dramatic films comprised 67 percent of total American production; documentary categories the remaining 33 percent. In 1908, the production of narrative forms increased to 96 percent of total output, and, in 1909, 97 percent.[48]

Small-Time Vaudeville

With the remarkable growth of the nickelodeon after 1906, vaudeville ceased to be the primary American exhibition outlet for motion pictures—although many middle-class Americans continued to know the movies as a vaudeville act, not as a nickelodeon attraction. But the relationship between film and vaudeville does not end in 1906; rather it is quickly renewed.

The ease with which a nickelodeon could be established in a busy, big-city shopping area—one needed only a storefront, projector, chairs, and films—caused the number of nickelodeons in some cities to reach saturation levels within a very short time. As early as April 1907, for example, the *Variety* correspondent in Atlanta was reporting "the Electric Theater [nickelodeon] craze is being overdone here."[49] Nickelodeon owners found they had to compete vigorously for patronage and

---

48. Sebastian de Grazia, *Of Time, Work, and Leisure* (Garden City, N.Y.: Anchor Books, 1964), p. 419.
49. *Variety*, April 6, 1907, p. 18.

search frantically for something to differentiate their theater from their rivals'. Adding more films to the program was difficult because of a scarcity of new films—American producers were simply unable to keep up with the demand for movies spawned by the nickelodeon explosion.[50]

Many nickelodeon managers turned to vaudeville acts as a means of making their establishments more appealing and of stretching out their programs without the addition of more films. *Moving Picture World* noted in November 1907, "a vaudeville act or two. . . has been a means of doubling the receipts of many picture theatres."[51]

Some entrepreneurs discovered that by moving their nickelodeon operations into converted legitimate theaters or by building large-capacity theaters especially for movie-vaudeville shows, they could increase their seating capacity, patronage, *and* ticket prices. Many people, particularly middle-class patrons, were willing to pay an additional nickel or dime to see a show in more comfortable and genteel surroundings than those offered by the typical nickelodeon.[52] By 1909, a hybrid entertainment form had emerged. Small-time vaudeville, as it was called to distinguish it from the "big-time" vaudeville of Keith, Proctor, et al., combined several reels of film with an abbreviated vaudeville program. The environment of the small-time was a large ornately decorated theater—the kind of place in which a middle-class patron would feel at home. But the admission scale, ten to fifty cents, also accommodated the former nickelodeon devotee.

Small-time vaudeville was so successful that by August 1909, *Moving Picture World* was predicting that the "store-room" shows would soon disappear, their place being taken by "especially built theatres, seating five hundred to a thousand, most of them giving a mixed bill of vaudeville and motion pictures."[53] Small-time vaudeville also produced a new generation of motion picture entrepreneurs, the first to build fortunes on movie exhibition. William Fox purchased his first movie theater in 1906 in Brooklyn. By 1910 he operated a circuit of fourteen small-time theaters in the New York area. Marcus Loew, another New Yorker, went from penny arcades to nickelodeons to small-time vaudeville. By 1909, he had one of the largest circuits of small-time theaters in the country—twelve theaters in New York City alone. It was with

50. Record, at 1499, *United States v. Motion Picture Patents Company,* 225 F. 800 (E.D. Pa. 1915).
51. *Moving Picture World*, November 16, 1907, p. 593.
52. *Moving Picture World*, August 29, 1908, p. 152.
53. *Moving Picture World*, August 28, 1909, p. 280.

the profits from small-time vaudeville that both Fox and Loew were later able to expand into motion picture production and distribution.

Conclusions

The relationship between vaudeville and film does not end with the rise of small-time vaudeville; the two industries remained closely tied into the 1930s. But this brief examination of their interaction until 1910 and of the emergence of vaudeville in the late nineteenth century allows us to see the importance of vaudeville to the early history of American cinema both in terms of specific industrial practices and in terms of the more general model vaudeville provided as a popular entertainment form.

Perhaps the most obvious effect of the movies' use as a vaudeville attraction was that the nascent motion picture industry was provided with a huge middle-class audience, probably numbering around a million persons each week. The failure of the Raff and Gammon scheme for marketing the Vitascope demonstrates the rapidity with which motion picture exhibitions spread across the United States and Canada; by the beginning of the 1896–97 vaudeville season, in the fall of 1896, motion pictures were stellar attractions in dozens of vaudeville theaters. Contrary to the view held by some film historians that this early interaction between film and vaudeville represents a low point in film history, vaudeville can be seen as providing the infant film industry with stability at a crucial time in its development. Motion picture production was thrown into turmoil in 1897 by the first of many patent infringement suits brought by Thomas Edison against his competitors. The patent wars continued for more than a decade, but the years 1897–1902 were ones of particular uncertainty for American producers. Fortunately, the producers did not have to tie up their resources in exhibition, since they had but to provide films and projectors to vaudeville theaters, not the exhibition site itself.

The use of film in vaudeville almost certainly conditioned the types of films made during the first decade of screen exhibition. Trick films, comic and dramatic narratives, travelogues, and news films all had predecessors in vaudeville visual novelties. Moreover, film producers catered to the interests and expectations of vaudeville audiences much more than film historians have acknowledged. The films shown in vaudeville in the years after 1896 were not brief snippets which vaudeville audiences invariably found dull, but, as the success of travel subjects and news films of the Spanish-American War demonstrate, quite varied in their appeal.

Despite the fact that many working-class persons were added to the motion picture audience during the nickelodeon "explosion" between 1906 and 1908, vaudeville's connection with the film industry does not end there. Rather, the two entertainment forms were quickly re-united in small-time vaudeville. It is small-time vaudeville that provides an important link between the storefront theaters and the picture palaces of the 1910s.

Thus, vaudeville provided a model in a general sense for the motion picture industry. First, vaudeville provided the film industry with a marketing model. Vaudeville was the first American popular entertainment form to recognize the fact that the American social class system was not rigid and fixed but fluid and, further, that the largest possible audience could be obtained by appealing to middle-class interests and tastes, while removing attendance barriers to audience groups both above and below. The ticket price range of vaudeville was such that most Americans could afford to attend at least occasionally, but the environment and accoutrements of vaudeville rivaled those of the most luxurious legitimate theaters, and hence, appealed to the more affluent patron.

Vaudeville provided film with a presentational model. The vaudeville program was modular rather than ensemble, each act serving a specific function on the bill and appealing to specific audience interests. Even with the advent of the feature film, movie theaters used this model—first, of course, in the inclusion of vaudeville acts on the bill, but even after vaudeville's demise movie theaters continued to run not only the feature attraction, but comic shorts, travelogues, newsreels, and other cinematic "acts."

Finally, vaudeville provided the film industry with a model of industrial organization. Long before the Motion Picture Patents Company and the "major" and "minor" studios of the 1920s and 1930s, vaudeville demonstrated the advantages to a show business enterprise of both vertical and horizontal integration. By forming circuits of theaters, vaudeville managers were able to secure the services of performers under long-term contracts. When competition among circuits threatened to drive up the salaries of performers, Keith and the other vaudeville magnates formed a trade organization to divide up territories among the circuits to prevent competition and "regularize" salaries. This organization (the Vaudeville Managers Association) further controlled the industry and performers by setting up its own booking agency (United Booking Offices) through which every performer had to arrange his or her route, and to which 5 percent of his/her salary had to be paid as a "booking fee." The vaudeville performer became an employee of a large industrial combine and was totally dependent upon it for the opportunity to practice his craft. Such trade and labor practices were not lost upon the early movie moguls.

RUSSELL MERRITT

Nickelodeon Theaters, 1905–1914: Building an Audience for the Movies

In its short heyday, the nickelodeon theater was a pioneer movie house, a get-rich-quick scheme, and a national institution that was quickly turned into a state of mind. Its golden age began in 1905 and lasted scarcely nine years, but during that time it provided the movies their first permanent home, established a durable pattern for nation-wide distribution, and—most important—built for the motion picture an audience that would continue to support it for another forty years. Even after its decline, it survived in popular legend as a monument to movies in their age of innocence: the theater primeval that showed movies to an unspoiled and uninhibited audience of children and poor people. How the nickelodeon was portrayed in movie histories, how sharply it was believed to contrast with the postwar years of the movie palace and expensive studio production, is evident in the terms used to identify it. James Agee, for example, writing from the perspective of his own childhood, turned the nickelodeon into a populist shrine, cataloguing its delights in the style of a Whitman poem. He recalled "the barefaced honky-tonk and the waltzes by Waldteufel, slammed out in a mechanical piano; the searing redolence of peanuts and de-mirep perfumery, tobacco and feet, and sweat; the laughter of unrespectable people having a hell of a fine time, laughter as violent and steady and deafening as standing under a waterfall."[1]

More recently, Edward Wagenknecht in *The Movies in the Age of Innocence* painted an unblemished portrait of Chicago nickelodeons as they appeared to him in his youth, a portrait more detailed than Agee's but no less affectionate. As other histories have shown, the nickelodeon era has been the epoch of film history easiest to sentimentalize.[2]

Theatre Unique on 14th St., New York City

1. James Agee, "Comedy's Greatest Era," *Life*, September 3, 1949, reprinted in Agee, *Agee on Film: Reviews and Comments* (New York: Mc Dowell, Obolensky, 1958) pp.6–7.

2. See the introduction to Edward Wagenknecht, *The Movies in the Age of Innocence* (Norman: University of Oklahoma Press, 1962). Other accounts of the nickelodeon can be found in the standard film histories of the silent era: Terry Ramsaye, *A Million and One Nights* (New York: Simon and Schuster, 1926); Benjamin B. Hampton, *A History of the Movies* (New York: Covici, Friede, 1931); Lewis Jacobs, *The Rise of the American*

Few historians would claim that his nostalgic view of the nickelodeon is pure fabrication. Even those who discount the innocence of the prewar years might find it hard to resist the allure of the vintage five-cent theater. The novelty was real, the appeal obvious, the popularity undeniable. But this portrait, two-dimensional and static, is patently incomplete. The purpose of my inquiry is to define that theater more sharply and, more important, to satisfy two nagging questions. First, how did theater operators finally attract the middle-class audiences so reluctant to peer inside the early movie houses? Second, when did the industry itself, originally supported and paid for by the working class, determine to abandon that audience for the broader, more affluent white-collar trade?

No one, to my mind, has answered these questions satisfactorily, least of all those historians who suppose that the middle-class moviegoer got started with features and World War I. By 1914, the middle-class audiences were, in fact, already in the theaters waiting for the spectacles and movie stars that would follow. The seduction of the affluent occurred, I will contend, in the preceding years, between 1905 and 1912, in precisely that theater supposedly reserved for the blue-collar workers.

"Democracy's Theater"

The nickelodeon itself was a small, uncomfortable makeshift theater, usually a converted dance hall, restaurant, pawnshop, or cigar store, made over to look like a vaudeville emporium. Outside, large lurid posters pasted into the theater windows announced the playbill for the day. For ten cents—nickelodeons were seldom a nickel—the early moviegoer went inside and saw a miscellany of brief adventure, comedy, or fantasy films that lasted about an hour. Movies were always the main attraction, but enterprising managers followed the formula created by William Fox and Marcus Loew in 1906, and enhanced their programs with sing-alongs, inexpensive vaudeville acts, and illustrated lectures.

Film (New York: Teacher's College Press, 1939); Kenneth Macgowan, *Behind the Screen* (New York: Delacorte, 1965). But these sources seldom go beyond a cursory description of nickelodeon exhibition. There is no American equivalent to the detailed study of British film exhibition found in Rachael Low, *The History of the British Film, 1906–1914* (London: Allen & Unwin, 1949). The nickelodeon era, for the most part, has been ignored in the current literature of film history, but two important studies have recently been made available: Garth Jowett, "Media Power and Social Control: The Motion Picture in America, 1896–1936" (Ph.D. diss., University of Pennsylvania, 1972); and Joseph H. North, *The Early Development of the Motion Picture, 1887–1909* (New York: Arno, 1973), a reprint of a 1949 doctoral dissertation. Important primary documents and contemporary descriptions of nickelodeons have been collected in George Pratt, *Spellbound in Darkness* (Greenwich, Conn: New York Graphic Society, 1973).

The show customarily began with a song, usually one of the popular ballads of the day—"Sunbonnet Sue," "Bicycle Built for Two," "The Way of the Cross," or perhaps "Down in Jungle Town"—or else a patriotic anthem. Hand-colored magic lantern slides illustrated scenes from the song and a final slide projecting the lyrics encouraged the audience to join in the chorus. The manager might then present his first movie, or bring on a live comedian, a dog act, or perhaps a ventriloquist; or else he might go straight to his most prestigious act: the illustrated lecture. Nickelodeon lecturing became for a time a lucrative business, with increasing care taken to recruit authentic "professors," preachers, and world travelers with exotic stories to tell. For the movies, a large black projector—a Vitascope Special or a Selig Polyscope if the theater were licensed—was set up in the back, either closed off in a separate room or enclosed inside a metal booth. Potted palms and gilded marquees were less essential, but popular, ways of adding "class" to the common show.

By 1910, when the nickelodeon craze had reached its peak, more than ten thousand of these theaters had sprung up across the country, creating demands for between one hundred and two hundred reels of film every week. "On one street in Harlem," wrote a *Harper's Weekly* journalist, "there are as many as five nickelodeons to a block, each one capable of showing to one thousand people an hour. They run from early morning until midnight, and their megaphones are barking before the milkman has made his rounds."[3]

If we may believe the most conservative estimates, by 1910 nickelodeons were attracting some 26 million Americans every week, a little less than 20 percent of the national population. In New York City alone, between 1.2 and 1.6 million people (or more than 25 percent of the city's population) attended movies weekly, while in Chicago, the nickelodeon craze reached 0.9 million persons (an astonishing 43 percent of that city's population). National gross receipts for that year totaled no less than $91 million.[4]

The lion's share of that audience came from the ghetto, a fact that nickelodeon commentators never tired of discovering. The label used over and over again by journalists commenting on the five-cent movie

3. Barton Currie, "The Nickel Madness," *Harper's Weekly* 51 (August 24, 1907): 1246. The theater statistic is from Hampton, *History of the Movies*, p. 58. *Moving Picture World* (hereafter to be referred to as *MPW*), December 5, 1908, p. 523, quotes an unnamed article by Glenmore Davis in *Success Magazine* claiming six thousand nickelodeon theaters in existence across the country in 1908.

4. "Moving Pictures and the National Character," *Review of Reviews* 42 (September 1910): 315–20. Michael Davis, *The Exploitation of Pleasure* (New York: Russell Sage Foundation, 1911), pp. 8–9, is slightly more conservative. He estimates that 900,000 New Yorkers attended movies weekly in 1910.

house, usually written with a delighted air of having discovered the exact phrase, was "democracy's theater." A Russell Sage survey revealed that in 1911, 78 percent of the New York audience consisted of members "from the working class" at a time when the worker had been effectively disenfranchised from the older arts. "You cannot go to any one of the picture shows in New York," wrote Mary Vorse for the *Outlook* in 1911, "without blessing the moving picture book that has brought so much into the lives of the people who work."[5] "They will stay as long as the slums stay," wrote Joseph Medill Patterson. "For in the slums they are the fittest, and must survive."[6]

The custodians of the poor took for granted that movies were made for the immigrant, the working man, children, and the unemployed. "If Tolstoi were alive today," the *Nation* claimed, "it is not unlikely that he would find in the movies a close approximation to his ideal of art. The Russian's ultimate test of a work of art was to appeal to the untutored but unspoiled peasant ... the man who is today the nickel theater's most faithful customer." Municipal censorship of one-reelers was under constant attack by civic groups who called it class legislation, calculated to impose harsher standards on the poor man's theater than on that of his wealthier counterpart. Many welfare agencies, seeing the nickelodeon's appeal, followed the lead of Jane Addams at Hull House and used movies as part of educational and rehabilitation programs for the poor. The United States Navy, which at that time enlisted over five thousand immigrants per year, began in September 1910 to manufacture a series of recruiting films that played in nickel theaters throughout New York and in recruiting stations across the country.[7]

5. Mary H. Vorse, "Some Picture Show Audiences," *Outlook* 97 (June 24, 1911): 442. The Russell Sage survey is in Davis, *Exploitation of Pleasure* pp. 8–9. Garth S. Jowett, "The First Motion Picture Audiences," *Journal of Popular Film* 3 (Winter 1974): 39–54, quotes reports from social workers in Boston, Pittsburgh, and Homestead, N.Y., which also demonstrate the preponderance of working-class people in nickelodeons.

6. Joseph Medill Patterson, "The Nickelodeons: The Poor Man's Elementary Course in the Drama," *Saturday Evening Post* 180 (November 23, 1907): 38.

7. "A Democratic Art," *Nation* 97 (August 28, 1913): 193. For the anticensorship arguments, see "Un-American Innovation," *Independent* 86 (May 22, 1916): 265; "The White Slave Films," *Outlook* 106 (January 17, 1914): 121; and U.S., Congress, House, Commitee on Education, *Hearings, A Bill to Establish a Federal Motion Picture Commission*, 63d Cong., 2d sess., 1914, 2, pt. 2: 197–98. For navy recruiting films, see "Moving Pictures and the National Character,"p. 317; and Arthur Dutton, "Where Will the Navy Get Its Men?" *Overland Monthly* 53 (March 1909): 233. The statistic for 1910 immigrant naval recruits, a figure representing 12 percent of all naval recruits, comes from "The Report of the Bureau of Navigation," *The Annual Reports of the Navy Department, 1911* (Washington, D.C.: U.S. Government Printing Office, 1911), p. 305.

To that audience, movies meant escape in the most literal sense. Amidst the famous horrors of overcrowded tenement barracks, sweatshop work that paid coolie wages, and continuing typhoid epidemics, movies were treated as a simple refuge—a variant of the racetrack, the lottery, the fortune-teller's, or the saloon. Movies offered the worker a chance to come in from the cold and sit in the dark.

He was not particularly interested in art—or in acculturation. When D. W. Griffith started directing at the Biograph studios in 1908, his most important competition came from heavyweight prize fights and French chase comedies. Films such as these demanded no great power of concentration; the comedy plots—if they can be called that—were simple and direct, uncomplicated by subtleties of character delineation or subplot. The fast-moving action usually rose in a straight line from one climax to another, resolving itself in a beating or an explosion. No one who leafs through the pages of *Moving Picture World* and reads the plot descriptions of new films can overlook the incredible stress on violent slapstick and knockabout humor. Vitagraph's *When Casey Joined the Lodge*, reviewed July 4, 1908, features two Irishmen at a lodge initiation fighting each other with bricks and tossing sticks of dynamite under lodge members, cops, and innocent bystanders. Three weeks later, Vitagraph followed up with *A Policeman's Dream* in which two boys awaken a daydreaming patrolman by setting him on fire.[8] Neither the policeman nor the boys are beaten, an exceptional outcome. In other comedies for July, 1908: a political candidate has dirt and paste thrown over him, then his wife beats him;[9] partygoers fall into a young man's room when a floor caves in and they are beaten;[10] a gentleman "endeavoring to be polite to all mankind" inadvertently wreaks havoc on a town through his awkwardness and receives "many an unkind blow and boost for his trouble."[11]

Later historians would claim that such films worked as part of the immigrant's acculturation to American society, entertaining guides to the values and customs of the new world. But, in fact, few movies of this period performed such a task. For all their popularity with American audiences, they revealed little about America. Indeed, the majority of them were produced in France: exports of the Pathé Frères Company, who single-handedly released more films in the United States

8. *MPW*, July 25, 1908.
9. *The Candidate*, Pathé-Frères.
10. *Noisy Neighbors*, Pathé-Frères.
11. *Too Polite*, Gaumont.

than the major American companies combined; *film trucs* from Georges Méliès; slapsticks and travelogues from Gaumont.[12] But even when they came from the United States, one-reelers seldom worked with the particularities of American stereotypes, landscapes, or social themes. Rather, the films were offered as spectacles that induced the onlooker to marvel at the unnatural, whether in the form of a slapstick chase, a comic dream, a wondrous adventure, or a historic disaster. Those who saw them did not learn much; it was rather the act of going to the movies that mattered most. By perceiving what was general in their own situation, immigrants could identify with others who shared that situation. Like the societies, the schools, and the press, the nickelodeon was a means through which the immigrants came to know each other.

Exhibitors Aspire to the Middle Class

But this portrait of the nickelodeon audience, like the portrait of the nickelodeon theater, is misleading because it is drastically incomplete. The five-cent theater may have been widely regarded as the working man's pastime, but the less frequently reported fact was that the theater catered to him through necessity, not through choice. The blue-collar worker and his family may have supported the nickelodeon. The scandal was that no one connected with the movies much wanted his support—least of all the immigrant film exhibitors who were working their way out of the slums with their theaters. The exhibitors' abiding complaint against nickelodeon audiences—voiced with monotonous regularity in trade journals, personal correspondence, and in congressional testimony—was that moviegoers as a group lacked "class." A movie customer wearing a suit or an officer's military uniform was a momentous event; a car parked outside the theater was reason for a letter to *Moving Picture World*. By contrast, certain kinds of workers were discouraged and occasionally even banned from the movies. An

12. Cf. "What Is An American Subject?" *MPW*, January 22, 1910, p. 82, in which an anonymous reporter counted forty films released the previous week, half of which, he noted, were produced abroad. Of those produced in the United States, he counted no more than ten with American themes, "that is, themes 'racy of the soil' and distinctly American in characterization, scenery, and surroundings. The other subjects were such as might have been made in Europe." The report concluded "that the American subject, even after a year's plugging away, does not seem to have secured a predominant part in the film program of the moving picture theaters of the United States."

Comet Theatre, New York City

extreme example is the case of the shantytown nickelodeons at the
Portsmouth and Charlestown naval shipyards that favored military
officers with reduced admission prices while they refused admittance
to enlisted men. Writing sympathetically of this policy, a trade editor
reasoned: "One way to keep trouble out of a theater is not to admit
it in the first place. . . . The roughhouse germ is present to a greater
or less extent in every squad of sailors. The manager has reason to
know in advance whether they are friend or foe, and therefore one
cannot blame a manager in Portsmouth or any other place for using
his discretionary powers, whether it involves the livery of Uncle Sam
or Johnny Bull or anybody else."[13]

Not until the secretary of the navy threatened a naval boycott of all
nickelodeons in Boston and Portsmouth and Governor Eugene Foss
of Massachusetts signed a bill prohibiting discrimination against military recruits in places of amusement did the operators relent and agree

13. *MPW*, June 3, 1911. The shipyard nickelodeon quarrel was reported in *MPW*,
June 3, 1911, p. 1246, and June 10, 1911, p. 1321.

to take back the enlisted men. Meanwhile, big-city nickelodeon operators were cautioned against earning reputations as ethnic theaters, and given three ground rules for attracting a "mixed" house: operators should avoid booking programs heavily slanted toward any one nationality, avoid ethnic vaudeville acts, and eliminate all songs in foreign languages.[14] Embarrassed by their regulars, ambitious managers constantly sought ways to attract the larger, middle-class family trade currently the domain of vaudeville and the legitimate stage.

The thirst for affluence and respectability helps explain the curious locations of the original nickelodeons. Even when they were working-class entertainment, the most important nickelodeons were seldom built in the worker's community or in his shopping area. Instead, they customarily opened in business districts on the outer edge of the slums, fringing white-collar shopping centers, accessible to blue-collar audiences but even closer to middle-class trade.

Boston as a Case Study

A study of nickelodeon theaters in Boston will dramatize this phenomenon. While not necessarily a "typical" American metropolis, Boston offers a useful and convenient case study of a city that early established itself as a large and important East Coast film market. Thanks to its reputation as a theatrical crossroads (it had already become illustrious as a testing ground for New York plays, as the headquarters for B. F. Keith's vast chain of vaudeville theaters, and as the town that introduced continuous performances), its nickelodeons were reported and analyzed in unusually full detail throughout the trade press. As a consequence of these reports and the constant attention given nickel theaters by local social workers, church groups, and the city political machine, Boston provides one of the most influential and best-documented collections of nickel theaters in the nation.

Boston's movie theaters were strung out along three strategic locations in the city's downtown shopping area. At one end seven theaters clustered around Scollay Square and Bowdoin Square—nearer expensive Beacon Hill townhouses than Italian and Irish tenements in the North End. This was Boston's original nickelodeon district, where in 1905 Mark Mitchell built Boston's first movie theater—the Theater Comique at 14 Tremont Row—and where Boston's first movie theater chain set up its main offices.

From this point, the nickelodeons were stretched out in a long line

14. *Motography* 7 (February 1912): 24.

along Tremont Row and Washington Street, where they operated side by side with the downtown B. F. Keith vaudeville houses and the major legitimate theaters. Although Washington Street commanded the highest building rentals in the city ($30,000 per year for lots ranging from twenty-five hundred to four thousand square feet), the steady flow of business made this the most prosperous and the most fiercely competitive theater district in town. Shoppers coming out of C. F. Hovey's or Meyer Jonasson department stores could select from the Bijou Dream, the Pastime, the Gaiety, or the Park without having to cross the street. The Unique and the New Washington were one block away from the "elegantly appointed" Bradford Hotel and down two blocks from the stylish Hotel Touraine. Two nearby legitimate theaters—the Shubert at 265 Tremont and the Boston at 539 Washington— were constantly complaining to the New York *Dramatic Mirror* about the cheap competition luring away their theater regulars. To meet the threat, the Shuberts began to show ten-cent movies at their Globe Theatre during the slow 1909 summer months—an unheard-of practice among Boston's expensive legitimate houses and one that created a bitter nickelodeon price war at the Eliot Street corner of Washington Street.

Past the hotel district and Chinatown, down in the city's skid row, Boston's third group of nickel theaters were coiled around Castle Square and lower Washington Street where, run-down and poorly tended, they fit in with the gray South End landscape. Sandwiched in with local saloons, pool halls, and cheap hotels, these honky-tonk theaters were the principal targets of municipal reformers and the mayor's office. The working-class family trade avoided these theaters for the most part, hopscotching over them to attend the more remote but better-tended theaters in the north. Mainly, the Castle Square theaters were taken over by the flotsam residing in the dives along Tremont and Shawmut, or the transients from the local boardinghouses. Several of the nickelodeons were used as sleeping quarters; police raids on the Paradise and Dreamland were considered commonplace.[15]

As a location, the South End was notorious as a graveyard for nickelodeons, where, despite cheap building rates, the theaters suffered the poorest record of survival. Theaters in the district changed hands constantly; successful operators to the north regarded the area as a quarantine zone, preferring to expand their own movie empires to the

15. The notable exception to this rule was the Idle Hour at Castle Square. For blacks living in the Kirkland Street neighborhood, the Idle Hour was virtually the only theater in town that permitted an integrated audience on the main floor. In fall 1910, a group of local black businessmen bought the theater outright and operated it (renamed the Pekin) for a year before it went out of business.

suburbs and the wealthy Back Bay. The idea of constructing quality nickelodeons in the South End, if it was considered, was never tried. Even further from consideration was the possibility of building theaters further south, in the South Roxbury shopping districts or near the South End factories where the catchpenny exhibits, smaller vaudeville houses, and cheaper legitimate theaters stood. Like the North End, the South End was strictly off-limits for ambitious nickelodeon entrepreneurs.

What makes this statistic startling is that there was a group of theaters in the South End neighborhood which demonstrated that catering to the ethnic family trade was economically feasible. These were the South End's three venerable first-class theaters—the Columbia, the Castle Square, and the Grand Opera House—which started showing movies to fill in the days when they weren't presenting live melodrama and variety acts, and ended by switching over to movies altogether. All three theaters demonstrated that it was possible to cater to ethnic, working-class clienteles and maintain a successful business. The Columbia, for instance, at 978 Washington Street, the South End's largest and most elaborate melodrama house in 1895, was alternating between movies and vaudeville shows ten years later, and worked on the Irish family trade by featuring ethnic acts and Irish songs between films. The Castle Square, home of the South End's single opera company in the 1890's, became a movie house in 1907, but continued with Yiddish plays in the summer for the growing Jewish community along the Pleasant Street neighborhood and North Roxbury. These were precisely the paths the new theater operators chose not to follow. The new movie theaters were determined to crash the new neighborhoods and stay out of the old ones.

Their horizons were sharply limited: the choleric opposition to the garish common shows prevented them from entering the suburbs, nor could managers obtain licenses to build in the wealthy Back Bay area or along Boylston Street. The exclusive Back Bay shopping thoroughfares on Newbury Street or Huntington Avenue were also off-limits. But even so, the most aggressive movie managers were pushing in these directions too, and by the beginning of World War I, even these cultural havens gave in to the onslaught of the dread Philistines.[16]

16. Theater addresses are found in the Boston *City Directory, 1910*; for remarks on the nickelodeons I have depended on the New England and Boston correspondent's report to *MPW* which began October 1, 1910, and continued more or less weekly throughout 1910 and 1911. See also Frederic E. Hayes, "Amusements," in *The City Wilderness*, ed. Robert A. Woods (Boston, 1899), for South End theaters. Donald C. King, "From Museum to Multi-Cinema," *Marquee* 6 (Third Quarter 1974): 5–22, provides a useful, lavishly illustrated history of Boston theaters from 1794 to the present.

The pattern was similar in New York City, Chicago, Philadelphia, and St. Louis.[17] Exhibitors and producers anxious to cover their investment made no major effort to advance the industry through the working class itself. Few if any films stressed ethnic ties, few chronicled adventures of immigrants—their arrival in the New World, life in tenements, or, until D. W. Griffith appeared, working conditions in shops or factories.[18] No one with prominent ethnic features was permitted in leading roles; the American blue-eyed, brown-haired beauty was required, whether playing an Italian street singer, a Sioux Indian maiden, a Spanish duenna, or a Gibson Girl. In the midst of a strange new audience, the industry clung to the vestiges of the safe old theatrical patterns.

The old world, in this case, meant the vaudeville theater. Vaudeville, decaying since 1900 in the wake of the nickelodeon's popularity, had in effect provided the unwilling model of exhibition for the energetic new rival. Just as, five years later, movie exhibitors would use the legitimate theater as a guide to learn how to exhibit feature films, so, in 1908, nickelodeon owners preyed on vaudeville houses for methods of exhibiting movie shorts. We have already seen one example of this: the nickelodeon locations we have described were determined less by proximity to their clientele than by proximity to the beaten path of vaudeville houses. Many nickelodeons were in fact converted vaudeville houses; others were built next door to them. When managers decided on mixing their short films with an illustrated song, a guest lecture, and variety acts, they were merely plotting variations of the vaudeville routine. Vaudeville's continuous performances and gingerbread architecture were also readily adapted to the new shows. Most important, when exhibitors imagined the ideal audience, they usually

17. For a description of New York nickelodeon locales, see Russell Merritt, "The Impact of D. W. Griffith's Moving Pictures from 1908 to 1914 on Contemporary American Culture" (Ph.D. diss., Harvard University, 1970), pp. 106–08. Contemporary accounts of nickelodeons in Philadelphia and Chicago may be found in the pages of *MPW*. Although no systematic, updated study of these theaters has yet been made, provocative essays on individual theaters and surveys of city theater history may be found in the pages of *Marquee*, the journal of the Theatre Historical Society.

18. For example, a detailed search through *MPW* film synopses published from March 9, 1907, the magazine's inaugural issue, through December 1908 revealed that of 1,056 American-produced films reviewed, a total of eight films specifically concerned the immigrant or the poor: *The Life of a Bootblack* (Essanay, 1907); *Smuggling Chinese into the U.S.A.* (Goodfellow, 1908); *The Eviction* (Selig, 1908); *The Little Match Girl* (Goodfellow, 1908); *The Rag-Picker's Christmas* (Goodfellow, 1908); *New Way to Pay Old Debts* (Lubin, 1908); *Old Isaacs, the Pawnbroker* (Biograph, 1908); and *A Mother's Crime* (Vitagraph, 1908). The two largest French companies—Pathé-Frères and Gaumont—contributed another seven films on the subject.

thought of the vaudeville audience—a cross section of urban and suburban American life. They preferred this old audience to the new, unfashionable audience that had discovered them. To follow the guidelines set up by vaudeville houses became the path of least resistance.

Luring the Family Trade

The problem was how to lure that affluent family trade, so near and yet so far. The answer, at times conscious but more frequently a matter of convenience, was through the New American Woman and her children. If few professional men would as yet, by 1908, consider taking their families to the nickelodeon, the woman on a shopping break, or children out from school, provided the ideal lifeline to the affluent bourgeoisie. Statistically, women and children numbered only 30 percent of the New York audience, even less than that during performances after 8 P.M., but they commanded the special attention of both the industry and its censors. In a trade hungry for respectability, the

Maintaining audience decorum

middle class woman was respectability incarnate. Her very presence in the theater refuted the vituperative accusations lodged against the common show's corrupting vulgarity.[19]

Theaters spared few efforts to woo her. Soon after Boston's Theatre Premier established the policy of giving free admission tickets to women for prenoon shows, the Olympic reacted by charging women and children half fare at all screenings and thereby set the precedent that virtually all the major Boston nickelodeons adopted. By the end of 1910, women and children were charged half fare in all of Philadelphia's nickelodeons while, with growing frequency, exhibitors' complaints about the movies took the form of gallant defense of the female's tender sensibilities.[20]

Women were no less venerated in the nickelodeon movies themselves. Original screenplays in particular reveal a preoccupation with women's stories. Female protagonists far outnumber males, dauntless whether combatting New York gangsters, savage Indians, oversized mashers, or "the other woman." In the best genteel tradition, audiences were spared scenes of debauchery and criminal acts; the outdated moral code of the Victorian era that required vice to be punished and virtue rewarded became an inflexible law throughout this period. "Saloons and other places of evil repute should not be shown or else shown so briefly [as] to carry small effect," warned an early screenwriter's manual. "Keep away from the atmosphere of crime and debauchery and avoid as much as possible the showing of fights, burglaries, or any other infraction of the laws. The juvenile mind is receptive and observant ... If you write clean and decent stories, you do not have to bother about the Board of Censorship. If you want to revel in crime and bloodshed you must be careful to keep the actions of your character within the unwritten law.[21]

The pressure to keep movies "popular" was thus offset by pressure to keep them "respectable." Film producers drew heavily on the literary lions—Zola, Daudet, Poe, Tolstoi, Dumas, Hugo, Twain, de Maupassant, and Shakespeare—for film "classics." At times, the tension between the two conflicting impulses yielded bizarre results. When in 1910 Vitagraph filmed Sophocles' *Elektra* in one reel, exhibitors were told to "BILL IT LIKE A CIRCUS—IT WILL DRAW BIGGER CROWDS THAN

19. For the attendance of women and children, see Committee on Education, *Hearings*, pp. 121–22. For more information on children's attendance, see *Survey* 35 (May 9, 1914).

20. Price reduction reported in *MPW*, January 21, 1911, p. 146 and March 4, 1911, p. 728. For Philadelphia's statistic, *MPW*, June 3, 1911, p. 1245.

21. Epes W. Sargent, *Technique of the Photoplay* (New York: Moving Picture World, 1913), pp. 133–34.

ANY FILM YOU HAVE EVER HAD."[22] In Louis B. Mayer's Orpheum, Pathé's *Passion Play*, "the life of Christ from the Annunciation to the Ascension in twenty-seven beautiful scenes," was followed the next week by *Bluebeard, the Man with Many Wives*. Both were successful.[23]

But the more sophisticated and plausible lures came from the new blood drifting into the film production studios. Although he came from a family and circumstances profoundly different from those of the theater manager, the early director and writer of dramatic films had aspirations of his own that also worked to attract the white-collar worker to the movies. Griffith's own perspective—and in this regard he is typical of such film directors as Sidney Olcott, Allan Dwan, and Frank Powell—was one of a bourgeois, native-born theater man, proud of his old American stock, comfortably living on a family income ranging from $800 to $1,000 per month when the national average was under $600 per year.[24] Filmmakers told the stories they knew best, and inevitably, as they became articulate, their films revealed their own middle-class background. Their perpetual quest for acceptance among their own kind provided special pressure to return to figures and motives approved by the guardians of popular culture.

For better or for worse, the five-cent movie, like the theater that housed it, was effectively dropping out of the hands of its original audience. For the immigrant, movies were becoming more and more part of his assimilation into American life. Moviemakers, like the nickelodeon operators, were out to satisfy the broader, more demanding audience of their peers.

By fall 1913, the concerted effort had finally begun to pay dividends. As the comfortless thrills of watching movies on wooden chairs gave way to deluxe motion picture theaters and as movies lengthened from one to four reels, the movie clientele imperceptibly began to change. Journalists wrote continually—and critically—about the "new public" and the "quicker-minded audience" that had discovered the movies and forsaken the theater and library. Residential neighborhoods, militant in their resistance to nickelodeons in 1908, gradually softened to the pressure of aggressive entrepreneurs and permitted construction of nickelodeons on their main streets. The climax came in June 1914, when a ten-reel version of Giovanni Pastrone's *Cabiria* was shown at the White House to President Wilson, his family, and members of the

22. Quoted in Wagenknecht, *Movies in the Age of Innocence*, p. 64.

23. Bosley Crowther, *Hollywood Rajah: The Life and Times of Louis B. Mayer* (New York: Holt, Rinehart and Winston, 1960), pp. 30–31.

24. Linda Arvidson, *When the Movies Were Young* (New York: Dover, 1969), p. 134. By 1910, Griffith's royalty checks averaged $900 and $1,000 per month.

cabinet. The president of the United States had gone to see a movie. Who could hope to hold out after that?

The movies did not lose the immigrant and blue-collar worker, but as new theaters invaded the suburbs and movies were shown in legitimate houses, the social stigma attached to the nickelodeon all but vanished. The most reliable estimates suggest that, in sheer numbers, movie attendance practically doubled during the nickelodeon era, increasing from twenty-six million persons per week in 1908 to at least forty-nine million in 1914.[25] Although women and children were still the most discussed groups of patrons, adult males statistically outnumbered both groups combined; Frederic C. Howe estimated that 75 percent of the national movie audience was adult male.[26] Makeup and size of audiences must have differed considerably from matinee to evening and from weekend to weekday (on Saturday afternoons, it was commonly conceded, schoolchildren reigned supreme in movie theaters everywhere). But among contemporary commentators, no one has been found to contradict the prevailing sentiment that movies were attracting "the better crowd." About the new audience, Walter P. Eaton in the *Atlantic* wrote:

You cannot, of course, draw any hard and fast line which will not be crossed at many points. In Atlanta, Georgia, for example, you may often see automobiles parked two deep along the curb in front of the motion picture theatre, which hardly suggests an exclusively proletarian patronage.[27]

In the *Outlook* Howe wrote:

There is scarcely a village that has not one or more motion picture houses. . . Men now take their wives and families for an evening at the movies where formerly they went alone to the nearby saloon.[28]

Boston's New Theaters

This new clientele had not arrived by chance. That it was aggressively wooed by movie entrepreneurs eager to break existent social barriers may be seen by the rapidly shifting patterns of prewar movie exhibition. The Boston theater district, which in 1910 was restricted

---

25. Frederic C. Howe, "What to Do with the Motion-Picture Show: Shall It Be Censored?" *Outlook* 100 (June 20, 1914): 412; Committee on Education, *Hearings*, p. 65; "Moving Pictures and the National Character," pp.315–20.

26. Howe, "What to Do with the Motion-Picture Show," p. 413.

27. Walter P. Eaton, "Class-Consciousness and the 'Movies,'" *Atlantic Monthly* 115 (January 1915): 49–50.

28. Howe, "What to Do with the Motion-Picture Show," p. 413.

to two downtown thoroughfares, gained considerable new ground by the outbreak of World War I. New movie theaters opened in virtually every major residential neighborhood surrounding the city. By the end of 1913, Dorchester, Roxbury, Cambridge, Somerville, Newton, Belmont, and Watertown had all succumbed to the rising movie fever and had permitted construction of motion picture theaters on their main streets. *Moving Picture World* treated the steady flow of news reports like dispatches from advancing front lines. "For the first time in the history of the town," it reported on December 14, 1913, "the selectmen of Brookline, Mass., have decided to grant a license for a photoplay show." Several months earlier the same correspondent reported victory in Brighton; a nickelodeon would finally open in that wealthy suburb after three years of opposition by Mayor John F. Fitzgerald. Most remarkable of all, in Boston's exclusive Back Bay community, the city's wealthiest residential district and its cultural hub, no less than three movie houses opened during the same year. The Back Bay had been kept intact through January 1913, but within eighteen months, moviegoers were watching features at the First Spiritual Temple, which the wealthy socialite Mrs. M. S. Ayer and her friends had converted into the Exeter Street Theatre; at the St. James, one block down from Boston's Symphony Hall; and at the Potter Hall, an opera house converted to movies after its 1910 opera season had failed.[29]

Meanwhile, Boston's downtown nickelodeon district, still stretched out along Washington Street and Tremont Street, grew in another direction—skyward. The movie cathedral was still several years away, but the trend toward bigger, more elaborate theaters was unmistakable to anyone reading the frequent theater reports made to the press. The Beacon, adorned with a gigantic spinning globe over the entrance that sparkled in the dark, opened its brass doors with *The Fall of Troy* on February 19, 1910, to a full house of eight hundred persons. Four years later, the same corporation built the Modern, a Gothic marvel with over one thousand seats, flying buttresses, and a door made to look like a cathedral portal. Nathan Gordon's Scollay Square Olympia opted for Florentine Eclectic. Passing under a golden statue of Victory, arms outstretched and belly protruding with a luminous clock, the Olympia's customer entered a vestibule decorated with Florentine murals, a ceramic tile floor, and a ticket booth resembling a Renaissance confessional. The theater claimed a seating capacity of eleven hundred, one

29. Henry Archer, *MPW's* New England correspondent, made steady reports on these new residential theaters throughout 1913 and 1914. See particularly his reports in issues dated March 14, 1914; May 2, 1914; May 16, 1914; and May 30, 1914.

of the largest in the city, but its special pride was the blue, gray, and gold draperies that hung from the boxes, balcony, and gallery railings, monogrammed with the letter O.[30] Not to be outdone, two Washington Street nickelodeons—the Joliette and the Park—drastically enlarged and refurbished their interiors with grandiose displays of their own.[31]

These enlarged theaters stiffened the downtown competition, but the most fearsome and far-reaching threat came from another quarter, originally indifferent to the ten-cent movies, reluctant to exhibit them, but willing to make the move when nickelodeon competition made it necessary. Driven out of the stage business by movies, several legitimate theaters had begun to show their own two- and three-reelers, and in so doing, they had diverted a considerable percentage of the audience the nickelodeons had sought for themselves. "The public," admitted a trade journalist ruefully, "evidently likes to go to a regular theatre which is playing moving pictures and vaudeville in preference to the regular photoplay theatres, even if the shows given are not better. Everyone knows that the Globe is a 'lemon' as a straight dramatic house, but reports go to state that it knocked out nearly $1,000 per week clear profit when showing the cinematographs last summer."[32]

In increasing numbers, audiences discovered that they could watch movies without going to the nickelodeon. By the end of 1913, the National Park, and Potter Hall theaters had abandoned legitimate drama altogether in favor of two- and three-reelers, while the Tremont, the Shubert, the Cort, and Opera House included occasional feature films in their regular theatrical season. The climax came on November 23, 1914, when B. F. Keith announced that the Boston, the city's oldest, largest, and most prestigious playhouse, would henceforth become a full-time movie theater. The gala premiere, by invitation only, featured William Farnum and Tom Santschi in *The Spoilers*. Even Senator Henry Cabot Lodge was there.[33]

Altogether, the number of Boston movie theaters increased more than 30 percent during the nickelodeon years, growing from thirty-one theaters in January 1907 to forty-one theaters in January 1914. In practically every case, the new theaters, with their enlarged seating capacities and more ornate decoration, were started in more prosperous and more exclusive business areas than those of their predecessors. No instance has been found of a Boston movie theater opening between

30. *MPW*, November 26, 1910; January 17, 1914; July 25, 1914; *Boston Globe*, April 2, 1914; July 1, 1914.
31. *MPW*, June 20, 1914; December 5, 1914; *Boston Globe*, December 3, 1914.
32. *MPW*, December 17, 1910.
33. *MPW*, December 5, 1914; *Boston Evening Transcript*, November 24, 1914.

1910 and 1914 in an area that could be described as a working-class community—Castle Square, the North End, the South End, or North Roxbury. The seduction of the affluent was taking place in thoroughfares closer to home.

Prestigious trappings for movies were nothing new. For the well-to-do, private screenings at society balls were chic novelties since the 1897 Paris Charity Bazaar which caught fire and caused the famous scandal; when Nora Saltonstall threw her annual gala at Boston's Copley Plaza Hotel, the *Globe* called the five reels of silent comedies a diverting but familiar social entertainment. Schools, charity balls, churches, and civic clubs projected movies eagerly supplied by exchange men anxious to launder the nickelodeon's shabby reputation. But, of course, this was not moviegoing in its customary sense. Society and the movie operator agreed that these were special activities, exceptional performances that created goodwill without interfering with the day-to-day commercial enterprise or compromising social position.

Legitimate theaters, by contrast, were seen as places where the affluent could watch movies on a regular basis, unembarrassed, at full fare. When such theaters began screening movies, they were immediately recognized as an enemy force which Boston's most important nickelodeon owners were eager to join. Marcus Loew, B. F. Keith, Nathan Gordon, and Mark Mitchell, by 1914 Boston's four most important nickelodeon owners, started systematic raids on legitimate theaters in order to bring them into their movie chains. At the same time, smaller operators who could not afford to purchase or lease legitimate theaters revamped their nickelodeons to resemble "first-class" houses in both appearance and format. Owners went out of their way to recruit managers with background in legitimate theater management, and modified the old format borrowed from vaudeville to give their shows the new look of the legitimate stage.

One important consequence of this invasion was that a social hierarchy, nonexistent among movie theaters in 1910, was rapidly developed by World War I. Patron and exhibitor alike began to rank theaters according to size and quality, discriminating between first-class theaters and the nickelodeon. The most expensive theaters worked conscientiously to disassociate themselves from the cheap theaters even as they encouraged comparisons with legitimate playhouses, while the public quickly adopted a double standard in regard to movie houses whereby films permitted in one kind of theater were not allowed in the other. When, for instance, the five-year-old National Board of Censorship was described by its chairman, Frederic C. Howe, in 1914, its jurisdiction was limited to five- and ten-cent theaters, enabling the

dollar theaters to play films—like the white slavery cycle and sex education shorts—the NBC prohibited from nickelodeons.[34] First-class
theaters gained other trade advantages too, notably first-run, exclusive
engagements in exchange for higher rental fees, that helped single them
out from second-run, cheaper theaters which, if they played the same
films, played them weeks later, frequently opposite other second-run
theaters showing the same bill.

The Nickelodeon's Demise

When, during the war years, production companies of the Motion
Picture Patents Company collapsed, they took the nickelodeon down
with them. Frozen out by the new independent production companies
who regarded one-reelers as outmoded, nickelodeons either enlarged,
changed format, or died. As early as 1914, trade journals spoke of the
five-cent theater as an endangered species. "We cannot close our eyes
to the fact," wrote Stephen Bush, "that theaters with small capacity
using mostly single reels are going out of business all around us."[35]
Salvage efforts took many forms, but the most important operators
saw the handwriting on the wall. Not until 1928, with the coming of
sound, would there be another such massive effort to renovate, build,
and dump movie houses as occurred in 1913 and 1914.

But, by then, the job of building an audience for the movies was
about finished. Without feature films and refined theaters, it is unlikely
that the middle-class audience would have long remained. But the
nickelodeon and its one- and two-reelers had in fact performed the
initial task generally credited to imported features, movie palaces, and
World War I. Mostly, it was the work of immigrants who would go
on to control production as they had exhibition. As film manufacturers
their names—Zukor, Loew, Laemmle, Fox, Mayer, the Warner—would
become nearly as famous as the stars they promoted. But even as
anonymous nickelodeon operators they moved the industry in the
direction that would remain unchanged for another generation.

34. Howe, "What to Do with the Motion-Picture Show," p. 414.
35. W. Stephen Bush, "The Single Reel II," *MPW*, July 4, 1914, p. 36

Part II
Struggles for Control, 1908–1930

In little more than a decade, motion pictures had developed from a novelty into an industry of national dimensions. Exhibition had grown by leaps to become the largest branch of the industry. Business was wide open and free-wheeling; it took relatively little capital to enter the field, and thousands of small entrepreneurs vied to make quick profits. An exchange system had been established, enabling theater operators to rent rather than buy both domestic and foreign films. Although marketing was still in its embryonic stage, demand for motion pictures continued unabated. For millions of Americans, the movies had become a regular and important source of entertainment, despite the admonitions of churchmen, social reformers, and theater critics. Patent warfare, however, stymied growth and prevented the industry from reaching its full potential. Only a handful of producers existed, whose energies were devoted more to protecting their patent claims than to the business at hand. The impulse behind the warfare was to lessen competition: to create barriers to entry for outsiders and to consolidate control from within. Taking their cue from other industries of the day, motion picture pioneers put aside their differences in 1908 to form a monopoly called the Motion Picture Patents Company.

The Motion Picture Patents Company

The formation of the Motion Picture Patents Company in 1908 was the result of a peace settlement between two hostile factions—one led by the Edison Manufacturing Company and the other by the American Mutoscope and

103

Biograph Company—that had been fighting each other to
establish hegemony of their respective patents. The MPPC
did not produce motion pictures, but was established as a
patent pool to hold the patents belonging to Edison, Biograph, and their allies that covered motion picture film,
cameras, and projectors. There were ten constituent members of the company, including virtually every leading producer and importer of motion pictures and manufacturer
of equipment. As the government later charged, the goal of
the MPPC was to destroy competition between the member companies, to exclude others from entering the business, and to monopolize the marketplace.

As a business, the Trust, as the MPPC came to be called,
issued licenses and collected royalties. All segments of the
motion picture industry were involved: (1) production of
raw film; (2) manufacture of motion pictures; (3) manufacture of projecting equipment; (4) film distribution; and (5)
exhibition. In return for licenses granting certain companies
the right to manufacture projectors, the Trust exacted a
royalty of $5.00 per machine. To use one of these projec-
tors, an exhibitor paid a royalty of $2.00 a week. The
MPPC issued licenses to produce pictures only to its members who were required to purchase all their film requirements from the Eastman Kodak Company, and, with the
exception of Edison, pay a royalty on each foot of film
acquired. Edison and Biograph, as owners of all the stock
in the MPPC, were the principal beneficiaries of this royalty scheme.

It was the ingenious way these agreements interlocked
that revealed the monopolistic intentions of the Trust. On
the production level, the MPPC kept the market to itself
by summarily rejecting all applications for licenses and by
denying newcomers the right to purchase Eastman Kodak
film stock. Competition from abroad was curtailed by limiting the amount of footage its one-and-only licensed importer could bring into the country. By controlling the film
supply, the MPPC could maintain its pricing schedule to
distributors, thus guaranteeing profits for its members. On
the distribution level, the MPPC licensed only enough
exchanges to distribute on a national basis. The others
would presumably have to close their doors because of a
dearth of product. On the exhibition level, the tying agree-

ment that required exhibitors to use licensed films on their licensed projectors enabled the MPPC to enforce the payment of projector royalties and, at the same time, prevent theaters from showing outlaw films.

The Trust did not attempt to create an absolute monopoly or to swallow the industry whole; it controlled selected parts, thinking that the remainder would collapse. With the exception of Pathé Frères, European producers were excluded from membership. And the Trust licensed only around two-thirds of the six thousand movie theaters. It licensed most exchanges at first, but later branched out to distribute on its own. Quality was not necessarily a factor; the public wanted "movies." But because the MPPC ignored segments of the market, it inadvertently created a widening gap between supply and demand, a gap that independents were only too happy to fill, as will be explained.

This outside competition exacerbated the MPPC's relationship with its exchanges. From the start, license violations were detected all over the country. Most had to do with the handling of outlaw films, but exchanges sometimes provided indifferent services, pocketed the two-dollar royalties, or opened theaters of their own which they gave preferential treatment. By 1910, the Trust had had its fill of such behavior and decided to go into distribution by organizing the General Film Company. It did so by the simple expedient of buying out the licensed exchanges. Faced with the implied threat of having their total supply of films cut off—the only source of a distributor's livelihood—licensed exchanges quickly capitulated. Only one licensed exchange balked—William Fox's Greater New York Film Company. Fox refused to sell, went into production, and brought suit against the MPPC. The result was the case *United States v. Motion Picture Patents Co.* that would formally dissolve the monopoly. By then competition and other factors had killed it anyway.

The MPPC's rationale for forming General Film was to provide better service to exhibitors and the public. Altruism was not the major factor, however; General Film offered a higher degree of monopoly control. Anything done by the MPPC to make its service more attractive increased goodwill and strengthened the company's position. Moreover, an exchange system controlled by the MPPC would be sure to collect all the royalties and to prevent licensed film from reaching illicit dealers. But most important, the MPPC could enjoy distribution profits. Licensed exchanges had never been required to share their profits with the MPPC or to pay a royalty. They were allowed the privilege of distributing MPPC films in return for collecting the controversial projector royalties.

Although the district court in 1913 ruled that the MPPC was illegal, the beneficial aspects of the MPPC should not be overlooked. The MPPC brought stability to the industry; endless litigation ceased when Edison and Biograph declared a truce. Licensed producers could thereafter invest their capital with a greater degree of safety to improve motion picture production. Now that producers knew where they stood in the eyes of the law, they could go about their business unmolested. The exodus to California began soon after, where producers could operate the year round and take advantage of the varied scenery. Theater owners, who were assured a steady supply of product from the MPPC, could invest their money to improve buildings and equipment. And in distribution, General Film definitely improved the chaotic conditions in the marketplace. First of all, it inaugurated the system of "zoning" so that theaters in a particular location would not show the same pictures simultaneously. Second, it established a differential pricing policy. Film rentals were formerly based on footage and age—the longer and newer the film, the higher the rental. General Film added another factor—the size and location of the theater. Rentals thereafter became standardized according to the class of theater and scaled in price, a practice that continues to this day.

Motion Picture Production, 1909–1912

The accepted account of motion picture production during the heyday of the MPPC goes like this: Since the raison d'être of the Trust was the collection of royalties, it used patent rights to enforce strict barriers of entry in production, distribution, and exhibition. The whole system hinged upon filling the playing time of theaters. Since demand was incessant—theaters required up to an average of four new films per day—it was in the best interest of the MPPC to mass-produce films at low costs in standard lengths of

1,000-foot reels. To stabilize output, the industry devoted its energies to the production of narrative films.

During this period, the industry shifted from the director system of production to a multiple director-unit system. One director and his staff could easily bring in a single reel each week. Since more profits could be had from more product, manufacturers followed the simple expedient of expanding the number of director-units in their firms. Each unit was a fully integrated work force that contained the personnel needed to make a motion picture. Vitagraph, for example, employed ten directors in 1910 at its studio in Brooklyn. Talent was drawn from the studio's stock company which contained nearly one hundred players. The expanded stage area permitted four or five productions to be shot simultaneously to meet a three-reels-a-week schedule.

To assume that MPPC producers churned out a homogeneous product would be simplistic. The single reel remained a constant (although split reels of around five hundred feet were produced as well), and production costs

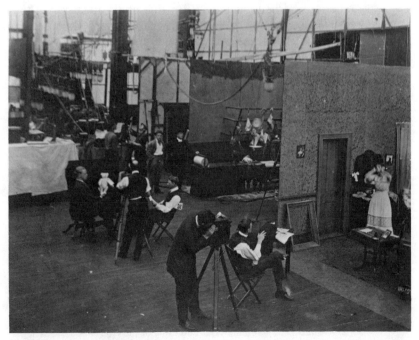

Production at the Edison Studio

had to remain within the limits dictated by the MPPC's uniform selling price. But audiences did express preferences, which the trade press duly reported in its columns and through its reviews. And social reformers kept a vigilant eye on motion picture content.

In turning to the production of narratives, producers raided popular magazines, famous novels, and successful plays for plots which they altered to fit a fifteen-minute time frame. Action films of all sorts were the most popular subjects, and among these, westerns topped the list. Westerns necessitated exterior filming, spacious expanses of unpopulated countryside, costumes, and cowboys, Indians, and horses. For a while "ersatz" westerns including *The Great Train Robbery* (1903) were produced in rural New Jersey, but as audience expectations increased, authentic locale became crucial.

The legend has it that outlaw producers fled to Southern California to escape the ubiquitous detectives and lawyers of the Trust. Lewis Jacobs, for example, says, "The safest refuge was Los Angeles, from which it was only a hop-skip-and-jump to the Mexican border and escape from injunctions and subpoenas."[1] But this myth must be put to rest. Trust producers led the way. As Richard Dale Batman points out, "Within twenty-four hours after signing the papers that made him an official member of the patents company, Selig sent out a touring company consisting of Director Francis Boggs, six actors and actresses, and a cameraman. For the next thirteen weeks, the company made pictures in the South and Southwest and in late March arrived in Los Angeles."[2] The peace provided by the MPPC allowed its producers to work the year round unhindered and thus to supply product for an expanding market. Unlike the production centers in New York and Chicago, the Los Angeles area had a temperate climate and varied scenery that could provide authentic settings for on-location action pictures—"Westerns in the mountains, Arabian pictures in the desert, sea stories at the beach, and a weird concoction of Indian-Spanish dramas in front of the missions," says Batman. By 1910, most MPPC produc-

1. Lewis Jacobs, *The Rise of the American Film* (New York: Teachers College Press, 1939), p. 85.
2. Richard Dale Batman, "The Founding of the Hollywood Motion Picture Industry," *Journal of the West* 10 (October 1971): 610.

ers had sent companies to the area where they were shortly joined by such newcomers as Bison, Nestor, Lux, Eclair, Fox, and IMP.

Resistance to the MPPC

Harassment of outlaw producers was not as incessant or as brutal as is often claimed. As mentioned earlier, the MPPC expected that those outside its sphere of operations would eventually wither away. Had demand for motion pictures stabilized, the MPPC might have had the industry to itself, but demand increased. The independent movement began almost simultaneously with the MPPC. In 1909, a Chicago distributor by the name of Carl Laemmle retaliated against the MPPC by importing pictures from excluded European producers and by going into production to form the Independent Motion Picture Company. For film stock he used Lumière's, which was now available in the United States. As other newcomers entered the scene, Eastman Kodak, deciding that its affiliation with the MPPC was legally and politically dangerous, abrogated its contract in 1911 and placed its film stock on the open market.

By 1912, the independent movement was strong and well organized. To enter the market, independents decided to fight the Trust on its own terms—namely, to provide complete programs of single reelers to theaters. Exchanges were organized to create national distribution networks, and producers were lined up to supply them with a steady supply of product. The movement coalesced around two distributors, Universal and Mutual, each of which had a dozen or so producers aligned with it. By aggressively promoting their pictures, luring talent from MPPC producers, and keeping attuned to audience tastes, these entrepreneurs succeeded in gaining a foothold. But the market they serviced along with General Film was one for short subjects. New developments were taking place during this period that would relegate all these companies to secondary positions in the industry.

The Rise of the Feature Film

A second wave of independents entered the scene around 1911. They offered audiences something different, something special that distinguished their product from the reg-

ular fare—feature films. To the trade, a feature film came
to mean a multiple-reel narrative with unusual content and
high production costs that merited special billing and advertising. An anomaly up until now, longer films had been
typically distributed as serials, because the distribution
system of the MPPC was set up to handle a standardized
product. Vitagraph, for example, released its four-reel version of *Les Misérables* over a three-month period in 1909.

Adolph Zukor has generally been credited with inaugurating feature films. Historians have characterized him as a
visionary who had a passion for quality and who single-
handedly fought the Trust to bring his dreams to fruition.
In 1912, by releasing *Queen Elizabeth*, a French import
starring Sarah Bernhardt, he proved to the industry that
the feature film would go over with the public. This
account is seductive, to say the least. However, a survey of
feature films distributed in the United States during this
period reveals that features were by no means a novelty.
In fact over twenty had been exhibited before *Queen Elizabeth*, several of which were hits.[3]

The influx of features actually began in 1911 as independents tested the waters with European imports. Classical epics from Italy, such as *The Fall of Troy*, *Dante's
Inferno*, and *Jerusalem Delivered*, led the way. *Dante's Inferno*, a Milano Film production imported by Pliny P.
Craft, enjoyed two-week runs in New York, Washington,
and Boston where it played legitimate houses and commanded a ticket price of seventy-five cents. This picture
received a license from the Trust, oddly enough. In 1912,
months before the arrival of *Queen Elizabeth*, Craft
released another Milano epic, *Homer's Odyssey*. Craft gave
the picture special treatment. To promote the fact that
Milano had spent $200,000 to reconstruct an entire Greek
city, he took out an eight-page spread in *Moving Picture
World* and inaugurated a national promotional campaign.
He again booked legitimate theaters, but ticket prices were
now jacked to $2.00. In the lobbies he hawked plaster busts
of Homer, postcards, and souvenir programs. Craft applied
the techniques that had served him well formerly as a

3. James J. Wiet, "A Listing of Feature Films Prior to 1914," Unpublished MS (Madison: University of Wisconsin, 1977).

publicist for William Cody's Wild West Circus. It would
be fair to suggest that these experiments signaled a major
industry shift, which was not lost on those like Adolph
Zukor who were eager to take the plunge.

However, marketing posed a problem. Features required
a special and individualized promotional effort to recoup
their high production costs. Distributors—General Film
and independents alike—handled short subjects exclusively
for programs that might change daily. And they also dealt
with nickelodeons, for the most part, which were too small
to generate much revenue. Clearly, a new distribution system had to be devised.

At first, producers and importers used the state's rights
method, which involved selling the marketing rights to the
feature territory by territory. The buyer, who could be a
local distributor or theater owner, would then rent out the
picture for a flat fee. This method, however, presented little
opportunity for the producer or importer to capitalize on
an unusual hit, with the result that rights were later sold
either for a limited time rather than in perpetuity, or else
on a percentage basis.

Roadshowing was another distribution method used
nearly from the outset. In roadshowing, the producer or
importer exhibited the picture himself. He would book a
theater on a percentage-of-the-gross basis and then take
over the actual operations for the run. This method worked
best with important legitimate theaters. But only the strongest attractions could be handled this way. Although state's
rights selling and roadshowing were basically different, they
were not mutually exclusive. An entrepreneur might first
roadshow his picture in big cities, where most of his revenue was generated, and later sell the film territory by
territory.

From 1912 to 1914, nearly three hundred features were
distributed using these methods. This total was evenly
divided among imports and American productions. Since
the risk of importing a film was less than that of producing
one, an endless number of companies were formed for the
sole purpose of exploiting a single feature. After the film
exhausted its potential market, the company would fold.
Most European countries, in addition to Italy, were heavily
into feature film production. To name just a few of the

many producers, there was Deutches Bioscope in Germany, Great Northern in Denmark, Film d'Art, Eclair, and Gaumont in France, and Hepworth and Barker in Great Britain. Of the importers, George Kleine, a member of the Trust, was the most successful. In 1913 alone, he had four big hits: *Quo Vadis?*, *The Last Days of Pompeii*, *Anthony and Cleopatra*, and *The Betrothed*.

American producers followed the tack of reproducing Broadway plays and adapting masterpieces of literature. The rationale is easy to understand. The legitimate theater was prestigious, having a long and close association with the affluent middle class. By producing a hit, an entrepreneur could minimize his risks, because the play had already generated favorable publicity. Broadway plays and popular classics were different from the regular movie fare and, as quality product, attracted a wider audience, one that could afford to pay more than a nickel or dime for a ticket.

For exhibition outlets, producers initially booked small-time vaudeville houses. A hybrid form, small-time vaudeville presented films and variety acts in equal proportions. Since a program might consist of four or five single reelers, theater managers found it easy to substitute a feature. By 1914, the economic potential of the feature film had influenced exhibition to the extent that in New York about one-fifth of the legitimate houses were playing features and charging $1.00, "Broadway prices," for tickets. The Strand, the most famous of the early motion picture palaces built expressly for showing motion pictures, opened in New York that year. Samuel F. "Roxy" Rothapfel managed the three-thousand-seat house and on opening night, April 14, 1914, presented a program that would set the standard for deluxe exhibition through the 1920s. For openers, the orchestra played a rousing rendition of the national anthem followed by the Hungarian Rhapsody No. 2. Then came a topical film, a travelogue accompanied by a tenor, and a Keystone comedy. Concluding the prelude, the Strand Quartet sang a number from *Rigoletto*. Finally came the "headliner," the Selig production of *The Spoilers* in nine reels, starring William Farnum.

The feature-length film became the norm for most producers by 1915. If anyone doubted the economic potential of the innovation, D. W. Griffith's *The Birth of a Nation* proved the clincher. Its New York run opened at the Liberty Theater on March 3, 1915, and continued for forty-four consecutive weeks at a $2.00 admission price. The exhibition format, consisting of reserved seats, scheduled performances, orchestral accompaniment, souvenir programs, costuming of ushers, intermissions, and the like, consolidated all the deluxe presentation practices of the day. The picture eventually ran for 802 performances in New York. Meanwhile, it roadshowed in leading theaters throughout the country and in Europe, breaking records everywhere.

The Star System

Myth has it that the star system was introduced by the independents in their battles against the Trust. A conservative enterprise, the MPPC manufactured a standardized

Lillian Gish in D. W. Griffith's *The Birth of a Nation* (Epoch Producing Corporation, 1915)

product with anonymous actors. The fear was that public
acclaim for performers might lead to demands for higher
salaries. Actually, the star system evolved during the heyday of the Trust, although not all members embraced it.
MPPC producers certainly understood the commercial
value of stars. The industry competed with other forms of
entertainment to attract the disposable income of the public, and it was plain to all that the star system operated
successfully in vaudeville, legitimate theater, and burlesque.
As early as 1909, the Edison Company publicized its acquisition of important theatrical talent from Broadway
producers David Belasco, Charles Frohman, and Otis Skin-
ner. Rental catalogues of the company contained lengthy
descriptions of their careers. In 1910, Kalem and Vitagraph
introduced lobby card displays containing pictures of their
stock companies. By then, trade papers regularly featured
stories about the "real lives" of movie players, among them
Mary Pickford, Ben Turpin, Pearl White, and Florence
Turner.

Independents though were probably more aggressive
showmen. Carl Laemmle, for example, stole Florence Lawrence from Biograph with an offer of a larger salary. She
was formerly known as "the Biograph Girl,"; Laemmle
rechristened her "the IMP Girl" and hit the road. On tour
with his star, he would plant stories in local newspapers
announcing that the Biograph player had died in a streetcar
accident. He then took out ads declaring that the stories
were nothing but rumors spread by the Trust. Florence
Lawrence was alive and well and could be seen in the
forthcoming IMP production of . . .

Stars provided a means of differentiating product and
even boosted sales, but the single-reel program inhibited
profits. Both General Film and the first independents marketed single reelers to generate quick turnover. Pictures
that changed daily could not benefit from individualized
promotion or word-of-mouth publicity. But the feature film
and the distribution system it engendered changed all that.

Producers turned to the legitimate theater for their first
stars. By 1913, any number of companies had emerged
to transform Broadway fare into motion pictures. Adolph
Zukor's Famous Players in Famous Plays is historically the

most important. Zukor's early successes include *The Count of Monte Cristo*, starring James O'Neill, who had toured with the play on and off for nearly thirty years; *The Prisoner of Zenda*, starring James Hackett; and *Tess of the D'Urbervilles*, starring Minnie Maddern Fiske. (All originated as novels and were dramatized for the stage, a regular practice of the time.) Zukor's competitors were the Broadway Film Company, Belasco's Motion Picture Drama Company, Playgoer's Film Company, De Luxe Attractions Company, and the All Star Feature Corporation, among others. Some of the international stars appearing in foreign imports were Max Linder, Nijinsky, Mme Réjane, Asta Nielsen, and Helen Gardner, in addition to the "Divine" Sarah Bernhardt.

For the industry to develop stars of its own, players had to appear in enough pictures to gain a following. Many of the first stars trained in the theater—provincial stock and touring companies, mainly—but the movies made them celebrities. They soon replaced Broadway idols who were often too old and too heavy to photograph well and ill suited to the demands of the new medium.

Of all the devices used to generate business, the star system was by far the most effective. In its fully developed form, the star system affected all three branches of the industry. A star's popularity and drawing power created a ready-made market for his or her pictures, which reduced the risks of production financing—an insurance policy of sorts, but also a production value and a trademark enhancing the prestige of the producer. As a result, stars became the prime means of stabilizing production. Stated another way, the production process revolved around stars—the narrative, acting, settings, and lighting were all manipulated to enhance the qualities of the star beloved by the fans. In distribution, the star's name and image dominated the marketing strategy and provided the basis of bargaining rental price. And in exhibition, the costs of supporting the system with its astronomical salaries, big budgets, and elaborate promotion campaigns were passed on to the public in the form of higher ticket prices.

Acting suddenly became the best-paid profession on earth, for some. Companies aggressively competed for the

Charlie Chaplin in *Behind the Screen* (Mutual, 1916)

big names, and did the salaries skyrocket: $100, $500,
$1,000, and, for the brightest and most illustrious, Mary
Pickford and Charlie Chaplain, $10,000 a week! The system
worked because the public endorsed it. As will be
discussed below, stars became a means to dominate the
market. But producers were not the only ones to understand the economic importance of stardom. Pickford,
Chaplin, and Douglas Fairbanks used star appeal as leverage to gain control of their work and to share fully in the
profits from their pictures. They graduated from the ranks
of contract players to become independent producers. In
1919, they joined forces with D. W. Griffith to form United
Artists, a distribution company, and operated entirely on
their own in competition with the major firms. The founding of United Artists marked the apex of the star system
in one line of its development (ch. 6).

The Rise of Paramount

The influx of feature films cried out for efficient distribution. State's rights distribution and roadshowing were satis-

factory techniques to exploit one picture at a time, but if producers ever hoped to expand and regularize their output, a better method had to be found. A national distribution system already existed to handle shorts, but how to create one for feature films? A former General Film exchangeman by the name of W. W. Hodkinson devised a way. In 1914, Hodkinson convinced eleven regional state's rights exchanges to join forces by forming Paramount Pictures Corporation, the industry's first national distributor of feature films. Hodkinson's plan guaranteed a steady supply of product because Paramount would help producers finance and advertise their pictures with advance rentals from the exchanges. In return, the company would charge producers a distribution fee of 35 percent of the gross to cover operating costs and a built-in profit margin. This innovative scheme attracted the best producers—Zukor's Famous Players, Jesse L. Lasky Feature Play Company, Bosworth, and Morosco—who signed long-term franchise agreements granting Paramount exclusive rights to their pictures.

Hodkinson geared the company to release 104 pictures a year, enough to fill the playing time of a theater that changed bills twice a week. Exhibitors contracted for the entire Paramount program, a practice known as block booking. Though block booking would later be much abused, selling poor films on the strength of the good, the practice at its inception worked to everyone's satisfaction. Hodkinson also codified prevailing practices into a system that graded houses from first-run to fifth, depending on size, condition, and location (from downtown in large cities to village). As an incentive to buy the Paramount line, theaters received protection from simultaneous showings in their areas.

Although production costs now ranged from $10,000 to more than $30,000, Paramount's distribution grosses soon reached the unprecedented amounts of $100,000 to $125,000 per picture. To accommodate the growing audiences, a wave of theater construction began across the country. And as the "feature craze" spread, other national distributors entered the market: Lewis Selznick's World Film Corporation, Metro Pictures, Triangle Film (which had D. W. Griffith, Thomas Ince, and Mack Sennett as producers), VLSE (which released the product of Vitagraph,

Lubin, Selig, and Essanay, former MPPC members who converted to features), Universal, and the Fox Film Corporation.

This tremendous expansion of the movie business convinced Zukor that Paramount and its producers should merge, not only to effect economies of scale in production, but also to capture a greater share of the market. Famous Players in its third year of existence earned over $1 million in profits, yet this money merely whetted Zukor's appetite. Hodkinson vetoed the idea, arguing that the three branches of motion pictures—production, distribution, and exhibition—should be kept separate. In his view, better pictures, better distribution, and better theater management would result if a lively independence existed among them.

But Zukor was not to be denied. In a series of intricate maneuvers, the details of which are lost to history but outlined in a Federal Trade Commission complaint in 1927, Zukor launched a takeover that set the industry on its ears. After secretly acquiring Paramount stock, Zukor, in June 1916, had Hodkinson deposed. Then he merged Famous Players with Jesse Lasky's studio. Separately they might be the first- and second-ranked producers in the country; together as the Famous Players-Lasky Corporation, they were in a class by themselves. Paramount became the distribution subsidiary of the new company. When Zukor completed his consolidations and acquisitions, in December 1917, he had created the largest motion picture company in the world.

Zukor would not go into exhibition as long as he could maintain a strategic hold on the market with his stable of stars. He had long since abandoned his original plan to use personages from the legitimate stage. His new stars and artists were those on whom the movie public had conferred stardom. His greatest prize was Mary Pickford; others in his illustrious stable were Douglas Fairbanks, Gloria Swanson, William S. Hart, Fatty Arbuckle, Pauline Frederick, Blanche Sweet, Norma and Constance Talmadge, Nazimova, and directors Cecil B. De Mille, D. W. Griffith, and Mack Sennett. With most of the best talent in the industry under his control, Zukor could dominate the field.

Motion picture pioneers Adolph Zukor and Marcus Loew

Implementing the next stage of his thinking, Zukor increased film rentals and expanded his production program, so much so that by 1918, Paramount distributed 220 features, more in one year than any one company before or since. Although Famous Players-Lasky had the greatest array of talent around, a major portion of its output was decidedly second-rate. But by using the distribution practice of block booking, Zukor ensured that these pictures would be rented to exhibitors at a profit.

Resistance to Zukor: First National

The star system clearly erected barriers to entry into the industry. Stars by their very nature were scarce commodi-

ties. They could be developed at great expense or lured
from other studios at an even greater cost, but in either
case it became increasingly difficult for the smaller
producer to compete against the likes of Famous Players-
Lasky, Fox, and other established firms. And although
exhibition had been growing by leaps, powerful producer-
distributors still called the tune.

An exhibitor backlash to this situation occurred in 1917,
when a Los Angeles exhibitor, Thomas Tally, conceived
an idea to strengthen the theater owner's position vis-à-vis
the producer's. If first-run exhibitors from every metropolitan area in the country joined forces to finance independent production and to distribute the films in their respective regions, they could assure themselves a steady supply
of outstanding product. If this supply could be
supplemented with films from other producers, the likes of
Zukor might be ignored altogether. First National Exhibitors Circuit was the result. Twenty-six of the country's
important exhibitors signed up as franchise holders. In total
they owned over 100 theaters, 30 of which were first-run
in key cities. First National would not waste money buying
or building studios; rather, it would use its considerable
purchasing power to capture the biggest box office names.
It proved its determination by plucking Charlie Chaplin
from Mutual and then Mary Pickford from Paramount
with $1 million contracts in 1918. By then, the franchise
holders controlled nearly 200 first-run houses and approximately 60 subsequent-run houses, as well as more than 350
theaters controlled under subfranchise agreements. First
National was indeed becoming an aggressive opponent.

The Battle for Theaters

First National's control of the biggest theaters in the
major metropolitan areas soon posed an ominous threat to
the rest of the industry. These theaters were the first-run
houses, and their importance was enormous. Their proximity to large concentrations of population meant that they
received the bulk of the business. No picture could earn a
profit without first-run showings. Typically, a producer
received up to 50 percent of his total rental from these
theaters, usually within six months after a picture's release.

Further, a successful first-run showing became the greatest selling point for distributors in dealing with the thousands of small-theater managers throughout the country. In short, control of these theaters meant control over access to the screen. And if First National increased production to fill the playing time of its theaters, the market for Zukor's pictures would diminish.

Zukor, as a result, went into the theater business. The fear of First National was not his sole motivation, however. The retail branch of the business had become the steadiest money-maker in the industry. It was not inherently speculative like motion picture production because the public had come to regard the movies more as a necessity than a luxury. Once the decision was made, Zukor moved in a big way. With $10 million from a Kuhn, Loeb & Company stock flotation in 1919, Zukor terrorized First National's ranks by buying options, intimidating theater owners, and awing local bankers from New England to Texas. Zukor's roving representatives were soon dubbed "the wrecking crew" and "the dynamite gang" by theater owners. His biggest victory in a long series of battles with First National occurred in 1926, when he acquired controlling interest of Balaban & Katz, which operated ninety-three theaters in and around Chicago and was First National's tower of exhibition strength. Zukor now owned or controlled over a thousand theaters, which he consolidated under the name Publix Theaters Corporation.

By adding exhibition to its production-distribution activities in 1919, Zukor's company became completely integrated. But others were soon forced to follow suit. First National added production to its distribution-exhibition arms by building a giant studio in Burbank, California, in 1922. Marcus Loew, meanwhile, who owned a chain of a hundred theaters, had bought an impoverished producer-distributor called Metro in 1920. Going deeper into production in 1924, he purchased first the Goldwyn Pictures Corporation and then the Louis B. Mayer unit. The trend continued. Fox Theaters Corporation, one of the most important chains in the country, embarked on a spree calling for the construction of thirty first-run theaters, each seating between four and five thousand.

By the mid twenties, the skeleton of the motion picture

industry's organizational structure that would characterize it for the next two decades had become apparent. After having undergone a series of major adjustments, the result of the decline of the MPPC, the industry after World War I saw the consolidation of its production, distribution, and exhibition branches. With their studios, national systems of distribution, and large chains of important theaters, fewer and fewer companies had come to assume more and more power. In 1925, Paramount, First National, Loew's, and Fox were the major entities. The movement toward consolidation would continue, bringing two additional companies to the fore—Warner Bros. and RKO. The story of their arrival is tied in with the advent of sound.

The Industry as Big Business

By the twenties, the movies ranked as a major industry. Its captains were an exceptional breed of showmen who, by exploiting the star system and feature films and by dreaming up bold and imaginative promotion techniques, enabled the movies to surpass every other branch of show business. Competition was particularly damaging to the professional theater and vaudeville. In 1908, over three hundred touring companies had crisscrossed the nation bringing live theater to almost every town of significant size. The number of legitimate houses had numbered around fifteen hundred. By the middle twenties, most of these houses had either closed their doors or been converted to movie theaters. As the road died—and there were causes in addition to the movies—professional theater became concentrated primarily on Broadway whose houses increased in number from sixteen in 1910 to seventy in 1928. Vaudeville was killed off entirely.

The motion picture industry had stabilized and in its organization resembled typical American industries—its production, distribution, and exhibition branches corresponded to the manufacturing, wholesaling, and retailing activities of other firms. And like its counterparts, the motion picture industry was vertically integrated in the main, with a handful of companies doing the lion's share of the business. Production was centralized in Hollywood now, where the studio system had developed into an efficient means of mass-producing large numbers of feature films revolving around stars. Distribution was highly structured, with every house in the country classified as to run and serviced, in turn, at precise intervals to capture every possible dollar. And in exhibition, the industry "adapted the then-dominant practice for mass marketing, the chain store strategy," says Douglas Gomery, to reach a weekly audience of nearly eighty million (ch. 9).

The twenties witnessed an unprecedented boom in theater construction that made the exhibition branch the fastest growing in the industry. The motion picture palace typified the age. These sumptuous and ornate buildings seating fifteen hundred and more were built in every town of over a hundred thousand population. These were the flagship theaters of the big chains and integrated companies. Not only did they occupy prime real estate in the main business districts, creating a strong asset base for their owners, but they also charged the highest prices and attracted the biggest crowds.

To finance this expansion, the industry turned to Wall

Grauman's Chinese Theater, Hollywood

Street. Until the twenties, motion picture companies, in general, had to finance their operations from within. Business was conducted on a cash-in-advance basis, which under the block-booking system meant that exhibitors had to pay 25 percent of the rentals upon signing the contracts and the remainder as each picture was delivered. Conventional bank loans to movie companies during these years were rare. But the impressive profit records during the post–World War I boom convinced bankers and financiers that the industry had reached maturity. Banks began to make available to the leading companies both commercial and long-term credit on customary trade terms. Investment houses underwrote stock issues which by 1926 would bring the invested capital of the industry to over $1.5 billion. By 1927, the seven largest firms had become publicly held corporations, and their preferred and common stocks regularly traded on the New York and Chicago stock exchanges.

More than national in scope, the American film industry dominated the foreign market. World War I was the turning point, says Thomas Guback: "European film industries had either been disrupted or forced out of business, creating a vacuum into which American pictures flowed, often at alarming rates" (ch. 17). But economics also played a part. Virtually the entire cost of making a motion picture is incurred in shooting the negative; incremental costs for the manufacture of positive prints are negligible in comparison. To put it another way, a motion picture might be expensive to produce, but relatively cheap to reproduce for physical distribution (advertising and promotion costs excluded). Because the domestic market contained a large number of theaters—about half the world's total—American pictures handled by the major companies could at least regularly break even at home before being marketed abroad. And because it cost little to prepare a silent picture for foreign distribution (e.g., by translating the intertitles), American films enjoyed a competitive advantage; they could easily undersell the local product. Although European nations established import barriers for cultural as well as economic reasons, their efforts were largely ineffective. Moreover, foreign film producers could not achieve reciprocity in the United States. The vertical integration of the

American industry and certain monopolistic trade practices guaranteed that the domestic market would be open only to the Hollywood product.

To protect its interests, the industry formed a trade organization in 1922, known as the Motion Picture Producers and Distributors of America. The post–World War I years witnessed great social change in the country, a loosening of moral bonds, among other things, that was reflected in the movies. A significant and vocal segment of the public blamed the industry as the perpetrator. And when a series of scandals involving well-known movie personalities rocked Hollywood in the early twenties, a host of civic, patriotic, and religious organizations cried out for censorship of some kind. In 1921 alone, censorship bills were introduced in thirty-seven state legislatures. Several states and municipalities had already enacted restrictive motion picture legislation. If more censorship boards had been created having legal sanctions, the whole distribution and exhibition pattern of the industry would have been thrown into disarray with disastrous financial consequences. Since the entrenched firms had most to lose from the situation, they created the MPPDA for their mutual protection. Taking the lead from professional baseball, which had hired Judge K. M. Landis as "czar" to clean house, company heads hired an outsider with high public standing to lend dignity and respectability to their industry. They chose a midwesterner with a solid middle-class background by the name of Will Hays. As chairman of the Republican National Committee, Hays ran Warren Harding's successful presidential campaign in 1920 and served as postmaster general in the administration. Hays had not only important connections in Washington, but also impeccable credentials. He was an elder in the Presbyterian church, a teetotaler, and a non-smoker. Moreover, he was adept at public relations.

As his principal task in the $100,000-a-year job, Hays had to defuse the censorship movement. He established the Public Relations Committee as a forum and invited influential religious and civic leaders to discuss how to improve motion pictures. It did the trick; criticism of the industry subsided for the remainder of the decade.

Under Hays, the MPPDA performed the usual functions of trade organizations. In addition to monitoring public opinion, it lobbied to keep foreign markets open to American films, to create harmonious trade relations among the branches of the industry, and to resist interference of any kind, most particularly in the form of antitrust actions.

The Advent of the Talkies

When American Telephone and Telegraph salesmen first made the rounds of the major companies, they found no takers for their new sound equipment. Prudent studio chiefs were not about to tamper with a flourishing business. Producers had extensive inventories of silent pictures. Their studios were designed for the production of only such pictures, and theaters throughout the country were built and equipped for them. Actors in whom producers had made huge investments were trained in making silents. The change to sound would involve not only scrapping millions but investing corresponding amounts in sound equipment. Moreover, the Western Electric sound system of AT&T was far from perfect. Yet, within three years, the conversion to the talkies was so sweeping that a silent picture could not be found anywhere except in small towns and rural areas.

Film historians have long accepted two traditional accounts of the sound revolution. The first was presented by Benjamin Hampton in his *A History of the Movies*, published in 1931. Hampton stated that around 1926, the novelty of motion pictures had worn off. Mediocre pictures, high ticket prices, and competition from radio were having an effect on the box office. "Something was needed to stimulate interest in the screen. . . . What could that be? Better pictures? More vaudeville acts? Or what? The movies found the answer to its problems," says Hampton, "and found it in the characteristically romantic manner that has always been the industry's principal charm."[4]

The hero of his story is Warner Bros. In 1925, the studio had neither the funds to acquire first-run houses nor the clout to secure access to the theater chains of the giant companies and was slowly dying. Near despair, Warner

4. Benjamin B. Hampton, *A History of the Movies* (New York: Covici, Friede, 1931), p. 374.

somehow secured bank financing to experiment with the Vitaphone sound system of Western Electric. In 1926, Warner debuted its Vitaphone program. The public was interested, but not enthusiastic, but "by the spring of 1927, the movement of the public toward talkies was unmistakable; by the autumn of 1927 it was a stampede."[5] The cause of the revolution was *The Jazz Singer*, which reaped a fortune and launched Warner on its course to greatness.

Hampton implies that Warner's success was a result of the company's prescience—Warner discerned that the audience was "ready" for the talkies. Lewis Jacobs, in his *The Rise of the American Film*, published in 1939, gives a different explanation; the company experimented with sound in a desperate attempt to ward off bankruptcy. With the premiere of *Don Juan*, the first feature with synchronized musical accompaniment, Warner discovered a solution to its financial problems. The major companies resolved to fight the "Warner Vitaphone peril," but after the release of *The Jazz Singer*, "the audience reacted riotously," throwing the entire industry into panic and forcing the entrenched companies to adopt sound.[6] This account characterizes the industry as behaving in a primeval manner. The market is irrational and capable of creating chaos and confusion. The audience too is irrational for it responds riotously to the novelty of the talkies. Thus, the industry was swept into a new era by cataclysmic forces.

These theories are not substantiated by evidence and provoke many questions. For example, how could a nearly bankrupt company finance costly experiments with sound? If Warner did not own a theater chain, as Hampton says, how did it secure first-run access for its Vitaphone pictures? If the industry was thrown into chaos, as Jacobs asserts, how was it that Paramount, Loew's, and the other majors made extraordinary profits on the heels of Warner Bros.? And, lastly, could one film, *The Jazz Singer*, create a revolution that would transform the industry?

Douglas Gomery, in his ground-breaking reinterpretation of the era, provides a much more rational explanation for these events (ch. 10). With evidence drawn from corporate

5. Ibid., p. 383.
6. Jacobs, *Rise of the American Film*, pp. 297–301.

records, legal cases, and trade papers, Gomery places the
coming of sound into a realistic context consonant with
the business practices of the period. His underlying
assumption is that businesses act in such a way over the
long run as to make the highest possible profits and that
technological innovation is one way to achieve this end.

Gomery utilizes this theory to analyze how and why the
industry converted to sound when it did. The theory of
technological innovation posits three stages of development—invention, innovation, and diffusion. Motion pictures with synchronized sound required the invention of
many complex components—the microphone, the amplifier,
speakers, and the like. Although entrepreneurs during the
early years of the industry attempted to mechanically link
sound to motion pictures using the phonograph, it took
the huge resources and experimentation of "outside" firms
such as the Western Electric laboratory of AT&T to create
a satisfactory sound system. Western Electric did not originally set out to invent sound motion pictures, it should
be noted; its sound system was an amalgamation of devices
devised for many purposes. Western Electric was constantly searching for ways to generate new sources of profits, and sound motion pictures were but one course to
pursue.

The innovation stage occurs when innovations are
adapted for practical use. By adopting a new technology a
firm can potentially reap great profits if it is first on the
market. But innovation requires special managerial talent,
financing, and a strategy. Gomery describes why Warner
Bros. *and* the Fox Film Corporation, rather than the majors, took the lead. Warner and Fox developed separate
strategies to assault the market, which reflected their relative strength in the industry and required years of planning
before reaching fruition.

Warner, for example, innovated with sound as part of an
overall plan to strengthen its position in the exhibition
market. The company was by no means on the verge of
bankruptcy in 1926, but in the midst of an expansion program under the guidance of Wall Street financier Waddill
Catchings. It already owned a prosperous production operation in Hollywood, a worldwide distribution system, and
even a small theater chain. Exhibition posed a problem

in this era of mergers, which sound technology might help solve. Motion picture palaces typically presented a mixed entertainment program consisting of live stage acts as a prologue and the main feature accompanied either by an organ or a full-sized pit orchestra. Warner decided to introduce programs of comparable quality but in sound by producing shorts of popular vaudeville acts and features with synchronized musical accompaniment. Sound motion pictures would permit the independent theater owner to compete with the opulent downtown houses owned by the chains and thus guarantee exhibition outlets for the Warner product. Accordingly, in April 1926, Warner formed the Vitaphone Corporation in association with Western Electric to make sound motion pictures and to market sound reproduction equipment.

Warner lost $1 million in 1926, but as Gomery points out, the loss was anticipated, short term, and incurred to finance the expansion program. He also emphasizes that the studio continued producing silent pictures in case the experiment with sound failed. In other words, Warner did not put all its eggs in one basket.

Beginning with the theatrical season of 1926–27, Warner presented the first of several full-length Vitaphone programs. Audience response was favorable. Meanwhile, the company initiated an all-out sales campaign to convince exhibitors to install sound-reproducing equipment. If theaters other than its own were wired for sound, Warner could enjoy long-term profits. This effort paved the way for the wide distribution of *The Jazz Singer* after its October 6, 1927, premiere. The movie played in many large cities, breaking records everywhere, and signaled the general acceptance of sound motion pictures. By being the first to innovate, Warner earned extraordinary profits, which were used to solidify its position in the industry. Beginning in September 1928, the company went on a spending spree, the likes of which had never been seen even in the movie business. By the end of 1930, Warner had acquired First National, the Stanley chain of three hundred theaters, and had boosted its assets from $5 million to $230 million, to become among the greatest of all movie companies. Fox Film Corporation also grew apace as a result of its innovation.

The third stage of development is diffusion, when the technology is widely adopted by an industry. The majors did not fight "the Vitaphone peril" or any other. Instead, they adopted a wait-and-see attitude; in February 1927, they agreed to postpone making the conversion for a year unless they collectively agreed to move sooner. In the meantime, they would study the situation. Thus, once Paramount, Loew's, and the lesser companies reached a decision in May 1928, the switchover proceeded rapidly and smoothly. Elaborate contingency plans had been formulated, with the result that the transformation to sound technology was completed within fifteen months.

The major companies signed long-term exclusive contracts with AT&T to secure the necessary equipment both to produce sound motion pictures and to exhibit them. It seemed that AT&T had the entire industry sewn up, but its preeminent position did not go unchallenged. RCA had also developed a sound system, called Photophone, and to exploit it had created a full-blown, vertically integrated motion picture giant, the Radio-Keith-Orpheum Corporation. Founded in October 1928 as a holding company, RKO merged Joseph P. Kennedy's Film Booking Office, the Keith-Albee-Orpheum circuit of vaudeville houses, and Photophone into a firm containing three hundred theaters, four studios, and $80 million of working capital. RCA thereupon charged AT&T with unlawful restraint of trade. After reaching an out-of-court agreement in 1935, the two companies cross-licensed their sound patents to restore amicable relations. By 1943, RCA was supplying about 60 percent of all sound equipment.

The advent of the talkies was thus directly responsible for the emergence of two additional major companies. Because fresh capital was required to finance the acquisition of sound equipment, the construction of soundproof studios, the hiring of new talent, and experimentation in the new medium, production costs rose to an average of $375,000 in 1930, as against $40,000–$80,000 a decade earlier. The changeover to sound cost the industry an estimated $500 million. The majors, which by then had established alliances with leading Wall Street banks and investment houses, had no difficulty making the transition, but the smaller entities were not so fortunate. Many independent producers and exhibitors simply closed their doors or sold out to the big theater chains. By 1930, the transformation of the industry into a virtual oligopoly had been completed.

ROBERT ANDERSON

The Motion Picture Patents Company: A Reevaluation

Film historians have portrayed the Motion Picture Patents Company as an avaricious monopoly. Terry Ramsaye's *A Million and One Nights* (1926), Benjamin Hampton's *A History of the Movies* (1931) and Lewis Jacobs' *The Rise of the American Film* (1939) have long been the standard reference sources for scholarship pertaining to the formation and business conduct of the Patents Company. These texts consistently present the MPPC as a thoroughgoing villian, designed both to collusively maximize profits and to eliminate competition by establishing prohibitive barriers to entry through patent pooling. The contributions of the MPPC to the development of the American film industry are discussed in negative terms: the failure of a repressive and conservative oligopoly to stifle the dynamism of the "people's theater," the art form of the twentieth century, the American motion picture. Owing to the recent availability of material housed at the Thomas A. Edison National Archives in West Orange, N.J., the Federal Archives and Records Center in Philadelphia, Pa., and the Library of Congress in Washington, D.C., the above one-sided interpretation of the Patents Company can be both challenged and repudiated.

From 1909 until its court-ordered demise in 1915, the MPPC radically altered, upgraded, and codified American film production, dis-

Adapted from "The Motion Picture Patents Company," Ph.D. dissertation, University of Wisconsin, 1983.

tribution, and exhibition. The Patents Company was responsible for ending the foreign domination of American screens, increasing film quality through internal competition, and standardizing film distribution and exhibition practices. But, and perhaps most significant, by aligning the small disorganized film companies into a combination of licensed manufacturers, the MPPC succeeded in transforming the fledgling American motion picture business into an internationally competitive industry.

From the Kinetoscope period to 1907, American film manufacturers were operating under the spectre of patents litigation. Thomas A. Edison, the renowned inventor and head of the Edison Manufacturing Company, set the tenor for the pre-MPPC era by instituting innumerable patent infringement lawsuits against each of his domestic rivals—the American Mutoscope and Biograph Company of New York, the Essanay Company of Chicago, the Lubin Company of Philadelphia, the Selig Polyscope Company of Chicago and the Vitagraph Company of New York. The expenses of these litigation suits crippled American film production. Unable to expand or reinvest in their studios, the various film-manufacturing firms remained small and disorganized.

The Edison Company's distrust of an open marketplace for motion picture manufacture and sale increased after the public's interest in the novelty of the Kinetoscope abated. As early as 1902, distributors and exhibitors were notified by the Edison Manufacturing Company that unless they handled Edison projectors and film exclusively they would not be protected from litigation.[1] Throughout the period, the Edison Company's emphasis on exclusivity continued to intensify. Dealerships promoting films manufactured by firms other than Edison became ineligible for the discounts, benefits, incentives, and legal protection which the Edison affiliates received.[2] Although contending that it was "not our intention to 'hog' the business in any way," the Edison Company demanded loyalty from its affiliates.[3] As such, all independent American film manufacturers outside the control of the Edison Manufacturing Company were viewed as a threat to Edison's hegemony over the domestic market.

Thomas A. Edison has been presented as the motivating force behind the establishment of the Motion Picture Patents Company. This is

---

1. William Gilmore, vice-president of Edison Manufacturing Company, to Edison Dealers and Exhibitors, November 17, 1902, George Kleine Collection, box 18, Library of Congress (hereafter cited as GKC).

2. Edison Manufacturing Company to George Kleine, August 15 and 24, 1904, GKC, box 18.

3. Edison Manufacturing Company to George Kleine, March 25, 1907, GKC, box 18.

incorrect, as the actual impetus to form the Edison licensing system, the model for and short-lived predecessor of the MPPC, came from Edison's opponents. Tired and financially depleted by the interminable legal wrangling over patent rights, manufacturers began to propose a mutually beneficial cessation of hostilities to the Edison Manufacturing Company. Realizing the virtual impossibility of circumventing Thomas Edison's crucial camera patents by means of invention (although both Vitagraph and Selig Polyscope pretended to have done just that),[4] concerned manufacturers contacted the Edison Manufacturing Company in early 1907 regarding the feasibility of a licensing agreement.

Thomas Armat, holder of several key projector patents and head of Armat Moving Picture Company, suggested a five-dollar-a-week royalty scheme to be exacted on exhibitors as a means of "getting back" at those "people who have been more or less unfair to the Edison Company."[5] Frank Marion, co-founder of the newly formed Kalem Company, conceded that Edison had "a practical monopoly on picture taking" and hoped for a "royalty proposition" to enable his company to commence manufacture in the United States.[6] By May 1907, a merger plan, recognizing the validity of the Edison patents, was being promoted by Essanay, Kalem, Pathé Frères of France, Selig, and Vitagraph. Even the notorious film duper Sigmund Lubin was asked "to enter and behave himself." Edison's traditional nemesis and patents rival, the American Mutoscope and Biograph Company, was not considered as a licensee.[7]

Edison, on the advice of his legal counsel, elected to exclude American Mutoscope and Biograph from the licensing proposal in order to divide the American film industry into two distinct camps, those favoring royalty payments to the Edison Company and those against.

4. Albert Smith to George Kleine, June 22, 1907, GKC, box 18. Frank Marion to George Kleine, March 14, 1907, GKC, box 29. George Kleine to unknown person, March 25, 1908, GKC.

5. Thomas Armat to Melville Church, attorney for Edison Manufacturing Company, April 1, 1907, Motion Picture Patents Company Files, Edison National Historic Site (hereafter cited as ENHS).

In January 1908, Edison would reject Armat's suggestion to control the projecting machine business: "Armat's ideas are too colossal. He is impracticable [sic]." Frank L. Dyer to William E. Gilmore with addenda by Edison, January 31, 1908, ENHS.

6. Frank Marion to George Kleine, March 11, 12, and 14, 1907, GKC, box 29. Marion succinctly states, "So far as Kalem is concerned it is royalty or Canada for us." George Kleine to Frank Marion, March 14, 1907, GKC, box 29.

7. George Kleine to William Gilmore, May 5, 1907, GKC, box 18. Letters from George Kleine to William Pelzer, attorney for Edison Manufacturing Company, May 8 and 11, 1907, GKC, box 18.

The strategy of the Edison officials was twofold; the growth of the licensees would strengthen Edison's control of the market while simultaneously eliminating Biograph as a serious competitor. George Kleine, co-founder of Kalem and an importer of European films, suggested that all applicants be admitted as Edison licensees, but the Edison attorneys rejected this plan. The acknowledged purpose of the licensing agreement was to "preserve the business of present manufacturers and not to throw the field open to all competitors."[8]

By establishing themselves as a finite and controlled film oligopoly under the auspices of Edison patent protection, the Edison licensees hoped to make entrance into the marketplace by additional domestic manufacturers a highly improbable occurrence. Therefore, as a prototype for the MPPC, the business policies and procedures of the Edison licensees acquires added significance.

The chaotic nature of the 1907–8 Edison license period can best be exemplified by an overview of the Kalem Company. Established in April 1907 by George Kleine, Samuel Long, and Frank Marion (hence the nomenclature Kalem, K-L-M) the company began filmmaking "under cover" in an attempt to avoid being sued by Edison over patent infringement. As the licensing process accelerated, Kalem applied to Edison only to be notified that the Vitagraph Company and an Edison attorney demanded Kleine's removal from the company prior to licensing.[9]

George Kleine, in his capacity as an importer, had previously rejected Edison's offer of a license and instead had joined with Biograph and Thomas Armat in conducting a vocal and well-publicized campaign against the evils of the Edison "trust" in *Show World, Moving Picture World, Views and Film Index*, and the *Chicago Tribune*.[10] After

8. William Pelzer to George Kleine, May 14, 1907, GKC, box 18. "The points you suggest for consideration seem to be all right with the exception of point 3 which refers to the issuance of licenses to *all* applicants. I do not think that the other manufacturers would agree, nor do we think it advisable to grant licenses to all applicants."

Frank Marion to George Kleine, February 26, 1908, GKC, box 29. "The position which had been announced as a sort of general working principle by the Edison Mfg. Co. that they would license American manufacturers who were making films when the Circuit Court of Appeals handed down its decision in 1907 . . ."

9. Frank Marion to George Kleine, February 26 and March 31, 1908, GKC, box 29. George Kleine to Frank Marion, March 2 and April 1, 1908, GKC, box 29. Samuel Long to George Kleine, March 3, 1908, GKC, box 29. George Kleine to Samuel Long, April 1, 1908, GKC, box 29.

10. Affidavit of George F. Scull in *Edison Manufacturing Company v. Kleine Optical Company*, May 7, 1908, pp. 16–23, ENHS, legal box 173. George Kleine to *Views and Films Index*, March 13, 1908, GKC, box 26.

consultation with his colleagues, Kleine sold his share of Kalem to Long, and the company entered into the standard royalty arrangement with Edison. Even though the licensed manufacturers began to turn a profit and expand their production facilities, the continuation of litigation between the Edison faction and the Biograph, Kleine, and Armat forces created a high degree of tension and uncertainty regarding the stability and future of the American film industry.[11]

But the open schism between the Biograph and Edison forces was not the only inhibitory factor on the industry; the distribution and exhibition branches of the motion picture business continued to court short-term profit at the expense of long-term development. Despite appeals from the Edison affiliates, the film exchanges both condoned and promoted subrenting, price cutting, the large-scale importation of foreign films, and the projection of damaged, "rainstorm," and "junk" films. More concerned with immediate profit than the long-term effects of the declining quality of exhibition, countless theater owners ignored the Edison Company's guidelines and continued to purchase and vend damaged and bootlegged prints. These abuses proved too ingrained, widespread, and profitable to be rectified in a divided marketplace.

Concurrent with the decline in the quality of film distribution, the reputation of the nickelodeon theaters also began to deteriorate. *Moving Picture World* virtually dismissed the entire nickelodeon crowd as riffraff when it declared that "the odiom attached to the name 'nickelodeon' [is] such that any person of refinement look[s] around to see if he is likely to be recognized by anyone before entering the doors."[12] Edison Company executive Frank Dyer concurred when he labeled the nickelodeons as "house[s] of assignation" where "all kinds of immoral practices were made."[13] By 1908, the American film industry appeared to be at the crossroads of either reform or collapse.

The animosity between the various film manufacturers erupted into a crescendo of claims and counterclaims when Biograph acquired the patent rights to the Latham loop at an auction held by the Anthony Scoville Company.[14] For a number of months motion pictures had been divided into two classes, Edison/licensed/trust or Biograph/in-

11. Record, at 1714 and 1723, *United States v. Motion Picture Patents Company*, 225 F. 800 (E.D. Pa. 1915), (hereafter cited as Record). J. Stuart Blackton, Record, p. 1883. George K. Spoor, Record, pp. 1987–88. Sigmund Lubin, Record, pp. 3047–48.

12. "The Combine and Its Policy," *Moving Picture World*, January 16, 1909, p. 57 (hereafter *MPW*). See also "The Nickelodeons," *Variety*, December 14, 1907, p. 33, and "An Amazing Growth," *New York Dramatic Mirror*, March 28, 1908, p. 4.

13. Record, p. 1508.

14. Fredrick Anthony, Record, pp. 2065–74. Thomas Stephens, Record, pp. 2075–80.

Essanay Studio, Chicago. Courtesy Bruce Torrence Historical Collection, c/o First Federal of Hollywood

dependent/antitrust, and owing to restrictions set by the Edison Company no exhibitor was authorized to obtain both kinds. Kleine in an open letter to the nation's nickelodeon managers described the industry as "practically [existing] in a state of revolution" and called on the Edison forces to sell or rent their product to the independents.[15]

Aware that the Edison Company was overtly maneuvering to squeeze the independents out of the market, Biograph retaliated by purchasing the Latham loop patent and serving injunctions on all the manufacturers affiliated with Edison. The loop was dismissed by Edison's legal counsel as having "nothing to do with moving picture films" and being "nothing but a joke in the business," but when its validity and applicability were upheld by the circuit court in Trenton, New Jersey, industry insiders realized that yet another round of protracted and expensive lawsuits was in the offing.[16] By summer 1908, both Edison and Biograph were willing to compromise to avert further litigation.

Biograph and Edison board members met behind closed doors in May 1908 to discuss the feasibility of creating "A Plan to Reorganize

15. George Kleine to Motion Picture Exhibitors, March 1908, GKC, box 26.
16. General Press Release by Frank L. Dyer, general counsel for the Edison Manufacturing Company, March 9, 1908, GKC, box 26. Thomas Stephens, Record, p. 2080.

the Motion Picture Business of the United States." The four-page working paper turned out by this committee outlined the ground rules for the merger of the Biograph and Edison interests into Corporation "X." This behind-the-scenes meeting, subsequently denied at each and every antitrust trial, established the following set of guidelines for the yet-to-be-named Motion Picture Patents Company:

Manufacturers will pay to the Edison and Biograph interests 1/2¢ per foot royalty on all films marketed in the United States. Exhibitors will pay to the same interests a royalty running from $1.00 to $5.00 weekly for each motion picture projecting machine in use by them, the amount to be based upon the seating capacity of the exhibitor's theatre.

A corporation is to be formed which we will call "X," it's [sic] capital stock "Y."

The business of Corporation "X" will be the renting of films, sale of machines and other items usual in the trade.

Manufacturers will sell exclusively to Corporation "X."

Corporation "X" will buy films from the manufacturers only. . . .

Corporation "X" will rent films and is not to sell them.

Corporation "X" will not buy films from any manufacturer who does not maintain the conditions agreed to.

The Board of Directors of Corporation "X" is to be composed of one representative of each manufacturer.

The Board of Directors will determine upon the cities of the United States which have been active in the film rental business and select from existing rental exchanges in each city one to three which are to receive an offer of purchase as hereinafter provided, these to be thereafter maintained as rental offices to Corporation "X."

The total number of agencies so selected is not to exceed fifty in the United States.

No fixed rental prices are to be established.

No theatre will be forced to pay a sum for film rental which is oppressive, the elastic scale acting in favor of those that need consideration.

Theatre owners engaged in evil practices can be disciplined.

Films can be withdrawn from the market when their condition becomes bad.

Open competition among manufacturers will continue.[17]

Thomas Edison was so thoroughly satisfied by the development of the meeting with Biograph that in June 1908 he announced to the press that there would soon be a "square deal for everybody," with everybody making money and getting a full return upon his investment of brains, money and labor. The "Wizard of Menlo Park" told reporters

17. "A Plan to Reorganize the Motion Picture Business of the United States," unsigned, May 1908, GKC, box 37.

that he was "willing to admit that the French are somewhat in advance
of us. But they will not long maintain their supremacy. Americans in
any department of effort are never content to stay in second place."[18]
Edison could afford to exude an air of confidence in the American
spirit, as the soon-to-be-consummated MPPC licensing agreement excluded every foreign manufacturer but Pathé Frères.

The collusive nature of the "Plan to Reorganize the Motion Picture
Business of the United States" and its adoption as the blueprint for
the Motion Picture Patents Company is blatantly obvious. Not surprisingly, given the Edison Company's dogged determination to control, or at the very least to be viewed as the guiding force of, the
American film industry, Edison garnered the major concessions. The
Edison Company's decided mistrust of competition manifested itself
in the clause limiting the number of manufacturers eligible to participate in the MPPC to those producing films by March 1908. Since
these firms were either already licensed by Edison or affiliated with
Biograph, the MPPC assured the Edison Company the long-sought-
after maintenance of the status quo. Now all outside competition would
violate the MPPC's sixteen key patents on cameras and projectors and
be subject to legal prosecution.

Not satisfied with the lion's share of the benefits from patent production, the about-to-be-announced MPPC contracted with the Eastman Kodak Company, the only manufacturer of commercial quality
35mm raw film stock in the United States, to deal exclusively with
them.[19] By the fall of 1908, the Edison licensees, the Biograph group,
and Eastman Kodak assumed they were on the threshold of a mutually
profitable and advantageous new era in American film manufacture.

The creation of the MPPC did not occur in a vacuum. The MPPC
was modeled not only on aspects of this Edison licensing agreement
and the short-lived Film Service Association, but also on large-scale
industrial enterprises of the day. Patent pooling, for protection and
profit, was a trademark of big business in turn-of-the-century America
and particularly of rapidly expanding and technologically oriented firms

18. "A Square Deal for All is Thomas Edison's Promise," *Variety*, June 20, 1908, p.
12.
19. Harry N. Marvin, Record, pp. 23–25. Petitioner's Exhibit No. 133, "Agreement
between Motion Picture Patents Company, the Edison Manufacturing Company and
the Eastman Kodak Company," Record, pp. 558–82. Petitioner's Exhibit No. 225, "Eastman Kodak Company," Record, p. 1223. Ralph Cassady, Jr., "Monopoly in Motion
Picture Production and Distribution, 1908–1915," *Southern California Law Review* 32
(Summer 1959): 333–35. Reese V. Jenkins, *Images and Enterprise* (Baltimore: Johns
Hopkins University Press, 1975), pp. 282–85.

such as A. B. Dick, Bell Telephone, Standard Oil, International Harvester, General Electric, and Westinghouse. The advantages accrued by acquiring and pooling patents for these diverse industries were basically the same, to effectively restrain, limit, or shut out the competition that would be inevitable if the various patents were held by firms or interests outside of or in opposition to the goals of the patents pool.

The field of electronics is illustrative of the type of model the MPPC patterned itself after. From 1897 to 1911, General Electric merged with numerous small firms (amongst them Edison Electric Company) in order to control their patents and prevent competition with its own product. Then in an agreement with its chief rival, Westinghouse Electric Company, General Electric established a "board of patent control" where both corporations exchanged patents rights internally and in effect constructed prohibitive barriers of entry for nonaligned companies.[20] The development of the MPPC can be viewed as the logical adoption of contemporary state-of-the-art business theory and practice to the vagaries of the domestic film industry.

When the heads and representatives of the Armat, Biograph, Eastman Kodak, Edison, Essanay, Kalem, Kleine, Lubin, Pathé Frères, Selig, and Vitagraph companies convened in New York in mid December 1908 to announce the charter of the Motion Picture Patents Company, the proceedings were largely a formality. Staged for the benefit of the newspapers and trade magazines, the meeting presented little new information to the signatories. The substantive matters of structure and control of manufacture, distribution, and exhibition had been decided on from one to seven months previously.

It would be foolhardy to contend that the Motion Picture Patents Company was formed for altruistic purposes. As a capitalist enterprise the MPPC was designed to maximize profits. Ending the chaos which engulfed the film industry became the means to guarantee the desired ends—increased profits and stability. Patent pooling and the incorporation of the above-mentioned industrial model were recommended as the legal solution to both the economic and organizational woes besetting the motion picture industry. While the intentions of the MPPC were hardly altruistic (1. profit maximize; and 2. improve the business), the effect of the Patents Company's accomplishing its primary goal was the marked expansion of all three branches of the American film industry.

20. Floyd L. Vaughan, *Economics of Our Patent System* (New York: Macmillan, 1926), pp. 52–58 and 69–100. Richard Caves, *American Industry: Structure, Conduct, Performance* (Englewood Cliffs, N.J.: Prentice-Hall, 1977), pp. 22–30.

Aware that the industry was on national display, the MPPC presented its exclusive licensing policy as the logical means to regulate and protect the hitherto floundering American motion picture industry. [For a description of the MPPC licensing and royalty schemes see the introduction to Part II—Ed.] George Kleine, in particular, anticipated the need for a strong public relations campaign both to help deflect "the first wild yell of protest against the octopus" and to "impress the public with the growing dignity of the moving pictures."[21] In spite of the Patents Company's preplanned effort to legitimate their new organization by repeatedly associating it with "the commanding genius" of Thomas Edison, the influential trade papers split on the "Trust" and began a heated pro and con debate in the print media.[22]

For every branch of the American motion picture industry, 1909 represented a year of unprecedented change and growth. The Patents Company's attempt to control, through interlocking agreements, all the aspects of the industry (i.e., the production of raw film, the manufacture of motion pictures, the manufacture of projecting equipment, distribution, and exhibition) failed due to the volatility of the marketplace. Exhibitors skirted and bent Patents Company regulations by mixing licensed/Trust film with the product of the newly created unlicensed/independent manufacturers. Although reviewers and critics for the trade magazines complained of the poor quality of the independent productions, moviegoers appeared unconcerned with the nuances of the patents question or the subtleties of filmmaking and continued to patronize "mixed," licensed, and unlicensed nickelodeons throughout the country.[23]

Historians have tended to focus on the so-called conservative nature of the Patents Company officials, the arbitrariness of the licensing agreements, and the threat posed by the Patents Company's detectives, while overlooking the ground-breaking innovations of the MPPC. Prior to the formation of the Trust, the American market was controlled by foreign manufacturers. The handful of existing American manufacturers lacked confidence in the future of the motion picture. To obtain

21. George Kleine to Frank L. Dyer, December 16, 1908, GKC, box 27.
22. "Film Consolidation a Fact," *New York Dramatic Mirror*, December 26, 1908, p. 8. "The Policy of the Associated Film Manufacturers," *MPW*, December 26, 1908, p. 520. "Manufacturers Assume Control of All Moving Pictures, Motion Picture Patents Co. Establishes a Dictatorship and Film Service Association Disbands," *Variety*, January 16, 1909, p. 13. "The Motion Picture Patents Company" and "The Independent Movement," *Nickelodeon*, February 1909, pp. 36–40.
23. "Independents," *New York Dramatic Mirror*, October 25, 1909, p. 16. "The Qualities of Imported Films," *MPW*, November 6, 1909, p. 635. "Reviews of Independent Films," *New York Dramatic Mirror*, June 25, 1910, pp. 20–21.

the twin goals of domestic hegemony and growth in manufacture, the Patents Company licensed all of the American manufacturers then in existence and embarked on an aggressive policy of competition, both with the foreign film manufacturers and between themselves.

The Patents Company removed price as a consideration for the exhibitor by establishing a uniform rental rate for all licensed film. For the first time, what differentiated a Selig from a Biograph and from a Vitagraph was not the price but the quality of the individual film.[24] The MPPC's conception that "the manufacturers should compete among themselves strictly along the line of quality" ended the deleterious effects of price cutting.[25] This, in turn, encouraged the manufacturers to terminate the production of cheaply made films and instead concentrate on the upgrading of production values film by film.[26] By their decision to "work for merit," actively competing amongst themselves for the exhibitors' dollars, the Patents Company significantly advanced the motion picture as both an art form and a mass-produced commodity.[27]

The licensed companies manufacturing the films most in demand prospered and expanded. By 1911, *Moving Picture World* estimated that 80 per cent of the world's motion pictures came from American manufacturers.[28] This phenomenal turnaround in international production occurred as a result of the expanded production schedules initiated by the MPPC. By gaining control of the American market for American product, the Trust permanently altered the future course of domestic and international film production.

At a time when the motion picture was on trial before the American public, the Patents Company ended the outright sale of film. This curtailed the projection of damaged and old prints and ushered in the policy of motion picture rental which continues to the present. The MPPC also initiated a systematic policy of theater renovation in a dedicated attempt to "end the day of the dingy moving picture room." In addition, the Trust joined with the newly created National Board of Censorship in a concerted effort to upgrade cinematic standards and produce films that were "educational, moral [and] cleanly amusing."[29]

24. Record, pp. 2152–53.
25. Frank L. Dyer to George Scull, January 23, 1909, ENHS.
26. "Film Consolidation a Fact," p. 8.
27. Telegram from William Selig to George Kleine, May 14, 1911, GKC.
28. "American Film Abroad," *MPW*, November 4, 1911, p. 357.
29. Motion Picture Patents Company, "Their Policy and Procedure," *MPW*, April 3, 1909, p. 401. "Licensed Theatres to be Inspected," *New York Dramatic Mirror*, April 3, 1909, p. 13. "Picture Theatre Inspection," *New York Dramatic Mirror*, April 10, 1909, p. 15. "Censorship Board," *MPW*, March 20, 1909, p. 335.

And finally, the Patents Company secured fire and accident insurance for all of its licensed theaters. While the acquisition of insurance may sound somewhat trivial, in 1909 it was considered a highly progressive and "remarkable" step for the industry.[30]

Significantly, the Patents Company's innovations were imitated by the independents, and these improvements helped to expand the interest in and acceptance of the motion picture in American society. The independents' implementation of flat rental rates based on cost per foot, exclusive programs, and minimum rental amounts were all derived from policies pioneered by the MPPC. These innovations stabilized and benefited both the licensed and independent fields. By returning the lion's share of the profits to the manufacturers, these policies encouraged standardization and expansion.

The effectiveness of these policies is illustrated by the growth of the three branches of the industry, whether independent or licensed, from 1909 to 1913. By 1913, the number of domestic motion picture theaters had more than doubled. The independent houses increased from an estimated 2,500 screens in 1909 to 8,306 in 1913. Over the same period the licensed houses expanded from 4,000-plus to 6,877.[31] The MPPC's innovations, dismissed by subsequent historians as being either insignificant or conservative, actually revolutionized the American film industry. By the conclusion of 1909, the Patents Company was envisioning competing for the European market, while the independents were organizing to take the domestic market away from the Trust.[32]

Despite the strenuous efforts of the Patents Company to halt conflicting service and the projecting of licensed film in unlicensed theaters, the distributors continued both to profit by and to practice these methods. Disillusioned by the repeated abuses, loss of profits, and the seeming impossibility of enforcement, the MPPC embarked on a plan to systematically purchase or cancel their affiliated exchanges and establish a single "model exchange."[33] The decision of the MPPC to

30. "Insurance for Picture Houses," *New York Dramatic Mirror*, April 10, 1909, p. 14. Advertisement, "Motion Picture Patents Company," *New York Dramatic Mirror*, April 24, 1909, p. 24. Letters to and from Dyer and Mingle and Ward, March 9–26, 1909, ENHS. Enclosed in the correspondence is the Fire Inspection Report devised by the MPPC for evaluating theaters.

31. Record, pp. 3026–32. Brief for the defendants, *U.S.A.* v. *M.P.P.C.*, pp. 94–95, ENHS, box 10.

32. William Selig to MPPC, November 4, 1909, GKC. Selig toured Europe and visited all of the film manufacturers in England and on the Continent. This ten-page letter is his report. "Moving Picture Men Start War on Trust," *New York World*, May 7, 1909, copy in GKC, box 37.

33. Cassady, "Monopoly in Motion Picture Production and Distribution," p. 356.

vertically integrate manufacture and distribution laid the cornerstone for the Hollywood film industry of the 1920s, 1930s, and 1940s.

In a document entitled "Detail of a Plan Under Which Licensed Manufacturers and Importers Will Take Over the Licensed Rental Business of the United States," the blueprint for the formation of the General Film Company was presented to the Patents Company leadership.[34] Announced officially in mid April 1910, the GFC had been in the planning stages since the formation of the MPPC. In December 1909 the MPPC had canvassed exhibitors regarding the number of reels exhibited each week and the price paid for service.[35] Within two months of the survey, Sigmund Lubin declared: "The Patents Company is going into the exchange business." Lubin regarded the MPPC's interest in distribution as natural, as "merely the process common in industrials of cutting out the middlemen."[36] For Lubin, the structure of the MPPC/GFC licensing arrangement illustrated contemporary corporate America. Whether the company be in electronics, oil, or farm machinery, vertical integration had proven the most efficient method to keep profits within the parent company. Why wouldn't the same formula prove effective for the motion picture industry?

At the time of the General Film Company's formation, MPPC distribution consisted of sixty-nine rental exchanges which operated on a licensor-licensee basis and remained independent of Patents Company ownership. Within twenty months, General Film acquired fifty-eight of the sixty-nine rental exchanges (ten of the sixty-nine met with cancellation, and William Fox's Greater New York Film Rental Company continued operation as a licensee of the MPPC). General Film has been accused of purchasing its network of fifty-eight exchanges through policies of price cutting, discrimination, intimidation, and the withholding of film from licensees unwilling to sell.[37] Actually, those exchanges that were acquired by GFC received adequate financial compensation and in numerous instances substantially more than what the owners estimated the business to be worth.[38]

34. Three-page document, "Details of a Plan under Which Licensed Manufacturers and Importers Will Take Over the Licensed Rental Business of the United States," GKC, box 26.

35. "Observations by Our Man about Town," *MPW*, April 17, 1909, p. 411. "Patents Co. Wants to Know All about Rental Business," *Variety*, February 26, 1910, p. 14.

36. "Jersey Corporation Spells Freeze Out to Film Renters," *Variety*, February 26, 1910, p. 14.

37. Vaughan, *Economics of Our Patent System*, p. 55.

38. J. A. Schuchert, Record, pp. 2010–11. Robert Etris, Record, p. 2063. Albert J. Gilligham, Record, p. 2208. Ike Van Ronkel, Record, p. 2233. Fred C. Aitken, Record, p. 2337. P. J. Scheck, Record, p. 2395. John F. Hennegan, Record, pp. 2697–99.

Whether the distributors associated with the MPPC greeted the establishment of the General Film Company as a favorable development is debatable, but the exhibitors did and virtually unanimously. A parade of theater owners testified that prior to the GFC, they were unable to advertise films, establish fixed programs, obtain nonconflicting service, select the films and only the films they wished to exhibit, determine the age of the film, or receive impartial, dependable distribution. The formation of the General Film Company alleviated these problems for the licensed exhibitor.[39]

From 1910 to 1915, the General Film Company introduced such industry-wide innovations as film rental and return, standardized exhibition, regularized pricing, uniform distribution rates, classification of theaters by size and location, and the establishment of runs and clearances. Perhaps most significant, the Patents Company's distribution "experiment" transferred control of film distribution away from the exchangemen to the manufacturers.[40] This "experiment" resulted in film manufacturers' controlling motion picture distribution through the ownership of exchanges from 1910 until the present.

Presented to posterity as a failure, the General Film Company during its lifetime modernized film distribution by eliminating distributor favoritism, standardizing print quality, and enforcing the return of rented film. In January 1915, *Motography*, a trade journal "free and independent of all business or house connections or control," offered the following unsolicited editorial on the GFC:

In spite of the few disgruntled customers common to all lines of business, the General Film Company has unquestionably been a beneficent influence in the business. It brought order out of chaos, offered the exhibitor his choice of competing brands, gave the public a really balanced program—in short, performed all the functions of an efficient clearing house. And it did it without destroying that competition which is the life of trade.[41]

But that assessment was written in 1915. By the 1920s, the credit for the innovations introduced by the GFC had been expropriated by others—primarily Hollywood studio heads Adolph Zukor, Carl Laemmle, Lewis J. Selznick, and William Fox.

The MPPC/GFC's innovations did not concern William Fox in 1912. The cancellation of Fox's Greater New York Film Rental Company

39. George Cohen, Record, pp. 1930–33. Harry Marsey, Record, pp. 1998–99. Matthew Hansen, Record, p. 2054. Alton Tredick, Record, p. 2256. James B. Clark, Record, pp. 2590–91. C. R. Jones, Record, p. 2627.
    40. Record, pp. 3234–35.
    41. "An Imaginary Bonanza," *Motography*, January 17, 1915, p. 13.

distribution exchange by the MPPC resulted in the initiation of a restraint of trade lawsuit against the Patents Company under the provisions of the Sherman Antitrust Act. The case, heard in the District
Court of the United States for the Eastern District of Pennsylvania,
concluded on October 1, 1915, when Judge Dickinson ruled that the
MPPC went "far beyond what was necessary to protect the use of
patents on the monopoly which went with them" and was therefore
illegal. A higher court dismissed the Patents Company appeal and
officially terminated the existence of the firm in 1918. While this accurately summarizes the legal demise of the MPPC, the reasons behind
the internal collapse of the Patents Company are substantially more
revelatory of why "the Trust" failed in the marketplace.

The failure of the Motion Picture Patents Company to control the
domestic marketplace was based on the invalidity of its own basic
operating premise. The Edison Manufacturing Company had wrongly
assumed that the American motion picture industry could be controlled, regulated, restricted, and protected through patent pooling and
licensing. The Edison Company leadership hypothesized that all of the
ingredients necessary to be a viable mass market filmmaking concern—
i.e., access to raw film stock, studios, cameras, projectors, distribution
exchanges, and exhibition outlets—were capable of being linked to either
patent royalties or licensing schemes. The incorporation of the Edison
company's faulty premise into MPPC policy gradually undermined
and ultimately destroyed the Patents Company.

The Patents Company's faith in its own power to create arbitrary
barriers to entry, designed to exclude non-patents-owners and nonli-
censees, was without substance in fact. On paper, the exclusionary
policies of the MPPC seemed feasible, but in the volatile American
motion picture marketplace they proved illusory. This was a fatal mis-
calculation.

The MPPC leaders considered the licensing and royalty plans so
"airtight" that they failed to anticipate any long-range resistance to
their industry-wide takeover. When opposition to the MPPC developed, the Patents Company was caught unprepared. The MPPC's response was litigation. But in combating the mushrooming independents, the litigation was simply too slow. The subpoenas and injunctions
did not deter the independents, as the independents controlled from
one-quarter to one-third of the domestic marketplace. The Patents
Company's decision not to license the "small fry" distributors and
exhibitors had proved to be extremely shortsighted.[42]

---

42. Unsigned two-page letter to Frank Dyer, September 17, 1909, ENHS.

The Patents Company's litigation-oriented strategy failed to provide the protection, control, regulation, and restriction its leaders had anticipated. Designed to guarantee the exclusive control over all aspects of the motion picture manufacture, the patent-pooling scheme proved an abysmal failure. While the Patents Company waited for its detectives to gather more evidence on the infringing independents, the independents took control of the American marketplace without relying on camera patents, licenses, attorneys, or operatives.

Specifically, the demise of the MPPC can be attributed to the following factors: the defection of Eastman Kodak (1911), the loss of European revenue caused by World War I (1914–16), the advent of the feature film (1912), and the Patents Company's exclusive reliance on internal financing. Each is worthy of analysis.

The Patents Company depended upon its exclusive contract with Eastman Kodak to act as a deterrent to the independent/unlicensed manufacturer entering into film production. The Trust's 1909 attempt to prevent the importation of raw 35mm stock through national tariff legislation failed,[43] but the quality and quantity of the European film stocks could not compete with the pictorial excellence, volume, or price of the Eastman product. However, owing to the bargaining between independent sales agent Jules Brulator and George Eastman, the contract with the Patents Company was modified to allow the sale of film to unlicensed as well as licensed manufacturers beginning July 1911. Within twelve months, the number of theaters exhibiting independent film grew by 33 percent or to virtually one-half of the theaters in the United States (6,571 licensed vs. 6,298 unlicensed).[44] This fifty-fifty split of the domestic market continued for the remainder of the Patents Company era. Not fatal, in and of itself, the defection of Eastman Kodak legitimized the cause of the unlicensed manufacturer and gave the entire independent movement a psychological lift.

When Edison and Biograph announced the plan for the formation of the MPPC to their licensees in 1908, the grand design was predicated on the elimination of all unlicensed competition. When this did not occur, the General Film Company was incorporated both to remove undesirable distribution practices and to establish further control over the market. The primary intent of this action was to diminish competition, but this too failed to happen.

The Patents Company's increase in litigation costs, when coupled with the cessation of royalty payments in September 1913, triggered

43. Sigmund Lubin to MPPC, June 23, 1909, ENHS.
44. Defendants Exhibits Nos. 157, 158, and 159, Record, pp. 3026–35.

division and outright animosity between the licensees. The royalty payments for the years 1909–13 totalled approximately $3,850,000, but the profits from the royalties were divided one-half to Edison, one-third to Biograph, and one-sixth to Armat.[45] For the eight nonstock-holding members, the lion's share of the profits were taken out before they had access to or could benefit from them. When the collection of royalties terminated in September 1913, of the over $1,000,000 collected in that year, the breakdown to the licensees was as follows:

Essanay	$ 20,843.13
Kalem	19,773.91
Kleine	8,974.28
Lubin	25,659.47
Méliès	3,445.60
Pathé Frères	27,660.96
Selig	22,815.41
Vitagraph	32,702.03
	$161,874.79

or less than 20 percent of the profits divided eight ways.[46]

Even though the legal counsel for the MPPC cautioned the various members to "hang together or hang separately," the licensees felt that the breakdown of the payment of skyrocketing legal costs at one-third MPPC, one-third GFC, and one-third jointly by the ten defendants assigned an equal burden of debt to all the companies, while the profits had been divided between Edison and Biograph.[47] The tension within the company surfaced when both George Spoor of the Essanay Company and George Kleine threatened to sue Edison for past "damages." By 1914, the facade of corporate unity was crumbling.

Concurrent with the MPPC's internal wrangling, the outbreak of World War I and the rise of the feature film unexpectedly altered the precarious balance of the American film industry. Since 1909, when William Selig traveled to the Continent to gauge the level of European filmmaking and the market potential for the MPPC, the Patents Company had shipped significant quantities of film abroad. Albert Smith, president of the Vitagraph Company, testified in 1913 that the volume of motion pictures he exported to Europe and Russia was twice the amount of Vitagraph product distributed domestically.[48] Several other

45. J. J. Kennedy to Edison Manufacturing Company, September 22, 1909, ENHS.
46. MPPC to George Kleine, September 13, 1913, GKC.
47. MPPC to George Kleine, December 21, 1914, GKC.
48. Albert Smith, Record, pp. 1723–33.

of the Patents Company firms, such as Lubin, also relied on the European market to supply a profit margin for their corporations. When this market deteriorated with the advent of hostilities, the internationally oriented manufacturers of the MPPC suffered a greater loss of revenue than the independents who continued to concentrate on the American market.

The standard interpretation of the demise of the MPPC revolves around the Trust's conservative response to the shift of production from the East Coast to Hollywood, the star system, and the rise of the feature film. While the first two alleged causes are without any basis in fact, as Biograph, Essanay, Kalem, Lubin, Selig, and Vitagraph established studios in California and the Patents Company employed and advertised internationally renowned contemporary stars, the contention that the Trust failed to understand the significance of the feature film is valid. The debate generated within the MPPC by the emergence of the feature film centered on two predominant themes: (1) the Edison Company did not want to exhibit unlicensed product in GFC-supplied theaters, particularly those houses which contracted for "exclusive" top-of-the-line service; and (2) the Patents Company officials considered "feature subjects of more than five reels . . . [as] too long for the average picture theaters."[49]

Licensed film importer George Kleine demonstrated the domestic marketability of ten-reel-plus European epics with *Quo Vadis?, The Last Days of Pompeii,* and *Anthony and Cleopatra*. These three films grossed $1,183,428.16 in licensed theaters from April 1913 to October 1914. Despite these impressive figures, the MPPC continued to claim that "the future [would] be the old regular program with film not longer than three reels."[50] Both Sigmund Lubin and Kleine pleaded with Biograph and Edison to allow the GFC to distribute independent features on a regular basis, but, despite some exceptions, the Edison Company's leadership remained recalcitrant and continued to insist on the integrity of the exclusive licensed program.[51]

But the myopic failure to recognize the potential of and audience interest in the feature paled beside the nearsighted policy of refusing to accept financing from Wall Street investment bankers. The MPPC

49. Memorandum from GFC, 1913, GKC.
50. J. A. Berst to George Kleine, July 8, 1914, GKC, box 4. Memorandum from GFC, 1913, GKC. "The unquestionable success of *Quo Vadis?* convinces us that in the handling of masterpieces no better plan can be used than that adopted by Mr. Kleine, namely: putting out these films under rigid restrictions to a limited number of large theatres on a percentage basis."
51. J. A. Berst to George Kleine, July 21, 1915, GKC, box 24.

Robert Henderson-Bland and Alice Hollister in *From the Manger to the Cross* (Kalem, 1911)

became unable to retain either its talent or its competitive posture, because of its exclusive reliance on money generated internally. As we have seen, the Patents Company was adversely affected by the disappearance of increasing amounts of its profits into the endlessly escalating quagmire of litigation. Rather than risk debt, the MPPC operated solely on the profits accrued from the previous year. Ostensibly sound fiscally, this balanced budget approach to the volatile domestic film marketplace presented the MPPC with severe monetary restrictions.

The MPPC was well aware that the demand for pictures came from two sources: the popularity of the subjects and the drawing power of the star.[52] By 1914, these two criteria became virtually indistinguishable. In dealing with Wall Street, the independents acquired the necessary outside capital to lure the best MPPC talent into their camp. Far from being fiscally irresponsible, the independents' decision to acquire talent with money loaned by Wall Street guaranteed the nec-

52. Record, pp. 2433 and 2466. Record, p. 2570.

essary box office interest in their product. Star power became synonymous with box office success. The MPPC realized this simple equa-
tion, but because of its balanced budget approach, lacked the requisite
revenue to compete with the Wall Street-backed, free-spending independents.

Following the verdict of the government's antitrust case against the
MPPC in October 1915, the Trust "obituaries" printed in the trade
papers proclaimed the public demise of the Patents Company. As a
result of the loss of the continental European market, the loss of their
top talent, the expense of feature film production, the psychological
effect of the court decision, and fatigue, one after another of the former
licensed manufacturers closed up their motion picture studios and
quietly retired. Being unable to compete with the Wall Street-financed
independents, the majority of the former MPPC manufacturers literally just gave up. To illustrate the precipitous decline of the MPPC,
Biograph slid from manufacturing 267 films in 1914 to halting production and releasing only 27 reruns in 1916.[53] By the conclusion of
World War I, only George Kleine, Pathé Frères, and Vitagraph's Albert
Smith and J. Stuart Blackton remained active in the motion picture
field.[54]

Perhaps the most sardonic epitaph for the Patents Company was
presented in Washington, D.C., in 1928. At a gala function, Thomas
A. Edison received the Congressional Medal "for illuminating the path
of progress through the development of inventions that have revolutionized civilization in the last century." The extensive three-page program notes chronicling the "notable events and achievements" in the
wizard's life failed to mention his association with either the Edison
Film Company or the MPPC.[55]

The contributions of the Motion Pictures Patents Company to the
development of the American motion picture industry—expansion and
standardization in production, distribution, and exhibition—have been
downplayed. The legacy of the Patents Company became that of conservatism, collusion, and repression. Rather than depicting the MPPC
as a response (both successful and unsuccessful) to a unique set of
historical circumstances (virtual chaos), historians have instead chosen
to vilify the "Trust." This distorted view needs to be reassessed by
contemporary film scholars.

53. Eileen Bowser, "Production Patterns of the Biograph Company, 1907–1916." Unpublished monograph, 1981.
54. Annual Report of Legal Matters Affecting General Film Company, June 25, 1918,
GKC.
55. Program Notes Edison Dinner, October 20, 1928, GKC.

6

TINO BALIO

Stars in Business:
The Founding of United Artists

On January 15, 1919, the biggest names in motion pictures staged a revolt. Mary Pickford, Charles Chaplin, Douglas Fairbanks, D. W. Griffith, and William S. Hart issued a Declaration of Independence announcing their intention to form United Artists, a distribution company to be owned and operated exclusively by stars for the benefit of the great motion picture public. Hollywood was too cynical to take the revolt seriously. "Film magnates and a number of lesser stellarites in celluloid," said *Variety*, saw Adolph Zukor behind the whole affair in just another attempt to weaken First National.[1] Others prophesied that the all-star combination would soon be riven by jealousies and never get off the ground. One wag remarked, "So the lunatics have taken charge of the asylum." A more accurate assessment, however, comes from Arthur Mayer, who said "The founders of United Artists displayed the same brand of lunacy as Rockefeller, Morgan, and du Pont."[2]

The founding of United Artists marked the apex of the star system. For the first time ever, motion picture performers acquired complete autonomy over their work, not only in the creative stage of production but also in the exploitation stage of distribution. Pickford, Chaplin,

Adapted from *United Artists: The Company Built by the Stars* (Madison: University of Wisconsin Press, 1976), chaps. 1–3.

1. *Variety*, January 31, 1919, p. 58.
2. Arthur Mayer, "The Origins of United Artists," *Films in Review* 10 (1959): 390.

and their partners had risen from the ranks of contract players to reach the status of independent producers. As heads of their own production companies they controlled all artistic aspects of their work—from the creation of the scenario, to the selection of the director, to the final cut. By forming United Artists, they took over the functions of sales, promotion, advertising, and publicity. They would now have to finance their own pictures, a service other distributors had provided before, but in the process they could enjoy distribution profits in addition to production profits. The founders of United Artists attained this position by being the first among their ranks to perceive the economic implications of stardom and by becoming entrepreneurs to apply this knowledge to motion picture business.

The economics of the star system is discussed in chapter 14. In this chapter, I will describe the career of Mary Pickford, the trailblazer of the United Artists group, to indicate how her stardom changed the trade practices of the industry. I will then analyze the structure and operations of United Artists, which carried this system to its ultimate conclusion.

Gladys Mary Smith, the future Mary Pickford, was born in Toronto, Canada, in 1893. Her father died when she was four, leaving her mother, Charlotte, impoverished with three small children. After doing assorted jobs to make ends meet, Charlotte landed a small part in the local theatrical stock company and soon became a character actress in the troupe. Through Charlotte's influence, Gladys made her theatrical debut at the age of six, followed by the other children in succession. In 1901, the Smiths hit the road and toured for five years, living out of suitcases and playing one-night stands in the provinces. The big break came in 1906, when Gladys tried out for a children's role in David Belasco's production of *The Warrens of Virginia*. It was Belasco, the eminent Broadway impresario, who suggested she change her name when he hired her for $25 a week.

After playing a long run in New York and a year on tour, Pickford was "at liberty," as they say in the theater. The story goes that out of desperation she presented herself to D. W. Griffith at the Biograph studio for a job to help support her family. Although the movies were considered theater's "bastard child" and held in low esteem by thespians, Pickford swallowed her pride and accepted the going wage of five dollars a day. But Pickford has provided another explanation, that on the stage she was "too old to play children and too young for the ingenue or young girl type. In pictures I played anything and everything."[3] It is commonly believed that at Biograph, Pickford played

3. Mary Pickford, "My Own Story," *Ladies Home Journal*, August 6, 1923, p. 16.

Mary Pickford, child actor

mostly young girl roles, but actually Griffith cast her to play almost every kind of woman in comedies, romances, action adventures, dramas, and period pieces.

Pickford's special appeal on the screen was evident from the start. Before her name began to appear in the credits, audiences had already identified her as "the girl with the long curls" or as "Little Mary," the character name most often used in her films. So with a foresight that would characterize her entire career she went to the Biograph executives to suggest that they capitalize on her drawing power by building her up in the press. They refused. As reported by the *New York Dramatic Mirror*, Biograph believed it was not the personality of particular players that made for successful motion picture production but rather "first the story, second the direction, and third, competent people as a class and not as individuals."[4] Biograph's policy might have also resulted from the expectation that if players' names were publicized they would ask for higher salaries, which is of course what happened.

But Carl Laemmle, a scurrying independent producer, could not afford to play it conservatively. An offer of $175 a week in December 1910 lured Mary to his Independent Motion Picture Company, where she became a headliner. Apparently, Mary came as part of a package because a publicity photograph of the IMP stock company shows that Charlotte, sister Lottie, and brother Jack were also in Laemmle's employ. Laemmle is given credit for releasing Mary Pickford's name to the public, but she most probably was known by name at Biograph. Upon joining IMP, she was featured in *Moving Picture World*'s weekly "Picture Personalities" column, in which it is clear that she was by no means an unfamiliar face: "Miss Pickford is an artiste of the highest rank in a field where there are very few of her kind. She is one of the three brilliant stars in the motion picture firmament, rising to the top of her profession while too young to sign a contract." Such praise after only a year and a half in the movies! The column continues with a description of Pickford's acting style, and provides a clue to her sudden popularity:

The essence of Miss Pickford's charm is born in her. She has a vigorous, winning personality that pervades her work and carries over into the audience a sympathetic interest in all she does. "There she is," means "we are glad to see *you*, little Mary, no matter what part you are playing." This direct interest is due to a certain youthful spontaneity in the movements of the actress as well as in her facial gestural expression. It seems as though she was not acting at all, but was simply having a good time. It is also due to her possessing that

4. *New York Dramatic Mirror*, July 16, 1910, p. 14.

sort of beauty which goes with a healthy physique, in this case spiritualized by an unusually active intelligence. Back of her spontaneity and youthful charm there is a highly trained and subtle art which makes Miss Pickford a veritable queen of comediennes; and back of that there is a thoroughly modern and progressive spirit unrestrained by worn out conventions. Miss Pickford's acting is entirely within the lines of the new art. She is intelligent and gracious, but her greatest charm lies in the fact that she seems to be perfectly natural in any role that she assumes.[5]

Laemmle promoted the Pickford pictures to exhibitors in a series labeled "Little Mary Imps" and used them as bait for his entire line. For reasons difficult to determine, Pickford left IMP within a year. After a brief stint at Majestic, she returned to Biograph in 1912. The following year she was back on Broadway, again with Belasco, but now playing the difficult role of a blind girl in *A Good Little Devil*. Mary recognized something unusual about the audience; movie fans were flocking to the theater to see her in person. This phenomenon was not lost on Adolph Zukor, who convinced her to join his Famous Players Film Company to star in the film version of the play.

So far in her brief career in the movies, Pickford had made approximately 150 pictures, all one-reelers, the vast majority of which were directed by D. W. Griffith at Biograph during the formative years of his development. By the time Mary started on her first feature, she had learned the entire art of motion pictures as it then existed from the master himself. Mary's starting salary with Famous Players in 1914 was $20,000 a year, a sizable sum by any standard in this period. Barely twenty-one, Mary quickly became Zukor's most effective box office attraction, and her salary was boosted to $1,000 a week. With *Tess of the Storm Country* in 1914, she became a household word. Sid Grauman, a San Francisco exhibitor, once referred to her up in lights as "America's Sweetheart." It was an apt description and the title stuck.

The implications of this fame were not lost on Mary or on her mother, who now had taken on the duties of manager, professional coach, and administrator of finance for her daughter. After the formation of Paramount, Famous Players features were released along with the output of other leading producers in blocks large enough to fill the playing time of a theater for an entire year. In contracting for the Paramount program, an exhibitor paid the same rental for the Pickford pictures as for the less popular films. Although the practice of block booking was standard in the industry, it changed when Mary's mother heard salesmen say, "As long as we have Mary on the program,

5. *Moving Picture World*, December 24, 1910, p. 1462.

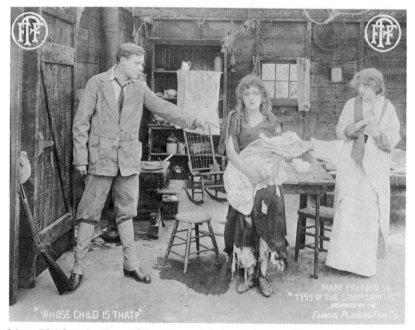

Mary Pickford in *Tess of the Storm Country* (Famous Players, 1914)

we can wrap everything around her neck"—that is, exhibitors would buy the entire Paramount output to get the Pickfords. If her daughter's neck was that strong, she reasoned, Mary was entitled to more money. As Benjamin Hampton says, "Although Mrs. Pickford did not realize it, she was registering the first important protest against the program system of film rental which in various forms, had been in existence since the organization of screen shows. Unconsciously, she was inaugurating a movement toward new methods of distribution and exhibition."[6]

Zukor passed the problem to Paramount's president, W. W. Hodkinson. Mrs. Pickford's demands had to be met. Mary was given a new contract with Famous Players dated January 15, 1915, which called for her to make ten pictures a year for a weekly salary of $2,000 and half the profits of her productions. The money would not come from Paramount coffers, however, but from exhibitors. Hodkinson decided to sell the Pickford pictures as a series and charge more for them on the average than other pictures in the regular Paramount

6. Benjamin B. Hampton, *A History of the Movies* (New York: Covici, Friede, 1931), p. 148.

program. This apparently slight departure from the program system, says Hampton, "made possible the high salaries that were to come to actors, the increase in admittance prices to the great theaters that were to be built, and the enthusiastic endorsement of both by the public."[7]

Hodkinson's distribution plan proved so successful that, within the year, Mrs. Pickford suggested her daughter's salary could be raised still further to $1,000 a day, $7,000 a week! Hodkinson balked. Such a salary would so inflate production costs that rentals would have to be doubled or even trebled. Exhibitors could not be kept in line at those terms; the answer was no. Rather than lose Mary, Adolph Zukor seized the opportunity to depose Hodkinson and make Paramount a subsidiary of a new corporate entity, Famous Players-Lasky, with himself at the helm. He could now deal with Mary on his own.

Mary Pickford was given a new contract on June 24, 1916. The contract still exists and is part of the United Artists Collection at the Wisconsin Center for Film and Theater Research.[8] It is a remarkable document, containing the full panoply of benefits and perquisites that have been devised to reward stardom. On this date, Mary Pickford left the ranks of contract players to become an independent producer. Adolph Zukor created a separate production unit called the Pickford Film Corporation, installed himself as president, and appointed Charlotte Pickford treasurer to represent Mary's interests. In essence, Famous Players-Lasky became Mary Pickford's partner in the firm. Pickford signed a two-year contract agreeing to produce six pictures a year. Her previous contract had called for ten a year. The reduction meant that Mary could devote more time to the quality of each production; it also might have been a response to audience demand. Fewer films would make the product more scarce and possibly sustain demand on a longer basis. Pickford's compensation was 50 percent of the profits against a guarantee of $1,040,000, which was payable at the rate of $10,000 every Monday during the life of the contract. As additional compensation, she received $300,000 to be paid in two equal installments at the end of each year and a bonus of $40,000 for the time she spent considering scripts during the period of contract negotiations. To make certain that the accounts were properly kept, she was to be provided with a monthly accounting. As a further check on finances, Mrs. Pickford was granted the authority to approve all expenditures.

The contract gave Pickford more control over her work such as the

7. Ibid., p. 148.

8. Memorandum of Agreement between Pickford Film Corporation and Mary Pickford, June 24, 1916, United Artists Collection, Wisconsin Center for Film and Theater Research (WCFTR), Madison.

right to select her directors and her supporting players, but in certain matters she had to share authority. If she was dissatisfied with a role selected for her, the final determination rested with the board of directors. The final cut of the negative was subject to the approval of an officer of the company and the director, in addition to Pickford; controversies were to be resolved by the judgment of two of the three. In the realm of advertising, however, she was granted the right of approval and, of course, was given "chief prominence," that is, her name alone was to be used on all advertising and promotional materials and in larger letters than any other element.

The list of perquisites included a studio for her sole use in New York called Mary Pickford Studio; parlor car accommodations for herself, her mother, and a maid when traveling to California to shoot during the winter; and a private secretary.

To market the Pickford product, Zukor formed a special distribution subsidiary, called Artcraft. Her pictures were to be sold no longer as a series, but one by one, separate and apart from the Paramount program—the contract insisted that Mary's films shall "in no way be used to influence the sale or lease of other motion picture films." Artcraft supplied the production financing in the amount of $160,000 minimum per picture. The money came from exhibitors in the form of advance film rentals, a standard practice. The distribution fee of 27.5 percent was at the low end of the normal industry scale, which ranged from 25 to 40 percent, so that close to the maximum was allocated to the producer from the distribution gross.

Mary Pickford became the first star to produce her own pictures and to win a considerable degree of control over her work. To place her achievement in perspective, we can compare her contract with Jimmy Cagney's at the height of his career at Warner. According to Robert Sklar, Cagney signed his best deal in 1938. The contract allowed him to make eleven pictures over a four-year period at a compensation per picture of $150,000 plus 10 percent of the gross over $1.5 million. He received star or co-star billing and the right of approval over stories.[9] That's it. Cagney at his prime was little more than a highly paid contract player. The movement toward oligopoly control had been complete by 1930, and one result was a power shift over creative matters in favor of the studio executive.

Rentals for Pickford's Artcraft releases as a result of her new contract

9. Robert Sklar, "The Fighting Actor: James Cagney vs. Warner Bros," paper presented at Mostra Internazionale del Nuovo Cinema Conference, Pesaro, Italy, December 13, 1982.

"America's Sweetheart"

had to be trebled to yield $300,000 or more per picture, just as Hodkinson had predicted. Exhibitors grumbled at first, but soon fell into line. Mary Pickford's Artcraft pictures marked some of the finest achievements of her career. Among these were *The Pride of the Clan* and *The Poor Little Rich Girl*, both directed by Maurice Tourneur; two Cecil B. De Mille hits, *A Romance of the Redwoods* and *The Little American*; and *Rebecca of Sunnybrook Farm, A Little Princess,* and *Stella Maris,* directed by Marshall Neilan. Her popularity now taxed the human imagination for explanation:

Because all the world is her lover and what is more remarkable, her lover has been true to her lo! these many years. She has had a thousand imitators, not one of whom has come anywhere near taking her place in the hearts of the people who go to see her on the screen no matter what she does. Because she has dignity as well as charm, brains as well as beauty, artistry as well as personal magnetism, and because she seems to have discovered the secret of perpetual youth.[10]

With Pickford content, at least for a while, Zukor continued his plans for industrial expansion. Unlike other industries of the day, such as oil, steel, sugar, tobacco, and railroads, which grew by consolidating competing companies, Famous Players-Lasky followed a new course. Rather than merging other producers and distributors into his company, Zukor absorbed the strength of his competitors—their talent. With stars, Zukor could dominate the market and name his price for their pictures. Exhibitor backlash occurred in 1917 with the formation of First National. To prove its determination, First National in 1918 plucked Charlie Chaplin from Mutual and then Mary Pickford from Zukor. Both were reputed to have received $1 million contracts, but this figure does not tell the whole story. In Chaplin's case, First National agreed to finance eight two-reelers for $125,000 each, salary included, and split the profits. In Pickford's, the agreement was for three features at around $250,000 each, salary included, plus half the profits. Both were charged a distribution fee of 30 percent, and both were given bonuses for signing the contract; $15,000 to Chaplin and $50,000 to Mary's mother for her "good offices."[11] Since, by the end of 1918, First National controlled over two hundred first-run houses, Pickford and Chaplin were assured revenues of at least $1 million a year, perhaps even $2 million a year. But Pickford and Chaplin received more than money; the First National contracts gave the two of them complete authority over their work. They now became independent producers in every sense of the term.

To retain Pickford, Zukor would have had to increase her salary 50 to 100 percent and jack rentals accordingly. He faced a dilemma: either decision—letting Mary go or raising rentals—would strengthen First National's position. He decided to do the former, but early in 1919, rumors abounded of a merger between Famous Players-Lasky and First National. The addition of a large theater chain to Zukor's empire would mean the dissolution of an attractive outlet for independent production. Complaints about the star system were also filling the air. Richard A. Rowland, president of Metro Pictures, had proclaimed that "motion pictures must cease to be a game and become a business." Metro, he said, would thenceforth desist from "competitive bidding for billion-

10. Undated article, Clipping File, Daniel Blum Collection, WCFTR.
11. Hampton, *History of the Movies*, pp. 180, 192.

dollar stars" and devote its energies to making big pictures based on "play value and excellence of production."[12] This state of affairs precipitated the forming of United Artists. As Mary Pickford said, "We are on the defensive, and many people have asked us why we didn't do this thing long ago. The answer to this is that we were never forced to do it until now. But now, with possibility of the merger of distributors looming before us, a combination that threatens to dominate the theaters of the United States, it becomes necessary for us to organize as a protection to our own interest."[13]

Their fears were borne out when the Federal Trade Commission in 1927 completed its investigation of Famous Players-Lasky for alleged infringement of antitrust laws. In one of its findings, the FTC stated that Adolph Zukor, in 1919, "endeavored to form a combination with First National by which the latter would produce no films, exhibit no films other than those produced by Famous Players-Lasky Corporation, and finally become subsidiary to or merge with, Famous Players-Lasky Corporation."[14] The merger did not go through, as it turned out, but that did not stop Zukor. After failing to lure First National's officers to his company, he continued to struggle for control of the industry by attempting to acquire First National theater franchises. And this battle he won.

W. S. Hart, although in on the early planning stages of United Artists, decided that discretion was the better part of valor, and remained with Famous Players-Lasky rather than take the risks of going independent. Zukor helped him to reach this decision by offering him $200,000 per picture to stay put. The others, meanwhile, had conferred with the man they hoped would head the new distribution organization. William Gibbs McAdoo had been head of the Federal Railroad Board during the war, secretary of the Treasury before that, and was a son-in-law of President Wilson. Pickford, Fairbanks, and Chaplin had come to know McAdoo well during the Third Liberty Loan drive when the three stars toured the country selling millions of dollars worth of bonds to support the war effort. McAdoo declined the invitation, but suggested that if Oscar Price, his former assistant on the railroad board, were named president instead, he would gladly serve as counsel for the company. This satisfied everyone; McAdoo, in the words of an editorial in *Moving Picture World*, would bring "prestige second to that of no other businessman in the country . . . his association marks

12. *Moving Picture World*, January 4, 1919, p. 53.
13. *Moving Picture World*, February 1, 1919, p. 619.
14. *In re* Famous Players-Lasky Corp., 11 FTC. 187 (1927).

another step in the progress of the business side of the screen, and it goes without saying his voice will have large influence in many quarters where large influence sometimes is very necessary."[15] For a while, anyway, the skeptics would be silenced.

United Artists was a cooperative venture in every respect. To finance the company's operations—opening exchanges, hiring salesmen, and the like—each of the founders agreed to purchase $100,000 of preferred stock. In return for equal units of common stock, each agreed to deliver a specified number of pictures to the company. Griffith was required to direct his, and the others were to play the leading roles in theirs. McAdoo was issued a unit of stock in consideration of his becoming general counsel.

The common stock had cumulative voting power, enabling each stockholder to elect his or her own representative to the board of directors and thus have a direct hand in the management of the company. To prevent UA from slipping from the original owners, the company was given the prior right to repurchase the common stock in the event a stockholder wanted to sell his interest to an outside party. And to further stimulate the cooperative spirit of the venture, and as a gesture of mutual trust, the owners adopted an unwritten law stating that no proposal, policy, or decision could be effected without unanimous consent.

A key feature of the distribution contracts stipulated that each picture was to be sold and promoted individually. Block booking was out. In no way could one United Artists release be used to influence the sale of another UA product. Merit alone would determine a picture's success or failure. The distribution fee was set at 20 percent in the United States and 30 percent elsewhere. If in the future the company gave one owner better terms, a "most-favored-nation" clause guaranteed similar adjustments in the other contracts. These fees were well below what Famous Players-Lasky and First National had been charging, because United Artists was created as a service organization rather than an investment that would return dividends. Profits would accrue to the owners as a result of the company's securing the best possible rentals for their pictures. With this in mind, the owners reserved the right to approve through their representatives in the home office all contracts with exhibitors.

During the early years of UA's existence, its owners delivered some of the finest pictures of their careers. The premiere UA release was Douglas Fairbanks' *His Majesty, the American*, which was released on

15. *Moving Picture World*, February 15, 1919, p. 899.

September 1, 1919. Fairbanks went on to produce such spectacular hits as *The Mark of Zorro* (1920), *The Three Musketeers* (1921), *Robin Hood* (1923), and *The Thief of Bagdad* (1924). Pickford's best-remembered pictures were *Pollyanna* (1920), *Little Lord Fauntleroy* (1921), a remake of *Tess of the Storm Country* (1922), and *Rosita* (1923). Griffith delivered *Broken Blossoms* (1919), *Way Down East* (1921), and *Orphans of the Storm* (1922), among others. Chaplin came through with the influential *A Woman of Paris* (1923) and his acknowledged masterpiece, *The Gold Rush* (1925).

Despite this record of excellence, which earned for the company the reputation as the Tiffany of the industry, United Artists was soon in a precarious position. From the outset, there existed a product shortage. To operate efficiently, the company was geared to release one picture a month—three pictures a year from each of the owners. The weekly overhead of $25,000 to maintain the sales organization necessitated such a schedule. But at the beginning Chaplin and Pickford still owed pictures on their contracts with First National, and these could not be rushed. Within days after the company's founding, Griffith also became a First National producer by signing a three-picture deal; he needed money to finance his UA commitments. Only Fairbanks was free to work for the new company. But even after the completion of these outside obligations, production progressed slower than anticipated. Chaplin, for example, decided to produce full-length features exclusively, rather than continue with two- or three-reelers. The others began producing on a grand scale. Encouraged by the reception of *The Mark of Zorro*, Fairbanks determined that his métier was costume spectaculars. *The Three Musketeers*, *Robin Hood*, and *The Thief of Bagdad* were among those that resulted. Production costs rose accordingly: Fairbanks' *His Majesty, the American* (1919) had cost $300,000, whereas *Robin Hood* (1923) cost $1.5 million. Nor was he the only producer with mounting costs. Pickford's *Pollyanna* (1920) cost $300,000, and *Dorothy Vernon of Haddon Hall* (1924) cost $750,000; Griffith's *The Love Flower* (1920) cost $300,000, and the budget for *Way Down East* (1921) reached $1 million. These big-budget pictures, of course, took longer to make.

Personal factors also have to be considered. In 1920, Doug and Mary postponed production to become husband and wife. In Pickford's case, one must also add the decision to change her screen image. After producing the remake of her favorite Famous Players picture, *Tess of the Storm Country*, Pickford painstakingly prepared for a new phase of her career—she wanted to establish a more mature screen character. In 1923, at the age of thirty, Pickford departed from her adolescent roles by playing a Spanish street singer in *Rosita*. She announced to her fans, "While I still play the part of a young girl, it is a distinct departure from the little-girl roles with which I have been associated in the past. I wear my hair up throughout the production with the exception of one scene. . . . I would be grieved to think that I am giving up little-girl roles forever. They have been so closely associated with my career and have meant so much to me that so long as I feel that I can play them convincingly, I shall hope to return to them from time to time if the proper story offers itself."[16] *Rosita* was directed by Ernst Lubitsch, who was brought over from Germany to assist with the transition. After the returns indicated a financial and critical success, Pickford began work on *Dorothy Vernon of Haddon Hall* in 1924. Like *Rosita*, it was an expensive costume picture with everything handled in a lavish style. Although the picture was also financially successful,

Doug and Mary

16. Pickford, "My Own Story," *Ladies Home Journal*, September 9, 1923, p. 128.

Pickford decided to check in with her audience by conducting a survey in *Photoplay* asking the public to decide which roles she should portray. The appeal brought twenty thousand letters from all over the world and nearly every one beseeched Mary to return to the "lovable character of youth" which she had rendered classic.[17] Her fans suggested such roles as Cinderella, Alice in Wonderland, Heidi, and Anne of Green Gables. Since the public would not let Mary Pickford grow up, she acquiesced for the while by producing *Little Annie Rooney* the next year.

The freedom of the stars to manipulate their screen images led to the rise of production costs, which in turn exacerbated the problem of production financing—the main cause of the product shortage. As pointed out earlier, the owners had to provide their own financing in the new arrangement. Because banks considered independent production a highly speculative enterprise, production loans were at first practically impossible to procure. This in itself made producing for United Artists a hazardous affair. But the company's sales policy further compounded the risks. UA's product could not be sold a season in advance of production, as was the output of the larger corporations using the block-booking method of distribution. Because pictures were sold to exhibitors separately on an individual contract, not only was a greater effort required of the sales staff, but also it took longer to exhaust the market for each picture. A UA producer would be well into his third picture before he could hope to recoup his investment on the first. In short, the owners did not have the unlimited capital needed to fill the company's requirements. Nor could the owners look to United Artists for financing. The option of selling stock in the company to the public was rejected from the outset, lest control of UA pass to outside parties. And conventional loans from banks in the form of lines of credit did not exist because the company had yet to operate in the black and lacked collateral. The owners, as a result, were on their own.

Despite the perils, D. W. Griffith chose to go public by forming D. W. Griffith, Inc., and selling stock to raise capital. Pickford and Fairbanks turned to exhibitors for assistance, a less risky alternative. UA's sales force knew the market for their pictures and could go to theater owners and say, "We'll give you the next Fairbanks picture providing you help finance it by paying your rental now." These monies were advanced to the producers without interest on a weekly basis. But in order to protect itself, the company could advance to its owners no

17. James R. Quirk, "The Public Just Won't Let Mary Pickford Grow Up," *Photoplay*. Undated article, Clipping File, Daniel Blum Collection, WCFTR.

more than $200,000 on each picture, which meant that they still had to invest heavily in their own productions.

The problem became more acute when the owners switched to big-budget pictures. To recoup these growing investments, rentals had to be raised. There was a limit, though, to what exhibitors would pay even for the most sought-after pictures. UA, as a result, introduced a percentage method that called for a guaranteed base rental and a split of box office receipts over a specified figure, depending on the picture, theater, and town. This method worked best for the first-run houses, and boosted sales. However, because much of the earnings could not be collected until after the play dates, the percentage method did not solve the problem of production financing.

In any event, this type of financing could not be relied on for long. The exhibition field was in a state of flux. More and more theaters were being acquired by the big chains or were forming alliances to secure better terms. In the early days, UA's pictures played in many second-rate theaters; in some areas of the country, the company was shut out completely.

Slowly, the attitude of banks changed. Loan officers were beginning to discover what theater owners had known all along, namely, that a Mary Pickford feature or a Chaplin comedy warranted a triple-A rating. So, in 1923, when UA did not have sufficient funds to advance Pickford $150,000 for the completion of *Rosita*, she could turn to the Mutual Bank of New York. UA negotiated the loan for her, which carried an interest rate of 6 percent. As security, Mutual demanded not only a first lien on the producer's share of the gross, which was to be expected, but also that UA deposit its operating funds with the bank for the duration of the loan.

But UA's resources were modest; it could do little to nurture the owners' productions, let alone those of outside producers. John Barrymore stayed away from the company for this reason, and negotiations with other stars got nowhere until they could be persuaded to take the risks of independent production. The fact of the matter is that during the first five years of UA's existence only two outside stars of any great importance distributed through the regular channels of the company—Alla Nazimova and George Arliss.

The product shortage meant that United Artists regularly lost money. When the deficit reached $213,000 in 1922, the distribution fee had to be raised from 20 to 22.5 percent to generate more revenue. It wasn't that the owners' pictures were unsuccessful—in fact, during 1921, UA had three big hits on its roster, Griffith's *Way Down East*, Fairbanks' *The Three Musketeers*, and Pickford's *Little Lord Fauntleroy*, which grossed $1.8 million, $1.5 million, and $900,000, respectively. But the company lacked the volume of business to offset the expenses of an operation that now reached a world market.

Several schemes were tried to augment production. Bringing in other big names as partners was not a possibility since they were either tied to the majors or, as noted above, had no stomach for the risks of independent production. UA therefore tried to attract stars of lesser magnitude to the ranks of independent production, forming a subsidiary distribution company called Allied Producers and Distributors so as not to tarnish the United Artists name. The owners of UA put up their own money to capitalize Allied and hired a separate sales staff to dispel from the minds of exhibitors any idea that the two companies' pictures were connected. But because the invitation to join Allied Producers did not include a guarantee of production financing, the anticipated rush never materialized.

Nor did other schemes work, with the result that UA's deficit had grown to $500,000 by 1924. Declining fortunes and prospects of a bleak future created dissension among the owners over sales policy and management. Griffith was particularly distraught; of his nine UA releases, *Way Down East* was the only one to make money. The blame did not rest necessarily with United Artists, as he claimed—although his pictures did not outsell Fairbanks' spectaculars, they grossed just as much as Pickford's on the average. The failure can be attributed to the high overhead expenses of Griffith's fully equipped Mamaroneck studio with its large permanent staff. Nonetheless, the credit line of Griffith's company had been fully extended, leaving him little choice but to accept a three-picture production deal from Paramount. This was his last hope to stay afloat.

Zukor had removed a major prop from United Artists, perhaps for good. Losing Griffith intensified the perennial product crisis, and the company was not in a position to attract other producers. It was only a matter of time, according to the trade press, before Pickford and Fairbanks would follow Griffith's lead and the insatiable Paramount would swallow up UA. But Pickford, Fairbanks, and Chaplin were not yet ready to give up their independence. The problems were serious, but not insurmountable. Besides, they were resourceful people. Once they had found someone with the know-how to reorganize the company, they could return to devoting their talents to making pictures. And there was never any questions in their minds as to who that person should be.

Joseph M. Schenck, producer and entrepreneur, was brought in as a partner in 1924 to replace McAdoo and Price who had long since departed. Schenck was named chairman of the board, and given authority to reorganize the company. Schenck brought three stars with him under contract—his wife, Norma Talmadge; his sister-in-law, Constance Talmadge; and his brother-in-law, Buster Keaton.

To solve the product crisis, Schenck formed Art Cinema Corporation to finance and produce pictures for UA distribution. This company was owned by Schenck and his associates and was not a UA subsidiary. Art Cinema took over the Hollywood studio belonging to Pickford and Fairbanks, named it United Artists Studio, and went into production, delivering to UA over fifty pictures. Among them were *The Son of the Sheik* (1926), starring Rudolph Valentino; *The Beloved Rogue* (1927), starring John Barrymore; *Evangeline* (1929), starring Dolores Del Rio; and *Du Barry, Woman of Passion* (1930), starring Norma Talmadge. In addition, Schenck personally produced three Buster Keaton masterpieces, *The General* (1927), *College* (1927), and *Steamboat Bill, Jr.* (1928).

Adding producers to the lineup was one way to reach the break-even point; another was to streamline operations. UA's worldwide distribution system would always be costly to maintain because the number of pictures in release would be relatively small. If Schenck could cut the overhead, or better still, discover an alternative method of distribution, the company would begin to reap handsome profits.

Schenck lighted on such a solution after conferring with his brother Nick, who was then vice-president and second in command at Loew's. The brothers realized that their companies had complementary problems. United Artists had the prestige that the Loew's young subsidiary, Metro-Goldwyn-Mayer, needed to bolster its image in the marketplace; MGM had the efficient distribution system. Why not combine, they said; everyone's doing it. The Schencks proposed forming a new corporation having the name United Artists/Metro-Goldwyn-Mayer, Inc., with the sole function of distributing the UA and MGM product. The Schencks were not contemplating merger per se; United Artists would retain its corporate identity by releasing its product separately. The proposal called for UA and MGM to transfer their assets to the new corporation in exchange for equal shares of voting stock.

When the deal was presented to United Artists in November 1925, Chaplin was the only one who would not agree to it. Pickford and Fairbanks had certain reservations at first, but Joe Schenck persuaded them to trust his judgment. Chaplin objected to the duration of the contract, which tied UA to the new corporation for fifteen years. Should it incur losses, he would be held liable, he feared. Also, Chaplin had little respect for MGM, which he referred to as "three weak sisters."

Chaplin remained adamant, and the deal had to be called off. According to *Variety*, Chaplin did not want to be associated with a "trust." The so-called merger, it reported Chaplin as saying, "would have been but a club for Metro-Goldwyn to force exhibitors into line, using the 'block booking' as a means to foist its film 'junk' on the exhibiting market."[18]

To survive the battle for the theaters, UA had no choice but to go into the exhibition business as well. The company was never in danger of being shut out from first-run houses, which generated the bulk of the business; UA's quality pictures were always in demand. But a power shift had been occurring in the negotiations over rental terms. As a theater circuit acquired more and more first-run houses, its bargaining position improved. It could ask for and get scaled-down terms.

Without Chaplin, but presumably with his blessings, Schenck, Pickford, Fairbanks, and Goldwyn formed United Artists Theatre Circuit, Inc., in June 1926. This was a publicly held company, also separate from United Artists, whose purpose was to construct or acquire first-run theaters in the major metropolitan areas. This move forced the important theater chains to recognize UA as a forceful competitor with the result that they accommodated UA's pictures. The United Artists Theatre Circuit is still in existence today operating a nationwide chain of theaters.

Schenck's success in reorganizing United Artists was trifling compared with what he envisioned. Given the forces within the industry toward amalgamation, it was only natural for him to propose combining the distribution company, theater circuit, Art Cinema, and the UA production units into one vertically integrated organization. More surprising, however, was his proposal, in January 1929, to merge with the Warner Bros. distribution arm as well. The new company would be called United Artists Consolidated. Under this arrangement UA owners would make a fortune on increased profits and dividends, Schenck promised.

United Artists did not become a part of the Warner empire, nor did it subscribe to Schenck's plan to consolidate the UA group. The extant corporate records are silent on these matters, but if reports in *Variety* are accurate, it was Chaplin again who obstructed the deal. His immediate response was that if the merger with Warner took place, he would withdraw and distribute his pictures on his own. Soon, Pickford and Fairbanks began to waver when it became obvious that as a result of the underwriting for the consolidation, control might pass to the

18. *Variety*, December 2, 1925, p. 27.

banking interests, leaving them without a voice in the company they helped create. Schenck, thereupon, had to call off the negotiations. United Artists would remain what it was founded to be, what Chaplin doggedly insisted on its being, a distribution company for independent producers.

Schenck's reorganization made its impact in 1928. UA began the year with a $1 million deficit and ended it with a $1.6 million surplus. Its worldwide gross that year came to $20.5 million, $10 million more than in 1925, when Schenck had joined the company. Net profit for 1929 came to $1.3 million. By 1932, UA had retired all of its preferred stock and accumulated a surplus of $2.5 million.

Despite the unsettling effects of the Depression, the motion picture industry by 1932 had stabilized. It had undergone a series of upheavals brought about by the battle for the theaters, the merger movement, and the sound revolution. The next sixteen years would be an era of oligopoly. Schenck's reorganization had created a niche in which United Artists could function effectively.

As United Artists entered this new era, a different breed of independent filled its ranks—the "creative" producer. Epitomized by Joseph Schenck, the creative producer operated in much the same way as the head of a major studio, only on a much smaller scale. Schenck chose suitable properties for his stars, oversaw the development of their scripts, secured the financing, and supervised production. The pictures made as "Joseph M. Schenck Productions" reflected his concepts overall, rather than those of the stars, directors, and screenwriters in his employ. Schenck's stars may have participated in the profits, but they functioned as junior partners at best in the production process. Every prominent producer who released through United Artists from 1930 to 1950 was this type of operator—to wit, Samuel Goldwyn, David O. Selznick, Alexander Korda, and Walter Wanger.

Of the original quartet that formed United Artists, only Chaplin remained active as a producer, the others having retired from the screen. The star system was now under the firm control of the major studios. The talkies required the talents of stage-trained performers, which Hollywood hired literally by the hundreds. Salaries for new stars ranged from $1,000 to $7,500 per week, far surpassing what Broadway could offer, but in return the studios demanded obeisance as stipulated by the option contract. As a result of vertical integration, the majors could call the tune. Scratched from the repertoire was the actor-producer.

7

JANET STAIGER

Blueprints for Feature Films: Hollywood's Continuity Scripts

The manufacture of Hollywood feature films in the 1930s and 1940s included the use of detailed scripts called continuities. These continuities provided a scene-by-scene description of the proposed film: camera angles and distances, action, dialogue, and additional information for production crews. These scripts, of course, were related to the written form of stage plays. However, their relationship to the finished film was much different from that of the drama script to a theatrical performance. The continuity script was a precise blueprint of the film for all the workers.

The continuity script assumed its special format in order for manufacturers to maximize their profits. To achieve optimum profits required production methods which would employ efficient and cost-effective work processes. At the same time, to attract consumers, the product needed to meet a certain standard of quality. Although these two aims were present from the earliest introduction of films, the shift from a one-reel (one-thousand-foot) film to the multiple-reel film increased pressure for a new type of script. In turn, the continuity script as it was organized in later years permitted the style of these films to develop in a particular direction. In other words, the style of the Hollywood film is bound tightly to a certain mode of production.[1] My

1. The mode of production for filmmaking includes far more than the continuity script and planning and writing practices; it includes division of labor, hierarchies of management, work practices, technologies, and physical capital. The linkage suggested is between only one part of the mode and the film product. This linkage was not inevitable since other economic practices or standards of product quality might have produced very different work practices and styles.

173

project in this essay will be to trace the transformation of the dramatic script into the continuity script and to describe how the continuity script then ensured the stylistic characteristics favored by the film-makers.

One-Reel Films and Their Mode of Production

From the first years of filmmaking in the United States, manufacturers used two methods in making their product. The first was generally applied to documentary subjects and news events. A cameraman would select the subject matter, stage it as necessary by manipulating any mise-en-scène and people, select options from available technological and photographic possibilities (type of camera, raw film stock, lens, framing and movement of camera, etc.), photograph the scene, develop, and edit it. In the case of traveling shows, the cameraman might also project the finished product. In this mode of production, the cameraman conceived and executed the filming of a sequence of actions. Advance planning was minimal, and a script as such was seldom—if ever—written down.

In the second method—which was generally used for narratives, variety acts, and trick films—the manufacturers increasingly employed two key workers: a director who took over much of the staging activities, and a cameraman who continued to handle the photographic aspects of the work.[2] In this mode of production, other workers (such as writers who thought up ideas for narratives, scenic artists who painted background flats, set construction and property workers, and costumers) filled out an array of support staff who helped share the work load so that the company could make more films faster. This method of filmmaking approximated theatrical production with the exception of the cameraman's insertion into the division of labor. Scripts if written were bare outlines of the action.

Disadvantages to this system surfaced however. Filmmakers quickly realized that they saved time and money if all the scenes to be shot at one place or on one set were done at the same time rather than

2. During the first years, a single individual—for example, Edwin Porter at Edison—would assume both of these jobs; on Porter's work see: Charles Musser, "The Early Cinema of Edwin Porter," *Cinema Journal* 19 (Fall 1979): 1–38. Production descriptions after 1908 (when trade information proliferates with the appearance of all-film trade papers) suggest that the split was common at that point. I would estimate the split began after 1904–6 as the exchange system and nickelodeon boom encouraged manufacturers to increase product output. Splitting the work allowed faster production with several individuals handling parts of the preparation, shooting, and assembly steps.

photographing them in the order in which they were to appear in the final film. After the crew photographed all the scenes, the director could reassemble them into the proper order. A prepared script became useful, then, to ensure the most efficient shooting order.

Moreover, the director's primary duty in his reassembly process was to structure a narrative in which an initial cause produced a chain of effects which ended in a "satisfactory" resolution. This the filmmakers believed achieved a clear, logical—and realistic—story. For example, in 1904 Kleine Optical Company set out its esthetic standards:

> The first requisite of a perfect film is photographic excellence. No matter how exciting the action, how thrilling a climax or how interesting a bit of scenery may be, it is undesirable if the photography is poor.
>
> The next desideratum is continuous action. There should be no lagging in the story which it tells; every foot must be an essential part, whose loss would deprive the story of some merit; there should be sequence, each part leading to the next with increasing interest, reaching its most interesting point at the climax, which should end the film.[3]

The goal of continuous action (pertinent events only, linked causally through time and space) derived from a belief in perceptual continuity as the basis of causal logic in the physical world. Narrative continuity, verisimilitude, dominance, and clarity (visibility—and later audibility) became primary standards of the well-made product. This conception of quality was at first no problem for filmmakers to achieve because if the film failed in its logic the manufacturer could either pay the costs to shoot an additional plot element or else send out the film as it was—a bit jumbled by standards of the best narrative.

This approach to film production received a setback as film distributors and exhibitors increasingly adopted one reel as the standard length of a film. As the exchange system developed and nickelodeon theaters proliferated, manufacturers turned out films which were priced by the foot and sold in a standard size for convenient pricing and handling. Without a script, it became difficult to provide a narrative with the requisite beginning, middle, and end. A 1911 trade paper critic pointed out that one of the major causes of inadequate narratives was the limitation of reel length: as filmmakers tried to fit the story into the thousand-foot limit, there seemed to be abrupt connections and sudden conclusions. Arguing that the length of the film should

---

3. "About Moving Picture Films," *Complete Illustrated Catalog of Moving Picture Films, Stereopticons, Siides, Films* (Chicago: Kleine Optical Company, October 1904), pp. 30–31, rpt. in George C. Pratt, ed., *Spellbound in Darkness: A History of the Silent Film*, rev. ed. (Greenwich, Conn.: New York Graphic Society, 1973), pp. 36–37.

not be standardized so strictly, the critic wrote: "There is too much evidence of 'cutting up' and 'cutting off' to the detriment of the continuity of the pictures, and this slaughtering of the subject only increases the ambiguity of the whole."[4] The problem for the producers, then, was to ensure complete narrative continuity and clarity despite the footage limitation.

The solution was to pay more careful attention to preparing a script which provided narrative continuity prior to actual shooting. In that way the director could make an initial estimate of the footage for each scene and add up all the scenes to check in advance that the scenes would not exceed the footage limit. In the early 1910s, instructions to free-lance writers repeatedly cautioned them to choose stories which could be presented within one reel (and, after 1912, two and three reels). Descriptions of shooting practices in the same period indicate that rehearsals served in part to precheck the scenes' lengths and that action would be compressed if necessary to meet the predetermined footages. One of the work functions of the cameraman was to calculate a precise footage length after every take which was then matched to the length specified by the script. If the scene ran in excess of its limit, it might be reshot. Tricks to get more narrative within footage limits included quickening entrances and exits of characters or "discovering" them in the scene. Intertitles and crosscutting were additional techniques used to eliminate or abbreviate action.[5]

Thus, both efficient production (shooting out of order) and a standard of clear, continuous action governed the preparation of the script. In a 1909 description of the standard film script, a trade paper writer set out its typical format: the title, followed by its generic designation ("a drama," "a comedy"), the cast of characters, a two-hundred-word-or-less "synopsis" of the story, and then the "scenario"—a scene-by-

4. "The Ambiguous Picture—Some Causes," *Moving Picture World* (hereafter *MPW*) 8 (January 7, 1911): 4. Note the implicit standards of a good narrative: "continuity" and clarity.

5. Clara F. Beranger, "The Photoplay—A New Kind of Drama," *Harper's Weekly* 56 (September 7, 1912), 13; Eustace Hale Ball, *The Art of the Photoplay* (New York: Veritas Publishing Company, 1913), pp. 28, 38–39, 52–53; Ernest A. Dench, *Making the Movies* (New York: Macmillan, 1915), pp. 2–3; C. G. Winkopp, *How to Write a Photoplay* (New York: C. G. Winkopp, 1915), p. 9; J. Berg Esenwein and Arthur Leeds, *Writing the Photoplay* (Springfield, Mass.: Home Correspondence School, 1913), p. 200; Frances Agnew, *Motion Picture Acting* (New York: Reliance Newspaper Syndicate, 1913), p. 79; John B. Rathbun, "Motion Picture Making and Exhibiting," *Motography* 9 (May 31, 1913): 405–8; Epes Winthrop Sargent, "Technique of the Photoplay," *MPW* 9 (August 12, 1911): 363–64; Esenwein and Leeds, *Writing the Photoplay*, p. 180. On crosscutting, see note 13 below.

scene account of the action including intertitles and inserts.[6] This scenario script would ensure that the standard of significant narrative action would be met within the footage requirement. It also provided the crew with all the story settings so that shooting out of order was faster, easier, and safer, and, hence, cheaper. With this mode of production, the manufacturer achieved both the aims of efficient production and a quality product.

Although descriptions of, and advice about, this working procedure were common in trade literature, it should be cautioned that the practice of shooting from a scenario script was not a requirement. A "stage director," filming a Civil War story on location in suburban Chicago in 1909, explained:

> I expect to call this piece "Brother Against Brother," but we don't always know until we see how they [the films] turn out. The idea is that the Union captain has taken his own brother prisoner as a spy, and then is compelled to have him shot. I don't know exactly what we'll do with it yet. We may have the Union captain commit suicide rather than shoot his own brother. We'll have to work this out later.[7]

Since at this point in history each narrative event was equivalent to a single shot (or tableau), and since the one-reel film was a linkage of fifteen to thirty shots, it was possible for the director to carry the parts of the story in his head throughout the length of the three- to six-day production schedule. It was necessary only that the director meet the footage requirements and handle the nonsequential shooting order.

If films produced by U.S. manufacturers had remained in this style and at this length, it seems probable that work practices would have continued in this manner with some preplanning incorporated within simple scripts. However, two major changes occurred: first, the idea of quality changed between 1908 and 1917, and, second, the standard length of the film increased during the same period. Both of these changes caused the manufacturers to shift from the scenario script to the continuity script.

The Quality Hollywood Film, 1908–17

With the formation of the Film Service Association in early 1908 followed by the Motion Picture Patents Company later that year, the attention of the manufacturers shifted from patent litigation to product

6. Archer McMackin, "How Moving Picture Plays are Written," *Nickelodeon* 2 (December 1909): 172–73.

7. W. W. Winters, "Moving Pictures in the Making," *Nickelodeon* 1 (January 1909): 25–26.

improvement and industrial stabilization (by eliminating competition). One result of these industrial events was the emergence of film reviewers in trade papers which took this new medium seriously. These writers, as well as the workers' associations which started in the early 1910s, provided an arena for discussions of filmmaking: general esthetics, innovations, realism, and conventions borrowed from other media. The trade groups functioned to standardize styles of representation. Retaining the initial requisites of visibility, verisimilitude, and "continuous action," the film industry after about 1908 chose new stylistic techniques to achieve these criteria until, by about 1917, the style of the Hollywood film had accumulated a complex set of standard procedures: cut-ins, crosscutting, systems of screen direction, matches-on-action, and so forth.[8] Beginning about 1908, these techniques continued to intensify the need for a written, preproduction layout, a blueprint of the film, in order to ensure that the standard would not be violated. By the end of this transitional period in 1917, the continuity script had become a standard working practice. Three stylistic goals, with the accompanying techniques to achieve them, were to affect the scriptwriting procedures.[9]

Continuity of Time and Space

Connected to the concept of "continuous action" is the implicit assumption that reality is itself continuous in time and space. Hence,

8. Several points should be made about this representation of events. First, uneven development occurred. Thus, the time period of 1908 to 1917 should be seen as a transitional one between the first style (up to about 1908) and the second style—the classical Hollywood film—which was fairly solidified by 1917. Obviously, instances of the shifts I will describe occurred in isolated cases prior to 1908. I am interested here not in "firsts" but in trends. In addition, this is not to be understood as a maturation from a primitive style since the first narrative films had a very particular and distinct style: the first period's films can be analytically described just as the later films can be grouped on the basis of a set of stylistic characteristics. Rather, the historical movement is a transformation from the first stylistic period to a second one. The two periods shared an interest in the overall criteria of "continuous action," verisimilitude, and clarity but diverged in stylistic techniques. Moreover, these stylistic techniques should not be thought of as neutral devises to be plucked from an array of available devices but instead are defined within larger historical and semiotic systems.

9. In the following I will be focusing on explicit statements by the trade about the standards, emphasizing the rationales for the techniques chosen. (Unfortunately, space does not permit discussion of the ideological implications of this discourse.) Explicit statements, however, do not indicate what was actually occurring in the films. For that I am relying on Kristin Thompson's chronology and extended discussion of the standardization of the Hollywood film style, which analyzes these techniques within the films. See her sections in David Bordwell, Janet Staiger, and Kristin Thompson, *The Classical Hollywood Cinema: Film Style and Mode of Production to 1960* (London: Routledge & Kegan Paul, 1985).

the reviewers argued that disjunctive time or space was unrealistic: "Jumpy and abrupt action will destroy almost completely the sense of illusion. It will all seem unreal and unconvincing."[10]

One problem, of course, was that the spectator did not have the days or years to watch the pertinent narrative events in their alleged time and space frame, nor would such a presentation highlight that chain of events. In the first period (1896–1908), condensation and elimination of time and space were standard solutions to consolidating the key action sequences, and prior literary and dramatic techniques were accepted conventions to construct a coded continuity. The early filmmakers translated book chapters and dramatic acts into scenes separated by dissolves, fades, and intertitles. These punctuation devices were often replaced during the transitional period (1908–17) by direct cuts between scenes even though the scenes were not spatially or temporally contiguous. By 1912 explicit conventions existed to cue such deletions:

One of the most objectionable of these blunders is failure to properly account for lapses of time or distance. The spectator receives a mental shock that is unpleasant and confusing when he sees a character transported in a flash from one spot to another, or from one period of time to another without any caption or exit to prepare the mind for the change. It is some seconds usually before he can readjust his mind to the new situation, and this makes for loss of interest. The fault is so easy to guard against, as has been pointed out many times in these and other columns that it is now almost criminal carelessness on the part of directors to ignore it. The simple expedient of having a scene continued until after the exit of the characters who are to appear in the next scene, if only for a second or two, prepares the spectators' minds for the change to come. Starting the next scene before the transported characters appear in it has a similar effect. When these are impossible, captions should be used.[11]

As the writer noted, intertitles could serve to cover narrative gaps and to signal temporal and spatial deletions, although this critic seemed to prefer solutions based on staging.

Another common problem was to indicate a lateral shift in space. Techniques of matching action and maintaining screen direction became conventional mechanisms to signal continuous time displaced to an adjacent location. For instance, a 1911 *New York Dramatic Mirror* review of *The White Rose of the Wilds* (Biograph) praised its editing:

10. Epes Winthrop Sargent, "The Photoplaywright," *MPW* 25 (July 17, 1915): 479.

11. "Spectator," "Spectator's Comments," *New York Dramatic Mirror* (hereafter *NYDM*) 67 (February 14, 1912): 28.

One of the most striking features of the production, to the experienced eye, is the almost perfect mechanical precision with which each scene is timed; it all goes like oiled clockwork and there are no jarring moments. In several instances the joining of scenes, where an entrance is made through a door and we instantly see the act completed on the other side, the action is so carefully put together that it seems the same movement. This is closely approaching perfection in the technique of picture directing.[12]

Frame cuts (where a figure exits at the frame line and then immediately enters the frame on the next shot) and later matches-on-action became effective cues for continuous time while introducing new space.

A third problem was to show relevant actions occurring simultaneously but in different places. Although split screens and elaborate sets were sometimes used, the technique of cutbacks (the period term for crosscutting) was a cheaper and faster production technique. By 1909 reviewers called for crosscutting to show parallel actions developing in situations other than chases. By the early teens, crosscutting was also supposed to provide emphasis, to avoid censorship problems, to stimulate suspense, to eliminate unnecessary action, and to cover continuity gaps.[13]

With the increasing complexity of a coded continuity, and its association with the "quality" film, the mode of production faced greater demands on its system of memory. Staging entrances and exits, matching movements to adjacent spaces, maintaining conventions of screen direction, and correlating parallel actions were more certain if workers kept a record of what was done. But records done on the spot without considering potential conflicts with succeeding setups were inefficient. Thus, a written script done in advance with descriptions of each shot and its adjacent shots provided a long-term cost advantage. It was cheaper to pay a few workers to prepare detailed scripts incorporating continuity solutions than to let a crew work it out on the set or by later retakes. The fact that in later years these scripts became known as "continuities" is traceable to the emphasis Hollywood filmmakers placed on the script's ability to prearrange the conventional cues to temporal and spatial relations.

---

12. "Reviews of Licensed Films," *NYDM* 65 (May 31, 1911): 31. Also see: "Reviews of Licensed Films," *NYDM* 65 (March 1, 1911): 31; Epes Winthrop Sargent, *The Technique of the Photoplay*, 2d ed. (New York: Moving Picture World, 1913), pp. 16–17.

13. Reviews from 1909 excerpted and reprinted in Pratt, *Spellbound in Darkness*, pp. 59–60; Epes Winthrop Sargent, "The Technique of the Photoplay," *MPW* 9 (August 26, 1911): 525; Epes Winthrop Sargent, "The Photoplaywright," *MPW* 18 (December 20, 1913): 1405.

Verisimilitude

Logical, temporal, and spatial continuity were, in a sense, already aspects of a standard of verisimilitude. Another aspect of verisimilitude was the matching of character actions and mise-en-scène to ideologically determined conceptions of reality. One of the earliest thrusts of advertising was that films presented realistic images of the world. For example, the 1903 Edison catalogue promoted *Life of an American Fireman* on the following grounds:

In giving this description to the public, we unhesitatingly claim for it the strongest motion picture attraction ever attempted in this length of film. It will be difficult for the exhibitor to conceive the amount of work involved and the number of rehearsals necessary to turn out a film of this kind. We were compelled to enlist the services of the fire departments of four different cities, New York, Newark, Orange, and East Orange, N. J., and about 300 firemen appear in the various scenes of this film.

From the first conception of this wonderful series of pictures it has been our aim to portray *Life of an American Fireman* without exaggeration, at the same time embodying the dramatic situations and spectacular effects which so greatly enhance a motion picture performance.

. . . This film faithfully and accurately depicts his thrilling and dangerous life, emphasizing the perils he subjects himself to when human life is at stake.[14]

Edwin S. Porter's *The Life of an American Fireman* (Edison, 1903)

14. *Edison Films*, Supplement 168 (Orange, N.J.: Edison Manufacturing Company, February 1903), pp. 2–3, rpt. in Pratt, *Spellbound in Darkness*, pp. 29–30.

By the early 1910s, a standard of authenticity in details provoked critics and spectators to point out inconsistencies or lapses in verisimilitude. A 1911 reviewer faulted Biograph's *His Daughter* because "the old father's fall was not convincing, and the girl's intention to leave the town was told only by the subtitle, as she ran out bareheaded and with no traveling equipment." Indians with vaccination marks, heroines that picked up pencils to write notes which were then shown in ink, and soldiers with anachronistic uniforms or improperly displayed insignia and flags were singled out as examples of unrealistic details which if noticed might break the illusion of the narrative story.[15]

A standard of verisimilitude not only contributed to intensive historical research and explicit descriptions of mise-en-scène in the scripts, but also promoted a shift from painted backdrops and general lighting (i.e., lighting merely to achieve proper exposure) to three-dimensional sets and realistic and dramatic lighting. By 1911, reviewers were praising both moves. The *New York Dramatic Mirror* claimed: "Artificial stage methods have been discarded by every successful company. Everywhere the tendency is toward truthful and compelling simulation of real life."[16] Or another reviewer on the lighting for *Five Hours* (Rex):

> A notable feature of this photoplay is the light. It comes from where it should come from. This is a most desirable feature in moving pictures, the high lights and shadows are so carefully adjusted as to perfectly mold the figures, bringing them out in clear relief from the background. They are human beings, not photographs. The photographic superiority of this release and its charm of naturalness make it a veritable gem.[17]

Two elements of lighting are praised. The first is a realistic motivation for the source of the light, such as fireplaces, lamps, and windows. Second, there is an emphasis on effects such as back- and side-lighting which molded the figures and separated them from the (narratively) less consequential background. Shifting from the initial standard of photographic visibility, filmmakers proceeded to adopt lighting schemas which suggested real depth within the two-dimensional photographic image.

Achieving such lighting effects was easy if the set was used only once, but returning to it for other setups required matching the exact

15. "Reviews of Licensed Films," *NYDM* 65 (March 1, 1911): 31; Robert C. McElravy, "The Importance of Details," *MPW* 15 (January 11, 1913): 145; "Doings in Los Angeles," *MPW* 12 (June 15, 1912): 1014.

16. "Spectator," "Spectator's Comments," *NYDM* 66 (December 27, 1911): 28. Also see, for example, "*The Scarlet Letter* (IMP)," *MPW* 8 (April 22, 1911): 881–82.

17. L. R. H[arrison], "*Five Hours*: A 'Rex' Gem," *MPW* 8 (April 1, 1911): 699. Also see: "Eclair Photography," *MPW* 8 (March 18, 1911): 586.

details of the lighting across gaps of work time. In addition, the demand for verisimilitude in character actions and mise-en-scène stimulated research and meticulous attention to set and costume details from shot to shot. Again, the answer was a detailed blueprint—a carefully constructed script.

Narrative Dominance and Clarity

Intertwined with continuity and verisimilitude was the standard of narrative dominance and clarity. Carefully cued time and space organization, foregrounded figures, and authentic details all promoted the illusion of a natural causality. But because the story dominated the rest of the elements of the film, techniques which facilitated its clarity might supersede these other two standards. It is this higher standard which promoted a shift to "analytical editing" in which a continuous narrative action in one place is, nevertheless, broken up into a series of shots (i.e., an establishing shot is followed by two-shots, close-ups, shot/reverse shots, and so forth).

In the early stylistic period, two violations of the integrity of a unified narrative action were inserts and character visions. In the case of inserts, a closer shot of an object (often a letter) superseded the practice of one-shot-per-scene. In a sense, the narrative advantage of ensuring the visibility of and attention to the object isolated from the mise-en-scène overrode the spatial consistency of the initial setup. Returning to the previous setup reanchored the object within the established tableau. Since the reason for such an insert was to provide the narrative information of what a character saw to the film spectator, often these inserts were point-of-view shots with such secondary cues as a mask simulating a keyhole or binoculars.

Character visions, such as the dream of the fireman in *Life of an American Fireman* (1903), were created by showing the action of the mental image simultaneously with the character who was thinking about it. Visions, whether dreams, memories, or mental constructions of anticipated events, provided narrative information about character motivation and, in the case of memories, about prior narrative events. However, the subjective portion of the image violated the unity and verisimilitude of the original space and time. With both inserts and visions, temporal and spatial continuity and verisimilitude stood aside as narrative clarity dominated the organization of the images.

These two violations of spatial and temporal consistency probably weakened the insistence on the tableau, or one-shot-per-scene, style. In addition, a shift in acting styles contributed to the movement toward analytical editing. Contemporary observers cite a significant change in acting styles starting about 1908. One of the more important trade critics, Frank Woods of the *New York Dramatic Mirror*, noticed a shift from acting with extravagant gesture to a subtler style based upon the Film d'Art imports. There was also at this time a general change in the acting style in the legitimate theater.[18] By mid 1909 companies such as Edison and Selig Polyscope, as well as the *Mirror*, were promoting a particular acting style:

> We call your attention to the absence in our [Edison's] dramatic productions of extravagant gesture and facial expression, which frequently mar the dramatic effect of a powerful situation or climax.
>
> Intelligent interpretation of a part requires that the play of varying emotions shall be conveyed by correct facial expression and that quiet, tense action shall supplant burlesque gestures and attitudes.[19]

In an advice sheet to its players, Selig Polyscope wrote: "Use your eyes as much as possible in your work. Remember that they express your thoughts more clearly when properly used than gestures or unnatural facial contortions. . . . Do not use unnecessary gestures. Repose in your acting is of more value. A gesture well directed can convey a great deal, while too many may detract from the realism of your work."[20] A *Mirror* review of Biograph's *The Unchanging Sea* (1910) stated that: "Every thought and feeling has been expressed with wonderful force, but with scarcely a gesture and with perfect naturalness."[21] With this emphasis on facial gestures and eyes, compositions framed closer to the player would improve visibility and, thus, narrative clarity.

Within a couple years, filmmakers were composing the film image so as to cut off players' feet. One handbook writer in 1912 remarked about the "American foreground" in which principal characters were framed from the knees or waist: "The American producers were first

---

18. "Spectator," "Spectator's Comments," *NYDM* 67 (January 31, 1912): 51–52; "Where Honor Is Due," *NYDM* 67 (January 31, 1912): 58. Also see: H. F. Hoffman, "Cutting Off the Feet," *MPW* 12 (April 6, 1912): 53. On contemporary acting styles see: G. C. Ashton Jonson, "A London Theatre Libre," *Drama* 1 (February 1911): 123; I. G. Everson, "Young Lennox Robinson and the Abbey Theatre's First American Tour (1911–1912)," *Modern Drama* 9 (May 1966): 74–89; Sandy Boynton, "The History of American Acting: A Detour," *Yale/Theatre* 8 (Spring 1977): 104–11.

19. Untitled, *Edison Kinetogram* 1 (August 16, 1909): 6.

20. "Pointers on Picture Acting," Selig Polyscope Co., 1910, rpt. in Kalton C. Lahue, *Motion Picture Pioneer: The Selig Polyscope Company* (New York: A. S. Barnes, 1973), p. 63. Edward Branigan points out that the emphasis on eyes as expressing the character's thoughts lays the groundwork for the eye line match. I am very grateful to him for this and other helpful comments.

21. "Reviews of Licensed Films," *NYDM* 63 (May 14, 1910): 20. Also see: "Reviews of New Films," *NYDM* 62 (December 22, 1909): 16.

to see the advantages of concentrating the spectators' attention on the face of the actor."[22] Moreover, filmmakers were inserting "bust pictures" (close-ups). As a trade paper writer explained in 1911:

Bust pictures, which are enlarged views of limited areas, are useful in determining action that might be obscure in the larger scene. It not only magnifies the objects but it draws particular attention to them. . . .

Many points may be cleared in a five-foot bust picture which would require twenty to thirty feet of leader to explain, and the bust picture always interests. Sometimes in a newspaper illustration a circle surrounds some point of interest, or a cross marks where the body was discovered. The bust picture serves the same purpose and answers, as well, for the descriptive caption that appears under a cut.[23]

The close-up and the restrained acting style complemented and promoted one another. Not only did the subtler gesture suggest a closer view but a closer view encouraged that style. The promotion in the film industry of the star system after 1910–11 should also be considered as a factor in this stylistic change.

It is entirely possible that had the film product remained at the one-reel length the demands for continuity, verisimilitude, and narrative dominance and clarity could have been met without resorting to the continuity script. Matching mise-en-scène, lighting, and action for an eighteen-minute film—even one with analytical editing and cross-cutting—is one thing; doing that for one seventy minutes or longer is another.

The Diffusion of the Multiple-Reel Film

A complete analysis of the economic grounds for the shift to multiple-reel films is not possible here, but some indication of the pertinent causes is important in understanding the changing screenwriting practices. The concept of a "feature" film dates back to the introduction of film as a product in the entertainment field. Edison, for example, advertised *The Great Train Robbery* (1903) as a "great *Headline Attraction*." The term "feature" was initially a marketing judgment that

22. James Slevin, *On Picture-Play Writing: A Hand-Book of Workmanship* (Cedar Grove, N.J.: Farmer Smith, 1912), p. 86.
23. Epes Winthrop Sargent, "Technique of the Photoplay," *MPW* 9 (August 5, 1911): 282. Note that the appeal is to saving length with this technique and that a comparable function in the newspaper is given as a justification. Also see: "The Reviewer," "Views of the Reviewer," *NYDM* 68 (September 18, 1912): 24, in which the writer, invoking a standard of verisimilitude, argues that the "close view" is "natural, as in life one does not see the entire form of a person with whom he is in close relation."

a film merited special billing and advertising. At first, its definition depended not on length but on a conception of how the film fit into the exhibitor's overall program. The advantage of a feature film was that the exhibitor could advertise its appearance as special and thus could justify a special increase in the admission price.[24]

In striving to satisfy the exhibitors' desire for feature attractions, studios remade famous plays and novels as well as hired famous writers and dramatists. *Passion Play* in 1897 was an early feature film which ran three reels, and Edison produced *Uncle Tom's Cabin* (one reel) in 1903. In this early period, with little attention to copyright, directors and others in the companies freely "borrowed" plots from the masters. Massive exploitation, however, waited until one producer set the example. Pathé released a three-reel version of *Passion Play* in France in 1906 and in the United States in 1907. A success in both countries, it stimulated several films and the formation of Film d'Art, a production company. Film d'Art purchased stories from famous French writers and employed famous players from the Comédie Française and established scenic artists and musicians.[25] An explicit appeal was made to the values of established literature and theater.

The development of the multiple-reel film in the United States is closely related to such adaptations of novels and plays. Increasingly, feature films came in longer than one-reel lengths. In October 1909, Pathé released *The Drink*, a two-reel drama; Vitagraph released in parts a four-reel version of *Les Misérables* over three months (September to November 1909), and then a three-reeler of *Uncle Tom's Cabin* in July 1910.[26] In June 1911, *Moving Picture World* cited the following productions as being filmed in two- and three-reel lengths: *The Fall of Troy, A Tale of Two Cities, Enoch Arden, The Battle of the Republic, The Maccabees,* and *Faust.* "We cannot do justice," the article continued, "to the subjects especially worth while in a thousand feet of

24. For a more detailed analysis of the causes of the multiple-reel film, see Janet Staiger, "The Hollyood Mode of Production" (Ph.D. diss., University of Wisconsin–Madison, 1981). *Edison Films,* Supplement 200 (Orange, N.J.: Edison Manufacturing Company, January 1904), pp. 5–7, rpt. in Pratt, *Spellbound in Darkness,* pp. 34–36. Also see Kleine's advice to exhibitors in "About Moving Picture Films," rpt. in Pratt, *Spellbound in Darkness,* pp. 36–37. "The Kinetogram," *Edison Kinetogram* 3 (September 1, 1910): 2; W. Stephen Bush, "Feature Programs," *MPW* 14 (November 9, 1912): 529.

25. Ralph Cassady, Jr., "Monopoly in Motion Picture Production and Distribution, 1908–1915," *Southern California Law Review* 32 (Summer 1959): 375–76; Georges Sadoul, *Histoire de l'art du cinéma: Des origines à nos jours,* 3d ed. (Paris: Flammarion, 1949), pp. 71–73.

26. Pratt, *Spellbound in Darkness,* p. 86; "Spectator," "Spectator's Comments," *NYDM* 65 (February 1, 1911): 29.

Norma Talmadge and Maurice Costello in *A Tale of Two Cities* (Vitagraph, 1911)

film. The play, even with the aid of the spoken word, takes from two to three hours to present, and cannot be condensed into a pantomime, which must be rushed through in generally less than thirty minutes."[27] In August the trade papers noticed that two-reelers were more common and the audience would attend them more than once:

The filming of some great opera or a popular literary or dramatic or historical subject requires more than a reel. . . . The larger production likewise makes a deeper impression on the memory and to that extent advertises itself much better than the shorter one-reel affair. . . .

27. "Higher Ideals," *MPW* 8 (June 17, 1911): 1355.

[The best way to raise prices] in the general run of moving picture houses is the two and three and four-reel production. With better and bigger pictures the public will readily see the fairness of bigger prices.[28]

In September in the regular column reviewing notable films all those selected for special attention were multiple reelers: *Foul Play* (Edison, three reels, based on a novel by Charles Reade), *David Copperfield* (Thanhouser, three reels, from Charles Dickens' novel), and *The Colleen Bawn* (Kalem, three reels, from the Irish play by Dion Boucicault).[29] With the trade writers emphasizing the profit advantages of longer films, producers increased their output. The successful importation of *Dante's Inferno* (five reels), *The Crusaders* (four reels), and *Jerusalem Delivered* (four reels) in the same year encouraged a view that length was not an inhibition, but rather a stimulation, to profits. At this point stage stars were also beginning to appear in filmings of their famous performances. In 1911, Cecil Spooner played his *The Prince and the Pauper* (Edison), Sidney Drew directed and acted in his *When Two Hearts Are Won* (Kalem), and Mabel Taliaferro appeared in a three-reel version of her *Cinderella* (Selig). The independent Powers hired Mildred Holland who performed her stage play *The Power behind the Throne*.[30]

One commentator writing in October 1911 stated: "No feature [multiple-reel] film, of which we have any knowledge, has been produced from an original scenario."[31] Although undoubtedly an overstatement, the close connection between the adaptation of a famous play, novel, opera, and short story into film and the increasing length of films is important. The longer film enabled a more detailed reproduction of these classics which were well known to a middle-class audience. With stage stars doing filmed versions of their famous plays, the longer film could nearly duplicate the theatrical experience and, even with higher than normal admission prices, the moving pictures could effectively compete with the legitimate stage.

With longer films, production times lengthened into weeks rather than days and the number of scenes multiplied per reel. The necessity

28. "Facts and Comments," *MPW* 9 (August 19, 1911): 436.

29. "Reviews of Notable Films," and W. Stephen Bush, "Standard Fiction in Films," *MPW* 9 (September 30, 1911): 954–56, 950–53.

30. W. Stephen Bush, "Do Longer Films Make Better Show?" *MPW* 10 (October 28, 1911): 275; "Another Step Forward," *MPW* 9 (July 22, 1911): 102; "Mabel Taliaferro on New Years," *NYDM* 66 (December 13, 1911): 29; "Mildred Holland in Pictures," *MPW* 10 (December 16, 1911): 881.

31. W. Stephen Bush, "Do Longer Films Make Better Show?" *MPW* 10 (October 28, 1911): 275.

to maintain continuity, verisimilitude, and narrative dominance and clarity for the five- and six-reel film while keeping down costs and production time intensified the need for a more detailed script. The scenario script used casually by filmmakers for the one-reelers became a prerequisite for efficient multiple-reel production. Had the manufacturers been less interested in full profit maximization or had the industry standards of "excellence" been otherwise, then the manufacturers might have developed some other scriptwriting procedure. But with those economic and ideological practices, the continuity script became the most acceptable work process.

Multiple-Reel Films and Their Mode of Production

The detailed continuity script was standard practice by 1914. Continuity scripts and associated paperwork varied little from studio to studio owing to their standardization through trade paper discussion of the formats. As a result, continuities from the New York Motion Picture Company are typical.[32] Each of this firm's production scripts had a number assigned to it which provided a method of identifying the film even though its title might shift. A cover page indicated who wrote the scenario, who directed the shooting, when shooting began and ended, when the film was shipped to the distributors, and when the film was released. The next part of the blueprint was the "Complete Picture Report" which summarized production information in more detail. Following that was a list of titles and intertitles and an indication as to where they were to be inserted in the final print. (Intertitles were usually rewritten after editing and printed separately.) At the end, the entire cost of the film was broken into a standard accounting format. The aim was to monitor the production for efficiency and economy.

A location plot preceded the script. This plot listed all exterior and interior sites along with shot numbers, providing efficient cross-checking and preventing lost production time and wasted labor. The cast of characters followed. Typed portions listed the roles for the story, and penciled in were the names of the people assigned to play each part. After a one-page synopsis of the action, the shot-by-shot script began. Each shot was numbered consecutively; included were the shot's

32. Aitken Brothers Papers, 1909–39, boxes 1–9, Scripts and Scenarios, TS and MS, State Historical Society of Wisconsin and Wisconsin Center for Film and Theater Research, Madison. Thomas Ince's studio (one of the studios of the New York Motion Picture Company) is a good example of the use of the continuity script coupled with a division of labor; see Janet Staiger, "Dividing Labor for Production Control: Thomas Ince and the Rise of the Studio System," *Cinema Journal* 18 (Spring 1979): 16–25.

location and a brief description of sets, properties, and costumes. Camera distances were specified, as well as any unusual effects in the lighting or cinematography. Scenes were broken into separate shots, and crosscutting was fully detailed. All action was specified. Temporary intertitles were typed in, often in red ink, where they were to be inserted in the final version. Since these scripts were often used on the set, penciled over each shot was a scribble marking the completion of that shot, and sometimes on the side was a hand-written number—probably the actual footage taken. The continuities also included postshooting instructions such as cutting and coloring directions.

The writing departments of the companies prepared these scripts. By at least 1911, all the licensed and the major independent firms had a writing department turning out original material as well as a scenario editor and staff to read and select free-lance submissions. Although they were never entirely shut off, reliance on free-lance submissions decreased after 1912 as the regularized, institutionalized sources of stories from adaptations and in-house writers became standard. (Also important were judicial decisions in 1909–11 which made companies liable for copyright infringement. Thus, firms preferred to deal with recognized authors rather than risk purchasing a plagiarized script from an unknown.)

About 1913, another division in writing responsibility became common: a separate set of technical experts began rewriting all the stories. Although the companies might hire famous writers to compose original screenplays, their material was then turned over to these technicians who put it into continuity format. These writers knew not only the continuity format and stylistic demands of the film but also the particular needs of the individual studios in terms of cost of sets, standing sets, star and stock personalities, directorial and staff areas of skill, and so on. Such a tactic provided the studio with a standardized script whose format was familiar to everyone and which was most likely to utilize the studio's physical capacities and labor force to best advantage.[33]

The division of writing responsibility around 1913—some writers specializing in creating stories, others in rewriting—produced experts in further subdivisions of scriptwriting. For instance, Vitagraph described its scenario department in 1912: "Several experienced writers are employed besides the Scenario Editor, to furnish original plays or reconstruct those accepted from outside sources. In addition to the

33. On the standard rewrite, see: "The Technical Difficulties of Scenario Writing," *Reel Life* 3 (November 15, 1913): 3; "Noted Authors to Write for Mutual," *MPW* 19 (January 3, 1914): 29; "The Listener Chatters," *Reel Life* 4 (April 18, 1914): 6; Epes Winthrop Sargent, "The Photoplaywright," *MPW* 23 (January 23, 1915): 510.

Scenario writers, title and sub-title draughtsmen are an adjunct." In 1915 the call for such intertitle specialists increased, with one scenario writer suggesting as a source "the trained newspaperman or woman, one preferably skilled in the difficult art of writing head lines."[34]

The story department soon took over the director's authority for much of the story selection, writing, and rewriting. In 1913 and 1914, the shift began seriously to reduce the director's input in those areas. Lawrence McClosky, scenario editor for Lubin in 1913, said that "now the director does not see the scenario, until it is handed to him for production, complete in every detail. . . . Under our system a script goes to a director in perfect form. He can immediately go to work on it. Four or five experts of our staff have read and discussed every phase of the script and every effort has been made to eliminate any flaws of structure." Lubin also split the department into three sections dealing with submission, reading, and technical rewriting. McClosky emphasized that a director could argue about and have the script's material changed before it went into production and that the director still had power to shape the project. He called the purpose of the procedure "to pave the way for the director."[35]

It is important to remember that the continuity script was also used by the production managers and other technical experts as a blueprint to plan sets, costumes, locations, and labor force. Detailed preshooting preparation in these areas became standard procedure by 1914. Once the producer, director, and story department selected a story and the continuity writers put it into continuity format, the assistant director in cooperation with the production department used the script to construct a scene plot, a costume plot, and a players' plot. This design "breakdown" allowed individual departments to plan their work and on that basis to estimate costs. The individual estimates were totaled, and if they exceeded the budget for the film, expenses were trimmed accordingly. Once the budget and related sets, costumes, and labor supplies were approved, work on construction and hiring could start.[36]

34. S. M. Spedon, *How and Where Moving Pictures are Made by the Vitagraph Company of America* (Brooklyn, N.Y.: Vitagraph Company of America, [1912]), [p. 29]; William E. Wing quoted in William Lord Wright, "For Photoplay Authors, Real and Near," *NYDM* 74 (July 14, 1915): 30.

35. Frederick James Smith, "The Evolution of the Motion Picture IV: From the Standpoint of the Scenario Editor," *NYDM* 19 (June 4, 1913): 15; E. W. S., "Changes in Lubinville," *MPW* 16 (May 24, 1913): 790; "For Those Who Worry o'er Plots and Plays," *Motion Picture News* 7 (June 21, 1913): 16.

36. This move was part of a larger, complex centralization and specialization of the management and work structure of the studio. See Staiger, "Hollywood Mode of Production." For a period description of the change, see "Putting the Move in the Movies," *Saturday Evening Post* 188 (May 13, 1916): 14–15, 96–98, 100–101.

The Hollywood film as it developed required the continuity script to allow it to expand its length while maintaining production efficiency and ideologically determined stylistic practices. Had the Hollywood film not increased in length or taken on the style that it did, the continuity script might have been unnecessary or else taken a different form.

Finally, it should be noted that the continuity script which seemed so vital to the sound period of the 1930s and 1940s actually was a well-established procedure by at least 1915—in conjunction with the diffusion of the multiple-reel film. Interestingly, when filmmakers added dialogue for the sound film, the Academy of Motion Picture Arts and Sciences included as part of its Research Council's projects the task of standardizing the new continuity scripts. It wrote in 1932:

As a result [of the change to talking films] the placement, order, numbering and display of the various parts [of the script]—dialogue, action, set description, camera instructions, etc. vary widely among the studios and are constantly subject to change. This unnecessarily complicates the work of those who handle the scripts during production. . . .

Proposed: To conduct such surveys as may be necessary to establish the basis for the various present practices. To correlate this information and secure general agreement on a recommended form of script that will be most legible, graphic, and convenient in practical use by actors, directors, writers, executives and the various production departments.[37]

Thus, Hollywood—as it had from the mid-teens—once again acknowledged the crucial function of the continuity script within its mode of production and style of film practice.

37. "Proceedings of the Research Council," *Academy of Motion Picture Arts and Sciences Technical Bulletin*, Supplement no. 19 (December 23, 1932).

The Movies as Big Business

With so much attention given to the film as art, it is not easy to view the motion picture business through the eyes of those who saw it as nothing more than a business opportunity—a chance to invest with the promise of high returns. Yet, even the art of the film was influenced by investment houses, banks, and lawyers—for artists often lived or died on the success or failure of these institutions—and no one can come to a full understanding of the history of film without understanding how the business was financed. This is exactly what the next selection explains. It is a prospectus prepared by the investment house of Halsey, Stuart & Co., and its purpose was solely to attract investors to the securities of the leading motion picture firms. In this light, the movies were placed on the same level with the oil or steel industries.

The Halsey, Stuart & Co. prospectus provides a good indication of the structure of the industry at the apex of the silent era. When this document was published the industry had stabilized, and even the most conservative banks—National City, Manufacturers Trust Company, the Irving Trust Company, and the National Bank of Commerce—had established commercial banking relations with the soundly managed movie concerns.

The well-known investment banks, observing the burgeoning movie industry, vied to handle new security issues of the major companies. The great expansion of the industry during the 1920s was facilitated by the underwriting of stocks and bonds by Wall Street and La Salle Street financiers and their purchase by the public. Among the investment banks most prominently involved in the movie business were J. & W. Seligman and Co.; Bankers Trust Company; Kuhn, Loeb & Company; Goldman, Sachs & Co.; Hayden, Stone & Company; and Dillon Read & Company.

The Halsey, Stuart prospectus describes those characteristics of the movie business most admired by financiers—characteristics that encouraged the massive infusion of capital into the industry during the 1920s. It tells much about the economic climate of the country also, reflecting the optimism of those bull market days when only endless expansion of enterprise was seen on the horizon.

The prospectus is an interesting document in many respects, sometimes amusing and at other times annoying. It links the growth of the industry not to the creative efforts of Edwin S. Porter, D. W. Griffith, Charlie Chaplin, and the artists who won the hearts of the public, but to industrialists like Thomas Edison and George Eastman. The prospectus praises not film's value as a medium of human expression, but the industry's vertically integrated structure, assembly line production techniques, efficient worldwide distribution system, air-conditioned movie palaces, and conservative accounting practices. In its enthusiasm, the prospectus inflates attendance figures, ignores the nefarious ways of some of the industry leaders in capturing control of the business, and glosses over the implications of America's domination of the world's screens. But similar criticisms could be made of prospectuses describing other industries. Here, the movies are seen as a business, pure and simple. And since financing played an inexorable role in the growth and direction of the industry, it must be understood.

HALSEY, STUART & CO.

The Motion Picture Industry as a Basis for Bond Financing

Motion pictures, meeting at popular prices the universal demand for recreation and amusement, have quickly become an essential part of modern living. People everywhere look to them for their relaxation, their entertainment, and increasingly for their general information and education. Without doubt the "Movies" are today one of the best known of all things American, both in this country and abroad. And yet the great Motion Picture Industry back of the movies—now a major ranking industry in the United States—has until very recently been comparatively unknown in its investment aspects.

It is time that the American people, who know and appreciate their "Movies" so well, should, as investors, become better acquainted with the Motion Picture Industry, its tremendous proportions, its financial structure, its prospects. And as the investor goes backstage, literally "behind the screens," to examine this vibrant new industry which makes possible his favorite form of recreation and education, he will not only find an industry of much larger dimensions than he anticipated, but one which is much more efficient, much better integrated, and more thoroughly seasoned than he could have imagined.

The motion picture industry has grown to its present rank among the great industries of the United States in a brief period of thirty years. But more surprising than even that rapid growth is the fact that

Prospectus, May 27, 1927.

195

in little more than one generation it has developed into a well-knit, efficiently organized industry.

Any critical appraisal of the motion picture business today will bring out the fact that it is an industry already quite thoroughly "in line" with the best methods of industrial organization and technique. While it is a relatively new industry, it is nevertheless a mature industry. And while it is still growing tremendously, its present development is being achieved along lines closely paralleling the expansion of our great veteran industries.

The integration of manufacturing, wholesaling, and retailing is already well advanced. This condition is not confined, as in some industries, to just one all-dominating corporation, but at least a half-dozen of the leaders in the motion picture field are now established as complete units of operation.

Very effective trade associations have been organized in this industry. It occupies an advanced position regarding public relations. It ranks high in its success in the arbitration of disputes.

The motion picture industry has stablizied itself and won much prestige in recent years through its progressive theater-building program. The big companies have always been strong in earnings, and now their asset situation has been much strengthened. Real estate, in the form of substantial theaters and office properties, bulks large in the typical balance sheet. In fact the motion picture concerns bid fair to become among the most extensive chain owners of business locations in the whole country.

In the production phase of this industry, standardized methods have been established; modern systems of cost control are the rule; conservative policies regarding depreciation are in vogue; film inventory values, based on the cost of producing pictures, are written off rapidly after each release date. And backing up all this is the present program of high-grade research into the economic as well as the mechanical problems of future development.

A Growth Chart of the Industry

If a comprehensive chart could be made to depict the growth of the motion picture industry, all of its graphic lines would start near the zero point about 1896, and rise to points of impressive magnitude by 1926.

The line representing motion picture theaters, for instance, would show approximately 20,000 of these buildings in the country at the present time, while in 1900 there were practically none devoted to pictures exclusively.

Employment figures for this young industry would show that in 1926 more than 350,000 persons found work in its various branches, whereas in 1900 only a few venturesome spirits had dared to think of motion pictures as a sole source of income.

Our chart would show, as well as possible, that the manufacture of motion picture films, which was close to the zero point in 1900, now exceeds 1,250,000,000 feet per year; consumes, incidentally, more silver in their manufacture than is used by the United States Mint; and dominates the film markets of the world.

The invested capital in the motion picture industry was also insignificant in the early years, but by 1926 the investment totaled a billion and a half dollars.

Historical Aspects

The "living picture" had been foretold and its coming cherished since before the Christian era. Early Chinese literature has frequent references to it. In medieval times a most enthusiastic prophet was Italy's great artist, Leonardo da Vinci.

Even the basic principle—"persistence of vision"—upon which the motion picture depends for its effect of continuity, had been known and commented on for centuries. As early as 1824 Peter Roget (better known as the compiler of his famous "Thesaurus") did some precise work in applying this law of human sight.

But many significant discoveries had to be made in widely divergent fields, and many devices were yet to be perfected before the genius of the late nineteenth century could tie them all together and bequeath to the fortunate people of the twentieth century a successful motion picture. Photography had to be perfected by men like Daguerre and Niepce. Engineering difficulties had to be solved by such experimenters as Dr. Plateau of Ghent and Franz von Uchatius of Austria. The electric motor was to be needed; many things in modern chemistry had to be understood. No wonder the people of the world waited long for their motion pictures, and no wonder they received them with great enthusiasm when at last they became a reality.

It is interesting to note what a variety of unrelated purposes inspired progress in the one line of speed photography. A Frenchman named Sellers [Coleman Sellers was American—Ed.], for instance, contributed much through his efforts to get a living picture record of his two small sons performing such commonplace acts as driving nails. On the other hand, Leland Stanford, in America, sponsored a still greater advance because he was willing to spend money without limit to prove, in support of a now-famous bet, that all four feet of a racing horse were completely off the ground at certain phases of its stride.

From Roget to Edison there was no letup in the search for effective devices that would present pictures to the eye in rapid succession. Some worked with parallel revolving discs, others with the hollow cylinder, and still others with crude mechanisms resembling the paddle-wheel. In each case a series of pictures was so placed that when the mechanism revolved they would be seen in quick sequence through prepared slots, or peepholes. These early impractical motion picture machines were known by the various names Phenakistoscope, Zoetrope, and Kinematoscope.

Edison and Eastman Important Figures

But the practical motion picture had to await Thomas A. Edison's development of the electric camera in 1888, and the perfection by George Eastman of a flexible film, the same year, which would feed rapidly through both the camera and an exhibition machine. A remarkable coincidence is that neither of these men knew of the work of the other, yet within a few months their contributions had been joined in the production of the first motion picture on modern principles. Still this was only a one-man "peep show" and eight years more were to elapse before a satisfactory projector was developed and an actual screen performance could be shown to an excited audience in the city of New York.

The year 1896, then, is generally regarded as the beginning of the business of motion pictures. Prior to that the penny arcades with their little "peep shows" had been the only commercial use made of this principle. It is significant that the people had up to that time believed that this would be its final use. Now quickly followed the appearance of "nickelodeons," and the screen production of novelty pictures.

The real business of the motion picture had to await still another milestone, however, before it could give promise of becoming a first-rate industry. That was the development of another brand-new idea—the scenario—telling stories in picture form. Like all new ideas, it came slowly. First there were little skits and episodes, but gradually the exhibitors and producers sensed the great fact that it would be narratives, plots, and events which would take with the public in a big way and make the motion picture a commercial success. But all this required another ten years, during which time the movies were used principally to supplement other forms of entertainment. Then, the first "feature" pictures were produced, and the moving picture immediately took its place as a complete entertainment on its own merit.

Organization of the Industry

The motion picture industry resembles in its organization most typical American industries. There are the three phases of production, distribution, and exhibition, which correspond, roughly, to the manufacturing, wholesaling, and retailing activities common elsewhere. Until quite recently these various services were rendered by more or less independent concerns specializing in their respective fields. But economies of production, and the theater demand for an all-year supply of pictures of standard trademark quality have tended to force consolidation in the production end. Exhibitors, too, have found great economy in the maintenance of theater "chains" for the routing of films and large-scale buying. The result is that we now have fully a thousand different theater groups in the United States which represent at least one-half of the seating capacity of the country.

A still further integration of the industry became inevitable as the larger of these chains of theaters felt the need for a dependable supply of high-grade pictures and secured an amalgamation with suitable producing organizations. Similarly, at the other end, leading producers required an assured outlet for their immense producing programs. Hence there has developed in the industry nearly a score of these "complete" producing-distributing-exhibiting organizations, which represent perhaps two-thirds of the motion picture business in the United States, and constitute a well-balanced and seemingly well established state of competitive equilibrium.

Just as the consolidation of the motion picture industry has tended to parallel that in other well-developed industries of the nation, so has its organization into trade associations. In fact, the motion picture industry has been more successful in this line than has almost any other major industry.

Five years ago, as is already well known, the forward-looking motion picture companies got together and organized the Motion Picture Producers and Distributors of America, calling Will H. Hays, former postmaster general of the United States, to be the president of the association. Mr. Hays has proved a genius of the first order and his organization has accomplished great things for the motion picture industry. Its chief activities have been: (a) improvement of public relations, (b) promotion of business comity within the industry, (c) encouragement of better business practice, such as standardized budgets, uniform cost accounting, uniform contracts, and the arbitration of disputes.

The arbitration system between buyer and seller in the motion picture industry has, in fact, become so successful that it is now being studied widely as a model for other lines of enterprise. The public relations work of the Hays association is widely known and very deservedly so. No industry has ever "gone to the people" so effectively. One of the principal aims of its public relations work has been to improve motion picture standards and service to the public.

The Hays regime in motion pictures has been so eminently successful that the member corporations recently underwrote the program for another term of ten years. Motion Picture Producers and Distributors is an entirely voluntary organization. Its membership has grown from nine at the time of organization to twenty-four at the present time, representing 90 percent of the producing end of the industry.

Production

In motion picture production America is not only an outstanding leader in the world today, but dominates the world market as in practically no other line of enterprise. We supply 90 percent of the motion pictures consumed abroad, reaching more than seventy foreign countries. In return, this foreign market contributes as film rentals something like $75 million per annum, estimated by some authorities to be approximately 25 percent of the total income of the production end of the American industry. The importance of this immense foreign market as a stabilizing element can hardly be overestimated, and the prospects for future growth which it entails are entirely beyond present comprehension. The United States is practically the only country at the present time whose market possibilities have even been charted, while competition abroad, as will be pointed out later, is not the fearsome specter which it is in many lines.

Approximately 12 percent of the American motion picture films are produced in New York City and environs; the rest is practically all a product of Southern California, principally of the Hollywood community. The great concentration of film production within that small geographical area is a distinctive feature of this industry. But that concentration constitutes the best assurance of the United States that its present paramount position in world picture production will be maintained indefinitely. The history of other great industries, such as pottery, meat-packing, and steel, has demonstrated how relatively immovable a great production center can be when once the specialized labor, the production equipment, and the marketing habits of the people have become centered in, and directed toward, some one locality.

Hollywood—World Center of the Industry

Hollywood now holds a larger share of the motion picture talent, of producing paraphernalia, and enjoys a more complete dominance in this industry than ever was experienced by Trenton in pottery, Pittsburgh in steel, or Chicago in meat-packing.

It was not mere chance that established the motion picture industry in Southern California. War conditions, it is true, favored American production in the early years, and hence indirectly the Hollywood area. But the actual localization of production there came through a process of pure competitive selection in which the geographical advantages favorable to producers in that region literally forced competing directors and their companies to come to California—and Hollywood.

The advantages of dependable sunshine, permitting outdoor production without delays, and of great variety in scenery at close range (the ocean on one side, the deserts, mountains, and forests in other directions), so that the sequence of almost any picture can be suitably filmed with but little cost for travel—all have militated to establish Hollywood as the center of the motion picture world. Moreover, such natural endowment can never be exhausted by exploitation. Hence the Hollywood advantage is neither imaginary nor ephemeral, and there is no present likelihood of its losing its commanding position, either in America or for the world at large.

There have been rumors as to great postwar competition soon to be expected from Europe, especially out of Germany and France. But the facts do not warrant any precipitate fears along this line. Both of the above countries have produced good films, and their art work is, in some cases, outstanding. But in neither country, nor in any one country for that matter, save Japan, can local producers find a sufficient theater market to make sure that they can recoup on production costs for a heavy schedule of feature pictures. Ambitious manufacturers abroad must therefore look to the American market. Yet the American market is preempted by American pictures, as good as the world affords. While 425 foreign pictures were sent to this country in one recent year, only six were successful in winning a showing in American theaters.

Factory-Studios Are Great Industrial Plants

Motion picture production does not classify with exactness as a manufacturing process, but it combines elements of what is commonly known as manufacturing, with "assembling." Motion pictures are produced by a process of photographing the scenes and sequences needed to build up an effective story. More and more, this takes place within the walls of great studios where, on one huge "lot," are assembled the

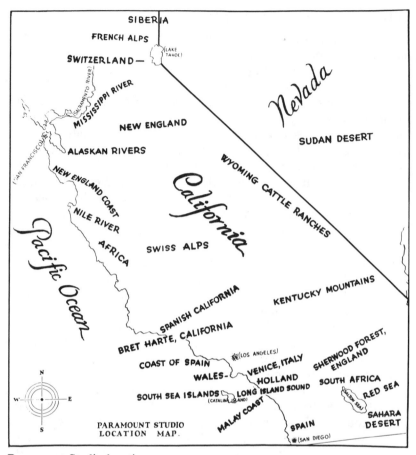

Paramount Studio location map

large variety of buildings and equipment needed in the manufacture of pictures.

In the early days, because everything in this industry was highly experimental, these studios were more or less flimsy and inexpensive. But now production requirements are so constant, so multifarious and extended, that large substantial buildings of brick and stone have been required to take their places. The visitor today to one of these immense studio-factories finds it laid out along paved streets on an extensive campus. The latest western "plant" of this sort to be erected cost $2 million.

The largest buildings on a movie lot are its great enclosed stages— most of them have several—of such large area and height that outdoor conditions can be simulated in any "corner," and numerous feature

Fox Movietone Studio, Beverly Hills

pictures be in process simultaneously. Then there are huge electric plants, laboratories of the most modern sort, carpenter shops big enough to accommodate the hundreds of workers, sculpturing and modeling plants on a factory scale, dressing rooms and bungalows to remind one of a residential suburb, general supply warehouses, administration buildings, etc.

Production Standards Are High

The very high standards of artistry now required in motion picture production, and the immense costs involved, tend to place this business in the hands of large-scale companies—producers who can afford expensive machinery, finance million-dollar plants, and carry monthly budgets, as one typical firm does, of as much as $400,000.

The American output of feature pictures is at present about 750 per annum. These will average in length from seven to twelve, thousand-foot reels. Of "short subjects"—comics, newsreels, etc.—there are perhaps two and a half times as many items, but they will average not more than two reels apiece.

The average cost of feature films ranges from $25,000 to $250,000, with the great spectacles which call for historical backgrounds, expensive costuming, and many actors, costing a million or more.

A marked tendency exists among these large companies to run a production schedule of fifty or more strong features per year. This is because they wish to provide as completely as possible for the weekly-release needs of their controlled and client theaters.

The human element plays a large part in picture production, but the following figures on the personnel of a representative organization show that not all the workers are actors, by any means. This particular company gives employment to about 1600 people. Only sixty-two of these are "stars" and featured players, while ninety are writers, eighty-five directors and assistants, fifty-five cameramen. Carpenters, painters, electrical workers, modelers, and wardrobe assistants employed by this firm run into three figures each.

The big problem in motion picture production, as in any type of profitable manufacturing business, is to control costs. This has received much attention in the industry in recent years. A typical "cost analysis" comprehending the expense items of a feature-picture budget will show: labor, 35 percent (made up of actors, 25 percent, directors, cameramen, etc., 10 percent); raw material, 37 percent (including scenarios, 10 percent, raw film, 5 percent, costumes, 3 percent, scenic sets, 19 percent); rent and transportation, 8 percent; and other factory overhead, 20 percent.

The Economics of Star Salaries

So much publicity has been given to the high cost of "stars" that one is surprised to learn, from such figures as the above, that the total actor cost (including the stars) of most films runs under 25 percent. Admittedly it is a big item and has to be watched with the same care as any important cost item in a competitive plant. Delays in picture production must be rigidly guarded against. But time economy is being effected with unusual skill. The production schedule of each picture is minutely blueprinted in advance so that the "shooting" of the various parts may be accomplished with the utmost conservation of salary costs.

Whatever change of emphasis from actor to play which the future may hold, the "stars" are today an economic necessity to the motion picture industry. In the "star" your producer gets not only a "production" value in the making of his picture, but a "trademark" value, and an "insurance" value, which are very real and very potent in guaranteeing the sale of this product to the cash customers at a profit. It has been amply demonstrated that the actual salaries (not the mystical exaggerations) paid to motion picture actors, however famous, are determined by the law of supply and demand in exactly the same way as are the rewards of executives in the business world.

The motion picture "star" of great box-office pulling power must possess a successful combination of (1) personality, (2) acting technique, (3) photographic ability, and (4) that unnameable capacity to grip the public imagination. This combination is rare, and the rewards of its fortunate possessors will doubtless always be among the highest in the business world.

Much of the former uncertainty in picture production has been eliminated. Not only have producers gone into the retail field and thus made sure of a fair "hearing" for their pictures, but the art of production itself has been mastered in a new way. Picture "direction" has become a science, and enough showmanship is now guaranteed for every picture to give it a genuine appeal. Demand has been analyzed and charted so that the "manufacturer" today produces to a relatively known market.

Distribution

The distribution phase of the motion picture industry, though overshadowed by the more spectacular nature of film production on the one side, and theater exhibition on the other, is still a matter of tremendous importance. It is, in fact, of relatively more importance than the comparable jobbing service in other lines of business. Distribution in this industry embraces three important phases: (1) physical deliveries and redeliveries, including the repair, renovation, and replacement of films; (2) the sales work—which is in reality the securing of rental contracts for specific datings; and (3) advertising—directed to theaters through trade papers, and to the public through posters, newspapers, and magazines.

The production phase of a motion picture is not completed when the first negative is finished at Hollywood. From this negative a large number of "positives," or exhibition films, must be made before there can be any distribution. These positives are printed off in various parts of the world, but principally in New York, which is the distributing center of the industry. Probably one hundred positives are made for the average feature film, and these are then consigned with orders to the various exchange cities in the United States and abroad. The film products of a dozen large integrated companies which have both producing and exhibiting facilities are handled through a branch-office arrangement in some thirty or forty "key" cities. About the same number of "state's rights" distributing organizations operate on a national scale, but they usually buy the exclusive territorial rights on films from "independent" producers, and in turn sell exhibition rights to the theaters, either for a flat price or on a percentage basis.

Jackie Coogan similarity contest

Product Paid For as Delivered

The hard necessity of financing the motion picture industry within itself during its early years tended to force the distribution business to operate on a cash basis. In fact, a great deal of it is, and has always been, on a cash-in-advance basis, with a customary 25 percent down-payment upon the signing of contracts by theaters for the running of prospective pictures. In any case, the films go out to practically all theaters on a C.O.D. basis, with transportation both ways paid by the exhibitors.

Distribution contacts with individual theaters are made through traveling salesmen out of the district offices, while the more important "chains" are sold direct from headquarters. Rental prices are arrived at in two ways. Bargaining prevails within limits, but it is the custom to apportion the expected revenue from a picture to different areas and let that determine the rental charge. The distribution of motion pictures is complicated, but it is also made relatively more important than in most industries, by the fact that there are "first-run" theaters which must be served on schedule ahead of the second-, third-, and fourth-run houses. In fact, the dating and routing of motion picture films requires a very high degree of precise handling. Yet making quick connections and delivering without exception in time for the advertised datings of the films is a standard of performance religiously adhered to in this phase of the industry.

Exhibition

No phase of the motion picture industry has shown a more amazing growth in the last few years than the exhibition end. There are several reasons for this. First, the coming of the era of great pictures made it possible for the first time for the theater manager to charge such admission prices as would permit him to accumulate revenue with which to build suitable "palaces of entertainment." Second, the development of chain theater groups and the integration of the large motion picture companies brought a higher grade of talent to the problems of theater management and construction. Third, and as a sequel to this, the exhibitors launched a very definite policy of catering to the pleasure of the patrons.

The "Show Windows" of the Industry

The success of any motion picture "feature" depends to a very large extent upon its opportunity for showing in certain populous centers, and its reception there. Second only to Broadway's treatment of a picture, the thousands of outlying theater managers are influenced by the acclaim given to new films at their own nearest metropolis. Hence it is now the custom to have a "prerelease" showing at a leading New York theater for every film of great importance, and a "first-run" showing for all feature pictures at strategic de luxe houses over the whole country. These first-run houses are regarded by the production end of the business as their "show windows." This is why producers have given so much attention of late to getting control of representative houses in this class. It is plainly imperative that if large production costs are to be compensated for, or profits made, the producers with a heavy schedule of pictures must be able to give them an extensive early showing in these prominent theaters which set the style, so to speak, for the country.

The first-run theaters get their films and are protected in the exclusive showing of them over a specified contract period. Then each picture goes to the second-run theaters according to the terms of their contracts, and so on to the lesser houses, at an ever-decreasing rental

Foyer of Tebbett's Oriental Theater, Portland, Oregon

charge. American theaters, for the most part, buy their films well in advance of showing.

Annual Attendance Gain Forcing Expansion

The 20,000 motion picture theaters in the United States at the present time represent approximately two-fifths of the world's total. The number of American theaters has been almost constant in recent years in spite of the fact that the seating capacity of the country has shown a substantial annual increase. The explanation is that the quality and size of motion picture theaters have been improving at a remarkable rate. In ten years the old store-building type of theater has given place almost entirely to commodious houses of distinctive design and elaborate appointments. This tendency originated among the downtown theaters in the great cities, but the vogue of the new de luxe theater has now spread to the smaller cities and towns and into high-grade residential sections everywhere.

The present seating capacity of motion picture theaters for the nation is estimated at 18,000,000, with the weekly attendance registering

Auditorium of Tebbett's Oriental Theater, Portland, Oregon

somewhat above 100,000,000—close to the total population of the
United States. More remarkable still is the fact that there is a 15 percent
to 20 percent annual gain in motion picture theater attendance. This
phenomenally high percentage increase of business in the picture industry has been made possible in the past by the great improvements
in the motion pictures themselves, by continued advances in photography and projection technique, by the development of professional
movie acting, and by the new heights of attainment in the art of staging
plays for the screen. The prospect for keeping up this patronage increase in the future is very bright, with "talking" movies, color pictures,
and stereoscopic effects just beginning to get hold of the imagination
of the public.

The Appeal of the De Luxe Theater

Nothing has done more to enlarge the motion picture theater audience during the present decade than the new type of theater construction. This will be written down as the era of the advent of big de
luxe motion picture houses. It is certain now that the standard picture
theater in America is to be much more of a real "palace" than prog-
nosticators in the early part of the century could possibly have guessed.

The American public has spoken a decided preference for luxury in its houses of entertainment. The old converted store-building theater cannot compete successfully any more, partly because the new and larger houses can afford to furnish better music and better talent in their entertainment, and partly because they bring to their patrons, of whatever status in life, a few hours each day of something besides entertainment—of genuine luxury in living.

These new attractions of the motion picture theater and its improved entertainment are not only holding the old type of theater patrons, but drawing largely from new groups—the music lovers, the church people, "society"—bringing new throngs to the theaters and creating an irresistible demand for more seating capacity.

New building activities in the motion picture line have been unprecedented for a number of years. Still the net gain in seating accommodations is not nearly so great as appears on the surface. This is due to the above-mentioned transition in the type of theaters. It is estimated that with the opening of each new "palace" theater (of large seating capacity), from one to three of the old store type close their doors and revert to former industrial uses.

Annual Admissions Estimated at $750,000,000

The present investment in motion picture theaters in the United States is estimated at $1,250,000,000. The current annual building program for the country runs into impressive figures, but much of this is required for the replacement of antiquated "movie" houses. Such impressive investment figures for the industry have been possible because of the fact that the motion picture theaters are dispensing a commodity which the people of America and of the world regard as a necessity in modern living, and which they are willing to buy in large quantities, for cash. The present annual intake of the motion picture box offices in the United States is conservatively estimated at $750,000,000.

Admission charges to the motion picture theaters have gone up markedly along with the increase in the quality of entertainment. Nevertheless they still remain within the reach of the great masses of the people, who have not only shown themselves willing to pay the price of good motion picture entertainment, but to add whatever reasonable surcharge is necessary to provide that luxurious atmosphere so much appreciated in the new picture palaces.

The new theater-building program is practically all of the de luxe type. This is fortunate for the industry. The large theater is a great economy in operation. Many of the operating costs, such as for supervision, advertising, and film rental, may be not materially higher for a 5,000-seat theater than for one with but 1,000 seats. There is a limit to size economy, of course, but when due care is given to seat arrangement and acoustics, this limit is not reached under 4,000 to 6,000 capacity in the average metropolitan area.

The de luxe theater of good location and under able management is a money-maker from the very start. Its opening is an event of importance in the community. Capacity crowds are assured for the first weeks of its operation, and maximum earning power is thus attained at once for this type of investment.

Site Values Appreciate

The danger of obsolescence is a matter of prime concern for fixed capital in almost every line of industry. Yet obsolescence is a small risk in the modern motion picture theater. It is less of a hazard than in most types of manufacturing plants, for instance, where the equipment may go out of date on short notice, with the discovery of new methods. Moreover, the new large movie house is always built with a regular theatrical stage, so it can handle any type of entertainment for which there may be a demand.

From the investor's standpoint the de luxe type of modern motion picture house is almost invariably in a strong position on the score of appreciating realty values. The modern theater is located in populous centers where the increment in real estate values must ordinarily be very substantial. Theater bonds thus have the virtues of other well-placed real estate securities, and in addition, because they are sponsored increasingly by the operators of large chains, and by the great producing-distributing organizations of the industry, they take on industrial prestige as well.

It is conservative to say that few commodities of general consumption have come on the market in recent years which the people have bought with such fervor as they have the product of the modern de luxe motion picture house. That makes the de luxe theater an investment of high order. It makes it, first, a paying investment; and second, because this demand rests upon an insistent human desire for entertainment, and upon a universal need for relaxation in these times of strenuous industrial activity, a permanent investment of real quality.

Looking Ahead in the Industry

The present is reassuring. But what of the future for this great industry which no less an authority than the director of the United States Bureau of the Budget has ranked as fourth in the whole country, while it is still scarcely thirty years of age? What are the prospects for further expansion? And what is the probability that its present popularity and patronage will be maintained?

Every survey of the situation indicates promising conditions ahead. The fundamental human desire for entertainment, the urgent need for recreation and for surcease from the dull routine of factory and office, is most certainly not going to diminish greatly in the near future. Moreover, the motion picture will doubtless increase in its ability to compensate for the drabness of modern industrial life.

The early prospects for adding "depth" to motion pictures—the stereoscopic effect—is a good omen for the industry. This alone will increase the interest and usefulness of nearly all films. Color photography as applied to motion pictures is now a reality and will, of course, be exploited on the screen in a way that will help the box office. In addition, this development promises to expand the usefulness of motion pictures in several directions outside the drama, particularly in education, art, and nature-study.

The "slow movie" has proven to have tremendous value outside the realm of entertainment. It is quite sure to become the most effective means for coaching in physical education and athletics. It will certainly have a wide usefulness in all forms of teaching, both in industry and in formal education.

Importance of the "Talking Movie"

Another pending development, whose importance no one dares even to conjecture, is the talking picture. Two firms have recently perfected the "Vitaphone" and the "Movietone," respectively. The Vitaphone is based upon the principle of synchronizing phonograph records with motion picture projection, while the Movietone depends upon the photography of sound. In this case both the sound record and the visual record are carried on the same film and released by passing through the projector. Each of these processes appears to be basically sound and of large potential significance in expanding the service of the films. Their first great usefulness is the capacity to bring the highest grade singing and orchestral music—now available as an accompaniment to the films in only the largest centers—into every theater of the country.

The "talking" movie will revolutionize the importance of newsreels and the like. It will increase immensely the historical importance of pictures of notable events. Appealing to both the eye and the ear, it will be able to teach history, geography, social relations, and practically every phase of human knowledge in a more effective way than we have known before.

The motion picture has already "introduced" the peoples of the world to each other. The talking movie will make them acquainted. Perhaps no other modern invention or industrial development can do so much to build international good will, and hence for the expansion of international commerce.

The possibilities of the motion picture in education have long been realized by forward-looking people, and during the past ten years the broad foundations for this expansion have been laid. Now, with the added possibilities in "slow" and talking pictures, we seem about ready to reach out in the field of education on a large scale.

Great universities like Columbia and Harvard are inaugurating courses in the use and technique of pictures. Other educational leaders like the Yale University Press are sponsoring "motion picture textbooks." Several of the leading dramatic companies are turning out a substantial by-product of educational films, while two or three large companies have been organized to specialize exclusively in this line. One of the most significant of all present efforts is that of the Eastman Kodak Company, which is sponsoring an impressive campaign of investigation and research into the problems of popular education through motion pictures.

Many state and city school systems are launching ambitious programs. Ohio, for instance, according to its director of visual education, will require, after September 1927, that all its first-class high schools be equipped with picture projectors and material.

Foreign Trade Follows the Film

There are vast uncharted opportunities ahead for the expansion of motion pictures into industrial, governmental, religious, and health work. American export manufacturers, as well as foreign competitors, have been amazed by the tremendous business-building potency of the foreign showing of American pictures. What the people of the world see their screen heroes wear, and eat, and use, they want for themselves. They demand these things at their stores. Business follows the film much more dependably than it follows the flag. Hence the government and industrial leaders are bound to use motion pictures on a vastly larger scale, both for advertising purposes at home, and to carry American goods abroad.

The Red Cross pioneered in the use of motion pictures for health work. Industry has proven their great usefulness in putting over "safety-first" programs and welfare work. Now comes the American College of Surgeons with the announcement that they will explore scientifically the possibilities of the films, both for teaching the healing arts to the students of medicine and for reaching the general public.

Paramount in foreign lands

No "Saturation Point"

It is impossible now to even think of the "saturation point" for motion pictures. To draw the line on "a picture a day" would be, to say the least, meaningless. With health, education, government, recreation, religion, and entertainment all making their appeals and rendering their services through this medium, it can hardly fail to become as universal an experience as reading from the printed page. It does not seem extravagant to prophesy that the motion picture will come to be regarded as almost as necessary to healthful living as the food which the people eat and the clothes they wear.

The industry behind all this promises to be and will long continue as one of the most serviceable to mankind. In turn it cannot fail to afford a field of unsurpassed opportunity for investment.

A Sound Basis for Financing

The motion picture industry has passed through its experimental period. There has been no perceptible slowing down in its money-making possibilities, but the decade since 1914 (the advent of big feature programs) has seen this industry take giant form, and shape itself along accepted lines of business organization. Production has been systematized during this period until the making of a picture today in one of the great studios is an impressive example of industrial efficiency.

Accounting and other control devices have been worked out to meet situations that were absolutely unique to this industry. The budget system for cost control in film manufacture has proven now to be as dependable a system of forecasting as one finds in many other industries.

The average man may have been led to believe that pictures of even the large companies are produced on a "hit-or-miss" basis; that a certain amount of money is spent in the mere hope that it will come back when the film is released. On the contrary the important and expensive films are sold in advance at the beginning of the year. Many of these pictures are even contracted for before production starts on them, so the company actually knows fairly well what its return is going to be before the filming gets under way. This being the situation, there is constant progress toward cost control, and budgets become increasingly significant. The money plans for a picture not only prescribe its maximum cost allowances, but they reflect a conservative estimate of its minimum net earning capacity.

The need for better inventory methods, balance sheet standards, and for contract forms which would prove equitable in both directions, long constituted serious problems in this industry. But recently these have been ironed out in an effective way.

One noticeably strong feature of motion picture inventory policy is that the entire value of the films which a company owns is written off its books within twenty-four months of their first release. Approximately 80 percent of this is charged off during the first year, regardless of what has been earned or the prospects for continued revenue. When it happens that a film has a long earning life, or proves to have rerun value later on, the entire earnings beyond the first two years, aside from distribution costs, are thus seen to be pure profit. In one recent case a film with a successful record five years ago, which was brought out and rerun to the new generation of theater-goers, netted more than $1,000,000 to its owners. And note that this film had been carried on the books of the company for several years as a nominal asset of but one dollar.

Scientific management and modern research methods have produced striking results also on the exhibition side of the motion picture industry. One illustration is concerned with that natural seasonal handicap—the falling-off of patronage during the hot months of midsummer. To overcome this, the de luxe houses installed refrigeration plants and advertised themselves as "the coolest spots in town." This policy completely reversed the situation in some cities and gives promise of becoming generally successful. Attendance charts for the above places now show an actual bulge in July and August. Moreover, cooling systems have been devised which are financially available to the small houses, down to 300–500 seating capacity, and in many cases are being installed by them.

Strong Banking Position

The bankers of the country have given ample testimony within recent years to their belief in the present soundness of this industry. Whereas formerly the business was compelled to depend almost entirely upon its own resources and financial ingenuity, the leading companies are all able now to obtain both commercial and long-term credits on customary trade terms. Numerous large financial undertakings in the motion picture industry have been consummated by financial houses of high standing. Approximately $200,000,000 in motion picture securities have been financed through Wall and LaSalle streets in the last twenty-four months.

A conspicuous development in financial literature has recently taken place along this line. Stories regarding the business end of motion picture production and distribution are now appearing in leading periodicals with a frequency commonly accorded other industries of leading rank. Both the stocks and bonds of motion picture concerns have been accepted for listing on the New York Stock Exchange, and the trading in these securities at the present time bulks into figures of real magnitude.

The motion picture industry has become the beneficiary in recent years of added confidence from many different directions. Local bankers in all parts of the country have come to see that theater construction on the present large scale and of the present type is not only good for employment but good for land values in any section of the city. Similarly, they have observed that the location of a de luxe theater in almost any type of community tends to draw high-class trade and very definitely improves business conditions there.

Independent moneyed men are turning to the motion picture industry. They have long sensed its great earning possibilities, but now, in addition, they have observed the results of conservative stabilizing policies such as are reflected in an ever-increasing percentage of fixed assets in the balance sheets of all the great motion picture companies.

They have been reassured by the expanding and apparently permanent nature of the industry's foreign trade. They have been impressed by the proven earning capacity of modern theater buildings, while the sinking fund provisions that are almost invariably a part of a theater mortgage lend added attractiveness.

Finally, there is a great tribute of public confidence contained in the list of sixty thousand individual shareholders of seven motion picture issues now traded on the New York Stock Exchange, and in the ever-increasing volume of such bonds which are being absorbed by American investors. Manifestly, the great American public, which enjoys so much the phantasy on the screen, has begun to be thoroughly intrigued by the vision of earnings and profits "behind the screen."

9

DOUGLAS GOMERY

U.S. Film Exhibition:
The Formation of a Big Business

In his basic summary and reinterpretation of the creation of America's twentieth-century industrial order, noted business historian Alfred D. Chandler argues:

The modern industrial enterprise—the archetype of today's giant corporation—resulted from the integration of the processes of mass production with those of mass distribution within a single business firm. The first "big businesses" in American industry were those that united the types of distributing organization created by mass marketers with the types of factory organization developed to manage the new processes of mass production.[1]

Such a transformation occurred in the American film industry in a twelve-year period from the end of World War I (1918) to the coming of the Great Depression (1930). Historians have written much on how Hollywood giants perfected the mass production of narrative motion pictures. We know far less, however, about the other half of Chandler's schema: mass marketing. Basically during the 1920s, each major movie corporation created a network for world distribution, and developed a large chain of theaters, principally in the United States. I have written about the question of world distribution elsewhere;[2] here I shall analyze

1. Alfred D. Chandler, *The Visible Hand* (Cambridge, Mass.: Harvard University Press, 1977), p. 285.
2. See Douglas Gomery, "Economic Struggle and Hollywood Imperialism: Europe Converts to Sound," *Yale French Studies* 60 (Winter 1980): 80–93.

how the American film corporations constructed and utilized ownership of theaters to garner greater profits, power, and control. I argue
that the American film industry adapted the then-dominant practice
for mass marketing, the chain store strategy, for "retailing" motion
picture entertainment, thus integrating the film industry into the mainstream of mass-retailing, big-business practice.

During the 1920s, in the United States, the chain store emerged as
the dominant mode for mass marketing goods and services: groceries,
hardware, sundries, gasoline, clothing, and so on. Each outlet was able
to offer a consumer a standardized product, at a price much lower
than prevailing rates available from "independent mom-and-pop" operations. Economies of scale and monopsony (buying) power provided
the sources for reduced costs. To maximize profits (the difference between price and input costs), owners of chains hired skilled executives
and experts in accounting and inventory control. Operating from a
central office, management partitioned the firm into fundamental departments, then increased the speed and regularity of operations, and
consequently pushed each unit to perform its specialty at maximum
efficiency and minimum cost. Simultaneously, the chain purchased
more outlets, reaped greater economies of scale, and secured more
monopsony power. Relying on large accounting departments for information on all phases of the enterprise, ownership and management
minimized waste and maximized profits, growth, and power. For example, during the 1920s, chain drugstores (selling medicines, sundries,
and food) more than doubled in number using such tactics; chain
clothing stores quadrupled. The Atlantic and Pacific (A&P) grocery
chain became America's largest. In 1912, A&P controlled only four
hundred outlets. Less than two decades later, the total exceeded fifteen
hundred, and A&P accounted for more than 10 percent of all food
sold in the United States. Alfred Chandler argues that the development
of the chain store strategy constituted the most important marketing
innovation in the United States during the first half of this century.[3]

Motion picture theater chains originated on a regional level, typically
within the environs of a single metropolitan area. Prior to World War
I, there still existed broad differences in the spectrum of motion picture
entertainment offerings across the United States. Gradually thereafter,
a half-dozen of the more profitable regional organizations established

3. Thomas C. Cochran, *Two Hundred Years of American Business* (New York: Delta,
1977), pp. 116–117; Godfrey M. Lebhar, *Chain Stores in America, 1859–1962* (New
York: Chain Store Publishing Co., 1963), pp. 24–64; Walter S. Hayward and Percival
White, *Chain Stores* (New York: McGraw, 1928), pp. 1–14; Chandler, *Visible Hand*,
pp. 233–39.

a definable set of industrywide trends: Loew's in New York City, Grauman in Los Angeles, Skouras in St. Louis, among others. But the most successful regional chain—in terms of profitability and growth—could be found in Chicago. Between 1918 and 1925, the Balaban & Katz (hereafter B&K) organization managed to overtake all rivals and completely dominate America's second largest city as well as a significant portion of the central United States. B&K controlled nearly one-eighth of the potential market for motion picture entertainment in the United States at that time. Profit rates matched any growth industry during the bullish 1920s. President Sam Katz strove to make B&K as successful as earlier Chicago-based chain store operations: Sears & Roebuck and Walgreen Drugstores. But Katz faced a formidable constraint. Since B&K entered the Chicago exhibition scene much later than its rivals, he could not contract for the most popular motion pictures. Others held exclusive rights for Chicago. Intially B&K could obtain only state's-rights or subsequent-run films. Katz and his associates, the Balaban brothers, Barney and Abe, thus had to formulate an alternative strategy to draw patrons to B&K theaters. The firm's success rested, I shall argue, on a combination of *nonfilmic* innovations for marketing motion picture entertainment.

Sam Katz recognized that during the early part of this century important socioeconomic changes were taking place in American cities. The innovation of rapid transit (elevated and surface lines) enabled the middle class (in terms of income) to move to the periphery of cities, or into politically independent suburbs. In response, B&K constructed its first picture palaces in the western, northern, and southern environs of the fan-shaped metropolis of Chicago. Each of these new "suburban" areas possessed its own central business/recreation district, about five miles from the lakefront location of Chicago's downtown. B&K first built a large (nearly 3,000-seat) theater in the Lawndale neighborhood (West Side), another in Uptown (North Side), and finally on the South Side in Woodlawn. Together these three operations proved so profitable that B&K could internally generate the funds necessary to erect a 4,000-seat theater on a prime spot in downtown Chicago. Moreover, once this matrix of four picture palaces was in place, no Chicagoan needed to spend more than a half-hour to travel to a B&K theater—using inexpensive elevated or streetcar transportation. Therefore as B&K acquired more theaters, required travel time fell to a quarter-hour. Only then did B&K seek control of a majority of downtown operations. Katz had discovered that B&K could monopolize exhibition in one city by controlling a small number of picture palaces in certain locations: outlying business centers as well as downtown. Ownership of *all* outlets provided neither an optimal investment strategy, nor maximum profits.[4]

B&K began its entertainment offerings with the theater building itself. All B&K picture palaces presented a decorative spectacle—modeled on European palaces and/or the homes and retreats of America's upper class. Sam Katz and his staff of architects did not invent ornate theater design, but did operationalize and standardize its utilization for motion picture audiences. As patrons reveled in the architectural excess, few noticed that each structural detail provided a specific function in the profit-maximizing plan of B&K. The exterior of each theater served as a massive outdoor advertising display. Vertical electric signs, sometimes one hundred feet tall, and marquees flashed the theater's name and offering in three colors. At this time, when the majority of American residents had only recently been wired for electricity, this spectacle of "bright lights" tendered a unique attraction in itself. In contrast, the ornate facades and stained glass windows behind the sign and marquee served to remind moviegoers of older, more traditional structures such as churches or halls of government. Inside, B&K provided space so all ticket holders could wait protected from the unpredictable Chicago weather. Those lingering customers could gaze at spectacular foyers, a painting gallery, and listen to live music. An intricate network of passageways enabled a staff of forty ushers to comfortably facilitate the entry and exit of seven thousand people in ten to fifteen minutes. Finally, B&K provided numerous auxilliary services which became attractions in themselves: clean, spacious restrooms, and free supervised child care services.[5]

The preceding analysis has focused on the placement and design of physical capital. Katz was also very much concerned with labor inputs. He attempted to systematize all employee actions. Management specified all duties, and experimented to find the least-cost solution for each task. Such control over all employee behavior enabled B&K to

4. Paul F. Cressey, "Population Succession in Chicago, 1898–1930," *American Journal of Sociology* 44 (1938): 58–61; Homer Hoyt, *One Hundred Years of Land Values in Chicago* (Chicago: University of Chicago Press, 1933), pp. 225–31; Douglas Gomery, "The Picture Palace: Economic Sense or Hollywood Nonsense," *Quarterly Review of Film Studies* 3 (Winter 1978): 29–32.

5. *Moving Picture World,* October 5, 1918, p. 67; "Uptown Theatre," *Marquee* 9 (Second Quarter 1977): 1–27; *Motion Picture News,* April 9, 1921, pp. 2485–86; John W. Landon, *Jesse Crawford* (Vestal, N.Y.: Vestal Press, 1974), pp. 36–39; R. W. Sexton and B. F. Betts, eds., *American Theatres of Today* (New York: Architectural Book Publishing Co., 1927), pp. 1–13.

keep its total wage bill to a minimum. Except for unionized musicians, stagehands, and projectionists, Katz and his experts hired individuals for proper appearance, trained him/her to efficiently perform assigned duties, and paid very low wages by using teenagers and women and/or blacks whenever possible. For example, ushers had to be white male college students of a specified height and weight. B&K managers trained these young men in how and when to address all types of patrons, provided the appropriate behavior for all emergencies, and fired anyone who accepted or even ungraciously refused a gratuity in any form. Maintenance workers were usually low-paid blacks. Katz's experts knew how many janitors and maids it took to clean a certain size floor, and let go any employees who did not match the accepted standards. Such standardization, although quite paternalistic in a largely antiunion era, guaranteed a certain definition of quality, much like country clubs and fine hotels which utilized similar labor policies. The generation of such a "clean, respectable" image became the cornerstone in B&K's successful attempt to attract more and more middle- and upper-middle-class patrons to movie entertainment.[6]

As Katz and his staff sought methods to make optimal use of location, physical capital, and labor, they helped introduce an important new technology to American culture. In 1917 B&K opened the first air-cooled movie theater in the United States. Prior to the construction of the Central Park theater, movie houses either shuttered during warm-weather months, or opened to small crowds. Chicago had become a center for invention and innovation in artificial cooling because its meat-processing firms required large refrigerated spaces. By 1917, a carbon dioxide system had been perfected to chill such spaces, but this process demanded expensive apparatus and thus could be utilized only by firms with a sizable, guaranteed cash flow. B&K possessed large spaces (auditoriums and foyers), and the revenue necessary to make such an investment worthwhile. By 1925, B&K had added a dehumidification system, thus offering a truly air-conditioned environment—the first available to the middle class. Prior to this, only owners of large factories and the rich could afford cool, dehumidified environments. Not unexpectedly, B&K theaters drew larger crowds during the summer months. Katz and his advertising experts capitalized on this comparative advantage and widely advertised this unique creature comfort. Such efforts proved so successful that B&K theaters became

6. Carrie Balaban, *Continuous Performance* (New York: A. J. Balaban Foundation, 1964), pp. 54–56, 95–100; Barney Balaban and Sam Katz, *The Fundamental Principles of Balaban and Katz Theatre Management* (Chicago: Balaban and Katz, 1926), pp. 36–73.

a source of civic pride—the most "advanced" in the United States at that time.[7]

Finally, Katz never tendered *just* motion pictures in B&K theaters. The show included live entertainment *and* motion pictures—in nearly equal proportions. In fact, when B&K still could rent only state's-rights and subsequent-run films, Katz hired and/or developed vaudeville talent, mounted spectacular stage revues unrelated to the movies being shown, bathed these spectacles in extravagant lighting effects, and created a reputation for "stage show" entertainment. In time, these presentations, using the industry jargon of the time, grew more popular than all but a handful of the movies B&K could ever present in one season. As B&K grew to dominate the Chicago market, the Hollywood producer-distributors begged Katz to take their most popular works, and profits expanded even further. Such shows were expensive, but to cover fixed costs, B&K rotated shows—with no significant loss in popularity. In fact, throughout the 1920s, *Variety*, the dominant industry trade paper, often argued that B&K "presentations" offered better "entertainment value" than most motion pictures Hollywood produced.[8]

Not unexpectedly, by 1923, several large Hollywood producer-distributors sought to merge with B&K in order to acquire a significant outlet for their motion pictures. More important, these movie corporations sought to bring Sam Katz and his management team to New York to head up their chain of theaters and institute the Balaban & Katz strategy on the national level. Katz shrewdly played one company off against another to achieve the best deal for B&K and himself. In November 1925, B&K merged with industry giant Famous Players-Lasky. Katz obtained complete autonomy to run the newly formed Publix theater chain. Within three months, Katz had centralized all power in his New York office, changed a majority of theater names to Paramount, begun to promote the Publix symbol in national magazines, and aggressively sought to buy and/or take over more houses. In the Katz organization scheme, all power flowed from the top. Orders were simply passed down to regional, district, and house managers. And this system worked: by 1930 Publix had become the most profitable theater chain in cinema history. The other major circuits, Loew's, Warner, RKO, and Fox, imitated Katz's marketing strategies and management procedures as best they could. Consequently, it is necessary to understand the workings only of the Publix chain system in order

7. Oscar E. Anderson, *Refrigeration in America* (Princeton, N.J.: Princeton University Press, 1953), pp. 222–24; Margaret Ingeles, *Willis Haviland Carrier* (New York: Country Life Press, 1952), p. 64; "Heating, Ventilating, and Cooling Plant of the Tivoli Theatre," *Power Plant Engineering* 26 (March 1, 1922): 249–55; *Variety*, June 10, 1925, p. 31.

8. *Variety*, April 12, 1923, p. 30; July 12, 1923, p. 27; November 1, 1923, p. 26; November 8, 1923, p. 21; December 8, 1923, p. 37; September 23, 1925, p. 32.

to comprehend the major changes which took place in the mass marketing of motion pictures in the United States during the late 1920s.[9]

Katz and his staff of experts in New York decided which films to show, stage shows to mount, employees to hire, equipment to buy, and advertising to display. For example, a staff of real estate specialists planned where to construct any new Publix theater. Underlings studied traffic patterns, population movements, the relative distribution of income, recreation habits, and other socioeconomic data before recommending the placement, size, and design of a new theater. Publix permanently retained architects C. W. and George Rapp, who worked so well in Chicago. And all existing and future deluxe theaters were air-conditioned; only small neighborhood houses were exempt. Katz instituted the labor policy first established in Chicago: politeness, but no tips, efficiency, and low wages. Management developed instructions for all situations, all emergencies. Managers, hired more for their record-keeping than "show business" skills, had to construct detailed reports of financial transactions and nonfinancial activities each week. With this data central office efficiency experts calculated elaborate charts and guides for use in future decision making. Sam Katz strove to make Publix as scientifically managed and optimally efficient a chain store operation as there existed in the United States at that time.[10]

All deluxe Publix houses presented films and stage shows. To facilitate the booking of feature films, shorts, and newsreels, Publix accountants accumulated in-house data on all revenue situations, and projected the potential gross for each filmic offering. Specialists, also based in New York, planned all facets of Publix stage presentations, even designing all lighting cues for every theater the unit would visit. Concepts followed from the formulae which had worked best in Chicago. By 1928, Publix had become the largest employer of vaudeville talent in the United States. (Executives in the New York office also engaged organists and pit orchestra members, but these musicians did not move with the presentation units.) Katz sought to develop popular performers, set up elaborate mise-en-scènes, and spread these costs over several hundred theaters. Here Publix effectively minimized costs

9. *Variety*, October 23, 1925, p. 27; June 26, 1929, p. 5; August 7, 1929, pp. 3–10; *Wall Street Journal*, June 11, 1927, pp. 1, 4; *The Film Daily Yearbook, 1927* (New York: Film Daily, 1927), pp. 649–71; *The Film Daily Yearbook, 1931* (New York: Film Daily, 1931), pp. 823–44.

10. Howard T. Lewis, ed., *Cases on the Motion Picture Industry* (New York: McGraw, 1930), pp. 519–21; Joseph P. Kennedy, ed. *The Story of the Films* (Chicago: A. W. Shaw, 1927), pp. 265–72; *Variety*, August 7, 1927, p. 19; *Film Daily*, January 14, 1926, p. 1; February 26, 1926, p. 1; July 26, 1926, pp. 1–2.

using economies of scale and monopsony power, the classic tools of a chain store operation.[11]

In Chicago, B&K advertised widely, but seemed to gain no comparative advantage. On a national scale, Katz was sure Publix could not rely on so crude an instrument as "word of mouth." So he hired a score of the practitioners of the advertising and publicity arts. Imitating other successful chain store enterprises, they attempted to sell the Publix trademark as an assurance of quality. The theme became, "You don't need to know what's playing at a Publix house. It's bound to be the best show in town." For each specific presentation/motion picture combination offered by the chain, specialists in the New York office prepared a manual containing advertisements, suggestions for their maximum exposure, and descriptions of devices to promote the program. The major Hollywood producers also supplied a "press kit," but Katz required all Publix managers to employ only in-house materials. Each local manager could select advertisements most appropriate to his market, and then execute the campaign within strict guidelines laid down from the New York office. All extraordinary expenses for advertising were planned and executed from New York.[12]

The innovation of sound motion pictures during 1928 did not disrupt Publix—as some film historians have lead us to believe. In fact, this technical change enabled the Publix system to function even more efficiently. With sound, Katz could have popular vaudeville arts and/ or presentations filmed, standardize the product, and eliminate travel and setup costs. Quickly, such filmed entertainment replaced live performance in all but the very largest Publix houses. Only the Paramount theater in New York, and the Chicago theater continued to offer a new stage show each week. Orchestras and organists were fired, for further savings—far greater than any extra costs involved in renting and showing the new sound motion pictures. By September 1929, Publix's product had become all sound, more standardized, more easily controlled, and even more profitable. Katz invested this surplus profit into more outlets. By May 1930, Publix controlled 1,200 theaters, dominating the southern United States, New England, and the states of Michigan, Illinois, Minnesota, Iowa, Nebraska, and the Dakotas. Through Famous Players Canadian, Publix extended its hegemony to Canada. At

11. Kennedy, *Story of the Films*, pp. 275–77; Lewis, *Cases on the Motion Picture Industry*, pp. 516–19; Arthur Mayer, *Merely Colossal* (New York: Simon and Schuster, 1953), pp. 106–11; *Film Daily*, April 8, 1926, pp. 1, 6; Ben M. Hall, *The Best Remaining Seats* (New York: C. N. Potter, 1961), p. 207.

12. *Variety*, August 7, 1929, pp. 4, 10, 189; *New York Times*, June 25, 1927, p. 15; Mayer, *Merely Colossal*, pp. 107–80.

its apex in 1930, Publix was the largest, most profitable, and most powerful motion picture circuit in cinema history.[13]

Late in 1930, the film industry was hit by the Great Depression. Average attendance began to fall—from an estimated eighty million per week to fifty million in 1933. Three of the large movie theater organizations, Publix, Fox, and RKO, went into receivership, and had to be reorganized. Historians point to this as the death knell of chain power. Theaters were even sold! The Publix chain would fall to fewer than one thousand houses by the mid 1930s. But in fact all circuits survived intact, and would go on to their most profitable period between 1936 and 1946. Reorganization and receivership ultimately meant very little because the federal government propped up and indirectly subsidized the major chains, Publix as well as Loew's, Fox, RKO, and Warner, from 1933 to 1935. The National Recovery Administration (NRA) allowed, and even encouraged, these chains to directly exercise the monopolistic power and procedures they had informally developed during the late 1920s.[14]

On June 16, 1933, the National Industrial Recovery Act (NIRA) established the NRA to initiate and monitor codes for "fair competition" for all U.S. industries. In exchange for acceptance of such a code, each industry gained an exemption from prosecution under all existing antimonopoly legislation. In 1932, Sam Katz had resigned as head of the Publix chain because of a disagreement over the best strategy to use to combat declining theater revenues. But his successor, Y. Frank Freeman, and other officers, as well as all heads of the other major chains, quickly embraced the NRA's offer of freedom to exercise monopolistic power. All pushed for a code which ratified the practices which had worked so well during the growth years of the late 1920s. Only small, unaffiliated exhibitors bemoaned this unequal treatment. But in time the small exhibitors gave in. Only the double-feature policy of exhibition remained a legal practice under the NRA's motion picture code.[15]

Quickly the five large chains, and their producer-distributor owners,

13. *Variety*, September 26, 1928, p. 19; May 29, 1929, p. 30; May 14, 1930, p. 4; *Film Daily*, April 8, 1929, p. 1; April 16, 1929, pp. 1, 4.

14. *Variety*, March 18, 1931, p. 20; April 29, 1931, p. 7; *Film Daily*, November 18, 1930, pp. 1, 4; April 10, 1931, pp. 1–2; August 20, 1931, p. 1.

15. L. S. Lyon, et al., *The National Recovery Administration* (Washington, D.C.: Brookings, 1935), p. 11; Arthur M. Schlesinger, Jr., *The Coming of the New Deal* (Boston: Houghton Mifflin, 1958), pp. 98–99; Ellis Hawley, *The New Deal and the Problem of Monopoly* (Princeton, N.J.: Princeton University Press, 1966), pp. 53–72; Louis Nizer, *New Courts of Industry* (New York: Longacre Press, 1935), pp. 64–302; *Variety*, June 6, 1933, p. 7; June 13, 1933, p. 5; June 20, 1933, p. 5; December 12, 1933, p. 5.

moved to formally establish what later became known as the "first-run zone clearance" system for distribution and exhibition. The famous Paramount antitrust case voluminously documented just how well that system worked.[16] Katz had developed the basis for the system as he adapted his chain store methods to all-sound motion picture offerings.

But this period of grace lasted only two years. In May 1935 the Supreme Court declared the NRA unconstitutional. The immediate effect on film exhibition practice proved minimal. The corporations had been reorganized, excess debts eliminated, and the "first-run zone clearance" system firmly entrenched. Independent exhibitors did institute alternative competitive behavior specifically outlawed under the NRA code: premium giveaways (dishes, glasses, even bicycles), and/or games (screeno, horserace night, or bank night). Yet since the small exhibitors could never command exclusive first or second runs of the films from the major companies—those affiliated with the five large chains—they were doomed to remain insignificant in terms of profits and power. But, in the longer run, the information gathered during the NRA would prove the undoing of the large theater chains. In 1937, the Roosevelt Administration switched to a strategy of aggressive but selective antitrust prosecutions as the best method by which to combat renewed hard times. In 1938, the Justice Department filed against the five major film companies principally because of their monopolistic behavior in film exhibition. The case would go on for a decade and ultimately see the chains separated from the producer-distributors. But by then the question for motion picture theater chains would not be the optimal way to grow and maximize profits, but how best to adjust to a powerful competitor, television. New and different forms of business strategy would be employed to meet that challenge.

In conclusion, I have argued that during the 1920s, film exhibition became a true big business by adopting the strategies of chain store retailing. Prior to World War I, movie exhibition was a set of regional, not nationwide enterprises. Business practices followed the patterns of nineteenth-century U.S. capitalism as set by small partnership enterprises. Sam Katz, first with Balaban & Katz and then Publix, brought twentieth-century business practices to movie exhibition by adopting the methods of large retailing corporations. Publix, then others, operated in a national market, employing coordinated advertising and an identifiable trademark. Scale economies, monopsony power, and innovations in business organization enabled chains to effect signifi-

16. *United States v. Paramount Pictures*, 334 U.S. 131 (1948).

cant reductions in costs. Air-conditioning and elaborate stage shows, as well as popular motion pictures, drew large crowds and generated sizable revenues. Then expansion proceeded in orderly fashion: costs fell, demand increased, profits rose, more theaters were acquired, and so on. Film exhibition took on the characteristics of growing, prosperous big business of the 1920s. When the Great Depression struck, the chains survived—and even prospered—because the federal government, through the NRA, openly sanctioned their monopolistic behavior. Instead of the informal collusion and exploitation which had taken place during the growth period of the 1920s, the chains could operate—after mid 1933—free from the threat of antitrust prosecution. This guaranteed the survival and prosperity of the newest of American big businesses until after World War II.

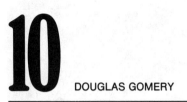

DOUGLAS GOMERY

The Coming of Sound: Technological Change in the American Film Industry

The coming of sound during the late 1920s climaxed a decade of significant change within the American industry. Following the lead of the innovators—Warner Bros. Pictures, Inc., and the Fox Film Corporation—all companies moved, virtually en masse, to convert to sound. By the autumn of 1930, Hollywood produced only talkies. The speed of conversion surprised almost everyone. Within twenty-four months a myriad of technical problems were surmounted, stages soundproofed, and theaters wired. Engineers invaded studios to coordinate sight with sound. Playwrights (from the East) replaced title writers; actors without stage experience rushed to sign up for voice lessons. At the time, chaos seemed to reign supreme. However, with some historical distance, we know that, although the switch-over to talkies seemed to come "overnight," no major company toppled. Indeed the coming of sound produced one of the more lucrative eras in U.S. movie history. Speed of transformation must not be mistaken for disorder or confusion. On the contrary, the major film corporations—Paramount and Loew's (MGM)—were joined by Fox, Warner, and RKO in a surge of profits, instituting a grip on the marketplace which continues to the present day.

Moreover, sound films did not spring Minerva-like onto the movie screens of twenties America. Their antecedents reached back to the founding of the industry. We need a framework to structure this im-

229

The Jazz Singer at the Warners' Theatre

portant thirty-year transformation. Here the neoclassical economic theory of technical change proves very useful. An enterprise introduces a new product (or process of production) in order to increase profits. Simplified somewhat, three distinct phases are involved: invention,

230

innovation, and diffusion. Although many small-inventory entrepreneurs attempted to marry motion pictures and sound, it took two corporate giants, the American Telephone & Telegraph Corporation (AT&T), and the Radio Corporation of America (RCA), to develop the necessary technology. AT&T desired to make better phone equipment; RCA sought to improve its radio capabilities. As a secondary effect of such research, each perfected sound recording and reproduction equipment. With the inventions ready, two movie companies, Warner and Fox, adapted telephone and radio research for practical use. That is, they innovated sound movies. Each developed techniques to produce, distribute, and exhibit sound motion pictures. The final phase, diffusion, occurs when the product or process is adopted for widespread use. Initially, the movie industry giants hesitated to follow the lead of Warner and Fox but, after elaborate planning, decided to convert. All others followed. Because of the enormous economic power of the major firms, the diffusion proceeded quickly and smoothly. During each of the three phases, the movie studios and their suppliers of sound equipment formulated business decisions with a view toward maximizing long-run profits. This motivation propelled the American motion picture industry (as it had other industries) into a new era of growth and prosperity.

Invention

Attempts to link sound to motion pictures originated in the 1890s. Entrepreneurs experimented with mechanical means to combine the phonograph and motion pictures. For example, in 1895 Thomas Alva Edison introduced such a device, his Kinetophone. He did not try to synchronize sound and image; the Kinetophone merely supplied a musical accompaniment to which a customer listened as he or she viewed a "peep show." Edison's crude novelty met with public indifference. Yet, at the same time, many other inventors attempted to better Edison's effort. One of these, Léon Gaumont, demonstrated his Chronophone before the French Photographic Society in 1902. Gaumont's system linked a single projector to two phonographs by means of a series of cables. A dial adjustment synchronized the phonograph and motion picture. In an attempt to profit by his system, showman Gaumont filmed variety (vaudeville) acts. The premiere came in 1907 at the London Hippodrome. Impressed, the American monopoly, the Motion Picture Patents Company, licensed Chronophone for the United

States. Within one year Gaumont's repertoire included opera, recitations, and even dramatic sketches. Despite initially bright prospects, Chronophone failed to secure a niche in the marketplace because the system, relatively expensive to install, produced only coarse sounds, lacked the necessary amplification, and rarely remained synchronized for long. In 1913, Gaumont returned to the United States for a second try with what he claimed was an improved synchronizing mechanism and an advanced compressed air system for amplification. Exhibitors remembered Chronophone's earlier lackluster performance and ignored all advertised claims, and Gaumont moved on to other projects.

Gaumont and Edison did not represent the only phonograph sound systems on the market. More than a dozen others, all introduced between 1909 and 1913, shared common systems and problems. The only major rival was the Cameraphone, the invention of E. E. Norton, a former mechanical engineer with the American Gramophone Company. Even though in design the Cameraphone nearly replicated Gaumont's apparatus, Norton succeeded in installing his system in a handful of theaters. But like others who preceded him, he never solved three fundamental problems: (1) the apparatus was expensive; (2) the amplification could not reach all persons in a large hall; and (3) synchronization could not be maintained for long periods of time. In addition, since the Cameraphone system required a porous screen, the image retained a dingy gray quality. Therefore it was not surprising that Cameraphone (or Cinephone, Vivaphone, Synchroscope) was never successful.

It remained for one significant failure to eradicate any further commercial attempt to marry the motion picture and the phonograph. In 1913, Thomas Edison announced the second coming of the Kinetophone. This time, the Wizard of Menlo Park argued, he had perfected the talking motion picture! Edison's demonstration on January 4, 1913, impressed all present. The press noted that this system seemed more advanced than all predecessors. Its sensitive microphone obviated traditional lip-sync difficulties for actors. An oversized phonograph supplied the maximum mechanical amplification. Finally, an intricate system of belts and pulleys erected between the projection booth and the stage could precisely coordinate the speed of the phonograph with the motion picture projector.

Because of the success of the demonstration, Edison was able to persuade vaudeville magnates John J. Murdock and Martin Beck to install the Kinetophone in four Keith-Orpheum theaters in New York. The commercial premiere took place on February 13, 1913, at Keith's Colonial. A curious audience viewed and listened to a lecturer who praised Edison's latest marvel. To provide dramatic evidence for his glowing tribute, the lecturer then smashed a plate, played the violin, and had his dog bark. After several music acts (recorded on the Kinetophone), a choral rendition of "The Star-Spangled Banner" stirringly closed the show. An enthusiastic audience stood and applauded for ten minutes. The wizard, Tom Edison, had done it again!

Unfortunately this initial performance would rank as the zenith for Kinetophone. For a majority of later presentations, the system functioned badly—for a variety of technical reasons. For example, at Keith's Union Square theater, the sound lost synchronization by as much as ten to twelve seconds. The audience booed the picture off the screen. By 1914, the Kinetophone had established a record so spotty that Murdock and Beck paid off their contract with Edison. Moreover, during that same year, fire destroyed Edison's West Orange factory. Although he quickly rebuilt, Edison chose not to reactivate the Kinetophone operation. The West Orange fire not only marked the end of the Kinetophone, but signaled the demise of all serious efforts to mechanically unite the phonograph with motion pictures. (The later disc system would use electronic connections.)

American moviegoers had to wait nine years for another workable sound system to emerge—and when it did, it was based on the principle of sound on film, not on discs. On April 4, 1923, noted electronics inventor Lee De Forest successfully exhibited his Phonofilm system to the New York Electrical Society. De Forest asserted that his system simply photographed the voice onto an ordinary film. In truth, Phonofilm's highly sophisticated design represented a major advance in electronics, begun when De Forest had patented the Audion amplifier tube in 1907. Two weeks later Phonofilm reached the public at large at New York's Rivoli theater. The program consisted of three shorts: a ballerina performing a "swan dance," a string quartet, and another dance number. Since the musical accompaniment for each was non-synchronous, De Forest, whose brilliance shone in the laboratory rather than in showmanship or business, generated little interest. A New York Times reporter described a lukewarm audience response. No movie mogul saw enough of an advancement, given the repeated previous failures, to express more than a mild curiosity.

In fact, De Forest never wanted to work directly through a going motion picture concern, but go it alone. Consequently, legal and financial roadblocks continually hindered substantial progress. De Forest tried but could not establish anywhere near an adequate organization to market films or apparatus. Movie entrepreneurs feared, correctly, that the Phonofilm Corporation controlled too few patents ever to guarantee indemnity. Still, De Forest's greatest difficulties came when he attempted to generate financial backing. This brilliant individualist failed ever to master the intricacies of the world of modern finance. Between 1923 and 1925, Phonofilm, Inc., wired only thirty-four theaters in the United States, Europe, South Africa, Australia, and Japan. De Forest struggled on, but in September 1928, when he sold out to a group of South African businessmen, only three Phonofilm installations remained, all in the United States.

It took AT&T, the world's largest company, to succeed where others had failed. In 1912, AT&T's manufacturing subsidiary, Western Electric, secured the rights to De Forest's Audion tube to construct amplification repeaters for long-distance telephone transmission. In order to test such equipment the Western Electric Engineering Department, under Frank Jewett, needed a better method to test sound quality. After a brief interruption because of World War I, Jewett and his scientists plunged ahead, concentrating on improving the disc method. Within three months of the armistice, one essential element for a sound system was ready, the loudspeaker. The loudspeaker was first used in the "Victory Day" parade on Park Avenue in 1919, but national notoriety came during the 1920 Republican and Democratic national conventions. A year later, by connecting this technology to its long-distance telephone network, AT&T broadcast President Harding's address at the burial of the Unknown Soldier simultaneously to overflowing crowds in New York's Madison Square Garden and San Francisco's Auditorium. Clear transmissions to large indoor audiences had become a reality. Other necessary components quickly flowed off Western Electric's research assembly line. The disc apparatus was improved by creating a single-drive shaft turntable using 33 1/3 revolutions per minute. Ready in 1924, the complete new disc system included a high-quality microphone, a nondistortive amplifier, an electrically operated recorder and turntable, a high-quality loudspeaker, and a synchronizing system free from speed variation.

In 1922, in the midst of these developments, Western Electric began to consider commercial applications. Western Electric did advertise and sell the microphones, vacuum tubes, and loudspeakers in the radio field, but Jewett's assistant, Edward Craft, argued that more lucrative markets existed in "improved" phonographs and sound movies. Employing the sound-on-disc method, Craft produced the first motion picture using Western Electric's sound system. To *Audion*, an animated cartoon originally created as a silent public relations film, he added a synchronized score. Craft premiered *Audion* in Yale University's Woolsey Hall on October 27, 1922. He followed this first effort with more experiments. On February 13, 1924, at a dinner at New York's

Astor Hotel, Craft presented *Hawthorne*. This public relations film showing Western Electric's plant in Chicago employed a perfectly synchronized sound track. By the fall of 1924, the sound-on-disc system seemed ready to market.

Laboratory success did not constitute the only criterion which distinguished Western Electric's efforts from those of De Forest and other inventors. Most important, Western Electric had almost unlimited financial muscle. In 1925, parent company AT&T ranked with U.S. Steel as the largest private corporation in the world. Total assets numbered over $2.9 billion; revenues exceeded $800 million. At this time America's national income was only $76 billion, and government receipts totaled only $3.6 billion. Western Electric, although technically an AT&T subsidiary, ranked as a corporate giant in its own right with assets of $188 million and sales of $263 million, far in excess of even Paramount, the largest force in the motion picture industry at the time. If absolute economic power formed the greatest advantage, patent monopoly certainly added another. AT&T spent enormous sums to create basic patents in order to maintain its monopoly position in the telephone field. Moreover, AT&T's management actively encouraged the development of nontelephone patents to use for bargaining with competitors. For example, between 1920 and 1926 AT&T protected itself by cross-licensing its broadcasting-related patents with RCA. In turn, RCA and its allies agreed not to threaten AT&T's monopoly for wire communication. In particular, in the cross-licensing agreement of 1926, AT&T and RCA contracted to exchange information on sound motion pictures, if and when required. Thus by 1926, AT&T had control over its own patents, as well as any RCA created.

Using its economic power and patent position, Western Electric moved to reap large rewards for its sound-recording technology. As early as 1925, it had interested and licensed the key phonograph and record manufacturers Victor and Columbia. Movie executives proved more stubborn, so Western Electric hired an intermediary, Walter J. Rich. On May 27, 1925, Rich inked an agreement under which he agreed to commercially exploit the AT&T system for nine months.

Innovation

Warner Bros.

Warner Bros. would eventually be the company to innovate sound motion pictures. However, in 1925, Warner ranked low in the economic pecking order in the American film industry. Certainly brothers Harry, Albert, Sam, and Jack had come a long way since their days as nickelodeon operators in Ohio some two decades earlier. Yet in the mid 1920s, their future seemed severely constrained. Warner neither controlled an international system for distribution, nor owned a chain of first-run theaters. The brothers' most formidable rivals, Famous Players (soon to be renamed Paramount), Loew's, and First National, did. Eldest brother Harry Warner remained optimistic and sought help.

In time, Harry Warner met Waddill Catchings, a financier with Wall Street's Goldman, Sachs. Catchings, boldest of the "New Era" Wall Street investors, agreed to take a flyer with this fledgling enterprise in the most speculative of entertainment fields. Catchings correctly reasoned that the consumer-oriented 1920s economy would provide a fertile atmosphere for boundless growth in the movie field. And Warner seemed progressive. The four brothers maintained strict cost accounting and budget controls, and seemed to have attracted more than competent managerial talent. Catchings agreed to finance Warner, only if it followed his master plan. The four brothers, sensing they would find no better alternative, readily agreed.

During the spring of 1925, Harry Warner, president of the firm, formally appointed Waddill Catchings to the board of directors, and elevated him to chairman of the finance committee. Catchings immediately established a $3 million revolving credit account through New York's National Bank of Commerce. Although this bank had never loaned a dollar to a motion picture company, not even the mighty Paramount, Catchings possessed enough clout to convince president James S. Alexander that Warner would be a good risk. Overnight Warner had acquired a permanent source for financing future productions. Simultaneously Warner took over the struggling Vitagraph Corporation, complete with its network of fifty distribution exchanges throughout the world. In this deal Warner also gained the pioneer company's two small studios, processing laboratory, and extensive film library. Finally, with four million more dollars that Catchings raised through bonds, Warner strengthened its distribution system, and even launched a ten-theater chain. Certainly by mid 1925 Warner was becoming a force to be reckoned with in the American movie business.

Warner's expansionary activities set the stage for the coming of sound. At the urging of Sam Warner, who was an electronics enthusiast, the company established radio station KFWB in Hollywood to promote Warner films. The equipment was secured from Western Electric. Soon Sam Warner and Nathan Levinson, Western's Los Angeles representative, became fast friends. Until then, Walter J. Rich had located no takers for Western Electric's sound inventions. Past failures had made a lasting and negative impression on the industry leaders, a belief shared by Harry Warner. Consequently, Sam had to trick his older brother into even attending a demonstration. That screening, in May 1925, included a recording of a five-piece jazz band. Quickly Harry and other Warner executives reasoned that if the company could equip their newly acquired theaters with sound and present vaudeville acts as part of their programs, they could successfully challenge the Big Three. Then, even Warner's smallest house could offer (1) famous vaudeville acts (on film); (2) silent features; and (3) the finest orchestral accompaniments (on disc). Warner, at this point, never considered feature-length talking pictures, only singing and musical films.

Catchings endorsed such reasoning and gave the go-ahead to open negotiations with Walter J. Rich. On June 25, 1925, Warner signed a letter of agreement with Western Electric calling for a period of joint experimentation. Western Electric would supply the engineers and sound equipment; Warner the camera operators, editors, and the supervisory talent of Sam Warner. Work commenced in September 1925 at the old Vitagraph studio in Brooklyn. Meanwhile, Warner continued to expand under Waddill Catchings' careful guidance. Although feature film output was reduced, more money was spent on each picture. In the spring of 1926, Warner opened a second radio station and an additional film-processing laboratory, and further expanded its foreign operations. As a result of this rapid growth, the firm expected a $1 million loss on its annual income statement issued in March 1926.

By December 1925, experiments were going so well that Rich proposed forming a permanent sound motion picture corporation. The contracts were prepared and the parties readied to sign, but negotiations ground to a halt as Western Electric underwent a management shuffle. Western placed John E. Otterson, an Annapolis graduate and career navy officer, in charge of exploiting nontelephone inventions. Otterson possessed nothing but contempt for Warner. He wanted to secure contracts with industry giants Paramount and Loew's, and then take direct control himself. Hitherto, Western Electric seemed content to function as a supplier of equipment. Catchings saw this dictatorial stance as typical of a man with a military background unable to adjust to the world of give-and-take in modern business and finance. Unfortunately for Warner, AT&T's corporate muscle backed Otterson's demands.

Only by going over Otterson's head to Western Electric's president, Edgar S. Bloom, was Catchings able to protect Warner interests and secure a reasonable contract. In April 1926, Warner, Walter J. Rich, and Western Electric formed the Vitaphone Corporation to develop sound motion pictures further. Warner and Rich furnished the capital. Western Electric granted Vitaphone an exclusive license to record and reproduce sound movies on its equipment. In return, Vitaphone agreed to lease a minimum number of sound systems each year and pay a royalty fee of 8 percent of gross revenues from sound motion pictures. Vitaphone's total equipment commitment became twenty-four hundred systems in four years.

As *Variety* and the other trade papers announced the formation of the alliance, Vitaphone began its assault on the marketplace. Its first goal was to acquire talent. Vitaphone contracted with the Victor Talking Machine Company for the right to bargain with its popular musical artists. A similar agreement was reached with the Metropolitan Opera Company. Vitaphone dealt directly with vaudeville stars. In a few short months it had contracted for the talent to produce the musical short subjects Harry Warner had envisioned. So confident was Vitaphone's management that the firm engaged the services of the New York Philharmonic Orchestra. Throughout the summer of 1926, Sam Warner and his crew labored feverishly to ready a Vitaphone program for a fall premiere, while the Warner publicity apparatus cranked out thousands of column inches for the nation's press.

Vitaphone unveiled its marvel on August 6, 1926, at the Warners' Theatre in New York. The first-nighters who packed the house paid up to $10 for tickets. The program began with eight "Vitaphone Preludes." In the first, Will Hays congratulated the brothers Warner and Western Electric for their pioneering efforts. At the end, to create the illusion of a stage appearance, Hays bowed to the audience, anticipating their applause. Next, conductor Henry Hadley led the New York Philharmonic in the Overture to *Tannhäuser*. He too bowed. The acts that followed consisted primarily of operatic and concert performances: tenor Giovanni Martinelli offered an aria from *I Pagliacci*, violinist Mischa Elman played "Humoresque," and soprano Anna Case sang, supported by the Metropolitan Opera Chorus. Only one "prelude" broke the serious tone of the evening and that featured Roy Smeck, a popular vaudeville comic-musician. Warner, playing it close to the vest, sought approval from all bodies of respectable critical opinion. The silent feature *Don Juan* followed a brief intermission. The musical accompaniment (sound-on-disc) caused no great stir because it "simply replaced" an absent live orchestra. All in all, Vitaphone, properly marketed, seemed to have a bright future.

That autumn, the *Don Juan* package played in Atlantic City, Chicago, and St. Louis. Quickly Vitaphone organized a second program, but this time aimed at popular palates. The feature, *The Better 'Ole*, starred Charlie Chaplin's brother, Sydney. The shorts featured vaudeville "headliners" George Jessel, Irving Berlin, Elsie Janis, and Al Jolson. These performers would have charged more than any single theater owner could have afforded, if presented live. The trade press now began to see bright prospects for the invention that could place so much high-priced talent in towns like Akron, Ohio, and Richmond, Va. By the time Vitaphone's third program opened in February 1927, Warner had recorded fifty more acts.

As a result of the growing popularity of Vitaphone presentations, the company succeeded in installing nearly a hundred systems by the end of 1926. Most of these were located in the East. The installation in March 1927 of apparatus in the new Roxy theater and the attendant publicity served to spur business even more. Consequently, Warner's financial health showed signs of improvement. The corporation had invested over $3 million in Vitaphone alone, yet its quarterly losses had declined from about $334,000 in 1925 to less than $110,000 in 1926. It appeared that Catchings' master plan was working.

John Otterson remained unsatisfied. He sought to take control of Vitaphone so that Western Electric could deal directly with Paramount and Loew's. To accomplish this he initiated a harassment campaign by raising prices on Vitaphone equipment fourfold, and demanding a greater share of the revenues. By December 1926, Western Electric and Warner had broken off relations. Simultaneously, Otterson organized a special Western Electric subsidiary called Electrical Research Products, Inc. (ERPI), to conduct the company's nontelephone business—over 90 percent of which concerned motion picture sound equipment.

Realistically Warner, even with Catchings' assistance, could not prevent Otterson from talking with other companies—even though exclusive rights were contractually held by Warner. However, only Fox would initial an agreement. The majors adopted a wait-and-see stance. In fact, the five most important companies—Loew's (MGM), Universal, First National, Paramount, and Producers Distributing Corporation—signed an accord in February 1927 to act together in regard to sound. The "Big Five Agreement," as it was called, recognized that since there were several sound systems on the market, inability to interchange this equipment could hinder wide distribution of pictures and therefore limit potential profits. These companies agreed to jointly adopt only the system that their specially appointed committee would certify, after one year of study, was the "best" for the industry. As further protection, they would employ no system unless it was made available to all producers, distributors, and exhibitors on "reasonable" terms.

Otterson needed to wrest away Warner's exclusive rights if he ever hoped to strike a deal with the Big Five. To this end, he threatened to declare Warner in default of its contractual obligations. Catchings, knowing such public statements would undermine his relations with the banks, persuaded Warner to accede to Otterson's wishes. In April 1927, ERPI paid Vitaphone $1,322,306 to terminate the old agreement. In May, after the two signed the so-called New License Agreement, Vitaphone, like Fox, became merely a licensee of ERPI. Warner had given up the exclusive franchise to exploit ERPI sound equipment and lost its share of a potential fortune in licensing fees.

Now on its own, Warner immediately moved all production to several new sound stages in Hollywood. While the parent company continued with its production program of silent features, Vitaphone regularly turned out five shorts a week, which became known in the industry as "canned vaudeville." Bryan Foy, an ex-vaudevillian and silent film director, now worked under Sam Warner to supervise the sound short subject unit. At this juncture, Vitaphone's most significant problem lay in a dearth of exhibition outlets for movies with sound. By the fall of 1927, six months since the signing of the New License Agreement, ERPI had installed only forty-four sound systems. ERPI was holding back on its sales campaign until the majors made a decision. Warner would later charge that ERPI had not used its best efforts to market the equipment and had itself defaulted. This accusation and others were brought to arbitration and, in a 1934 settlement, ERPI was forced to pay Vitaphone $5 million.

As the 1927–28 season opened, Vitaphone began to add new forms of sound films to its program. Though The Jazz Singer premiered on October 6, 1927, to lukewarm reviews, its four Vitaphoned segments of Al Jolson's songs proved very popular. Vitaphone contracted with Jolson immediately to make three more films for $100,000. (The four Warner brothers did not attend The Jazz Singer's New York premiere because Sam Warner died in Los Angeles on October 5. Jack Warner took over Sam's position as head of Vitaphone production.) Bryan Foy pushed his unit to create four new shorts each week, becoming more bold in programming strategies. On December 4, 1928, Vitaphone released the short My Wife's Gone Away, a ten-minute, all-talking comedy based on a vaudeville playlet developed by William Demarest. Critics praised this short; audiences flocked to it. Thus Foy, under Jack Warner's supervision, began to borrow even more from available vaudeville acts and "playlets" to create all-talking shorts. During Christmas week, 1927, Vitaphone released a twenty-minute, all-talking drama, Solomon's Children. Again revenues were high, and in January 1928, Foy moved to schedule production of two all-talking shorts per week.

Al Jolson and Eugenie Besserer in *The Jazz Singer* (Warner Bros., 1927)

Warner had begun to experiment with alternative types of shorts as a cheap way to maintain the novelty value of Vitaphone entertainment. Moreover, with such shorts it could develop talent, innovate new equipment, and create an audience for feature-length, all-sound films. In the spring of 1928, with the increased popularity of these shorts, Warner began to change its feature film offerings. On March 14, 1928, it released *Tenderloin*—an ordinary mystery that contained five segments in which the actors spoke all their lines (for twelve of the film's eighty-five minutes). More part-talkies soon followed that spring.

Harry Warner and Waddill Catchings knew the investment in sound was a success by April 1928. By then it had become clear that the *The Jazz Singer* show had become the most popular entertainment offering of the 1927–28 season. In cities that rarely held films for more than one week *The Jazz Singer* package set records for length of run: for example, five-week runs in Charlotte, N.C., Reading, Pa., Seattle, and Baltimore. By mid February 1928, *The Jazz Singer* and the shorts were in a (record) eighth week in Columbus, Ohio, St. Louis, and Detroit, and a (record) seventh week in Seattle, Portland, Ore., and Los Angeles. The Roxy even booked *The Jazz Singer* package for an unprecedented second run in April 1928, where it grossed in excess of $100,000 each week, among that theater's best grosses for that season. Perhaps more important, all these first-run showings did not demand the usual expenses of a stage show and orchestra. It took Warner only until the fall of 1928 to convert to the complete production of talkies—both features and shorts. Catchings and Harry Warner had laid the foundation for this maximum exploitation of profit with their slow, steady expansion in production and distribution. In 1929, Warner would become the most profitable of any American motion picture company.

The Fox-Case Corporation

As noted above, only the Fox Film Corporation had also shown any interest in sound movies. Its chief, William Fox, had investigated the sound-on-film system developed by Theodore W. Case and Earl I. Sponable and found it to be potentially a great improvement over the cumbersome Western Electric disc system. Theodore Case and Earl Sponable were two recluse scientists. In 1913, the independently wealthy, Yale-trained physicist Case established a private laboratory in his hometown of Auburn, New York, a small city near Syracuse. Spurred on by recent breakthroughs in the telephone and radio fields, Case and his assistant, Sponable, sought to better the Audion tube. In 1917 they perfected the Thalofide cell, a highly improved vacuum tube, and began to integrate this invention into a system for recording sounds. As part of this work, Case met Lee De Forest. For personal reasons— envy perhaps—Case turned all his laboratory's efforts to besting De Forest. Within eighteen months, Case labs produced an improved sound-on-film system, based on the Thalofide cell. Naively, De Forest had openly shared with Case all his knowledge of sound-on-film technology. So as De Forest unsuccessfully attempted to market his Phonofilm system, Case quietly constructed—with his own funds—a complete sound studio and projection room adjacent to his laboratory.

In 1925, Case determined he was ready to try to market his inventions. Edward Craft of Western Electric journeyed to Auburn, and saw and heard a demonstration film. Craft left quite impressed. But after careful consideration, he and Frank Jewett decided that Case's patents added no substantial improvement to the Western Electric sound-on-disc system, then under exclusive contract to Warner. Rebuffed, Case decided to directly solicit a show business entrepreneur. He first approached John J. Murdock, the long-time general manager of the Keith-Albee vaudeville circuit. Case argued that his sound system could be used to record musical and comedy acts—the same idea Harry Warner had conceived six months earlier. Murdock blanched. He had been burned by Edison's hyperbole only a decade earlier, and De Forest a mere twenty-four months before. Keith-Albee would never be interested in talking movies! Executives from all the "Big Three" motion picture corporations, Paramount, Loew's (MGM), and First National, echoed Murdock's response. None saw the slightest benefit in this latest version of sight and sound.

Case moved to the second tier of the U.S. film industry—Producers Distributing Company (PDC), Film Booking Office (FBO), Warner, Fox, and Universal. In 1926, Case signed with Fox because Courtland Smith, president of Fox Newsreels, reasoned that sound newsreels could push that branch of Fox Film to the forefront of the industry. In June 1926, Smith arranged a demonstration for company owner, founder, and president William Fox. The boss was pleased, and within a month helped create the Fox-Case Corporation to produce sound motion pictures. Case turned all patents over to the new corporation, and retired to his laboratory in upstate New York.

Initially, William Fox's approval of experiments with the Case technology constituted only a small portion of a comprehensive plan to thrust Fox Film into a preeminant position in the motion picture industry. Fox and his advisors had initiated an expansion campaign in 1925. By floating $6 million of common stock, they increased budgets for feature films and enlarged the newsreel division. (Courtland Smith was hired at this point.) Simultaneously Fox began building a chain of motion picture theaters. At that time Fox Film controlled only twenty small neighborhood houses in the New York City environs. By 1927, the Fox chain included houses in Philadelphia, Washington, D.C., Brooklyn, New York City, St. Louis, Detroit, Newark, Milwaukee, and a score of cities west of the Rockies. To finance these sizable investments, William Fox developed close ties to Harold Stuart, president of the Chicago investment house of Halsey, Stuart. Meanwhile, Courtland Smith had assumed control of Fox-Case, and, in 1926, initiated the innovation of the Case sound-on-film technology. At first all he could oversee were defensive actions designed to protect Fox-Case's patent position. In September 1926, exactly two months after incorporation, Fox-Case successfully thwarted claims by Lee De Forest, and a German concern, Tri-Ergon. For the latter, Fox-Case advanced $50,000 to check the future court action.

At last, Fox-Case could assault the marketplace. Although Smith pushed for immediate experimentation with sound newsreels, William Fox conservatively ordered Fox-Case to imitate the innovation strategy of Warner and film popular vaudeville acts. On February 24, 1927, Fox executives felt confident enough to stage a widely publicized demonstration of the newly christened Movietone system. At ten o'clock in the morning, fifty reporters entered the Fox studio near Times Square and were filmed by the miracle of Movietone. Four hours later these representatives of the press corps saw and heard themselves as part of a private screening. In addition, Fox-Case presented several vaudeville sound shorts: a banjo and piano act, a comedy sketch, and three songs by the then-popular cabaret performer Raquel Mueller. The strategy worked. Unanimous favorable commentary issued forth; the future seemed bright. Consequently, William Fox ordered sound systems for twenty-six of Fox's largest first-run theaters, including the recently acquired Roxy.

However, by this time Warner had signed nearly all popular entertainers to exclusive contracts. Smith pressed William Fox to again consider newsreels with sound. Then, Smith argued, Fox Film could offer a unique, economically viable alternative to Warner's presentations, and move into a heretofore unoccupied portion of the market for motion picture entertainment. Furthermore, sound newsreels would provide a logical method by which Fox-Case could gradually perfect necessary new techniques of camerawork and editing. Convinced, William Fox ordered Smith to adopt this course for technological innovation. This decision would prove more successful for Fox Film's overall goal of corporate growth than either William Fox or Courtland Smith imagined at the time.

Smith moved quickly. The sound newsreel premiere came on April 30, 1927, at the Roxy in the form of a four-minute record of marching West Point cadets. And despite the lack of any buildup, this newsreel elicited an enthusiastic response from the trade press and New York-based motion picture reviewers. Quickly Smith seized upon one of the most important symbolic news events of the 1920s. At eight in the morning, on May 20, 1927, Charles Lindbergh departed for Paris. That evening Fox Movietone News presented footage of the takeoff—with sound—to a packed house at the Roxy. Six thousand persons stood and cheered for nearly ten minutes. The press saluted this new motion picture marvel and noted how it had brought alive the heroics of the "Lone Eagle." In June, when Lindbergh returned to a tumultuous welcome in New York City and Washington, D.C., Movietone News cameramen also recorded portions of those celebrations. Both William Fox and Courtland Smith were now satisfied that the Fox-Case system had been launched on a propitious path.

That summer, Smith dispatched camera operators to all parts of the globe. They recorded the further heroics of aviators, beauty contests, and sporting events, as well as produced the earliest filmic records of statements by Benito Mussolini and Alfred Smith. Newspaper columnists, educators, and other opinion leaders lauded these latter short subjects for their didactic value. Fox Film's principal constraint now became a paucity of exhibition outlets. During the fall of 1927, Fox Film did make Movietone newsreels the standard in all Fox-owned theaters, but that represented less than 3 percent of the potential market. More extensive profits would come as Fox Film formed a larger chain of first-run theaters. In the meantime, Courtland Smith established a regular pattern for release of Movietone newsreels, one ten-minute reel per week. He also increased the permanent staff and established a worldwide network of stringers.

In addition, Smith and William Fox decided again to try to produce vaudeville shorts and silent feature films accompanied by synchronized music on disc. Before 1928, Fox-Case released only one scored feature, *Sunrise*. The two executives moved quickly. By January 1928, Fox had filmed ten vaudeville shorts and a part-talkie feature, *Blossom Time*. During the spring of 1928, these efforts, Fox's newsreels, and Warner's shorts and part-talkies proved to be the hits of the season. Thus in May 1928, William Fox declared that 100 percent of the upcoming production schedule would be "Movietoned." Simultaneously Fox Film continued to wire, as quickly as possible, all the houses in its ever-expanding chain and draw up plans for an all-sound Hollywood-based studio. Fox's innovation of sound neared completion; colossal profits loomed on the horizon.

The Rise of RKO

Only RCA offered Warner, Western Electric, or Fox any serious competition. In 1919, General Electric and Westinghouse had created RCA to control America's patents for radio broadcasting. Like rival AT&T, GE conducted fundamental research in radio technology. The necessary inventions for what would become RCA's Photophone sound-on-film system originated when, during World War I, the U.S. Navy sought a high-speed recorder of radio signals. GE scientist Charles A. Hoxie perfected such a device. After the war, Hoxie pressed to extend his work. Within three years, having incorporated a photoelectric cell and a vibrating mirror, he could record a wide variety of complex sounds. In December 1921, GE executives labeled the new invention the Pallo-Photophone.

To test it, Willis R. Whitney, head of the GE Research Laboratory, successfully recorded speeches by Vice-President Calvin Coolidge and several Harding Administration cabinet members. At this point, GE executives conceived of the Pallo-Photophone as a marketable substitute for the phonograph. During 1922 and 1923, Hoxie and his assistants continued to perfect the invention. For example, they discovered that the recording band need not be 35 millimeters wide. A track as narrow as 1.5 millimeters proved sufficient, and thus freed sound to accompany a motion picture image. Simultaneously other GE scientists, Chester W. Rise and Edward W. Kellogg, developed a new type of loudspeaker to improve reception for the radio sets General Electric manufactured for RCA. Late in 1922, Whitney learned of Lee De Forest's efforts to record sound on film. Not to be outdone, Whitney ordered Hoxie and his research team to develop a sound reproducer that could be attached to a standard motion picture projector. In November 1923, Hoxie demonstrated such a system for GE's top executives in an almost perfect state. However, by that time, Whitney and his superiors sensed that De Forest's failure to innovate sound motion pictures proved there existed no market for Hoxie's invention. Whitney promptly transferred all efforts toward the development of a marketable all-electric phonograph. GE successfully placed its new phonograph before the public during the summer of 1925.

One year later, because of Warner's success, Whitney reactivated the sound movie experiments. At this point he christened the system "Photophone." By the end of that year, 1926, GE's publicity department had created several experimental short subjects. Quickly GE executives pondered how to approach a sales campaign. However before they could institute any action, Fox sought a license in order to utilize GE's amplification patents. Contemplating the request, David Sarnoff, RCA's general manager, convinced his superiors at GE that RCA should go out on its own, sign up the large movie producers Paramount and Loew's, and not worry about Fox. The GE high brass agreed and assigned Sarnoff the task of commercially exploiting GE's sound movie patents.

Sarnoff easily convinced Paramount and Loew executives to seriously consider RCA's alternative to Western Electric's then monopoly, even though RCA had yet to publicly demonstrate Photophone. Presently the "Big Five Agreement" was signed. Sarnoff immediately went public. On February 2, 1927, Sarnoff demonstrated Photophone for invited guests and the press at the State theater in GE's home city of Schenectady, New York. Musical short subjects featuring a hundred-piece orchestra impressed all present. Nine days later Sarnoff recreated the event for more reporters at New York's Rivoli theater. Here two reels of MGM's *The Flesh and the Devil* were accompanied by a Photophone recording of the Capital theater orchestra. Then three shorts featured the Van Curler Hotel Orchestra of Schenectady, an unnamed baritone, and a quartet of singers recruited from General Electric employees. A *New York Times* reporter praised the synchronization, volume, and tone. Sarnoff, in turn, lauded Photophone's ease of installation and simplicity of operation.

In private, Sarnoff tried to convince the producers' committee of his company's technical and financial advantages. The producers had established three specific criteria for selection: (1) the equipment had to be technically adequate; (2) the manufacturer had to control all required patents; and (3) the manufacturer had to have substantial resources and financial strength. Only two systems qualified: RCA's Photophone and Western Electric's Vitaphone. At first, the producers favored RCA because it had not licensed any movie concern, whereas Western Electric had formal links to Warner and Fox. In October 1927, Sarnoff proposed an agreement which called for a holding company, one-half owned by RCA and one-half by the five motion picture producers. All of GE's sound patents would be vested in this one corporation. Sarnoff demanded 8 percent of all gross revenues from sound movies as a royalty. The producers countered. They sought individual licenses and fees set at $500 per reel. For a typical eight-reel film (90 minutes) with gross revenues of $500,000, the 8 percent royalty would be $40,000; at the new rate the amount came to $4,000, a savings of $36,000.

Sarnoff reluctantly acceeded to the per reel method of royalty calculation, but stubbornly refused to grant individual licenses. On the other hand, the motion picture corporations held fast to their belief that they should play no role in the manufacture of the apparatus. They wanted a license only to produce and distribute sound films. For two months the two parties stalemated over this issue. Late in November 1927, John Otterson of Western Electric stepped forward and offered individual licenses. Western Electric's engineers had made great progress with their sound-on-film system, and there no longer existed exclusive ties to Warner. Consequently, in March 1928, the movie producers, with all the relevant information in hand, selected Western Electric. Each producer—Paramount, United Artists, Loew's, and First National—secured an individual license and would pay $500 per reel of negative footage. All four signed on May 11, 1928. Universal, Columbia and other companies quickly followed. The movie producers had adroitly played the two electrical giants off each other and secured reasonably favorable terms.

Sarnoff reacted quickly as the tide turned toward Western Electric.

First General Electric purchased (for nearly $500,000) 14,000 shares of stock of the Film Booking Office from a syndicate headed by Joseph P. Kennedy. This acquisition guaranteed Photophone a studio outlet. FBO was the only producer with national distribution which was not linked in talks with Western Electric. Next Sarnoff formed RCA Photophone, Inc. Sarnoff now controlled production facilities and the necessary sound technology. To generate significant profits, RCA needed a chain of theaters.

In 1928, the Keith-Albee vaudeville chain controlled such a chain. Faced with declining business in vaudeville, Keith-Albee executives developed two approaches. First they took over the Orpheum vaudeville chain, and thus merged all major American vaudeville under one umbrella. The new Keith-Albee-Orpheum controlled two hundred large downtown theaters. Second, Keith-Albee acquired a small movie company, Pathé, just to hedge its bets. When Sarnoff approached the owners of the new Keith-Albee-Orpheum they were more than ready to sell. Sarnoff quickly moved to consolidate his empire. FBO and Pathé formally acquired licenses for Photophone. FBO and Pathé executives supervised the addition of music-on-film to three features, *King of Kings, The Godless Girl,* and *The Perfect Crime.* Upcoming sound newsreels and vaudeville shorts were promised. However, these films would be useless unless Sarnoff could wire the Keith-Albee-Orpheum theaters with Photophone equipment. Warner, Fox, and Western Electric had taken almost two years to eliminate all the problems of presenting clear sounds of sufficient volume in large movie palaces. As of this point Photophone had yet to be tested in a commercial situation. And Sarnoff and his staff would need at least six months to iron out technological problems. Promised first in April, then July, commercial installations commenced in October 1928. In the meantime, Sarnoff used a low installation price and sweeping prognostications of future greatness to persuade a shrinking number of prospective clients to wait for Photophone equipment.

That October, Sarnoff legally consolidated RCA's motion picture interests by creating a holding company, Radio-Keith-Orpheum (RKO). Sarnoff became president of the film industry's newest vertically integrated combine. The merger united theaters (Keith-Albee-Orpheum), radio (NBC), and motion pictures (FBO and Pathé, subsequently renamed Radio Pictures in May 1929). Although late on the scene, RCA had established a secure place in the motion picture industry. RKO released its first talkies in the spring of 1929, and Photophone could battle Western Electric for contracts with the remaining unwired houses.

Gradually during the 1930s, RCA Photophone would become as widely accepted as Western Electric's system.

Diffusion

The widespread adoption of sound—its diffusion—took place quickly and smoothly, principally because of the extensive planning of the producers' committee. Since an enormous potential for profits existed, it was incumbent on the majors to make the switchover as rapidly as possible. Paramount released its first films with musical accompaniment in August 1928; by September its pictures contained talking sequences; and by January 1929, it sent out its first all-talking production. By May, one year after signing with ERPI, Paramount produced talkies exclusively and was operating on a level with Warner and Fox. In September 1929, MGM, Fox, RKO, Universal, and United Artists completed their transitions. Those independent production companies which survived took, on average, one year longer.

Elaborate plans had been laid by the industry to facilitate diffusion. In Hollywood, the Academy of Motion Picture Arts and Sciences was designated as a clearing house for information relating to production problems. The local film boards of trade handled changes in distribution trade practices. And a special lawyers' committee representing the major producers was appointed to handle disputes and contractual matters with equipment manufacturers. For example, when ERPI announced a royalty hike, the committee initiated a protest, seeking lower rates. Unions presented no difficulties. The American Federation of Musicians unsuccessfully tried to prevent the wholesale firing of theatrical musicians; Actors' Equity, now that professionals from the Broadway stage began to flock west, failed to establish a union shop in the studios. All problems were resolved within a single year; the industry never left an even keel.

ERPI's task all the while was to keep up with the demand for apparatus. It wired the large, first-run theaters first and then, as equipment became available, subsequent-run houses. Installations were made usually from midnight to nine in the morning. For example, in January 1930, ERPI installed more than nine systems each day. To facilitate the switchover, Western Electric expanded its Hawthorne, Illinois, plant, and ERPI established training schools for projectionists in seventeen cities and opened fifty district offices to service and repair equipment. Many smaller theaters, especially in the South and Southwest, could not afford ERPI's prices and signed with RCA, or De Forest. As late as July 1930, fully 22 percent of all U.S. theaters still presented silent versions of talkies. That figure neared zero two years later.

The public's infatuation with sound ushered in another boom period for the industry. Paramount's profits jumped $7 million between 1928 and 1929, Fox's $3.5 million, and Loew's $3 million. Warner, however, set the record; its profits increased $12 million, from a base of only $2 million. A 600 percent leap! Conditions were ripe for consolidation, and Warner, with its early start in sound, set the pace. It began by acquiring the Stanley Company, which owned a chain of three hundred theaters along the East Coast, and First National. In 1925, when Waddill Catchings joined the Warner board of directors, the company's assets were valued at a little over $5 million; in 1930 they totaled $230 million. In five short years, Warner had become one of the largest and most profitable companies in the American film industry.

Not content merely to establish RKO, David Sarnoff of RCA set out to sever all connections with General Electric and Westinghouse and acquire sound manufacturing facilities of his own. The first step in this direction was the acquisition in March 1929 of Victor Talking Machine Company and its huge plant in Camden, New Jersey. In the process, RCA secured Victor's exclusive contracts with many of the biggest stars in the musical world. By December 1929 Sarnoff had reached his goal. RCA was now a powerful independent entertainment giant with holdings in the broadcasting, vaudeville, phonograph, and motion picture industries.

William Fox had the most grandiose plan of all. In March 1929, he acquired controlling interest in Loew's, the parent company of MGM. Founder Marcus Loew had died in 1927 and left his widow and sons one-third of the company's stock. Nicholas Schenck, the new president, pooled his stock and that belonging to corporate officers with the family's and sold out to Fox at 25 percent above the market price. The new Fox-Loew's merger created the largest motion picture complex in the world. Its assets totaled more than $200 million and an annual earning potential existed of $20 million. Fox assumed a substantial short-term debt obligation in the process, but during the bull market of the late twenties he could simply float more stock and bonds to meet his needs.

Adolph Zukor of Paramount, meanwhile, added more theaters, bringing Paramount's total to almost one thousand. He also acquired a 49 percent interest in the Columbia Broadcasting System. Then, in the fall of 1929, he proposed a merger with Warner that would create a motion picture and entertainment complex larger than Fox-Loew's and RCA combined. Catchings and Harry Warner were agreeable, but the new U.S. attorney general, William D. Mitchell, raised the red flag. If that merger went through, the industry would be dominated by three firms. As it happened, though, it was to be dominated by five. After the stock market crash, William Fox was unable to meet his short-term debts and had to relinquish ownership of Loew's. The oligopolistic structure of the industry, now formed by Warner, Paramount, Fox, Loew's, and RKO, would continue to operate well into the 1950s. The coming of sound had produced important forces for industry consolidation, immediately prior to the motion picture industry's first crisis of retrenchment—the Great Depression.

Bibliographical Note

This article is based on a series of articles I wrote between 1976 and 1980. The innovative activities of Warner Bros. are analyzed in "Writing the History of the American Film Industry," *Screen* 17 (Spring 1976): 40–53. For a separate discussion of the experiences of Fox and RCA, see "Problems in Film History: How Fox Innovated Sound," *Quarterly Review of Film Studies* 2 (August 1976): 315–30, and "Failure and Success: Vocafilm and RCA Innovate Sound," *Film Reader* 2 (January 1977): 213–21.

The reaction of the industry at large can be seen in two distinct stages. I treat the initial reluctance and waiting in "The Warner-Vitaphone Peril: The American Film Industry Reacts to the Innovation of Sound," *Journal of the University Film Association* 28 (Winter 1976): 11–19. For general acceptance and prosperity, see "Hollywood Converts to Sound: Chaos or Order?" in Evan W. Cameron, ed., *Sound and the Cinema* (Pleasantville, N.Y.: Redgrave, 1980), pp. 24–37.

A complete list of my publications on the coming of sound can be found in Claudia Gorbman, "Bibliography on Sound in Film," *Yale French Studies* 60 (Winter 1980): 276–77.

Part III

A Mature Oligopoly, 1930–1948

Structure of the Industry

By 1930, the motion picture industry had become, in economic terminology, a mature oligopoly. The merger movement had run its course, with the result that five companies dominated the screen in the United States. The largest was Warner Bros. with its one hundred subsidiaries; the wealthiest was Loew's, Inc. (ch. 13), the theater chain that owned Metro-Goldwyn-Mayer (ch. 12); and the most complex and far-flung was Paramount. These and two other giants with equally formidable holdings, RKO and Twentieth Century-Fox along with their allied theater enterprises, became known as the Big Five. All were fully integrated: they produced motion pictures, operated worldwide distribution outlets, and owned chains of theaters where their pictures were guaranteed a showing.

Operating in a sort of symbiotic relationship with the Big Five were the Little Three: Universal, Columbia, and United Artists. Universal and Columbia had their own studios and distribution facilities and were useful to the majors during the 1930s and 1940s in supplying low-cost pictures to facilitate frequent program changes and double features. United Artists, the smallest of the eight, was unique; it was solely a distribution company for a small group of elite independent producers.

These major companies held monopolistic control of a type that is "frequently hard to trace and appraise, and though more or less consistently evolved, that varies endlessly in methods or application and degrees of effectiveness," in the words of Robert A. Brady. "One might regard the movie industry as dominated by a semicompulsory

253

cartel," Brady adds "or even a 'community of interests' of
the type that typically stops short of the more readily in-
dictable offenses under usual Anti-Trust procedure."[1] By
pooling their interests, acting in concert, and establishing a
market cartel, the majors succeeded in holding onto their
power until the Supreme Court in 1948 and television
brought this era of the movies to a close.

With stables of stars, writers, directors, producers, cameramen, and other artists and technicians, each of the
majors (with the exception of UA) produced from forty to
sixty pictures a year. Although in total their productions
represented around 60 percent of the industry's annual
output, practically all the class-A features, the ones that
played in the best theaters and generated the most revenue,
were made and distributed by these eight companies. Competition among the companies in the area of production
was minimal. They vied with each other in acquiring story
rights and creating stars, but not for the services of the
established talent. They regularly loaned one another high-
priced stars and technicians on mutually satisfactory terms.
Independent producers, for the most part, were not accorded this right or had to pay premium rates.

The eight majors exercised even greater power in distribution; they collected about 95 percent of all film rentals
paid to national distributors. This oligopolistic situation
further helped to keep independent producers in a subordinate position. In order to secure financing from banking
institutions, independents had to guarantee national distribution and access to better-class theaters. Only then could
their pictures stand a chance of making a profit. But the
Big Five, which owned extensive theater chains, gave preferential treatment to one another's pictures and closed an
important segment of the market to outside product.
Moreover, through the use of such trade practices as block
booking and blind buying, the majors preempted the playing time of the key theaters nationwide.

It was in the area of exhibition that the Big Five had the
greatest strength. Of the eighteen thousand theaters operating in the United States in 1945, the five integrated com-

1. Robert A. Brady, "The Problem of Monopoly," *Annals of the American Academy of Political and Social Science* 254 (November 1947): 125.

panies either owned or controlled only three thousand, but this number represented the best first-run houses in the metropolitan areas. The ownership of these first-run outlets carried overwhelming economic power in that they accounted for nearly 70 percent of the nation's box office receipts. The Big Five competed with one another at the first-run level in the large cities, but in the neighborhoods and smaller towns, the situation was different. In building their chains, the Big Five acquired theaters in different regions of the country—Fox's chain was located in the Pacific and Rocky Mountain states; Paramount's in the South, New England, and greater Chicago; Loew's in New York City and Ohio, and so forth. Because each major company wanted to distribute its films nationwide, they exhibited one another's pictures in noncompetitive areas as a matter of course. In this "community of interests," a hit motion picture was profitable for all the integrated companies.

The monopolistic structure of the industry was challenged by the Department of Justice, culminating in 1938 in the antitrust case *United States v. Paramount Pictures, Inc., et al.* The case reached the Supereme Court ten years later, after thousands of pages of testimony and exhibits, two consent decrees, two lower-court decisions, and appeals. In a landmark decision, the Court held that the Big Five were parties to a combination that had monopoly in exhibition as a goal. One result was that the five integrated companies were directed to divorce their theater holdings from the production-distribution ends of their business. The proceedings, along with the rise of television, brought an era to a close.

Effects of the Depression

Sound staved off the Depression in the motion picture industry for well over a year. But when the novelty of the talkies wore off in 1931, box office receipts plummeted and Hollywood felt the effects of a disabled economy. Warner, after realizing profits of $17 million in 1929 and $7 million in 1930, lost nearly $8 million in 1931; Fox suffered a loss of $3 million after a $9 million profit the year before; and RKO's $3 million surplus from 1930 turned in to a $5.6 million deficit. Paramount remained in the black that year,

but Zukor saw his company's profits fall from $18 million
to $6 million, and by 1932 he had a deficit of $21 million.
By 1933, Paramount, with its 501 subsidiaries, went into
bankruptcy; Fox underwent reorganization; and RKO was
thrown into receivership. Warner, battered by losses of $14
million in 1932 and $6 million in 1933, was fighting to
stay afloat. Of the majors, only Loew's had not yet shown
a deficit; however, its earnings plunged from $10 million
in 1930 to $1.3 million in 1933. As for the minors, Uni-
versal had gone into receivership; Columbia and United
Artists were wounded, but not down.

Admission prices were slashed, audiences shrank—average weekly attendance dropped from an estimated eighty
million in 1929 to sixty million in 1932 and 1933—production costs more than doubled because of sound, and revenues from foreign markets dwindled, but these factors in
themselves did not cause the collapse. It resulted from the
companies' having overextended themselves, first in the
ferocious battle of the majors for control of the country's
theaters in the 1920s and then in the tremendous capital
investment in studios and theater equipment required for
the conversion to sound. In short, the Big Five could not
meet their fixed cost obligations, which means, simply,
they did not have the cash to pay their mortgage commitments, short-term obligations, and the heavy charges on
their funded debts.

Correspondingly, the common stock value of these majors was reduced from a 1930 high of $960 million to $140
million in 1934. Theater after theater went dark. Paramount found it cheaper to close many of its unprofitable
smaller houses than to pay overhead costs. The company
also shut down its Long Island studio and laid off almost
five thousand employees who had been earning between
$35 and $50 a week. The number of unemployed and un-
derpaid extras in Hollywood became a national scandal.
Wages for those lucky enough to find work dropped from
$2 a day to $1.25. When President Roosevelt declared a
nationwide bank moratorium in March 1933, studio heads
announced to their artistic personnel that everyone earning
over $50 a week would have to take a salary cut of 50
percent for two months.

Such was the state of the motion picture industry at the

Gold Diggers of 1933 (Warner Bros.)

dawn of the New Deal. In a comprehensive attempt to revive industry, President Roosevelt drafted the National Industrial Recovery Act (NIRA), which became law in June 1933 and was administered by the National Recovery Administration (NRA). Its general aim was to promote cooperative action among trade groups. The act assumed that collective action was superior to cutthroat competition and that members of the business community would be willing to put aside selfish interests for the good of the nation. It stipulated that industries were to draw up codes of fair competition enforceable by law. Business could ignore antitrust laws but, in return, had to make concessions such as guaranteeing labor the right of collective bargaining and establishing minimum wages and maximum hours.

Code of Fair Competition for the Motion Picture Industry

The Code of Fair Competition for the Motion Picture Industry was signed into law on November 27, 1933. Reflecting the vertically integrated structure of the industry, it regulated trade practices among producers, distributors,

and exhibitors and established guidelines for labor-management cooperation. By acting in concert through the offices
of the Motion Picture Producers and Distributors of America, the industry trade association, the major companies
imposed their will on the code.

They succeeded, most importantly, in receiving government sanction for the trade practices that they had spent
ten years developing through informal collusion. These
trade practices comprised the block-booking system, clearance and zoning, and admission price discrimination. All
had been used to wrest the greatest possible profits from
the market and to keep independent exhibitors in a subordinate position.

Block booking was without doubt the most contested
trade practice in the business. All the majors sold their
pictures in blocks of varying size, usually consisting of an
entire season's output. These were offered to exhibitors on
an all-or-none basis before the pictures had actually been
produced. In contracting for these blocks, exhibitors were
required to take short subjects as well. This practice, the
forcing of shorts, together with block booking, was known
as full-line forcing. As a congressional investigating committee remarked, "This is the only industry in which the
buyer, having no idea of what he is buying, underwrites
blindly all the product offered him."[2]

The independent theater owner was not against block
booking as such, since he needed a large number of pictures
to fill the playing time of his theater, which probably
showed double bills and changed programs two or three
times a week. But he did vigorously object to having all of
the pictures of a company foisted on him regardless of
their quality or desirability. Compulsory block booking did
not exist for the circuits affiliated with the majors, it
should be noted. The majors negotiated selective contracts
allowing them to play only the best of each other's pictures.

Block booking enabled the major studios to function at
capacity with the assurance that even the poorest picture
would be bought. This, in turn, helped them secure a flow

2. U.S. Temporary National Economic Committee, *The Motion Picture
Industry: A Pattern of Control* (Washington, D.C.: U.S. Government
Printing Office, 1941), p. 31.

of production financing. As a long-term policy, block booking in preempting exhibition playing time stifled competition by closing the market to independent producers and distributors.

Before it was endorsed by the NRA, block booking had been attacked by consumer groups, Congress, and the Federal Trade Commission, in addition to the independents, so in drafting the Motion Picture Code, the majors made a few concessions in the hope of quelling the controversy. But the block-booking system remained pretty much intact.

The majors also succeeded in protecting the favored status of their theaters by controlling the clearance and zoning boards. The boards took over the function of local film boards of trade, established before the NRA and dominated by the Big Five, to arrange theaters in a particular territory into a marketing pattern consisting of run, clearance, and zoning. Theaters first showing newly released pictures were designated first-run. Located in the large metropolitan areas and owned mainly by the circuits affiliated with the majors, these theaters accounted for nearly 50 percent of all admissions. Neighborhood houses and those in surrounding towns had the subsequent right to show pictures and were designated second-run, third-run, and so on. Clearance referred to the number of days that had to elapse before a picture having closed in one theater could open in another. Zoning referred to the geographical area over which clearance restrictions applied. Since the value of a motion picture to an exhibitor depended on its novelty, the granting of excessive clearance to first-run theaters had the effect of increasing their drawing power and keeping patronage in subsequent-run houses at comparatively lower levels.

Practically every legal action independent exhibitors or the government filed against affiliated circuits contained charges of inequitable clearance and zoning. With the creation of the clearance and zoning boards, the majors now had the power to adjudicate these matters for themselves.

The same held true for complaints of admission price discrimination which would be heard by the grievance boards. In licensing their pictures to exhibitors, distributors stipulated minimum admission prices. This eliminated price rivalry among theaters and captured optimum reve-

nue from rentals. The affiliated circuits, which operated
first- and second-run theaters primarily, had a vested interest in seeing later-run independent theaters subjected to
strict admission price control since if these houses cut
prices they would draw off customers. At the outset of the
Depression, independents, to attract patrons, offered prizes,
coupons, two-for-one admissions, and the like, which indirectly reduced prices of admission. To prevent these practices, grievance boards were vested with extraordinary
power. They could punish exhibitors found violating admission price code provisions by ordering a boycott by the
distributors.

On May 27, 1935, the Supreme Court in a unanimous
decision invalidated the NIRA. The immediate effect on
the motion picture industry was slight. It had come through
the Depression virtually intact. Business improved steadily
after 1933, and within two years all the companies were
once again earning profits, with Loew's the undisputed
leader. By 1935, Paramount and Fox had undergone reorganization. In 1936, after selling off its theaters, Universal
came out of receivership. RKO was not stabilized until
1940. Just as important, the industry's monopolistic trade
practices continued in force without significant alteration.

Double Features

As mentioned above, the Depression spawned new exhibition practices which were introduced by independents
to prop up sagging box office and to compete with first-run
theaters. Although games like Screeno, Banko, and Bingo
were comparatively short-lived, double features made a
lasting impact on the industry.

Until the 1930s, the accepted movie program consisted
of a feature and a few shorts. Around 1931, independent
theaters in New England began presenting double features
as a form of price cutting to draw more patrons. The lure
was two for the price of one. The practice spread and,
although affiliated theaters at first refused to budge, they
eventually followed suit, with the result that by 1935 most
theaters outside first-run played double bills.

The wide acceptance of double features changed the
character of exhibition, presented many perplexing distribution problems, and, more important, put a heavy burden

upon production facilities. In the long run it did not affect attendance figures. As more and more theaters in a given area adopted this practice, business was no better than it would have been if all the exhibitors had continued to show only single features. A significant reason was that few exhibitors could afford to pay the rentals of two quality pictures on a single bill. An exhibitor typically showed one strong attraction and one cheap class-B picture.

Hollywood, therefore, adopted a differential pricing policy to deal with distribution: flat fees for class-B pictures and percentages for the class-A product. Although flat fees were set low out of necessity, producers could predict with great accuracy the amount of revenues B features could generate and scale production costs accordingly. Class-A pictures remained the staple of the industry. By selling them on a percentage-of-the-gross basis, companies assumed the risks, but in so doing, could benefit from surges at the box office. Revenues from second features might have been small in comparison, but on the plus side, cheapies allowed the studio to operate at full capacity and provided an inexpensive training ground for new talent.

Theaters playing double features required twice the product, obviously. The Big Five did not possess the capacity to fill the playing time of all the theaters, not even with the Little Three in addition. There remained a gap, albeit small, between supply and demand. This situation explains the existence of Poverty Row, a group of tiny studios in Hollywood that ground out small budget genre pictures for the lower half of double bills in theaters usually located on the wrong side of the tracks. Republic, Monogram, Grand National, and Producers' Releasing Corporation were the important ones, but a host of others made brief appearances. As a group, however, Poverty Row had marginal impact on the business.

Motion Picture Production and Vertical Integration

Mae Huettig has described the structure of the Big Five as "a large inverted pyramid, top-heavy with real estate and theaters, resting on a narrow base of intangibles which constitute films" (ch. 11). This structure had far reaching effects on the quantity, quality, and content of motion

pictures. Owning chains meant that the majors had, first of
all, to fill the playing time of their houses. Most of their
subsequent-run houses played double features which
changed at least twice a week. Some theaters required up
to three hundred pictures a year. Hollywood, as a result,
geared itself to producing two types of pictures—the class A
with name stars, lavish sets and costumes, and big budgets,
and the class B, cheapies produced on a shoestring. It
would not have been profitable for the studios to make
class-A product exclusively, nor did they have the financial
resources or artistic personnel to do so. At most, each studio could produce from fifty to sixty features a year, with
the result that the Big Five played one another's pictures as
a matter of course. As noted earlier, this was possible because the affiliated chains were located mainly in different
regions of the country.

Despite all the publicity given to Hollywood, the headquarters of the industry was in New York. As Lillian Ross
put it,

Almost two years before, I had become interested in *The Red
Badge of Courage* and I had been following its progress step by
step ever since, to learn what I could about the American motion
picture industry. Now, three thousand miles from Hollywood, in
an office building at Forty-fifth and Broadway, I began to feel that
I was getting closer than I ever had before to the heart of the
matter.[3]

In offices such as these, company executives made many
crucial decisions affecting production. Because most of the
Big Five's money was invested and made in the bricks and
mortar branch of the business, exhibition had an important voice in formulating policy. Power went to those closest to the principal sources of income, says Huettig. Basically, exhibition exerted a conservative influence. Theaters
were acquired through the sale of bonds and other forms
of long-term financing, an indebtedness requiring fixed
payments. The head of exhibition, as a result, wanted to
play safe with proven stars and popular genres. The head
of distribution would indicate the number of pictures required for the following season, predicated on the needs of
the company's own theaters and the output of the competi-

3. Lillian Ross, *Picture* (New York: Avon, 1969), p. 247.

tion. He likely urged the filming of a popular novel, a well-known comic strip, or a Pulitizer Prize play, on which thousands had aleady been spent on advertising by others. Then the chief executive, that is, the president, determined the total production budget, based on the company's overall performance. Loew's might spend as much as $28 million a year; a smaller company like Columbia, $7 million to $8 million. Next, he divided the budget among the "A" and "B" groups and finally the individual pictures. After the distribution department had prepared a release schedule, the studio took over. To repeat, company executives, not artistic personnel, decided the types of pictures to be made, the number in each cost category, and so forth.

Hollywood motion picture production is characterized as the studio system. It developed during the rise of the feature film and typified the production process of the major firms throughout the silent era. Sound modified the system somewhat, but it remained essentially intact until the fifties.

Studios were organized by departments. At the top of the hierarchy stood the studio chief, who usually carried the corporate title of vice president. Primarily concerned with business affairs, he negotiated contracts with stars, smoothed out labor problems, ensured that the studio operated efficiently, and acted as liaison with New York. Louis B. Mayer functioned in this capacity at MGM; Darryl Zanuck at Twentieth Century-Fox; and Jack Warner at Warner.

The studio chief might also function in a dual capacity as head of production or delegate this responsibility to another executive. In either case, the beginning stage of the production process involved the selection of properties for story ideas. To assist in these decisions, the story department, which had offices in Europe, New York, and Hollywood, sifted through novels, Broadway plays, short stories, and original ideas for suitable material. Properties would then be assigned to associate producers (or executives with similar titles) who carried them through to completed motion pictures. Irving Thalberg, the head of production at MGM, had ten associate producers under him, each a specialist in certain kinds of pictures—sophisticated comedies, action films, genre pictures, and even animal stories. They

were not independent agents, but surrogates for the production chief, executing his wishes and concepts. By the
end of the 1930s, most studios had organized their production departments in this manner with each associate producer being given the responsibility of making around six
pictures a year.

Once approval was given on a project, the associate producer's task was to supervise the writing of the screenplay.
Scripts typically went through several stages of development: a scenario—a short story version around twenty-five
pages long; a treatment describing each major scene; and
finally the shooting script containing a breakdown of the
scenes into shots and dialogue. Seldom did one screenwriter create a screenplay. More likely, a different writer or
even teams of writers were assigned to each successive
stage. Like everything else at the studio, screenwriting had
its specializations; some writers were hired for their skill in
plot construction, some for comic effects, and others for
polishing dialogue.

Completed script in hand, the production chief now assigned director and cast. For the top stars, the scripts were
tailor-made from the start. Directors, too, might have been
assigned beforehand and even consulted during the final
stages of script preparation, but only a few, such as Ernst
Lubitsch, John Ford, or Michael Curtiz, were afforded this
courtesy. The staff director shot the script as written. He
had no control over budget, casting, or editing. The concept
of one man/one film existed only as it related to the production chief. Thalberg, for example, thought of the completed film as raw material. After sneak previews, he
ordered entire scenes reshot and altered endings for greater
audience appeal.

In the production and postproduction phases, other departments such as art direction, costumes, makeup, cinematography, editing, and down the line to special effects,
publicity, and so on would contribute to each picture as
required. In this fashion, MGM made its forty pictures a
year, utilizing a work force of six thousand who were
members of twenty-seven departments.

Nothing so much characterized Hollywood production
as the star system. The economic rationale for using stars
has been previously noted. Thalberg added a new twist

to it. He reasoned that if one star helped ensure a picture's success, a "galaxy" of two, four, or even eight would increase its chances. The question to be answered now is how Hollywood developed its talent. We can dismiss the myth that potential stars were discovered working behind soda fountains around Hollywood and Vine streets or performing as bit players in extravaganzas. The studios left little to chance (ch. 14). If a performer showed promise, the producer cast him or her in different roles and measured audience reaction to each performance. Fan mail, sneak previews, and exhibitor evaluations indicated market response as did reviews in trade papers and box office grosses. Once the correct narrative formula was found, the image of the star would be fixed. Thereafter, the star would play the same role over and over with little variation until audience interest waned. When this happened the star's career would come to an unhappy end unless, of course, a new image could be found.

The best performers chafed at being stereotyped. Repeating the same role deadened the spirit and prevented a talented actor from reaching his full potential. Studios justified their policies with the explanation that developing a star required enormous expenditures of money. To tamper with success would be foolhardy. Regardless, they could dictate policy by enforcing the provisions of the option contract. Used for stars, feature players, and important production personnel, this contract tied talent to the studio for a fixed term, usually seven years. At yearly intervals, the studio had the option of renewing or dropping the contract. If renewed, the person received an increase in salary as previously specified. This type of contract placed talent in a subservient position; they were employees who had to perform as the studio wished. "Difficult" people could be disciplined by being loaned out to appear in pictures that had little chance of succeeding.

Since production revolved around stars, publicity and promotion took on dimensions greater than the individual motion picture. Hollywood glamour, the life-styles of stars, and studio comings and goings were all hyped to maintain interest in the public mind.

The publicity department handled press releases, interviews, and press agent activities. It was organized like the city room of a newspaper. The department head functioned as editor, making assignments and reviewing finished copy before it was released. Special items such as new contracts, salaries, and hard news stories about the studio and stars were his special domain. When a suicide or messy divorce occurred, he had to use public relations of a high order to protect the reputation of the studio and to salvage a career. Working under the department head were the unit reporters who covered the big pictures and built up new players, and publicists who were assigned to individual stars. Since the publicist was concerned with the proper image, he oversaw the clothing, makeup, and general appearance of his charge on all public appearances. During interviews, he often fielded questions the star found difficult or the studio wanted to avoid. The remainder of the publicity department specialized in creating fashion layouts, in serving as liaisons with fan magazines, and planting stories with Louella Parsons, Hedda Hopper, and other gossip columnists. Hollywood was the third largest news source in the country, outranked only by Washington and New York. Three hundred correspondents representing fan magazines, newspaper syndicates, and periodicals sent news all over the United States and abroad. Even the Vatican had a correspondent in Hollywood.

Of all the outlets for publicity, the fan magazine was the most voracious. *Photoplay*, *Modern Screen*, and *Silver Screen*, the largest magazines, each had monthly circulations of nearly a half million. Marriage, divorce, romance, children, and death were their favorite topics. Greta Garbo, Carole Lombard, Errol Flynn made the best copy, and child stars, especially Shirley Temple, Deanna Durbin, Judy Garland, and Mickey Rooney.

The still photography department supplied the iconography. Photographs were the physical artifacts of the motion picture experience. For all productions, photographs were taken of key scenes for use in lobby displays, advertising, and poster layouts. Glamour portraits, a staple of the department, reached the level of "objets d'art." In the hands of such skilled photographers as George Hurrell and Clarence Bull, these portraits captured, in a single still, the essence, the image of the star, what the film took ninety minutes to establish. By the thousands these stills went out

George Hurrell with Bette Davis on the set of *The Little Foxes* (RKO, 1941)

each week to fans, magazines, and newspapers where they were eagerly consumed.

The Production Code Administration

Vertical integration, monopolistic trade practices, and the mode of production were all influential in shaping the form and content of the product. These factors were inherent in the system. But because Hollywood geared its product to reach a mass audience, it was particularly susceptible to outside intimidation in the form of censorship. It should be remembered that the motion picture did not enjoy the constitutional guarantees of freedom of speech until 1952.

Salacious motion picture content and Hollywood scandals combined to ignite a public outcry for censorship during the early twenties, leading to the formation of the Motion Picture Producers and Distributors of America in 1922. As a result of adept public relations work on the part of its president, Will Hays, reformers were mollified with the assurance that the industry could effectively regulate itself. The Committee on Public Relations was the means Hays used to achieve his goal. After being formally absorbed into the MPPDA in 1925, the committee conducted a study of the specific rejections and deletions made by state censorship boards. These were codified in a document entitled "Don'ts and Be Carefuls." The list of "Don'ts" contained eleven items that could not be shown on the screen such as white slavery, miscegenation, sexual perversion, and ridicule of the clergy. The list of "Be Carefuls" comprised twenty-six subjects such as international relations, arson, murder techniques, rape, first-night scenes, the use of drugs, and excessive and lustful kissing. Hays asked for voluntary compliance because an enforcement machinery was thought to be repugnant to producers.

The vagueness of the code spurred Martin Quigley, a Catholic layman and publisher of the influential trade magazine *Motion Picture Herald*, to improve on it. He enlisted the assistance of Daniel A. Lord, a Jesuit priest who had been technical advisor on *The King of Kings*, to draft a new, more detailed version. The Motion Picture Production Code was completed in 1930 and with Hays' urging adopted by MPPDA members. To see that the code was implemented, the Studio Relations Committee was empowered to work with producers throughout all stages of production from the writing of a scenario to the final editing of the picture.

Up until the Depression, producers were fairly conscientious in abiding by the Production Code, but when box office attendance plummeted in 1932–33, they introduced more explicit and violent subject matter into their pictures in an attempt to attract patrons. Moreover, producers were not sure that the 1930 code really represented and reflected with the public wanted. The Catholic church cried out in protest, as did Protestant and Jewish organizations. The Catholics were the most militant and declared war against the industry by forming the Legion of Decency in 1934 with the goal of boycotting offensive pictures until the industry created a mechanism to enforce the Production Code. At the height of its crusade, more than eleven million church members signed pledges of support.

The Legion of Decency exerted irresistible economic pressure. Faced with the potential loss of revenue from such a large group of patrons at a time when the industry was practically bankrupt, the majors decided to act. On July 1, 1934, Will Hays and the board of directors of the MPPDA amended and amplified the Production Code. Joseph I. Breen was placed in charge of the Production Code Administration, the successor to the Studio Relations Committee, and having considerably more clout. His find-

Scarface: Shame of the Nation (United Artists, 1932), starring Paul Muni, Ann Dvorak, and George Raft

ings were subject to review only on appeal of the presidents of MPPDA companies. Breen's department would scrutinize all scripts and pictures with the knowledge that each release had to have the Hays Office seal of approval before it could be exhibited in affiliated theaters. Any member violating this rule was subject to a $25,000 fine. Without access to these theaters, of course, no picture with a budget of any consequence could return its investment, let alone earn a profit.

The Catholic church called off its threatened boycott and, along with other religious groups, decided to give the industry another chance at self-censorship. The church, however, apparently had misgivings about the "Breen Office" because in 1936, it began to systematically review and classify motion pictures on its own. But the Production Code Administration succeeded beyond a doubt. By 1937, it would review nearly every picture exhibited in the United States each year.

The Production Code and the operation of the Breen Office are described by Ruth A. Inglis (ch. 15), a staff member of the Commission on Freedom of the Press. Centered at the University of Chicago and consisting of prominent professors and administrators in higher education, the commission investigated the industry in 1947 to discover how the motion picture could reach its full potential as an art form and as a medium for the enrichment of society. The results were published in Inglis' report, *Freedom of the Movies*.

Although the report's recommendations were too idealistic for easy implementation, two were ultimately acted upon—First Amendment guarantees were granted to the motion picture and the vertically integrated companies were broken up. These recommendations obviously were not new. Nor did their implementation create a renaissance for the movies, as some had hoped. Nonetheless, the commission's overall critique of the Production Code's effect on motion picture content remains valid. The commission agreed with critics of the industry who complained that the motion picture avoided any serious treatment of significant social, political, and moral issues. But it did not make a whipping boy out of the Breen Office. The report accused the industry of hiding behind the Production Code to avoid

trouble from pressure groups. In other words, the timidity
was self-serving. One can add that the enforcement mechanism helped guarantee that the screen would remain non-
controversial—for a picture to play in a theater owned by
the Big Five, it had to receive the Hays Office seal of
approval. In essence, the five majors exercised censorship
over the entire industry. An independent producer who
hoped to establish his name and business by treating such
important social problems as race relations or extremist
politics could be kept out of the market.

The Production Code was a moralistic document, yet in
the opinion of the commission, the code defeated its own
purpose by making it impossible for pictures to treat sex
naturally and honestly. And lastly, the report asked why
screenwriters must invent "compensating moral values"
when they are lacking in real life.

Thus, prodded by the Catholic Legion of Decency, Hollywood directed its powers of persuasion to preserving traditional concepts of morality. For the next generation, the
industry would produce the "family" film, which addressed
itself to the undifferentiated mass audience. Motion pictures might be technically polished and contain so-called
expensive production values, but they would not deal in
an honest fashion with the pressing concerns of an enlight-
ened citizenry.

The Labor Movement in Hollywood

The development of the studio system of production is
inextricably linked to the rise of organized labor. As each
step in the production process became departmentalized
and further subdivided, competing unions fought to win
jurisdiction over new work functions and to codify responsibilities. At the heyday of the era in 1946, labor was organized into forty-three distinct craft and talent groups.
The largest union group was the International Alliance of
Theatrical Stage Employees (IA), which had thirteen locals
and over ten thousand members in Hollywood. IA controlled virtually every craft required to shoot a movie. The
Conference of Studio Unions (CSU), with a membership
of seven thousand, controlled the preshooting crafts. Talent
was organized into the Screen Actors Guild, the Screen

Writers Guild, the Screen Directors Guild, and the American Federation of Musicians. Office employees, story analysts, publicists, and others were organized into white-collar unions.

Like labor movements in other industries, Hollywood's was characterized by jurisdictional fights, turbulent labor-management conflicts, racketeering, and political agitation. Until the days of the NRA, Hollywood's industrial relations were harmonious, in the main. Labor peace was achieved by the signing of the Studio Basic Agreement in 1921, when the producers formally recognized five important unions and agreed to a mechanism for the arbitration of industrial conflicts. Labor won better working conditions and more pay, but the studios succeeded in keeping an "open shop," meaning that employees did not have to be union members in order to work. This fact pretty much nullified the effectiveness of a strike since the studios could readily hire replacements.

The formation of the Central Casting Corporation, also in 1926, improved the lot of Hollywood extras. Movie-struck people from around the country had flocked to Los Angeles in the hope of breaking into pictures. A small percentage found occasional work but only a handful steady employment. Extras were subjected to all kinds of abuses such as high employment agency fees, underpayment of wages, overwork, maltreatment, and other forms of exploitation. In turn, they were the source of many social problems. To avert a national scandal, Will Hays commissioned the Russell Sage Foundation to study the situation. Central Casting, a nonprofit agency financed by the MPPDA companies, was the result. As the name implies, the organization functioned as a clearinghouse; extras could now call in rather than make the daily trek to the studios, which were located miles apart. Wages and working conditions improved somewhat, but not employment opportunities. Central Casting failed in one major respect; it did not find a means to discourage the thousands of aspirants so that a residual of trained extras could enjoy at least a semblance of regular employment.

Stirrings among the talent groups, especially the actors, led to the creation of the Academy of Motion Picture Arts and Sciences in 1927. Conceived by Louis B. Mayer, the

Academy was a company union that embraced five categories of filmmakers: producers, directors, actors, writers, and technicians. These employees apparently were given sufficient rewards to forestall serious labor organizing among their ranks for five years.

But when studios instituted the salary cut after the 1933 bank holiday, and attempted to blame their financial difficulties on high-priced talent, things changed. In drafting the NRA code, companies wrote in provisions barring star raiding, curbing the activities of agents, and limiting the salaries of creative artists. The reaction in Hollywood was the formation of the Screen Writers Guild in April 1933 and the Screen Actors Guild later that June. Together they bombarded Washington with telegrams, held mass meetings, and launched publicity campaigns opposing the control of salaries on any basis other than free competition among producers. As the deadline approached for the signing of the code, they threatened to strike. Eddie Cantor, representing the Screen Actors, spent Thanksgiving with President Roosevelt, a meeting that later resulted in the permanent suspension of the obnoxious provisions in the code. However, the guilds failed to receive recognition as bargaining agents for the actors and writers or to substantially improve the status of their members in the industry.

The studios readily acceded to the demands of the craft unions and the army of stagehands and technicians organized by IA. They received a reduction in hours, an increase in wages, and greater job security. These concessions cost management relatively little, since the salaries paid to these workers constituted a small percentage of the cost of production. As Larry Ceplair and Steven Englund remark, "On the surface, industry management appeared liberal and farsighted in granting concessions to well-established unions and technicians vital to the movie-making process. When the creative personnel who, if organized, might challenge the studio system, however, formed guilds, management proved intransigent, shrewd, and unscrupulous."[4]

4. Larry Ceplair and Steven Englund, *The Inquisition in Hollywood: Politics in the Film Community, 1930–1960* (Garden City, N.Y.: Anchor Press/Doubleday, 1980), p. 18.

Although stars earned salaries in excess of six figures, the plight of the regular actor was not as fortunate. The typical weekly wage was $66. The workweek, however, consisted of six days. Actors often worked past midnight and then were ordered to report back to the studio at 8 A.M.; they did not receive overtime compensation or premium pay for Sunday and holidays. Nor did an actor enjoy continuous employment. He would be paid only for those days actually worked during a shooting schedule that stretched several weeks. Needless to say, there was no machinery guaranteeing the impartial arbitration of disputes for those under contracts.

For screenwriters, exploitation took the following form, which is described by Leo Rosten:

> For two decades [1921–41] the movie writers in the low salary brackets (of whom where are plenty) were not given the protection of minimum wages or minimum periods of employment. They were discharged with no advance notice; their employment was sporadic and their tenure short-lived. They were laid off for short-term periods, under contract but without pay. They worked on stories on which other writers were employed, without knowing who their collaborators (or competitors) were. Their right to screen credits was mistreated by certain producers who allotted credit to their friends or relatives or—under pseudonyms—to themselves. They were frequently offered the bait of speculative writing without either guarantees or protection in the outcome.[5]

The passage of the National Labor Relations Act in 1935 theoretically gave unionization another boost in that the act restored many of the labor provisions of the invalidated NRA code and specifically authorized collective bargaining. Hollywood producers, like management in other industries, simply ignored the act. Finally, after two years, the actors threatened a massive strike. This won recognition for the Screen Actors Guild on May 15, 1937. Low-salaried players received most of the initial benefits. The contract set minimum rates of pay, guaranteed continuous employment, and stipulated twelve-hour rest periods between calls. Although successive contracts won concessions for all classes of performers, the relationship of the actor to the production process remained unaltered; in fact, it

5. Leo Rosten, *Hollywood: The Movie Colony and the Movie Makers* (New York: Harcourt, Brace, 1941), p. 136.

was never an issue. The concessions had relatively minor economic impact on the studios, which accounts for the ready acquiescence.

Recognition for the Screen Writers Guild came only after a protracted and acrimonious battle. Under the leadership of John Howard Lawson, a militant minority drew up a platform that went far beyond the bread-and-butter issues of the Actors Guild. Lawson's group wanted the screenwriter to share creative authority in the production process. In the studio system, the screenwriter was typically an employee who wrote for hire, just another cog in the wheel. The platform had three goals: (1) a union strong enough to back its demands by shutting off the supply of screenplays; (2) alliances with the Dramatists Guild and other writers' organizations so as to be able to stop the flow of all story material at the source; and (3) remuneration on a royalty basis that would give authors greater control over the content of their work by making them part owners of the movies based on their scripts.

Debate over the platform split the ranks of the screenwriters. Conservatives consisting of the older, elite writers saw the amalgamation plan as a dilution of their privileged status. For this and ideological reasons, they revolted to form a rival union, the Screen Playwrights, in 1936. Seizing the opportunity to squelch the militants, the studio chiefs recognized the Screen Playwrights almost immediately and signed a five-year pact. The Screen Writers Guild countered by filing a representation suit with the National Labor Relations Board. The NLRB held elections and certified the Screen Writers Guild on August 8, 1938, as the sole bargaining representative of motion picture writers. But because of recalcitrance on the part of producers, it took three years to hammer out the terms of recognition. A guild shop was finally established in May 1941. Needless to say, none of the goals of the original platform was realized. The studios agreed to ban speculative writing, set a minimum wage, and make the guild sole arbiter of screen credits, but they would have nothing to do with elevating the creative status of the screenwriter.

In its dealings with talent groups, Hollywood proved to be a belligerent and devisive foe; to keep the labor force in line, the studios adopted the tactic of collusion. Although craft workers and the rank-and-file laborers received certain

economic benefits from the NRA, the open shop remained
intact. A fight over jurisdiction launched by IA in 1933
seemed to cripple the labor movement, whereupon the studios and rival craft unions successfully crushed the strike.
As strikebreakers were brought in to fill vacancies, IA
members flocked to join other unions to save their jobs.
Afterward, IA ceased to function in Hollywood.

The next year, however, IA installed a new president,
William B. Browne, the former head of the Motion Picture
Machine Operators Union in Chicago. To act as his personal representative, Browne appointed fellow Chicagoan
and professional hoodlum William Bioff. The arrival of
this team introduced a new wrinkle to the Hollywood labor
scene—racketeering. To reinstate his union, Browne used
IA's deadliest weapon; he appealed to the theater projectionists and succeeded in closing down all the houses in
the Paramount chain after a dispute with that studio in
1936. Although Paramount immediately buckled, Browne's
price for a strike settlement was high—a closed shop agreement for all IA's former members not only at Paramount
but throughout the entire industry. Feeling the pressure,
the studios capitulated. As a result of the agreement, IA's
membership jumped from thirty-three to twelve thousand.

Browne and Bioff thereupon instituted a "defense fund"
by levying a 2 percent assessment on every IA paycheck
and set about to increase IA's hegemony by instituting a
series of jurisdictional fights. In their dealings with the
studios, they used the potent threat of a projectionist strike
to extract $100,000 bribes from company heads in return
for either reducing wage demands or not making them at
all. Throughout the years of Hollywood's labor troubles,
"the role of the studios was far from that of an innocent
bystander," in the words of John Cogley. "As employers,
the studio chiefs were very much involved in behind-the-
scenes manipulations, playing one [labor] group against the
other. When bribes were paid to Willie Bioff, it was the
studio bosses who paid them. . . . They [later] acknowledged that by agreeing to the Browne-Bioff 'arrangements'
about wage-cuts and increases, the movie companies had
saved approximately $15 million."[6]

6. John Cogley, *Report on Blacklisting I: The Movies* (Fund for the
Republic, 1956), p. 52.

Browne's and Bioff's activities came to light when labor lawyer Carey McWilliams urged that the California Assembly investigate IA. McWilliams charged that Bioff was a former member of the Capone mob and had been arrested and questioned in connection with at least two murders in Chicago—both victims were trade unionists who had challenged Browne's and Bioff's control of IA locals. Hearings were held in 1937 but no formal action was taken by the Assembly. Afterward, columnist Westbrook Pegler revealed that Bioff had run a brothel on Chicago's South Side and that he was convicted for pandering (though he never served).

Subsequent investigations on the part of the U.S. Treasury Department led to charges of extortion against Browne and Bioff in 1941. In the same action, Joseph Schenck, head of Twentieth Century-Fox, was indicted on a charge of income tax evasion for concealing a company bribe of $100,000 to the pair. Browne and Bioff were sentenced to ten and eight years, respectively. Schenck was found guilty of perjury, for which he received a prison sentence of one year and a day.

With Browne and Bioff out of the way, progressive trade unionism now had a chance. Under the leadership of Herbert Sorrell, a group of twelve non-IA unions formed the Conference of Studio Unions in 1941. This coalition originally consisted of unions peripheral to the industry, but grew rapidly to encompass most preshooting crafts such as painters, carpenters, decorators, and electrical workers. Originally the business agent for the painters' union, Sorrell was a radical and aggressive labor leader who emphasized bread-and-butter issues and collective strength. To those in Hollywood who considered IA a corrupt and reactionary force, the emergence of CSU marked a long step forward in the labor movement. To studio executives, however, Sorrell spelled trouble. The Wage Stabilization Act froze salaries for the duration. Afterward, they anticipated that Sorrell would call a strike demanding excessive wage increases and other costly concessions.

To contain Sorrell's influence, the studios conspired to exploit one of the many jurisdictional disputes that characterized the warfare between the CSU and IA from the beginning. In 1945, the Association of Motion Picture Producers, the Hollywood affiliate of the Hays Office, refused to recognize a change in affiliation of the interior decorators who voted to join the CSU. Although Sorrell successfully appealed to the War Labor Board, the AMPP ignored the ruling. Perceiving this as a portent of the studios' behavior after the war, Sorrell launched a strike in March 1945 that lasted eight months. The studios retaliated by hiring IA replacements. Warner, in particular, opted for more violent tactics by employing thugs, tear gas, fire hoses, and the studio's private police and fire departments to disrupt picket lines.

The strike, meanwhile, took on ideological overtones. Roy Brewer, who was sent in by IA International to take over and direct strategy, labeled the strike "political" and distributed a barrage of leaflets attacking Sorrell for his "Communist associations" and support of "Communist causes." Coming from a scandal-ridden union, these political attacks proved ineffective at first. The strike ended in a stalemate, with most of the issues relegated to arbitration, which settled nothing.

Sorrell thereupon called another strike in 1946 over yet another jurisdictional dispute with IA. By now, Brewer's red-baiting began to pay off. The end of hostilities marked the beginning of the cold war in foreign affairs and a conservative backlash against the legacy of the New Deal on the domestic front. In catch-up moves to offset the wartime wage freeze, workers in most industries struck in droves, prompting management to use any and all means, including anti-Communism, to weaken organized labor. Hollywood executives fought labor militancy by collaborating more closely with Brewer to lock out CSU members and to hire IA scabs. Brewer, for his part, further consolidated his power by aligning with right-wing patriotic groups, most notably the Motion Picture Alliance for the Preservation of American Ideals. This strike dragged on for three years, CSU picket lines dwindling as members deserted to IA and the assurance of work. Meanwhile, the antilabor cause was given a boost when the House Committee on Un-American Activities investigated the alleged Communist infiltration of the film industry in 1947 (ch. 18). By 1949, Sorrell and other left-wing labor leaders were purged from all Hollywood unions, and the democratic labor movement in the film industry came to an end. Roy Brewer and the IA, with the approval of the studios, now dominated the labor scene in Hollywood.

Effects of World War II

The Foreign Market

As hostilities spread in Europe and the Orient during the thirties, American film companies saw their foreign markets dwindle. Spain was the first casualty of the industry, following the outbreak of the Civil War in 1936. By 1938, Japan had occupied parts of China, Manchukuo, and the Kwantung Peninsula. Nearly half of the Far Eastern market soon came under Japanese control.

In the wake of the German Anschluss, the industry retreated from Austria, Czechoslovakia, Norway, and Occupied France. Continental Europe, where the majors had done over a quarter of their worldwide business in 1936, practically vanished as a market by 1941. The only business conducted on the Continent during the war was with neutral Sweden and Switzerland.

Of greater consequence was Great Britain, the principal outlet for American films abroad. Revenues fell off alarmingly after war was declared in September 1939. The Nazis began to bomb London and other English cities, which necessitated the evacuation of more than three million people. Until the threat of air attack subsided, theaters remained closed. By 1940, however, all but about 10 percent of the country's forty-eight hundred movie theaters were open once more, providing escape and relaxation from danger and war related work. Average weekly attendance in Great Britain increased from nineteen million in 1939 to more than thirty million in 1945, and gross box office receipts nearly trebled.

Although business in Great Britain did not suffer, U.S. companies could not share in the bonanza because of currency restrictions. Immediately following the declaration of war, Britain reduced the amount of sterling that American distributors could remove from the country; half of their former revenues, or $17.5 million, could be taken out in 1940, and only $12.9 million in 1941.

Currency restrictions such as those imposed by Great Britain were nothing new to American distributors. They had long been subjected to quotas, taxes, contingents, and tariffs of all varieties. The rise of nationalism in Europe was one cause; another was protectionism for national film industries. Although the Americans had successfully fought these protective measures in the past—with the help of the U.S. government, it should be noted—the war severely damaged the foreign film market (ch. 17).

To offset conditions in the war-torn European countries, Hollywood turned to Latin America. There, although the industry had a near monopoly, the market had never been fully exploited. The Department of State aided Hollywood's cause by creating the Office of the Coordinator of Inter-American Affairs (CIAA) in October 1940. Its objective was to promote the Good Neighbor Policy and to initiate programs that would combat pro-Axis sentiment in South America. CIAA opened its Motion Picture Division almost immediately, under the directorship of John Hay Whitney.

Whitney's first goal was to convince the industry to abolish the stereotyped bloodthirsty Latin-American villain from its movies and to produce films having Latin-American themes and locales. His second was to neutralize propaganda flowing into Argentina, Brazil, and Chile from Axis wire services, features, newsreels, and documentaries. Whitney created the Newsreel Section for this purpose, and by 1943, the CIAA had shipped to South America more than two hundred newsreels produced in cooperation with Paramount, Pathé, Universal, Fox, and Hearst's News of the Day. These pictures reached an audience of more than eighteen million by 1944, according to CIAA estimates.

Business in Latin America improved steadily during the war, but not as much as expected. Several factors help explain this: first, shipping between the two continents operated erratically and less frequently than before; second, the films on war subjects, which Hollywood churned out in great numbers at the beginning, had little mass appeal;

Wallace Beery as Pancho Villa in *Viva Villa!* (MGM, 1934)

and third, national film companies, especially in Mexico, stepped up their own production.

The Domestic Market

By the time America entered the war, it was apparent to the industry that it would have to rely on the domestic market. Fortunately, conditions at home created a boom in business. Dollars were plentiful, while commodities were not. Movies were the most readily available entertainment. Although gasoline restrictions hurt attendance in some rural areas, the integrated companies, whose theaters were more favorably situated, flourished. Domestic film rentals for the eight majors jumped from $193 million in 1939 to $332 million in 1946. As *Variety* noted, "Every night was Saturday night" at the movies. B pictures, low-grade pictures, pictures featuring unknown players—all commanded an audience. Weekly attendance by the end of the war reached ninety million, the highest ever.

As business improved, pictures ran longer and longer to

capacity houses, with a significant result. The eight majors released 388 pictures in 1939, but only 252 in 1946. Twentieth Century-Fox, Paramount, and Warner cut the production of B pictures in 1942. Although the decision was motivated in part by wartime rationing of film stock, it became apparent early on that more and more dollars could be earned from fewer and fewer top-grade films. Production costs rose during this period, to be sure, but not as fast as profit margins. Paramount's earnings, for example, soared from $10 million in 1941 to an incredible $44 million in 1946.

The industry continued to operate during the war unfet-

James Cagney in *Yankee Doodle Dandy* (Warner Bros., 1942)

tered by government controls of any sort. Roosevelt recognized the importance of the industry from the outset, stating, "The American motion picture is one of our most effective mediums in informing and entertaining our citizens. The motion picture must remain free insofar as national security will permit. I want no censorship of the motion picture."[7] Nonetheless, no unanimity existed as to the specific role Hollywood should play.

Wartime film production emanated from three sources: (1) government agencies with their own production units; (2) federal agencies that contracted with private firms: and (3) Hollywood. To provide direction and organization to meet the needs of the armed forces, the federal bureaucracy, and the public, the Coordinator for Government Films operated out of the Office of War Information headed by Elmer Davis. The industry appointed the War Activities Committee to coordinate its efforts. As a first objective, the committee arranged with exhibitors nationwide to provide free playing time for government films.

Tensions existed from the start. The OWI pushed Hollywood to increase its output of war films, even though about one out of every four pictures produced during the 1941–42 season related in some way to the war effort. Moreover, the OWI believed that fluctuations in the war necessitated closer supervision of motion picture content. Officials complained that Hollywood typically depicted Americans as living lavishly and seemingly oblivious to the great sacrifices being made abroad. Our allies felt that characterizations of their countrymen were distorted. Both wanted the motion picture to be self-conscious, attuned to the realities of the time.

The industry, however, was attuned to the audience and looked to the box office as a gauge to determine preferences. After all, the public could also receive news and information from the other media. Hollywood learned from experience in England that after three years of fighting, audiences were rejecting the steady diet of war films in favor of entertaining, escapist pictures.

Issues were never resolved. In 1943, the OWI came under attack from Congress. Some of its members charged

7. Quoted in "Hollywood in Uniform," *Fortune* 25 (April 1942): 92.

that government-sponsored films, such as the *Why We Fight* series, were nothing more than political propaganda for a Roosevelt fourth term. The OWI's budget was slashed in 1944, and the War Activities Committee took over the entire job of coordination. Hollywood's product showed a pronounced trend toward lighter and mellower diversion.

The machinery created by the majors carried them to the crest of prosperity in 1946. Paramount's profits for that year have already been stated. Earnings for the other members of the Big Five were: Twentieth Century-Fox, $22 million; Warner, $19 million; Loew's, $18 million; and RKO, $12 million. Afterward, the industry underwent a period of retrenchment, reappraisal, and reorganization.

MAE D. HUETTIG

Economic Control of the Motion Picture Industry

Some Questions to Be Answered

Despite the glamour of Hollywood, the crux of the motion picture industry is the theater. It is in the brick-and-mortar branch of the industry that most of the money is invested and made. Without understanding this fact, devotees of the film are likely to remain forever baffled by some characteristics of an industry which is in turn exciting, perplexing, and irritating. Emphasis on the economic role of the theater is not meant to belittle the film itself. Obviously it is the film which draws people to the theater. Nevertheless, the structure of the motion picture industry (a large inverted pyramid, top-heavy with real estate and theaters, resting on a narrow base of the intangibles which constitute films) has had far-reaching effects on the film itself.

This may seem farfetched. Most writers on the motion picture industry rather studiously avoid its duller aspects, i.e., those dealing with the trade practices, financial policies, intercorporate relationships, etc. But the facts indicate clearly that there is a connection between the form taken by the film and the mechanics of the business, even if the connection is somewhat obscure. It is true, as one student has pointed out, that "the issues involved are not peculiar to the motion picture

Abridged by the editor from *Economic Control of the Motion Picture Industry* (Philadelphia: University of Pennsylvania Press, 1944), pp. 54–95.

285

industry."[1] Despite this lack of uniqueness, the problems of organization, intercorporate relationships, and financial policy in the motion picture industry deserve more than passing mention. The attitude of the industry itself toward discussion of these problems has not been completely candid. A great reluctance to disclose factual information with respect to its operations has unfortunately characterized most of the leaders of the industry.

Among the many questions which lack a reliable answer are: How many people attend movies? How often? How large is the industry in terms of invested capital and volume of business? What is the annual income of all theaters? How many theaters are owned by what groups? What type of film is most uniformly successful? What is the relationship between the cost of films and their drawing power? Little is known of the industry's place in the broader pattern of American industry, or its method of solving the specialized problems of commercial entertainment. There are few reliable statistics available (and of these none is compiled by the industry itself) with regard to these questions.

What Is the Economic Importance of the Industry?

There are various ways of measuring the role of an industry in our economy. The indices most commonly used are: (1) volume of business, (2) invested capital, and (3) number of employees. The value of such criteria is limited, since comparison between all types of industries produces results too general to be significant. However, in the case of the motion picture industry, these indices are valuable as a means of delimiting its economic importance and recording some basic information regarding its size. This question assumes importance partly because the industry itself seems to be under some misapprehension with respect to the answer. It may well be true, as Will Hays frequently says, that the motion picture is a great social necessity, an integral part of human life in the whole civilized world, but this value is in no way minimized by an accurate statement as to the industry's economic importance. "Standing well among the first ten (or the first four) industries in this country" [for a similar statement, see ch. 8, for example—Ed.] has so often prefaced the remarks of industry spokesmen as to indicate that the facts are not generally known.

Here, then, let it be noted that insofar as size of industry is measured by dollar volume of business, the motion picture industry is not only

1. Howard T. Lewis, *The Motion Picture Industry* (New York: Van Nostrand, 1933), p. xiii.

Hell's Angels première at Grauman's Chinese Theater, Hollywood. Courtesy Bruce Torrence Historical Collection, c/o First Federal of Hollywood

not among the first ten, it is not even among the first forty. It is surpassed by such industries, to name only a few, as laundries, hotels, restaurants, loan companies, investment trusts, liquor, tobacco, and musical instruments.

Viewed thus as a part of our national economy, the motion picture industry is not a major bulwark. There are forty-four other industries, out of the total of ninety-four industrial groups enumerated by *Statistics of Income* (Bureau of Internal Revenue), that reported a larger gross income in 1937 than did the combined motion picture producing and exhibition corporations. In terms of employment, the motion picture industry accounts for somewhat fewer than two hundred thousand persons in all three branches of production, distribution, and exhibition.

When motion picture corporations are compared with those in other branches of the entertainment field, another story is presented. The entire field of commercial amusement, including billiard halls, bowling alleys, dance halls, etc., is dominated by the motion picture industry.[2] Motion picture corporations, constituting 44 percent of the total number of amusement corporations in 1937, accounted for 78 percent of the gross income and 92 percent of the total net income of the group. This should prove what has long been suspected and probably needs little proof: that movies are the favorite form of entertainment for most Americans.

Production versus Exhibition

From the point of view of the moviegoing public, one of the most important questions about the industry is: who decides what films are made; or, as it is more commonly put, why are films what they are? From the industry's point of view, too, this question of the kind of product released is ultimately its most important single problem. Quality of product is increasingly vital now that the motion picture business is settling down into a semblance of middle age, devoid of the novelty appeal it formerly had.

The answer to the question posed above is in the relationship among the various branches of the industry. By virtue of the division of labor within the business, film distributors and exhibitors are much more closely in touch with the moviegoing public than are the producers, and they trade heavily on their advantageous positions. From their seat in the box office they announce that so-and-so is "poison at the box office," that what the public wants is musicals or blood-and-thunder westerns, that English stars murder business, and that sophisticated farce comedies leave their audiences completely cold.

Broadly speaking, and omitting the relatively unimportant inde-

2. In 1938, amusement corporations constituted roughly 2 percent of the entire number of active corporations filing income tax returns. The gross income of all amusement corporations was slightly over $1 billion, or less than 1 percent of the total gross income ($120 billion) of all corporations filing returns. Net income (less deficit) of amusement corporations was $52 million. Bureau of Internal Revenue, *Statistics of Income*, 1939.

pendent producers, the relationship among the three branches of the industry may be described in two ways. First, there is the relationship between a major producer and theater operators not affiliated with his company. Second, there is the relationship *within* a major company among the various departments of production, distribution, and exhibition. The intracompany relationship is the more important with respect to the kind of films made, since contact within the organization is much closer than contact between the unaffiliated exhibitors and producers. The unaffiliated exhibitors are not generally consulted by producers with respect to the nature of the films to be made. However, they occasionally make their views known through advertisements in the trade press and probably express their opinions quite freely in talking with the sales representatives of the producers. Most of their arguments are ex post facto, however, and affect the future lineup of product negatively, or not at all.

On the other hand, the sales and theater people *within* the integrated companies are extremely important in determining the type of picture to be made, the number of pictures in each cost class, the type of story, etc. It is not intended to give here a detailed account of the manner in which these decisions are reached, but in general the procedure is as follows: The person in charge of distribution announces the number of films wanted for the following season. This figure is presumably based on some estimate of what can be profitably sold, but it is also related to the needs of the company's own theaters for product. The chief executive announces the amount of money available for the total product. The amounts vary among the individual companies from $7 or $8 million for the smaller companies to $28 million for Loew's. The next step is the division and allocation of the total amount to groups of pictures. The names given these classes vary, but the grouping is in accordance with the quality to be aimed at as defined by the amount of money to be spent. That is, there are the "specials" and the more ordinary "program" features. There are "A" pictures and "B" pictures. The latter are designed, more or less frankly, to meet the need for the lesser half of the double feature program. Once the allocation of production funds is made, the next step is that of determining the budgets for the individual pictures within each group. The amount spent on a given picture is presumably related in some way to the anticipated drawing power of the particular combination of talent and production values planned for the given picture. After the detailed budget is worked out, a tentative release schedule is prepared for the use of the sales force (distribution). From this point on, the problems belong primarily to the production department.

Note what this cursory outline reveals. Company executives, i.e.,

On the set of Samuel Goldwyn's *Dead End,* directed by William Wyler (United Artists, 1937)

theater, sales, and production people, determine the following: the number of pictures to be made, the total amount of money to be spent, the distribution of the funds among the various classes of pictures, the budgets of the individual pictures, and the dates when the pictures are to be finished.

It is not meant that all such issues are decided by ukase and handed down from the front office to the production staff. The interdepartmental conference technique is customary, with every department chief valiantly defending his own position. At work are all the usual subterranean factors which determine where power ultimately rests. There are, however, certain objective factors which are present to some degree in each of the five large majors. These tend to give decisive policy-making power regarding the kind of films made to the groups farthest removed from production itself, i.e., the men in distribution and theater management.

The objective factors are found in a prosaic listing of the various sources of income to the five principal companies. In approximate order of importance, they are: (1) theater admissions, (2) film rentals, (3) the sale of film accessories, and (4) dividends from affiliated companies. The relative importance of each source varies for the individual majors, but in almost every instance the chief single source of income is theater admissions. Although there is an inseparable connection between the quality of films and company earnings from film rentals and theaters, the division of functions within the company structure operates to give the preponderance of power to those nearest the principal source of income, i.e., the theaters. Furthermore, the earning power of a given chain of theaters depends not so much upon the quality of films made by its parent company as on the quality of films in general. If successful films are available, the dominant group of affiliated theaters in a given area generally has preferential access to them, regardless of which major produced them. In other words, the successful theater operations of each of the majors depend largely on the return from the theaters. But successful theater operation for a major company is not directly dependent on the quality of its own pictures, although this contributes, of course. By virtue of the regional division of the theater market, there is in effect a pooling of the product; the affiliated theaters in their separate areas have access to the best pictures available. Consequently, competition in the production of pictures has no real parallel in the theater organization. A good picture, i.e., one successful at the box office, redounds to the benefit of each of the theater-owning majors since each shares in the box office. This interdependence seems a unique characteristic of the motion picture business. In other industries, an exceptionally good product is feared and disliked by other producers or sellers of similar goods. But of the small group of dominant movie companies, it is really true that the good of one is the good of all.

The production and exhibition phases of the business behave toward each other like a chronically quarrelsome but firmly married couple and not without reason. The exhibitor group controls the purse strings;

it accounts for more than nine-tenths of the invested capital and approximately two-thirds of the industry's income. Nevertheless, it requires films. Consequently, the conflict between the two groups more nearly resembles a family quarrel than is ordinarily true of trade disputes, since the essential interdependence between production and exhibition is recognized by all. To a theater operator there is no substitute for "celluloid." Conversely, the producers of movies have no real alternative to the theaters as outlets for their product. The normal interdependency between supplier and customer is accentuated in the motion picture industry by the combination of functions within the same corporate framework. But difficulty results from the fact that while the selling of entertainment is a commercial process, making films is largely creative and artistic in nature. Moviemakers, like artists in other fields, are generally inclined to experiment with new techniques and are not above wanting to interpret or affect their surroundings. Exhibitors, on the other hand, may not know much about the art of the film, but they know what has been good box office before. Consequently, theirs is the conservative influence; they are the traditionalists of the trade, exerting their influence in the direction of the safe-and-sound in film making.

Structure of the Industry

As a result of the dominance of the integrated companies, the structure of the motion picture industry cannot be described along simple functional lines of production, distribution, and exhibition. Each of the major companies is a replica of the industry in all its activities. In addition to the five majors, there are approximately six or seven producing-distributing concerns (principally Universal, Columbia, United Artists, Monogram, Republic, and Producers' Releasing Corporation) and a large number of exhibition companies. These, in turn, are divisible into two groups; the individually operated theaters and the chains of four or more theaters.

The Majors

The best single source of information about the major motion picture companies is the Securities and Exchange Commission, with which registration statements and annual reports are filed. These provide considerably more factual data than have ever before been available to outsiders, making it possible to delineate the structure of the companies and their relationship to each other with respect to size, volume of business, their financial policies, profitability, executive remuneration.

Examination of the list of subsidiaries reported by any one of the five large companies indicates that the production of films is merely one of many activities and not necessarily the most important. Warner Bros. Pictures, Inc., for example, lists 108 subsidiaries. They include the following: a film laboratory, Brunswick Radio Corporation, and a radio manufacturing subsidiary, a lithographing concern, a concern that makes theater accessories, ten music-publishing houses, real estate companies, booking agencies, several broadcasting corporations, a company called Warner Bros. Cellulose Products, Inc., theater management companies, recording studios, and a television company—all this in addition to a film-producing unit and numerous theater subsidiaries, controlling approximately 507 theaters.

Loew's, Inc., consists of approximately seventy-three subsidiaries controlled more than 50 percent, plus twenty additional corporations in which effective control was disclaimed. The subsidiaries are primarily theater concerns, but include distribution companies, vaudeville-booking agencies, music-publishing houses, and several realty concerns. In fact, three of Loew's most important subsidiaries are registered with the SEC as real estate corporations. Control without majority ownership of the stock in many of the theater subsidiaries operates either through written agreements or through acquiescence of the remaining stockholders. In practice, this generally means that the owners of the theater have agreed to share control with Loew's in exchange for a franchise to exhibit Loew's pictures.

Paramount Pictures, Inc., is the most complex of the five, although its activities are apparently less ramified than Warner's. Whereas it originally bought out entire circuits of theaters, financing most of the purchases with bonds, reorganization in 1935 brought with it many changes in policy and structure. Today, most of its theater enterprises are partnerships; Paramount participates but does not exercise complete control. This is borne out by the fact that only 95 of its 203 subsidiaries are controlled 50 percent or more. Decentralized theater operations have been the approved policy at Paramount since the failure in 1933 of an attempt to manage in detail some 1,600 theaters from New York. It is estimated that at least half of Paramount's theaters are now run by their original owners on a part-ownership and contract basis, and that Paramount's average interest in its theaters is somewhat less than 70 percent.

The smaller producing companies are less complicated in structure and less far-flung in their activities. However, even concerns like Columbia Pictures and Universal Pictures operate twenty-eight and thirty-four subsidiaries, respectively. Most of these are distribution units. Universal Pictures Corporation is itself a subsidiary of Universal Corporation, a holding company which controls almost all its common stock. Both Universal Corporation and Columbia Pictures Corporation are managed by voting trusts.

The diversity of functions demonstrated by the large movie companies is reflected in the executive personnel, that is, the directors and officers of the companies. If the production of movies is but one aspect of the corporate existence, it follows that representation will be given to the other activities in some proportion to their importance. Take Paramount, for instance. Its board of directors includes the following: Harvey D. Gibson, banker, affiliated with the New York Trust Company, Manufacturers' Trust Company, the Textile Banking Company, etc.; A. Conger Goodyear, manufacturer and financier; John D. Hertz, partner in Lehman Brothers, founder of the Yellow Cab Company; Maurice Newton, partner in Hallgarten and Company, investment banker with diverse interests in tobacco, rubber, petroleum, and real estate. The president of Paramount is Barney Balaban, a Chicago theater man; vice-president is Frank Freeman, also originally a theater operator. Chairman of the executive committee is Stanton Griffis, broker and partner in Hemphill, Noyes. Mr. Adolph Zukor, the company's founder, occupies the somewhat honorific post of chairman of the board of directors.

The structure of the major companies is important because there is a real and direct connection between the way in which they are set up, the kind of people who run them, and the kind of films produced. This is the reason for emphasis on the fact that the capital assets of the dominant companies are so largely land, buildings, and real estate. Where the investment takes this form, it is not surprising that the executive personnel should consist of men skilled primarily in the art of selecting theater sites, managing real estate, and financing operations, rather than of talented producers.

The balance sheets of the five theater-owning majors show that from half to three-quarters of their total assets are "land, buildings, and equipment." On the other hand, for the two producing-distributing companies (Universal and Columbia), this proportion is under 15 percent.

In itself, the fact that the majors' assets are chiefly theaters, i.e., real estate, might have little significance. However, most of the theaters were acquired with the aid of bonds and other forms of long-term debt. The policy of debt financing has been of great importance in the history of the industry. More than 30 percent of the total invested capital in the seven major motion picture companies is borrowed. The case of several individual companies is even more extreme. Nearly half of the total capital of Warner and Paramount, for example, is borrowed. Thus, it is no accident that the principal corporate officers of four out of the five big majors are bondholders or their representatives. Debt financing has had many important ramifications affecting the stockholders, dividend policies, and internal corporate practices. Most important, however, to the moviegoer, is this fact: The production of films, essentially fluid and experimental as a process, is harnessed to a form of organization which can rarely afford to be either experimental or speculative because of the regularity with which heavy fixed charges must be met.

Originally, the motive behind the acquisition of theaters by producing companies may have been the need for the security represented by assured first-run exhibition for their films. Today, however, the majors derive most of their income from their theaters, and production is less important as a source of revenue than exhibition. In fact, the chief advantage of continued control over production and distribution is that it enables them to maintain their advantageous position as favored theater operators. Thus, the production of films by the major companies is not really an end in itself, on the success or failure of which the company's existence depends; it is an instrument directed toward the accomplishment of a larger end, i.e., domination of the theater market. This does not mean that there is no attempt to make successful films or that film production is itself unprofitable (although three of the five largest major companies have regularly incurred losses in production); it means simply that the principal concern of the men who run the major companies is their theaters.

The relative importance of production as a source of income to the majors is shown in Table 1. The analysis is incomplete because the amounts obtained in film rentals from foreign markets are not included. However, even adding the 35 percent generally imputed to the foreign market by industry spokesmen does not substantially alter the argument.

These same figures are of interest for what they reveal of the relative strength of each of the large majors in the realm of production, insofar, at least, as film rentals reflect the demand for a given company's product. Taken in conjunction with the film rentals of the non-theater-owning majors, the distribution of business among the various producing units is as shown in Table 2.

It is quite apparent that there is no direct correlation between the

TABLE 1
Income from Domestic Film Rentals as Percent of Total Volume of Business
Five Major Motion Picture Companies, 1939

Company	Domestic Film Rentals	Volume of Business	Film Rentals as Percent of Volume of Business
Loew's	$ 43,227,000	$112,489,000	38.4
20th Century-Fox[a]	33,150,000	53,752,000	61.0
Warner Bros.	28,917,000	102,083,000	28.3
Paramount	28,227,000	96,183,000	29.3
RKO	18,190,000	51,451,000	35.3
	$151,711,000	$415,958,000	36.4

[a]The case of Twentieth Century-Fox differs somewhat from that of the other majors. During a complicated reorganization in 1933, control of the Fox theaters changed hands, ending up eventually in General Theatres Equipment Corporation. This company, in turn, was controlled by Chase National Bank. Fox, newly merged with Twentieth Century in 1935, possessed a 42 percent stock interest in General Theatres Equipment Corporation. The company's income from theaters takes the form of dividends on the stock interest and is therefore not comparable to the amounts listed as income from theaters for the other majors.

TABLE 2
Gross Film Rentals from Distribution within the United States
of Ten Motion Picture Companies, 1939

Loew's	$ 43,227,000	21.5%
20th Century-Fox	33,150,000	16.5
Warner Bros.	28,917,000	14.4
Paramount	28,227,000	14.0
RKO	18,190,000	9.1
Universal	14,161,000	7.0
United Artists	13,478,000	6.7
Columbia	13,194,000	6.5
Republic	6,160,000	3.1
Monogram	2,532,000	1.2
Total	$201,236,000	100.0%

numbers of theaters owned by a given major and its income from film rentals.[3] Paramount, for example, has more theaters than any of the other majors, but its income from film rentals is substantially lower than that of three other companies with fewer theaters. The difficulty of interpretation here is increased by the fact that individual companies may have varying policies with respect to film rentals charged their

3. Theater holdings of the major companies are approximately as follows:

Paramount	1,239
20th Century-Fox	517
Warner Bros.	507
RKO	222
Loew's	139
	2,624

affiliated theaters. For instance, in one company it may be desirable for the controlling group to show greater profitability in theater operations than in production; accordingly, low film rentals may be charged up against the theater department. However, there is no way of allowing for factors of this kind. We can only take the figures at their face value, keeping in mind complications arising from metaphysical accounting practices.

If there is no direct correlation between theater ownership and income from film rentals, what is the chief value of the integrated form of organization? If a company owning relatively few theaters can earn more from its films than one with many theaters, why does it bother with theater operation at all?

From the producers' standpoint, theater ownership is valuable for two reasons. Theaters function as a kind of insurance policy, in that (1) they provide first-run exhibition, and (2) they offer a minimum market for films which might otherwise not be well received. This market is difficult to evaluate, but it is unlikely that the affiliated theaters of a given company account for more than 25 percent of its total film rentals. Paramount, for example, the largest theater owner, is said to receive approximately 25 percent of its film rentals from its own theaters. It is reasonable to assume that the other majors, with substantially smaller theater holdings, receive an even smaller proportion of their total film rentals from their theaters. Loew's received approximately 10 percent of its total film rentals from its affiliated theaters. None of the major companies receives a dominant share of its film rentals from its own theaters. They could not, in other words, guarantee great success for films which would otherwise find no market, but they do act as a partial buffer against complete failure.

To summarize: The major motion picture companies engage in a variety of activities. The production of films is one such activity, but not the most important one with respect to the amount of corporate income for which it is directly responsible. This is reflected in the fact that executive personnel of the large majors is chiefly financial and composed of real estate men rather than experts in the realm of production. Control of the producing companies passed into the hands of the present financial group when they became primarily theater concerns, with the consequent emphasis on problems of financing theater expansion and real estate operation. Today, approximately two-thirds of the total capital of the majors is invested in theaters. Furthermore, most of their income is derived from theaters. There is, however, no apparent connection between the number of theaters controlled and the profitability of the company's producing activities. The highest-grossing films are produced by the major with the fewest theaters, i.e., Loew's. From the point of view of the producing groups within the majors, the chief advantage of having affiliated theaters is the assurance of a minimum market. From the point of view of the theater departments within the majors, however, the advantage of having production facilities is incalculably great. It gives superiority over competing unaffiliated theaters, whose choice of product is always secondary to that of the dominant major in any given area. Thus the chief advantages of integration are in the domain of exhibition.

What Kind of Theaters Do the Majors Own

The value of theater ownership is not a function of number only but of location, size, and quality as well.

Average seating capacity of all theaters in the United States is 623. The deluxe metropolitan houses, most of which are affiliated with the major producing companies, have an average seating capacity of 1,445; the theaters owned by independent circuits average 897 seats, as compared with an average of 515 for the independently owned theaters. For the theater group as a whole, ownership of seating capacity is reported to be as follows: Of a total of approximately 11 million seats, affiliated theaters have 22 percent; unaffiliated circuits, 27 percent; independently operated theaters (fewer than four theaters operated by the same individual or group of individuals), 51 percent.

The situation in a specific area is described in figures recently published by the New York Film Board of Trade. The total number of theaters in the greater New York area in 1940 was 1,208. Of this number, 197 or 16.3 percent were affiliated with the major producers. Their theaters contained 28.4 percent of the total number of seats in the area, averaging nearly 2,000 seats per theater, as compared with an average seating capacity of 1,093 for independent chain theaters and 777 for individually owned theaters. It is relevant to note that the affiliated theaters provide the major producers with nearly 70 percent of their entire film rentals from the New York area. Since film rentals usually represent a percentage of the box office gross, it is reasonable to conclude that the affiliated theaters probably received a proportionate share of the total theater receipts for the area.

A further point to be made in this connection concerns the location of the theaters owned by the major producing companies. Seating capacity is highly concentrated in the large metropolitan centers; 2.5 million seats out of the total of approximately 11 million were in thirteen cities with population of over 500,000 each.

These thirteen large cities have 2,251 theaters located therein and, while housing almost one-fourth of the total seating capacity in the entire country, represent only 14 percent of the number of theaters. In other words, a very large number of the theaters in the United States are small theaters in small towns.[4]

As a result of this concentration of large theaters in the metropolitan centers, 60 percent of the total film rentals of the major producing companies was derived from the exchange areas containing the thirteen cities with population over 500,000.

The most important aspect of theater ownership, however, arises out of the differentiated nature of the theater structure. Just as various products may be distinguished from each other on the basis of price or quality, so, in the case of theaters, can the distinction be made almost entirely in terms of the "run" that each has. "Run" refers to priority rights in the showing of films for the particular community in which the theater is located. The first, second, and third runs account for all but a small proportion of total theater receipts. First-run theaters receive a share of the business altogether disproportionate to their number as well as to their size, although this latter disparity is less marked.

Most first-run houses are owned by the five major companies. They own or control the operations of 126 out of 163 first-run theaters in the twenty-five largest cities of the country. Only 37 first-run theaters in the entire country are independently owned and operated. The number of first-run theaters each controls, through either ownership, management contract, or pooling arrangement with a competing distributor, is distributed as follows:

Company	Number of Controlled First-run Theaters
Paramount	29
Warner Bros.	28
20th Century-Fox	26
Loew's	24
RKO	19
Nonaffiliated	37
Total	163

To summarize: The theaters owned by the major companies are

4. Motion Picture Producers and Distributors of America (the Hays Office), Annual Report of Theater Service Department, February 1939.

among the largest in the industry, located for the most part in the metropolitan centers, and include 77 percent of the important first-run houses.

Why Are the First-Run Theaters Important?

First-run theaters are important because: (1) they receive the bulk of the business; (2) producers receive a substantial proportion of their total film rentals from first-run showings; (3) control of these important theaters is, in effect, control over access to the screen; (4) last, and probably least important, they provide a testing ground for the pictures by means of which the prices to be charged for individual films may be determined.

The precise importance of the first-run theaters varies from city to city. In general, the larger the city, the less the relative importance of the first-run, and the more important the neighborhood houses. In New York and Philadelphia, for example, the first-run theaters provide between 20 and 30 percent of the total film rentals, whereas in Atlanta and Kansas City they provide well over 50 percent of the total. The importance of the first-run houses appears to depend on the nature of the theater control situation in each particular city. In Philadelphia, for example, where the first-run theaters account for less than 30 percent of the film rentals, Warner Bros., the dominant company in that area, owns not only first-run houses but also many subsequent-run houses. It has 8 large theaters in Philadelphia and 183 others in Pennsylvania. None of the other majors has a first-run outlet in Philadelphia.

In this situation the relevant question is not how much of the gross comes from the first-run theaters, but how much comes from the affiliated theaters. Philadelphia is almost entirely Warner territory by virtue of the absorption in 1929 of the Stanley Company, one of the most powerful theater circuits in the country. Over 75 percent of all film rentals from the Philadelphia area is derived from affiliated theaters, which means, in this case, Warner theaters. In Atlanta, on the other hand, over 80 percent of the total film rentals comes from first-run theaters, of which there are five. Paramount owns four; Loew's, one.

The extent to which the majors absorbed other than first-run theaters in any given area apparently depended upon the nature of local moviegoing habits. Moviegoers in large decentralized cities tend increasingly to patronize neighborhood theaters, with a consequent reduction in the relative importance of the first-run movie palace. In such situations, the majors extended their theater ownership to include the subsequent-run houses, the source of most of the patronage. In Atlanta, and most of the smaller cities, however, patronage is concentrated in the deluxe theaters. Unaffiliated theaters are permitted to retain that portion of the total volume of business which remains for the subsequent runs. Nearly three-quarters of the total film rentals paid by Atlanta theaters are derived from affiliated houses.

In New York City, on the other hand, first-run theaters produce not more than 20 percent of the total. Of the total subsequent runs, affiliated theaters produce in the neighborhood of 80 percent. For the city as a whole, affiliated theaters of all runs produce nearly 70 percent of all film rentals. Thirteen percent of the total film rentals paid in the United States are from New York City.

To summarize: It is very likely that in all but the largest cities of the country the first-run theaters provide well over 50 percent of the total revenue, in some areas as much as 80 percent. Where this is the case, the theater holdings of the majors are confined to first-run theaters. In that type of theater situation in which movie attendance is dispersed through neighborhoods, the theater interests of the majors are more extensive, including strategically located subsequent-run houses. In any event, the net effect of theater ownership by the major producing companies (with respect to income from the production of films) is that they are their own best customers. They provide themselves and each other with the bulk of the market for films.

By no means less important than the revenue offered by the first-run theaters is the power which accompanies their ownership. This power rests upon the peculiarities of the market for films and is tantamount to authority to decide what films may reach the public. Originally the first-run theater developed out of the willingness and ability of enterprising theater owners to pay higher rentals for the first showings of better quality films. It then had the effect of stimulating competition among producers for access to this important segment of the market. Today, owned by the major producing companies, first-run screen time is occupied almost entirely by their own pictures. As a market for independent producers (i.e., those other than the eight major companies) first-run theaters are virtually closed.

How was it possible for this power to be concentrated in such a small number of theaters? The answer to this question is partly in the realm of applied psychology. It involves the deeper question of why people go to the movies at all and why they go when they do. Inescapable is the fact that at least one factor in influencing moviegoing is the advance buildup given a picture, the barrage of publicity and exploitation which accompanies the release of a new film, the reviews by critics who see the film as it opens its run, and all the other multifarious activities of publicity agents. Great importance is attached to these activities by the people within the industry. Consequently, when an inexpensive picture achieves public acclaim without the preliminary fanfare usually reserved for the more costly pictures, it is called a "sleeper," a term which indicates that even the producer of the picture was taken by surprise.

A measure of the industry's faith in advertising is the estimated $110 million annually spent on it. Consequently, exhibitors the country over receive requests from their patrons: When is the next Super-Colossal going to show? When is Clark Gable's new picture coming here? They have heard; they know that the leading man in such-and-such a picture is actually in love with the star; they read fan magazines and columnists; they listen to radio programs devoted exclusively to Hollywood gossip—in a word, they care. Who are the exhibitors to ignore such a wealth of feeling? At first, the importance of first-run theaters was related to the public's appreciation of the material superiority of the theater, its greater comfort and beauty. This in turn gave greater earning power, permitting payment of higher rentals for the better films. The process whereby their influence was extended over moviegoers outside their immediate jurisdiction has been described as follows:

The new Palace theatres became liberal advertisers in newspapers and publishers responded by giving their shows publicity in news columns and reviews. The newspapers in thirty to fifty metropolitan centers throughout the country— key cities—circulate in all neighboring cities and towns, and the advertising and publicity of a first run in a key city create a demand for the picture in the surrounding district. Theatres in Long Island or New Jersey, for example, learned that a photoplay first shown at the Strand or the Rialto, in New York, would draw large audiences, while a film with no first run in the metropolis would attract little attention. Soon exhibitors everywhere in the United States followed the line of least resistance, giving preference to pictures with the prestige of key-city first runs, ignoring all others or renting them only at very low rates. Within a few years photoplays without first runs were not regarded by theatre-goers as first class, and unless a producer could obtain first runs his chance of making money grew very slim.[5]

As long ago as 1917, representative feature films, if given first-run exhibition, grossed from sixty to one hundred thousand dollars; without adequate first-run exhibition, earnings would drop thirty to forty thousand dollars, amounts which usually failed to cover costs.

5. Benjamin B. Hampton, *A History of the Movies* (New York: Covici, Friede, 1931), pp. 172–73.

The line of least resistance adopted by the exhibitors—that is, their refusal to book pictures other than those which had received big-city openings—was somewhat shortsighted, as it later turned out. It had the effect of forcing independent producers out of the field, making much simpler the task of the forces working toward control through integration. Obviously, if most exhibitors book only those pictures which receive first-run showings, then control of the first-run theaters is, in effect, control over all the others. Once the independent producers were denied access to the screen, the process of encirclement was complete: The major producers were also the major exhibitors. It was for them to say whose pictures would be shown.

The final result is clear. The majors show their own films and each other's. If the film of an independent producer gives promise of box office success, they may take over its distribution, showing it in their own theaters and selling it to nonaffiliated theaters. For this service they charge the producer a price which usually amounts to 35 percent of the total gross. Such, for example, is the arrangement whereby RKO distributed the product of the Walt Disney Studios, the beloved Mickey Mouse and Donald Duck cartoons, as well as the more recent feature-length pictures. Such product is, for all practical purposes, part and parcel of the rest of the merchandise distributed by the major; from the point of view of the nonaffiliated theater owner, it is immaterial that the production was independent. His access to it is subject to exactly the same restrictions as surround all other films released by the major; it does not compete independently with the product of the majors.

The exhibition policy of the first-run theaters is analyzed in the petition of the federal government in its recent antitrust suit against the majors. Data collected by the Department of Justice show that, for the exhibition years 1934 through 1937, not less than 95 percent of all pictures shown in the first-run metropolitan houses of each of the majors consisted of the releases of the eight companies. Over 99 percent of the films exhibited in Loew's first-run theaters were released by the majors. "As a result," the petition reads, "the independent producer does not have access to a free, open, and untrammelled first-run market in metropolitan cities in which to dispose of his pictures. Entrance to this market by an independent producer is only at the sufferance of (the defendants herein) who control it."[6] The petition neglects to add an equally important fact, namely, that with the closing of this market to the independent producer, the remainder of the market, the subsequent run is, in effect, also closed.

6. *United States v. Paramount Pictures, Inc., et al.*, Petition, 1938, p. 71.

As a control device, the development of strategic first-run theaters as the showcases of the industry proved remarkably effective. Ownership of these relatively few theaters gave control over access to the market; this enabled other sources of supply to be shut out with a consequently enhanced value for the remaining product. Add to this the fact that ownership of these theaters carries with it the bulk of the theater receipts, and the rationale behind the structure of the motion picture industry becomes clear.

Relationship between the Big Five and the Little Three

It might be asked, why are the three smaller companies (Universal, Columbia, and United Artists) included in the category of the majors? (This usage is accepted by the industry at large and all government agencies dealing with it.) They own no theaters, they account for but fractional shares of the industry investment, they receive proportionately little of the total business. What makes them major companies? There seems to be but one reliable criterion here—they have access to the screens of the first-run theaters owned by the Big Five.

No one studio today turns out enough pictures to provide a year's supply of films for a double feature program. First-run theaters showing double features on a weekly change policy use from seventy to one hundred films a year. Subsequent-run theaters, most of which run films no longer than three days and play double features, may use three hundred feature films annually. Since, as has already been indicated, the theaters are the chief source of income for most of the integrated majors, their need for good box office films is sufficiently great to warrant opening their screens to the product of other producers on occasion. This also explains, in large measure, why Hollywood as a whole rejoices when a successful picture appears, regardless of which studio produced it. A good picture, as almost anyone in Hollywood can tell you, is one that makes good at the box office. The box office, in part at least, belongs to each of the five majors, although in varying degrees in different regions. For example, the Philadelphia theater situation is dominated by Warner. A picture made by Metro (Loew's producing company) when exhibited in the Philadelphia area appears in Warner theaters. Loew's has little choice in the matter; all the first-run theaters in Philadelphia belong to Warner Bros. It is therefore to the advantage of Warner for Loew's to release successful pictures since it means good business for Warner theaters. Loew's, it should be noted, benefits doubly from a successful picture: first, in the form of box office receipts of its own theaters, and, second, in the form of higher film rentals from other theaters.

No studio in Hollywood today produces more than sixty-five feature films a year. With the exception of United Artists, most of the companies release between forty-five and fifty-five features; hence, the need of the theater-owning majors for the product of other companies. The need is not merely for film, but for films of a special type—for the most part, inexpensive class-B pictures to make up the lesser half of the double-feature program. This use of fill-in pictures is quite apparent from the fact that so few of the films of the smaller companies are given first place on the program.

To summarize: The demand for films is greater than the output of any one major company. While giving preference to its own films in all instances, each of the theater-owning majors needs supplementary product from two or more of the other companies. If, by some miracle, double features were to cease, a substantial part of the market for the films of Universal and Columbia would disappear.

Role of the Majors in Production and Distribution

Although the total number of active motion-picture-producing corporations is variously cited as 246 (*Statistics of Income* 1937), 100 (*Standard Statistics*), and 83 (*Biennial Census of Manufacture* 1937), the importance of the eight majors with respect to volume of production is perhaps best indicated by the following analysis. Five of the majors make 100 percent of the newsreels produced; the eight majors released 396, or 85 percent of the total, of 452 feature films released in 1939. The 1939–40 *Motion Picture Almanac* lists, under the heading "Motion Picture Production Organizations," the names of seventy-three companies. Of this total, the number actively engaged in producing feature films (including the seventeen independent producers whose pictures are released by the majors) is very small, probably not more than thirty. A check of the names of the independents against a list of all features released in 1939 reveals that only ten of the independent companies named had produced any features whatsoever during this period.

Four of the smaller companies distributed the product of these ten, namely: Republic Pictures, Monogram Pictures, World Pictures, and Victory Pictures. Their combined releases amounted to fifty-six features, of which Republic released twenty-one, Monogram twenty, World Pictures twelve, and Victory Pictures three. These numbers, however, are misleading as a guide to the importance of their productions, since it is very unlikely that any substantial number of these pictures played in the larger city theaters. Almost all the pictures were inexpensive westerns, aimed at a market which holds little interest for the majors.

Virtually the entire market for feature films and newsreels is supplied by the releases of the major companies. The estimate made by officials of the Motion Picture Producers and Distributors of America that the majors account for 80 percent of the value of total film production probably errs in the direction of understatement, since with rare exceptions the amount of money spent by the independents on their productions is fractional compared with the majors.

The theater people, however, maintain firmly that no film which has box office merit has any difficulty in finding a first-run release, that the eagerness of theater owners for attractive films is so great that it would be impossible for any combination of producers to keep worthy independent product off the market; furthermore, that the theater-owning majors would probably be the first to book any potentially successful films produced independently since they would thereby profit from increased theater receipts. This suggests that there may be reasons, other than market restraints, which account for the predominant role of the majors' product. It also raises the question, what is worthy product?

Right or wrong, it is a fixed belief in Hollywood and throughout the motion picture industry that the quality of a film is generally commensurate with its cost. Theater operators following this line of reasoning tend to value the product of a given company in accordance with the amount spent (this, it might be noted, is an additional factor in any explanation of the premium on extravagance of which Hollywood is so proud). Without, at the moment, examining this assumption too closely, let us look at the figures on production budgets of the several companies.

Loew's spends $28 million annually on its program of feature films; Twentieth Century-Fox, Paramount, and Warner spend approximately $23 to $25 million. RKO allows $20 million for its feature films. Universal and Columbia, on the other hand, spend $11.6 million and $8.8 million, respectively. As it happens, the order in which the companies are named is exactly the order in which they rank in terms of the amounts they receive in film rentals (see Table 2).

The breakdown for Loew's shows that approximately $28 million was spent on forty-one feature pictures. Six of these, or 14.5 percent, cost more than a million dollars each; over half of the total number of films cost more than $500,000 each. None cost as little as $100,000. The average cost per picture was $683,000.

As proof of the importance attached to the cost of films by the industry, witness the advertising of Loew's in the trade press. For example, the release of *Ziegfeld Girl* was announced in a double-page spread as follows:

Take Your Seats, America!

You've got a date with the girls from the Follies! M.G.M. has kept its promise to top "The Great Ziegfeld"!

It took money to do it! It took months of planning, months of dreaming dreams! With No Expense Spared! M.G.M. proudly presents "The Ziegfeld Girl." It is a Pageant of Stars and Song and Spectacle! Ten marquees could not hold its names in lights! James Stewart. Judy Garland. Hedy Lamarr. Lana Turner. And countless other great entertainers and Girls! Girls! Girls! Darlings in diamonds, honey-haired blondes, red-heads, brunettes. M.G.M. combed America for its most famous beauties. Celebrated models, famed faces from the magazine covers. Never such a wealth of feminine loveliness! Spectacular musical numbers one after another! "Minnie from Trinidad," "You Stepped Out of a Dream," and others. More than you'd find in a whole season of Broadway musicals!

Lights! Curtain! Bravo!

Lest it be thought that this advertisement is unrepresentative, here is Republic's announcement to the trade of one of its extraordinary attractions. This is also a double-page spread in several colors. In large letters, the banner is: "Gene Autry's First $500,000 All-Star Production, *Melody Ranch*, 'Exhibitors Everywhere Can Play *This* One with Confidence.'"

It should not be inferred from this that lavish spending is a surefire formula for successful film production. If success is measured in terms of the return-per-dollar-invested, the quickies turned out by Universal and Columbia are frequently ten times more profitable than the all-star spectacles of Metro or Fox. In fact, a tabulation of the earnings of a season's output by one of the more extravagant producers reveals that of a total of forty-nine films, fourteen did not return their negative cost. Of the fourteen, eight had cost more than $1 million each.

Thus it appears that the answer to the question, what makes a major producer, runs as follows: The major producers are those whose product has access to the first-run theaters of the country. This access in turn depends partly on the amount of money spent on a production. Only in part, however, since the money is important merely for what it will buy in the way of talent and production values. Thus, having, let us say, $500,000 available for investment in a picture is no guarantee of a first-run release for the finished picture unless talent of recognized standing in the trade can be obtained. For instance, John Hay Whitney is a recurrent investor in film productions. He does not undertake to make films himself; he enters into an arrangement with a producer of great prestige in the Hollywood community, David O. Selznick, whereby he advances the funds for the production of *Gone with the Wind*. His financing, Selznick's production, and a cast of widely publicized talent suffices to secure a release through Loew's, on terms profitable to all concerned. The point is that the money is not more important in this situation than the fact that a producer of Selznick's status is undertaking to make the picture. Almost any of the established actors, directors, etc., are willing and eager to appear in a Selznick production. Money alone might not suffice to obtain big-name actors for a picture unless the persons in charge of the production also had the confidence of the talent groups.

The obstacles in the way of securing talent for independently produced pictures are twofold in nature: first, and most obvious, are the contractual commitments of the established players. These contracts do not bind the artists entirely; they generally provide that the company holding the contract has the power to determine the productions in which the person may work. This serves several purposes. In the first place, if the artist is already famous and important, the employing studio regards him or her as a "property," the value of which might easily be impaired by injudicious appearances in unsuccessful movies, or in roles which contradict a carefully nurtured public sentiment about the actor. This factor is quite important in shaping the decisions on lending of players. In the second place, salaries of valuable personnel as fixed by contract are so high, in many instances, that their cost places them beyond the reach of most independent producers.

The contract system provides an additional means of controlling talent. For example, when it is considered desirable to punish an actor, he may simply be lent to an independent producer for a picture generally regarded as certain not to succeed. This is the Hollywood equivalent of Siberia, and undoubtedly an effective means of discipline.

An additional important obstacle in the way of securing established talent for the independently produced pictures is the artists' fear of jeopardizing their status. The fear may center on the questionable success of the picture. If no major release is obtained for the picture, it is destined for the low-grade markets represented chiefly by the cheaper theaters specializing in horse operas and lurid sex dramas. Appearance in such pictures is almost certain to decrease the actor's bargaining power with the major producers. Stars firmly established or with promising careers seldom venture into independent productions. For the most part, actors in this class of product are either still unknown or passé.

Such are a few of the factors affecting the availability of talent to the independent makers of films. The recital may not be complete; certainly the majors deny any monopolistic hold on the market for artists. The facts, however, are indisputable, regardless of the interpretation as to cause. During the years between 1933 and 1939 the seven major producers loaned to each other a total of 2,005 actors, directors, writers, and cameramen. To independents, a total of 180 loans was made. Whatever reluctance the companies may have to lending their personnel to independents is, of course, reinforced by the unwillingness of the artists themselves to work at lower rates of pay than their contracts provide. In fact, it is customary, when a major lends another company one of its stars, for the price paid to exceed the regular contract rate by as much as 75 percent. In other words, the borrowing company pays not only the salary of the star during the period of the loan, but also a pure rent to the lending company. This extra charge is justified as a means of compensating the home studio for the idle time of contract players, i.e., the time during which they are paid by the home studio but not used.

It should, perhaps, be repeated here that none of the obstacles described has any reality for those so-called "independent" producers whose pictures are released through the majors. For example, Selznick

David O. Selznick's *Gone With the Wind,* directed by Victor Fleming: Vivien Leigh, Clark Gable, and Olivia DeHavilland (MGM, 1939)

was able to borrow Clark Gable from Metro for *Gone with the Wind*. A major release is, in itself, sufficient to obtain working capital, production facilities, and personnel. One of the first bankers to take an interest in film production said long ago that he would lend the entire cost of production to a producer who has "a good distributing contract in a good distributing organization."

That the situation had not changed appreciably is evident in the following news item:

Bankers financing film production report a sudden increase in applications for loans from off-the-lot producers [independent producers]. . . . Pressure for loans is stronger than it has been in many years. Financial men say, however, that it is easier to grant a $50,000 loan than $15,000. Virtually all applications for small budget films are being turned down as unjustified by prospective returns. Big loans are more readily granted because pictures in that category are usually intended for a major release which must be set before the banks advance the usual 50 percent of the cost.[7]

This, as the moviegoer often has occasion to say, is where we came in. The circle is complete. The independent producer is, by definition, one whose pictures are not distributed by the majors. Without such distribution and access to the first-run theaters, his market is extremely limited. This, in turn, makes both talent and capital shy of appearing in independent productions. Hence, independently made films are rarely considered fit for exhibition in metropolitan theaters where audiences have, by now, developed a modicum of sophistication.

Because the product of the independents is not considered fit for extensive exhibition, the principal market for films belongs to the major companies. If the reasoning seems circuitous, the facts are even more so.

7. *Variety*, September 10, 1941.

Portrait of a Vertically Integrated Company

FORTUNE

Metro-Goldwyn-Mayer

Metro-Goldwyn-Mayer, largest of 124 subsidiaries owned by Loew's, Inc., is a corporation devoted exclusively to the business and the art of producing moving pictures. Its plant—fifty-three acres, valued at a trifling $2,000,000—is in Culver City, California, on the dusty outskirts of Los Angeles, opposite three gasoline stations and a drugstore. In operation, the plant presents the appearance less of a factory than of a demented university with a campus made out of beaverboard and canvas. It contains twenty-two sound stages, a park that can be photographed as anything from a football field to the gardens at Versailles, $2,000,000 worth of antique furniture, a greenhouse consecrated to the raising of ferns, twenty-two projection rooms, a commissary where $6,000-a-week actors can lunch on Long Island oysters for fifty cents, and a Polish immigrant who sometimes makes $500,000 a year and once spent the weekend with the Hoovers at the White House. On MGM's Culver City lot there is room for the practice of 117 professions, but the colored shoeshine boy outside the commissary considers himself an actor because he frequently earns a day's pay in an African mob scene. When he is neither acting nor powdering the brown suede riding boots of an Oklahoma cowboy who has just learned how to play polo, the shoeshine boy is likely to be the chauffeur of one of MGM's sixteen company limousines.

MGM's weekly payroll is roughly $250,000. On it are such celebrities as Marion Davies ($6,000), Norma Shearer, the three Barrymores, who

From vol. 6 (December 1932), pp. 51–58+.

get about $2,500 a week each, Clark Gable, Jean Harlow, Joan Crawford, Buster Keaton, Robert Montgomery, Marie Dressler (whose pictures take in more than any of the others'), Helen Hayes, Jimmy Durante, Conrad Nagel, Ramon Novarro, Wallace Beery, small Jackie Cooper, who makes $1,000 a week, John Gilbert and, until very recently, Greta Garbo. Miss Garbo is likely soon to return from Sweden where she recently retired after amassing a fortune of $1,000,000. If she does return, she will doubtless have a chance to make another million. Actors' salaries are only a small part of MGM's outlay. The biggest and most expensive writing staff in Hollywood costs $40,000 a week. Directors cost $25,000. Executives cost slightly less. Budget for equipment is $100,000 a week. MGM makes about forty pictures in a year, every one a feature picture or a special feature. Average cost of Metro-Goldwyn-Mayer pictures runs slightly under $500,000. This is at least $150,000 more per picture than other companies spend. Thus Metro-Goldwyn-Mayer provides $20,000,000 worth of entertainment a year at cost of production, to see which something like a billion people of all races will pay something more than $100,000,000 at the box office. *Motion Picture Almanac*, studying gross receipts, guesses at a yearly world total movie audience of nine billion.

For the past five years, Metro-Goldwyn-Mayer has made the best and most successful moving pictures in the United States. No one in Hollywood would dream of contradicting this flat statement. In *Film Daily's* annual critical consensus of the ten best, MGM scored fourteen times in the past five years (last year *A Free Soul, Min and Bill, The Sin of Madelon Claudet*) as against ten for United Artists and eight for Paramount. In *Motion Picture Almanac's* ranking of the fifteen box office leaders of 1931, MGM led with five (*Trader Horn, Susan Lenox, Politics, Strangers May Kiss, Reducing*). MGM bids fair to show the same statistical success in 1932. Very few people know why this is true. It may be luck. It may be the list of MGM stars, vastly the most imposing in what moving picture people describe, significantly, as "the industry." It may be MGM's sixty-two writers and eighteen directors. It may be MGM's technicians, who are more numerous and more highly paid than those of MGM's competitors. It may be Irving Thalberg—Norma Shearer's husband. If no one in Hollywood knows the reason for MGM's producing success, everyone in Hollywood believes the last. Irving Thalberg, a small and fragile young man with a suggestion of anemia, is MGM's vice-president in charge of production. The kinds of pictures MGM makes and the ways it makes them are Irving Thalberg's problems. He is what Hollywood means by MGM.

Mr. Thalberg's earnings of $500,000 a year have come mostly from a unique bonus arrangement explained later. His actual salary is now only $110,000. But despite recent cuts MGM's costs begin with a battery of "executives" who get as much as railroad presidents. As for "artists," it was at MGM that Pelham Grenville Wodehouse was employed for a period of a year in which he later admitted, with the intention of being politely grateful, he had been paid $2,000 a week for doing nothing. It was not, however, Mr. Thalberg who hired Maurice Maeterlinck to stay at a Pasadena castle and write a scenario—which MGM will never use—of which the hero was a bumblebee. It is frequently asserted that as many as ten of MGM's staff of writers may be set to work simultaneously, in groups of two or three, on the same story. There are said to be unproduced stories in MGM's files which cost $1,000,000. Because Mr. Thalberg thinks a superspecial about Soviet Russia would be popular, $200,000 has been given to scenarists who have nonetheless been unable to fabricate one. A picture called *The Bugle Sounds* and another one appropriately entitled *The March of Time* have cost $250,000 or more apiece and have been postponed.

Mr. Thalberg's methods, however, would be infinitely more comical if they were a little less efficacious. It was Mr. Thalberg who decided, to the great advantage of his company, that MGM pictures should have not one star but two, like *Red Dust* or *Faithless*, or a whole galaxy, like *Grand Hotel* or *Rasputin*. It was Mr. Thalberg who caused retakes—the immensely expensive process of remaking pictures when they have theoretically been completed—to be an integral part of MGM procedure, instead of a last resort for correcting particularly appalling blunders. The $20,000,000 of MGM's money that slips through Mr. Thalberg's thin and nimble fingers usually returns to them, but Mr. Thalberg really has better things to think about than the familiar legerdemain of profit and loss. His brain is the camera which photographs dozens of scripts in a week and decides which of them, if any, shall be turned over to MGM's twenty-seven departments to be made into a moving picture. It is also the recording apparatus which converts the squealing friction of 2,200 erratic underlings into the more than normally coherent chatter of an MGM talkie.

Most of MGM's executive offices are in a white wooden building near the shabby colonial façade that faces the three gasoline stations. Mr. Thalberg's beaverboard sanctum is on the second floor, flanked by a fire escape that leads onto a viaduct to his private projection room (with three desks, two pianos, and twenty-seven velvet armchairs). It is usually not much before ten o'clock when Mr. Thalberg's black Cadillac squeezes through the iron grille gates of the studio and stops under the catwalk to his projection room. By this time there are people all over the lot who want words with him.

He enters—a small, finely-made Jew of about thirty-three, changeable as the chameleon industry in which he labors. He is five and one-half feet tall, and weighs 122 pounds after a good night's sleep. This lightness, in calm moments, is all feline grace and poise. In frantic moments he appears as a pale and flimsy bag of bones held together by concealed bits of string and the furious ambition to make the best movies in the world. He seats himself, in his modern, beaverboard office, at a massive, shiny desk, in front of a dictograph which looks like a small pipe organ and partially hides a row of medicine bottles. Before him are huge boxes of cigarettes, which he never opens, and plates of apples and dates into which he sometimes dips a transparent hand. Squirming with nervous fervor in the midst of his elaborate apparatus, he speaks with a curiously calm, soft voice as if his words were a sort of poetry. He describes parabolas with one hand and scratches his knee with the other. Rising, he paces his office with stooped shoulders and hands clasped behind him. This reflective promenading he learned from Carl Laemmle, Sr., who discovered Irving Thalberg when, recently released from a Brooklyn high school, he was an office boy in the Broadway shop of Universal Pictures.

There is naturally no chance that Mr. Thalberg's activities will fall into routine. His efforts follow no pattern whatsoever, except that they consist almost exclusively of talk. He deals with actors, whose simple wants of avarice or vanity he finds it easy to appease. He deals with writers, with whom he seldom commits the unpardonable blunder of saying: "I don't like it, but I don't know why." He is ceaselessly aware of Dolores Del Rio's gifted husband, Cedric Gibbons, who designs MGM scenery and of the tall, twittering hunchback Adrian, who drapes MGM's loveliest bodies. He deals with M. E. Greenwood, the gaunt studio manager, who used to be an Arizona faro dealer and now tells MGM's New York office how much the company has spent every week and how much to place on deposit for MGM's account at the Culver City branch of Bank of America. Through Mr. Greenwood, and sometimes more directly, Irving Thalberg observes the two thousand of the skilled but unsung: "grips," assistant camermen, "mixers," cutters, projectionists, carpenters, unit managers, artisans, seamstresses, scene painters. Often he calls a group of these underlings into the projection room to consider pictures with him.

Mr. Thalberg must know how to focus all this talent. Beginning with an Idea. Ideas are the seeds of motion picture production—the most valuable commodity in Hollywood—Ideas for whole films, Ideas for episodes, Ideas for a single scene. At RKO the brilliant, young new chief, David Selznick, spends his days and nights grasping at Ideas. Working for Paramount in New York, George Putnam (spouse of Amelia Earhart) is paid to do nothing except have Ideas. Men get huge salaries for generating and sifting Ideas. Mr. Thalberg gets the hugest. He had the Idea that the sleek Park Avenue romance *Tinfoil* needed a worldly sort of actress who wasn't to be found on MGM's payroll. Presto, came another Idea—he borrowed Tallulah Bankhead from Paramount. Tallulah Bankhead whose eyelids, according to the costumer Adrian, "are so heavy they look like the fat little stomachs of sunburned babies." It was RKO's Selznick's Idea that a great success could be achieved by putting all three Barrymores—Ethel, Lionel, John—in one picture. But Mr. Thalberg had no sooner heard of it than it clicked with him and he promptly snatched Ethel (who preferred MGM anyway) from Selznick's all but completed grasp—with a bid of $2,500 a week. And then he immediately set two scenario writers to achieve another Idea—a script which would allow the Barrymores to agitate their eyebrows and twitch their nostrils without at any time pretending a sexual interest in one another which might offend a priggish public. The result was *Rasputin.* To direct this Russian pageantry it was naturally Mr. Thalberg's Idea to appoint the crafty, understanding Slav, Richard Boleslavsky, late of the Moscow Art Theatre, author of *The Way of a Lancer.* Had the Barrymore script been an adventurous, outdoor affair, Mr. Thalberg would probably have selected W. S. Van Dyke, who directed *Tarzan* and *Trader Horn.* He has a versatile panel of directors to choose from: Howard Hawks, the realist who did *The Criminal Code;* Sidney Franklin, the cosmopolitan of *Private Lives* and *The Guardsman;* Sam Wood, specialist in light comedy, college, and football pictures; Edgar Selwyn, a masterly tearjerker; Clarence Brown, very tactful with veterans like Marie Dressler; Tod Browning, a connoisseur of the vicious, who directs best when the principal characters are deformed, as in *Freaks.*

Ideas permeate the studio structure and the Thalberg day. While Thalberg makes telephone calls, he authorizes Cedric Gibbons to spend $30,000 on a set for *Pig Boats* and orders his scenario chief, Sam Marx, to assign three new writers to the task of adapting *Reunion in Vienna.* In between conferences, in which he reveals himself as a person of opinions on underdone lovemaking or overdressed heroines, Mr. Thalberg gnaws a red apple and looks at rushes of *Tinfoil,* pronouncing half of them trash. With one eye on a copy of *Variety* he considers his casting director, Ben Thau, for the position left vacant by the suicide of gentle, masochistic Paul Bern, husband of Jean Harlow, and decides that *Tinfoil* had better be called *Faithless.*

The frantic morning terminates confusedly in Mr. Thalberg's regular lunch with his ten associate producers. These men are shock absorbers for Mr. Thalberg. It is obviously impossible for him to supervise all of MGM's forty pictures a year. Hence the associate producers. They advise and confer with writers during the preparation of scripts. When the script has been approved by Mr. Thalberg, they attempt to coordinate the efforts of writer, director, and cast. Without being able in most cases to act, write, or direct, they are supposed to know more about writing than either the director or the star, more about directing than the star or the writer. Matters of costs, sets, locations, cast, lighting, and the like are referred to them; all disputes, recriminations, and temperamental teapot tempests are for them to settle or assuage, unless they seem insoluble, in which case they are solved by Mr. Thalberg. MGM's associate producers are likely to work on two or three pictures simultaneously. They are the principal cogs through which Irving Thalberg causes MGM's wheels to spin. Each of these gentlemen gets $1,000 a week or more for communicating Mr. Thalberg's spirit. But as a class associate producers are extremely susceptible to nervous breakdowns which, it has been suggested, is due to the consciousness of enjoying great responsibility without sufficient authority and credit.

While the rest of the studio personnel is munching in the noisy commissary, the associate producers sit down to luncheon with Mr. Thalberg in the "Executive Bungalow," a squatty hut with a Cecil B. De Mille dining room. Hunt Stromberg, as "box office producer" par excellence, is the only one who, by contract, can work without Mr. Thalberg's approval. He handled Joan Crawford's celebrated trilogy *Modern Maidens, Blushing Brides,* and *Dancing Daughters.* Al Lewin is a college graduate and an ex-instructor of English at the University of Wisconsin. Thus set apart from his confrères, he gets such sophisticated jobs as *The Guardsman* and *Private Lives.* Bernie Hyman does animal stories and Bernie Fineman does genre pictures and curios like *Mata Hari;* Irish Eddie Mannix, who looks like a bulldog, is a master of action films such as *Hell Divers.* Marie Dressler, the most profitable star on the MGM roster, is intrusted during production to the supervisory discretion of Mr. Thalberg's brother-in-law, Larry Weingarten. The late Paul Bern used to oversee electric sex fables like *Susan Lenox, As You Desire Me, Grand Hotel,* and *Red Dust.* Harry Rapf, called "Mayer's sundial" because of his nose, played sad airs on the national heartstrings with *The Champ* and *The Sin of Madelon Claudet,* and is now having his nervous breakdown. All these associates—the somber, sagacious Jews, the lusty, impetuous Irishman—are professionally just so many extensions of Irving Thalberg's personality. He has much more to say to them than they to him. Only one important instance of impudence or rebuke to Mr. Thalberg has ever occurred at MGM. When he took to bouncing a twenty-dollar gold piece on his glass-top desk during conferences, his confrères cured this painful habit by hoarding similar coins for the same purpose. Chattering at lunch, Mr. Thalberg and his underlings resemble in their gloomy refectory the personnel of an agitated Last Supper, with Mr. Thalberg as a nervous Nazarene, free, however, from the presentiment that any of his disciples will deny or even contradict him.

His afternoon is as formless as his morning. To say that the manifestation of Mr. Thalberg's efforts at MGM consists of conversation is not so much a sidelight on the way movies are made as it is a comment on Irving Thalberg. He doesn't spend time making infinitesimal calculations because he is an artist, and an artist with a blank canvas to fill doesn't begin by marking off squares. He begins with instinct and checks his results with a meticulous sense of values. He is a stickler for results but he cannot be a stickler for plans. Even so with Irving Thalberg. Nowhere is his artistry more evident than in his expenditure of MGM money. "Look," he says, "a successful feature may take in ten million dollars at the box office. An unsuccessful one may take a million. If the difference is fifty or a hundred thousand dollars in production . . ." There is, so far as Mr. Thalberg is concerned, no more to be said. It is his artistic instinct which tells him when the extra fifty or one hundred thousand will broaden, like the beam of a projection machine, into an enormous profit. His extravagance has so far justified itself, and he by no means goes haywire with the exchequer. When J. B. Priestley thought *The Good Companions* was worth $50,000, Mr. Thalberg offered $25,000 and came away without the book.

When Mr. Thalberg leaves Culver City at dinner time he takes with him a large pigskin portmanteau, made to order for a peculiar purpose: carrying scripts. In Mr. Thalberg's house at Santa Monica, designed for him by art director Cedric Gibbons, there is a soundproof room. This is so that the sad growling of the Pacific, beside which he lives, shall not interrupt Mr. Thalberg's perusal of the contents of his portmanteau. Life *chez* Thalberg has the atmosphere of neither a saloon nor a dance pavilion. Mr. Thalberg drinks only occasionally, a rather silly release when it happens, and dances very little for one who foxtrots so expertly. The chatter of Mr. Thalberg's working day is replaced at night by an electric silence in which, pallid and intent, he performs the trick of dividing his brain into two parts. One part, reading a script, turns it into a moving picture; the other part watches this imaginary picture and, probably because it is so much like the conglomerate brain of fifty million other U.S. cinemaddicts, tells Mr. Thalberg with an astonishing degree of accuracy whether or not the picture is good. And when he doesn't wish to look at these imaginary pictures in his brain, he can look at real ones—in his own drawing room. Shifty and two-faced, like every other property in a beaverboard industry, this is a projection room in disguise, with a screen which pops up out of the floor. Mr. Thalberg's favorite diversion of nights, while the Pacific murmurs below, is to watch Metro-Goldwyn-Mayer talkies flicker above his hearthstone.

The cinema is both an industry and an art but it is also, more importantly, a new industry, a new art. The problems which confront a producer are somewhat like those which might confront a novelist if the secret of the alphabet had been discovered thirty years ago, except that his tools are more complex and more expensive. So far, very few people have grown up with the idea of expressing themselves, or anything else, in the cinema. They drift into what must remain, for them, "the industry" from journalism, the stage, drafting rooms, laboratories, or the camphorated closets of the wholesale fur business. They are animated thereafter by a defending scorn for an endeavor that has appealed, successfully, only to their avarice. There are a few people in Hollywood for whom the cinema carries a different invitation. For someone like Thalberg it is an avocation, a new language, a necessity. If he had ever had time to be profoundly interested in anything else, if he had been subjected to the complications of formal education or, even momentarily, failure, he would be infinitely less competent, because less focused, than he is. Tutored by a sharper master than adversity—success—he is now called a genius more often than anyone else in Hollywood, which means that the word is practically his nickname. He represents a new psychological type of power, which must be distinguished if you would understand the present age: a man of extremely nervous sensibilities who deals with nervous affairs in a nervous environment— and can keep on doing so. If moving pictures did not exist, Irving Thalberg might not be called a genius, but it is amusing to speculate upon what less glittering objectives he would have dissipated his furious creative concentration.

But MGM is neither one man nor a collection of men. It is a corporation. Whenever a motion picture becomes a work of art it is unquestionably due to men. But the moving pictures have been born and bred not of men but of corporations. Corporations have set up the easels, bought the pigments, arranged the views, and hired the potential artists. Until the artists emerge, at least, the corporation is bigger than the sum of its parts. Somehow, although our poets have not yet defined it for us, a corporation lives a life and finds a fate outside the lives and fates of its human constituents.

Metro-Goldwyn-Mayer came into existence in 1924. It is, from one aspect, the climax of an ancient and ludicrous feud. Back in the days when Norma Shearer was a Canadian schoolgirl, the late Marcus Loew owned a lot of movie theaters and Adolph Zukor was associated with him. Mr. Loew was none too fond of Mr. Zukor, and his disdain manifested itself in highly original ways. In board meetings Mr. Loew would divert himself by snapping match sticks at Mr. Zukor. When the Loew enterprises moved into handsome new offices Mr. Zukor, although he was treasurer, was not permitted a desk of his own and had to examine the expense accounts standing up. Later, when Adolph Zukor became head of the nearest thing to a movie production trust the industry has ever known— Famous Players-Lasky Corp.—he avenged himself on Mr. Loew by making it next to impossible for the Loew theaters to get Lasky pictures.

Marcus Loew, in short, had to develop his own production unit. In 1920 he acquired Metro Pictures Corp., started in 1915 by Richard Rowland, now a Fox production executive. Metro was making no money when Loew bought it, but shortly produced *The Four Horsemen of the Apocalypse,* in which Rudolph Valentino darted his first historic glances. Early in 1924 Loew's bought Goldwyn Pictures Corp., started in 1916 by the Selwyn brothers and the able pinochler Samuel Goldfish. Later in the year Mr. Nicholas M. Schenck, who was chief executive of Loew's, negotiated for the Louis B. Mayer Pictures Corp. Mr. Mayer did a great deal of talking on behalf of himself and his partners, Irving Thalberg and J. Robert Rubin. He talked so well that when the contract was signed the Mayer partners got not stock nor cash but a percentage of Loew's profits which changes according to how much of Loew's earnings are accounted for by MGM. And Mr. Schenck was satisfied because he got Messrs. Mayer, Thalberg, and Rubin as a unit all duly bound by contracts to work for Loew's (Mr. Thalberg's contract has five years to go).

As it turned out, this was an elegant deal for all concerned. In other words, the present-day Loew's stockholder is a partner of Messrs. Mayer, Thalberg, and Rubin, but these are not the only ones to share in the profits. Loew's reported that in 1931 president Schenck got a bonus of 2 1/2 percent of the profits, or $274,000, and treasurer David Bernstein one of 1 1/2 percent, or $164,000. This was in addition to salaries of $2,500 and $2,000 a week respectively.

Having acquired MGM, Mr. Schenck might have been content to watch it flourish with Loew's. Instead, when William Fox conceived great designs for the Fox Film Corp. and wanted Loew's theaters as well, Mr. Schenck sold his stock, which had a market value of $47,000,000, to Mr. Fox for $55,000,000. Mr. Fox also bought a large block from Marcus Loew's estate (he had died in 1927), getting a controlling total of 45 percent of Loew's stock. But the transaction, fortuitously, had small effect on the fortunes of MGM. For Mr. Fox's subsequent delusions of grandeur took the form of expanding the Fox chain of theaters and leaving the Loew's circuit strictly alone.

In 1930 Fox collapsed and the ruins were left in the hands of the Chase Bank. During the corporate turmoil which followed, the Law took action (under the Clayton Act) which delighted the hearts of Mr. Schenck and his MGM partners. Three eminent gentlemen were appointed as "trustees of the court" to oversee what had been the Fox holdings in Loew's. The trio which now faces Mr. Schenck at his stockholders' meetings, with 45 percent of Loew's in their pockets, are Thomas W. Gregory, onetime attorney general of the United States, John R. Hazel, onetime federal judge, and the redoubtable Bostonian Thomas Nelson Perkins. Mr. Schenck probably smiles at these "trustees in the public good" as he never smiled at Mr. Fox or the Chase Bank men. For he knows that, rather than true controllers, they are merely the arms of that benign agent (for Mr. Schenck) which put them there and will ultimately remove them—the N.Y. Federal Court. This leaves the partners of MGM in a most gratifying position where they can run the corporation for their own profit.

MGM happens to be the corporation which has gone through the Depression with less corporate trouble than any other in the industry. This is more than a coincidence. It is a symptom of MGM's internal amiability. Which, along with Mr. Thalberg and Greta Garbo, is another reason for MGM's success. Last summer, when Paramount had just reported the largest loss in cinema history, a quarterly deficit of $5,900,000, MGM was on the point of acknowledging that it would have had one but for the salary cut. Although a panic summer and a few pictures slightly below MGM standard were enough to account for the loss, Mr. Schenck and MGM's attorney and vice president, J. Robert Rubin, made one of their biannual visits to the Coast. After conferring with Mr. Thalberg and Mr. Mayer, however, Mr. Schenck and Mr. Rubin came away satisfied to let Mr. Thalberg continue producing as he sees fit, for the time being at least.

With the old régime of fur peddlers, secondhand jewelers, and nickelodeon proprietors who started all the major cinema companies except

RKO and Warner, MGM has now only one connecting link. He, Louis B. Mayer, is probably the most dignified personage in Hollywood. Mr. Mayer arrived in the United States from Poland before the turn of the century, helped his father with a New England ship-salvaging firm, and reached Hollywood, unlike most of the producers of his era, after owning only one theater (in Haverhill, Massachusetts). What he did own, however, was a profitable production and distribution business. By the time that his five year-old producing company became part of the Loew's merger, Mr. Mayer had already started to turn over the reins to young Mr. Thalberg, whom he had enticed away from Universal in 1923. Now, at about forty-five, Mr. Mayer is an MGM vice-president, but he probably does not spend more than half his time on matters closely pertaining to MGM. Mr. Mayer would like to have the entire industry reflect the Mayer prestige. One of his hobbies is the pretentious Academy of Motion Picture Arts and Sciences, which sets itself up as an arbitrator of Hollywood squabbles and gives annual awards for all kinds of cinematic excellence. It also satisfies Mr. Mayer to think of himself as the first producer who has gone far beyond mere cinema success, though it is not true that he was offered an ambassadorship, even to so modest a democracy as Turkey. Had it been offered, Mr. Mayer would now be in Ankara instead of Hollywood.

Mr. Mayer's entrance into politics was made through his acquaintance with a lady who is now chief of his secretariat, Mrs. Ida Coverman. Mrs. Coverman, then (and now) an ardent believer and worker in the cause of Republicanism, persuaded Mr. Mayer to take a financial interest in the gubernatorial election of 1924. The story goes that she introduced Mr. Mayer to Mr. Hoover when the latter was at Palo Alto after his term as secretary of commerce. Mr. Mayer did hard work in the 1928 campaign and he was doing more hard work for Hoover this autumn.

Mr. Mayer's rôle in the extremely public private affairs of MGM is almost identical with his rôle in his private life of public services. He is the diplomat, the man of connections. His affiliations with the White House (he is the only cinemagnate who ever spent a weekend there) give him a roundabout connection with the Hays organization—MGM can feel assured that such narrow-minded whims as overcome the censors will not be practiced unduly on MGM pictures. Whenever a prince of Siam or a South American ex-president visits Hollywood he is entertained by Mr. Mayer; this produces pompous publicity for MGM. Mr. Mayer's courtesies to U.S. senators and vice-admirals make it easier for MGM to borrow a battleship for *Armored Cruiser* or a fleet of navy planes for *Hell Divers*. And so far as MGM is concerned, the prospect of Mr. Hoover's defeat was not so appalling to Mr. Mayer as it might have been if he had not been so closely associated with William Randolph Hearst.

Not only MGM but the whole of Hollywood owes Mr. Mayer a debt—thus far expressed only in gratitude—for the maintenance of the Hearst connection. The truth is that Marion Davies' pictures cost MGM a great deal more than might seem, superficially, advisable. In rural districts, where there is a tendency to frown upon Miss Davies' lavish domesticity, her dramas do not draw so well as they did at one time. Her $6,000-a-week salary alone reaches a total in twelve weeks which would bring her productions near the borderline of loss. On the other hand, it would obviously be unwise for MGM to economize in the matter of Davies production. Hollywood understands that by obliging Mr. Hearst in the matter of Miss Davies Mr. Mayer is not only insuring Hearst support for his own productions but also preserving the rest of the industry from the indignation which the Hearst press would doubtless extend to the cinema as a whole if Miss Davies were to suffer some indignity.

Even within MGM, in the hours he devotes to studio affairs, Mr. Mayer's efforts fall into much the same category—of personal connections, intrigues, and affiliations. He is a commercial diplomat. Contacts and contracts are his specialty, and the latter are completely in his care at MGM. This is an exceedingly important branch of MGM's activities. In the cinema industry, no one of any consequence is employed without a written agreement of some sort. This is partly because the traditions of the industry are not those of banking, but much more because a company which gets a Jean Harlow wants to keep her and, conversely, Jean Harlow needs to be sure that a quick shift in public taste—or the suicide of her husband—won't stop her paycheck.

For example, Mr. Mayer was very glad to be able to sign John Gilbert on a five-year contract in 1927. A year or two later he was sorry he had done so. Mr. Gilbert, compelled to start making talkies when his own vocal equipment was as squeaky as experimental sound apparatus, was a far less valuable property in 1929.

As might be expected, Mr. Mayer resents the high salaries that go to MGM actors, but he sees little that can be done about it. It would be very pleasing to Mr. Mayer and to all other Hollywood producers if it were possible to prevent actors from demanding and getting all that they are worth at the box office. This is, in a word, impossible, and Mr. Mayer knows why. "If the major producers agreed not to pay a certain star more than, for instance, $800 a week," says Mr. Mayer, "some independent producer would offer him more, if he were worth more. Accordingly, there is no chance for the studios to combine to control actors' salaries. Besides, it would be illegal."

It is obvious that the process of contracts is a highly individual matter of bargain and barter, and beyond the routine of being tactful, diplomatic, and, so far as is legal, sly, Mr. Mayer can have no rules for his procedure. It is his business simply to get the most and give the least. Yet, so far as Mr. Mayer has a policy, his policy of bargain making must parallel Mr. Thalberg's policies of picture making.

There may be disagreements—Mayer, Thalberg, Schenck—but behind the disagreements there is an essential loyalty (a successful corporation does not necessarily inspire loyalty, but it certainly tends to inspire such loyalty as may be based on the human desire to create successfully.) And above the disagreements arises a great consistency which is not the policy of Thalberg or Mayer or Schenck but the policy of MGM. The various elements in this policy, which are the reasons for MGM's outstanding success in the past five years, we can now recapitulate:

First, there is that corporate smoothness, that amity among executives which we have mentioned above and which is so understanding that Mr. Mayer has felt free to rebuke Mr. Thalberg's wife for being "yellow" because she balked at working with director Reginald Barker on *Pleasure Bound.* Internally, MGM keeps just about the quietest of Hollywood's many mad households.

Second, there is Mr. Thalberg's heavy but sagacious spending. It is the most outlandish feature on MGM's face, and one of the most effective. There is no sign of its being submitted to economical plastic surgery. Utilizing a one-half square mile of inlaid floor, two thousand yards of gold cloth, and fifty pounds of beards, the picture *Rasputin* cost $750,000 long before its completion, and director Boleslavsky was so enwreathed in genuine, expensive Russian atmosphere that he was able to forget Lionel Barrymore's profane and scornful mutterings. MGM would seem to have shown conclusively that although vast expenditure is no guarantee of good results, economy is decidely *not* the secret of profitable movie production. Economy may be of great importance in the relatively constricted economics of the legitimate stage. But in the movies, as Mr. Thalberg observes, differences of hundreds of thousands in expenses are easily justified when they may make differences of millions in the "take."

Third, there is the kind of picture MGM makes with its money. All questions of MGM policy ultimately boil down to the fact that MGM is show business and in show business the show's the thing. MGM pictures vary from *Private Lives* to *Tarzan*, from *Smilin' Through* to *Fu Manchu*. But there is a certain common denominator of goodness which MGM expects and Mr. Thalberg tries to get out of Culver City. It is easier to state what this goodness is *not* than what it *is*. It is not innovation. MGM was the last of the big companies to adopt sound, and its most advanced camera technique has been borrowed from Russia, Germany, and France (of course Mr. Thalberg now sees to it that MGM sounds are as clear as bells and that its cameramen avoid the stodgier angles). It is not superior direction. Probably no MGM director is as gifted as Ernst Lubitsch or Josef von Sternberg, for instance, both of whom work for Paramount. It is not superior writing. MGM has the largest literary staff in Hollywood—its superiority, however, is debatable.

But when we consider acting, we strike a real clue to MGM's preeminence. Here arises a delicate question. Some people feel that movie celebrities really act; others stay convinced that, even in these sophisticated days, movie acting as a whole remains not so much acting as the exuding of personality. Now while there may be some dispute about MGM's acting, no one will deny that the MGM roster exudes more personality than any other in Hollywood. MGM has under contract at least a dozen of those hypnotic ladies who are asked to send their height, weight, bust dimensions, and autograph to dreamy admirers all over the country. And a half dozen male performers of equally mesmeric power. MGM can claim to have developed many of these, such as Shearer, Garbo, Davies, Harlow, Crawford, Gable, Gilbert (now trying a comeback), Montgomery, Novarro. It is currently developing Virginia Bruce, Dorothy Jordan, Myrna Loy, Karen Morley, Robert Young, Johnny Weissmuller, and others. And MGM does well by those luminaries it acquires with a reputation in advance, such as Wallace Beery, Marie Dressler, the Barrymores, and Jimmy ("Schnozzle") Durante, who among them do more acting of all sorts than the rest of the list combined. Irving Thalberg has lately made much of the fact that he is discarding the old "star" system. It is true that there are a diminishing number of pictures in the old movie tradition—pieces of utter whiffle for the display of some jerkwater matinee idol—and that there are more movies with an intelligent basis today than there were ten years ago. But what Mr. Thalberg substitutes for the "star" system is a galactic arrangement whereby two or more "stars" appear in one film: Davies and Montgomery in *Blondie of the Follies*, Garbo and Gable in *Susan Lenox*, Harlow and Gable in *Red Dust*, Bankhead and Montgomery in *Faithless*. So long as personality per se counts for so much at the nation's box offices, so long will some sort of star system, unit or multiple, persist. And so long as MGM keeps as much personality on tap as it has at present, so long can MGM hope to be well up in the Hollywood van. The day may come when a superb actor like Alfred Lunt will prove a bigger movie drawing card than the "cute" and widely heralded Robert Montgomery—if and when it does, the motion picture industry will make another story.

The glamour of MGM personalities is part of a general finish and glossiness which characterize MGM pictures and in which they excel. Irving Thalberg subscribes heartily to what the perfume trade might call the law of packaging—that a mediocre scent in a sleek flacon is a better commodity than the perfumes of India in a tin can. MGM pictures are always superlatively well packaged—both the scenes and personalities which enclose the drama have a high sheen. So high a sheen that it sometimes constitutes their major box office appeal. MGM's versions of *Grand Hotel* and *Strange Interlude* are cases in point. The consensus of critical opinion held that neither of these pictures had the dramatic value of the stage plays from which they were adapted. But for *Grand Hotel* Mr. Thalberg assembled the Barrymore brothers, Greta Garbo, and Joan Crawford, a quartette no movie addict could resist if they were playing *Charlie's Aunt.* Cedric Gibbons designed a circular staircase which is already more famous than that at Blois and, by way of contrast, Lionel Barrymore emitted the loudest belch in the history of the drama. The highly touted "unspoken thoughts" in *Strange Interlude* weren't very successful because the actors "mugged" the lines so violently, but Norma Shearer was never more subtly gowned, the great Clark Gable audience was delighted to see its hero as a real gentleman rather than a deluxe yegg, and the whole picture gave the hinterlands the idea that sex didn't need to be represented in terms of Marlene Dietrich's garters. Irving Thalberg's willingness to toy with such sophisticated stuff as *Strange Interlude* is encouraged by the fact that a large majority of Loew's and hence MGM's theaters are in urban centers and especially in greater New York. But in general he is betting on good taste as nationally salable, and if his actors' names are still more important than the themes they delineate, it remains true that Irving Thalberg treats both actors and themes with a fine eye for contour and polish. In this regard, the quality and texture of Miss Shearer's gowns for some drama of the *haut monde* can be compared with the quality and texture of the hippopotamuses that Mr. Thalberg hired for *Tarzan.*

The rule of the cinema industry, which is still too adolescent and eccentric to be subject to any formulas derived from its past, is that no company can long remain preeminent. Shifts in personnel, shifts in audience taste that contradict the taste of executives, overexpansion, vanity, have so far been effective to prevent any Hollywood producing organization from permanently besting its rivals. Hollywood expects the same rule to affect MGM. MGM's rivals would doubtless dearly love to cut MGM's throat; they are effectively restrained by the fact that they would cut off their noses if they did so. So long as MGM makes the best pictures in the United States, it is valuable to its competitors by filling their theaters better than they can do it with their own product. This is one of the basic rules of behaviorism in the cinema—which remains, among industries, a loud but somewhat furtive giant and, among arts, a young muse who appears to be a trollop.

Loew's, Inc., home office, 1540 Broadway, New York. Unknown to most movie fans, the unpretentious offices above the State Theater coordinated the operations of a $144 million entertainment empire controlling the glamorous production activities of the MGM Studio, an international distribution organization, and over one hundred theaters resting on some of the choicest real estate in the country.

The Loew's theater chain, though not the largest in the business, was consistently one of the most profitable—the result of Marcus Loew's genius for building in correct places. This rendering of John Eberson's design shows a theater meant to provide a little baroque splendor for Akron, Ohio.

Loew's 150 salesmen gathered each year at a convention to map strategy for peddling the next season's product to the country's 11,000 theaters.

Mayer presiding over ceremonies marking the merger of Louis B. Mayer Pictures and the Metro-Goldwyn Company, April 26, 1924. Pictured on the rostrum is Marcus Loew, founder and president of the parent company.

Construction begins on twenty-two sound-proof stages during the transition to the talkies. MGM expanded its studio operations in Culver City to accommodate fifty productions a year.

Irving Thalberg, MGM vice president in change of production, with Norma Shearer, John Gilbert, King Vidor, and Eleanor Boardman

MGM celebrities in *Dinner at 8*. Thalberg modified the star system to create a galactic arrangement whereby two or more stars were featured in a picture. The actor roster exuded more personality than any other studio's in Hollywood and boosted MGM's weekly payroll to $250,000.

330

An early directorial roster. Although the names changed, block booking kept the number constant.

The prop department contained, among other things, $2 million worth of antique furniture.

The costume shop. Every contributor to motion picture production, from seamstress to director, belonged to one of Hollywood's forty trade unions.

Box lunches for hungry extras. Central Casting Corporation handled the placement of extras. Two-thirds of the 20,000 extras earned less than $500 a year in the thirties.

The annual publicity and advertising budgets amounted to over $5 million.

Portrait of a Vertically Integrated Company

13 FORTUNE

Loew's, Inc.

Mr. Nicholas M. Schenck, for the last twelve years president of Loew's, Inc., is the author of that optimistic saying, "There is nothing wrong with this industry that good pictures cannot cure." It has been the easier for Mr. Schenck to say that about the movie business because Loew's picture-making unit, Metro-Goldwyn-Mayer, has for at least eight years made far and away the best pictures of any studio in Hollywood. Metro's gross revenue from film rentals has been consistently higher than that of other studios, and as a result Loew's, Inc., has been and still is the most profitable movie company in the world. So vital are Metro pictures to Loew's earnings that whereas Mr. Schenck, the undisputed boss of the whole shebang, received some $220,000 from his profit-sharing contract last year (over and above a salary of $2,500 a week), Mr. Louis B. Mayer, the employee who runs Metro, received $763,000 on his profit-sharing contract, over and above a salary of $3,000 a week. That's what Mr. Schenck and his board of directors are willing to pay for "good pictures."

When *Fortune* looked at Loew's in December 1932 [see ch. 12—Ed.], the whole story was devoted to Mr. Mayer's fabulous studio. Today, however, Mr. Schenck is faced with one or two problems, not then anticipated, which Mr. Mayer may not be able to solve for him singlehandedly. The chief one is the antitrust suit that the Department of Justice brought against Loew's and seven other major units of the movie industry in July 1938. Loew's, like its four biggest competitors,

From vol. 20 (August 1939), pp. 25–30+.

is engaged in selling and exhibiting, as well as in making pictures; and the government, on behalf of the small producers and independent theater owners who feel squeezed by this vertical trustification, seems resolved to break it into halves. The fight is proceeding to trial very, very slowly, but only the vagaries of the law, and not good pictures, will ultimately end it.

Another thing in the back of Mr. Schenck's mind is the fact that Metro pictures, while still possibly the most successful in the world, have recently been failing to make their customary splash in the trade. The absence of splash was loudly heard last fall, when the expensive superspecials *Marie Antoinette* and *The Great Waltz* were presented to an American public that has not even yet shown any inclination to return to Metro their negative costs. Jeanette MacDonald's *Broadway Serenade* and Joan Crawford's *Ice Follies of 1939*, coming along in the spring, helped to confirm the impression that Metro had struck a slump; so did the news that the touted *I Take This Woman* (Spencer Tracy and Hedy Lamarr) has been indefinitely postponed. In a company that had grown used to releasing a *Grand Hotel, Mutiny on the Bounty, Thin Man, Test Pilot, Boys' Town, Captains Courageous*, or their box office equivalents every month or so, the recent Metro crop of turkeys has not been reassuring. Insofar as this constitutes a problem for Mr. Schenck, he can hardly turn solely to Mr. Mayer, for it might be Mr. Mayer's fault. It is certainly Mr. Mayer's responsibility. But it has not been costing Mr. Schenck any sleep. The fact is that Metro's gross picture rentals, which reflect the average popularity of the studio's entire product of fifty or so pictures a year, are ahead of the 1938 gross to date by some $2,000,000. The number of exhibitors who are buying the product has also been steadily climbing. Hence if Metro is indeed in a serious slump, the only measure thereof is the volatile thermometer of Hollywood gossip. To be sure, Hollywood gossip is itself sometimes a hard business factor, in its effect on people in the industry.

The antitrust problem, though more tangible than the studio problem, has not troubled any Schenck sleep yet either. He believes that Loew's cause is just, and that the government will either drop its suit (which Assistant Attorney General Thurman Arnold denies) or lose it. Some people say that even if the five big chains were to be divorced from the five big studios, the effect might be to stimulate Loew's profits rather than to stop them. It would be a different sort of picture business from the one Mr. Schenck knows, however. A trust is a delicate thing to monkey with, and not even Trustbuster Arnold dares envision the result if he should bust this one. We can best tell what both he and Mr. Schenck are up against by looking at Loew's as a whole, to see how the richest of the movie trusts gets its ephemeral product made, distributed, exhibited, and turned into such surprising quantities of cash.

Although Loew's assets, some $144,000,000, are exceeded by those of Warner Brothers, its profits have for eight years been well ahead of those of any rival. Its gross revenues are also larger. In 1930 and 1937, on grosses of $129,500,000 and $121,800,000 respectively, it earned some $14,500,000. Last year, on a gross of $122,700,000, it earned just under $10,000,000; and even in 1933, the poorest movie year since sound, its profits were $4,000,000. With the somewhat special exception of Warner Brothers, Loew's was the only one of the five integrated "majors" to weather the Depression without bankruptcy, reorganization, or shake-up of any kind.

For a company with such a record, the home offices over the State Theater at Broadway and Forty-fifth Street, New York, are modest to the point of dinginess. Overshadowed by the Paramount Building and by many a flyspecked Times Square hotel, the sixteen-story Loew's building gives no hint of the size of the checks that are signed on its seventh floor. The executives, too, present what is for Broadway an almost conservative front. There are no fluted vests, but they are all well fed and healthy-looking with Florida tans, and are mostly free from that apprehensive quickness of speech and gesture that the uncertainties of show business stamp on so many of its votaries. For Loew's men, show business is not uncertain at all. And a surprising number count their service to Loew's in decades, not in years. Mr. Schenck himself, for example, has not worked for anyone else since 1906, and being a quiet, imperturbable, almost diffident man, he has succeeded in holding the loyalty and affection, as well as the services, of his executives. He still talks with an accent carried all the way from central Russia, which he left when he was nine, but it is unaccompanied by the bombast, the flailing gestures, the arrogance commonly associated with men who have reached large positions in pictures. Mr. Schenck has an uncanny eye for profitable pictures, and a genius for building theaters in the correct places. But he eschews any self-glorification. He plays the ponies for profit as well as for fun, and keeps a fast speedboat and an unpretentious yacht on Long Island Sound. The speedboat he uses mainly for commuting between Manhattan and his estate next to Walter Chrysler's at Great Neck. The estate is inhabited by Mr. Schenck, Mrs. Schenck (née Pansy Wilcox of Morgantown, West Virginia), and three daughters, who are their father's main interest in life. The Schenck ménage is a gracious place of unobtrusive luxuriousness, resembling an English country house in mood and having only one boisterous detail—a set of tremendous brass cuspidors labeled "Great Expectorations" in the bar.

Among the other veterans in the Loew's building are the secretary, Leopold Friedman (twenty-eight years of service with the company); David Bernstein (thirty-four years of service), vice-president and treasurer, and "one of the world's greatest financial minds," according to Nicholas Schenck; Charles C. Moskowitz (twenty-six years of service), plump, jowly manager of the metropolitan theaters, who has never married because he thinks a wife would interfere with his work; vice-president J. Robert Rubin (twenty-four years of service), the MGM studio's handsomely dressed eastern ambassador, general counsel, and literary properties man de luxe; Joseph Vogel (twenty-nine years of service), amiable, soft-spoken, philosophic manager of the out-of-town theaters. All told, the reigning executives of Loew's are a conservative group with traditions, and from them the company takes much of its character. No less an arch-Bostonian than Thomas Nelson Perkins has sat on the Loew's board of directors.

It would be an exaggeration to say that these men run Loew's, Inc., as coolly and conservatively as other men might run a bank. You know at once that you are dealing with an excited sort of business from the number of telephones on some of the executive desks, with which they have to play a kind of shell game whenever there is an incoming call. They not only concern themselves with the story buying, selling, and publicity aspects of pictures—subjects all garish enough—but are in control of such miscellaneous Loew's affiliates as two artists' booking services, a radio station (WHN), three music-publishing companies, and any number of those strange noctivagants known as talent scouts. Still, of the 125-odd subsidiaries of Loew's, Inc., that it is their duty to coordinate, at least a hundred are theaters, which is to say real estate. And by and large the language and psychology of business, not of art or of nonsense, set the tone of the New York office of Loew's, Inc. Conservative business at that. Loew's was the first picture company (1926) able to sell long-term debentures on the New York Stock Exchange, and $15,000,000 worth of Loew's ten-year bonds were sold three years ago (through Dillon, Read) at the lowest rate in the history of the industry, a trifle over 3.5 percent.

Marcus Loew

Some of the reasons for this conservatism stem from the present policies of the officers, but the most important ones are to be found in Loew's history. Twelve years dead, the founder of the company,

Marcus Loew, did certain things and avoided doing others that largely account for the organization's prosperity today. Marcus Loew was strictly a theater man. Reared on the streets of the East Side Manhattan ghetto, he sold newspapers when he was eight, entered the fur business, grew an aggressive black mustache, and presently bought his way into a company that Adolph Zukor had started to exploit peep-show motion-picture devices in penny arcades. Zukor's company opened its first showplace in Union Square, Manhattan, and made $20,000 the first year, while Marcus Loew headed a subsidiary company developing out-of town locations. No sooner had the venture been firmly established than the partners started wrangling, and the Automatic Vaudeville Co., as it was called, shortly dissolved. Loew was left with three penny arcades, including one in Cincinnati, and soon turned them into nickelodeons. The films of the period, which ran less than five minutes on the screen, were of deplorable quality, and the business was thoroughly disreputable. David Warfield, who had an investment in his friend Loew's enterprise, refused to let it be known that he had anything to do with the nickelodeons for fear of blighting his name on the stage. (Mr. Warfield, now seventy-two, is still a director of Loew's, Inc.) Loew rented vacant stores and lofts, at first, and furnished them with benches or secondhand chairs to seat the audiences. Later on he acquired regular theaters, and boosted attendance by cashing in on—as well as helping to inspire—the vaudeville craze. "Vaudeville and Pictures" was what the Loew houses offered, and it was ten years or so before the line was changed to "Pictures and Vaudeville."

To Marcus Loew, indeed, goes more than a little of the credit for the cinema's development as an adult medium of entertainment. Realizing early that the screen would never progress beyond the nickelodeon stage unless production improved, his constant demand was for pictures that told stories, pictures that were dignified, pictures that would appeal to a more intelligent public than the peep show addicts. When he was finally able to secure such pictures—from Zukor himself, among others—he began unloading nickelodeons and purchasing larger, tonier houses judiciously selected with an eye to population shifts and neighborhoods. Sometimes it was necessary to regenerate particular theaters before nice people would start going to them. Loew purchased an old harlot of a burlesque house called the Cosy Corner, in Brooklyn. The police had raided the place so often that it finally closed, and was taken over by the Salvation Army. Loew bought it for a song, fumigated it physically and then morally by putting on a troupe of Italian actors who played only Shakespeare and d'Annunzio. In a few months, as the Royal, it became the loftiest theater in the borough, and Loew was then able to introduce in it high-class vaudeville and pictures, to his future profit.

It was just after the war that the movie industry, dislocated by the zooming of production costs under the competitive influence of the star system, began to assume the vertically integrated shape it has today. First National, a circuit of exhibitors, began it, first by financing producers, and then by building a giant studio in 1922. Adolph Zukor had already merged Paramount (distributing) and Famous Players-Lasky (producing) in 1916; now he began to buy theaters, and by 1927 owned more than a thousand. Marcus Loew, who by 1919 had more than a hundred theaters, and whose Loew's, Inc., was a $25,000,000 company listed on the New York Stock Exchange, followed the trend. In 1920 he bought an impoverished independent producing and distributing company called Metro (then run by Richard Rowland) and poured $2,000,000 of his theater profits into it. Mr. Loew, soon afterward, acknowledged himself "surprised to learn how many things about picturemaking an exhibitor did not know." But in 1924 he went deeper into production by buying the Goldwyn Pictures Corp., from which the eccentric Sam Goldfish had already retired, and also the independent producing unit run by Louis B. Mayer.

With the Mayer company Loew's also took unto itself a new and subsequently controversial business practice. The chief assets of the Mayer company were the men in it, including Mayer himself, J. Robert Rubin, Irving Thalberg, and others whom Mayer had lured from other studios with the offer of profit-sharing bonuses. After the formation of Metro-Goldwyn-Mayer as a Loew's, Inc., subsidiary, the three among them were entitled (after dividends of $2 per common share) to 20 percent of Loew's net up to a withdrawal of $2,500,000, and 15 percent above that. In 1930 they divided a $2,200,000 melon on the $14,500,000 profits. As comparable payments ensued, certain stockholders began to doubt whether any men in the world were worth that much to any company, and suit was brought in 1938 to revoke the bonus contracts. But it was proved as definitely as anything of the kind can be that Messrs. Mayer, Rubin, and Thalberg had been indispensable, and that Loew's mounting profits depended largely on their efforts. At any rate, Mr. Sidney Kent, president of Twentieth Century-Fox, testified that his company would be glad to have them on his lot if they could be weaned away. The profit sharers—including Messrs. Schenck, Arthur Loew, and Bernstein, who have contracts of their own—were made to repay some $528,000 to the company; but the reason for that was a mere bookkeeping error, as Judge Valente made perfectly clear. Today, with additional contracts made this year, the bonuses of fourteen executives on both coasts average about 20 percent of net, Mr. Louis B. Mayer leading the field with 6.77 percent.

Marcus Loew died in 1927, leaving an estate of more than $10,000,000 and a staff of executives trained for years in his conservative—for the picture industry—methods. During the late twenties, when Paramount, Fox, and Warner were borrowing money to buy or build as many theaters as they could get, Loew's sat tight with its chain of ten dozen or so high-class houses. "The day of reckoning will come," Mr. Schenck kept saying, resisting the pressure to join his competitors' spree. Indeed it did. When box office receipts dropped in the Depression, Fox, Paramount, and the others were left holding a bagful of inflated real estate and debt. The greater part of the industry went down in a dismal heap of bankruptcies, lawsuits, shake-ups, and reorganizations, in which control passed largely to Wall Street. Loew's, however, stood like Gibraltar, keeping its theaters and its financial independence as well.

There was a period, to be sure, when Loew's independence was in serious doubt. In 1929 William Fox bought a 45 percent interest in the company, obtained mainly through purchase of stock from the Loew estate, Nicholas Schenck, and other executives. There was some idea of eventual merger, and Fox put a couple of directors on the board. But he never got around to interfering with the Schenck management. Before he had the chance, his own huge chain of theaters was in the most absorbing difficulties, and on top of that the government as an antitrust measure sued to restrain him from voting his Loew's stock. The stock was sequestered and three directors "in the public interest" went on the board. After Fox was dethroned from his own company, his Loew's stock reverted to the Chase Bank and other creditors, and has since been disposed of gradually in the open market. Nobody owns so much as 10 percent of Loew's 1,600,000 shares of common or 137,000 shares of preferred today.

Loew's strength in the Depression—a dividend was paid in every year—was only partly due to Mr. Schenck's caution in the matter of the theaters. There was only one year, 1932, when the profits from the theaters ($5,000,000 that year) exceeded the profits from the studio ($3,000,000). The rest of the time it was just the other way around. For while the theater chain had been keeping itself within handy and profitable limits, Metro-Goldwyn-Mayer had been setting the industry by the ears. Getting off to a good start after 1924 with *He Who Gets Slapped, The Big Parade,* and the Garbo-Gilbert silents, the new sixty-three-acre studio at Culver City rapidly became encrusted with more stars and triumphs than Hollywood had seen in one place since the great Wallace Reid days of the old Paramount lot. And Culver City had something else that Paramount had never had. This was a studio chief whom all Hollywood united in calling a production "genius," the small, pale, nervous youth named Irving Thalberg. To his golden touch with stars and stories Metro's amazing profits were almost universally ascribed. Thalberg, by attempting with a good deal of success to oversee every consequential production on the lot, drove himself to a physical breakdown, and although he took things a little easier thereafter, he died three years later, in September 1936. In examining the Loew's of 1939, it is logical to begin with the rich heritage of Culver City that Thalberg left behind.

Star Factory

"They won't miss him today or tomorrow or six months from now or a year from now," a studio executive remarked at Thalberg's funeral. "But two years from now they'll begin to feel the squeeze." With the release of *Goodbye, Mr. Chips,* MGM parted with the last picture that Irving Thalberg had anything to do with, and his admirers, a group that includes many who never knew him, have been pointing out symptoms of the squeeze for about a year. After his illness there was, of course, a determined effort to fill his shoes. There has been a long parade of would-bes—David Selznick (*David Copperfield, Tale of Two Cities*), Hunt Stromberg (*Maytime, The Thin Man*), and Mervyn LeRoy (*Wizard of Oz*), among others—and the Culver City lot today burgeons with characters who believe themselves to be undiscovered second Thalbergs. Thalberg is almost as pervasive an influence at Culver City today as he was in his lifetime. Recent errors of executive judgment are ridiculed in his name, and compared with the master's performance in similar situations. During his illness, Deanna Durbin and Fred Astaire were tested at Culver City, and turned down. On the subject of Astaire, some hapless underling scrawled on his report card, "Can't act; slightly bald; can dance a little." The Irving Thalberg Building, which harbors the executives, is super-air-conditioned and hermetically sealed. This, the wags allege, is so that the ghost of Thalberg can't get in to see what his successors are doing.

But if MGM no longer has a Thalberg, it still has a weekly studio payroll of $615,000 and a production force of six thousand people. Among these are the twenty-six MGM stars, which the trade has been told are "more stars than there are in heaven." They are headed by the veterans Crawford, Shearer, William Powell, Garbo, and Gable, and include Loy, Donat, Spencer Tracy, Eddie Cantor, the Marx brothers, Robert Taylor, James Stewart, Rosalind Russell, Jeanette

MacDonald, Nelson Eddy, Hedy Lamarr, Mickey Rooney, Wallace Beery, and Lionel Barrymore. There are fifty-odd featured players; eighty writers, among them F. Scott Fitzgerald, Ben Hecht, Anita Loos, and Laurence Stallings; the Class I directors, like Jack Conway, Victor Fleming, W. S. Van Dyke, Robert Z. Leonard, King Vidor, Sam Wood, Frank Borzage, H. S. Bucquet (a graduate of the shorts department and the current white hope of the studio), Norman Taurog, Clarence Brown, and George Cukor. There are the usual host of grips, maids, artists, flacks, and other proletariat, among them such unclassifiables as the man who, during the recent making of *The Wizard of Oz*, stood by the men's room to make sure that none of the many midgets employed in that picture fell into the full-sized commodes. There are also the executives.

Chief of these, of course, is Mr. Louis B. Mayer himself. Now fifty-four, Mr. Mayer is essentially a businessman, although in that capacity he does a good deal of informal acting and is sometimes known as Lionel Barrymore Mayer. In an effort to induce Jeanette MacDonald to unfreeze for her songs in *Maytime*, for example, he called her to his office and sang *Eli Eli* to her on the spot. He is also a tireless pinochle player and rumba dancer, and the possessor of a tough and energetic physique. A hard-shell Republican, he got a lot of kudos in the old days through his friendship with Hoover, which no doubt helped to reconcile the inner Mayer to sharing so much of the credit for Metro pictures with Thalberg. Perhaps he misses his kudos today. But, being a good businessman, he has not tried to fill Thalberg's shoes himself. His job remains what it was, to oversee the entire studio, to handle the delicate diplomacy of contract negotiations, and to refer the tougher problems to Mr. Schenck, whom he calls "The General" and with whom he talks on the telephone two or three times a day. Mr. Mayer, perhaps the most feared man in Hollywood, is also responsible for the general lines along which Metro pictures are constructed. Unlike the rest of the world, these have not changed since the days when Mr. Mayer was a White House guest.

The chief of these policies is a ringing faith in the star system. Metro has created most of its own stars, and has even recreated a few (William Powell, Wallace Beery) whom other studios had virtually given up. How costly the making of a star can be is illustrated by *I Take This Woman*, already mentioned as having been shelved after considerable production expense. Because Hedy Lamarr is potentially a very valuable property, Metro dropped the money rather than get her off to a bad start. (Of course, the picture may yet be completed and titled, say the wags, *I Retake This Woman*.) But the making of a star, although it calls for a judicious selection of material to begin with, also imposes penalties on the star's casting thereafter. Metro pictures are more often vehicles than stories. Mr. Rubin and his aides are constantly combing the world for creative matter of all kinds, and they pay the best prices for it, but many of their best story buys are twisted out of recognition to fit expensive reputations. Even history can be bent to Metro's purpose, the most conspicuous recent example being Norma Shearer's *Marie Antoinette.*

Naturally there is no issue of taste or social conscience to be raised by this timidity; but there is a question of studio morale. Since the ingredients of a successful picture are nothing but people and ideas, an atmosphere of courage and inventiveness can be just as vital to a studio as a chestful of contracts for stories and stars. Many Hollywood gossips believe that the recent series of Metro fiascos can be traced to a decline in morale. In spite of the slogan on the executive walls—"Don't let Metro's success go to your head"—a good deal of complacence can be sniffed in the Culver City air. Mr. Mayer's executive staff—Eddie Mannix, Sam Katz, Ben Thau, Joe Cohn, and Al Lichtman—is an honest and competent group, but, like Mr. Mayer himself, some of them have been there an awfully long time. The studio manager is sufficiently unpopular to convince Mr. Schenck that he must be a good one, but he happens to be Louis Mayer's brother. Not that Mr. Mayer practices nepotism as extravagantly as some other studio heads, even if—having a nephew and two nieces on the payroll—somewhat more literally. But the gossips agree that a lot of the energy that used to go into good pictures seems to be going somewhere else. Leaving some rushes of his last picture, one of the twenty-three Metro producers yawned. "Really," he was heard to say, as he made for a telephone to see how they were running at Santa Anita, "really, I suppose I've got to find a production I can really interest myself in."

But we are here dealing with intangibles; and there is obviously no good evidence yet that Metro, like Paramount before it, has passed its prime. It should be pointed out that all studios have suffered and survived slumps, including Metro itself. And the tangible evidence of the whole product shows no slump at all. Metro has figured about as heavily in the annual Academy Awards in the last two years as it ever did, and in 1938 it produced four of the "Ten Best Pictures" (*Boys' Town, Marie Antoinette, The Citadel,* and *Love Finds Andy Hardy*) selected by *Film Daily*'s poll vote of critics all over the country. For the coming season about fifty pictures are scheduled on a studio budget of $42,000,000. This, as usual with Metro, is the highest per-picture budget in the industry, and probably the proportion of hits, duds, and break-evens will not change very much. This summer (always a movie low spot) Metro has already released a big hit in *Goodbye, Mr. Chips*, made in its English studio. *Tarzan Finds a Son* also looks like a big grosser, as do the forthcoming *Lady of the Tropics*, *Wizard of Oz*, and—to be sold by Metro, though made by David O. Selznick— *Gone with the Wind*. Meanwhile the studio is getting from three to five times the negative cost out of its Dr. Kildare and Hardy Family series, which are produced for less than $300,000 apiece and have struck a new note in screen fare by being quiet, homely, pleasant, and increasingly successful.

Bricks and Mortar

The health of the studio is, of course, of prime importance to Mr. Schenck. Of his $122,700,000 gross revenues last year, around $75,000,000 came from film rentals, as did some $7,000,000 of his $10,000,000 profits. But his other assets, if less spectacular, are more reliable. Between Loew's on the West Coast and Loew's on the East there is not only a difference of 3,000 miles, but a gulf in the method of doing business. Of the business that Marcus Loew started, there are now 125 Loew's theaters in the United States and Canada, of which 76 are in or near New York City and the rest scattered throughout the country. There are another 28 theaters abroad. Of the total, Loew's owns more than half outright, the others being either controlled, leased, or managed. The total depreciated theater investment is about $62,000,000 and the theater profits, which have been remarkably steady, amounted to about $3,000,000 last year.

Approximately half the Loew's U.S. theaters are first-run houses; the rest are subsequent-run with double features, or with double features and Screeno, depending on the location and the strength of the product allotted them. The salaried theater manager, who makes from $75 to $100 a week, is given some initiative in deciding whether some added attraction beyond pictures is needed to satisfy his clientele, but his pictures are all booked for him by Loew's. Even the Screeno question would probably be taken up with Charles Moskowitz (in charge of the theaters in the New York area) or Joe Vogel (who supervises the houses outside of New York). Since the mechanics of theater management are comparatively simple, consisting mainly of seeing that the projection and sound equipment is in good order, that the cooling system works properly, and that the personnel is properly uniformed and properly deferential, the manager's job is one of bookkeeping, of public relations, and, more important, of film "exploitation." In this he is assisted up to a point by the MGM publicity department, headed by Mr. Howard Dietz, the well-known musical comedy librettist. He also has the guidance of Oscar Doob, who directs theater advertising for Messrs. Moskowitz and Vogel. But he is expected to think up publicity tricks of his own, and to maintain pleasant relations with newspapers and others.

What it means to "exploit" a run-of-the mill picture can be judged from inspecting an "Exhibitor's Service Sheet," which is sent out to the managers of all theaters, Loew's and others, some time in advance of the film exhibition dates. Take, for example, the service sheet for *Bridal Suite,* a "hilarious romance" with Robert Young, Annabella, Walter Connolly, Billie Burke, and others. This twelve-page booklet contains newspaper stories with headlines like "Love Laughs at Psychiatry in Comedy Attraction," "Too Many Gags Kill The Story, Avers Director," and "Robert Young Says Comedy Role Is Lazy Man's Job . . ." There is also an assortment of "catchlines"—"Howl Bent For Laugh Heaven, Four Zanies Tangle With Cock-Eyed Love!" is typical. Then two prepared newspaper reviews—"Teaming Annabella and Robert Young, *Bridal Suite* made its romping debut on the screen of the . . . . . Theatre last night." This material is sent out in mat form without charge by the MGM film exchanges, but exhibitors must pay for colored posters and display material like white paper wedding bells to hang in the lobby, arrows saying "THIS WAY TO THE BRIDAL SUITE," and chastely printed mailing cards announcing that "Annabella and Robert Young will be At Home. . . . You are cordially invited to attend," with the footnote "Regular Admission Prices Will Prevail." In addition to all the foregoing, there are admonitions that exhibitors secure the "cooperation" of hotels and have bellboys page fictitious couples in the lobby and summon them loudly to the "bridal suite." Another exploitation scheme suggested is the construction of "peephole and shadow-box displays" in the theater lobby and adjacent store windows. "There is bound to be a natural curiosity where the title *Bridal Suite* is concerned," the sheet explains. "Nor is it necessary to become suggestive or nearly indecent in order to make box-office capital . . ."

Of course Mr. Dietz gets out other types of publicity, too, and it is only fair to say that Mr. Doob himself might well chuck out press books of the *Bridal Suite* type, which are designed for small-town exhibitors. Mr. Dietz, for example, confected the much-admired *Pygmalion* advertising campaign, in which the figure of George Bernard Shaw, as being known to a wider public than any of his works, was shrewdly exploited. Mr. Dietz's department is a big business in itself, spending about $2,500,000 a year. So, for that matter, is Mr. Doob's, which spends another $3,000,000 on advertising alone. It is Mr. Dietz's emissaries who instruct exhibitors all over the country in the technique of securing free newspaper space; but Mr. Doob's men think up the local exploitation angles for the Loew houses.

Meanwhile Messrs. Vogel and Moskowitz are constantly prodding the Loew managers, too. As buyers, Messrs. Vogel and Moskowitz actually see every picture that comes out of the eight major studios—some 350 to 400 a year. This ceaseless viewing also helps them decide how to exploit each one. "We shout the good ones and gumshoe the bad ones," says Mr. Moskowitz. It was Mr. Moskowitz who recently got every theater manager in the metropolitan area to a meeting at 12:45 A.M. to discuss ways and means of fighting the competition of the World's Fair. A Brooklyn theater manager struck a novel blow in this fight. When Denys Wortman, dressed as George Washington, was traveling in a stagecoach from Washington to Flushing to help open the fair, the Brooklyn man, who was playing *Stagecoach* at the time, hitched his own banner-covered stagecoach onto Wortman's equipage, so that the whole parade seemed to be advertising the picture.

To make any generalizations about overhead or earnings of an "average" Loew's theater is impossible on account of the spread that exists between first- and subsequent-run houses, to say nothing of variables such as good and bad pictures, weather conditions, and seasonal fluctuations in attendance. For example, the Penn Theatre in Pittsburgh, operated by Loew's as a partly owned affiliate, is a first-run house seating 3,300. Rent, taxes, depreciation, interest on bonds, and amortization total $5,500 per week, and operating expenses (including salaries of $1,500) come to $3,600 weekly. The Penn exhibits only the highest quality "A" features, and selects fifty-two pictures a year from the total output of MGM, Warner's, Paramount, and United Artists. Film rentals in houses like the Penn are invariably on a percentage-of-gross basis, with the theater paying over to the distributor a portion of the total receipts taken in during the run of the film. Thus *Sweethearts*, with Nelson Eddy and Jeanette MacDonald, grossed $25,000 at the Penn in one week, and the 40 percent rental came to $10,000. But at Loew's Lee Theatre, a subsequent-run house in Richmond, *Sweethearts* grossed $470 over the weekend, with the theater paying a rental of $190. The Lee has 600 seats, costs $740 a week to operate, including cost of films, and usually grosses no more than $950.

Little theaters like the Lee, however vital to their neighborhoods, are far less important to Loew's than its first-run houses, especially those in the big cities. In Rochester, New York, for example, where

Metro pictures are sold to twenty-five different theaters, Loew's owns just one first-run house, but that one customarily pays twice as much rental for a film as all the other twenty-four put together. Outside of New York, home of the big Loew neighborhood chain, there are only five Loew theaters that are not first-run. Still, the whole U.S. chain is only 125 houses strong. Other people own first-run houses, too; and a Metro picture, to break even on its domestic sales, must play something like eight thousand theaters. Which brings us to the problem of distribution.

Pig in a Poke

The trouble with the movie business, say statisticians, is that it is overseated and underproduced. The 16,250 theaters now open in the United States can seat about ten million people at once, whereas average attendance in 1938 was only eighty million a week. The average seat is thus occupied only two or three hours a day. But the first-run houses are nearly full most of the time, which means that the others are proportionately empty. Moreover, so many theaters change bills twice a week or more, and double features at that, that the four hundred features or less turned out by all eight major studios in the course of a year are scarcely enough to keep all the theaters going. In order to assure himself of "product," every exhibitor therefore has to make an annual contract for a steady supply of pictures. The studios, on their part, try to sell only to those exhibitors who will give them the fullest representation in each town. As a result there has grown up a bargaining system that makes the process of getting the pictures into theaters the most confusing part of show business. Over Loew's part in this confusion sits one William Rodgers, who took the job in 1936.

To call on the eleven thousand theaters with which Loew's is able and willing to deal, Mr. Rodgers sends out his hundred fifty salesmen early every summer, when the selling season begins. In trying to make annual contracts, the salesmen are under some handicap because, while they talk freely about Culver City's plans, they can guarantee nothing, not even a definite number of pictures. They used to guarantee a certain number of Gables, Crawfords, and perhaps one Marx Brothers, but Loew's found itself with so many unfulfilled contracts that Mr. Rodgers changed that. Now the sale is made on the basis of the previous season's performance, or what Mr. Rodgers calls "the integrity of our company." The salesmen don't have a price list either. What they offer, with wide variations depending on the strategic importance of the account, are four unnamed superspecials on which they want about

40 percent; perhaps ten lesser bombshells at about 35 percent; another ten at around 30 percent; and a residue of twelve or more program pictures—the "B's"—mostly at flat rentals. But the salesman's object is clear: to get the best available house in each neighborhood to contract for as many pictures as possible. If he can, the salesman insists on the exhibitor's taking the whole line; well over half of Metro's contracts are on that basis. Robert Benchley, Pete Smith novelties, and other shorts also figure in the deal. Through a slit in this poke can be seen a tip of the pig's ear. This is the cancellation clause, which permits the exhibitor to cancel up to 10 percent of the pictures after he has read the reviews.

This system, called block booking and blind selling, has of course been roundly attacked. The Neely bill now before the Senate would bar it altogether, and Claude Fuess, the headmaster of Andover, is one of the high-minded people who have written in support of such a measure, presumably from his experience as a picture buyer for the Saturday-night shows in the auditorium. Many an independent exhibitor objects to block booking, too. But the chain exhibitors apparently do not. It would seem more of an evil, perhaps, if the average exhibitor did not need two or three hundred pictures a year anyway, a number that could not represent much intelligent winnowing on his part even under the most favorable circumstances. And indeed the loudest exhibitor complaints are directed not at block booking as such, but at questions of priority rights to good releases, "clearance" (how soon afterward what rival gets what picture), and the percentage brackets to which the various releases are applied.

The blocked deals made by Mr. Rodgers' salesmen are mainly limited to five or six thousand independent theaters. These theaters account for about 40 percent of Metro's gross. There are also the deals made with the large independent chains (10 to 15 percent), and still more vital are those made with the five big chains of the "trusts." These deals Mr. Rodgers himself gets in on. Some 48 percent of the Metro gross comes from Mr. Rodgers' deals with Loew's, Paramount, Warner, RKO, and National Theatres (affiliated with Twentieth Century-Fox). The Loew chain alone, small as it is, accounts for 15 percent of Mr. Rodgers' gross. An interesting fact about the chains, which the government pointed out in its opening petition in the antitrust suit, is that except in metropolitan areas (the downtown deluxe theaters) they tend to complement rather than compete with each other. Loew is concentrated in New York State, Paramount in Canada, New England, and the South, Warner in Pennsylvania and New Jersey, Fox on the West Coast, and so on.

In such a setup, the big studios obviously need each other's chains very badly in order to get national distribution for their pictures. Mr. Rodgers makes the best deal he can with Joe Bernhard, head of the Warner chain, while Warner's sales manager Gradwell Sears is talking to Joe Vogel and Charles Moskowitz. When you add up all these Big Five deals, multiply them by repeated quarrels over preferred showing, clearance, percentages, and the dozen other points raised by each release, you get a very complicated situation indeed. It is so complicated that it is only natural to suppose that the boys would like to sit down together, all at the same table.

Although the government has been bloodhounding the industry for many years, nobody has ever yet found such a table. Nor is there any positive evidence that any sales manager, aggrieved by bad representation in a competitor's town, ever tries to use his own company's theaters as a club—that would be illegal, too. What probably happens is that the bargaining strengths of the various chains all cancel each other. At any rate, the battle for the best showings is settled in the long run by the comparative drawing powers of the different studio products. If the Loew chain were twice as big as it is, the gross revenues of Metro pictures would probably not be any bigger than they are.

The government claims that Mr. Rodgers sells his pictures to the big chains on terms more favorable than he gives to the independent exhibitors. Mr. Rodgers says it is the other way around. The considerations of priority and clearance are so shaded and complex that either claim would probably be impossible to prove. Naturally Mr. Rodgers gives theaters in the Loew chain a certain edge, which helps account for the Loew chain's impressive contribution to the Metro gross; and this may put *some* independent exhibitors at a disadvantage. But Mr. Schenck will challenge you to find a single independent who has been forced out of business by chain competition. And industry figures show that while the number of Big Five chain theaters in operation has been standing still, the number of independent theaters—especially the number affiliated with independent chains—has been increasing. Meanwhile Mr. Rodgers has been doing his bit to stave off the Neely bill and similar symptoms of "indie" agitation by a long-range appeasement program, instituted in 1936. Metro, the hard-dealing company that first broke the Balban and Katz refusal to make percentage deals in the Chicago area, now advertises itself to the trade as "the Friendly Company," and goes to great lengths to the end that no exhibitor can blame his losses on a Metro deal. Each of Mr. Rodgers' sales or district managers has a fund from which he can rebate on the spot to any exhibitor whose books show an unjust deal; Metro turns back several hundred thousand dollars a year on this account. Mr. Rodgers is also chairman of the industry's code committee, which is busy drawing up new trade practices, including a 20 percent cancellation clause.

The concentration of economic strength in Loew and its rival trusts is probably not very different from that observable in many other industries, and can certainly have happened without collusion. But the government, besides wishing to divorce the chains from the studios, brings the further claim that the big studios are not really competing with each other at all. This complaint takes us back to Hollywood. One of the commonest practices out there is the renting of stars by one studio to another. The lending studio usually charges about 75 percent more than the star's salary, as a contribution to the lender's burden of idle star time. For its part the borrowing studio gets the star it wants for no longer than it wants. An especially frequent borrower from Metro's opulent star stable has been Twentieth Century-Fox, of which Joseph M. Schenck, Nick's massive brother, is chairman of the board. The far-tentacled Mr. Mayer is also related to the Fox studio, through his son-in-law William Goetz. It is undoubtedly easier for Fox to borrow Spencer Tracy than it would be for an independent studio like, say, Republic; but that is not because of the managerial kinship. Both Metro and Spencer Tracy would certainly feel safer with Darryl Zanuck in charge, even if Republic paid in advance. And Mr. Mayer can still gnash his teeth when Darryl Zanuck produces a hit and gloat when he lays an egg—provided, of course, a Metro star isn't in it. At any rate, the practice of star pooling has proved so useful to Hollywood that it is difficult to envision the making of pictures without it.

A similar fogginess, indeed, envelops the vision of any part of the movie business in which the government's suit may be successful. Astronomical budgets, which give Metro pictures their high commercial gloss if nothing else, can be supported only by a nationwide (plus an international) market, and that means that the pictures must be sold to some kind of chains. On the other hand, a strong theater chain that could get nothing but a shoestringer's pictures, however artistic, would soon be financing another Lasky, Zukor, Goldwyn, or other successfully extravagant showman, and start the cycle all over again. The problem is so complicated that Mr. Arnold himself has no suggestions as to how his suit will improve matters, or what shape an ideal picture industry ought to take. But if a cleavage comes, and Mr. Schenck must decide between his theaters and his pictures, the theaters would presumably be sold. Steady earners though they are, they haven't the golden possibilities that Metro still has. It would then become Mr. Schenck's even more urgent duty to keep Metro ahead of the field with "good pictures." Perhaps his aphorism is the answer to this problem after all.

CATHY KLAPRAT

The Star as Market Strategy: Bette Davis in Another Light

Bette Davis became a star in 1933, playing the sexy ingenue in *Ex-Lady*. Warner touted her as the platinum blond coquette, the flirt destined to be the object of men's pursuit. Yet just two years later, in *Dangerous*, Davis' image had been completely changed–she became a vamp, a sexually aggressive seductress, a destroyer of men. What could have caused this radical change? The answer must be found in the broader inquiry into how the star system functioned in the American film industry during the 1930s and 1940s, the era of oligopoly control. We have recently come to understand the narrative significance of the star in classical Hollywood cinema. What is less well understood is the economic significance. Stars established the value of motion pictures as a marketable commodity. In economic terms, stars by virtue of their unique appeal and drawing power stabilized rental prices and guaranteed that the companies operated at a profit.[1]

To maintain this crucial economic function was the major preoccupation of the studio. Power flowed from the top in the studio system, and the production chief himself chose the roles for his stars and made the important career decisions. Although stars may have been well compensated, they were indentured employees, placed in a subservient position by the option contract. Stars were created, not discovered,

---

1. Unquestionably, there are other interventions which may also account for this change in roles. For example, the Production Code intoned against such blatantly sexual representations.

351

counter to popular myths. Entire departments functioned as components of star-making machinery. The scriptwriting department created vehicles for the star's screen persona. And in promoting the pictures, the advertising and publicity departments built up the uniqueness of the star by transforming his or her personal life to match the screen persona. The star system not only characterized the production process, but was inextricably linked to vertical integration. The question should now be rephrased to ask, how did distribution and exhibition affect what was presented on the silver screen?

The Economic Imperative

Although the industry had become vertically integrated by 1930 dominated by five companies, many marketing problems had yet to be resolved. Curiously, the majors had difficulty at first in controlling the price of their films. *Sales Management*, a trade journal of the period, characterized the situation in this manner: "Picture a product distributed to thousands of dealers serving well over 50 million consumers weekly, a product without a fixed price because its value cannot be determined in advance. Imagine too that there is no preordained market for this particular product and that the product is not tangible at all, but a series of moving shadows."[2]

The geographic location of the theater chains owned by the majors exacerbated the problem. For the most part, these chains were located in different regions of the country. For example, Warner owned the best houses in the Philadelphia area. Because they did the lion's share of the business, Paramount, Fox, and the other majors would regularly book these houses.[3] To achieve national distribution, therefore, the majors played one another's pictures. In other words, these companies did not compete on the exhibition level except in certain cities. Nonetheless, the major distributors and exhibitors had to bargain price. In practice, they bargained for a certain percentage of the box office gross. These terms, rather than flat rental, permitted the companies to benefit from the extraordinary box office results of a hit. But the question remained: How to determine the percentage?

To understand how the problem was resolved, we must first analyze some relevant economic principles. Let us return to the *Sales Management* quote. The quote implies that the stabilization of price is

2. A. Montague, "How the Wheels Go Around in a Motion Picture Sales Department," *Sales Managment* 56 (January 15, 1946): 52.

3. Mae Huettig, "The Motion Picture Industry Today," in Tino Balio, ed., *The American Film Industry* (Madison; University of Wisconsin Press, 1976), p. 245.

concomitant with a preordained consumer market, a market difficult to establish because of the intangible nature of film. According to Richard Caves, in his book *American Industry: Structure, Conduct, Performance,* product differentiation establishes a preordained consumer market for a product by creating distinguishing marks which the consumer can recognize.[4] Designer jeans present an exemplary case of this principle at work. Until Calvin Klein stuck his label on a pair of overalls, jeans were considered inexpensive heavy-duty pants fashioned from denim. After Klein's name differentiated his jeans from other now déclassé models, he could double the price. In other words, a consumer preference was established by the Calvin Klein label (the mark of differentiation), a preference which generated a preestablished market for his jeans. Theoretically, this market would then stabilize the product's demand curve, which is a measurement of the amount of the product (in this case jeans) buyers demand at various prices. Consequently, if demand for a product can be stabilized by a distinguishing mark of differentiation, then price too can be stabilized.

Caves implies that this strategy is especially compatible with the intangible nature of a product like film because, "differentiation is most effective when the product serves an ill defined personal need." And what could be more intangible that the series of moving shadows which constitute the commodity of film?

Whether designer jeans or film stars, the principle of differentiation operates in similar fashion. In fact, the evolution of the star system can be seen as a series of experiments along this line. At first, producers used their trademarks as differentiation. If an actor was acknowledged at all, it was in terms of the firm's trademark. For example, Florence Turner was known only as the "Vitagraph Girl."[5] However, company names seemed the same to fans, and consequently trademarks were not distinguishable.[6] Next, producers tried narratives. In 1911, *Motion Picture Story* (note the emphasis on story, not stars), one of the earliest fan magazines, asked its readers to choose their favorite film stories. Instead of the expected answers, the magazine was deluged with inquiries about favorite players.[7] The fact that audiences distinguished

4. Richard Caves, *American Industry: Structure, Conduct, Performance* (Englewood Cliffs, N.J.: Prentice-Hall, 1964), pp. 19–21.
5. For more information see Robert Cochrane, "Advertising Motion Pictures," in Joseph Kennedy, ed., *The Story of the Films* (Chicago and New York: A. W. Shaw, 1927).
6. Benjamin B. Hampton, *A History of the Movies* (New York: Covici, Friede, 1931), p. 92.
7. Gerald McDonald, "Origin of the Star System," *Films in Review* 4 (November 1953): 458.

films by stars became inescapable, and accordingly, the producers began to utilize talent as a successful strategy for differentiation.

This strategy is spelled out by Robert Brady who analyzed the monopolistic practices of the film industry in an article entitled "The Problem of Monopoly." As Brady explains, "Film projects the acting of the star, each one of which has some unique drawing power [or consumer demand] and each film in which the star displays his talent is a unique differentiated product."[8] Star differentiation dovetailed nicely with the standard industry practice of basing film rentals for future releases on the box office success of previous productions. Accordingly, if a star could generate and fix demand, then star differentiation offered a method of standardizing and predicting success and consequently stabilizing the price paid for such films.[9]

But consumer demand accomplished more than price stabilization; it actually encourages the producer to raise his prices. This phenomenon can be explained by the concept of demand elasticity. Demand elasticity measures the sensitivity of demand in relationship to quantity and changes in price. Theoretically, if demand can be fixed by product differentiation, it then becomes less sensitive to increases in price. Our Calvin Klein example illustrates this principles at work. Because of his name differentiation, Klein could charge more for his jeans without affecting the quantity demanded. In this case, the demand curve is termed inelastic, or insensitive to price increases.

The concept of demand inelasticity is pertinent to the problems of film exhibition and distribution posed at the outset of this chapter. The film producer had to market his product on two levels: to the exhibitor and distributor. If a picture contained a successful star, the exhibitor was willing to pay a higher price, thus demonstrating the principle of inelastic demand at work.[10] Of course, the exhibitor knew that the star would stimulate attendance at the box office. As pointed out elsewhere, theaters were classified according to runs. A picture would open at a first-run house which commanded the highest ticket price, and after a specified period of time elapsed, it would move to a second-run house with a lower tariff per ticket, and so on down the line. Consequently, if the audience could be aroused to see the film immediately upon release (i.e., at the first-run house), more money

8. Robert Brady, "The Problem of Monopoly," *Annals of the American Academy of Political and Social Science* 254 (November 1947): 131–132.

9. Howard Lewis, *The Motion Picture Industry* (New York: Van Nostrand, 1933), pp. 119 and 188.

10. Charles Skouras, "The Exhibitor," *Annals of the American Academy of Political and Social Science* 254 (November 1947): 29.

could be made per ticket. Just how much money these first-run theaters generated is suggested by the fact that although they comprised only 25 percent of the total exhibition seats, they returned over 50 percent of the box office receipts.[11] As we know, the majors controlled these theaters and received the bulk of their revenues from them. But the question is how? Through marketing mainly. Publicity campaigns revolved almost exclusively around stars and were geared to run concurrent with first-run release dates. Human interest stories, stunts, and ballyhoo would generate immediate interest in a new picture and thus funnel the audience in to the more expensive seats for the first-run house. In this manner did differentiation by star permit a firm not only to stabilize price but also to charge more for its product.

The Process Begins

If product differentation was the function of the star, the question now becomes, how did studios develop stars? Because the staple of the industry was narrative films the question should be rephrased: How were stars matched to narratives and thus to the scriptwriting, publicity, and advertising strategies of a studio? Once again, the principle of product differentiation applies: a producer could simply change the traits of his product to fit consumer demand. In practice, the industry would cast a player in different roles and test audience response to each. This response would be calibrated by fan mail, sneak previews, and exhibitor preferences. Audience reaction and box office grosses printed in trade papers also provided important market indicators and, as a result, we can reconstruct the process of fitting player to character. Bette Davis' career offers a convenient illustration. Her star persona was created at Warner Bros. where she ascended to stardom in 1935 and reigned as "Queen of Warner's," the top box office attraction, until the expiration of her contract in 1949.

Variety will be used as the data source. This trade paper regularly published box office grosses, annual lists of the biggest money earners, and reviews designed especially for the exhibitor. Together, they should provide an accurate index of audience response. I will concentrate on the early career of Bette Davis, the period from 1932 to 1935. She made five pictures, each one an experiment to determine the correct narrative match. As we shall see, when the audience reacted unfavorably, the studio cast her in a different kind of role. And when the audience reacted favorably, Warner built her star persona around that part.

11. Huettig, "Motion Picture Industry Today," p. 245

Bette Davis first created a stir in 1932, playing a blond coquette in *Cabin in the Cotton*. In her role as the rich spoiled flirt, Davis appeared in a scene·partially disrobed as she attempted to titillate and cajole poor sharecropper Richard Barthelmess (the film's star) into betraying his friends. Although Davis had only a featured part, she elicited a strong audience reaction. *Variety* predicted that Davis' vivid portrayal would create business for a film that otherwise would be but a moderate grosser.[12] Confirming the prediction, *Motion Picture Herald* said: "Miss Davis flashes through the picture in a manner that should send your patrons out of the theatre talking about her."[13] The picture did take off, but more important, *Variety* named Davis as a box office leader for 1932 on the basis of this role.[14]

Warner, therefore, decided to exploit Davis as a comely coquette. In 1933, she received star billing as the naive sexy blond in *Ex-Lady*. *Variety* verified the strategy in a prerelease publicity article which confirmed that Davis' popularity in *Cabin in the Cotton* provided her with the starring role in *Ex-Lady*.[15] In this film, Davis vacillates between becoming "the old fashioned woman" bound by the demands of her husband and the free-spirited alluring "modern woman." She chooses the latter, and in the process her anatomical attributes are once again foregrounded. Davis often appears partially attired, wearing only low-cut diaphanous nightgowns. However, the picture flopped. "*Ex-Lady* didn't materialize in anything,"[16] read the *Variety* epitaph, and Davis was excluded from the box office leaders chart of 1933. So much for the blond sex bomb.

For her next picture, Davis was loaned out to RKO in 1934 to play a featured role in *Of Human Bondage*. *Variety* described the role as something new: the vamp.[17] As defined by Molly Haskell, the vamp is "a woman who while exceedingly feminine and flirtatious is too ambitious and intelligent for the docile role society has decreed she play. . . . She remains within traditional society, but having no worthwhile project for her creative energies, turns them onto the only available material—the people around her—with demonic results."[18] In play-

12. *Cabin in the Cotton* review, *Variety*, October 4, 1932, p. 19.
13. Quoted in *Cabin in the Cotton* press book.
14. "Comparative Grosses," *Variety*, October 11, 1932, p. 35; also "Box Office Leaders for 1932," *Variety*, January 3, 1933, p. 25.
15. Celia Afer, "Accident Saves Bette Davis from Being Another Good Girl," *Variety*, May 28, 1933. p. 6.
16. "Comparative Grosses," *Variety*, May 9, 1933, p. 9.
17. *Of Human Bondage* review, *Variety*, July 3, 1934, p. 26.
18. Molly Haskell, *From Reverence to Rape* (New York, Penguin Books: 1974), p. 214.

ing the part of Mildred, Davis was no longer the glamorous flirt of
Cabin in the Cotton or *Ex-Lady*. Instead, Mildred drew upon the potentially destructive qualities of Davis as a flirt to create the hardened
tramp who seduces and destroys Leslie Howard, the star (see illus. 1).

Pandro Berman, who produced *Of Human Bondage*, must have realized that the latent powers Davis displayed in her previous roles
could be productively applied to the character of Mildred. In requesting
Davis, Berman believed she would be ideal for the part, which he said
"could make anybody on the strength of its sheer power and emotional
qualities, but will never under any circumstances be able to be considered a sympathetic role."[19] Mildred did make Davis: audience response was ecstatic. RKO too was ecstatic and in a special memo to
Hal Wallis, Warner's production chief, praised Davis' sensational performance both in the picture and at the box office.[20]

The correct match between narrative role and actor had now been
found. In fact, the fusion was so perfect that when Davis failed to
received an Academy Award nomination, Warner initiated a write-in
campaign on her behalf. Although the campaign failed, it was responsible for changing nomination procedures to allow for the write-in of
additional nominees by the membership.[21]

After *Of Human Bondage*, Warner cast Davis in *Bordertown* in a
role described by *Variety* as equalling or bettering her characterization
in *Bondage*.[22] Conceived as a vehicle for Paul Muni, *Bordertown* featured Davis once again as the sexually menacing destroyer of men.
Although *Bordertown* appeared on Warner's production schedule in
June 1934, prior to the release of *Bondage*, it is significant that Davis
was not cast as Marie until after her triumph. *Bordertown* went into
production with Muni and Davis in September 1934, which suggests
that the favorable audience response to *Bondage* designated the role
of Marie as the correct one for Davis.[23] *Variety*'s review supports this
assumption by predicting good box office because of good casting.[24]
But more interestingly, the ads placed by the studio begin to ask, "Who
will be the real star of the film: Bette Davis or Paul Muni?"[25] Similarly,

19. RKO Interdepartmental Memo from Pandro Berman to Frank O'Heron, November 9, 1933, RKO Archive, Los Angeles.
20. RKO to Hal Wallis, July 3, 1934, RKO Archive.
21. *Variety*, February 20, 1935, p. 3.
22. *Bordertown* review, *Variety*, January 29, 1935, p. 14.
23. Warner's Production Schedule, *Variety*, June 26, 1934, p. 29; also "*Bordertown*
in Production," *Variety*, September 11, 1934, p. 31.
24. *Bordertown* review, *Variety*, January 29, 1935, p. 14.
25. *Bordertown* advertisement, *Variety*, January 8, 1935, p. 35.

1. Mildred: a new type for Davis (*Of Human Bondage*)

QUIZ ON BETTE DAVIS

▼

2. The ballot box: one measure of audience response

359

the campaign books asked exhibitors to place signs in their lobbies asking the audience if Davis should be starred in this role (see illus. 2).[26]

The audience must have answered yes, because in August 1935, Warner began production on *Dangerous*, starring Bette Davis as the vamp. In this picture, Davis no longer performs in a secondary role. She plays the main character, Joyce Heath, the deadly seductress who destroys the lives of two men. It is clear that Davis was awarded this role on the basis of her success in *Of Human Bondage*. *Dangerous* did not appear on Warner's production schedule for 1934–35, so it must have been because of *Bondage* that the picture was added to the list.[27]

Variety predicted that *Dangerous* would perform well at the box office,[28] which was accurate, but more intriguing, Warner knew Davis would be a hit. Although *Dangerous* was produced in August, it was not released until the last week in December, the final week to qualify for an Academy Award.[29] This strategy suggests that the studio wanted to cash in on its discovery because the picture would be running precisely during the period of the nominations and awards. Indeed, Davis won the award for best actress and Warner began to profit from its new star. *Variety* confirms: "Bette Davis award pulmotors [*sic*] *Dangerous,* provides boost to the film . . . winning holdovers and topping average."[30] With *Dangerous*, the process of fitting actor to character is completed. In economic terms, we can say the differentiation of the star in the correct narrative role determined by audience response created a market for the film.

The Function of Advertising and Publicity

But the matching of actor and character was only the beginning of the process of differentiation. Once the correct role was determined, advertising and publicity took over to transform the star's personal life in accordance with the actions and traits associated with the star's screen character. The audience was assured that the star acted identically in both her "real" and "reel" lives. What we saw on the screen was not just an actress but Bette Davis, the vamp.

Fusing character and actor was executed by the studio's publicity department, which had as its overall task the creation and manipu-

26. *Bordertown* press book.
27. "Warner's Production Schedule," *Variety*, June 26, 1934, p. 29.
28. *Dangerous* review, *Variety*, January 1, 1936, p. 441.
29. "Films in Production," *Variety*, August 21, 1935, p. 28.
30. *Variety*, March 18, 1936, p. 6.

lation of the star's image. To begin, the department manufactured an authorized biography of the star's personal life based in large part on the successful narrative roles of the the star's pictures. The department would disseminate this information by writing features for fan magazines, press releases, and items for gossip columns. A publicist would then be assigned to the star to handle interviews and to supervise the correct choice of makeup and clothing for public appearances. Finally, the department had glamour photographs taken that fixed the important physical and emotional traits of the star in the proper image.[31]

A chronological investigation of this process at work in Davis' career reveals that from 1932 to 1934, the blond coquette period, fan magazines featured Davis wearing revealing blouses and bathing suits. Sporting thick false eylashes, illuminated by glamour lighting, Davis stared out at the reader in come-hither poses (see illus. 3).[32] And yet not much personal information was printed, an indication that Warner was still trying to determine the correct role for Davis. The little information reported stressed Davis' glamour differentiation. Stories included such items as: "The smallest waist in Hollywood" (1932),[33] "Becoming a platinum blond boosts her image" (1933),[34] and "My makeup secrets to enhance beauty" (1934).[35]

As previously noted, audiences did not react positively to this image. After *Of Human Bondage*, the depiction of Davis in magazines changes to accommodate her image as vamp. Significantly, many of these articles imply that her rise to stardom was the direct result of this picture. But more intriguing, articles also refute her previous incarnations as the blond bombshell. The "Universal Train Story," a Davis myth popular with the fan magazines, is typical. The story and its variations tell us that when Davis first went to Hollywood, Universal sent a representative to meet her at the train station. But the man saw no one who resembled a glamourous movie actress so Bette went unrecognized and unmet.[36] Another version recalls that Carl Laemmle, Jr., the head of Universal, considered Davis "about as attractive as Slim Summerville" (a skinny, homely comedian).[37] Simultaneously, the

31. Margaret Sullivan, "The Art of Selling the Star System: A Study of Studio Publicity," Unpublished manuscript (Madison: University of Wisconsin, 1977).

32. Bette Davis file, General Stills Archive, Clipping Files, Wisconsin Center for Film and Theater Research (WCFTR), Madison.

33. Ibid.

34. Ibid.

35. Ibid.

36. Ibid.

37. Ibid.

3. Davis' incarnation as glamour girl

iconography of her photographs changes. Publicity stills now portray her clothed in tailored suits, wearing little makeup (see illus. 4). After 1937, she is no longer blond. Gone also are the come-hither poses.

Articles in the fan magazines also naturalized the physical characteristics Davis employed to create her roles. One story tells us that Davis pops her eyes wickedly in *Dangerous* because as a little girl her face was badly burned, causing this disfigurement of bulging eyes![38] Another report attributes Davis' "staccato speech and pent up intensity" to her New England education.[39] And yet another account claims that Davis was naturally high-strung and offscreen "punctuated her expressions with body movements."[40]

Similarly, Davis' personal background became matched to her screen actions. She is now described as being "as forthright as a male" (in *Beyond the Forest* and *In This Our Life* she is explicitly associated with male actions), and a person who particularly enjoys riding horses (an action she performs in *Jezebel* and *Dark Victory*).[41] *Modern Screen* avowed that Davis was fiery, independent, and definitely not domesticated (all qualities she displayed in her films).[42] *Motion Picture Classic* portrayed her as hard-boiled and ruthless, determined to get what she wants (all traits which motivate many of Davis' actions in her vamp films).[43]

A parallel attempt was made to transpose character relationships from her films to her personal life. One article asked, "Will Bette wed George Brent?" and included a still from *Jezebel* showing the two embracing as evidence of this coupling.[44] In addition to *Jezebel*, Brent played opposite Davis as leading man nine times (see illus. 5). A tidbit in 1939 confided that Davis and Miriam Hopkins disliked one another; that year, they played rivals in *The Old Maid*.[45]

The campaign to shift actor to role can also be seen in newspaper advertising. During the 1932–33 season, ads regularly touted Davis as the sexy blond. After 1934, as expected, the ads change to exploit her vamp image. The economic principles related to product differentiation once again come into play. To repeat, product differentiation

38. Ibid.
39. Ibid.
40. Ibid.
41. Ibid.
42. George Benjamin, "That Marital Vacation," in Martin Levin, ed., *Hollywood and the Great Fan Magazines* (New York, 1970), pp. 110–12.
43. Bette Davis file.
44. Ibid.
45. Ibid.

Today—poised, glamorous, sophisticated. She breaks most of the rules of stars.

4. Davis reincarnates

364

BETTE DAVIS AND GEORGE BRENT
in

The Great Lie

5. Brent and Davis embracing from *The Great Lie*

allows the producer to change the nature of his product to respond to market conditions.[46] This principle is particularly relevant to the advertising practices of the film industry. Vertical integration permitted producers to control the advertising campaigns directed at both the public and the exhibitor. These campaigns took the form of press books, which contained promotional materials such as posters, lobby cards, publicity articles, and ads for planting in local newspapers as well as suggestions for exploitation. Designed and executed by the advertising departments of the distribution branches, press books were dispensed to exhibitors for each release. In addition, the advertising department prepared ads for trade papers using the exhibitor to book new releases.[47]

Warner's advertising strategy for the early Bette Davis pictures is predictable. To start with *Cabin in the Cotton* once again, the ads promoted the blond sex bomb image. Photos show Davis embracing Richard Barthelmess, the star. The exploitation campaign suggests publicizing Davis "the love expert" and "her flaming excitement" (see illus. 6)."[48] The press book for *Ex-Lady* advises giving Davis strong billing *especially* if the exhibitor played *Cabin in the Cotton*. Photos portray Davis clothed in low-cut dresses, reclining in bed, or looking sexily over her shoulder. The text refers to the "blond beauty" from *Cabin in the Cotton*.[49]

As expected, the character of the advertising begins to shift after *Of Human Bondage*. The centrality of this film to Davis' career as star is suggested by the evolution of the advertising campaign. The first ad appeared on June 10, 1934; Davis' name is printed in small letters underneath that of the film's star Leslie Howard.[50] As the positive returns came in, Davis' name increased in size. Ads in *Variety* emphasize this and promote Davis as a market sensation.[51] Ads now also insist that Davis is an actress and *not* a screen beauty.

For subsequent pictures, ad campaigns completely change to capitalize on Davis' image as the tough vamp. No longer does Davis appear in titillating costumes. Photos now project a tough, glaring image. Furthermore, ads begin referring to the traits and actions Davis exhibited in *Of Human Bondage*. For *Bordertown*, we read, "The manwrecker from *Of Human Bondage*," "The woman without a soul from

46. Caves, *American Industry*, p. 20.
47. Cochrane, "Advertising Motion Pictures," pp. 238–48.
48. *Cabin in the Cotton* press book.
49. *Ex-Lady* press book.
50. *Of Human Bondage* advertisement, *Variety*, June 10, 1934, pp. 50–51.
51. *Of Human Bondage* advertisement, *Variety*, July 17, 1934, p. 21.

6. Davis as love expert

Of Human Bondage," "This role is even stronger than *Of Human Bondage.*" Advertising also plays Davis against Paul Muni: "Who will give the best performance, Muni or Davis?" and "Muni in *Bordertown* or Davis in *Bordertown?*" are questions meant to tantalize the readers.[52]

Ads for *Dangerous* continue the process. One layout shows a picture of Davis with leading man, Franchot Tone, followed by Davis with Muni (from *Bordertown*), followed by Davis and Howard (from *Of Human Bondage*). The caption reads, "Bette Davis smacks 'em where it hurts!"[53] Note that the name associated with "smacking 'em where its hurts" is not that of a character that Davis portrays but rather Bette herself. Davis *is* these characters. Likewise, these ads link Davis to her previous films: "That woman's back in town again," "Manwrecking Bette is on the manhunt again," and "One look into Bette Davis' eyes and Tone joins Howard and Muni in succumbing to her fatal attraction." This strategy is even more obvious in the storyboard campaign. In a series of stills we see Davis accompanied by dialogue, presumably from the film. However, a closer examination discloses that her lines are not from the film but instead depict the actions she performed in her vamp films! "I'll destroy your ambitions, your hopes," Davis threatens.[54] By repeating such lines, the ads seem to be marketing more than star differentiation; they are also conditioning the audience to expect a specific plot structure. Expect to see Davis seduce and destroy men, the ads imply. The star's effect on narrative structure is important and will be discussed later.

A comparison of the ads in *Variety* directed to the exhibitor with the press book campaign designed for the public reveals the same plan at work. Exhibitor ads, however, play up box office figures, which we can interpret as a ploy to stabilize demand and to establish price.

Advertising strategy carried over into exploitation. Consisting of publicity stunts, contests, and feature stories for newspapers and magazines, exploitation was aimed at the public exclusively. A campaign began concurrent with the release of a new picture and attempted to generate immediate interest in the star. The goal, as stated earlier, was to funnel audiences into the more profitable first-run theaters. Like advertising, exploitation concentrated on the star's differentiation and reflected changes in audience response.

For *Cabin in the Cotton* and *Ex-Lady*, the campaigns emphasize

52. *Bordertown* press book.
53. *Dangerous* press book.
54. Ibid.

Davis' glamour. Feature stories discuss her makeup and low-cut gowns. A contest proposes designing dresses for "the alluring Miss Davis."[55] With *Bordertown* the focus is now on the vamp. One article begins with the information that Davis is the manwrecker from *Bondage* and then reports that Davis is ignoring her husband![56] The campaign for *Dangerous* becomes even more imaginative. Originally titled *Hard Luck Dame*, the picture was changed to *Dangerous*, presumably to capitalize on Davis as a "dangerous woman."[57] We are told that "she turns on the power and blows the fuses." Suggested stunts—the police can write tickets and the fire department plan inspections—should revolve around dangerous situations to exploit Davis behaving dangerously.[58]

To summarize, product differentiation based on the uniqueness of a star functioned as a strategy to stabilize the demand curve for the studio's output. Actions and character traits of the narrative provided the building blocks of differentiation. The correct role for a star was determined by market indicators, and once found, became the basis for constructing mythical accounts of the star's personal life. Through the use of advertising and publicity, the studio said, in effect, come not to see just Bette Davis, but to see Bette Davis who in real life is the personification of her screen role.

The Star and Narrative Structure

As might be expected, star differentiation had a profound effect on narrative structure and the screenwriting process. Classical Hollywood cinema is protagonist centered, and the standard practice was to cast the star as the protagonist. The goals and desires of the protagonist generally motivate the causal logic of the action and, consequently, the structure of the narrative, the components of which included plot, the behavior of the characters in their relationship to the star, as well as the settings for the action.[59] Thus, we can see that if the protagonist was constructed by the traits and actions of star differentiation, then the narrative was structured by the star.

Structuring a narrative around a star played a crucial role in the

---

55. *Cabin in the Cotton* press book.
56. *Bordertown* press book.
57. "In Production," *Variety*, August 21, 1935, p. 38.
58. *Dangerous* press book.
59. Stephen Heath, "Film and System: Terms of Analysis Part Two," *Screen* 16 (Summer 1975): 101; see also David Bordwell and Kristin Thompson, *Film Art: An Introduction* (Reading, Mass.: Addison Wesley, 1979), pp. 50–58.

production process by providing a framework to standardize and reproduce a star's pictures. Davis' vamp pictures typically contain a triangle consisting of Bette the vamp, a passive man (either her husband or fiancé), and the other man. As a passive counterpart to the bad Bette, they also contain a "good woman." Davis usually seduces and destroys one of the men; sometimes she destroys both. In propelling the action, Davis is the active agent who controls events. If another character (usually a man) threatens her control, she kills him.

Take *Dangerous*, for example. In the opening, we are introduced to Don Bellows, a successful young architect, on the way up. He has a warm and supportive fiancée ("the good woman") and leads an orderly if not contented life. Out on the town one evening, Don chances on a down-and-out alcoholic actress in a honky-tonk nightclub. It's Bette Davis. From here on, the logic of causality is set into motion as Davis becomes an angel of destruction. Don is immediately attracted to her. (Except for the ending, we see Davis only when Don goes to her, a narrative technique that suggests her powers of ensnarement.) Davis gets dead drunk; out of compassion, Don invites her to his country home for rest and rehabilitation. Davis thereupon sets out to manipulate the relationship; she lies about being unmarried and becomes the sexual aggressor. Once under her control, Don neglects his business, his career, and his fiancée. His formerly neat appearance degenerates into dishabille, as he loses one by one his job, his social standing, and his reputation. To underscore that Don is not an isolated case but part of a pattern, we learned from the outset that Davis is a jinx who has devastated many a man: she is dangerous. Cut to Davis' destitute husband. Formerly the president of his company, he is a bookkeeper living in a tenement, his downfall also caused by the fatal attraction to Davis. And when he interferes with Davis' plans by refusing to grant her a divorce, she attempts to kill him. This pattern of actions is repeated (with variations) in *Beyond the Forest, The Letter, In This Our Life,* and *Deception,* among others.

In addition to actions and characters, narrative settings are also affected by the presence of the star. In Davis' case, they often function to constrain her actions. For example, the antebellum era and mores established in *Jezebel,* and the suffocating small town in *Beyond the Forest* operate to repress Davis' desires, thus causing her to act against this confinement.

If the presence of a star made for standardized plots, it also simplified character development. In a conventional well-made narrative, character traits are revealed by the actions of the character as the drama unfolds. However, in Davis' pictures, characterization *precedes* narrative actions. Before Davis even appears on the screen in the above-mentioned pictures, the audience is informed that her character is contrary, hard to handle, and restless. Invoking these traits connects Davis to her previous roles and to published descriptions of her personality. It also creates expectations as to how the action will progress. In *The Letter*, Davis' mere presence in the picture establishes a certain probability. As the film opens, Davis empties a gun into a man at close range as he staggers down the veranda stairs. No motivation is provided, but we presume that the audience is familiar with the Davis persona and can accept her killing a man outright (see illus. 7).

This function of the star as a structural element of the narrative is confirmed by Rolf Rilla in his book on the contemporary practices of the day, *The Writer and the Screen*. Rilla says the main job of the screenwriter is to create vehicles for a star. Accordingly, the screenwriter had to be cognizant of the star's idiosyncratic traits (i.e., differentiation) and incorporate them into the characterization. A description of these traits could be drawn from the studio's publicity department and from scripts of previous productions. Lead roles had to conform to the code of screen conventions (the expectations of star differentiation) associated with the star. "Whatever the story of the film, character and relationships have to be explored along well es-

7. The outright murder in *The Letter*

tablished channels," says Rilla, who goes on to say that "the ability to permutate familiar situations is an essential prerequisite of the craft."[60]

The Practice of Offcasting

Permutating familiar situations for Davis extended into the practice of offcasting, which meant performing a role opposite from her differentiated image. For example, in *The Great Lie*, Davis was cast as the good woman instead of the vamp. However, the ads for this film *still* refer to Davis as the vamp. The copy reads, "*contrary* to the former Davis pattern, Bette Davis' new film does not find her killing anyone or acting nasty."[61] Similarly, an ad for *All This and Heaven Too*, another picture in which Davis is offcast, and ad shows a photo of Davis as the vamp from *Jezebel* (see illus. 8 and 9).

Offcasting is linked to two interrelated economic imperatives: the efficient deployment of resources (scale economies) and product variation. The law of scale economies states that the more units produced, the lower the cost per unit. Scale economies are related to the high overhead expense of employing stars. Davis' contract for 1942 specified a minimum salary of $200,000.[62] If Davis played in several films, the studio could amortize the expense. That's exactly what happened. In 1942, Warner starred her in three pictures, diffusing her salary to the per unit cost of $66,000.

If star salaries meant more pictures, then the output had to be varied. After all, would an audience pay to see Bette Davis in three vamp films in one year? Enter the practice of offcasting. With this practice, the studio diversified the traits of its product while at the same time invoking the familiar expectations associated with star differentiation. In other words, the picture was the same, but different. Offcasting became an important means to extend the box office potential of a star. Bette Davis was typically offcast as the good woman. In such films as *The Great Lie, Now, Voyager, The Old Maid,* and *All This and Heaven Too,* she is the active agent who attempts to neutralize the evil of a bad woman. Davis acts contrary to her former pattern. Instead of Davis as "manwrecker," it is the other woman in the film (usually the male character's wife) who is destroying the man. (Although the bad wife does not appear in *Now, Voyager,* we see the results of her

60. Rolf Rilla, *The Writer and the Screen* (London: W. H. Allen; 1973), p. 71.
61. Bette Davis file.
62. Bette Davis contract, August 17, 1938, Legal Files of Warner Bros. Story Purchase Department, WCFTR.

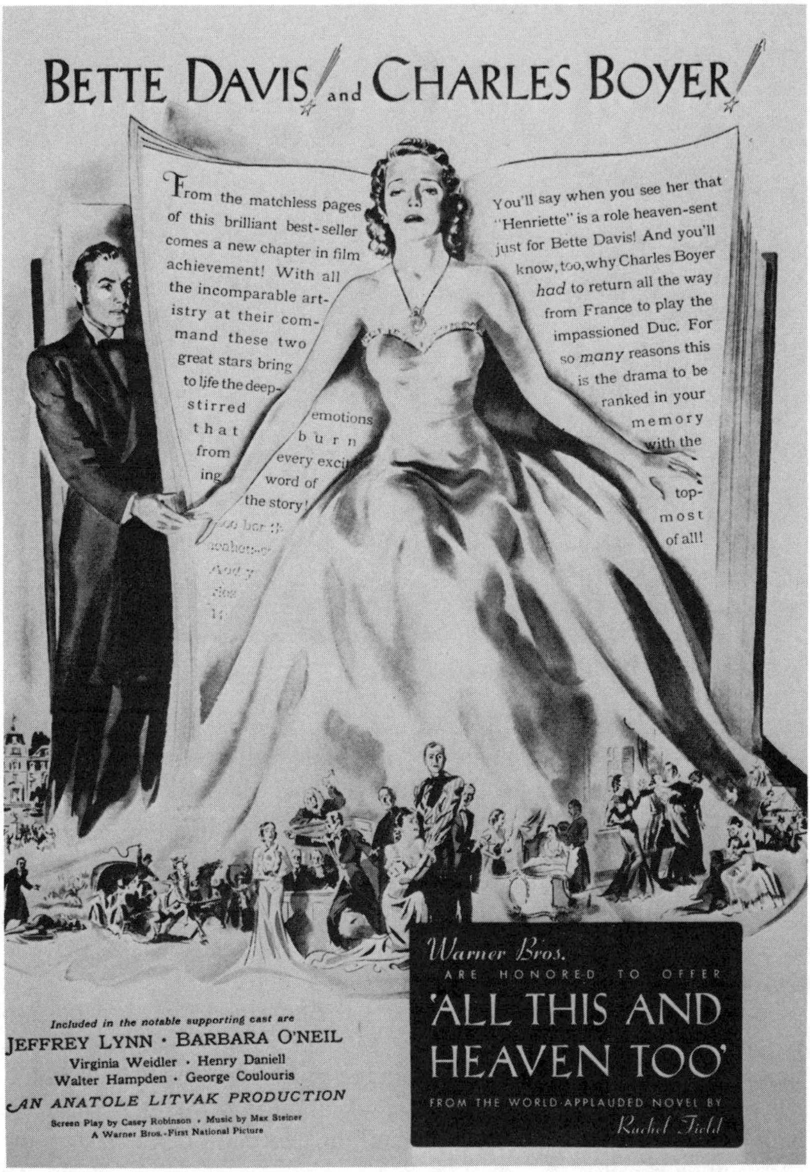

8. Different roles, same dress

9. Davis offcast as "the nurturer"

neglect in the lives of her husband and child.) Davis the compassionate nurturing woman is supportive of the male, but because she is honorable, refuses to break up the marriage. Then the male is eliminated from the plot, usually leaving behind a child. In the absence of the male, the structure shifts to the opposition of the two women. Who will become the "true" wife/mother of the husband/child? Davis, comporting herself according to the standards of the good woman, wins and finally becomes naturalized as wife/mother, displacing the bad woman.

This structure varies to encompass the combinations and permutations of Bette's image. In *A Stolen Life*, for example, she plays identical twins, both the good woman and the bad woman. In *Dark Victory*, her role of Judith Traherne is an amalgamation of the good and the bad. However varied, her roles play off the expectations created by the vamp image.

The experiment to offcast Davis began in 1937 with *That Certain Woman*; "She's a lady," we are told. The picture ranked number six at the box office for Warner that year, good enough to start a trend. Thereafter, the company alternated her roles. In 1940, Davis starred as the vamp in *The Letter* and the good woman in *All This and Heaven*

Too. In 1941 and 1942, she played the former role in *The Little Foxes* (on loan to Sam Goldwyn) and *In This Our Life,* and the latter in *The Great Lie* and *Now, Voyager.* All were top money earners.[63]

Off casting not only provided the variation to sustain audience interest, but also served to enhance the image of the star as a great performer. Portraying only one type of character made the star vulnerable to charges that she wasn't acting but "just being herself." (Of course, the industry wanted the audience to believe that Davis was her character, but not at the expense of casting doubt on her acting expertise.) However, once the studio offcast the star it could claim, "There are as many Bette Davises as there are Bette Davis-starring pictures! That's part of Miss Davis' greatness: the ability to make each character she plays stand by itself, a distinct and memorable triumph of screen acting."[64]

The Contract Controls

The function of the star system in the marketplace should now be clear. It is understandable therefore that the industry required a means of controlling the image of the star at the production level. The option contract did the job. This was a legal document that specified in standard clauses the conditions of employment. The term of the contract varied, but for important stars, it was usually seven years. In practice, the contract tied the star to the studio, but it was not reciprocal. The studio reserved the right of either dropping or renewing the contract every year. If the option were picked up, the star received an increase in salary as previously specified. This clause ruled out the possibility of a star's renegotiating his or her contract to capitalize on a sudden surge of popularity.

Other conditions were equally restrictive. The option contract gave the studio *exclusive* rights to a star's services. An actor agreed "to act, sing, pose, speak or perform in such roles as the producer may designate." If the star refused an assignment, the studio could sue for damages and extend the contract to make up for the stoppage. The contract also gave the studio control of the star's name and likeness in all matters relating to advertising and publicity. Prohibited from hiring a personal press agent, a star had to comply with the wishes of the studio's publicity department in matters relating to interviews,

63. Box office statistics from Nick Roddick, *A New Deal in Entertainment: Warner Brothers in the 1930s* (London: British Film Institute, 1983).

64. *The Corn is Green* Advertisement, *Motion Picture Herald* 159 (July 1945): 3.

public appearances, and image making. In short, the option contract gave the studio complete control over the image of the star.

An examination of Bette Davis' employment contracts at Warner reveals that she earned more money as her star ascended, but not more control over her work.[65] In joining the studio in 1931, she signed a standard player's contract and started out with a salary of $400 per week. The term was five years, renewable every six months for the first year and yearly thereafter, a provision that allowed the studio to dump her fast if it had made a mistake.

Of Human Bondage won her a new contract in 1934, just three years into the first. Acclaim brought only minor concessions from the studio, however; a raise in salary to $1,350 per week from $1,000 and feature billing.

Davis did not receive star billing until 1938. Now at the pinnacle of her career, she was rewarded in her third contract with a beginning salary of $3,500 per week. But the contract was also more restrictive by explicitly detailing her duties to the studio. Davis had to "perform and render her services whenever, wherever and as often as the producer requested." Significantly, these services included interviews, sittings for photographs, and the rest of the elements the studio could orchestrate in its differentiation strategy.

Subsequent contracts gave Davis more money and set a limit on the number of pictures she was required to make, but not much else. She never did earn the right to choose her roles or to have a say in her publicity. On the contrary, as Davis' name grew larger on theater marquees, the studio consolidated more control over her career.

Conclusion

As this case study demonstrates, the star functioned in a dual capacity for the film industry: to differentiate the product and to provide a framework for standardizing production. The strategy alleviated pricing difficulties in marketing motion pictures by creating an inelastic demand curve enabling the producer to charge higher prices for his product and to maximize profits. To maintain this function, the legal, advertising, publicity, and screenwriting departments of the studio were pressed into service. But this study describes more than marketing strategy; it suggests how the economic imperatives of the industry shaped the very nature of the product itself.

65. The Bette Davis contracts with Warner are dated December 24, 1931; December 27, 1934; August 17, 1938; June 7, 1943; February 4, 1946; January 27, 1949. Legal Files of Warner Bros. Story Purchase Department, WCFTR.

The Production Code

15

RUTH A. INGLIS

Self-Regulation in Operation

Like censorship or the operation of any mature judicial system, self-regulation involves an authoritative basis, a written code, administrative agencies, and a body of precedents interpreting the code.

The authority for self-regulation is implied in the legal articles of incorporation of the original Motion Picture Producers and Distributors of America, wherein it is stated: "The object for which the Association is created is to foster the common interests of those engaged in the motion picture industry in the United States

"by establishing and maintaining the highest possible moral and artistic standards in motion picture production;

"by developing the educational as well as the entertainment value and general usefulness of the motion picture;

"by diffusing accurate and reliable information with reference to the industry;

"by reforming abuses relative to the industry, by securing freedom from unjust or unlawful exactions, and by other lawful and proper means."

The Motion Picture Production Code and the Advertising Code are interpreted and applied by the Production Code Administration and the Advertising Advisory Council (sometimes called the Advertising Code Administration). Since June 1934, when the PCA was established officially under the direction of Joseph I. Breen, several amendments

Abridged by the editor from *Freedom of the Movies* (Chicago: University of Chicago Press, 1947), pp. 126–171.

have been passed and a body of cases interpreting the code has accumulated.

The Form and General Principles of the Code

Terry Ramsaye, the movie historian, has called the code "the motion picture industry's Magna Charta of official decency." Fundamentally, the complete code is a moralistic document. The word "moral" or its derivatives appears in it twenty-six times. Valuative terms like "sin," "evil," "bad," "right," and "good" appear frequently. Although divine law is mentioned only once, the language and reasoning of the code belong to moral philosophy rather than to social science.

In the "Preamble" the producers acknowledge and accept the public responsibilities associated with the control of motion pictures. At the same time they ask the public and public leaders for sympathetic understanding of the problems involved and for their cooperation in solving them.

The basic premise of the code is that the movies as entertainment and as art affect the moral life of a people. Although it is admitted that art in itself may be "unmoral," art as a product of a person's mind and as an influence upon those who come in contact with it is claimed to have "a deep moral significance." No proof is offered. The movies are charged with a special moral responsibility because of their wide appeal and peculiarly persuasive and effective qualities, which transcend those of books, plays, or newspapers. The radio is not mentioned. The code summarizes the point in the "Reasons Supporting the Preamble" as follows:

"In general, the mobility, popularity, accessibility, emotional appeal, vividness, straight-forward presentation of fact in the film make for more intimate contact with a larger audience and for greater emotional appeal.

"Hence the larger moral responsibilities of the motion pictures."

Three general principles are enunciated:

"1. No picture shall be produced which will lower the moral standards of those who see it. Hence the sympathy of the audience shall never be thrown to the side of crime, wrong-doing, evil or sin.

"2. Correct standards of life, subject only to the requirements of drama and entertainment, shall be presented.

"3. Law, natural or human, shall not be ridiculed, nor shall sympathy be created for its violation."

The first and third principles have similar implications and corollaries. Wrongdoing is not outlawed from the screen. Crime must not be presented alluringly, however, although sympathy for sinners is permitted. The important thing is that the distinction between right and wrong must never be blurred. No final source of authority for right and wrong is given except the specific prohibitions in the "Particular Applications." Fiction is frequently concerned with conflicting values and situations in which the choice between good and evil is not sharply defined. One might wonder if such plots do not present baffling problems in interpreting the general principles of the code.'The PCA has made no complaint.

The concept of "natural law" expressed in the third principle is, in our times, one which is more or less peculiar to the Catholic church. It does not mean that "natural" scientific laws like the law of gravitation may not be ridiculed, as Walt Disney cartoons frequently do. Rather, it is understood as a moral imperative. "By natural law is understood the law which is written in the hearts of all mankind, the great underlying principles of right and justice dictated by conscience." On the other hand, "human law" refers to "the law written by civilized nations." A significant corollary is: "The courts of the land should not be presented as unjust. This does not mean that a single court may not be represented as unjust, much less that a single court official may not be presented this way. But the court system of the country must not suffer as a result of this presentation."

The second principle constitutes one of the few positive sections of the code. It is a plea for using the film as a "powerful natural force for the improvement of mankind." The phrase "subject only to the requirements of drama and entertainment" provides latitude for the presentation of evil, which is made permissible by the commentary on the first and third principles. Later, in a section which logically belongs with the discussion of general principles, a distinction is drawn between sins which repel the normal audience and those which attract. The former—"murder, most theft, many legal crimes, lying, hypocrisy, cruelty, etc."—are less difficult to present unattractively, and the chief danger is that the young and impressionable may become hardened to them. Attractive sins like "sex sins, sins and crimes of apparent heroism, such as banditry, daring thefts, leadership in evil, organized crime, revenge, etc.," require more careful attention.

There follows a noteworthy statement to the effect that if it were possible to have theaters catering exclusively to mature audiences, greater freedom could be allowed. This is consistent with the basic premise that part of the need for regulating the content of films arises because they are a mass medium available to children as well as to adults. The possibility of a system of graded theaters will concern us later. For the present, we need note only the reasonable attitude which is taken. Granted the basic premises which are adopted, the rationale of the code is logical and the moral demands are temperate. Let us turn now to the specific rules and regulations embodied in the code.

Particular Applications

In contrast to the philosophical origin of the section on principles, the practical provisions of the code were empirically derived. They prohibit the kinds of content which, over the years, have caused trouble for the industry.

"PARTICULAR APPLICATIONS" OF THE CODE

I. CRIMES AGAINST THE LAW

These shall never be presented in such a way as to throw sympathy with the crime as against law and justice or to inspire others with a desire for imitation.

1. *Murder*
   a) The technique of murder must be presented in a way that will not inspire imitation.
   b) Brutal killings are not to be presented in detail.
   c) Revenge in modern times shall not be justified.

2. *Methods of crime* should not be explicitly presented.
   a) Theft, robbery, safecracking, and dynamiting of trains, mines, buildings, etc., should not be detailed in method.
   b) Arson must be subject to the same safeguards.
   c) The use of firearms should be restricted to essentials.
   d) Methods of smuggling should not be presented.

3. *The illegal drug traffic* must not be portrayed in such a way as to stimulate curiosity concerning the use of, or traffic in, such drugs; nor shall scenes be approved which show the use of illegal drugs, or their effects, in detail (as amended September 11, 1946).

4. *The use of liquor* in American life, when not required by the plot or for proper characterization, will not be shown.

II. SEX

The sanctity of the institution of marriage and the home shall be upheld. Pictures shall not infer that low forms of sex relationship are the accepted or common thing.

1. *Adultery and illicit sex*, sometimes necessary plot material, must not be explicitly treated or justified, or presented attractively.

2. *Scenes of passion*
   a) These should not be introduced except where they are definitely essential to the plot.
   b) Excessive and lustful kissing, lustful embraces, suggestive postures and gestures are not to be shown.
   c) In general, passion should be treated in such manner as not to stimulate the lower and baser emotions.
3. *Seduction or rape*
   a) These should never be more than suggested, and then only when essential for the plot. They must never be shown by explicit method.
   b) They are never the proper subject for comedy.
4. *Sex perversion* or any inference to it is forbidden.
5. *White slavery* shall not be treated.
6. *Miscegenation* (sex relationship between the white and black races) is forbidden.
7. *Sex hygiene* and venereal diseases are not proper subjects for theatrical motion pictures.
8. Scenes of *actual childbirth*, in fact or in silhouette, are never to be presented.
9. *Children's sex organs* are never to be exposed.

III. VULGARITY

The treatment of low, disgusting, unpleasant, though not necessarily evil, subjects should be guided always by the dictates of good taste and a proper regard for the sensibilities of the audience.

IV. OBSCENITY

Obscenity in word, gesture, reference, song, joke, or by suggestion (even when likely to be understood only by part of the audience) is forbidden.

V. PROFANITY (as amended November 1, 1939)

Pointed profanity and every other profane or vulgar expression, however used, is forbidden.

No approval by the Production Code Administration shall be given to the use of words and phrases in motion pictures including, but not limited to, the following: Alley cat (applied to a woman); bat (applied to a woman); broad (applied to a woman); Bronx cheer (the sound); chippie; cocotte; God, Lord, Jesus, Christ (unless used reverently); cripes; fanny; fairy (in a vulgar sense); finger (the); fire, cries of; Gawd; goose (in a vulgar sense); "hold your hat" or "hats"; hot (applied to a woman); "in your hat"; louse; lousy; Madam (relating to prostitution); nance; nerts, nuts (except when meaning crazy); pansy;

razzberry (the sound); slut (applied to a woman); S.O.B.; son-of-a; tart; toilet gags; tom cat (applied to a man); traveling salesman and farmer's daughter jokes; whore, damn, hell (excepting when the use of said last two words shall be essential and required for portrayal, in proper historical context, of any scene or dialogue based upon historical fact or folklore, or for the presentation in proper literary context of a Biblical, or other religious quotation, or a quotation from a literary work provided that no such use shall be permitted which is intrinsically objectionable or offends good taste).

In the administration of Section V of the Production Code, the Production Code Administration may take cognizance of the fact that the following words and phrases are obviously offensive to the patrons of motion pictures in the United States and more particularly to the patrons of motion pictures in foreign countries: Chink, Dago, Frog, Greaser, Hunkie, Kike, Nigger, Spig, Wop, Yid.

  VI. COSTUME
    1. *Complete nudity* is never permitted. This includes nudity in fact or in silhouette, or any licentious notice thereof by other characters in the pictures.
    2. *Undressing scenes* should be avoided and never used save where essential to the plot.
    3. *Indecent or undue exposure* is forbidden.
    4. *Dancing costumes* intended to permit undue exposure or indecent movements in the dance are forbidden.

  VII. DANCES
    1. Dances suggesting or representing sexual actions or indecent passion are forbidden.
    2. Dances which emphasize indecent movements are to be regarded as obscene.

  VIII. RELIGION
    1. No film or episode may throw *ridicule* on any religious faith.
    2. *Ministers of religion* in their character as ministers of religion should not be used as comic characters or as villains.
    3. *Ceremonies* of any definite religion should be carefully and respectfully handled.

  IX. LOCATIONS
    The treatment of bedrooms must be governed by good taste and delicacy.

X. NATIONAL FEELINGS
   1. *The use of the flag* shall be consistently respectful.
   2. *The history*, institutions, prominent people and citizenry of all nations shall be represented fairly.
XI. TITLES
   Salacious, indecent, or obscene titles shall not be used.
XII. REPELLENT SUBJECTS
   The following subjects must be treated within the careful limits of good taste:
   1. *Actual hangings* or electrocutions as legal punishments for crime.
   2. *Third-degree* methods.
   3. *Brutality* and possible gruesomeness.
   4. *Branding* of people or animals.
   5. *Apparent cruelty* to children or animals.
   6. *The sale of women*, or a woman selling her virtue.
   7. *Surgical operations.*

Enforcement and the Production Code Administration

On July 15, 1934, Joseph I. Breen was put in complete control of the administration of the code, the old Studio Relations Department having become officially the Production Code Administration. It became mandatory for member companies and those using the distribution or exhibition facilities of member companies to have their pictures passed by the PCA. The old system of handling appeals through the Hollywood Production Committee was abolished; henceforth all appeals were heard in New York City by the board of directors of the Motion Picture Producers and Distributors Association.

The "Resolution for Uniform Interpretation" as amended June 13, 1934, outlined the procedures of self-regulation as follows:

"1. When requested by production managers, the Motion Picture Producers & Distributors of America, Incorporated, shall secure any facts, information or suggestions concerning the probable reception of stories or the manner in which in its opinion they may best be treated.

"2. That each production manager shall submit in confidence a copy of each or any script to the Production Code Administration. . . . Such Production Code Administration will give the production manager for his guidance such confidential advice and suggestions as experience, research, and information indicate, designating wherein in its judgment the script departs from the provisions of the Code, or wherein from experience or knowledge it is believed that exception will be taken to the story or treatment.

"3. Each production manager of a company belonging to the Motion Picture Producers & Distributors of America, Incorporated, and any producer proposing to distribute and/or distributing his picture through the facilities of any member of the Motion Picture Producers & Distributors of America, Incorporated, shall submit to such Production Code Administration every picture he produces before the negative goes to the laboratory for printing. Said Production Code Administration, having seen the picture, shall inform the production manager in writing whether in its opinion the picture conforms or does not conform to the Code, stating specifically wherein either by theme, treatment or incident, the picture violates the provisions of the Code. In such latter event, the picture shall not be released until the changes indicated by the Production Code Administration have been made; provided, however, that the production manager may appeal from such opinion of said Production Code Administration, so indicated in writing, to the Board of Directors of the Motion Picture Producers & Distributors of America, Incorporated, whose finding shall be final, and such production manager and company shall be governed accordingly."

It is odd that neither the code nor the "Resolution for Uniform Interpretation" included any reference to penalties for violations of the code. Conformance would seem to be of a miraculously voluntary nature. The official "Foreword" of the code as it was released in the 1945–46 *Motion Picture Almanac* states:

"This service is rendered and this work conducted on a purely voluntary basis. No one is compelled to produce motion pictures in accordance with the Code regulations. No attempt is made to force producers to accept the service of the Production Code Administration. As a result, however, of almost fifteen years of day-by-day operations, during which time more than six thousand feature-length motion pictures and twice as many short-subject films, have been serviced by the Code Administration, there is evident on all sides, a ready disposition to conform to the regulations of the Code and to be guided in large measure by the judgment and experience of its administrators."

Where was the "ready disposition to conform" in 1932 and 1933? It would have averted the boycott by the Legion of Decency.

The $25,000 fine, which was the capstone of the machinery for self-regulation, has never been publicized by the MPPDA. Even when the resolutions regarding the fines for violating the production and advertising codes were passed, no official announcement was made. Whether intentional or not, news about the fines took the form of an open secret in the trade.

Specifically, the $25,000 fine was for producing, distributing, or exhibiting a picture lacking the approval of the Production Code Administration. This meant that noncode pictures could not be exhibited in theaters owned or controlled by MPPDA members. In view of the strength of the members of the MPPDA in the distribution and exhibition branches of the industry, the power of enforcing the code by means of such a measure is readily apparent.

Since March 30, 1942, the $25,000 fine has applied to production and distribution only, not to exhibition. The organization made no official statement on the subject at the time, but the following appears in the *Motion Picture Almanac* for 1944–45:

"Pictures approved by the P.C.A. are awarded a certificate. Through an amendment, enacted in 1942, of an earlier resolution, member companies of the Association are no longer in an agreement not to present in their theaters films which do not bear a 'Code Certificate.' Member companies, however, are pledged to maintain in their theaters moral and policy standards as exemplified in the Production Code and accompanying regulations."

In other words, noncode films would be acceptable in member theaters if they were as pure as films passed by the PCA. As yet, the independent producers have not adopted a code of their own or established an agency to administer it similar to that of the MPPDA. But if they should, and if the pictures were morally unobjectionable, presumably a member of the MPPDA could show them in his theaters without fear of penalty for having violated the code agreement of 1934. This legalistic distinction might spell the difference between conviction and acquittal for the MPPDA in any possible future antitrust case.

Until September 1946, the Amendment of 1942 made no practical difference because the change was not generally known in the industry. But when the code seal was withdrawn from *The Outlaw* because of violations of the Advertising Code, the Motion Picture Association [in 1945 the MPPDA became the Motion Picture Association of America—Ed.], according to *Variety* for September 11, 1946, released a statement that exhibitors "are under no obligation not to show the picture and no liability will attach if they do so." Some affiliated theaters played *The Outlaw*. The Amendment unquestionably weakened the enforcement mechanism of self-regulation.

The $25,000 fine has never been invoked. Or, if it has, that fact has not been made public. There may have been occasional violations. The magnitude and nature of the business make it likely that some major movie house during the last ten years has used a bootleg film for a day or two to fill in between major bookings, but there has been no policing of theaters to see if occasional bootlegging goes on. Nevertheless, it is safe to assert that, by and large, noncode films have not been exhibited to the theaters of MPAA members in the past.

Films passed by the PCA constitute the vast majority of the commercial entertainment motion pictures exhibited in the United States. Nontheatrical films, of course, are not included. Newsreels are not regulated by the PCA, but it handles all other kinds of short subjects. The few commercial films not coming under the purview of the PCA are of two kinds. The domestic variety is deliberately produced to violate the provisions of the code, this fact frequently being advertised in the lobby displays of the cheap theaters of the sex circuit where such pictures are exhibited. Others are foreign films, some of a similar cheap type but some of high artistic merit, which are exhibited in special theaters. The foreign films which have distribution in the movie houses of MPAA members must be approved by the PCA. In his annual report for 1938, Will Hays, president of the MPPDA, estimated that "approximately 98 per cent of all the pictures exhibited on the screens of America last year were submitted to and approved by this agency of the Association."

The PCA is financed separately from the other activities of the MPAA. A fee is charged for the services rendered in connection with each picture. The schedule of fees has never been made public, but it is based upon the total production cost of the pictures, the fee for expensive pictures being more than the fee for the less costly ones. The charge for short subjects is considerably less than for feature productions. The fee is the same no matter how many scripts are submitted. No charge is made for pictures which are rejected. Currently, foreign pictures are serviced for one-half the fee which would be charged for a domestic production in the same cost category. Within the United States, MPAA members and nonmembers are treated strictly alike so far as fees are concerned. However, if the PCA ever runs a deficit, the members must make it up. The small independent companies are a nuisance because they occasionally go bankrupt, owing fees to the PCA.

Self-Regulation of Advertising, Titles, and Newsreels

Shortly after the adoption of the Production Code in 1930, the directors of the MPPDA adopted an advertising code which set forth the following principles:

    1. We subscribe to the Code of Business Ethics of the International Advertising Association, based on "truth, honesty and integrity."

2. Good taste shall be the guiding rule of motion picture advertising.
3. Illustrations and text in advertising shall faithfully represent the pictures themselves.
4. No false or misleading statements shall be used directly, or implied by type arrangements or by distorted quotations.
5. No text or illustration shall ridicule or tend to ridicule any religion or religious faith; no illustration of a character in clerical garb shall be shown in any but a respectful manner.
6. The history, institutions and nationals of all countries shall be represented with fairness.
7. Profanity and vulgarity shall be avoided.
8. Pictorial and copy treatment of officers of the law shall not be of such a nature as to undermine their authority.
9. Specific details of crime, inciting imitation, shall not be used.
10. Motion picture advertisers shall bear in mind the provision of the Production Code that the use of liquor in American life shall be restricted to the necessities of characterization and plot.
11. Nudity with meretricious purpose, and salacious postures, shall not be used.
12. Court actions relating to censoring of pictures, or other censorship disputes, are not to be capitalized in advertising.

The Agreement for Uniform Interpretation states that all advertising copy is to be submitted to the MPAA and that disapproved material shall not be used. In cases of disagreement between the publicity director of a company and the Advertising Code Administration, the final decision is to be made by the president of the MPAA. As with the Production Code, the penalty for violations is not mentioned. However, in March 1935, the MPPDA adopted a resolution establishing a fine of not less than $1,000 or more than $5,000 for violation of the Advertising Code. Fines have been levied less than half-a-dozen times during the last ten years.

The work of the Advertising Code Administration (ACA) has received the hearty cooperation of most of the industry. Quickly realizing the danger of sensational advertising and publicity, most studios took individual steps to avoid it shortly after the creation of the Hays organization in 1922. It is revealing that the Legion of Decency made little complaint against movie advertising in 1934.

The Advertising Code Administration was directed by John J. McCarthy, a veteran motion picture advertising man, until his death in 1937. Gordon White is now the director, and, as always, the men connected with this work are experienced in the ways of motion picture exploitation. Offices are maintained in Hollywood and New York City, and rapid service is given. Frequently material is brought in by messengers, and a judgment is given while they wait. All material is submitted in triplicate, one copy being returned to the studio, one being kept by the office which handles it, whether in Hollywood or in New York, and the third being sent to the other office. Thus the two offices keep in close touch with each other.

Proportionately, the number of revisions and rejections of advertising and publicity is remarkably small. In a twelve-year period more than 97 per cent of the material received immediate approval.

In supervising advertising and publicity at its source, the ACA uses the most practical but not the most effective means of control. Although the exhibitor usually relies upon what is furnished by the studio, he may change the material or use his own. The exhibitor's own copy may contravene the Advertising Code. In order that the public may not confuse the advertising of the sex circuit theaters with that of the members of the MPAA, there are unwritten agreements or informal arrangements with many newspapers that unsuitable motion picture advertising will not be accepted.

Although not mentioned by the Advertising Code, the ACA and the PCA cooperate to prevent advertising in pictures. This is a matter of policy on the part of the major companies. Some advertising in films is inevitable, as it would be both costly and unrealistic for the studios to make artificial props of typewriters, automobiles, and other common articles. Although occasionally high-pressure publicists for national products try to inject their sponsors' wares into films and at times bribe studio employees to achieve their ends, every effort is made to avoid unnecessary close-ups of radios and other items showing the name of the product, outdoor scenes showing advertising signs or billboards, and dialogue mentioning trade names. Exhibitors especially are opposed to this kind of advertising. On the other hand, some independent producers do not agree with general industry policy in this matter and prominently display advertised products in their films. Walter Wanger's *Scarlet Street* is a recent example.

The Production Code provides that "salacious, indecent, or obscene titles shall not be used." To prevent the simultaneous use of identical or harmfully similar titles of motion pictures and to establish priorities, the Title Registration Bureau was established in 1925. Ten years later the bureau also assumed the function of preventing the use of morally unacceptable titles. Fewer than 1 percent of the new titles are rejected. Examples of rejected titles are *Killing Is Convenient, The Hell You Say, Ten Little Niggers,* and *Guilty Love.*

The bureau's file of released pictures includes over forty thousand titles, and priority is claimed for approximately eleven thousand titles in its file of unreleased pictures. Controversies are settled by arbitration. The bureau operates an elaborate system of files so that the status of any title can be determined almost instantly.

Newsreels are not mentioned in the Production Code and are exempt from routine PCA regulation. However, a member of the New York staff of the MPAA, Arthur DeBra, attends a showing twice a week of all the major newsreels which are released. He advises the companies regarding any difficulties which he can foresee. They are free to disregard his advice, but their desire to avoid trouble encourages them to take advantage of his wide experience with the reactions of public groups. The fact that certain subjects are always handled with care indicates that some more or less informal self-regulation exists. For example, even during political campaigns, the lameness of President Roosevelt was never clearly shown. As a matter of fact, the managers of the different newsreels are known to cooperate closely in production problems, and they probably have some kind of gentleman's agreement which has never been made public. Nevertheless, the newsreels have avoided the systematic control characteristic of other theatrical films.

Now that we have described all the aspects of self-regulation in general terms, a more detailed examination of the Production Code Administration is in order.

The Structure and Functions of the PCA

The headquarters of the Production Code Administration are located in the MPAA offices in Hollywood. A smaller branch in the New York office handles films which are produced in the eastern area. The staff consists of a director and a corps of approximately ten assistants, seven or eight in Hollywood and two or three in New York. Usually the assistants are young men with some experience in the industry; a few, but not all, are Catholic.

The director of the PCA is Joseph Ignatius Breen, a former Catholic newspaperman who became interested in the industry through Martin Quigley. Before the Legion of Decency campaign he was on the MPPDA staff in a subordinate capacity. To meet the crisis brought about by the Legion, Breen was given the opportunity to administer the code. He replaced Dr. James Wingate, a former New York motion picture censor who had assumed Colonel Joy's position as head of the old Studio Relations Department when the latter resigned to accept an executive position in the industry. The lack of effective means of enforcing the code made it impossible for either the persuasive charm of Joy or the stern demands of Wingate to achieve success. Breen had the approval of the Catholics and the enforced cooperation of the industry. To a remarkable degree, he has maintained the confidence and respect of both groups.

No small measure of Breen's success is attributable to his personality. Opinions may differ as to the influence of Mr. Breen on motion pictures, but it is clear that he has a peculiar combination of qualities which are ideal for his position. Because of his fairness, reasonableness, and courage, he commands a position of respect among the producers. He is generally liked as an honest, witty Irishman, whose enjoyment of life disqualifies him for the usual censor stereotype. He knows the business thoroughly and is always eager to offer suggestions to help a producer save a picture. He "walks the streets at night" trying to think up ways to circumvent the code, that is, to preserve both the entertainment and the moral values in pictures. On the other hand, Breen can be tough and is able to oppose the most influential figures in Hollywood.

He operates the PCA as a service organization for the producers. Although technically they are required to submit only final scripts and finished prints of the pictures to the PCA, close cooperation at every point in the production process is to their mutual advantage.

No efficient producer would consider buying the movie rights to a questionable novel or play without consulting the PCA regarding the possibility of making an acceptable movie of it. Members of the staff of the PCA see all New York plays as they open and prepare opinions on their suitability as movie material. A negative opinion means that the play has little chance of reaching the screen without such drastic changes as to make the use of the title virtually a fraud upon the public. The PCA also encourages producers to submit original stories for suggestions and criticisms before the first screen adaptation is written. Decisions are rendered within seventy-two hours.

When each picture first comes to the office, it is assigned to two members of the staff who prepare reactions to it independently. If they disagree, or if the picture is likely to present unusual difficulties, Breen handles it himself. As improved scripts are written, they are submitted so that any necessary changes may be made as early as possible. Although conferences and telephone consultations are frequent, PCA judgments and opinions are transmitted by letter so that there is a written record of the decisions concerning each picture.

In addition to preventing the filming of scenes which would certainly contravene the code, the PCA points out danger spots or scenes which must be filmed with care to avoid objectionable qualities. Sometimes the PCA recommends "protection shots" so that if the original scene proves suggestive or objectionable, the second version of the scene made in another manner may be acceptable. Sometimes "protection shots" are made to facilitate foreign distribution.

In considering scripts, casting is often important to the PCA. Innocent-sounding lines take on additional meaning when spoken by certain actors and actresses. Mae West's invitation to "come up and see me sometime" is a good example. As a means of self-protection, the PCA ends each advisory letter with the reminder that the final decision is given after viewing the finished picture.

During the actual filming of a picture, arrangements are made to have a representative of the PCA on the set while difficult scenes are being shot. Sequences which present problems are discussed and ways of making them acceptable are suggested. All lyrics of songs are checked to make sure that they do not violate the provisions of the code. Some companies also submit dancing costumes, but this is optional.

Final judgment is rendered upon a review of the finished picture. If it is acceptable, a code seal of approval is given. This and the certificate number must appear on the main title of each picture.

The PCA does not keep final scripts, but it does maintain a record of the exact footage of the films which receive the code seal. This, and the fact that Breen's office gets reports on deletions from most censor boards, make it virtually impossible for any producer to change a film after the seal has been given without knowledge of the fact's reaching Breen.

The PCA in Action

Breen and his staff analyze stories with reference to their theme and their details. The acceptability of the theme is judged first. For such evaluative purposes, the theme of a picture can be determined by asking what problem confronts the leading characters and stating how the problem is solved. If the characters find their answers in moral ways, the theme of the picture is usually acceptable. If the characters find it necessary to murder or steal or commit adultery or break some other social taboo or law, the story is unacceptable unless proper compensating moral values and elements of punishment are present.

Three illustrations can be cited. They come from the testimony of Mr. Francis Harmon, now vice-president of the MPAA, before a congressional hearing in 1940 on a bill to prohibit compulsory block booking. They are quotations from letters in the PCA files. The material within the brackets is Mr. Harmon's:

CASE A

[NOTE.—This opinion dated February 28, 1940, addressed to a member producer, seems to have resulted in decision not to proceed with a motion picture based upon this novel. No revision of the objectionable story has been submitted to the Production Code Administration.]

February 28, 1940

MR. ———

ADDRESS ———

DEAR MR. ———:

We have read the novel entitled ———, by ———, which you have been kind enough to submit to us for our judgment, and greatly regret to report that the story, as it stands, is not acceptable from the standpoint of the Production Code, and that a motion picture based upon it would have to be rejected by this office.

The book contains three elements, apparently basic to the present story, which are at the same time basically objectionable under the Code.

(1) The male lead, J———, commits adultery in flagrant fashion. The Code says that adultery as a subject should be avoided. When adultery is absolutely necessary for the plot, there must be ample compensating moral values, in the nature of a strong voice for decency, of pointed suffering, of actual punishment of the guilty. We fail to find these values in the story we have read.

(2) Illegal drug traffic and its effects are portrayed. The Code says that "Illegal drug traffic must never be presented." The reason given is as follows:

"Because of its evil consequences, the drug traffic should not be presented in any form. The existence of the trade should not be brought to the attention of audiences."

You will readily realize that this is a clear-cut prohibition.

(3) J——— commits murder, and there is no indication whatever of any punishment for this crime. While there is no need of showing the process of law, there must be some accounting for the crime.

There are some objectionable minor details which need not be enumerated at this time.

If you can see your way clear to revise this story in its fundamental form, we shall be happy, of course, to consult with you.

Cordially yours,

JOSEPH I. BREEN

CASE B

[NOTE.—Attached letter dated February 15, 1940, submitted by member company. On November 14, 1939, a "synopsis" was submitted and rejected "on the ground that marriage is frivolously treated and both bigamy and adultery are presented without any compensating moral values." These problems were discussed with producer November 16, 1939. A "story treatment" was submitted January 3, 1940, in which some difficulties had been met through plot changes. The attached letter points out additional changes still required . . .]

February 15, 1940

MR. ———

ADDRESS ———

DEAR MR. ———:

We have read the first draft, dated February 12, 1940, of the script for your proposed production titled ———, and regret very much to report that we cannot approve this material in its present form because of the suggestive flavor of the final sequence wherein it is pointedly, and rather crudely indicated that L—— and A—— are going to bed together.

In addition, we direct your attention to the following details:

Page 27: There seems to be an excessive amount of drinking in a number of scenes. Kindly make sure to limit all drinking to a minimum absolutely required for characterization and plot motivation.

Page 37: We presume there will be no suggestive reactions to the playing of "Lets Put Out the Lights and Go to Bed."

Page 79: In order to avoid objectionable innuendo, there must be no break in W——'s line, "I can hardly wait—er—to see Bermuda."

We shall be glad, of course, to examine the revised version of this story. In any event, our final judgment will be based upon our review of the finished picture.

Cordially yours,

JOSEPH I. BREEN

CASE C

[NOTE.—Two very objectionable films, dealing with marijuana were submitted to the Production Code Administration—one in Hollywood, the other in New York. Both were rejected. The attached opinion refers to the film submitted in New York. About 25 thoroughly objectionable films, sold singly rather than in blocks, pollute the stream of distribution and exhibition. Some of these pictures were submitted to, and rejected by the Production Code Administration while others were never submitted. None of these was made by a member of the Motion Picture Production Code Administration.]

June 15, 1938

Re: ———

MESSRS. ———

ADDRESS: ———

GENTLEMEN:

Yesterday afternoon at your request we reviewed your feature picture, ———, to determine its suitability for Certificate of Approval from this Association under the Production Code.

This is to advise you that this film, both in general theme and in detailed treatment, violates numerous provisions of this Code and, therefore, cannot be approved.

You have here the story of a girl who goes to a beach party where purveyors of marijuana and other illegal drugs give her and the other young people present at the party their initial experience with drugs of this harmful character. There are a number of scenes portraying the lustful embraces, suggestive postures, and acts of passion which follow the use of these cigarettes, and, likewise, sequences showing several of the girls undressing and going in swimming in the nude. One of the girls is drowned, and your female lead, as a result of an illicit sex affair with the boy who accompanied her to this party, becomes pregnant. The boy, in an effort to secure money needed to marry her, becomes an employee of the dope ring and is killed by an officer during an attempt to catch a group of smugglers who are illegally bringing into the country a quantity of dope for the ring.

The leaders of the dope ring persuade the girl to leave home to have her baby and getting her into their clutches make her in time their star salesman for dope. Later, through spite, she takes the lead in a scheme to kidnap a child from her sister, only to learn after the child has been snatched that it is her own baby which her sister had adopted. When your lead returns to the gangsters' hideout where the chiid is being held, she is shown first taking a hypodermic injection of dope and then committing suicide—dying a few moments after she enters the hideout and finds the gang leaders in the custody of the law.

One section of the Production Code provides that illegal drug traffic must never be presented. This is the central theme of your story.

Another section of the Code states that illicit sex, "sometimes necessary plot material, must not be explicitly treated, or justified, or presented attractively." A long series of decisions on the part of the Production Code Administration are to the effect that when illicit sex is shown there must be shown also compensating moral values. In our opinion, there are insufficient compensating moral values in this film.

Another section of the Code specifically states that "excessive and lustful kissing, lustful embraces, suggestive postures and gestures, are not to be shown." The sequences where the young men and the girls at the beach party under the influence of drugs are shown rolling around on the floor in one another's arms, exposing their persons unduly and giving play to their passions, seems to us a violation of this section.

Other sections of the Code specifically state that "complete nudity is never permitted" and "indecent or undue exposure is forbidden." Your picture violates these sections in the sequences wherein the girls are shown undressing, running out of the room across the beach sand, and bathing in the ocean in the nude.

Finally, the Association's special regulations re "Crime in Motion Pictures" state that "with reference to the crime of kidnapping * * * such stories are acceptable under the Code only when the kidnapping is (a) not the main theme of the story; (b) the person kidnapped is not a child; (c) there are no details of the crime of kidnapping; (d) no profit accrues to the kidnappers; and (e) where the kidnappers are punished." Since the victim of your kidnapping is a child your story definitely violates item "b" above.

The regulations re Crime likewise state that "suicide, as a solution of problems occurring in the development of screen drama, is to be discouraged as 'morally questionable' and as 'bad theatre' unless absolutely necessary for the development of the plot." Your female lead is guilty of a number of crimes and is shown committing suicide at the end of the picture.

In the light of these plain provisions of the Production Code we have no recourse save to decline to issue the Association's Certificate of Approval for this production. For your further information, you have the right to appeal from this adverse decision of the Production Code Administration to the Board of Directors of this Association. In the event you desire to appeal this decision, you should address a letter to this effect to Will H. Hays, President, Motion Picture Producers and Distributors of America, Inc., 28 West 44th Street, New York City.

Very truly yours,

PRODUCTION CODE ADMINISTRATION
By F. S. HARMON

The term "compensating moral values" is mentioned frequently in the letters. It is a concept which Breen has developed and which is an important factor in his administration of the code. The stupidity of most censorship may be traced to the lack of some such guiding principle. As George Bernard Shaw said, "the censor makes an office list of words that must not be used and subjects that must not be mentioned (usually religion and sex); and though this brings the job within the capacity of an office boy, it also reduces it to an absurdity." Breen has avoided this pitfall, although there is a list of prohibited words and phrases.

Breen has stated that "the compensating moral values are: good characters, the voice of morality, a lesson, regeneration of the transgressor, suffering and punishment." The use of the concept makes easier a practical application of what Breen calls "a cardinal principle of the Code—namely, that *wrong must always be characterized as wrong, and not as something else.* Sin is not a mistake but a shameful transgression. Crime is not an error of frailty but the breaking of the law. Wrong is not pleasant but painful, not heroic but cowardly, not profitable but detrimental, not plausible but deserving of condemnation."

In his testimony Harmon cites the MGM picture *Conquest* as an example of how compensating moral values may make it possible to film otherwise unacceptable themes. His summary of the picture follows:

CASE D

CONQUEST (METRO-GOLDWYN-MAYER) CERTIFICATE NO. 3624

[NOTE.—This picture referred to by name with permission of producer.]

This historical romance (based upon a published novel) of the illicit love affair between Napoleon (Charles Boyer) and Countess Marie Walewska (Greta Garbo) was an outstanding film of 1937–38.

From the standpoint of the production code, the problem was to comply with the section stipulating that "Adultery, sometimes necessary plot material, must not be explicitly treated, or justified, or presented attractively." This film is a LEADING CASE, illustrating the principle, now well established in scores of pictures, that in order for an illicit sex affair not to be "justified" or "presented attractively," the dialogue and action must contain "adequate compensating moral values."

The following "compensating moral values" appeared in the finished picture as the result of constructive collaboration between the producer and the Production Code Administration over a period of more than 2 years during which 51 letter opinions were written, numerous conferences held, and four screenings of the film arranged:

"Compensating moral values"

(1) The day after Napoleon met the beautiful young Polish countess at a ball in Warsaw, and clearly became infatuated with her, two Polish patriots called upon her and her aged husband, suggesting that she yield to any advances Napoleon should make, and thus aid in securing Napoleon's signature to a decree reestablishing Poland as a nation. Dialogue and action were inserted in which the aged husband strongly resented the suggestion and challenged the patriots to a duel for implying that his wife's adultery would be justified on patriotic grounds.

(2) When the countess does go to Napoleon in an effort to secure concessions for her countrymen, the audience sees her start to leave the emperor's room, only to be pulled back by the amorous Napoleon. The surrounding circumstances indicated that she had made a serious effort to secure concessions and at the same time protect her virtue.

(3) When the countess returns home to her husband, after the affair, he condemns her action, refuses to live longer under the same roof with her, and goes at once to Rome where he secures annulment of the marriage.

(4) The next time the countess sees Napoleon she upbraids him for his conduct toward her, thereby establishing the fact that she recognized her own wrongdoing in committing adultery with him.

(5) When the soldier brother of the countess learns that his promotions in Napoleon's army have resulted in part from his sister's illicit affair with the emperor, he comes to see his sister, upbraids her severely, expresses humiliation, and leaves her in fury.

(6) When the countess comes to tell Napoleon that she is going to have a baby by him, the action was so arranged that Napoleon takes the lead in the conversation, and tells her instead of the marriage of state which Tallyrand has arranged for him with Marie Louise of Austria. The audience is made

clearly to understand that the man in the case has taken the woman when it suited his passion and cast her aside when it suited his conveniences. It is clearly indicated that the countess realizes this.

(7) Later when the countess brings her illegitimate son to see Napoleon on Elba, he overhears the little boy saying his prayers and asking God "to bless my father whom I have never seen." Later, the little boy, who has become a hero worshiper of Napoleon, tells him: "Gee, I wish you were my Daddy *** I have never seen my father," thereby heaping coals of fire on the head of the man who brought him into the world under such circumstances that his paternity was unrecognized. This scene constituted a powerful portrayal of the tragedy of illegitimacy.

Thus, through constructive collaboration during production the historical fact of this illicit love was not altered but the surrounding details were so handled as to indicate clearly to theater audiences that such conduct was wrong, that it brought tragedy in its wake, and that innocent persons suffered as a result.

After the acceptability of the central theme has been decided upon, attention is turned to the details of the story. Stories with passable themes may be rejected because of the number of questionable scenes and the amount of unacceptable dialogue. Most pictures have some details which have to be corrected. The great bulk of the work of the PCA is in the nature of giving attention to endless details. Several of the letters presented by Mr. Harmon illustrate that point. (Again, the comments in brackets are his.)

CASE E

[NOTE.—A story treatment of a few pages was submitted January 8 by this nonmember producer who distributes through a member company. Treatment was approved January 10, attention being called to various story points which seemed to require care. The attached opinion relates to suitability of script of a hundred pages or more. Due note was taken of the P.C.A. cautions set forth in this letter and completed film was approved March 18, 1940.]

February 16, 1940

MR. ———

ADDRESS ———

DEAR MR. ———:

We have read the script for your proposed production titled "———," and are happy to report this material seems to meet the requirements of the Production Code.

However, we direct your attention to the following details:

Scenes 32, 35, 36, and 44: Please bear in mind that the Code prohibits the showing of gun battles between criminals and law-enforcing officers. We recommend that a line be inserted to indicate that N—— is trying to shoot the *tires* of the police car and that N's shooting be held to a minimum and that he use but one revolver.

Scene 218: We presume there will be no gruesome details as to the injured boys.

Scene 287: We believe it would be well to have M—— wounded rather than killed by the police and, in Scene 288 contd. Page 130, he would be shown conscious, but perhaps limping, when he gets into the police car. This will change the dialogue at Scene 309 contd. Page 139, from indicating that M—— has been killed to his being wounded.

Scenes 291 *et seq.*: We assume that there will be no unacceptable exposure of A's person.

Scene 311 contd. Page 140: Please amplify L's speech to indicate that G—— has been arrested and will be punished also.

You understand, of course, that our final judgment will be based upon the finished picture.

Cordially yours,

JOSEPH I. BREEN

In the course of interpreting the code during the past ten years, Breen's office has established many precedents. In effect they constitute a body of regulatory law which has accumulated. In order to maintain a reasonable consistency in interpreting the various provisions of the code, a member of the staff of the PCA has compiled and annotated these precedents in the form of a loose-leaf notebook in which the treatment of various subjects is indicated. The topics are arranged alphabetically from "abdomens" to "zippers," and in each case relevant decisions are given. The book of annotations is a working tool for the staff of the PCA, a guide to policy in difficult cases, and enables the PCA to maintain a desirable flexibility in keeping with changes in the moral values of the American community. Since the annotations are not published, it is possible to reinterpret the code as conditions change and as new problems arise without calling public attention to this fact.

The portion of the annotations relating to the treatment of lawyers, judges, and courtroom scenes was included in a study published in the *American Bar Association Journal* in 1939. Under the heading "Professions" the following statements of policy are given:

"All of the professions should be presented fairly in motion pictures.

"There should be no dialogue or scenes indicating that all, or a majority of the members of any professional group, are unethical, immoral, given to criminal activities, and the like.

"Where a given member of any profession is to be a heavy or unsympathetic character, this should be off-set by showing upright members of the same profession condemning the unethical acts or conduct of the heavy or unsympathetic character.

"Where a member of any profession is guilty of criminal conduct, there should be proper legal punishment for such criminal conduct—such punishment to be shown or indicated clearly."

The specific policy regarding the portrayal of lawyers is indicated as follows:

"So long as stories are written, and plays and motion pictures produced, there will always be a considerable number which will deal with lawyers and court room scenes. The reason for this is that drama deals with 'conflict,' and there is much dramatic conflict present in the practice of the law, since lawyers are involved where issues and problems have arisen which need legal interpretation or solution.

"Sometimes dishonest, or shyster, lawyers appear in plays or motion pictures just as they exist in everyday life. Where dishonest or unethical lawyers appear in pictures, there should be shown also ethical and high principled lawyers who off-set the other type, and who condemn them. The lawyer who commits criminal acts should be punished properly for his misdeeds which are shown clearly to be wrong."

This study also gives us another glimpse into the way in which the PCA functions. The following quotations from letters to the producers are typical:

"Scenes 25, 26, and 27: The speeches by 'G' are much too general in that they indicate that all lawyers have to 'betray justice and the law' in order to be successful. All of this should be rewritten to get away from the present flavor."

Again . . . after reading a revised script a P.C.A. opinion said:

"We feel that some punishment should be indicated for the crooked attorney. This might be handled by having the judge in the court indicate that he is going to have this lawyer investigated by the Grand Jury or the Bar Association."

. . . following a personal conference between members of the P.C.A. and the producer of this picture, the P.C.A. wrote in part as follows:

"In our conference the other day we suggested that since the early portion of the story makes clear that both 'C' and 'B' are unethical in their legal practices, and that the latter as well, is crooked, this material might be objectionable to members of the legal profession.

"We suggested that the court room scene conclude with a dignified and vigorous condemnation on the part of the court. Upon reading the script we feel that such condemnation is essential.

"We further suggest that material be injected making it quite clear that 'B' realizes the wrongfulness of his criminal acts, and condemns himself for his past misdeeds and regenerates completely."

In December 1938, a film was rejected because it violated the section of the Production Code regarding human law. As the *American Bar Association Journal* study reported:

In this rejected film a witness to a motor accident who was called to the stand to testify in a civil suit, was shown unceremoniously fined by the judge without any charge being preferred against him. The judge was shown acting in a highly arbitrary manner in throwing this innocent witness into jail upon failure to pay a fine levied against him without any pretense of "due process of law."

The PCA wrote: "We're still of the opinion that this picture ridicules human law, presents the courts of the land as unjust, and tends to make the court suffer as a result of this presentation." Therefore, the picture was rejected.

The mechanisms of self-regulation are the Motion Picture Production Code and its Administration, the Advertising Code and its Administration, and the Title Registration Bureau. All are part of the Motion Picture Association and function as service agencies for the industry. Closely integrated with the motion picture production process, they enable the movie companies to discharge the responsibilities forced upon them by moralistic and other pressure groups with economy and dispatch.

Part IV

Retrenchment, Reappraisal, and Reorganization, 1948–

After the war, things were never the same for the movie industry. Beginning in 1947, the winds of ill fortune blew incessantly for ten years, during which weekly attendance declined by about one-half. The decline began even before television. When servicemen returned, the birthrate increased sharply; families with babies tended to listen to the radio at night rather than go to movies. Veterans swarmed into educational institutions, and studies cut into their leisure time. And because the country was at peace, goods and services were diverted to civilian purposes. Houses, automobiles, appliances, and other commodities were purchased in abundance, cutting in on disposable income.

Television began its real commercial expansion in 1948. The number of sets in use soared by more than 1,000 percent, from 14,000 in 1947 to 172,000 a year later. In 1949, the number went up to 1 million, in 1950 to 4 million, and in 1954 to 32 million. By the end of the fifties, nearly 90 percent of the homes in the United States had television sets. Simultaneously, the number of commercial television stations rose from 7 to 517. Television had grown to replace the movies as the dominant leisure-time activity of the American people.

With the precipitous drop in attendance, annual box office receipts declined from $1.692 billion in 1946 to $1.298 billion in 1956, or about 23 percent. Revenues declined more slowly than attendance, primarily because ticket prices rose by nearly 40 percent, from thirty-four cents to fifty cents on the average. Over four thousand

401

conventional four-wall theaters closed their doors during this period. The introduction of drive-ins, however, offset that loss. Nonetheless, since it was difficult to convert a movie house to another purpose, these former exhibitors were hard hit by the drop in real estate values.

On the production level, the gross revenues of the ten leading companies fell from $968 million to $717 million, or 26 percent in this period. Combined profits fell more precipitously, from $121 million to $32 million, or 74 percent. As a result, Hollywood underwent a period of retrenchment. Production was severely cut back as studios trimmed budgets. The stock system went by the boards. In an attempt to reduce overhead, actors, writers, producers, and directors were taken off long-term contracts or pared from the payrolls. Actors were particularly affected: in 1947, 742 were under contract; in 1956, only 229. The labor force shrank as well. Employment fell off from the postwar peak of twenty-four thousand in 1946 to around thirteen thousand ten years later.

The Impact of the *Paramount* Case

When the Supreme Court handed down its decision in the *Paramount* case in May 1948, it was heralded as a landmark victory for antitrust (ch. 20). The Court voted unanimously to uphold the general verdict of the district court. Block booking, the fixing of admission prices, unfair runs and clearances, and discriminatory pricing and purchasing arrangements favoring affiliated theater circuits were declared illegal restraints of trade and their future use by the eight defendants was prohibited. The Big Five were ordered to terminate all pooling arrangements and joint interests in theaters belonging to one another or to other exhibitors. The Supreme Court, however, rejected the competitive bidding mandate on the grounds that it would play into the hands of the buyer with "the longest purse." Concerning the charge of monopoly in exhibition, it suggested that the district court make a fresh start on the issue of theater divorcement and divestiture.

RKO and Paramount, apparently tired of the ten-year battle with the government, began negotiations for consent decrees. The Department of Justice rejected compromise

Television takes its toll on the neighborhood theater

proposals calling for the divestiture of selected theaters and insisted on the complete divorcement of the affiliated circuits from their production and distribution branches. Both decrees were approved by the district court in 1949 and contained these provisions: (1) the prohibition of unfair distribution trade practices, so that each picture would thenceforth be rented on a separate basis, theater by theater, without regard for other pictures or exhibitor affiliation; (2) the splitting of the existing companies into separate theater and producer-distributor companies with no interlocking directors or officers; (3) the divestiture of all theaters operated in pools with other companies, and of all theaters in closed towns, that is, where they had no competitors; and (4) the establishment of voting trusts to prevent shareholders in the former integrated companies from exercising common control of both successor companies.

The other three integrated companies—Loew's, Twentieth Century-Fox, and Warner—refused to go along with these decrees until the district court and then the Supreme Court left them with no alternative. Theater divestiture progressed irreversibly.

Concerning Columbia, Universal, and United Artists, some economists have argued that they should not have been made defendants in the case because they owned no theaters. The Little Three filed for a separate consent decree, not to extricate themselves from the case but merely to modify certain injunctions. The district court, however, subjected the three companies to the same price-fixing and trade practices prohibitions as it had the majors.

The motion picture industry underwent many revolutionary changes during the postwar period, and it may be impossible to separate the impact of the decrees from the shifts in audience demand and the rise of television. Nonetheless, Michael Conant, in his *Antitrust in the Motion Picture Industry*, has noted some immediate gains from the court action. First of all, the Big Five and the former affiliated circuits were forced to deal with each other at arm's length, creating more competition on the exhibition level. They could not give one another preferential treatment without the threat of possible contempt-of-court charges. Moreover, as publicly held companies, their officers and directors had the fiduciary responsibility to maximize profits by booking the best possible theater or picture. Since the independent exhibitor was no longer forced to buy a full line of pictures from a producer to get the ones he wanted most, he gained more control over his business. Many independents won earlier-run status and shorter clearances. In downtown metropolitan areas, where discrimination against independents was most acute, distributors gave all theaters of comparable size equal opportunity to bid on pictures for first-run exhibition.

On the production level, the *Paramount* decision enabled the Little Three to capture a larger share of the market. Because the majors could no longer usurp the playing time of the best houses through the practice of block booking, the Little Three had free access to all classes of theaters. Universal and Columbia, whose product had been relegated mostly to the bottom half of double bills, expanded production of class-A features, the former releasing such hits as *The Glenn Miller Story* and *Magnificent Obsession* and the latter, *From Here to Eternity* and *The Caine Mutiny*.

Access to first-run houses created a boom in independent production, and the beneficiary here was United Artists. In the period from 1946 to 1956, the number of independent producers more than doubled to around a hundred fifty. Other factors, most notably income tax breaks, also played a part. Within a decade, United Artists had grown to become a major company, releasing fifty pictures a year. By then most of the other companies emulated UA's mode of operation. Retrenchment had left them with idle studios and underutilized distribution systems. Having once created barriers to independent production, the majors now vied to provide financing and studio space to these producers and to handle their films.

Divorcement also affected motion picture content. Without first-run theaters, the Big Five lost its power to enforce the strictures of the Production Code Administration. Further undermining the code, the Supreme Court in a landmark decision read the movies into the First Amendment in 1952, and "extended to them the same protected status held by newspapers, magazines, and other organs of speech" (ch. 19). As a result, the PCA revised the code in 1956 to bar obscenity rather than controversial subject matter.

The new freedom of expression accorded to motion pictures, together with divorcement, gave rise to the "art theater." For the first time in over a generation, foreign films had equal access to the domestic market. Located mostly in metropolitan areas and in college and university communities, these theaters specialized in reissues of Hollywood "classics" and independently made American pictures with offbeat themes, in addition to foreign films. In 1950, less than a hundred such theaters existed, but by the mid sixties, the number climbed to over six hundred. No new construction was entailed; the typical art theater had formerly existed as a small subsequent-run house, the kind that was the first to feel the brunt of television. Rather than closing, this theater carved a niche for itself by exhibiting imported films and specialized product.

Although the *Paramount* decision restructured the industry, it by no means reduced the importance of the big companies. In 1954, ten producer-distributors (the eight defendants plus two minors, Republic and Allied Artists) collected most of the total domestic film rentals, as did ten companies (not all the same ones) in 1972. Conant has offered several explanations. First, the drop in production output by the majors was not offset by the increase in independent production. Consequently, the distributors already in business increased their rivalry to acquire product. This factor boosted distribution costs and affected profits. Second, film distribution is not an ease-of-entry business. To operate efficiently, a distribution company requires a nationwide or worldwide organization and enough cash to finance and distribute thirty to forty pictures a year. And since the market absorbed less and less product during the fifties, it could support only ten distributors at most. Lastly, the cost of film production rose as a result of color, 3-D, and wide screens, increasing the potential loss on any one picture and consequently creating greater market uncertainties.

The divorced theater circuits also fared well. As a result of divestiture, they sold off their weaker houses in small towns while retaining their large first-run theaters. Thus, despite the impact of television, average annual receipts per theater for many of the circuits actually increased. Moreover, their buying power guaranteed their prominence in the exhibition field. The independent exhibitor, on the other hand, the supposed beneficiary of the decrees, probably gained the least in relationship to the majors. Those who owned favorably situated theaters or had the capital to acquire drive-ins held their own or even prospered. But the small theater operator found no shelter in the decrees from the vicissitudes of the business brought about by television, shortages of product, and higher rentals.

Foreign Markets

With the decline of the domestic market, Hollywood's foreign operations took on greater importance. After World War II, the industry set about recapturing lost territories by releasing its tremendous backlog of pictures that had yet to be distributed abroad. The protective barriers established during the 1920s and 1930s had disappeared, and national film industries, with the exception of Great Britain's, had been totally disrupted by the war. Increasing the likelihood that the industry would dominate international business was Washington's regard for American motion pictures as an important propaganda weapon in the cold war.

Foreign governments, however, pressed just as vigorously to protect their impoverished economies. European nations were heavily in debt and could not afford the luxury of importing films when other commodities essential to their well-being were desperately needed. To stem the dollar outflow, foreign governments passed restrictions reminiscent of those after World War I, but the balance-of-payments problem added a new twist in the age-old battle with Hollywood: frozen funds. Since exhibitors and audiences alike preferred Hollywood's pictures to the domestic product, governments decided to allow them free entry on the condition that only a portion of their earnings could be taken out. Great Britain was the first country to adopt such a scheme by lifting its 75 percent import duty on pictures in 1948 and stipulating that for the next two years American companies could withdraw only $17 million annually from the country—all other earnings were frozen. France, Italy, and Germany instituted similar measures, with the result that the majors began investing in production abroad by constructing studios, purchasing story rights, and financing pictures. Frozen funds were but one of several factors contributing to the postwar phenomenon of runaway production, the others being the urge to film authentic locales, lower labor costs, and tax advantages. Currency restrictions gradually relaxed with the resumption of more normal international trade. Foreign governments turned to other measures to nurture and protect their domestic film industries, including such forms of financial assistance as prizes, production loans and credits, and subsidies.

The subsidy was found to be the most effective measure and was adopted by most European countries. Although subsidy plans differed in size and operation from country to country, their general purpose was the same—namely, to provide producers with monies in addition to revenues collected from normal distribution. These monies were usually generated by increasing ticket prices or entertainment taxes and allocated by a governmental or public agency.

Production subsidies were instituted to aid domestic filmmakers, but, as Thomas Guback points out, foreign subsidiaries of American companies quickly discovered how to conform to the provisions of the plans so as to become "national" producers of "national" films and gain access to European subsidies (ch. 17). Runaway production was stimulated, and at the same time the international scope of Hollywood's operations was broadened. In 1949, 19 American-interest features were made abroad; in 1969, 183. Guback estimates that "during the five years ending in 1972, about 45 percent of the 1,246 features made by U.S. companies were produced abroad."

Overseas, American film companies dominate the screen just as they do at home. They distribute the biggest box office attractions and capture the lion's share of the gross. Before the war, about a third of their revenue came from abroad; by the sixties, the proportion rose to over one-half. Thus, Hollywood's quest to capture a greater share of the foreign market to compensate for declining revenues at home was fulfilled. The ramifications of this expansion for the indigenous cultures of foreign nations, especially those of the developing countries, are considerable, as Guback's chapter clearly indicates.

The HUAC Hearings

Divorcement, television, and an embattled foreign market made for a beleaguered Hollywood at just the time it faced still another assault—now from the House Committee on Un-American Activities. HUAC actually made two assaults, holding hearings in both 1947 and 1951 on the alleged Communist infiltration of the motion picture industry. J. Parnell Thomas, head of the committee in 1947, intended to prove that card-carrying party members dominated the Screen Writers Guild, that Communists had succeeded in introducing subversive propaganda into motion pictures, and that President Roosevelt had brought improper pressure to bear upon the industry to produce pro-Soviet films during the war.

Hollywood's politics had been investigated twice before, by HUAC in 1939 and the Senate Interstate Commerce Committee in 1941. These were the first counterattacks by conservative forces against labor militancy in the guilds and the perceived antiisolationist themes in a number of prewar features. But a united front among producers in the aftermath of Pearl Harbor successfully blocked these intrusions by Congress. After the war, however, the political atmosphere in Hollywood changed. Anger over labor militancy, which had smoldered for years, culminated when the Motion Picture Alliance for the Preservation of American Ideals extended HUAC an invitation to resume the investigation of the industry. Founded in 1944, the Alliance was a militant right-wing organization dedicated to combating the impression that Hollywood was made up of "Communists, radicals, and crack-pots." For a host of reasons, not the least of which was opportunity for publicity, HUAC was more than eager to comply.

The hearings began on October 20, 1947, and lasted for two weeks. The first part took testimony from friendly witnesses, many of whom were members of the Alliance— Sam Wood, Ayn Rand, Roy Brewer, Robert Taylor, Mrs. Lela Rogers (mother of Ginger), and Adolphe Menjou. Jack L. Warner and Louis B. Mayer represented the top Hollywood executives. Chairman Thomas encouraged these witnesses to expound freely on the "Communist" problem in Hollywood, allowing them to read prepared statements, to use notes, and to slander individuals they deemed politically undesirable without fear of cross-examination and immune from subsequent suit or prosecution.

The second part focused on ten political activists, later dubbed the Hollywood Ten, who were leaders of the Hollywood left—John Howard Lawson, Dalton Trumbo, Albert Maltz, Alvah Bessie, Samuel Ornitz, Herbert Biberman, Edward Dmytryk, Adrian Scott, Ring Lardner, Jr., and Lester Cole. All were screenwriters, with the exception of Dmytryk, a director. The first to testify, and establishing a pattern followed by the other nine, Lawson announced that as a matter of principle he would refuse to answer the committee's question "Are you now or have you ever been a member of the Communist party?" by invoking the First Amendment. Like the "friendly" witnesses, Lawson had a prepared statement, but as he attempted to read it, Thomas repeatedly pounded his gavel for silence and then had him forcibly ejected from the proceedings. The other "unfriendly" witnesses also invoked the First Amendment. All ten were cited for contempt of Congress and subsequently went to the federal penitentiary.

Paul V. McNutt, former high commissioner to the Philippines, who had been engaged as counsel for the producers at the hearings, said, "It became apparent by the chairman's questions that the purpose of the hearing was to try to dictate and control through the device of the hearings, what goes on in the screens of America. It does not require a law to cripple the right of free speech. Intimidation and coercion will do it. Freedom simply cannot live in an atmosphere of fear. The motion-picture industry cannot be a free medium of expression if it must live in fear of a damning epithet 'Un-American!' whenever it elects to introduce a new idea, produce a picture critical of the status quo, or point up through a picture some phase of our way of life that needs improving."[1]

HUAC cried out against "Communist subversion" in filmmaking, but never proved the charge. The three films Hollywood produced about Russia during World War II— *Mission to Moscow* (Warner), *Song of Russia* (MGM), and *North Star* (Samuel Goldwyn)—were nothing more than friendly tributes to an ally who was valiantly holding off

Mission to Moscow (Warner Bros, 1943), one of the few pro-Russian pictures made during the war. Walter Huston, Manart Kippen, and Vladimir Sokoloff

1. Quoted in John Cogley, *Report on Blacklisting I: The Movies* (New York: Fund for the Republic, 1956), pp. 9–10.

the Nazi armies at Stalingrad. These pictures were released at a time when the U.S. Signal Corps produced another paean to Russian courage, a documentary entitled *The Battle of Russia*. Given the operations of the studio system, the chances were slim that any screenwriter could influence film content along party lines. The Hollywood screenwriter never had final say over what appeared on the screen. That was always the province of the studio producer, a point that was emphasized by both Jack Warner and Louis B. Mayer during their testimony. Were members of the Hollywood Ten subversives? Larry Ceplair and Steven Englund, in their persuasive study *Inquisition in Hollywood*, state: "There is no evidence to indicate that the Hollywood Reds ever, in any way, conspired, or tried to conspire, against the United States government, spied for the Soviet Union or even undermined any social institution in this country. . . . Nor did they ever try formally to propagandize Hollywood movies in the literal sense of 'subversion,' i.e., 'to undermine the principles of' or corrupt."[2]

Thomas, for reasons of his own, abruptly suspended the hearings after the Ten's testimony. Although the committee produced so little in the way of tangible evidence to support the thesis it had set out to prove, Hollywood, in typical fashion, panicked. Fifty leading motion picture executives emerged from a two-day secret session at the Waldorf-Astoria in Manhattan on November 24, 1947, to announce that members of the Hollywood Ten had by their actions "been a disservice to their employers," had "impaired their usefulness to the industry," and were suspended without compensation. More ominously, though, the executives invited Hollywood's talent guilds to help them eliminate the subversives in their ranks. So began the blacklist, which would hang like a pall over the industry for the next ten years. Television, foreign trade restrictions, antitrust prosecutions all had begun to undermine the profitability of Hollywood movies. The leaders of the industry found it in their economic best interests to capitulate to the Red Scare.

In 1951, HUAC investigated Hollywood a second time

2. Larry Ceplair and Steven Englund, *The Inquisition in Hollywood: Politics in the Film Community, 1930–1960* (New York: Anchor Press, 1980) p. 243.

(ch. 18). These hearings continued sporadically until 1954, during which time ninety prominent industry figures testified. The committee now wanted people to name others they knew as Communists; 324 were cited and blacklisted by the studios. HUAC's hold on public opinion had been considerably strengthened during the interim by a series of national and international events: the fall of China to the Communists, the first successful atomic explosion by the Soviets, the outbreak of the Korean War, the rise of Joseph McCarthy, and the conviction of Alger Hiss. The combined forces of these events helped the committee achieve its goal of eradicating liberalism and radicalism in Hollywood.

The hearings had a profound effect on motion picture content. After the war, the industry had showed an interest in social problem films that explored anti-Semitism, racism, and demagoguery. Many of these pictures had been critical and box office hits—*Gentleman's Agreement, Crossfire, All the King's Men,* and *Home of the Brave,* for example. But after the 1947 hearings, producers lost courage, and the percentage of social problem films declined. Hollywood emphasized "pure entertainment" for the duration of the hearings and in addition introduced a series of anti-Communist pictures as a sop to HUAC. The public showed little interest in the cold war fare; nearly forty pictures were made from 1947 to 1954, most of which lost money. As a public relations gimmick, however, the pictures helped restore Hollywood's image among the right-wing guardians of the industry.

The Rise of Independent Production

Independents have existed since the days of the Motion Picture Patents Company, but for the present purposes, we need begin this discussion only with the period of oligopoly control. As generally understood by the industry, an independent producer was a small company that secured its own financing and arranged for the distribution of pictures made under its supervision. An independent might have a contract with a distributor, but no corporate ties existed between the two firms. Each was separately owned and controlled. In terms of output, an independent might produce a single picture or operate on a long-term basis producing a few pictures annually.

Prominent independents who produced class-A features released through United Artists and, occasionally, through RKO. During the 1930s, only a handful of such producers were in business: Charlie Chaplin, Samuel Goldwyn, David O. Selznick, Walt Disney, Walter Wanger, the team of Merian Cooper and John Ford, plus a few others. Chaplin was the anomaly of the group. He not only produced his pictures using his own money, but wrote, directed, and starred in them as well—a one-man show. The archetypal operation, such as Goldwyn's and Selznick's, functioned as a major studio in microcosm. Like the studio chief, these men were concerned with financial matters, and like the line producer, they were responsible for overseeing all creative aspects of production. Because these men had long-time business and family connections with the majors, and because of their successful track records, they enjoyed a privileged status among independents. Established stars were available to them on loanout, financing could be secured from the leading banks, and with United Artists distribution, access to first-run houses could be theirs.

World War II brought new entrants into the field. Most had fled the production ranks of Hollywood, men such as Hunt Stromberg, David Loew, and Lester Cowan. Some were stars, such as Jimmy Cagney, and others were speculators of many stripes. The marketplace was one factor accounting for the sudden interest in independent production: the drop in production output caused by the shortage of studio personnel, together with the increasing demand for movies, had the effect of making independent production a less speculative venture. Another had to do with the Internal Revenue Service: the wartime income tax rates had badly eroded the take-home pay of high-priced talent. By operating his own independent production company, a producer, director, or actor in the top income tax bracket could reduce his effective tax rate from 80 to 60 percent. Moreover, under certain conditions, an interest in a completed picture could be sold as a capital asset, making the profit from such a sale subject to only a 25 percent capital gains tax.

Cagney's tax situation will illustrate the benefits of independent production. As a contract actor working for Warner, he made three pictures in 1941. Each grossed about $1.5 million in the United States. Since his take-home pay was based on profit participation, he earned over $350,000 that year. After taxes, however, the amount was reduced to a paltry $70,000. If he were to produce on his own just one successful picture a year, he would stand to make more money. Additional benefits would accrue as well: he could keep actors under contract; accumulate an asset position in completed pictures; and build a business for himself. More beguiling, he would not have to jeopardize his private financial resources.

Which brings up the matter of financing. During the thirties, an established independent obtained financing in the form of a residual loan from a bank, for example, the Bank of America. As a condition for the loan, the producer had to have a distribution contract and successful pictures in release. To provide security for his new project, he had to mortgage a number of his completed pictures as well as the proposed one and to pledge the residual profits from his films in current distribution. These conditions made it extremely difficult to break into the business and help explain why so few first-class independents existed in this period. To get started required private investment and/or loan guarantees and special concessions from a distributor. Take the case of David O. Selznick. Before going independent in 1935, he had been head of production at RKO from 1932 to 1933, pulling that studio out of its slump by producing such hits as *What Price Hollywood? A Bill of Divorcement*, and *King Kong*. During the following two years, as an MGM vice-president, he produced a remarkable string of pictures that included *Viva Villa! Manhattan Melodrama, David Copperfield*, and *A Tale of Two Cities*. However, Selznick had no proprietary interest in these pictures, so that in forming his production company, Selznick International, he had to raise over $3 million from private investors to embark on an eight-picture deal for United Artists release.

By the time Cagney turned independent, the situation had changed. The increased demand for motion picture entertainment during the war convinced the banks that any feature distributed by a leading company would always

return around 60 percent of its negative cost. This amount
became the limit the bank would loan and was available
at current interest rates. As Janet Wasko explains, "banks
followed this policy of lending a percentage of a picture's
negative cost without depending on past films to secure
a loan. In other words, actual production loans, rather than
residual loans were arranged."[3] Bank financing was known
as "first money," which meant that this loan was the first
to be paid off from the producer's share of the distribution
gross. First money, however, was the last money raised
by a producer. "Second money" in effect financed a picture.
Covering the remaining 30 to 40 percent of the budget,
and paid off after the bank loan, second money could be
secured in cash and/or deferments in the form of salaries,
studio credits, and film laboratory charges. To compensate
for the risk, a lender of second money—be he a financier,
distributor, or family friend—often demanded a profit participation rather than interest. "Completion money" guaranteed that should a picture go over budget, money would
be forthcoming to finish it. The bank and risk capital
groups, as a condition of their loans, demanded that a
producer secure such money since an uncompleted picture
is totally worthless. Completion money could be either a
bond signed by a financially responsible person or cash up
to 15 percent of the production cost held in escrow.

The loan was repaid in the following manner: in placing
the picture in release, the distributor collected rentals from
exhibitors, which in total was called the "distribution
gross" (as opposed to the "box office gross," the total
money collected by exhibitors). From this amount, the
distributor deducted the distribution fee, usually around 30
percent, to cover marketing and print costs, leaving the
"net producer's share," which went first to repay the bank
loan, then to those parties who had put up funds in second
position and, if needed, for completion. The allocation of
the net producer's share proceeded in this manner until
the negative was paid off, after which the profits would be
apportioned on some sort of formula basis to those with
deferred salaries, the producer, and other participants. This

3. Janet Wasko, *Movies and Money: Financing the American Film
Industry* (Norwood, N.J.: Ablex, 1982), p. 108.

is a simplified version of a complex procedure that does
not even begin to address all of the safeguards and techni-
calities built into such deals; nonetheless, in outline, this
procedure fairly typifies the method of production financing
for independents during the forties and in many cases afterward even to the present. As will be explained later, a
new form of financing would be used by the majors as
independent production supplanted the old studio system.

By 1945, there were nearly fifty independents in business.
Although the IRS closed a few tax loopholes, the number
burgeoned to over a hundred by the end of the decade.
Divorcement and divestiture, together with the abolishing
of block booking, provided an opening wedge. And the
breakdown of the studio system freed top-flight stars, directors, producers, and technicians from long-term contracts, enabling independents to bid for their services in an
open market. However, these advantages were offset by
the uncertainties of the marketplace brought about by
competition from television. Audience tastes and attendance habits were changing and complicated the problem of
evaluating the potential of new motion picture projects.
As a result, production loans from banks became more restrictive. George Yousling of the Security-First National
Bank of Los Angeles, a leading motion picture financier,
wrote in 1948 that in passing on a loan application, his
bank was concerned with two basic risks: (1) the completion of the picture; and (2) the repayment of the bank loan.
Concerning the former, the bank examined the cost consciousness of the producer, his track record, the experience
of the director, and the reputation of the cast and production staff. Negotiations would not begin, however, unless
the producer had a distribution contract and a completion
bond. Concerning repayment, the bank evaluated the box
office potential of the picture and reserved the right to
approve the script, cast, and budget. Further, it asked such
questions as:
1. Is it of an extremely controversial nature from the
   religious, racial, or ideological points of view?
2. Does it deal with immoral or other censorable
   matters?
3. Is it a story that has limited appeal and attraction in
   this country or abroad?

4. Is it one that requires location shooting, large groups of extras, or elaborate sets which may lead to heavy unforeseen expenditures through delays and construction problems?[4]

Why the bank adopted this attitude is understandable. After all, it was interested not as much in art as in protecting its investment and earning profits in the form of interest. But this attitude helps explain why the independents of the fifties and sixties were familiar faces—stars Burt Lancaster, Kirk Douglas, John Wayne, Elizabeth Taylor, and Danny Kaye, and directors William Wyler, Stanley Kramer, and Otto Preminger, to name a few—and why the product differed little if at all from typical Hollywood fare. When Frank Capra and partners William Wyler and George Stevens formed their independent production company, Liberty Films, in 1946, Capra predicted that independent productions would be different—they would have individuality. Of his company, he said, "Each one of these producers and directors has his own particular style of film making, his own individual ideas on subject matter and material, and the manner in which it should be treated. And each one, on his own and responsible only to himself, will as an independent producer have the freedom and liberty to carry out these ideas in the manner he feels they should be executed."[5]

A more critical assessment of the independent movement has been provided by Richard Dyer MacCann: "Independent production has been hailed as a kind of cure-all for what ails Hollywood, both artistically and commercially. It has been praised as a source of new freedom, new talent, and new ideas. But the departure from the old studio system is more apparent than real. And when independence does have some independence about it, the films that emerge are as likely to appeal to the lowest common denominator of taste as they did in the old days."[6]

4. George Yousling, "Bank Financing of the Independent Motion Picture Producer" (New Brunswick, N.J.: Graduate School of Banking, Rutgers University, 1948), pp. 30–31.

5. Frank Capra, "Breaking Hollywood's 'Pattern of Sameness,'" *New York Times Magazine*, May 5, 1946, p. 19.

6. Richard Dyer MacCann, "Independence with a Vengeance," *Film Quarterly* 15 (Summer 1962): 14.

Billy Wilder's *Some Like It Hot,* starring Tony Curtis, Jack Lemmon, and Marilyn Monroe (United Artists, 1959)

Another factor militated against change, in MacCann's opinion, and that was the growing power of the agent. Prior to the fifties, talent agents played a marginal role in the industry. At best, they succeeded in negotiating higher salaries for their clients during contract renewals. It was the studio that nurtured talent, selected properties for development, and took the long view. But during retrenchment, the studios abrogated these functions, finding it more efficient and more economical to deal with production on a picture-by-picture basis. Agents were quick to capitalize on the situation. As MacCann explains, "Instead of offering a script (or a writer) to a studio which already had a contract list of actors, or offering an actor to a studio well-staffed with writers, the agency would offer a combination—a 'package.' This usually consisted of a writer and his script, one or two stars, and even a director."[7] Since agents earned money by collecting a 10 percent commission on income from their clients, they were out to exact the best terms, which boosted production costs, so that mostly sure-fire projects were favored. The unconventional, experimental, or controversial film did not figure into their scheme of things either. All the top actors, writers, directors, and producers are today represented by such powerful agencies as International Creative Management, William Morris, and Creative Artists Agency.

As I have implied, independent production has become assimilated by the majors as an alternative to the studio system of production. The term "independent" no longer has meaning in this new context and is best used to describe the producer of documentaries, experimental films, and low-budget features that are handled outside the channels of mainstream Hollywood. In the realm of production, the majors function essentially as bankers supplying financing and landlords renting studio space. Distribution is now the name of their game.

United Artists became the prototype for the modern company. UA had always functioned exclusively as a distributor of independent production; it never owned a studio or had actors under contract. After the war, UA went downhill as a result of incessant wrangling on the part of its owners, mismanagement, and lack of capital. The threat of bankruptcy in 1951 convinced Mary Pickford and Charlie Chaplin, the two remaining stockholders, to turn over operating control to a management team headed by Arthur B. Krim and Robert S. Benjamin. The deal these two lawyers struck stipulated that if UA showed a profit within three years, they would be rewarded with half ownership of

7. Ibid, p. 15.

the company. Through a series of deft maneuverings that secured over $3 million in production financing, a full roster of pictures, and two big hits, *High Noon* and *The African Queen*, Krim and Benjamin put the company in the black in one year. Soon after, they bought out Pickford and Chaplin and owned the company outright.

Krim and Benjamin departed from the old United Artists' policy by going into production financing. Only in this way could the company build an asset base and be assured of a constant flow of quality pictures. By gaining the confidence and support of an increasing number of banking institutions, they initiated a broad financing program and thus were able to attract important producers, stars, and directors to the independent ranks. In 1957, UA's roster included fifty independents, among them such actor-producers as John Wayne, Frank Sinatra, Gregory Peck, Bob Hope, and Kirk Douglas; such director-producers as William Wyler, Stanley Kramer, and Otto Preminger; and such production units as the Mirisch Corporation and Hecht-Hill-Lancaster. Under Krim and Benjamin's management between 1951 and 1978, UA movies won ten Best Picture Academy Awards, including three consecutive Oscars in 1976, 1977, and 1978.

The majors each release around twenty pictures a year. Of these, maybe twelve are financed for worldwide distribution, three for domestic release, and five for foreign distribution. A company's total exposure might be $80 to $100 million a year. Production financing takes several forms, but the ones most often used are institutional financing from within—that is, the use of internally generated funds from production and distribution or money borrowed from commercial banks on a revolving loan basis—and guarantees of bank loans for individual pictures. In their dealings with the majors, banks no longer involve themselves in creative matters; they do not pass judgment on pictures but look to the company's net worth and overall earnings record.

Although product emanates from a variety of sources, but mostly from producers and talent agencies, it typically takes the initial form of a "package." The package is the seed of a motion picture deal. If a studio is interested, it will draw up a production-financing agreement setting forth the conditions of the deal. The project progresses in steps, the first of which is research and development. In this stage the screenplay is written and/or revised, a budget and production schedule are prepared, and the director and cast secured. These are the basic ingredients, known as the "above-the-line" costs, over which the distributor-financier has the right of approval. During this stage, the company may reimburse the producer for the "front money" he invested to put the package together and for overhead expenses to maintain his office staff and for the preliminary work on the script.

If the distributor does not approve any of the basic ingredients within a specified period of time, the producer has the right to place the project in "turnaround"—that is, to set up the project elsewhere to get it made. If the distributor gives the go-ahead, the project enters the preproduction period, during which a start date is set and the department heads and other "below-the-line" personnel are hired for the production and postproduction periods to physically make the picture.

The producer is usually given complete autonomy including the final cut, a right which is delegated to the director. However, certain conditions are imposed by the distributor: (1) the picture has to be delivered with a specified minimum theatrical running time; (2) the picture has to receive a specified rating from the Motion Picture Association; and (3) the distributor retains the rights of editing for television distribution, foreign exhibition, and foreign censorship.

In return for supplying complete financing, the studio receives all worldwide distribution rights to the picture in all media, gauges, and languages in perpetuity and acquires the ownership of the copyright and negative. The studio also receives all worldwide sound track album rights and music-publishing rights. In matters relating to remakes and sequels and ancillary rights to the underlying literary material, the studio might share joint control with the producer.

As a reward for the producer, he may be given up to 50 percent of the profits. He may also receive a producer's fee for performing certain administrative tasks during production, but, in general, he functions as a coventurer with the company and defers salary and other considerations until after the cash cost of the picture has been recouped. This method of remuneration exists for other creative personnel although some big stars are paid a large salary up front plus a percentage of the profits or in some instances a percentage of the gross—that is, a percentage of the distribution gross from the start of release.

The distributor-financier is the risk taker and will typically take 50 percent of the profits and charge a distribution fee of 30–40 percent of the gross. This fee goes to pay the costs of the company in selling and marketing the picture worldwide, but it is also a separate source of income if a picture is a hit since these overhead costs remain fixed. However, distribution income, extraordinary though it may be from a blockbuster, must be used to offset losses on other pictures. In other words, the distribution fee is used as a means to spread the risks of production financing. Over the years, more than half the pictures made have lost money. Not only have production costs risen, but so have the costs of marketing. Today, a typical $10 million picture might require another $10 million for prints and advertising. To explain the nature of this risk another way, we can look to the apportionment of box office receipts. From every hundred dollars taken in by theaters, the distributor collects as rentals around forty on the average. After the distribution fee and print and advertising costs have been deducted, only around fifteen dollars remain to cover negative costs. As a result, the distributor-financier dictates the ingredients in production, just as had the bankers before.

The above is a simplified version of a typical deal. The point to be stressed, however, is the dominant position of the majors in the industry. They alone have the resources to finance a steady flow of pictures and a sales force to market them aggressively around the globe. As explained earlier, the costs of entry for distribution are high, and given the limited demand for motion pictures worldwide, it is unlikely that newcomers will challenge the existing companies.

Responding to Television

As TV began to make inroads into movie audiences, Hollywood's first impulse was to maintain a strictly stand-off attitude toward the new medium. Television was a novelty whose attraction for the public would quickly wane, the hypothesis being "They'll get tired of it soon enough." The quality of TV programming supported this position; most network programs were produced on shoestring budgets and did not approach the technical polish of the Hollywood product. Moreover, the heads of the major film companies, several of whom had come up through the exhibition ranks, were not about to consciously damage the theatrical market—the one that had been the mainstay of revenues from the beginning.

Television, though, had a voracious appetite for programming, requiring talent, stories, people, and ideas to produce thousands of shows each season. Most prime-time programs were broadcast live, but to fill out their schedules, networks had to rely on film material. In the early days, they used old features and shorts from Republic and Monogram for about one-fifth of their program time. Local stations, possessing neither the facilities nor the financial resources for extensive live broadcasting, had greater needs.

Hollywood, as a result, saw the development of an entire subindustry after 1950, consisting of small independent production companies devoted to turning out series of low-budget telefilms, usually a half hour in length. Desilu Productions, the creation of Desi Arnaz and Lucille Ball, set the pace. "I Love Lucy" debuted in fall 1951 and soon became an immensely popular series drawing a weekly audience of thirty million. Arnaz had the foresight to film the program, a decision that earned for his company a fortune in residuals from reruns. Other important early producers were Ziv-TV Programs, Hal Roach Productions, and Revue Productions. Revue, a subsidiary of the powerful Hollywood talent agency Music Corporation of America, later metamorphosed into Universal Television and helped establish MCA as the present-day entertainment conglomerate.

Audiences did not tire of television, and upon realizing this, the majors adopted a new adage to replace the debunked hypothesis. To draw people back to the theaters, the tack became "We'll give them something television can't." Television viewing habits had become pretty much established by the fifties: a direct correlation existed between age and the amount of time spent watching the tube. The movies had lost most of the adult audience, for good

"I Love Lucy"

economic reasons: first, the cost of watching television for a consumer who had already purchased a set was negligible compared with the price of a theater ticket; second, frequent program changes provided variety; and third, television was convenient—it could be viewed in the most informal circumstances, without effort, and in the comfort of one's home. The motion picture industry, as a result, decided to differentiate its product and make the most of its natural advantages over its rival. It would exploit color, 3-D, and wide screens.

Innovation

Since television was in black and white, more movies would be made in color. During the early fifties, the percentage of features produced in color jumped from around 20 to more than 50 percent of total domestic output. Technological advances paved the way, most notably Eastman Kodak's introduction of Eastmancolor in 1950, a monopack system that greatly simplified all aspects of color cinematography.

Technicolor had dominated the field since 1935, when it perfected its famous three-color process. Simply stated, Technicolor utilized a three-strip camera for photography and the imbibition method for the making of prints. The camera was cumbersome, intricate, and expensive, and required a high light level for shooting. The imbibition process, similar to lithography, entailed the printing of the three primary colors in sequence by dye transfer to the film stock. In contracting to use Technicolor, a studio received a package consisting of the Technicolor camera, a cameraman who also functioned as an advisor to the production cinematographer, and a color consultant who worked with the art director, set decorator, and costume designer. Technicolor supplied the film and, of course, processed it in its own laboratories.

Although the company had regularly done over 90 percent of all domestic business in professional color cinematography, Technicolor's facilities were inadequate to meet the rising demand after the war. By 1948, Technicolor found itself with an incredible work backlog. The company processed nearly fifty films that year and had many more in the works. The problem rested in part with the imbibition process, which was slow under any circumstances. As Dudley Andrew has pointed out, "The overload of 1948 made for nine-month work estimates on any film lucky enough to be scheduled, and by this date there were contracts for color printing being written two to three years ahead of projected delivery time."[8]

Meanwhile, complaints from the industry had prompted the Department of Justice to file an antitrust suit in 1947 against Technicolor (and Eastman Kodak, supplier of Technicolor's film), charging restraint of trade and monopolization of professional color cinematography. Among the specifics, the suit alleged that Technicolor, by controlling certain patents, blocked Eastman Kodak from marketing professional monopack film and prevented studios from developing their own color photography systems. Eastman acquiesced to this arrangement, it was further alleged, because Technicolor agreed to purchase all of its film requirements from the company. The case did not go to court, but was concluded by the entering of consent decrees—Eastman in 1948, and Technicolor in 1950—requiring each firm to license specified patents, some royalty-free, and to furnish technical information to licensees. The issues of the case are complex and need not be presented here; however, an outside analysis of the case has argued persuasively that Technicolor by no means foreclosed Eastman from developing a professional single-strip color process, and that the introduction of Eastmancolor was the direct result of favorable market conditions.[9]

Eastmancolor components consisted of a monopack negative, print film, and intermediate film. Its great advantage was ease of handling. Designed for use in a standard camera, the singlestrip negative achieved the consistency and brilliance of Technicolor and was economical as well. Processing the Eastman film stock involved a photochemical

8. Dudley Andrew, "The Postwar Struggle for Color," *Cinema Journal* 18 (Spring 1979): 48.
9. *U.S. v. Technicolor, Inc., Technicolor Motion Picture Corp., and Eastman Kodak Co.*, No. 7507-M (S.D. Cal. 1947); see George E. Frost and S. Chesterfield Oppenheim, "A Study of the Professional Color Motion Picture Antitrust Decrees and Their Effects," *Patent, Trademark and Copyright Journal of Research and Education* (Spring 1960): 1–39 and (Summer 1960): 108–48.

procedure similar to black and white. Names such as Metro Color, Warner Color, and Deluxe Color that appeared on film ads and credit titles did not refer to the creation of new color processes—an intent of the antitrust action—but to the studio and/or lab that developed and printed Eastmancolor film. By 1954, the Technicolor camera was a thing of the past, but because Technicolor's imbibition process had decided advantages in making large numbers of release prints, the company continued in operation as a processor of Eastmancolor negative stock.

Color film production declined between 1955 and 1958, the novelty value having apparently worn off, but rose steadily again during the sixties to encompass nearly all feature work. An important influence was the conversion to color broadcasting by the networks after 1965. By then, television had become an important secondary market for Hollywood films as will be discussed later.

Innovating further to distinguish itself from TV, Hollywood experimented with screen size and depth illusion. The revolution began in 1952 with the introduction of Cinerama and 3-D. Although both were comparatively short-lived, they provided business a shot in the arm and, if nothing else, proved that the public was not literally chained to the television set.

Cinerama was launched at the Broadway Theater on September 30, 1952, with the presentation *This Is Cinerama*, a spectacular two-hour travelogue with scenes ranging from a gripping roller coaster ride to a plane trip through the Grand Canyon. Cinerama created a sense of depth by projecting an image in three segments with separate projectors on a broad curved screen. Stereophonic sound enhanced the realism of the experience.

The invention of Fred Waller, former head of Paramount's special effects department, Cinerama was more than a decade in the development. Waller unveiled a prototype called Vitarama at the New York World's Fair in 1939. Using a battery of eleven projectors and a concave screen, Waller exhibited a stunning industrial film telling the history of petroleum. Waller perfected the process for commercial use with support from Laurence Rockefeller in a venture called Vitarama Corporation. Stereophonic sound was incorporated into the system after the war by

Hazard Reeves, a sound engineer and industrial promoter. Reeves came up with the name Cinerama and formed a company, Cinerama, Inc., to test the market.

Not surprisingly, the industry initially viewed the innovation as a curiosity. To convert a single theater to Cinerama would be expensive—anywhere from $50,000 to $100,000—and the three-camera system would radically alter conventional production methods. It remained for an outsider, Lowell Thomas, the famed radio newscaster, to take the plunge. A demonstration in 1950 spurred him to acquire the exclusive rights to the process until 1957 and form Cinerama Productions Corp., with Merian C. Cooper as executive producer. A Hollywood veteran, Cooper had produced a number of pictures at RKO, including *King Kong*, and had founded another innovative company, Pioneer Pictures, which made the first three-color Technicolor feature, *Becky Sharp*, in 1935.

Since Cinerama could never supplant regular exhibition, the plan was to exploit it as a roadshow attraction. Presentations would be given in the best houses in the largest cities complete with reserved seats and top ticket prices. Only these conditions could guarantee long and profitable runs. But to equip a string of theaters required capital, and for this reason Thomas persuaded Louis B. Mayer, the former chief of MGM, to come in as board chairman. Mayer's presence did the trick; Bankers Trust loaned the company $1.6 million to convert theaters in Detroit, Chicago, Los Angeles, Pittsburgh, and elsewhere.

This Is Cinerama was enormously successful, eventually grossing more than $20 million. In New York, the picture played 122 weeks to an audience of 2.5 million, the longest run in the city's history. *Cinerama Holiday*, the second production, premiered in October 1953, and was just as popular. However, after the third, *Seven Wonders of the World* in 1954, Cinerama hit a slump. For one thing, audiences grew tired of the same travelogue format. The company contemplated narratives, but the three-camera system apparently posed an insoluble production obstacle. For another, high conversion costs kept the number of Cinerama theaters down, which meant that a picture had to play an incredibly long time before it could break even, let alone earn profits. Also, there were technical problems such as jiggling dividing lines between the three panels on the screen and uneven color matches. Although Cinerama developed a single-lens projection system which was first used in 1963 for the production of *It's a Mad, Mad, Mad, Mad World*, other wide-screen systems had already penetrated the market.

3-D hit the market on the heels of Cinerama, with the production of Arch Oboler's *Bwana Devil* in November 1952. Although ineptly made with color mismatches and scenes out of focus, the public loved this African adventure picture especially the moments when spears were seemingly thrown at the audience. The three-dimensional process was the innovation of Milton Gunzberg, his brother Julian, an opthalmologist, and Friend Baker, a Hollywood camera engineer. Dubbed Natural Vision, it utilized a camera with two lenses positioned like human eyes that shot a scene simultaneously on separate reels of film. In exhibition, two projectors cast the images on the screen so as to slightly overlap. Each projector was equipped with a special polarized filter. In viewing the picture, audiences wore spectacles with corresponding polaroid filters that fused the images stereoscopically.

The Gunzburgs tried to sell the majors on Natural Vision, but found no takers. It may have been that the studio heads were afraid of rendering their film libraries obsolete if 3-D caught on. A more likely explanation, however, was that they preferred others' taking the financial risks of promoting an untested innovation. As entrenched firms they had everything to gain and little to lose by following such a strategy.

Since the Gunzburgs had invested heavily in their process, they had no choice but to deal with a small-time independent producer, Arch Oboler. Oboler had had a long career in radio as a dramatist and worked in various capacities on three features before *Bwana Devil*. Financing posed a problem, and Oboler had to come up with $10,000 of his own plus borrowed funds to complete the picture. He even had to arrange distribution on his own, since no company was willing to touch it. But after the opening run in Los Angeles, United Artists came in with an offer to buy the picture for $500,000 plus a share of the profits. A deal was struck on January 13, 1953.

The success of *Bwana Devil* convinced Warner to experiment with the Natural Vision process. Their entry, *House of Wax*, starring Vincent Price, was a remake of the early thirties horror film *Mystery of the Wax Museum*. The picture opened on April 8, 1953, and grossed $1 million during the first week of its national release. As other studios joined the rush, Polaroid spectacles were being produced at the rate of six million per week. The Gunzburgs had exclusive rights to distribute the spectacles until July 1953, which they made the most of by purchasing them for six cents each and selling them to exhibitors for ten. In addition, the Gunzburgs received $25,000 per film plus 5 percent of the gross as royalty from producers.

Harry Warner boasted that everything would be 3-D in two years; his brother Jack's remark was more accurate: "It's a novelty, good for a fast buck at the box office." The boom was over by 1955. About forty pictures were made in Natural Vision and the other 3-D processes it spawned. With the exception of Warner's *Dial M for Murder*, directed by Alfred Hitchcock, nearly all contained rather puerile plots of the horror or adventure variety. 3-D systems had several drawbacks—dual projectors were difficult to operate in sync, and the spectacles proved to be a real annoyance to some—but clearly, the demise of 3-D was due to the industry's unwillingness to experiment with the truly creative potential of this innovation. Once the novelty had worn off, audience interest died.

CinemaScope was the one novelty to make a real impact on the industry. The innovator this time was a major studio, Twentieth Century-Fox. Its first entry, *The Robe*, opened at the Roxy in New York on September 16, 1953. After a week of sensational business, the picture opened in a hundred other cities with the same results. Here was the signal wanted by the other companies to jump on the widescreen bandwagon.

Like Cinerama and Natural Vision before it, Cinema-Scope was based on an outside invention, in this case, the anamorphic lens perfected in the twenties by Henri Chrétien, a member of the Paris Optical Institute. With this lens a camera could compress a picture image horizontally; a "compensating" lens on the projector could stretch it out on the screen. Spyros Skouras, the president of Twentieth Century-Fox, first learned of this process in December 1952, just after Cinerama and 3-D had hit the market. To Skouras, who had rejected these two processes as impractical, Chrètien's device seemed to offer several advantages: first of all, the lens could be fitted on existing equipment; second, less manpower would be needed on the set and in the projection booth; and third, the costs of converting theaters for projection would be modest, anywhere from $5,000 to $25,000.

Skouras had to act fast. The fortunes of his once-powerful company were declining. Poor earnings had already forced him to institute an executive salary cut ranging from 25 to 50 percent and brought charges of mismanagement from a minority stockholder group against him and Darryl F. Zanuck, the vice-president in charge of production. Skouras secured an option from Chrètien, and within three months he had the lens tested, settled on the patent rights, worked out numerous complex deals with equipment manufacturers here and abroad, and plunged his company into this new process, which he called CinemaScope. As perfected by Twentieth Century-Fox, CinemaScope utilized regular 35mm film that projected an image two and a half times as wide as it was high. A curved screen and stereophonic sound—four sound tracks·were magnetically printed on the film—approximated an illusion of depth.

Skouras realized from the outset that he could convince exhibitors to make the conversion only by guaranteeing them an adequate supply of product. As a result, he announced in February 1953 that Twentieth Century-Fox's future lineup would be in CinemaScope, exclusively. To finance the conversion, Skouras mortgaged the entire studio, the back lot, and all the real estate the studio owned and borrowed funds in the millions from the Chase Manhattan Bank and the Bank of America. In another effort to generate product, Skouras made CinemaScope available to all comers, an opportunity that MGM promptly took up. After the phenomenal success of *The Robe*, Universal, United Artists, Columbia, and Warner also signed pacts with Fox.

Although the larger theaters quickly accepted Cinema-Scope, many of the smaller ones balked at the expense. Partly to ensure quality exhibition of its films and partly to

protect its interest in equipment sales, Fox required theaters to purchase the complete package consisting of lenses,
screens, and speakers. The price tag on the stereophonic
sound system created the most resistance, so to stimulate
sales, Fox lowered the price in March 1954 and then
dropped the provision on stereo sound altogether. As a
result, over eleven thousand theaters had made the conversion by the end of the year.

After the premier of *The Robe*, Fox released twelve more
CinemaScope pictures in as many months, including *How
to Marry a Millionaire, Beneath the Twelve-Mile Reef*, and
Three Coins in the Fountain. These thirteen pictures
grossed $40 million; a year earlier, the forty-seven pictures
the company released brought in $40.9 million. Overall,
Fox's profits came to $16 million as compared with $8
million the year before.

Skouras' gamble paid off, but competition was soon on
the way. Paramount entered the wide-screen sweepstakes
with VistaVision in its production of *White Christmas*,

Michael Todd's *Oklahoma!* directed by Fred Zinnemann (Magna Theatre Corporation, 1955)

which premiered at Radio City Music Hall on October 20, 1954. That same year, Michael Todd, an independent producer, introduced a 65mm format process, Todd-AO. His first entry was *Oklahoma!* which was followed by *Around the World in 80 Days*, both smash hits.

We need not pause to describe the technical aspects of these two processes or the others that hit the market during this period—all these innovations brought people back to the movies. They did not resume their former moviegoing ways before television; customers became selective. As a result, the phenomenon of the "big picture" characterized business more and more. Up to 1954, only about one hundred pictures had grossed more than $5 million; in just the eighteen months after CinemaScope, over thirty had done so. For now, the "big picture" created a boom, but as a long-term production strategy, it was fraught with peril, as will be discussed later.

Collaboration

When television proved it was here to stay, the motion picture industry adopted the adage "If you can't whip 'em, join 'em." Collaboration took several forms. One was to produce filmed programming directly for the TV market. Of the established studios, Columbia was the first to move. In 1949, it converted Screen Gems, a subsidiary that produced theatrical shorts, into a television department. After a two-year period of experimentation, it produced programs for the "Ford Theater" and, in 1954, was responsible for the popular comedy series "Father Knows Best." Columbia never owned theaters and had earlier been consigned to producing mostly "B" features in the scheme of things. Now in the waning days of the studio system, the company could not afford to stand pat.

The entry of the majors into TV was tentative and imitated the example set by Walt Disney Productions. In April 1954, Disney signed a contract with ABC to produce a weekly hour-long series revolving around the Disneyland theme park. A special feature of the deal allowed Disney to devote six minutes of each hour to promote the company's current theatrical releases. It was this concept of using programming as both product and promotion that the studios found alluring. And after observing the overwhelming

success of the "Disneyland" show, the majors began producing series with their names in the titles such as "The
MGM Parade," "The Twentieth Century-Fox Theatre,"
and "Warner Bros. Presents." Sponsored by the respective
studios and containing commercials for forthcoming productions, these series represented advertising expenditures
and not sources of income. And they were not particularly
popular.

But finally the majors caught on to the potential of television and began producing regular filmed programs for
the networks. By the end of the fifties, most of the prime-
time shows emanated from Hollywood. Thereafter, the
working relationship between the film industry and commercial broadcasting would be between Hollywood (the
supplier) and New York (the exhibitor). For the networks,
filmed programming served as a form of quality control
in which acting and directing errors could be edited out
and poorly rendered scenes reshot. As episodic series proliferated, broadcasting live from New York presented more
and more of a problem. Studio space being at a premium,
casts had to rehearse in rental halls and offices around the
city. Before airing, they could be given but one full dress
rehearsal. During this single rehearsal, set construction for
other programs might be in progress. The resulting pressures on everyone were tremendous, creating a high probability for error. In 1953, the crossover from live to filmed
production began. For producers of television, film production offered the possibility of residuals. Programming could
be preserved for future syndication as broadcasting times
of stations increased to include afternoon and morning
hours and as commercial television systems developed
worldwide. As pointed out earlier, independents were first
to grasp this opportunity, but after the majors formed
alliances with the networks, they ultimately captured the
syndication market for themselves.

Another form of collaboration, meanwhile, had been the
supplying of old features and shorts to television. Monogram and Republic had released their pictures to the new
medium almost immediately. The major companies held
out until December 1955, when RKO, deciding to withdraw from motion picture production, sold its film library
to a television programming syndicate for $15 million.

Two months later Warner sold its library to Associated Artists Productions for $21 million. Other companies followed suit, and by 1958, an estimated 3,700 features, mostly of pre-1948 vintage, had been sold or leased to TV for an estimated $220 million.

Because these libraries had been fully amortized, i.e., their production costs paid for, these sales were considered as windfall profits by the studios. However, as demand for theatrical film product increased, the majors discovered that they had undervalued their old films. During the early sixties, a run-of-the-mill feature leased to the networks fetched $150,000 for two showings, as compared with an average sales price of $10,000 per film for the RKO library in 1955. NBC started the bidding in 1961 when it bought a package from Twentieth Century-Fox to launch "Saturday Night at the Movies," the first weekly movie night on a major network. The package comprised pictures from the fifties, strong in color product from the CinemaScope days. NBC wanted to promote color broadcasting, and its parent, RCA, the sales of color television sets.

The studios were free to dispose of the pre-1948 libraries since they controlled television performance rights and all subsidiary rights to their pictures. However, in 1951, the Screen Actors Guild successfully negotiated an industry-wide contract requiring the payment of residual compensation to its members who appeared in features made after 1948 that were leased to television. In 1960, other principal guilds won similar concessions.

The average price for features jumped to $400,000 in 1965. The following year a new high was reached when ABC paid Columbia $2 million for *The Bridge on the River Kwai*. The picture was used by Ford Motor Company, the sole sponsor, to unveil its 1967 line. When *Kwai* aired on September 12, 1966, it made history; this nine-year-old film attracted an audience of sixty million, beating out such popular programs as the "Ed Sullivan Show" and "Bonanza" in the ratings.

Afterward, competitive bidding by the networks became hectic. Prices rose steadily, nudging the $800,000 mark by 1968, as the networks scheduled movies every night of the week. This figure was the average price for a regular feature in a package deal that allowed a network to air each

Sessue Hayakawa and Alec Guinness in David Lean's *The Bridge on the River Kwai* (Columbia, 1957)

picture twice. Hits and blockbusters commanded much higher prices.

By now, television had become a regular secondary market for theatrical films. Conventional theatrical exhibition had been considered the primary source of revenues, with anything from TV just "gravy." But as relations between the two industries stabilized, television income became expected and planned for. Few new film projects were put into production without assessing their potential on TV, and a TV sale was used as collateral in obtaining financing. Television distribution typically began eighteen months after the end of the theatrical run, first to the networks and then to local stations.

Demand for feature films reached the point of drawing two networks, ABC and CBS, into motion picture production. ABC signed a co-production deal with MGM, while CBS went into production on its own, by forming a sub-

sidiary later known as Cinema Center Films. Distribution
was handled in the first case by Cinerama, and by National
General, a theater chain, in the latter.

Demand also created a new type of collaboration, the
made-for-television movie (MFT). An outgrowth of experiments in long-form television programming by MCA in
the late fifties, the MFT developed into two formats, the
single-night feature and the multinight miniseries. Both
were designed as inexpensive alternatives to the escalating
costs of theatrical features. MCA, the innovator of these
forms, had started out as a talent agency, becoming the
most powerful in the industry after the war. During the
fifties, it expanded into television by forming Revue Productions and then into motion pictures by acquiring Universal Pictures. In the process, MCA purchased
Paramount's pre-1948 film library, Universal Studios, and
Decca Records to become the biggest producer in Hollywood. MCA moved into MFTs in 1965, when NBC signed
a contract for more than sixty pictures over the next five
years. Called "World Premiere," the NBC series was
launched in 1966 with *Fame Is the Name of the Game.*

Production costs for MFTs were kept low, around
$500,000 an hour, with financing provided by the networks.
Shooting schedules were accordingly short, sixteen to
twenty-five days for a typical ninety-minute MFT in 1967,
compared with fifty to seventy days for a theatrical feature.
MFTs were broadcast twice. Costs were usually recouped
the first time, through the sale of commercial spots; the
second time around was all profit. Afterward, the MFT
reverted to the producer who earned income through domestic and foreign syndication.

The MFT soon eclipsed the theatrical feature as a prime-
time staple. Confronted with seven movie nights a week
during the 1968–69 season, audiences became selective and
ratings dropped. Some movies were considered too racy,
too violent, and too specialized for the mass television
audience. Nevertheless, aggressive bidding for theatrical
films, the entry into motion pictures by the networks, and
the production of MFTs combined to create a glut on the
market that proved nearly catastrophic. In 1968, the networks had sufficient product to get them through 1972 and

stopped bidding on theatrical films. The majors, meanwhile, had adopted a big-budget philosophy, spurred on by
The Sound of Music in 1965, and had come to depend on
big television revenues. There was more than enough
product to meet the needs of exhibitors, which meant that
in 1968, producers suffered staggering losses. The newcomers—ABC, CBS, and National General–lost collectively
over $80 million and dropped out of the business. In Hol-
lywood, only Disney and MCA escaped unscathed; the
other majors absorbed losses ranging from $15 to $145
million. Fox and Columbia were potential candidates for
receivership, and MGM cut back drastically on production
and stopped distributing its own films. Under pressure
from the banks, companies were forced to streamline operations, share studio facilities with competitors, distribute
jointly abroad and, most important, stop making
blockbusters.

After the retrenchment ended in 1972, the majors
emerged healthy as ever. Thereafter, they produced fewer
and fewer films each year, slowly tipping the supply-de-
mand relationship vis-à-vis the networks in their favor.
Prices paid by the broadcaster skyrocketed: $7.5 million for
The Deep, $15 million for *Alien*, and $10–$13 million for
any Clint Eastwood or Burt Reynolds film. Other factors
strengthened Hollywood's position. Competition among
the networks heightened after the emergence of ABC as a
viable competitor to CBS and NBC. In the battle for ratings, bidding for favorable programming of all types intensified to the benefit of producers. By the end of the seventies, the stranglehold of the networks on distribution of
mass entertainment also began to weaken as new technologies developed. Pay-TV, cable television, satellite transmission, and videotape and videodisc were all designed to
distribute entertainment product outside existing network
channels. These developments plus the advent of superstations and quasi-networks of independent stations served
to open new markets for filmed product. As David Londoner concludes his analysis, "The Changing Economics of
Entertainment," in the future "the networks should be
swimming upstream and the program suppliers downstream" (ch. 22).

The Industry in the Age of Conglomerates

Today the motion picture industry is alive and well. The companies that were parties to the *Paramount* antitrust suit still dominate business; their structure and operations changed, however, as the industry entered the age of conglomerates. Beginning in the fifties, American business as a whole underwent a period of consolidation as large numbers of firms merged and as corporate control and decision making became centralized among a relatively few companies. Mergers had been common to business before this time, but growth had proceeded along rational lines. A book publisher, for example, might have merged with another publisher, or a steel company might have acquired an appliance manufacturer. After World War II, however, a new type of corporate entity came into being—the conglomerate, which can be defined in a broad sense as a diversified company with major interests in several unrelated fields of endeavor. An example of such a firm is Gulf & Western Industries, which started out as a producer of automobile bumpers, and spread into such diverse fields as zinc mining, sugar, cigars, real estate investments, and as we will see later, motion pictures. In 1960, Gulf & Western's total assets were a modest $12 million; by 1968, the total came to $3 billion. Manufacturing companies led the way, but other industries such as insurance, broadcasting, newspapers, retail distribution, and utilities also caught the merger fever.

The motion picture industry was not immune to this movement: in 1966, Paramount was absorbed by Gulf & Western; in 1967, United Artists became a subsidiary of Transamerica Corporation, a "multiservice" organization engaged in insurance and financial services; in 1969, Warner was taken over by Kinney National Services, a conglomerate originally engaged in car rentals, parking lots, building maintenance, and funeral homes which then branched out into the entertainment field to create Warner Communications; and in 1969, MGM was acquired by Las Vegas developer Kirk Kerkorian, who put the studio into the hotel and casino business. More recently, United Artists changed hands again by merging with MGM to form MGM/UA Entertainment Company, Twentieth Century-Fox was bought by oilman Marvin Davis, and Columbia sold to Coca-Cola.

Observers of the industry have complained that motion picture companies are now being run by "outsiders" who lack any traditional respect for their studio's history, institutions, and products. The new industry leaders are bland finance men interested only in the bottom line and not in quality product. One critic has gone so far as to say that conglomerization has tended "toward a resurgence of concentration and centralization" and "toward a greater homogenization of product"; and that "cultural bias, distortion, and instability tend to be the result."[10]

The first response to these criticisms should be the reminder that profits have always been the first and foremost concern of motion picture companies. The second is that these criticisms are simplistic. Before rushing to judgment we might want to know why motion picture companies were prone to conglomerate takeovers, how a studio performed before and after, and other factors that might explain the structure and operations of the industry.

We can begin by quoting a truism by A. D. Murphy of *Variety*: "Neither a film producer-distributor nor an exhibitor can claim some Divine Right of staying in business; staying alive in business is the perpetual problem of every individual company."[11] The majors learned some valuable lessons from the 1969–71 recession in Hollywood. The first is that attendance worldwide has stabilized in size for all practical purposes, meaning that the market can support only a finite number of productions. The majors, as a result, cut back on production; in 1969 they released 225 pictures, but by 1977 the number had fallen to nearly half that. Which brings up the matter of costs. Production costs declined for only a brief period as producers hoped to emulate such low-budget youth-oriented hits as *Bonnie and Clyde* (1967), *The Graduate* (1967), and *Easy Rider* (1969). But after *The Godfather* broke the all-time box office record in 1972, the big-budget policy came back to roost. As a result, production costs for a typical motion picture rose

10. Joseph D. Phillips, "Film Conglomerate 'Blockbusters,'" *Journal of Communication* 25 (Spring 1975): 171.

11. A. D. Murphy, "Distribution and Exhibition: An Overview," in Jason E. Squire, ed., *The Movie Business Book* (Englewood Cliffs, N.J.: Prentice-Hall, 1983), p. 248.

Easy Rider, starring Dennis Hopper and Peter Fonda (Columbia, 1969)

from around $2 million in the early seventies to around $11 million today. Simultaneously, advertising and promotion costs have escalated enormously; outlays for these items have sometimes matched negative costs.

The second lesson is that only a few pictures, perhaps ten a year, will capture most of the box office dollars. To quote A. D. Murphy again, "There's just no getting around the fact that the film hits draw the available business like magnets. When there are several strong films, a mediocre picture becomes a box office dud, and a weak release is a box office bust."[12] The long and short of it is that motion picture production is a risky business, some say a crap shoot. It is indeed, since not even half the pictures earn back their negative and marketing costs from theatrical distribution. Factors such as these might well account for why no new producers or distributors have successfully challenged the majors.

As a third lesson, the majors learned to offset the risks of production by cutting operating costs, by adopting defensive marketing tactics, and by diversifying. To reduce

12. Ibid, p. 250.

overhead, companies closed branch offices, combined studio facilities, and merged foreign distribution operations. New marketing practices were designed to go beyond traditional channels of distribution to exploit the entire leisure-time field. Book tie-ins, novelizations, sound tracks, and the merchandising of toys, games, and clothing created additional "profit centers" to amortize production costs. These nontheatrical sources of income together with television revenues are known collectively as ancillary income. If a blockbuster fails, ancillary income could soften the blow; if the picture catches on, ancillary income might soar as well. Supergrossers, such as *Jaws, Star Wars, Close Encounters of the Third Kind*, and *E.T.*, have literally changed the structure of their parent companies. Extraordinary profits cannot entirely be plowed back into production in today's market because of the limited demand for product and because of the difficulty of putting together the necessary ingredients—stars, properties, directors, etc.—to make a commercial picture.

Jaws (Universal, 1975), directed by Steven Spielberg: Robert Shaw and Richard Dreyfuss

The industry, as a result, has diversified. Twentieth Century-Fox, for example, purchased a Coca-Cola bottler, a ski resort, and a savings and loan company; Warner Communications, a toy company and a manufacturer of video games; MCA, two publishing houses and a Coca-Cola bottler; and Columbia, a pinball machine manufacturer. By providing protection against business downturns in a specific area, diversification, in turn, has had a stabilizing effect on motion picture companies. If some have turned into conglomerates in the process, survival, nothing more, need be inferred.

With this prologue, we can now examine more closely the conglomerization of the industry. Conglomerization has proceeded in three ways: motion picture companies were either taken over by huge multifaceted corporations, absorbed into burgeoning entertainment conglomerates, or became conglomerates through diversification. Paramount and United Artists are examples of the first, Universal, Warner, and Disney, the second, and Twentieth Century-Fox, Columbia, and MGM, the third. Although each company deserves individual analysis, we will present a cross section of the industry.

Paramount was nearly moribund in 1966. Barney Balaban, its president, was in his seventies, while the average age of the board of directors was not far behind. The studio experienced continued production losses, shied away from telefilm production, and was anything but aggressive in its dealings with the networks. Moreover, the studio's assets base had been seriously eroded. To augment earnings, Paramount had sold off its pre-1950 film library, television stations, and the venerable Paramount Building in New York's Times Square. After a $125 million takeover, Gulf & Western chief Charles Bluhdorn installed himself as president, overhauled management, introduced fiscal controls, and restructured the company. Over the next five years, he strengthened production by opening the studio's doors to independent producers, moved seriously into television by acquiring Desilu Productions, cut foreign distribution overhead by joining forces with Universal overseas to form Cinema International Corporation, and embarked on an ambitious acquisitions program. By the time Paramount released *The Godfather* in 1972, the company was once again a going concern. A string of hits thereafter has transformed Paramount into one of the most consistently profitable companies in the business. On economic terms, if nothing else, Gulf & Western's takeover proved beneficial.

Unlike Paramount, United Artists was in excellent shape at the time of its merger with Transamerica. UA had set an earnings record of $13.6 million in 1966, owned an extensive film library, and had strong ties with the creative community. Under the leadership of Arthur Krim and Robert Benjamin, the company's continued growth seemed assured, in the opinion of Transamerica. UA, in turn, saw the merger as an opportunity to strengthen the value of its common stock and thereby aid its plans for diversification. The merger, in other words, was a love match. UA's stock, valued at $175 million, was exchanged for an equal amount of Transamerica's in the takeover; two years later the stock had risen in value to over $500 million. However, in 1970, UA was caught up in the industrywide recession and posted a loss of $35 million and wrote off another $50 million. UA was blamed for Transamerica's nine-month profit slide of 45 percent and for a decline in its stock from $27 to $11 a share. After bailing out UA to the tune of $20 million, Transamerica abandoned its hands-off policy by clamping fiscal controls on UA's operations, set up a computerized information program to project motion picture profits, and required UA's top executives to report all financial moves to a Transamerica line vice-president.

This bailout can be considered an example of cross-collateralization—the practice of using profits from one line of business to support another line. Critics of conglomerates claim that this practice is anticompetitive: "Because the large conglomerate generally enjoys abnormally high profits in at least some of its markets, it may expand its power by coupling such non-competitive profits with an ability to shift marketing emphasis and resources among its various market," says former FTC staff member Willard Mueller.[13] In the case of United Artists, cross-collateraliza-

13. Willard F. Mueller, "Conglomerates: A 'Nonindustry,'" in Walter Adams, ed., *The Structure of American Industry* (New York: Macmillan, 1977), pp. 463–64.

tion happened only once; elsewhere in the industry, we do not know if the practice has been used. It is unlikely though, since all the majors under conglomerate control rebounded quickly from the recession and once again became moneymakers for their parent companies.

United Artists staged a dramatic recovery beginning in 1971. Earnings in 1974 came to $10 million and were rising. In 1975, they came to $11.5 million and in 1976, $16 million. In 1977, United Artists had the best year ever racking up $469 million in revenues, but immediately thereafter, Krim, Benjamin, and three top executives resigned to form Orion Pictures, a financing and distribution company that became linked to Warner Communications. Relations between Transamerica and its motion picture subsidiary had been deteriorating steadily. UA's top executives owned stock options in Transamerica. The problem was that UA's performance had little impact on the movement of Transamerica's stock. Transamerica was so large that even during the best of years, UA contributed only about 12 percent of the conglomerate's total earnings. To make matters worse, Transamerica as a whole had performed rather poorly throughout much of the decade. From 1974 on, Krim and Benjamin suggested remedies to the situation but all were rejected; Transamerica insisted on a uniform salary schedule for all its executives. Without Krim and Benjamin, UA's independent producers lost confidence in the company. United Artists floundered. After the disastrous critical reception of Michael Cimino's *Heaven's Gate* in 1980, the company was forced eventually to write off nearly all the $40 million production cost. There would be no cross-collateralization this time. Transamerica wanted out of the motion picture business and sold United Artists to Kirk Kerkorian, the owner of MGM, who merged the two studios to form MGM/UA Entertainment Co.

Gulf & Western and Transamerica are examples of conglomerates that are composites of companies whose products and markets are unrelated. Warner Communications and MCA can be classified as product extension types of conglomerates in that their subsidiaries are functionally related but deal in products that do not compete with one another. The operations of Warner Communications are described in chapter 21.

As an example of a motion picture company that has diversified in businesses primarily outside the entertainment industry, we can look to Twentieth Century-Fox. During the sixties, the studio's policy under Darryl Zanuck's stewardship was to produce the big-budget picture. *The Sound of Music* set the pace, having been produced at a cost of $10 million in 1965 but grossing $100 million in rentals during the next two years. Subsequent blockbusters such as *Dr. Doolittle, Hello Dolly!* and *Tora! Tora! Tora!* failed miserably, however, plunging the studio into near bankruptcy. After deposing Zanuck in 1969, the studio installed Dennis Stanfill, a finance specialist, as the new president in charge of production. As a solution to the mismanagement of the past, Stanfill announced the policy of creating "separate profit centers" out of corporation operations to offset the risks of producton.

Stanfill cut back on production in 1971 and set limits on feature film budgets. The following year, Stanfill began diversifying by creating several music-recording companies. Through radical executive reorganization and consistent cost-conscious measures, Stanfill reduced the company's debt from $125 million to zero in the thirty-six-month period from 1971 to 1974. With the $12 million profit from 1974, Stanfill invested in a French motion picture chain, and when the hit picture did come along—*The Towering Inferno* and *Young Frankenstein*, for example—Fox branched out further by acquiring TV stations.

To devote his energies to the diversified interests of the company, Stanfill moved up to chairman of the board and chose Alan Ladd, Jr., to replace him as the president of Fox's feature film division. It was Ladd, of course, who was responsible for *Star Wars*. By April 1978, *Star Wars* grossed $216 million, setting an industry record. With money literally pouring into the company coffers, Stanfill purchased Coca-Cola Bottling Midwest ($27.5 million), Aspen Skiing Corporation ($48.6 million), Magnetic Video ($7.2 million), and the Pebble Beach Corporation ($77 million).

It should be clear from this brief overview that the motion picture industry has not fallen victim to rapacious conglomerate takeovers. In at least two cases—that of Paramount and Warner—the takeovers have substantially benefitted the film companies, transforming them from moribund and lethargic entities into thriving concerns. The transformation took place as a result not of such anticompetitive devices as cross-collateralization and reciprocity but of innovative management techniques, new organizational structures, and new methods of conducting business.

Conglomerization is just one of several factors that must be considered to understand the industry. In updating his study of the *Paramount* Decrees, Michael Conant examines all facets of the business and concludes that a much freer market exists today as a result of the Supreme Court decision (ch. 20). But when critics fret about the supposed power of the majors, are they really concerned with competition or are they lamenting the poor quality of the product? Unfortunately, having more producers and more distributors in the market place would not change the character of the motion picture. Film is an art; in the hands of Hollywood, however, it is also a commodity, produced, distributed, and exhibited to make a profit. Concluding a book on the industry with this reminder may seem odd, but the fact has yet to take root.

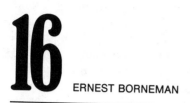

ERNEST BORNEMAN

United States versus Hollywood: The Case Study of an Antitrust Suit

The suit was first filed on July 20, 1938. Thurman Arnold was then in charge of the Department of Justice's Antitrust Division, and his brief, charging the majors with twenty-eight separate offenses, paired the principal objective of theater divorcement with the secondary objective of "abolishing all monopolistic practices in the motion picture industry." He asked for a permanent injunction, the appointment of trustees, and a court order canceling all contracts violating these objectives, while the defendants, on their side, steadily denied the very existence of monopoly. But in March 1939 the distributors, on their own, established a new Trade Practice Code which went some way toward meeting the government's purpose. In August 1939, however, Thurman Arnold ruled the new code illegal. In June 1940 the actual trial began, after thirteen postponements, and ended three days later with an adjournment to permit negotiation between the defendants and the plaintiff. For all practical purposes the case, in this manner, was "settled out of court," for in October of the same year a "consent decree" was published which was, in effect, a compromise, offering minor concessions to the government in exchange for the major concession of leaving theater control in the hands of the "Big Five."

Sight and Sound 19 (February 1951), pp. 418-20+, and (March 1951), pp. 448–50.

The defendants interpreted this temporary consent decree as a permanent approval of their trade practices, and were considerably put out when the government began to negotiate for a new decree. Thurman Arnold had become an appeals judge, and the majors had come to believe that the Justice Department had lost interest in them when, in August 1944, the assistant attorney general, Robert L. Wright, moved for a trial. On October 8, 1945, the trial opened in Foley Square.

For twenty days Robert L. Wright hurled some three hundred documents, secretly and felicitously collected, at the startled galaxy of defendants' counsels. Letters from exhibitors, carbons of contract forms, witnesses' transcriptions, and an FBI investigation of five hundred towns of fewer than 25,000 inhabitants were included in the plaintiff's prima facie case. Concentrating on "divorcement," the government did not press charges of monopoly, but left them open for a possible appeal to the Supreme Court.

The charges had not changed very greatly during the twenty-five years that had passed since the Federal Trade Commission, in 1921, had filed its first complaint against the predecessors of today's defendants, and the brief filed then might just as well have served Mr. Wright on the day he opened his attack upon the defendants at Foley Square:

> On July 22, 1919, the board of directors of Famous Players-Lasky Corporation . . . for the purpose of . . . block-booking, as distinguished from the lease of individual pictures, and for the purpose of intimidating and coercing to lease and exhibit films produced and distributed by Famous Players-Lasky Corporation adopted a . . . policy of building, owning or otherwise controlling theatres, especially . . . first-run theatres in key cities. . . . Therefore it is made difficult for the small and independent producers or distributors of films to enter into or remain in the moving picture industry or market, or to lease indivdual pictures on merit.

The period to which this 1921 brief referred was known in the industry as "the battle for the theaters." Strong-arm men and purchasing agents sent out by the majors became known among independent exhibitors as the "dynamite gang" and the "wrecking crew." Hundreds of exhibitors who had been in the industry since its infant days were driven out of business by methods which neither side in the battle now cares to remember. In 1920 the few remaining independents began to combine into the first of today's exhibitors' organizations, the Motion Picture Theatre Operators of America. For many a gaudy month the battle seesawed from coast to coast. The exhibitors held their ground as long as they owned it; they lost it when First National, largest of the exhibitors' organizations, was broken by Famous Players-Lasky.

They lost it, characteristically, because Zukor bought out the key members of the pool, one after the other, till the whole organization collapsed from the inside. Sam Katz, the head of the Balaban and Katz theater chain in Chicago, who had carried the spearhead of the battle against Famous Players by advocating the transformation of the company into a fully integrated production-distribution-exhibition organization able to compete with Zukor on his own ground, at long last himself joined Famous Players. The battle which had begun as a maneuver for the maximum number of theaters, regardless of location and size, then suddenly began to veer round to a strategy for the acquisition of so-called "first-run" theaters (i.e., theaters large enough and sufficiently well appointed to serve as showcases where new productions could be presented at special prices).

Since the operating costs of large and small theaters do not differ as much as their admission prices, and since the public seemed willing to be grossly overcharged for the right of seeing a new film earlier than their neighbors, the first-run theaters henceforth became the keystones of the majors' theater empire. "Approximately 50 percent of the revenue for a film is derived from first-run showings within six months from the date of the release of the picture," said the Federal Trade Commission in 1921. This rate has not basically altered since.

But the blame for the growing rigidity of the industry did not entirely rest with the majors. The independent exhibitors themselves, with the small businessman's preference for a sure thing, helped to strengthen the majors' monopoly over production by refusing to show pictures made by the independent producers. Since the independent producer, by dint of the majors' distribution monopoly, could not possibly obtain first-run exhibition, he had no chance of obtaining any run at all, and if exhibitors refused to show films which had not had the benefit of first-run exhibition, the whole attempt to produce independently became futile.

In point of fact, this meant that control of the total theater field became vested in a diminutively small number of first-run theaters, and the monopoly control by the first-run houses allowed the forcing of prices in all other houses, regardless of whether these subsequent-run houses were actually owned by the majors or not.

Control of first-run theaters meant, in effect, control of the screen, and the process of doling out licenses designating this theater as first-run and that as second-, third-, fourth-, or nth-run was the means by which the control over the whole of the motion picture industry was first achieved, and is still maintained. The regional assignment of "runs" became known as "zoning," while the temporal assignment of runs was known as "clearance." These two terms were the hinges upon which the whole argument turned.

During the trial the majors contended that since none of them owned more than a very small fraction of the nation's theaters, they could not be held individually responsible for any monopoly control of the market. Conceding this to be true, the government argued that although none of the defendants owned sufficient theaters to control the market singly, all of them together owned enough first-run theaters to exert a monopoly in conjunction, and that no proof of actual conspiracy had to be provided since, in effect, the very existence of the majors was sufficient to exclude all competition. Collectively, the government claimed, 3,137 theaters, or 70 percent of the nation's first-run market, were controlled by the majors, and 437 of these theaters were being operated under "pooling arrangements"—that is to say, two or more theaters, normally in competition, were being operated as a unit whose policy was controlled by the majors.

Theater pools, operated by renegade independents, had a way of breaking the morale of the exhibitors' united front. Pool operators frequently specified that none of the pool members might acquire other theaters within their area without first offering them for inclusion in the pool. In this way, the pool had a tendency to expand and perpetuate itself, and this expansion was further favored by the pool's willingness to lease any of its theaters to any "independent" exhibitor in return for a share of the profits. Frequently, the mere threat by one of the Big Five, or by one of the big pools, to erect a theater in a given area therefore made it necessary for the independent to buy up the projected theater—and in many cases the terms of purchase made by the distributor or the pool might well contain references to certain concessions which, in effect, might henceforth make the independent exhibitor a part of the distributor's network.

There was no way, short of voluntary surrender to the majors, by which an exhibitor could raise the status of his theater from, say, third- to second-run, or second- to first-run. In October 1938, the NRA, in the draft for a new code embodying a standard license agreement, said: "Only in the motion picture business does the situation exist where individuals of creditable standing, with large investments, are unable to purchase in the open market the products which they desire and need for the conduct of their business." In June 1946, during the trial at Foley Square, a brief submitted, significantly enough, not by the exhibitors but by the Society of Independent Motion Picture Producers, enlarged upon this concept by saying: "In other lines of merchandising, if a store is given an 'exclusive' or a priority on some item, it by no means follows that it also has the same rights to all competitive items produced by other competing manufacturers. (A first-run house is first-run not only for one of the majors, but for all of them.) . . . No other theatre may become first-run by the ordinary competitive technique of paying more for the privilege of a first-run. . . . As in a caste system, a theatre is either born into the aristocracy or not."

If the owner of a second-run house was willing to extend first-run privileges to a picture produced by someone other than one of the majors, he had to be prepared to do without any of the majors' pictures henceforth. In other words, he had to be prepared to go out of business. This, as a matter of fact, could happen for even slighter reasons than cooperation with independent producers or distributors. In December 1939, the firm of South Side Theatres completed a 1,050-seat deluxe house at a cost of $80,000 at Inglewood near Los Angeles. The house was expected to obtain second- or third-run rights and to pay its way with admission prices of 30 or 35 cents, but the distributors were unwilling to grant any but fifth-run rights, which, at an admission price of 15 cents, made it impossible for the owner to make ends meet. So, the house remained closed and store facilities in the same building, which were to be rented to other firms, also remained vacant.

At the trial, when the government recounted cases of this kind to prove that the whole system of assigning "runs" was tantamount to a conspiracy in restraint of trade, the majors replied that the only thing of value which they, as distributors, had to sell was the right to exhibit a picture and that the spatial and temporary exclusiveness of this right was the essence of the thing that was being bargained for. To this, the government replied that it would be perfectly legal for a distributor to sell theater B a film to be played on a date any given number of days behind theater A, but that it was illegal for the distributor and theater A to agree on the number of days before the film would become available to theater B.

When the "Little Three" companies (those having an integrated production-distribution setup but not active as exhibitors) were trying to dissociate themselves from the "Big Five" during the trial by saying that since they owned no theaters they could not possibly be guilty of conspiracy in the exhibition field, the government replied that they had been guilty of perpetuating the monopoly of the Big Five by favoring the latter's theaters over those operated by independent exhibitors, and that the method used to perpetuate the monopoly had been the offering of more favorable terms of clearance and of smaller blocks of product to the theaters affiliated with the Big Five.

This method of selling product unseen, in advance, and in more or less sizable blocks had been the exhibitors' second complaint for more than thirty years. At the third session of the Seventy-sixth Congress, during the hearings before the Committee on Interstate Commerce in the House of Representatives, Miss Jeannette Willensky, secretary of the Independent Motion Picture Theatre Owners of Eastern Pennsylvania, explained the exhibitors' view of this process of block booking and blind selling with a degree of blandness never since equaled:

Columbia promises to make a minimum of thirty-two and a maximum of forty . . . the work sheet states that the program will be selected from properties of the company and from additional outstanding stories acquired during the year. First National-Warner Brothers Pictures will make twenty-seven. Only numbers appear on the contracts and work sheets. If you buy from First National, you get numbers 951 to 977. If you buy from Warner Brothers, you get numbers 901 to 927. And the distributor also reserves the right to alter the prices and terms of four pictures, by merely giving a notice to the exhibitor. . . . Fox Pictures will make a maximum of fifty and a minimum of forty. . . . The names of features will be given in the trade journals during the year. . . . R.K.O. will make forty-five pictures, identified only by numbers 601 to 646. No description of the subjects. Universal will make thirty-six pictures, founded on published works . . .

The designation of play dates by the distributor has always provoked the most bitter opposition among exhibitors. Theater attendance varies from day to day in a fairly regular pattern: Monday, Tuesday, Wednesday, and Thursday each contribute 10 percent of the week's gross; Friday provides 15 percent, Saturday 20 percent, and Sunday 25 percent. If the distributor made a cash deal and specified Monday to Thursday as the days of the week on which the exhibitor was licensed to show the picture, the exhibitor naturally felt bitter. If, on the other hand, the distributor made a percentage deal, and specified Friday to Sunday as play dates, the exhibitor felt rooked for different reasons.

The Department of Justice, in its proposed findings of fact, said on June 22, 1946:

The differentials in admission prices set by a distributor in licensing a particular picture in theatres exhibiting on different runs in the same competitive area are calculated to encourage as many patrons as possible to see the picture in prior-run theatres where they will pay higher prices than on subsequent runs. The reason for this is that if 10,000 people of a city population are ultimately to see the picture—no matter on what run—the gross revenue to be realized from their patronage is increased relatively to the increase in numbers seeing it at higher prices in prior-run theatres. In effect, the distributor, by the fixing of minimum admission prices, attempts to give the prior-run exhibitors as near a monopoly of the patronage as possible.

During the trial the majors held that all these practices, though they might occasionally turn to the disadvantage of an odd exhibitor, were essential to the survival of the industry. To this the government replied that if the faithful application of the Sherman Act would really lead to the ruin of the industry, it would be up to the defendants to petition Congress, as the proper legal body, to grant them the right to maintain a special monopolistic position, but that the Department of Justice was not authorized to alter the Sherman Act so as to keep the defendants in business.

On New Year's Eve in the midst of tin whistles, paper streamers, and funny hats, the court quietly slipped in its final decree. Most of the press ignored it, and the *Herald Tribune,* one of the few papers to notice it at all, came out with a five-inch boner headlined "Eight Film Companies Cleared of Sherman Law Charges." Six days later, before plaintiff and defendants had found time to study the decision, the whole case threatened to blow up with the compliments of the season. The man who had thrown the firecracker into Foley Square was Abram F. Myers, general counsel of two of the independent theater owners' associations, who announced his intention to call upon the House Judiciary Committee with a request to investigate "actions and connections" of one of the judges of the statutory court. Alleging that Judge Henry W. Goddard's wife was the owner of a theater leased to two of the defendants, Warner and Paramount, he asked for investigation of the "lengthy delays in the case agreed to by one of the judges," and the alleged "indulgence" of the same judge toward defense counsel's "delaying tactics."

Immediately the government announced its decision to appeal to the Supreme Court, the defendants announced their intention to take cross-appeals, and the independent theater owners, who probably had more at stake than either of the contending parties but had so far been able only to give gratuitous advice as "friends of the court," now announced their intention to intervene actively by petition to the Supreme Court. Everybody knew, however, that no industrialist had been sent to prison in more than forty-five years for a violation of the antitrust laws, and the degree of unconcern within the industry was most clearly indicated by the almost rock-steady tenor of the majors' stocks. The maximum drop after the announcement of the decision was about one-fourth of a point, and the enforcement of the court's judgment was seen as so distant as to leave things pretty much as they were under the consent decree.

As in all previous trials, the government had failed to obtain its main objective—theater divestiture—on which all other measures of relief were ultimately dependent. What it had got was a whole grab bag of odd concessions which went just a little beyond the terms of the consent decree but had the strange effect of being more violently attacked by the exhibitors, who were supposed to have been the main beneficiaries, than by the majors, the unwilling benefactors.

Technically, the court held the defendants' claim that they had a legal method of doing business, based on their copyright, to be untrue and the method, as such, to be illegal. The decree, in so many words, declared that the defendants had "unreasonably restrained trade and commerce in the distribution and exhibition of motion pictures and attempted to monopolize such trade and commerce." But in effect, while condemning the method by which the defendants had acquired their theaters, the court allowed them to retain control over them, regardless of whether the process of acquisition had been valid or invalid under the Sherman Act. Moreover, the fact that the court had allowed the defendants a free hand with respect to the theaters they owned, while ordering them to sell films to all other competitors on an auction basis, was immediately attacked not only by the independent exhibitors, but also by those semiindependent theaters and chains of theaters which had in the past reached a working agreement with the majors. Instead of full divorcement of exhibition from distribution and production, the court had thrown out the whole discussion of production monopolies and had offered only limited restrictions upon selected distribution practices. Instead of devising a more effective method of arbitration between distributors and exhibitors, the court had washed its hands of the entire arbitration system. Instead of declaring the whole practice of clearance and zoning invalid, the court had substituted competitive bidding on individual pictures for block booking in groups of five. Instead of making the system of competitive bidding compulsory on a national basis, the court had made it optional by limiting it to "competitive areas." This was a compromise which pleased no one.

"As far as the relief aspects of the case are concerned, the defendants might as well have written the decision themselves," said the assistant attorney general. The government had defined a monopoly as restriction of trade and had recommended dissolution of the monopoly as "the traditional judicial method used to restore competition in industries dominated by combinations." The court had rejected this definition and had chosen instead to define monopoly as *conspiracy* in restraint of trade. While the government had been concerned with the effect, the court had dealt only with the motive; the result was that the defendants were allowed to maintain control wherever the government had failed to prove that such control had arisen from their "inherent vice," or from their explicit "purpose of creating a monopoly." The court, in fact, went so far as to specify that "ownership by a single defendant of all first-run theatres" was no monopoly if such ownership was the result of the independent exhibitors' "lack of financial ability to build theatres comparable to those of the defendants." This definition knocked hell out of the government's whole argument, for it had been the very lack of this financial ability that had given rise to the complaint of restricted competition. The question of "inherent vice" had never entered the government's case, and was therefore felt to be entirely beside the point.

Following the same line of logic, the court had dismissed the complaint of monopoly against the defendants "based upon their acts as producers." "None of the defendants," the court said bluntly, "has monopolized ... to restrain trade or commerce in any part of the business of producing motion pictures." In the limited sense in which the court had defined monopoly, this was perfectly true. The government's point, however, was not that the defendants, as producers, had attempted to monopolize the studios, but that their triple function as producers, distributors, and exhibitors had allowed them to prevent independently produced films from obtaining distribution comparable to that of their own. The government had, therefore, petitioned for dissolution of production from distribution, as well as for dissolution of distribution from exhibition. The court, having dismissed the first, had logically to refuse the second.

The independent exhibitors, siding with the government, complained that, although the court appeared to have frozen the defendants' theater holdings, it had in fact allowed them to strengthen their hold upon the theater market. Even the clause calling for the divestment of part-owned theaters was felt to be capable of a second interpretation: if a distributor owned 95 percent or more of a theater he was allowed to maintain control of it, and if he owned less than 95 percent he did not automatically have to divest himself of it either but could, on the contrary, petition the court to acquire the whole of it, by claiming that the acquisition did not "unduly restrain competition." If competition was defined as "financial ability" to build or maintain theaters, and if restraint upon competition was defined as "inherent vice," the distributors might well be expected to succeed in obtaining complete control of the theater market with the approval of the very court which had been called to break that control.

Not only were the independent and semiindependent exhibitors concerned, but the "Little Three," who at the beginning of the trial seemed least concerned with its results, suddenly became extremely disturbed about the provision that permitted the Big Five to retain their theaters, but prohibited the lesser defendants from acquiring or building theaters without court approval.

And even the independent exhibitors, who by the spirit of the decree were the only ones allowed to acquire new theaters, were dissatisfied because they had been allowed to do so even before this decision. The decision's only result, that they could see, was the sudden inflation in the asking price of theaters available for purchase and of real estate plots suitable for the erection of new theaters.

As for auctioning each picture individually rather than selling all of them en bloc, the exhibitor's first reaction was fear of rising film rentals. When unlimited block booking had been replaced, under the consent decree, by limited block booking in groups of five, the rentals had gone up so drastically that many of the smaller independents had been driven out of business. Now that the expense of auctioning and trade-showing each picture individually had been made compulsory in competitive areas, the exhibitors, aside from the competitive forcing of prices to be expected, saw themselves faced with the possibility of being continually outbid by the majors' affiliated theaters. Some independent exhibitors foresaw the majors' bidding as high as 75 percent per film, even at the risk of taking losses, just to keep control of the theaters in a given area. Other exhibitors, who under the old system had obtained special privileges owing to their long establishment in business, now saw the possibility of their being unable to compete with large theater chains, who were certain to try to buy up all theaters unable to meet the new film rentals.

Even recourse to arbitration was not viewed with too much hope by the independents. Unable to afford legal counsel of the same caliber as the majors, the small exhibitor had learnt, even under the consent decree, to desist from arbitration and be content with whatever the majors cared to offer him, rather than to invite their ill will by entering into legal battles with them.

Nor were the majors themselves entirely happy. Pointing out that the court decision had specifically named only eight companies and their subsidiaries, they asked whether the decision had any bearing at all upon the industry as such: whether it would, if and when it became law, be applicable, for instance, to such smaller distributors as Republic, Monogram, and SRO, and whether these companies might not be allowed to beat the majors at their own game by acquiring theaters and developing a system of clearances, franchises, formula deals, and all the other tricks of the trade, while the majors themselves were specifically enjoined from pursuing any and all of these practices.

But the distributors' worst fear, and the main reason for their cross-appeal to the Supreme Court, was the possibility that the decision, if permitted to stand on the government's appeal, would constitute a prima facie case of conspiracy for any independent theater owner who might care to bring private litigation against them. The decree, therefore, did not merely threaten them with a possible loss of income in the distant future, but put them in imminent danger of millions of dollars of damage claims stretching back through the whole period prescribed by the statutes of limitation.

Small wonder, then, that the Supreme Court, when it came to rule on the various appeals and cross-appeals, found itself with nothing else to do than to throw out all six key issues of the statutory court's decree—theater divestiture, joint ownership of theaters, franchises, cross-licensing, auction bidding, and arbitration. Most important, however, it ruled against the whole principle of defining restraint of trade in terms of *intent* and defined it instead in terms of *effect*.

"It is," said the Court in a ruling specifically addressed to the Griffith Circuit, "not always necessary to find a specific intent to restrain trade or to build a monopoly in order to find that the anti-trust laws have been violated. It is sufficient that a restraint of trade or monopoly results as a consequence of a defendant's conduct or business. . . . So it is that monopoly power, whether lawfully or unlawfully acquired, may itself constitute an evil and stand condemned under Section 2, even though it remains unexercised. . . . We remit to the district court not only that problem but also the fashioning of a decree which will undo as near as may be the wrongs that were done and prevent their recurrence in the future."

This, for the first time in the history of the case, was a decision so clear-cut that two of the defendants did not even bother to wait for the district court to "undo the wrongs that were done" before they decided to compromise and apply for a new consent decree. The other three of the Big Five, however, decided to play for time and launch another series of appeals.

What followed was most instructive. Both groups, of course, now accepted the principle of divestiture, but whereas the three die-hard companies—MGM, Warner, and Twentieth-Century Fox—got little more than an extension till July 1953 to carry out the order of the Court, the two conciliatory companies—RKO and Paramount—succeeded in obtaining a major concession: after splitting themselves in two, the new production-distribution outfit was allowed in due course to reacquire theaters while the new theater-owning company was permitted in due course to produce films again.

This, of course, was a direct violation of the spirit of the Sherman Act and, if it proved anything, it proved once more how easily the purport even of the Supreme Court's decisions could be overruled by the weight of economic pressure; but it had also the farcical result of showing how fast the three diehards could run when they saw a good thing.

Warner was the first of them to apply for a consent decree of its own. Submitted to the trial court on January 4, 1951, the draft immediately raised a question which was to influence all further divorce argument—the question of who was to run the new companies. Would the three Warner brothers, for instance, be allowed to take charge of the three new production, distribution, and exhibition companies?

The government said no. Whereupon the three Skouras brothers, who run Twentieth Century-Fox, declared that they would agree only to a consent decree which left them in charge of the three new Twentieth Century companies to be set up.

By then, however, a much more serious problem had crept up which took the whole case back to its economic roots. RKO, which was now ready to implement its consent decree, found itself faced with a demand for immediate repayment of $8,500,000 worth of loans. Why? Because the production-distribution end of RKO had been operating at a loss all through 1950 and had been kept above water only by the profits of the theaters.

A quick look at its books told Warner's creditors that things, though less acute, were hardly satisfactory there either; for whereas the theater-owning wing had earned a fair 62 percent of the company's totals over the last ten years, the production-distribution end had earned a bare 32 percent of the net. Since the consent decree now proposed that all stockholders would receive one half-share in each of the new companies in exchange for each share in the old one, the question naturally arose whether the gains of the new theater company would continue to offset the possible losses of the new production-distribution company.

So much for the majors, their creditors, and their stockholders. As for the independent exhibitors, who might have been expected to be pleased now that they had at last obtained what they had asked for, the whole situation had been altered by the advent of television. Rightly, they now feared that the new production-distribution companies, unhampered by any loyalties to their one-time theaters or to any others, would now sell freely to television networks, 16mm users, and other nontheatrical buyers, leaving the theaters with a scarcity of films, an increase in competition, and an inflation of rentals.

From enemies of monopoly, the independents now turned into active monopolists, banding together to exert pressure on distributors not to sell pictures to television networks under threat of losing theater-owning customers. The Justice Department's Antitrust Division, once the theater owners' best friend, now became their worst enemy when it supported the television networks in their battle against theater pressure. And, to make the paradox complete, the independents now began to clamor for a reunification of the divorced majors so as to give the producer-distributors a new vested interest in theater ownership.

That made just about everyone unhappy. When the Justice Department, the Little Three, the theater pools, the large independents, the small independents, and the Big Five had all had their say, everyone thought that everything had been said that could be said. Then a new voice spoke up. The Internal Revenue Service, bland as only tax collectors can be, announced that the winners of treble-damage awards in successful antitrust actions brought by independent exhibitors against major distributors would have to declare their awards as personal profits and pay income tax on them at the top rate of 80 or 90 percent. This meant that if he failed to recover his costs, the exhibitor, after paying his attorney's fees, would probably find himself in the red as a result of seeing justice triumphant.

While the merry haha of the ultimate paradox went echoing down the Doric halls of the U.S. Courthouse, the silent man in the visitors' gallery silently got up and walked out to pay homage. Depositing his two quarters at the box office of his local theater, he became once again the consumer who foots the bill. All through the trial, the defendants contended that all their trade practices had been developed precisely so as to bring the best pictures at the cheapest price to the largest number of consumers, while the plaintiff contended that it had been precisely the public which had been most grievously harmed by the defendants' attempts to force prices and withhold pictures from competitive theaters. Neither plaintiff, nor defendants, nor the Court bothered to define what was meant by the "best" pictures. It was notable, however, throughout the trial, that whenever a defendant spoke of a "good" film he was in fact referring to one which had been expensive to produce, or which had grossed well at the box office. In either case, *esthetic value* or, to use the industry's own vocabulary, *entertainment value* had been identified with an economic category of sorts. If any single incident was required to point up the common failure of all parties concerned in the conflict, it was this failure to see the motion picture as something transcending the terms of economic categories.

For what happened to RKO and Paramount after they had begun to put divorcement measures into effect was far from reassuring. Without certainty of theatrical outlets, their distribution offices now began to exert more pressure than ever on the production staff to turn out "sure things" rather than "prestige items." This meant that whereas in the past there had been occasional scope for experimental films in which the production people could do their best work, divorcement had now removed the margin of certainty which theatrical outlets had once provided. Instead of better films, the public got routine grist from the celluloid mill.

The most salient comment on this situation was made by the *Stanford University Law Review*, which attacked the government's brief, the Supreme Court's ruling, the trial court's decree, and the two consent agreements alike on the simple grounds that a form of divorcement which left production at the mercy of distribution, and distribution at the mercy of vast theater circuits, was worse than no divorce at all.

Urging a separation of production from distribution and a breakup of all chains of theaters, the article termed the present system an "oligopoly" which would continue to monopolize the market by dint of the small number of distributors and their excessive power.

In this connection it is significant that the American Civil Liberties Union filed a motion asking leave to intervene as friend of the court on the ground that "the questions involved. . . are of paramount sociological importance and vitally affect . . . the general public in the attainment of maximum freedom and diversity of expression," and that this petition was denied by the court on the ground that "the interests of the public are amply represented by the government in this case."

The government's brief admitted that public interest was directly involved, inasmuch as the admission prices of all theaters, whether independent or controlled by the Big Five, were in effect controlled by the trade practices of the Big Five; but the very definition of "public interest" in these terms stood as an indictment of the whole procedure.

17

THOMAS H. GUBACK

Hollywood's International Market

When the Supreme Court ruled in 1915 that "the exhibition of motion pictures is a business pure and simple, originated and conducted
for profit," that was considered sufficient reason to refuse films protection as speech under the First Amendment. Today it certainly is
obvious, as it should have been then, that film is not just an ordinary
business, but one vested with social consequences because of its com-
municative powers. As such, film is a mixture of business and art.

It is the commercial aspect of film, however, that establishes the
priorities governing production decisions and is responsible for putting
on the screen the shadows that captivate and mesmerize us. By being
made in such an environment, motion pictures naturally support dominant thought patterns and are especially noncritical of the economic
system that nurtures them.

A unique attribute of a motion picture is that virtually its entire cost
is incurred in making the first copy. Duplicates require little additional
investment, and wide distribution hastens the flow of revenue to producers who are obliged to repay loans from banks and financiers. Be-

This article was abridged by the editor from a longer manuscript prepared especially
for this collection. For more discussion on the subject of the film industry's worldwide
operations see the following publications by Thomas Guback: *The International Film
Industry* (Bloomington: Indiana University Press, 1969); "American Interests in the
British Film Industry," *Quarterly Review of Economics and Business* 7 (Summer 1967):
7–21; "Film and Cultural Pluralism," *Journal of Aesthetic Education* 5 (April 1971): 35–
51; "Film as International Business," *Journal of Communication* 24 (Winter 1974): 90–
101; and "Cultural Identity and Film in the European Economic Community," *Cinema
Journal* 14 (Fall 1974): 2–17.

Poster of Michael Todd's *Around the World in 80 Days,* shot in Todd A. O.
(United Artists, 1956)

cause exported prints deprive the home market of nothing, while offering the producer a larger base on which to recoup his investment, it is not surprising that film has become a staple commodity in international trade.

Foreign markets are essential because a nation with productive capacities beyond its own needs is compelled to dispose of its excess wares abroad. Hollywood, however, exports films not primarily because it has product surpluses but because high production costs have made it difficult to recoup investments from the home market alone. The exploitation of foreign markets by the American film industry requires attention, for it demonstrates that film, in addition to being a commercial enterprise, is also a conveyor of values and myths.

Forging International Distribution Chains after World War I

World War I was a dramatic turning point for the United States because it changed our status from a debtor to a creditor nation. Between 1915 and 1920, the leading European nations became debtors to the United States, whereas at the beginning of the century over $3 billion of American securities had been held in Europe. The war redirected the international flow of capital, as surpluses in Europe were shot away at the fronts and American capital in the form of war loans and goods was sent abroad.

The motion picture was one product to benefit from these conditions. European film industries had either been disrupted or forced out of business, creating a vacuum into which American pictures flowed, often at alarming rates. In 1913, the last prewar year, some 32 million feet of motion pictures were exported from America; a decade later, the amount had more than quadrupled, and by 1925 it stood at 235 million feet. During these dozen years American film exports increased fivefold to Europe and tenfold to the remainder of the world, as the industry developed markets in the Far East, Latin America, and in a few parts of Africa.

It was possible for American films to achieve this dominance because they usually were amortized in the home market, which had about half the world's theaters, and thus could be rented abroad cheaply. Such a policy, of course, was a blow to foreign producers who suddenly found their own home markets glutted by American pictures. A result of the war, therefore, was that American distributors were able to gain control of the foreign field without competition. And by the time capital was once more available for production abroad, American films had obtained almost complete control of world markets.

The exports to Europe, however, were of special significance because they generated about 65 percent of overseas revenue. By 1925, a third of all foreign revenue came from the United Kingdom alone, where American films captured 95 percent of the market. In the same period, 77 percent of the features shown in France came from the United States, as did about 66 percent in Italy. America's entry was achieved often at the expense of foreign producers, by dumping, underselling, and block booking. The quality of European filmmaking was not a factor; on the contrary, Hollywood thought so well of foreign films that it brought directors and stars to America, and freely borrowed European production techniques.

Selling overseas extended American distribution chains around the globe, from which they have never retreated. Sidney Kent, general manager of Paramount Publix, could boast in 1927 that a "foreign negative is shipped to London and then to other countries and averages a hundred and forty-two prints, distributed among a hundred and fifteen foreign exchanges serving seventy-three countries," and that "titles are translated from English into thirty-six languages." In fifty-five countries, Paramount did enough business to warrant having its own offices and staff. Even at that time, it was evident that film was a very special kind of merchandise. As Kent explained:

Motion pictures are silent propaganda, even though not made with that thought in mind at all. . . . Imagine the effect on people . . . who constantly see flashed on the screen American modes of living, American modes of dressing, and American modes of travel. . . . American automobiles are making terrific inroads on foreign makes of cars [because] the greatest agency for selling American automobiles abroad is the American motion picture. Its influence is working insidiously all the time and even though all this is done without any conscious intent, the effect is that of a direct sales agency.[1]

Kent recognized fifty years ago what has since become a commonplace: "The American motion picture bears a great and direct relation to the American trade balance abroad." He meant trade in goods, but he could have included ideas.

In evolving a foreign investment policy in the 1920s, the government encouraged expansion of markets for American goods (and capital). A former U.S. trade commissioner in Europe was able to write that it "is the business of the United States Government" to put its information-gathering services overseas at the disposal of American businessmen because "success in foreign trade is based on a full knowledge of the needs and conditions in the foreign market. . . . We have . . .

---

1. Sidney R. Kent, "Distributing the Product," in Joseph P. Kennedy, ed., *The Story of the Films*, (Chicago and New York: A. W. Shaw, 1927), p. 206.

representatives abroad who look after our economic welfare as the diplomats look after our political welfare."[2] As an exportable commodity, therefore, the motion picture was aided along with other goods, and the pattern of assistance continues to the present day. Film also presents propaganda for the system it represents, and government, in turn, has helped the industry remove foreign barriers protecting national film industries from Hollywood's incursions. Thus, on the eve of sound, American films dominated the world market. It was not just that trade seemed to follow the film, but that film was (and is) trade. Bankers, at this time, finally recognized the financial vision of one of their number, A. H. Giannini, and began investing heavily in the film industry, thereby adding Wall Street's power to Hollywood's.

Especially irritating to foreign filmmakers was their inability to achieve reciprocity in the American market, or for that matter even to penetrate it. In 1913, the United States imported some sixteen million feet of motion pictures, but by 1925 the amount had fallen to about seven million feet. Foreign producers were "denied access . . . for the sufficient reason that this market can now [1926] be profitably reached only through one or more of a group of not more than ten national American distributors . . . each of which is busily engaged in marketing its own brand of pictures through its own sales or rental organizations, and through the theatres owned, controlled, or operated by one or more of this group."[3] In effect, the United States became virtually a closed market, with vertical integration and horizontal cooperation assuring that theaters would exhibit products of the major Hollywood companies first, and those of independents second. The small number of foreign films played mostly in metropolitan centers, where a handful of theaters catered to ethnic audiences. Until the early 1950s, foreign films remained unknown quantities to most Americans. Their seeming lack of box office appeal "proved" that it was the homemade variety that was "in demand."

Sound solidified the position of American films overseas. By adding to costs, sound made film production for small markets increasingly precarious. As films had to be amortized somewhere, producers who had access to large domestic markets obviously had an edge. As Forsyth Hardy has explained:

When films were silent and the Scandinavian producers could sell their films—as they did—all over the world, their achievement was remarkable in that they

2. Harry T. Collings, "United States Government Aid to Foreign Trade," *Annals of the American Academy of Political and Social Science* 127 (September 1926): 134, 135.

3. William Marston Seabury, *The Public and the Motion Picture Industry* (New York: Macmillan, 1926), p. 195.

were competing successfully with stronger units in larger countries. When sound reached the cinema . . . the mere survival of [their] filmmaking became remarkable.[4]

Resistance to Hollywood's Exports

In the mid- and late 1920s many foreign countries began to be concerned about the influx of American films. There were two major reasons for their concern. First, on the business side, American pictures preempted exhibition time and rendered locally made films greater financial risks. Consequently, few were produced. The development of talent suffered as well, for there was less certainty that one could profitably pursue a career in film alone. Efforts to produce films on low budgets sometimes led to a reduction in technical standards and artistic excellence, giving such pictures even less chance to succeed either at home or elsewhere in competition with Hollywood's slickly finished exports. There also was concern about the money drawn by American films from foreign countries, amounts that some believed ought to remain at home as long as no reciprocal income was derived from America. Germany, for example, hoped that restrictions on U.S. pictures would give its own pictures a greater chance for exhibition.

Second, on the cultural side, film was considered a great medium of information and persuasion, which not only selectively presented certain traits and ideals but also glamorized them, even if unintentionally. Hollywood's output pointed up American stories and myths, American products and values. In 1926 it was already being charged (by no less than a former general counsel of the Motion Picture Board of Trade in the United States) that "American producers are now actively 'Americanizing' England, her dominions and colonies, and all of Europe."[5] Indeed, the British Empire was being superseded by the American Empire. More than forty years later one could write of the consequences and say that "gunboat diplomacy is now an item in the antiquities showcase but communications diplomacy is a very thriving business."[6]

Germany was the first major market to take action against American pictures. In 1925 it introduced a contingent act governing film imports. Distributors were issued a permit to release a foreign film each time

4. Forsyth Hardy, *Scandinavian Film* (London: Falcon Press, 1952), p. ix.

5. Seabury, *Public and the Motion Picture Industry*, p. 198.

6. Herbert I. Schiller, *Mass Communications and American Empire* (New York: A.M. Kelley, 1969), p. 110.

they financed and distributed a German one. The United Kingdom, France, and Italy quickly followed Germany's example. In France, a limit was placed on the number of film imports, whereas in the United Kingdom and in Italy quotas on exhibition required that a certain percentage of screen time annually be devoted to locally made films. The Italian law set it at a conservative 10 percent; the British quota, in the Films Act of 1927, was progressive, beginning at 5 percent and rising to 20 percent in ten years' time. But constant production difficulties led, in Britain, to the making of cheap "quota quickies," preying upon the exhibitors' demands for any national picture to comply with the letter of the law. The Films Act of 1938 attempted to legislate these pictures out of existence by establishing a minimum cost test, while resetting the quota at 12.5 percent, with provisions to raise it to 25 percent by 1947.

In any event, the great wave of American film exportation that started after World War I produced retaliatory import quotas, distributor quotas, and screen quotas, designed either to control the number of such pictures on the market or to reserve a portion of screen time, however small, for domestic filmmakers. The objective was not merely to protect or stimulate domestic production, but also to prevent a medium of local artistic and cultural expression from being forced out of existence by the commercial strength of America's film industry. The sentiments of foreigners were convincingly summed up in a question once raised by a British government official. "Should we be content," he asked, "if we depended upon foreign literature or upon a foreign Press in this country?"[7]

Government-Industry Alliance

These menaces to American commercial interests prompted Hollywood to enlist the aid of the American government, an alliance that has continued to the present. In the late 1920s, the State Department interceded on the industry's behalf in France, Spain, Italy, Germany, Austria, Hungary, and Czechoslovakia (all of which were considering new or revised restrictions aimed at American pictures) by stressing that the building of foreign markets had involved large investments, and that these could be jeopardized by arbitrary measures restricting the distribution of American films. The State Department alleged, in defending Hollywood's trade policy, that foreign restrictions "intro-

7. Quoted in Political and Economic Planning, *The British Film Industry* (London: PEP, 1952), p. 43.

duce an element of commercial uncertainty and industrial instability to which American motion picture producers and distributors find it difficult or impossible to adjust themselves." In other words, the State Department along with American companies did not appreciate foreigners' trying to protect themselves in their own markets. The tribulations of foreign producers were conveniently overlooked with the argument that was to become standard whenever American film interests were threatened: "This government had adopted no restrictive regulations similar in any way to those enforced in certain foreign countries."[8] The statement created the impression that America was a free market, which it was not because the structure and policy of the industry in the United States quite effectively, without help from Washington, kept the home market for its own films.

Functioning as a sort of watchdog over the international affairs of the industry was the Foreign Department of the Motion Picture Producers and Distributors of America (MPPDA). It maintained contact overseas with the offices of member companies, with foreign government personnel responsible for cinema matters, and with officials of the Department of State and the Department of Commerce. The twofold duty of the department was to try to keep foreign distribution channels open for U.S. films and to inform Hollywood about censorship policies. A great deal was at stake, because until the beginning of World War II, American companies were deriving about a third of their revenue from abroad.

The Foreign Market after World War II

Film industries everywhere naturally felt the effects of World War II. By 1944, Hollywood's foreign market had been reduced to the British Empire, Latin America, and some neutral countries of little economic importance. Companies made every effort to maintain and enlarge their position in the United Kingdom, the most important foreign market, especially when the exhibitors' quota had to be abandoned in 1942 for five years. The war caused a drastic cutback in production in Britain and continental Europe. Afterward, though, opportunities for foreign filmmakers did not improve. Filmmaking equipment had been damaged or destroyed, and production capital became scarce as war-torn nations rebuilt their economies. Moreover, protective measures developed during the 1920s and 1930s were stripped away, leaving many countries cinematically defenseless. This factor was crucial

8. Quoted in Howard T. Lewis, *The Motion Picture Industry* (New York: Van Nostrand, 1933), p. 406.

because, with many markets closed to Hollywood during the war, a tremendous backlog of unplayed films had built up and were ready to be released abroad. In short, the war actually enhanced the status of the American film industry at the expense of others. Ground that foreign industries might have recovered was inevitably—sometimes irretrievably—lost.

The importance that the American film industry attached to its foreign markets became even more urgent after the war. In 1945, the MPPDA changed its name to the Motion Picture Association of America (MPAA), and the former Foreign Department took on new life as the Motion Picture Export Association. The MPEA was organized as a legal cartel under provisions of the Webb-Pomerene Export Trade Act of 1918. This legislation was one of the earliest government efforts to stimulate exporting by small and medium-sized firms at a time when few companies were concerned with foreign markets. The act permitted domestic competitors to cooperate in foreign trade by forming export associations that might otherwise have been held illegal under the Sherman Antitrust Act of 1890 and the Clayton Antitrust Act of 1914. This exemption allowed companies supposedly in competition in the American market to combine, to fix prices, and to allocate customers in foreign markets.

The act permitted the MPEA to act as the sole export sales agent for its members, to set prices and terms of trade for films, and to make arrangements for their distribution abroad. In bringing together the majors and allowing them to act in concert through a single organization, the MPEA presented a "united front" to the nations of the world, and by legal internal collusion prevented possible ruinous competition among American film companies overseas. The MPEA facilitated the international activities of its members by expanding markets and keeping them open, expediting transfers of income to the United States, reducing restrictions on American films through direct negotiations and "other appropriate means," distributing information about market conditions to members, and negotiating film import agreements and rental terms. The MPEA maintains a headquarters in the United States as well as an extensive network abroad. As Jack Valenti, MPEA/MPAA president (and former White House aide to Lyndon Johnson), has remarked: "To my knowledge, the motion picture is the only U.S. enterprise that negotiates on its own with foreign governments."[9] It is not surprising that the MPEA is called "the little State Department."

9. Jack Valenti, "The 'Foreign Service' of the Motion Picture Association of America," *Journal of the Producers Guild of America* 10 (March 1968): 22.

Baby Doll at the London Pavilion

Even before the war's end, plans were being made to recapture overseas markets for American media. As Allied troops liberated Europe, American motion pictures followed in their path, with exhibition arranged by the Bureau of Psychological Warfare. The Office of War Information was handling the distribution of U.S. films in France, Belgium, the Netherlands, and Italy, until American companies could reopen their offices. The propaganda value of such pictures was clearly recognized because, as a Department of Commerce representative explained, "Only the movies which put America's best foot forward will be sent abroad."[10] The cold war reinforced this stance. By assuming the role of world policeman, the United States instituted vigorous measures to prevent many countries dissatisfied with capitalism from drifting toward the left. For example, the Marshall Plan provided funds to bolster West European economies and to stimulate production and reconstruction. The exportation of American media materials was deemed essential to the government's effort because they favorably depicted the American system.

The length to which the United States was willing to go to protect its interests was revealed early in 1975. Previously unpublished State Department documents indicated that in 1948 President Truman was so concerned about a possible Communist election victory in Italy that he approved a top-secret recommendation that the United States "make full use of its political, economic, and, if necessary, military power" to prevent it.[11] Part of the American policy, aimed against popular election processes, involved combatting left-wing appeals in Italy with U.S. information programs. Obviously, American films had their role to play. The government vigorously assisted in their global distribution for political reasons, while the industry seconded that view because it was congruent with its economic aims. In 1950, Eric Johnston, MPEA/MPAA president, was able to write: "Many times I have talked with President Truman about the influence of American films abroad, and he has said he regards American films as 'ambassadors of good will.' "[12]

Thus the MPEA launched its postwar distribution campaign with the blessing and indeed the support of the government. The backlog of unplayed pictures, said Johnston, "flooded in, even more than the countries could absorb."[13] The results were described in a UNESCO report:

10. *Motion Picture Letter* [issued by the Public Information Committee of the Motion Picture Industry] 3 (September 1944) and 4 (February 1945).
11. *New York Times,* February 12, 1975, p. 9.
12. Eric Johnston, "Messengers from a Free Country," Motion Picture Association of America. The article also was published in *Saturday Review of Literature* 33 (March 4, 1950): 9–12.
13. U.S. Congress, Senate, Committee on Foreign Relations, *Hearings, Overseas Information Programs of the United States,* 83d Congress, 1st Sess., 1953, Pt. 2, p. 272.

The large number of cheap American films available . . . apart from adding to the dollar deficit, is only one of the factors prejudicing the development of national film production industries. These industries, unable to recover their outlay on the films which they produce, are stunted in growth and become unable to meet the demand of the national market. The exhibitors, therefore, are driven to depend for their existence upon foreign, largely American, films.[14]

However, European nations, in debt and with little or no dollar reserves, could not afford the luxury of importing American films when essential commodities were needed. These countries, therefore, had to develop measures to protect themselves and their film industries not only from American pictures but also from the substantial drain on hard currency that their exhibition entailed. This latter currency problem posed a new complicating factor: balance of payments. To stem the dollar outflow, foreign governments passed measures much as they had after World War I, but in addition they instituted currency restrictions freezing earnings generated by American companies. Hollywood preferred to settle for repatriation of a share and leave the remainder rather than refuse to export films and quit the markets altogether.

As a result, the MPEA, with State Department help, concluded a number of film trade treaties with foreign countries. One, the 1948 Anglo-American Film Agreement, allowed U.S. companies to withdraw annually only $17 million of their earnings (leaving more than $40 million each year to accumulate in blocked accounts), in exchange for access to the British market unhindered by import quotas. However, the pact permitted American companies to spend their frozen earnings in Britain to produce films, acquire story rights, and buy real estate and studios.

Similar terms appeared in the 1948 Franco-American Film Agreement, which allowed U.S. firms to withdraw up to $3.6 million annually in earnings, leaving about $10 million blocked each year. These frozen funds could be spent for joint production of films with French companies, construction of new studios, acquisition of distribution and story rights, and so on. The agreement also permitted 121 American films annually to enter France, although all the rest of the world's producing countries had to scramble for and divide among themselves a total of only sixty-five import permits. This obvious inequity reflected the mighty bargaining position of the MPEA and the State

14. The Film Centre, *The Film Industry in Six European Countries* (Paris: UNESCO 1950), p. 21.

Department, as well as the effect of Marshall Plan aid upon the affairs of many countries.

The 1948 pact, as advantageous as it was, replaced a May 1946 agreement which placed no limit on the importation of U.S. films and provided no obstacles to the dumping of old pictures. Known as the Blum-Byrnes agreement, and bitterly remembered even today by some French cinephiles, it demonstrated the "fine cooperation" between the State Department and the film industry, according to Eric Johnston. He believed as well at the time that the "best possible course is to continue the present policy of the State Department . . . which is based wholly on the traditional American belief in freedom of expression and communication".[15] The effect of the Blum-Byrnes agreement on the French industry was so grave that Committees for the Defense of the French Film were organized to draw public attention to it. Obviously the motive of the agreement was to make France a "free market" for the dumping of U.S. pictures, as Italy turned out to be when it received an average of over 570 American films annually in the first four postwar years.

Because the balance-of-payments problem affected other media as well, it was seen by our government as an obstacle to the broad dissemination of the American point of view by private means. To overcome this obstacle, the Informational Media Guaranty Program was established in 1948 as part of the Economic Cooperation Administration. The program guaranteed that the U.S. government would convert certain foreign currencies into dollars at attractive rates, provided the information materials earning the moneys reflected appropriate elements of American life. This was a decided advantage to Hollywood companies, for it allowed them to distribute and exhibit their films in difficult currency areas with complete assurance that some of the resulting revenue would become available in dollars. American films then went forward into the world with the rank of ambassador. From the inception of the IMG Program until mid-1966, American motion picture companies received close to $16 million under the currency conversion provision.

Changes in the Domestic Market after 1950

A number of forces intersecting in the early 1950s made a significant impact on the industry and its markets. Theater attendance declined drastically, first as suburban living, new forms of leisure, and an abun-

15. *Motion Picture Letter* 6 (February 1947).

dance of consumer goods altered the moviegoing habit, and then by the spread of television, which provided not only its own "free" entertainment but also old Hollywood films. Simultaneously, the industry underwent an upheaval brought about by the *Paramount* decision in 1948: the majors were forced to divorce their exhibition branches from their production-distribution companies; the affiliated theater chains had to divest themselves of some houses; and new procedures

Federico Fellini's *La Dolce Vita* (1959): Anita Ekberg

for marketing films were instituted. Thereafter, Hollywood production-distribution firms sought to maximize their own profits, rather than the profits of their exhibition subsidiaries, as they had done formerly. And since they were no longer obligated to turn out enough films to fill the playing time of company-owned theaters, production was cut back. Exhibitors, who were used to double features and frequent program changes under the old block booking system, now complained of product shortages.

This realignment of relations between the majors and the exhibitors allowed foreign films to penetrate the American market, and their broader distribution was linked with the rise of "art house" circuits. Not all imported films were "art," but many offered a striking alternative to Hollywood's slick products by revealing slices of life and dramatic elements that American films, following the strictures of the Production Code, had failed to develop. Imported films, moreover, were often made more on an artisan and less on a factory basis, and consequently seemed to present more personalized statements than the sanitized and anonymous Hollywood product. Italian neorealist films, the French *nouvelle vague*, and pictures such as Dreyer's *Ordet* in the mid-1950s revealed new dimensions of the cinema to American audiences, after which Hollywood's fare seemed anemic and inconsequential in comparison. Not a few foreign films were able to capitalize on sexual content and frankness, which the Production Code rendered taboo and which television could not deliver into living rooms. Responding to the obvious commercial appeal of sex, some Hollywood majors circumvented the code by organizing special distribution subsidiaries to bring such pictures into the American market for exploitation. Meanwhile, faced with a product shortage and declining attendance, exhibitors were told in 1954 by an executive of United Paramount Theatres that "it might be wise for [them] to consider ways and means of popularizing the foreign film" and "to establish an audience where there has been none before."[16]

Runaway Production

Ultimately, it was the American companies that imported films from abroad. The first attempts to acquire monies in blocked accounts abroad entailed such ingenious schemes as buying wood pulp, whiskey, furniture, and other commodities and selling them elsewhere for dollars. Producers also invested in ship construction and in a variety of other

16. *Variety*, September 29, 1954, pp. 3, 18.

noncinema fields, all with the assistance of the MPEA diplomatic corps. Soon, though, frozen funds were invested in filmmaking. Initially this often meant shooting American films on location overseas, which became known as "runaway production." (Other American industries, in the 1960s and 1970s, were to follow this pattern by moving their production facilities abroad.) In addition to providing authentic locales, foreign shooting provided the opportunity to hire workers whose salary scales were lower than Hollywood's. The impact on American film trade unions was so severe that the House Committee on Education and Labor finally was persuaded to hold hearings on the matter in 1961 and 1962.

By this time, however, runaway production had matured. Films were no longer merely shot abroad instead of on Hollywood's lots; rather, American investment was being channeled into pictures that met every legal requirement for being declared "British," "French," "Italian," or another nationality. The inducement for this existed in a range of production subsidization schemes that were inaugurated in Western Europe in the postwar years. Essentially, these programs recognized the economic vulnerability of private enterprise film production and sought to protect it by stimulants, one of which provided filmmakers with an increment of revenue above what they obtained by commercial means from the box office. This attempt to close the gap between production costs and ticket revenues was just another in a series of reformist schemes on the part of European governments to keep their film industries viable as commercial undertakings. In reality these programs served limited purposes and managed only to postpone for a couple of decades the coming to grips with the commercial aspect that dominates filmmaking in capitalist market-oriented economies.

Production subsidies quite openly were instituted to aid *domestic* filmmakers in European countries at a time when capital was short and American pictures dominated the screens. Subsidization laws, to ensure that aid would go to those who needed it, incorporated definitions of "national" producer and "national" film. However, incredible as it may seem, these laws did nothing to prevent foreign subsidiaries of American companies from conforming to the decrees so as to become "national" producers of "national" films. As a result, they had access to European subsidies and participated in programs designed to encourage European filmmaking. Understandably, some European producers were bitter over this latest intrusion. John Davis, president of the British Film Producers Association, put the matter quite bluntly twenty years ago:

[It] is obvious that the [subsidization] scheme would not have been put forward by the Government or accepted by the industry on the ground that the levy recoverable from the box office takings was required to support films made in this country by American subsidiaries.[17]

It was in the United Kingdom that the American companies concentrated their production efforts, although they also were active in Italy, France, and other countries.

It is impossible to determine the precise amounts paid as subsidies to foreign subsidiaries of American companies. However, it has been estimated that for every dollar-equivalent of subsidy paid in France to U.S. firms, two are paid in Italy and probably four in the United Kingdom. Moreover, probably little more than 10 percent of subsidy payments went to British production companies in the mid-1960s. In some cases of coproduction, American producers have been able to receive subsidies from three countries for a single film, covering as much as 80 percent of its cost. It is not surprising, then, that through the 1960s, American films financed abroad rose from an estimated 35 percent to 60 percent of the total output of U.S. producers. American interests reportedly produced 183 features abroad in 1969 at an estimated cost of $234.7 million, while 142 were made domestically for about $228.3 million. During the five years ending in 1972, about 45 percent of the 1,246 features made by U.S. companies were produced abroad, a decline prompted by rising salaries overseas and devaluation of the dollar.

Data released by the Italian industry reveal that in the decade up to 1967, American companies spent a yearly average of about $35 million to acquire and to finance Italian features, and to make their own films in Italy. In the United Kingdom, figures for the decade up to and including 1971 show that of 489 British first- or co-feature films exhibited in the two main theater circuits, about two-thirds were financed wholly or partially by American interests. In fact, U.S. firms were involved financially in almost five times more British films than was the British government's chosen banking instrument, the National Film Finance Corporation.

American investment in European films is now so complex that it is becoming increasingly difficult to identify precisely the sources of finance and the stage of production at which such money is injected. For example, pickup deals allow an American distributor to retard its

17. British Film Producers Association, *Fourteenth Annual Report 1955-1956*, p. 7.

investment until the picture is completed and approved. Should the transaction, then, be considered production financing or a distribution deal? Likewise, when an American company guarantees a foreign bank loan for a European producer, the question arises as to just where the ultimate seat of authority is and who has final control. About the only thing of which one can be certain is that commerce rules.

American Distributors Remain Dominant

The increased American investment in European films after the early 1950s necessitated bringing them into the U.S. market for exploitation, which meant a departure from the old policy of the major American distributors. British, French, and Italian interests tried to establish their own distribution chains in America, but American distributors were able to maintain a monopoly position in the domestic market, while simultaneously fortifying their worldwide distribution networks. As before, foreign films could profitably enter the U.S. market only by means of American companies, demonstrating that the situation had not changed in half a century. Data show that of those pictures earning $1 million or more in the U.S.-Canadian market during 1973, 65 percent of the rentals were earned by five distributors: Twentieth Century-Fox, Warner, United Artists, Universal, and Paramount. Another 29 percent or so were earned by five other companies: National General, Columbia, Buena Vista (Disney), MGM, and Cinerama Releasing Corporation.

Overseas, American distribution companies are just as potent. During 1972 in Italy, they released twenty-four Italian features that were among the biggest box office attractions in the country, prompting charges anew that the nation's film industry had been colonized by U.S. interests. During 1972 in France, 7 companies handling mainly American films received 42 percent (about $42 million) of all payments to distributors from exhibitors. The remainder of the distributors' gross was divided among 114 French companies. In the United Kingdom during 1970, seven American distributors were estimated to have received about 84 percent (more than $40 million) of all film rentals. Typically they handle, in addition to their own American and non-British pictures, about 40 percent of the British films on the market, a share that has increased substantially over the last quarter-century, owing to the corresponding rise of American investment in British pictures.

Revenues from Abroad

Probably no other major American business is so heavily dependent upon export trade as is the film industry. In the 1950s about 40 percent of the industry's theatrical revenue came from abroad; by the early 1960s, about 53 percent did. Not only is exportation of U.S. films essential to their producers, but, as we have seen, such pictures also are believed to create goodwill for America and its political-economic system. Furthermore, in view of recent U.S. trade deficits, it is claimed that American film earnings abroad make positive contributions to our balance of payments. The MPEA has estimated that the U.S. film industry remitted $342 million from abroad in 1972.

Data on foreign earnings of American companies and films, although far from being precise, do provide measures of their activity. Table 1 presents estimates of the total distribution gross received by eight member companies of the MPEA: Allied Artists, Columbia, MGM, Paramount, Twentieth Century-Fox, United Artists, Universal, and Warner. In terms of specific countries, the United Kingdom, which had been the best foreign market for American distributors until 1970, slipped to second place in 1971, and to fourth in 1973. Italy finally captured first position, while Canada moved from sixth in 1963 to second a decade later. West Germany and France rounded out the top five in 1973. Although variations such as those do occur, the rule holds that the top five markets overseas contribute between 40 and 45 percent of foreign revenues, and the top ten account for 65 percent. Foreign business is worth around $400 million annually, and it has grown in actual dollars. But, as *Variety* asserted: "Putting the world data to-

TABLE 1
Distribution Gross of U.S. Major Companies
($000,000)

Year	Foreign	Domestic	Value in Actual Dollars	Value in 1963 Dollars
1963	$293.0	$239.4	$532.4	$532.4
1964	319.9	263.2	583.1	575.5
1965	343.5	287.2	630.7	611.8
1966	361.5	319.5	680.9	642.1
1967	357.8	355.9	713.7	654.4
1968	339.0	372.3	711.3	626.0
1969	348.4	317.4	665.8	556.0
1970	360.4	381.3	741.7	584.4
1971	347.5	336.7	684.2	517.2
1972	388.8	426.4	815.2	596.7
1973	415.5	390.5	806.0	555.3

Source: *Variety,* May 15, 1974, p. 34.

gether, the net gain in world film revenues [for the American majors] over an 11-year period was, in 1963 constant dollars, less than $23,000,000 or about 4 percent and this was due to tiny expansion in the United States."[18]

Overseas the proliferation of television, motor cars, and weekend houses and the decline in the number of theaters have left their impact on earnings of American distributors, especially in Western Europe. Even with increased rental terms, the foreign market can hardly be called a growth area, and if expansion is to come at all, it must be in those regions where the theatergoing habit is in its infancy. Of course, these are also the regions in which television is being introduced, and although TV-set saturation is still low, the development of a movie audience will have to compete with video's attraction.

The Response of Developing Nations

A stagnation in established foreign markets was recognized in the early 1950s by Eric Johnston. He felt that some markets were yielding just about as much as they could, and that companies should not exhaust themselves trying to extract revenue from them when the effort could be better applied to virgin regions. In this way, the African continent became important for its economic potential, as it has been for its political position.

The achieving of political independence by many African peoples in the 1960s did not automatically ensure their autonomy, for they were confronted with neocolonialism from Europe and with political and economic intervention from the United States. In some cases, independence meant a restructuring in form, but not in substance, of film-marketing patterns that had existed during colonial rule, and the outcome was that film distribution continued to be dominated by foreign powers who paid scant attention to Africa's cultural identities.

The U.S. industry's first systematic effort to develop the African market took form after MPEA representatives toured the area in 1960. In April of the following year, the American Motion Picture Export Company (Africa) was established and began distributing films of seven Hollywood firms in the English speaking countries of Ghana, Gambia, Sierra Leone, Nigeria, and Liberia. In September 1969, the West Africa Film Export Company (which later changed its name to Afram Films, Inc.) was created to distribute films of its seven members in fifteen French speaking countries with a population of about sixty million.

After more than a decade of independence for many African coun-

18. *Variety*, May 15, 1974, p.34.

tries, hardly any have been able to develop a national cinema policy. In fact, cinematic relations *among* these nations barely exist, and it is still true that African filmmakers have to visit international festivals in order to see the works of their colleagues. As a result, American and European interests have imposed a de facto policy of their own. It is a decidedly commericial policy, with little concern for African peoples and their identities. The Senegalese filmmaker Mahama Traore has observed:

Distribution of films in Senegal does not reflect the needs of the people because what we receive are the latest commercial films from France, Italy, and America. It's really an imperialist and colonialist assault—those films are vehicles of violence, sex, and a culture that is alien to us, a culture into which we are not integrated and into which we in fact refuse to be integrated, because we want to remain ourselves.[19]

The Response of Industrialized Nations

Although cinematic problems seem to take their most acute form in developing nations, those in many industrialized countries are just as serious. The age-old resistance to U.S. intrusion takes current form along a wide variety of fronts, sometimes expressing itself as a rejection of private ownership altogether, sometimes merely as national or regional fervor seeking local commercial opportunities or independence.

In Europe, the European Economic Community has been seen by some as the core around which a European film policy could be built. The program might embrace not only financial measures to strengthen film industries of member states, but also a systematic way of coming to terms with American companies, films, and investments. This could entail the establishment of a European distribution firm to compete with American interests in Europe, and later in other areas as well. However, the only concrete result of the EEC so far has consisted of four directives on film calling for liberalization of trade and distribution among members. There has been no indication at all that EEC authorities are concerned about the large role played by the United States in members' film industries, nor has there been much attention directed to the cinema beyond some elemental commercial aspects. Missing has been a realization that a *European* film industry could not be built upon American investment and distribution.

Elsewhere in Europe, more direct steps were taken to challenge the American position. Among them was the establishment in the early

19. " 'Cinema in Africa must Be a School'—An Interview with Mahama Traore," *Cinéaste* 6 (1973): 33.

1970s of the International Federation of Independent Film Producers as an alternative to the International Federation of Film Producers Associations. The latter has been felt by many to be a spokesman for MPEA interests. In the United Kingdom, the Association of Cinematography, Television, and Allied Technicians called in 1973 for social ownership and worker control of the film industry, and urged nationalization without compensation of key interests, including all subsidiaries of American picture companies. In North America, the Council of Canadian Film Makers has recently urged nationalization of the theater holdings of Famous Players, Ltd. (owned 51 percent by Gulf & Western Industries), which operates more than a quarter of all the houses in Canada, and the inauguration of exhibition quotas for Canadian films.

Signs such as these occur regularly, suggesting that in both developing and industrialized nations there is a constant search to express, and sometimes establish through the cinema and other art forms, a national cultural identity. The purpose is not to compete in the making of films for international audiences, but to use the cinema to present or clarify the problems, lives, and aspirations of peoples.

Short-run economic benefits, however, mitigate these aspirations. American films overseas keep theaters open and contribute tax revenue. U.S. investment has also helped to stimulate filmmaking in a few countries, but on its own terms, as is evident in Great Britain whose film industry is essentially an appendage of Hollywood. We can only speculate about what kinds of pictures a *British* industry would make, if one could be created, turning back half a century of American domination. Jobs have been created and studios kept active with American money, but the slightest cutback can precipitate unemployment crises with the reminder that industries lose their autonomy when they become subservient to foreign corporations who have only their own interests at heart.

Nonetheless, foreign governments, indecisive about progressive solutions, have been reluctant to discourage American investment. Their inaction leaves the cinema in limbo caught between old revisionist policies that keep the film industries barely alive, and American power that implicitly chokes them. This dilemma feeds upon a myopic belief that the unhindered and free flow of communication is automatically beneficial to exporter and importer alike, and that any attempt to protect domestic cultural and social interests is a blow to international understanding. Of course, unrestricted communication can be destructive to indigenous cultures and can thwart people's chances to develop their own manners of expression.

Multinationals and Conglomerates

The American film industry's international stature must be placed in context and seen as part of the proliferation of multinational corporations and as part of the astonishing growth of U.S. private investment abroad, amounting to $107 billion by 1973, up from less than $12 billion in 1950. In this way, the film industry stands as just another segment of American business that has stretched its operations around the globe, seeking more and more places to market its goods, to return its investments, or to supply it with human and natural resources.

Several major film companies are now subsidiaries of huge conglomerates, meaning that theatrical film production and distribution have become small segments of parent firms engaged in a diversity of enterprises. Paramount Pictures, for example, was acquired by Gulf & Western Industries in 1966, not because it was thriving (actually Paramount was at the bottom of the barrel), but because it appeared to have substantial hidden wealth in its large, undervalued film library. Today, Paramount is part of the Leisure Time Group of G&W, which contributed less than 11 percent of its parent's total operating revenues in fiscal 1974. Revenues of theatrical films ($103 million) accounted for about 3.5 percent of G&W's total, and just a bit more than the $78 million the parent received from theater operations. In 1967, United Artists became a subsidiary of Transamerica Corporation, which was involved in car rentals, data processing, insurance, and various financial services. During 1973, UA's theatrical film rentals of $163.8 million represented less than 8 percent of Transamerica's total revenues. Universal's parent, MCA, received about 21 percent of its 1973 revenue from theatrical films' earnings of $87.5 million.

Companies such as Walt Disney Productions, Columbia Pictures, and Twentieth Century-Fox, which have not been acquired by conglomerates, have diversified into other fields. In 1974, Disney's film rentals brought in $90 million of its total revenue of $430 million; Columbia's generated $11 million of its $257 million total; and Fox's, $160 million out of $282 million.

As theatrical film earnings during the past quarter-century have diminished in size relative to other corporate pursuits, production has become geographically decentralized with, perhaps, up to half of our pictures being made abroad. Distribution, on the other hand, has become more centralized. In 1970, MCA (Universal) and Paramount formed Cinema International Corporation (a Dutch company) to distribute theatrical films of both firms outside North America. In 1973,

MGM withdrew from distribution completely and signed ten-year agreements with CIC and United Artists to handle its theatrical and television film library. As a report from the Security Pacific National Bank explained, "Hollywood has evolved into the international headquarters of the film industry. Financial and distribution functions are and will remain centered in the area."[20]

American film companies have forged a new empire rivaling those of former days based on spices and minerals, an empire in constant evolution, stretching around the world, and worth billions of dollars. Its impact on human minds can hardly be calculated. However, it is not only the qualitative aspects of film that should command our attention, enticing as they may be. The industry's shape today and tomorrow, as well as the images it produces, is the result of economic, political, and historical forces, unfolding and working themselves out.

20. "The Motion Picture Industry in California—a Special Report," *Journal of the Producers Guild of America* 16 (March 1974): 8.

JOHN COGLEY

HUAC: The Mass Hearings

Hollywood reacted to news of the impending investigation in 1951 with something like panic. A *Life* reporter wired her editor at the time that the movie people put her in mind of "a group of marooned sailors on a flat desert island watching the approach of a tidal wave." The industry was not sure it could take another investigation, which would inevitably bring on more "revelations" and bad publicity and might mean picket lines around the nation's movie houses. To add to this anxiety, business was spectacularly bad. In 1946 domestic film rental stood at a dizzy $400 million; weekly movie attendance climbed to an all-time record of eighty million. But by 1951 television was a going thing and movie attendance was in the lower depths of a decline that finally, about February 1953, leveled off at forty-six million.

In the lush days of World War II movie companies had expanded enormously, buying up vast studio facilities and adding to their rosters of high-priced talent. All the major studios had stockpiled costly films. Things looked black indeed. Although the slump lasted for seven years, its most severe effects were felt in the period between congressional probes. These were years marked by big layoffs and frequent theater closings. The movie companies were finding it difficult to get bank credit and dreaded the consequences of political controversy. What banker in his right mind would put up the money for a picture that might be picketed because one of its stars had the habit of signing petitions? Trouble had piled up on trouble for the moviemakers. When

From *Report on Blacklisting I: The Movies* (Fund for the Republic, 1956), pp. 92–117.

the government won an antitrust action and theater chains were separated from their distributor-producer owners, the industry—as *Fortune* magazine put it—"began to feel like a man with a loud humming sound in his head."

In March 1951, just before the hearings began, *Variety* reported that in New York, Joyce O'Hara, acting president of the Motion Picture Association, had met with studio advertising and publicity heads and announced that movie people who did not firmly deny communistic ties would find it "difficult" to get work in the studios after the hearings closed. The association had no intention of repeating the mistakes that had made Hollywood look foolish in 1947.

The House Committee on Un-American Activities was different too. In December 1949, J. Parnell Thomas was convicted of payroll padding and was later reunited with members of the Hollywood Ten in prison. If the film industry managed to salvage any consolation from that, it was short-lived. For this time the committee returned to the subject of Communism-in-Hollywood under new auspices (Georgia's John S. Wood had succeeded Thomas as chairman) and vastly changed circumstances.

In 1947 the wartime friendship between the United States and Russia was still a fresh memory. By 1951 U.S. soldiers were at war in Korea with the forces of two Communist powers, and the cold war with Russia was at its height. With the Hiss-Chambers, Klaus Fuchs, and Judith Coplon cases behind it, the nation was becoming ever more security conscious and, in the opinion of many, was afflicted with a bad case of political jitters. A senator named McCarthy was becoming a front-page fixture. And, above all, the House Committee itself had a spanking new policy implemented by its new research director, an ex-FBI man named Raphael I. Nixon. Nixon, comparing the 1947 with the later hearings not long ago, commended Parnell Thomas's work but said it was unfortunate that in 1947 the committee had focused its attack on movie content, "the weakest argument."

Parnell Thomas's pursuit of Communist propaganda in films admittedly had led the committee up a blind alley.[1] In Nixon's opinion, the 1947 committee could have centered a more pertinent and fruitful enquiry on the "prestige, position, and money" the Communist party

---

1. At the close of the 1947 hearings, J. Parnell Thomas announced that "at the present time the committee has a special staff making an extensive study of Communist propaganda in various motion pictures." The study was abandoned. Thomas also announced that at the next hearing the committee would have "a number of witnesses who will deal with propaganda in the films and techniques employed." These witnesses never materialized.

picked up in Hollywood. And that is what the committee went looking for in 1951.

Hollywood was chosen for a "broad base investigation," Nixon explained to a reporter, because of the volume of cooperation the committee got there. But a critical Democratic congressman whose district

"Crusade for Freedom"—Louis B. Mayer presiding at a Korean War rally on the steps of MGM's Irving Thalberg Building. Sitting behind the podium is production chief Dore Schary.

borders on the movie capital once suggested another reason. "The yearning for publicity on the part of some members of the Committee," he said, "could only be satisfied by the famous names a movie hearing would produce." Nixon recognizes that such charges were made against the committee but argues that it was the newspapers rather than the committee itself which put the emphasis on big names. "We couldn't overlook our responsibilities just because prominent people were involved."

By 1951, a number of prominent persons were begging the committee for a chance to testify, and the committee had to disappoint some of them. There were, first of all, the ex-Communists, who by now looked upon the hearings as the only public forum open to them. If they wanted to prove to the world that they had broken with the Party, they had to testify. And until they did prove this, they were unemployable in the studios. The committee welcomed them. But another class—persons who had never belonged to the Communist party but suffered from unfavorable rumors—were also eager to go on record as anti-Communist. Many wanted to be heard but, according to Nixon, Edward G. Robinson, Jose Ferrer, and the late John Garfield were the only three called where the committee had no proof of Party membership, past or present. Robinson requested a hearing. Garfield and Ferrer were subpoened because they had been "the subject of considerable interest on the part of private organizations."

At first the committee wanted Garfield and Ferrer to testify in private session. "But," Nixon said, "we were catching it all over—from George Sokolsky, Victor Riesel, and even from Ed Sullivan. No one came right out in print and said so, but there were intimations of payoffs. Mr. Moulder [congressman from Missouri] was subjected to criticism for stating that he thought Garfield was all right." Nixon also recalls that at the time some inexperienced anti-Communist groups were given to making loose, unsubstantiated charges, and the committee drew fire for not acting on the "leads" these groups provided. From the other extremity, the committee was attacked for "establishing blacklists."

Whether or not the committee was interested in "establishing blacklists," it is now beyond question that many who testified (or who refused to testify) found themselves "unemployable" after they appeared as uncooperative witnesses before the committee. During the scattered movie hearings of 1951, ninety Hollywood figures, almost all well established in their careers, appeared on the witness stand. They took a variety of positions. Ferrer and Garfield swore that they had never been Party members; their names did not appear in the committee's long lists of unfriendly witnesses published later. Thirty others like novelist Budd Schulberg and Sterling Hayden said they had been Party members and named people they knew as Communists. Their names appeared in the committee's 1952 annual report as "individuals who, through the knowledge gained through their own past membership in the Communist Party, have been of invaluable assistance to the Committee and the American people in supplying facts relating to Communist efforts and success in infiltrating the motion-picture industry."

One of these witnesses, screenwriter Martin Berkeley, named 162 persons he swore he knew as members of the Communist party. His list included Dorothy Parker, who had spent some time in Hollywood as a screenwriter, Donald Ogden Stewart, Dashiell Hammett, Lillian Hellman, Edward Chodorov, writer-producer, and Michael Gordon, now a Broadway producer. Berkeley had originally been named before the committee by Richard Collins. Berkeley later testified that after he learned Collins had mentioned him, he sent a "very silly" telegram to the committee. "I charged Mr. Collins with perjury and said I'd never been a member of the Communist Party, which was not true. I was not at that time a member and have not been for many years. [Berkeley left the Party in 1943.] Why I sent the telegram—I did it in a moment of panic and was a damn fool." But before Berkeley realized his "foolishness" and admitted there was truth to Collins' charge, several friends had begun to organize a defense fund for him. This campaign was under way when Berkeley sheepishly admitted that Collins had told the truth.[2]

Berkeley joined the Motion Picture Alliance for the Preservation of American Ideals after his sensational testimony and became a leading figure in the organization. An MPA spokesman said not long ago that the group relied more on Martin Berkeley than on any of its other members to identify Communists and "Communist sympathizers" in the movie industry.

During the hearings that followed the 1951 sessions, other cooperative witnesses who provided names for the House Committee included actor Lee J. Cobb, director Elia Kazan, and playwright Clifford Odets.

A list of 324 names was made available to the public by the House Committee in its 1952 and 1953 annual reports. Names of those cited

2. In later years Berkeley was cited by columnist George Sokolsky as a prime example of an anti-Communist who suffered unemployment for cooperating with the committee. Many in Hollywood, however, believe that by his erratic behavior Berkeley had made himself unpopular and it was this rather than his anti-Communism per se which caused his difficulties.

as Communists by cooperative witnesses were listed alphabetically. Everyone cited was blacklisted in the studios. But methods varied from studio to studio and from person to person, perhaps to avoid the "illegal conspiracy" which Paul V. McNutt warned against in 1947.

If the named people were under contract when they were identified or called to testify, their contracts were cancelled, bought up, or simply not renewed. If they were free-lance workers, usually their agents told them they could no longer find work for them, and they stopped receiving "calls." Most were urged by their agents or studio executives to "clear" themselves of the charges made against them, either by testifying fully before the committee or putting themselves in the hands of Roy Brewer or Martin Gang.

Larry Parks was the first Hollywood witness who decided to admit he had been a Communist. Parks was under the impression that it would be possible for him to testify without being required to name others he had known as Communists. While he was on the stand, committee counsel Frank Tavenner read off a list of names and asked the actor to tell what he knew about them. Parks hesitated. Then Congressman Charles Potter of Michigan and Committee Chairman Wood took turns with Tavenner in explaining to Parks why he had to involve others.

Congressman Wood told Parks, "I for one am rather curious to understand just what the reasons are for declining to answer the question." Potter added, "Now, I assume you share the belief that we share that an active member of the Communist Party believes in principles that we don't believe in, in overthrowing our Government by force and violence. Now, you say you would readily give information concerning a man you have knowledge has committed murder. Wouldn't you also give information to the proper authorities of a man you knew or a woman you knew or believed to be working to overthrow our Government by force and violence?" The actor pointed out that it was not yet illegal to be a Communist, but Potter answered: "So when we are drafting men to fight Communist aggression, you feel that it is not your duty as an American citizen to give the committee the benefit of what knowledge you might have . . ." Parks replied: "Well, yes; I wanted to do that. I think that there is a difference, Congressman, in my opinion. There is a difference between people who would harm our country and people who in my opinion are like myself, who, as I feel, did nothing wrong at the time."

Congressman Francis E. Walter of Pennsylvania (later chairman of the committee) came to the actor's rescue: "How can it be material to the purpose of this inquiry," he asked, "to have the names of people when we already know them? Aren't we actually, by insisting that this man testify as to names, overlooking the fact that we want to know what the organization did, what it hoped to accomplish, how it actually had or attempted to influence the thinking of the American people through the arts? So why is it so essential that we know the names of all the people when we have a witness who may make a contribution to what we are trying to learn?"

Tavenner answered Walter: "Although there is information relating to some of these individuals as to whom I had expected to interrogate this witness, some of them have evaded service of process, so that we cannot bring them here. That is one point. Another is that this committee ought to be entitled to receive proof of information which it has in its files as a result of its previous investigation relating to a matter of this kind. There would be no way to really investigate Communist infiltration into labor without asking who are Communists in labor. And the same thing is true here in Hollywood. Those are the reasons I think it is material."

Larry Parks made a last desperate plea: "Don't present me with the choice of either being in contempt of this committee and going to jail or forcing me to really crawl through the mud to be an informer, for what purpose? I don't think this is a choice at all. I don't think this is really sportsmanlike. I don't think this is American justice. . . . I think it will impair the usefulness of this committee to a great extent, because it will make it almost impossible for a person to come to you, as I have done, and open himself to you and tell you the truth. So I beg of you not to force me to do this."

Tavenner's reply is often cited as proof that the committee was "compiling a blacklist."[3]

"Mr. Parks," he said, "there was a statement you made this morning

3. In its 1953 annual report, the committee noted that, as a result of its work, and the greater "cooperation" received from the motion picture industry, "it can be stated on considerable authority that perhaps no major industry in the world today employs fewer members of the Communist Party than does the motion picture industry." It went on then to acknowledge that "particularly those individuals who have been identified under oath before the committee as one-time members of the Communist Party and who, in turn, invoked the fifth amendment in refusing to testify, have charged that the committee is compiling a 'black list.'

"The absurdity of this charge is obvious when is is considered that these individuals, of their own accord and volition, joined the Communist conspiracy, and that it is on their own personal determination that they have refused to affirm or deny sworn testimony placing them in the Communist Party."

The committee seemed to be describing how and why a "black list" was compiled, rather that how "absurd" it was to say that such a list did result from its hearings.

in the course of your testimony which interested me a great deal. This is what you said: 'This is a great industry. . . . It has a very important job to do, to entertain people; in certain respects to call attention to certain evils, but mainly to entertain.' Now, do you believe that persons who are in a position to call attention to certain evils ought to be persons who are dedicated to the principles of democracy as we understand them in this country? . . . What is your opinion as to whether or not members of the Communist Party should be in positions of power and influence in the various unions which control the writing of scripts, the actors, and various other things which we have mentioned during the course of this hearing?" Parks answered by agreeing with Tavenner that such people should not be "in any position of power" in the industry. Tavenner went further: "Or to influence the course which [the industry] takes?" Parks agreed again. "Then," Tavenner said, "we will ask your cooperation before this hearing is over in helping us to ascertain those who are or have been members of the Communist Party, *for that particular purpose* which we have mentioned" (emphasis added). Larry Parks, in executive testimony, later offered the committee the names it sought.

Reticence similar to Parks' was expressed by playwright Lillian Hellman. After she received her subpoena, she wrote to the committee:

Dear Mr. Wood:
As you know, I am under subpoena to appear before your committee on May 21, 1952.
I am most willing to answer all questions about myself. I have nothing to hide from your committee and there is nothing in my life of which I am ashamed. I have been advised by counsel that under the fifth amendment I have a constitutional privilege to decline to answer any questions about my political opinions, activities, and associations, on the grounds of self-incrimination. I do not wish to claim this privilege. I am ready and willing to testify before the representatives of our Government as to my own opinions and my own actions, regardless of any risks or consequences to myself.
But I am advised by counsel that if I answer the committee's questions about myself, I must also answer questions about other people and that if I refuse to do so, I can be cited for contempt. My counsel tells me that if I answer questions about myself, I will have waived my rights under the fifth amendment and could be forced legally to answer questions about others. This is very difficult for a layman to understand: But there is one principle that I do understand: I am not willing, now or in the future, to bring bad trouble to people who, in my past association with them, were completely innocent of any talk or any action that was disloyal or subversive. I do not like subversion or disloyalty in any form and if I had ever seen any I would have considered

it my duty to have reported it to the proper authorities. But to hurt innocent people whom I knew many years ago in order to save myself is, to me, inhuman and indecent, and dishonorable. I cannot and will not cut my conscience to fit this year's fashions, even though I long ago came to the conclusion that I was not a political person and could have no comfortable place in any political group.

I was raised in an old-fashioned American tradition and there were certain homely things that were taught me: To try to tell the truth, not to bear false witness, not to harm my neighbor, to be loyal to my country, and so on. In general, I respected these ideals of Christian honor and did as well with them as I knew how. It is my belief that you will agree with these simple rules of human decency and will not expect me to violate the good American tradition from which they spring. I would, therefore, like to come before you and speak of myself.

I am prepared to waive the privilege against self-incrimination and to tell you everything you wish to know about my views or actions if your committee will agree to refrain from asking me to name other people. If the committee is unwilling to give me this assurance, I will be forced to plead the privilege of the fifth amendment at the hearing.

In his reply, the chairman advised Miss Hellman that "the Committee cannot permit witnesses to set forth the terms under which they will testify."

In her testimony later, Miss Hellman invoked the Fifth Amendment.

In 1951 and 1952, the committee issued subpoenas in batches of fifteen or twenty to actors, writers, story editors, screen analysts, producers, and directors. The economic pressure to become a cooperative witness was not only implicit in the spreading blacklist, it was underscored by the apparent collaboration between studio executives and House investigators. Subpoenas were delivered in dressing rooms and in the legal offices of studios, though home addresses were known to the investigators who served the subpoenas. Many at first did not admit that they had received subpoenas. Later, as the numbers grew, the subpoenaed grouped together, raised money for lawyers' fees, and formed classes for legal consultation. A sense of shock was experienced by many when they were subpoenaed. One person described it this way:

Even though you know what takes place in that committee, you are so accustomed to respecting government in all its forms that your fear is enormous. Intellectually, you understand what's happening, but you can't control the fear. An insidious form of self-guilt sets in. You accept the views of the committee in spite of yourself. It's quite bewildering. Afterwards, you find yourself guarded and evasive whatever you do, wherever you go.

By the time the 1951–52 hearings were well under way, the Smith Act had been held valid by the Supreme Court.[4] Some of those subpoenaed in the spring of 1951 did not know whether they would be jailed or not. They knew that if they failed to cooperate with the committee there was absolute certainty that they would be blacklisted. The only real question, then, was what defense they might use to avoid imprisonment. The Ten had been jailed after depending fruitlessly on the First Amendment, and no other defense from a contempt charge for declining to answer questions before a congressional committee had been definitely established. The Fifth Amendment, with its clause protecting a witness against self-incrimination, appeared to many to be their only safe course.

This, however, carried with it a serious disadvantage. In 1950, the Supreme Court had decided in *Rogers v. U.S.* that a witness could not refuse to answer a question about the Party under the Fifth Amendment, once he had admitted Party membership. Since the committee made it clear during the Larry Parks hearing that after a man had admitted Party membership he was expected to name others he had known as Communists, witnesses who would not name others but wanted to stay out of jail had the choice of either denying Party membership and running the risk of perjury indictments, or of refusing to answer the question at all.[5]

4. Smith Act (Alien Registration Act of 1940) provides the following:

Sec. 2. (a) It shall be unlawful for any person—
1. to knowingly or willfully advocate, abet, advise, or teach the duty, necessity, desirability, or propriety of overthrowing or destroying any government in the United States by force or violence, . . .
2. with the intent to cause the overthrow or destruction of any government in the United States, to print, publish, edit, issue, circulate, sell, distribute, or publicly display any written or printed matter advocating, advising, or teaching the duty, necessity, desirability, or propriety of overthrowing or destroying any government in the United States by force or violence;
3. to organize or help to organize any society, group, or assembly of persons who teach, advocate, or encourage the overthrow or destruction of any government in the United States by force or violence; or to be or become a member of, or affiliate with, any such society, group, or assembly of persons, knowing the purposes thereof.

Sec. 3. It shall be unlawful for any person to attempt to commit, or to conspire to commit, any of the acts prohibited by the provision of this title.

All prosecutions under the Act have been on the basis of section 3 (conspiracy to advocate). After the release of the first group convicted under the Smith Act during the Foley Square trial, the government announced its intention to charge them with section 2, part 3.

5. It is beyond the competence and legal knowledge of the author of this report to venture an opinion on whether they were justified, according to this reasoning, to resort to the Fifth Amendment.

This meant that they also had to remain silent about accusations of disloyalty, espionage, and conspiracy which they were anxious to deny. Two witnesses named as one-time members of the Party, for example, insist they can prove they were serving overseas in the armed services when, according to the testimony of the House Committee hearings, they were supposed to be attending Communist party meetings in Hollywood.

To prepare witnesses and to keep them from answering questions that might cause them to lose their immunity privilege under the Fifth Amendment, teams of lawyers rehearsed their Hollywood clients by simulating the examinations they would be put to on the witness stand. Variations of the Fifth Amendment position were developed. For instance, Carl Foreman, who was the writer and associate producer of *High Noon*, invoked what later became known as the "diminished Fifth." He denied that he was a Party member at the time he was testifying but would not answer the question as to whether he had been a Party member at some previous date. Another variation was employed by producer Robert Rossen (*All the King's Men, Body and Soul, The Brave Bulls*). The first time he testified, Rossen invoked what came to be known as the "augmented Fifth." He said that he was not a member of the Communist party, that he was "not sympathetic with it or its aims," but declined to say whether he had ever been a Party member in the past. Eventually, though, those who invoked variations on the Fifth Amendment position found themselves as thoroughly unemployable in Hollywood as those who simply "took the Fifth," as the position came to be described.

Tension gradually increased in Hollywood. Once it was clear that the hearings were not to be stopped before the committee had unearthed every available witness who could provide it with names, pressure to give cooperative testimony was exerted on all sides. Families were divided. Some of the "unfriendly" witnesses moved to new neighborhoods to avoid the ostracism they felt certain they would meet once their testimony was publicized.

Among the prominent Hollywood figures subpoenaed by the committee was Sidney Buchman, a Columbia producer. Buchman had been an executive assistant to Harry Cohn, in charge of production at Columbia. He wrote the screenplays for *Mr. Smith Goes to Washington* and *Here Comes Mr. Jordan*, produced *The Jolson Story*, and wrote and produced *Jolson Sings Again*. As a Columbia executive Buchman had worked on films featuring many of Hollywood's top stars. When he testified before the committee on September 25, 1951, he took a position many unfriendly witnesses say they too might have taken had they believed the penalties would be as light as those later inflicted on Buchman.

Buchman testified that he had been a Communist but refused to name anyone he had known in the Party. He did exactly the thing which, according to precedent, should have meant a contempt citation. Observers were puzzled, until it was noted that Congressman Donald Jackson, California Republican, had left the hearing room in the course of Buchman's testimony but before the producer had refused to answer questions. This left the committee without a quorum and, consequently, unable to issue a contempt citation against Buchman for his refusal to give full testimony. Buchman's lawyer noted the lack of a quorum at the conclusion of the testimony.

Public curiosity about Buchman's good fortune was expressed in various sections of the press. The committee served Buchman with another subpoena, but this time he did not appear at the appointed time and was cited for contempt of Congress. On March 17, 1952, Buchman was indicted on two counts of contempt—for having failed to appear on January 25 and again on January 28. One count was later thrown out because Buchman had been cited twice on the basis of a single summons.

On March 25 District Judge T. Blake Kennedy in Washington, D.C., fixed the bond at $1,000 after the movie producer had been arraigned and pleaded not guilty. On May 9 a motion to dismiss the indictment was filed, argued, and denied. Ten months later, jurors were sworn and the trial started March 9, 1953. On March 10 a judgment of acquittal was entered on the first count. On March 12 the jury delivered a verdict of guilty. The jury was polled and Buchman was permitted to remain free on bond pending sentence. On March 16, 1953, Judge Kennedy sentenced Buchman to pay a fine of $150. The court suspended imposition of a prison sentence, and the defendant was placed on probation for a period of one year.

Edward Bennett Williams, Buchman's lawyer, says that Congressman Jackson left the hearing room at the fortuitous time because he had to drive Senator Potter of Michigan, a guest in his home, to the airport. Williams claims that the reason Buchman got off with such a light sentence was that the jury had been deadlocked, so the judge delivered what is known as an Allen charge: the judge was required to inform the minority in the jury to remember that the majority was acting according to its best lights and then to turn to the majority and repeat the same admonition in favor of the minority. However, says Williams, Judge Kennedy, for some unaccountable reason, became confused and delivered both charges to the minority members of the jury. After the judge realized this, he felt constrained to prevent any further complications in the case and decided to let Buchman off with a light sentence.

Buchman no longer works in the motion picture industry and is engaged in other business in New York City.

The first witness from Hollywood to invoke the Fifth Amendment was an actor named Howard Da Silva, who is as well known on Broadway as in Hollywood. Da Silva had appeared in the original cast of *Oklahoma!*, in *Waiting for Lefty, Golden Boy, A Doll's House*, and *Abe Lincoln in Illinois*. For years he had moved back and forth between the Hollywood studios and the New York stage. In 1939 he went to Hollywood for the film version of *Abe Lincoln in Illinois*. From then until March 1951, when he appeared before the House Committee, he played in about forty films, working at all the major studios and serving under contracts for periods at Warner Brothers and Paramount. He appeared in *The Lost Weekend, The Great Gatsby*, and *Keeper of the Flame*, among others. His income showed a continuous increase from 1939 to 1951.

During his 1947 testimony, Robert Taylor said he did not know whether Da Silva was a Communist but that he "always has something to say at the wrong time" at meetings of the Screen Actors Guild. After that, Da Silva had trouble. Between 1947 and 1951, he changed agents four times in an attempt to improve his lot. Again and again, his agents reported that film executives said, "We can't hire him—he's too hot." Da Silva managed to make some films after 1947 and even completed a co-starring role after he was subpoenaed. But on March 21, 1951, he appeared before the House Committee and said, "I object to being called to testify against myself in this hearing. I object because the First and Fifth Amendment and all of the Bill of Rights protect me from any inquisitorial procedure and I may not be compelled to co-operate with this Committee in producing evidence designed to incriminate me and to drive me from my profession as an actor."

After that Da Silva found no more work in Hollywood. He returned to New York and found roles in a few radio shows, but he was removed from this medium, too, almost immediately. His agent told him that the William Morris agency, which packaged a show he had been on, had received six letters from American Legion posts objecting to Da Silva's appearance.

Da Silva tried to return to Broadway, but again he ran into serious trouble. Two potential "angels" raised objections when he read for roles, and once a producer told him point-blank: "We can't use you because the theater will be picketed. It is a case of blacklist but I can't help it."

Witnesses who invoked the Fifth Amendment were banished from the studios in a variety of ways. Most studio executives, remembering Paul V. McNutt's warning about the illegality of an industry-wide "conspiracy," took pains to conceal the reasons for firings. Howard Hughes, then chief at RKO, furnished an exception. Paul Jarrico, a screenwriter, was working at the Hughes studio at the time he invoked the Fifth Amendment before the House Committee on April 13, 1951. Jarrico recently described his subsequent experiences in Hollywood this way:

> In my case the evidence that I was blacklisted was simple and unmistakable. On March 23, 1951, I was subpoenaed to appear before the House Committee on Un-American Activities. The serving of the subpoena was publicized by the Los Angeles press, most of the newspapers quoting me accurately as saying I was not certain yet what my position before the Committee would be, but "if I have to choose between crawling in the mud with Larry Parks or going to jail like my courageous friends of the Hollywood Ten, I shall certainly choose the latter."
>
> I was fired from my employment as a screenwriter at RKO that very day, forbidden to come onto the studio lot even to pick up my personal belongings. I appeared before the Committee on April 13, 1951, and was a most unfriendly witness. I not only exercised my privilege under the Fifth Amendment, I assailed the Committee for trying to subvert the American Constitution.
>
> I was subsequently informed by my agents, the Jaffe agency, that there were no further possibilities of my employment in the motion-picture industry, and on June 20, 1951, at their request, I released them from the obligation of representing me. Though I had worked as a screenwriter more or less steadily for almost fourteen years prior to the date on which I was subpoenaed, I have not been employed by any Hollywood studio since.
>
> In the spring of 1952, I became involved in a highly publicized legal controversy with Howard Hughes. As head of RKO, he had arbitrarily removed my name from a film called *The Las Vegas Story*, which had been my last writing assignment at RKO. I had been awarded a screen credit on this film by the Screen Writers Guild, which, under its collective-bargaining agreement, had exclusive authority to determine writing credits.
>
> Hughes sued me for declaratory relief, asserting that I had violated the morals clause by my stand before the Committee. I filed a cross-complaint, asking for damages. The Screen Writers Guild sued Hughes independently for breaching the collective security agreement. Hughes won, both as against the Guild and me. Successive appeals of the Guild were defeated and the Guild finally accepted a compromise in which it gave up its hard-won authority to determine credits solely on the basis of literary contribution. My appeals were also denied.

In the course of these suits and in the public statements surrounding them, Hughes made it very clear that he maintained and intended to maintain a political blacklist. *The New York Times* reported on April 7, 1952, that RKO "will operate on a curtailed production basis for an indefinite period . . . in a drastic move for time to strengthen a political 'screening' program to prevent employment of persons suspected of being Communists or having Communist sympathies." The *Times* quoted Hughes further as asserting that "every one" of eleven stories, selected as the best for filming out of 150 read by the studio over a period of six months, had to be discarded because "information concerning one or more persons involved in the past writing of the script or original story showed that those writers were suspected of Communist ideas or sympathies." Added Hughes: "All studios have at their disposal information concerning the people who have been connected with one or more of the well-known Communist front organizations."

At a meeting of the Motion Picture Alliance on May 15, 1952, according to the *Los Angeles Daily News*, Roy Brewer declared that not one of the witnesses who "hid behind the Fifth Amendment" in the previous year and a half of hearings had subsequently been offered employment in the film industry. Later, it became apparent in Hollywood that workers who had been named as Communists but had neither been called to testify nor come forth to answer the charges made against them were also blacklisted. Brewer confirmed this, too, in another public statement. In answer to a charge in *Frontier* magazine that he was "straw boss of the purge," Brewer replied that the only blacklist he knew of was the list "established by the House Committee on Un-American Activities containing names of persons who have not repudiated that [Communist] association by comparable testimony."

Though 324 people had been named between 1951 and 1954, when Hollywood's "mass hearings" ended, they were not all motion picture workers. Some had left town years before they were named, others were wives of studio employees, others were trade union or Communist party functionaries who had never held jobs in the industry. But, when these people are eliminated from the list of those named, 212 remain who were active motion picture workers, many of whom had never made their living in any other industry. These 212 do not work in the industry today, though there is a small sub-rosa effort on the part of a few producers to buy the services of some of them (at cut-rate prices!) and present their work to the public under some other name.

The blacklisting proceeded through 1951, 1952, and 1953. Those dropped by the studios were not limited to persons who could influence film content, or who would receive screen credit for their work. The

Jose Ferrer

Larry Parks

Lee J. Cobb

Elia Kazan

industry had accepted the committee's new emphasis on "prestige, position, and money."

For example, there is the case of composer Sol Kaplan, who had scored more than thirty pictures in Hollywood between 1940 and 1953. Kaplan received a subpoena while he was working on a Twentieth Century-Fox sound stage. He had never been publicly identified as a Communist. John Garfield, who denied before the committee that he had ever been a Communist, said in the course of his testimony that Kaplan was a friend of his. Though Kaplan had been under contract to Twentieth Century-Fox for one year, he was fired when this happened. Later he was reinstated on a week-to-week "probation" basis after he protested that many top studio executives (including the man who was firing him) were also friends of Garfield. Kaplan was subpoenaed in April 1953. Shortly before he was scheduled to testify, a Fox business executive in charge of the music department told him that his job, despite economy firings, was safe. During his testimony, on April 8, 1953, Kaplan challenged the committee to produce his accusers and invoked almost the entire Bill of Rights when he refused to cooperate.

After the hearing, he returned to work at Twentieth Century-Fox. The musician says that his colleagues looked surprised when they saw him in the studio. Nothing happened the first day, but on the second he was told to call one of Fox's top producers. The producer, who was a friend of Kaplan, told him that Darryl Zanuck, production chief of the studio, did not want to fire him. Congressman Clyde Doyle, Democratic member of the committee, the producer said, did not believe that Kaplan was a Communist. If Kaplan would appear privately before Doyle—which could be "arranged"—he might be able to keep his job at Fox. The producer added that "no one would even know you spoke to Doyle." Kaplan said that he would not consider taking such a position because he did not believe in "deals" where important principles were concerned. Fifteen minutes later he received a telephone call from the same executive who had assured him that his job would be safe in case of economy firings. A new order had made Kaplan's dismissal necessary, the executive told him. When Kaplan pressed him, the studio executive finally admitted that the musician was being fired for political reasons.

If the unfriendly witnesses before the committee suffered social ostracism and loss of employment, the cooperative witnesses also paid a price. Not only Communists but many non-Communists looked upon them as "informers" (or, as they were described in the official

Communist press, as "stool pigeons"). Everyone in the movie colony had seen the British officer contemptuously push the money across the table with his swagger stick in John Ford's classic *The Informer*. Everyone remembered how Victor McLaglen, as the Irish Judas, had picked it up. Also, many Hollywood liberals were bitter about the uses to which, in earlier days, the Communists had diverted their innocent goodwill to Party causes. Now, when they saw some of these same people playing the "informer" role, they found even more reason to turn on them. The remaining Communists did all they could to encourage the feeling.

For those who supplied the committee with the names it wanted, social life became extremely difficult. Richard Collins, for instance, remembers going to a Screen Writers Guild meeting after he testified where only a half-dozen persons were willing to speak to him. Meta Reis Rosenberg recalls being denounced as a "stool pigeon" by someone who shouted from the balcony of a La Cienega Boulevard art gallery. Many of the "friendly" witnesses tell stories of how they were insulted and avoided. The wife of one witness says that the only people who offered any sympathy or financial help during this period were members of the Motion Picture Alliance for the Preservation of American Ideals. "When we needed friends as we never needed them before, Ward Bond telephoned and asked how we were doing," she recalls gratefully. Rebuffed as they were by liberal Hollywood, a number of the cooperative witnesses completed the full circuit from the Communist party to the right-wing Motion Picture Alliance for the Preservation of American Ideals, where they were welcomed.

Social ostracism was not the only price paid by the ex-Communists who gave the committee "names" during the mass hearings. Some, especially the earliest witnesses, found they were on an informal "blacklist." Only after influential figures in the MPA, powerful individuals like Roy Brewer, and members of the House Committee began to exert pressure on the studios were the cooperative witnesses reemployed. In the beginning the studio heads were not sure that ex-Communists would find any more favor with the patriotic pressure groups than unfriendly witnesses.

But as the parade of ex-Communists to the witness stand lengthened, it became less difficult for them to find work, though in some circles it was felt that people who played the "informer" were beyond the pale. Even today there are some in the industry who, though they have no sympathy with Communism, feel so strongly about this that they are extremely reluctant to hire any ex-Communists and are adamant about not hiring specific ones.

Martin Gang, according to the blacklisted screenwriter who called on him, spoke of the danger of nationwide picketing by private organizations. That same month, October 1951, movie picketing began in Los Angeles by a group called the Wage Earners Committee. The Wage Earners Committee, according to its executive director, "had the humblest sort of origin." "In typical American fashion," a waiter, a telephone switchman, a small-restaurant owner, and a retired salesman formed the organization. The committee—which was later found by the National Labor Relations Board to have accepted financial assistance from an employer who "intended to establish and set up Wage Earners as an instrumentality to offset legitimate collective bargaining"—immediately declared its belief in the "inalienable rights of the individual, as opposed to regimentation, communization, or dictatorship in any form." Politically, it was opposed to "every candidate controlled by the Labor Boss" and pledged itself to give its support to "the honest candidates the Labor Boss is attempting to purge."

The Wage Earners began their attack by picketing a film written by one of those named as a Communist before the House Committee. They carried signs which read: "This picture written by a Communist. Do not patronize." Later the group focused its attack on the film version of *Death of a Salesman*. It picketed a theater where the picture was showing and handed out circulars attacking Arthur Miller, author of the play, Fredric March, the star, and the producer, Stanley Kramer. Picketing of other films followed.

Then the full force of the Wage Earners was turned against Dore Schary, production chief at MGM. Pickets carried signs reading: "Communists are killing Americans in Korea. Fellow travelers support Communists. Yellow travelers support fellow travelers. Don't be a yellow traveler." Another sign read: "Please do not patronize. This is an MGM picture. Dore Schary 'Boss' of MGM. See House Un-American Activities Report. . . See Calif. Tenney Committee Reports . . ." Page numbers were listed.

Meanwhile, a publication of the group, the *National Wage Earner*, listed ninety-two films "which employ commies and fellow travelers and contain subversive subject matter designed to defame America throughout the world." The executive director of the committee, R. A. McConnon, announced, in a mimeographed letter demanding retraction of statements published about his organization in *Daily Variety*, that the Wage Earners were dedicated to providing "revelations of the identities and operations" of "subversive propagandists" in the motion picture industry. The group would stop picketing, he declared, "if the Industry would make an honest, and resultantly effective, policing of the medium. And this must include the immediate cessation of all pictures in which Americans are pictured as being intolerant and prejudiced against any so-called minority groups." Representatives of the Wage Earners offered to consult with the studios about the content of motion pictures and the loyalty of artists considered for employment.

In the circulars distributed by members of the Wage Earners Committee, producer Kramer was characterized as being "notorious for his red-slanted, red-starred films." The "true facts" about Kramer, the WEC held, were that he "taught at the Los Angeles Communist training school in 1947" and had employed a certain number of performers with "Communist-front" records. (Kramer's "teaching" actually consisted of a single guest lecture given at the People's Educational Center, where he spoke on a technical aspect of motion picture making.) The Wage Earners belabored Fredric March with charges that had been made against him by the New York *Counterattack*—but ignored the fact that the actor later received a retraction and reached an out-of-court settlement with that publication.

Among the page references in the Tenney Committee reports cited against Dore Schary was a reprint of an article from the *Hollywood Reporter* describing the meeting of the Screen Writers Guild at which Schary announced the Waldorf policy. At the meeting, the trade paper reported, one of the Hollywood Ten had called Schary a "thief." The other references were to Schary's participation in several organizations designated by Senator Tenney as "Communist dominated." There was no indication in any of the references cited that the film executive was personally "subversive" or "disloyal." The case against him, whatever there was of it, was based solely on "association."

Schary and Kramer both filed suit against the Wage Earners Committee, on grounds of libel and, in Schary's case, of willful interference with contractual relations. Picketing by the Wage Earners was then stopped by court order.

In Washington, D.C., members of the Catholic War Veterans picketed Judy Holliday's *Born Yesterday*. Later, in New York, the Catholic veterans picketed her second picture, *The Marrying Kind*, and distributed leaflets describing her as "the darling of the *Daily Worker*." Miss Holliday, along with Garson Kanin, author of *Born Yesterday*, was listed in *Red Channels*. Her studio, Columbia Pictures, was alarmed by the picketing incidents. She had won an Academy Award for her first starring role and promised to be an extremely valuable and lucrative "property."

Columbia vice-president B. B. Kahane told a reporter not long ago that after the picketing started, he questioned the star and was completely satisfied that her loyalty was beyond challenge. Columbia was satisfied, but that was not enough to call off the picket lines. The film company enlisted the services of Ken Bierly, a former editor of *Counterattack* turned public relations consultant. Bierly's first job for Columbia was to "clear up the confusion about Judy Holliday." Soon after Bierly took over, the picket lines disappeared. Later, he told Merle Miller, author of *The Judges and the Judged*: "You might put it that I had something to do with getting the facts, the true facts to the right people."

It was not only a question of getting the "true facts" to the "right" people but also of getting them to a large number of Americans who had been led to believe that Judy Holliday was a suspicious if not subversive person. A public relations campaign was necessary if Columbia was to realize its investment in the star. Miss Holliday's future was turned over to a group of skilled publicists. Gradually the rumors about her were silenced.

On March 26, 1952, Judy Holliday went to Washington, D.C., the *Born Yesterday* locale, and testified before the Senate Internal Security Subcommittee. She admitted that she had been "duped" into supporting Communist front organizations but convinced the subcommittee she had always been anti-Communist. Senator Watkins asked her: "You watch it now; do you not?" Miss Holiday in accents reminiscent of Billie Dawn replied: "Ho, *do* I watch it now!"

Other veterans' groups threatened to take an active interest in Hollywood's employment practices. A California unit of Amvets asked studio heads to define their position regarding the hiring of persons suspected of disloyalty. But no further action was reported after a number of persons in the same organization denounced the move as a publicity scheme.

In November 1951, a Hollywood post of the American Legion sponsored a resolution to provide for the picketing of theaters showing pictures which carried the name or credit of "unfriendly" witnesses. The resolution was not adopted. Later, the same post sponsored resolutions before local and regional organizations of the Legion to establish a committee of the California department which would act as liaison with representatives of the film industry. The committee would be organized "for the purpose of conferring concerning any person now employed or contracted with, by such studio, who is a Communist, or whose acts, ideas, or ideals are inimical to the welfare of

Judy Holliday in the Broadway production of *Born Yesterday,* 1946

the United States, and, in the event a result deemed satisfactory to
the committee is not obtained, to take such other and further steps or
action as the committee may deem fit and proper, including lawful
demonstrations at such times and places as it may deem necessary to
carry into effect the purposes of this resolution." But these resolutions
also failed to pass.

 With all this adverse activity and with the threat of more to come, the Hollywood producers were feeling harassed and put upon. Their brave resolutions after the Waldorf Conference that the industry would not be "swayed by hysteria or intimidation from any sources" seemed less persuasive by the hour. The "mass hearings" of 1951 put Hollywood on the defensive, and the producers were feeling pressures from all sides.

RICHARD S. RANDALL

Censorship: From *The Miracle* to *Deep Throat*

On May 26, 1952, the Supreme Court of the United States announced its decision in the case officially known as *Burstyn v. Wilson* and declared that motion pictures are "a significant medium for the communication of ideas," their importance not lessened by the fact that they are designed "to entertain as well as inform."[1] In reaching this conclusion, the Court, in effect, read the movies into the First Amendment to the Constitution and extended to them the same protected status held by newspapers, magazines, and other organs of speech. The case, which had involved refusal by the New York State Board of Censors to issue an exhibition permit to Roberto Rossellini's forty-minute award-winning film *The Miracle*, was the first case of movie censorship the Court had considered in thirty-seven years. Together with an economic crisis in the medium, it helped to precipitate a revolution in the content of films that has probably not yet run its course.[2]

Before the *Miracle* case, a myriad of state and local boards of censors, invested with simple statutory authority to deny permits to films found offensive, had near life-and-death power over cinematic exhibition in

1. *Burstyn v. Wilson*, 343 U.S. 495, 501–2 (1952).

2. For background on censorship before the *Miracle* case and after it through the mid-1960s, as well as detailed examination of governmental censor boards during the latter period, see Richard Randall, *Censorship of the Movies: The Social and Political Control of a Mass Medium* (Madison: University of Wisconsin Press, 1968).

510

their communities. In its only previous consideration of movie censorship, *Mutual Film Corp. v. Ohio*, in 1915, the Supreme Court had found movies were "business, pure and simple . . . not to be regarded as part of the press of the country or as organs of public opinion."[3] As a simple commercial product rather than a constitutionally protected medium of speech, they could be regulated through prior censorship and be stopped before reaching their consumers in much the same way dangerous drugs or hazardous chemicals might; indeed, they were often compared to exactly those items of commerce.

Movies had also become subject to regulation by the industry itself through the Production Code Administration—the "Hays Office," as it was known in its early days. Run by the Motion Picture Producers and Distributors of America (now the Motion Picture Association of America), the organization of a handful of large companies known as the "majors," the agency imposed restraint on the content of films at the production stage. The industry had reluctantly embraced this arrangement in the early 1930s when it faced not only increased possibility of federal censorship and further proliferation of state and local censor boards, but also mounting pressure from many religious groups. Formation of a Roman Catholic reviewing and rating body, the Legion of Decency, and the threat of parish boycott of films constituted, in fact, the chief "gun behind the door." This triad of controls—industry self-regulation, organized religious pressure, and governmental censor boards—effected a censorial stability that lasted nearly a generation. The industry discovered it could live quite easily with these burdens because of the extraordinary profits from the "family" film, the chief product of a censored medium addressing itself to an almost undifferentiated mass audience in the 1930s and 1940s.

In the fifties, new constitutional freedoms and the rapid growth of television upset this equilibrium. The *Miracle* decision did not outlaw governmental censor boards per se, but it did provide a constitutional basis for challenging their rulings and those of the Federal Bureau of Customs in the case of imported films. Specifically, it held that a film could not be denied exhibition merely because it was found to be "sacrilegious." In one line of cases that followed, various other statutory censorial criteria, such as "harmful," "immoral," and "indecent," used freely by censors, were held unconstitutional. By a process of elimination, these decisions made it clear that obscenity would be the only permissible criterion for governmental prior restraint of movies. In a second and even more striking series of cases in the 1950s

3. *Mutual Film Corp. v. Ohio*, 236 U.S. 230, 244 (1915).

and early 1960s, many of them involving other media, the Court narrowed the concept of obscenity itself as a proscribable category.

While these new legal freedoms provided filmmakers with opportunities to explore themes, visual representation, and dialogue that had been off-limits for the family film, economic factors provided the necessity for doing so. With its enormous growth after World War II, television challenged and then in a short time completely usurped the older medium as the prime supplier of American family entertainment. While the number of sets in American homes was increasing fourfold in the fifties, movie admissions fell by 50 percent. For American production companies the crisis was made worse by the growing competition from inexpensively made foreign films, many of which were far more daring and imaginative in their content than the American product. In the fifties, American films were, in effect, acquiring the blessings of a new freedom at the same time that they were losing much of both their audience and their solvency.

These developments alone would have been enough to weaken the industry's own self-regulatory apparatus, but the authority of the Production Code had also been undercut as a result of an antitrust decree in 1948 requiring production companies to divest themselves of interest in theaters. Previously, five majors had controlled 70 percent of the first-run theaters in major cities and about 45 percent of all film rentals in the country. With such concentration, they possessed tremendous economic leverage on all other elements in the industry. In unhinging their power and forcing decentralization upon the industry, the decree indirectly cut the power of their creature, the Production Code.

The Censorship Interest

With the movies forced to find a new role among the media of entertainment and particularly to be something television was not, a radical change in the content of films was inevitable. No less so was that this change and the freedom that made it possible would come under attack from those who would find the new content threatening or believed it harmful. Two questions are appropriate here. What kind of depiction or cinematic representation has been found objectionable? And why? The first is the more easily answered. Over the years, more censorial attention has been given to the portrayal of sexuality and sexual immorality than to depiction of any other realm of everyday life. Almost every governmental censor board has been empowered to censor obscenity, and, in the pre-*Miracle* period, many were authorized

Anna Magnani in Roberto Rossellini's *The Miracle* (1948)

to ban or cut films their members thought to be indecent or immoral as well. Likewise, the industry's own Production Code proscribed a variety of erotic matter including "indecent or undue exposure," "intimate sex scenes violating common standards of decency," "justification of illicit sex relationships," and "obscene speech, gestures, and movements."[4]

Not all censorial interest has been directed at erotic matter, however. Many boards could and did censor the portrayal of criminal behavior, of racial, religious, or class prejudice, and of anything which, in their opinion, could be an incitement to crime or lead to a disturbance of the peace. The Production Code cast an even wider net. Detailed and protracted acts of brutality, cruelty, physical violence, or torture were not to be shown, nor was excessive cruelty to animals. Religion was not to be demeaned, and words or symbols contemptuous of racial, religious, or national groups were not to be used in ways that might incite bigotry or hatred. And, lest there be any doubt, "evil, sin, crime and wrong-doing" were not to be justified.

It would be a mistake to suppose that these various censorial standards were the work of a few Mrs. Grundys. The state and local laws that created censor boards were deliberate decisions, publicly arrived at, reflecting a response to widespread popular concern with what was being shown on the nation's screens. Much the same can be said for the creation of the Production Code Administration and the formulation of the code itself. In their breadth and scope the governmental and industry censorship standards reflected not only the awe in which the movies were held by most persons as a presumed shaper of ideas, attitudes, and even behavior, but also the range of concerns and values held by a large part of the nation.

The question of why there should be a censorship interest at all, that is, why certain content should be threatening or believed harmful, is less easily answered. Objections to obscenity, to take the most common object of censorship, are usually based on the assumption that it may lead to harmful results in the way of behavior, attitudes, or esthetics. Through its supposed appeal to the prurient interest, obscenity is assumed to incite or at least encourage illegal and possibly antisocial acts of a highly aggressive sort. Exposure to obscenity is thought to affect an individual viewer's moral values and thus, indirectly, those of family or community. As an unsightly and unpleasant visual experience to many of those who may be exposed, obscenity is said to

4. *The Motion Picture Code of Self-Regulation*, Motion Picture Association of America (undated), pp. 5–6.

constitute an assault on esthetics and taste and possibly an invasion of privacy and peace of mind in the case of involuntary exposure. Many who advocate censorship as a means of protecting against one or more of these alleged harms make distinctions based on the age of the person exposed, the degree to which the exposure is unsought or unsuspecting, and whether or not the material is "pandered."

Some critics of censorship have maintained that dubious censorial motives lie behind concern about these alleged harms. Those who would keep certain matter from the sight of their fellow citizens are said to be psychologically disturbed Anthony Comstocks driven less by their professed rational concern for the public and common good than by their own personal fears and anxieties. And, indeed, some sophisticated criticism of the censorial disposition suggests that it may be explained as a projection of repressions tightly imposed upon oneself as a means of controlling powerful but deeply recessed drives toward sexual expression and aggression. By censoring, according to this theory, one reaffirms self-control and increases the distance between the conscious self and disturbing impulses or temptations within.

A more sociologically oriented criticism of motives suggests that the quest to censor often involves the desire to have one's own values, morals, or cultural standards or those of the group or class to which one belongs reflected in public policy and taste. Accordingly, the status of one's group or class and, indirectly, of oneself is enhanced or diminished by the degree to which its moral, ethical, or esthetic standards or life-style is "in force." In this view, censorial motives, whether conscious or unconscious, are not limited to concern about erotic depiction but go beyond it to include concern about the representation of social, political, economic, religious, and esthetic ideas and values.

Clearly, censorship has always had a lunatic fringe where obscenity was seen in every unpunished adultery or in every four-letter word or décolletage. These censorial excesses and idiosyncrasies would seem to offer some confirmation of the psychological repression theory of censorial motives. Nor is there any lack of evidence of hypersensitivity to the depiction of status. Every year, the Production Code Administration and its successor, the Code and Rating Office, have received complaints, often running into the thousands, about the portrayal of some identifiable group of persons—lawyers, Hungarians, redheads, Moslems, glass blowers, South Carolinians, abstainers, men without undershirts, and so on. This steady outpouring of concern prompted one wit to observe that the only villain it was possible to portray safely in a movie was a white, Anglo-Saxon Protestant who was unemployed! It would be unfair, however, to dismiss all censorial concern as a matter of repressed desires or the defense of particularist status values. Worry about erotica or the depiction of violence is a concern that also appears to be reasonably held by many reasonable persons. Unfortunately, there is no conclusive evidence that such portrayal in the movies has or does not have harmful effects; hence, it is impossible to say how justified or unjustified some of the fears may be. That judgment must await the comprehensive and definitive studies that would indicate whether a steady offering of sex and violence is actually damaging or merely offensive to conventional sensibilities.[5]

In the meantime, whether based on rational and "common sense" opinion or concerns about status or one's own libidinal and aggressive drives, censorship pressures are unlikely to abate. They probably will continue to be felt by public officials and by those who make, distribute, and exhibit motion pictures. In fact, even were conclusive evidence to be found that obscenity is not harmful, it would be unlikely to have much effect on irrational censorial concerns. The remainder of this chapter will deal with censorship interest since the *Miracle* case and with how public officials and those in the industry have responded to and been affected by it.

Obscenity and Censorship in the Law

Following the *Miracle* decision, not only did the Supreme Court invalidate every substantive censorship criterion except that of obscenity, but it also placed censor boards under a set of rigorous procedural requirements. Today, a board of censors requiring prior submission of films must be prompt in its review and, should it deny a permit because of alleged obscenity, must take the matter into court immediately. Once there, it must carry the burden of proving that the film is, in fact, obscene. This is an important procedural distinction since, in effect, it reverses the crucial burden of proof, taking it from the defendant film proprietor and placing it upon the censors. Previously, a proprietor could not exhibit a film denied a permit unless he himself sued the board of censors and proved the film not obscene.

5. There have been many studies of the effect of erotica and violence in the media, including several involving movies, but the findings, though illuminating, are far from conclusive, at least as a basis for formulating definitive public policy on the matter. Among the more recent and systematic studies have been those conducted by the Commission on Obscenity and Pornography in 1969. The commission also reviewed earlier studies and related them to the more recent work. See *Report of the Commission on Obscenity and Pornography* (Washington, D.C.: U.S. Government Printing Office, 1970), pp. 139–263.

In order to prevent long, frequently delayed trials during which the film would, in effect, be suppressed, the Court has also required that the judicial decision be prompt.

The cumulative effect of the rulings cutting away the substantive ground of prior censorship and those imposing procedural rigor has been nearly to eliminate prior censorship as an institution. Denial of exhibition permits is now so difficult to sustain that many state legislatures and local city councils have abandoned prior censorship altogether. At the time of the *Miracle* decision, seven states—Kansas, Maryland, Massachusetts, New York, Ohio, Pennsylvania, and Virginia—and as many as eighty cities and towns, including Chicago, Milwaukee, and Detroit among the larger ones, had prior censorship boards. Today, only Maryland and a handful of cities maintain them. Occasionally new boards are proposed, but such attempts are often made for their symbolic value or arise out of sheer frustration with other methods of control. Very few have gotten beyond the debating stage. If prior censorship has any future at all, it will probably be more in classifying films for children and adolescents than in censoring them for adults. In fact, one of the few operating boards left today, the Dallas Classification Board, has powers only to classify. An additional and perhaps somewhat paradoxical result of the demise of prior censorship is that the number of formal prosecutions of exhibitors for showing obscene films and the number of instances of informal harassment of exhibitors have both increased markedly, reflecting a new accommodation of censorship pressures.

The narrowing of what is legally proscribable as obscenity has had an even more profound effect on the movies. This doctrinal change is probably one of the true revolutions of our time and is, of course, part of a larger cultural change in sexual attitudes and behavior, which it unquestionably helped to bring about. Strange as it may seem, the Supreme Court had not considered the obscenity question itself in any definitive way until 1957. That year, in two cases heard together—one involving the mailing of allegedly obscene magazines, and the other the sale of similar material in a bookstore—the Court reaffirmed that obscenity, being "utterly without redeeming social importance," was outside the protection of the Constitution. But it added, pointedly, that "sex and obscenity are not synonymous," and that the portrayal of sex in art, literature, and scientific works was entitled to the constitutional protection of speech and press. The test to be used in determining whether a particular book, magazine, or film was obscene was "whether to the average person, applying contemporary community standards, the dominant theme of the material taken as a whole appeals to the prurient interest."[6] This formulation, known in constitutional law as the *Roth* test, after the name of one of the defendants in the two cases, is still the basic yardstick for obscenity today. Its application in specific cases has been tortuous, however, and it is significant that in no major obscenity cases have the nine justices of the Court been unanimous. In a few, a majority has not even been able to agree on a theory for deciding the case.

In other cases following the 1957 decision, the Court appeared to add still another measure to be met before obscenity could be legally established—that of "patent offensiveness." Thus, in addition to the *Roth* test and the fact that a film, book, or magazine in question must be "utterly without redeeming social importance," it must also be "so offensive as to affront current community standards of decency."[7] With these tests, much of what was formerly thought to be obscene became constitutionally protected speech. Thus, speculation grew that the only proscribable obscenity left was so-called hard-core pornography.[8]

At the same time, the Court has spun out several exceptions to a hard-core standard. In one, involving prosecution of Ralph Ginzburg, publisher of the magazine *Eros*, the Court held that dealing with material that is not, in itself, hard-core pornography might nonetheless be punishable if the material were "pandered," that is, marketed as though it were legally obscene. In a second, the Court allowed that a different and broader test of obscenity might be applied where recipients of the communication were juveniles. These two exceptions to the hard-core standard introduce the important concept of "variable" obscenity—the idea that something may be obscene to one audience or in one mode of presentation but not another. A third exception was in the direction of further permissiveness and grew out of a prosecution of a man for possessing admittedly hard-core pornographic films discovered accidentally by police in a search of his home for evidence of illegal gambling. The Supreme Court held that mere private possession of hard-core pornography in one's home, in contrast to its public sale,

6. *Roth v. United States, Alberts v. California,* 354 U.S. 476, 484 (1957).

7. *Manual Enterprises v. Day,* U.S. 478, 482 (1962).

8. Exactly what constitutes hard-core pornography has never been established with much precision in the law or even in popular discussion, though it would appear to include depiction of actual and explicit sexual intercourse rather than suggested or simulated congress. It is also thought to include explicit depiction of various "perversions," such as masturbation, fellatio, cunnilingus, pedophilia, necrophilia, and bestiality. At least one Supreme Court justice, Potter Stewart, finds the hard-core concept a workable test for obscenity for the simplest of reasons: "I know it when I see it!" In the film trade, the distinction between hard-core and soft-core content has considerable meaning in the marketing of many "sexploitation" films. More will be said of this later.

exhibition, distribution, or dissemination, was not a punishable offense.

A major change in the obscenity doctrine and one having considerable bearing on the movies came in a set of decisions announced by a more conservative Supreme Court, led by Chief Justice Warren Burger, in 1973. In one case, involving the Paris Adult Theatre in Atlanta, the Court flatly rejected a position toward which many had thought it had been moving, namely, that even hard-core pornographic films might be shown publicly if the audience were consenting adults. The case involved *Magic Mirror* and *It All Comes Out in the End*, acknowledged to be obscene, which were shown to an audience of adults at a theater devoid of offensive advertising. A majority of the Court maintained that the right to have access to pornography was limited to the privacy of one's home and did not extend to commercial movie houses. According to Chief Justice Burger, a state could decide that "public exhibition of obscene material, or commerce in such material, has a tendency to injure the community as a whole, to endanger the public safety, or to jeopardize . . . the state's right to maintain a decent society."[9]

In a second case, *Miller v. California*, involving the mailing of pornographic illustrated books, the Court upheld the conviction of the sender and, in doing so, revised the test for obscenity in two important ways. First, it modified the requirement that proscribable obscenity must be "utterly without redeeming social importance," saying, instead, that "at a minimum, prurient, patently offensive depiction or description of sexual conduct must have serious literary, artistic, political, or scientific value to merit First Amendment protection."[10] Second, in a declaration that shook the entire film industry, the Court returned to an element in the original *Roth* test that had never been satisfactorily defined, "contemporary community standards," and held that "community" referred not to the national community, as many had supposed and as many civil libertarians had urged, but to the state or local community. Chief Justice Burger, again the spokesman for the majority of the Court, said that the nation was too large and too diverse for a single national standard to be "articulated for all fifty states in a single formulation, even assuming the prerequisite consensus exists." He added that it was unrealistic as well as constitutionally unsound to require that "the people of Maine or Mississippi accept public depiction of conduct found tolerable in Las Vegas or New York City.

9. *Paris Adult Theatre v. Slaton*, 413 U.S. 49, 69 (1973).
10. *Miller v. California*, 413 U.S. 15, 24 (1973).

... People in different states vary in their tastes and attitudes, and this diversity is not to be strangled by the absolutism of imposed uniformity."[11] A corollary of establishing the state or locality as the "community" whose standards are to be applied is that the local trial judge or jury would be the agent for making that determination rather than the higher courts. The fact that different juries might reach different conclusions about the same material would not mean that constitutional rights had been abridged, according to the Chief Justice. Such a differential outcome is "one of the consequences we accept under our jury system."[12]

Though the Court was again badly divided, 5–4, in these two cases, the decisions still number among the few times when as many as five justices were able to agree on a clarification of a major substantive aspect of the obscenity test. Three of the dissenting justices thought pornographic communication should be free of restriction unless it were made available to juveniles or were given "obtrusive exposure to unconsenting adults." A fourth dissenter, Justice William O. Douglas, reiterated his long-held position that there should be no restrictions on pornography at all except where shown to present a clear and present danger of precipitating illegal acts.

The Court has achieved greater consensus on the procedural aspects of the obscenity problem than on the substantive ones discussed above. As in the case of governmental censor boards, the justices have been careful to hold prosecutors and police to certain standards of due process in order to protect material which is alleged to be obscene but which might possibly be found not obscene later in a trial. A book, magazine, or film, for example, may not be seized by police unless there has been some prior, though not necessarily conclusive, judicial finding that it may be obscene. As a practical matter, this has meant that before a film may be confiscated as allegedly obscene, a judge must view it, usually by paying his way into the theater where it is being shown, and then must issue a warrant for its seizure as a possibly obscene item. Police may not seize films on their own judgment that they are obscene. In a 1973 case involving *Blue Movie*, the Burger Court also clarified this aspect of the obscenity problem. New York City policemen saw the film and summoned a judge who viewed it and, at its conclusion, signed a warrant for the arrest of the theater manager, projectionist, and ticket taker, and for seizure of the film to preserve it as evidence. The Court upheld this action on the theory

11. Ibid., 32.
12. Ibid., 26, n. 9.

that the confiscated reels were not the only print of the film; hence, the seizure did not constitute a prior restraint that would prevent any exhibition of the film while the obscenity question was pending trial.

Despite these more restrictive recent decisions, libertarian evolution of the obscenity doctrine is dramatically evident in a comparison of films that have been the object of obscenity censorship at various times since the *Miracle* decision and formulation of the *Roth* test. The major movie obscenity cases of the fifties involved films like *Game of Love, The Lovers, Lady Chatterley's Lover,* and *La Ronde.* Objections to these films had largely to do with their themes of sexual immorality. Few of them contained any nudity, and none involved four-letter words. Their offense was that they appeared to advocate, or at least not condemn, certain transgressions against established sexual values, usually adultery. This kind of cinematic depiction, sometimes referred to as ideological obscenity, is clearly no longer proscribable. It is fair to say that all idea content and advocacy in movies are protected today against an allegation of obscenity, no matter how morally offensive the ideas may be to some persons. Though presenting different problems, the major cases of the 1960s seem almost as quaint now as those of the fifties. In the early sixties, the controversies involved limited erotic nudity, such as brief glimpses of female breasts or buttocks; nonerotic nudity in the "nudie" or nudist camp genre that quickly sprang up and almost as quickly disappeared (actually became passé as a result of films with detailed erotic nudity); particular words in the sound track like *shit,* as slang for heroin in *The Connection* or *rape* and *contraceptive* in *Anatomy of a Murder;* and detailed simulated sexual violence as in the rape scene in *The Virgin Spring.* In the late sixties, the controversies more often than not involved simulated consensual sexual acts, as in the case of *A Stranger Knocks* and *491.* The latter, which includes a scene of a prostitute *about* to have intercourse with a large dog, was, like most of the controversial films preceding it, naively believed to approach the limits of cinematic freedom. None of these films and none of the objectionable categories of depiction— advocacy of immorality, nudity, four-letter words or other frank dialogue, simulated sexual acts—are likely to constitute the hard-core pornography that would be constitutionally proscribable for an adult audience today. In fact, in the trade today, detailed erotic nudity and simulated sexual acts are known as soft-core. Though this kind of cinematic depiction may occasionally provoke a prosecution or other censorial action today, it is unlikely that the Supreme Court would uphold a finding of obscenity based upon it.

Censorship cases in the mid-seventies are very likely to involve hard-core content, the kind represented in such films as *The Animal Lover* (where a woman actually has intercourse with a dog), *The Devil in Miss Jones, Behind the Green Door,* and *Deep Throat.* The last, the most financially successful pornographic film ever made, went into national distribution after a spectacular run in New York City. It became the object of obscenity actions in various cities and towns, including New York itself, where it was found obscene after a ten-day trial that accumulated more than a thousand pages of expert testimony and was covered on the front pages of the *New York Times.* The exhibitor was fined $100,000, which took most of his profits from a six-month booking. In its seventy-minute running span, the film encompasses fifteen nonsimulated sexual acts, including seven of fellatio, four of cunnilingus—one or both *de rigueur* in most hard-core films— and others requiring more imagination. The fact that *Deep Throat* has also been found *not* obscene in some trials in some communities is a striking indication of how radical an effect the evolving obscenity doctrine has had on movies.

It is not yet clear what long-run effects the 1973 Burger Court de-

Maria Schneider in *Last Tango in Paris,* directed by Bernardo Bertolucci (United Artists, 1972)

cisions will have. The requirement that depiction of sexual conduct must have "serious literary, artistic, political, or scientific value" may force producers of pornographic films to pay more attention to traditional story elements such as plot and character and may put an end to "loops"—pornographic shorts featuring sexual action only and totally lacking story and sometimes even credits or titles. Paradoxically, if the net result is to increase the quality of pornographic films, those films may become more widely attractive and have greater impact on viewers than anyone has yet imagined. The requirement that community standards be those of the state or local community could easily result in a film's being obscene in one city or state but not in another. This happened with *Deep Throat*, which was found not obscene in Binghamton, New York, and thus has been declared both obscene and not obscene in the same state! This "balkanizing" effect would not be unlike that which prevailed in the days of unrestricted state and local prior censorship, where rulings on a film often differed from one state or locality to another. Such a possibility is a disturbing one for an industry that must rely on national distribution of its product and, therefore, on some uniformity of the marketplace. These economic imperatives could result in the production of films that would satisfy the lowest common denominator of standards, that is, those of the most restrictive communities. This would be particularly likely in the case of large-budget features. On the other hand, though the Supreme Court has given emphasis to state and local standards, it has reserved the right to conduct its own review of a film. It was through just such an independent review that the Court unanimously found *Carnal Knowledge* not obscene in 1974, even though it had been judged so in Georgia presumably through local application of local standards.

Self-Regulation: The Rating System

Self-regulation by the movie industry has always had a between-Scylla-and-Charybdis status. It came into being and has continued in force in order to head off more restrictive governmental censorship and massive boycotts by organized groups. Yet, many people within the industry have never been happy with the economic burdens it often indirectly imposes, or with its limitations on creative energies. Before the antitrust decree of 1948, when the industry was still highly centralized, profits from the family film and the general economic power of the big companies helped to check dissident voices. These conditions ended in the fifties, and the Production Code gradually lost much of its power within the industry. Exhibitors, who could no longer be easily coerced into showing only films bearing the code seal, opened their theaters to nonapproved films. On the production side, a major company, United Artists, successfully defied the code by releasing Otto Preminger's *The Moon Is Blue* and *The Man with the Golden Arm* without seals. Tied to the censorship criteria of an earlier day, the code office was also unable to give the seal to such later leading films as *The Pawnbroker* (because of nudity), *Who's Afraid of Virginia Woolf?* (profanity), and the British-made *Alfie* (subject of abortion). These decisions further weakened its standing, and many advocated dropping self-regulation altogether as unworkable. To do so, however, clearly would have invited massive efforts to enact new governmental censorship, possibly at the federal level.

Faced with this dilemma, the MPAA revised the code in 1966, liberalizing its standards, and empowered the code office to affix the label

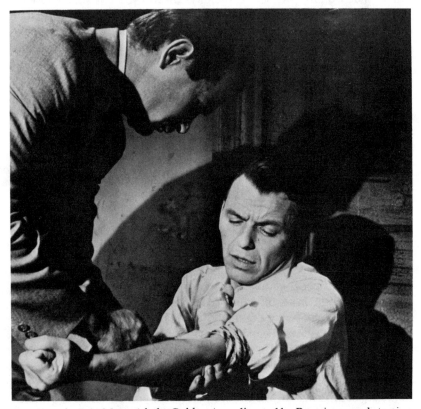

Otto Preminger's *Man with the Golden Arm,* directed by Preminger and starring Frank Sinatra (United Artists, 1956)

"Suggested for Mature Audiences" ("SMA") to certain films judged not suitable for children. The label marked a break in the industry's adamant opposition to any age classification of its films and was the forerunner of the present rating system. For those films affected, it appeared only in first-run advertising, and there was no arrangement at the exhibition level to give it effect at the box office. With these limitations, it soon proved unequal to the prime task of self-regulation, that of heading off outside censorship. Censorial pressures built up rapidly in the late sixties as an increasing number of films, including many of the widely distributed ones of the major companies, dealt with sexual themes and included nudity, detailed erotic behavior, and frank language. At the same time, the Supreme Court had expressly upheld the right of governmental censor boards to classify films for children and was exploring the concept of "variable" obscenity, with its implication that a film not obscene for adults might be proscribable if children and adolescents were in its audience. Thus, in 1968, two years after the Production Code had been revised and the "SMA" label established, the latter was dropped and, in near desperation, leaders of the industry embraced the idea of a full-scale rating system. Jack Valenti, the new president of the MPAA, and attorney Louis Nizer, the organization's respected general counsel, spent several months persuading major production, distribution, and exhibition elements to support a rating system and be willing to enforce it upon themselves. With a tentative consensus behind it, the MPAA inaugurated the system in November 1968, and the United States became the last major Western nation to have some kind of systematic age classification of motion pictures.

Under the system, American producers and the importers of foreign features submit their films before release to the MPAA's Code and Rating Office. The office, which has been headed successively by a former member of the Production Code staff, a psychiatrist, and a professor of mass communications, views each film and assigns one of four designations that have now become household symbols: "G" (general audience); "PG" (parental guidance suggested, indicating that some material may not be suitable for preteenagers); "R" (restricted, indicating that persons under seventeen may not be admitted unless accompanied by a parent or adult guardian); and "X" (no one under seventeen admitted). The specific criteria upon which these ratings are based have never been made public, and have apparently shifted over the years, mainly in the direction of greater permissiveness. Unsurprisingly, erotic content appears to be the chief concern in arriving at a rating, though violence may occasionally be taken into account. Of nearly three thousand films viewed and rated during the system's first six years, 1968–74, three-quarters were in the "PG" or "R" categories. The complete breakdown by percentage is "G," 20; "PG," 38; "R," 37; and "X," 5. Since the first years of the system, the percentage of "R" ratings has increased markedly and "X" ratings slightly. The percentage of "G" ratings has dropped considerably.

The enforcement responsibility, without which the system would be advisory only and probably largely ineffective in reducing censorship pressure, falls to exhibitors. Exhibitor cooperation with a system run mainly by production interests is voluntary and not always smooth. Attempts by the MPAA and production interests to coerce exhibitor cooperation through economic or other leverage would raise antitrust questions. The MPAA and the National Association of Theatre Owners, the largest exhibitor organization, estimate that about 80 percent of exhibitors work with the rating system. Among them are most of the large theater chains or circuits, many of which have enthusiastically supported the system from the beginning. Yet, even where exhibitors do cooperate, there are no reliable data today on the quality and thoroughness of box office enforcement. Some evidence indicates the enforcement may be linked to the existence of local pressures.[13]

The extent to which the system covers films in commercial release also bears on its effectiveness. Just as exhibitors cannot be coerced into bringing their admission policies into conformance with the ratings of the films they are playing, so, too, producers and importers cannot be required to submit their films for rating. The system does provide that a film not submitted may, in release, bear an "X"—the so-called self-applied "X." But a film not submitted for rating may not bear any other rating letter. Independent studies indicate that about 80 percent of the films in commercial release have been submitted for rating. Because these include most of those of the major producing companies and major importers of foreign features, about 90 percent of the exhibition bookings or "play dates" involve rated films. Further, since most of the largest theaters and biggest circuits play mainly major, rated productions, probably as much as 98 percent of the American moviegoing audience on a given day or night views rated films.

Like the Production Code before it, the rating system faces two additional problems: one having to do with the degree of evenhandedness with which it is administered within the industry, and the other

13. See Richard S. Randall, "Classification in the Film Industry," *Technical Report of the Commission on Obscenity and Pornography* 5 (Washington, D.C.: U.S. Government Printing Office, 1970), pp. 219–93.

the degree of credibility with the public at large. The first of these affects the amount of support attainable in a decentralized industry, the second the extent to which self-regulation is accepted as a substitute for other forms of censorship. Run by the MPAA, the trade association dominated by the major production companies, the rating system has been attacked by independent producers, importers of foreign films, and some other nonproduction elements in the industry as a tool by which major companies can throttle or at least inhibit competition. Where charges of favoritism are made, they usually have to do with the Code and Rating Office's having given an "R" or "X" to a film the proprietor of which thought it should have received a "PG" or "R," respectively. The economic consequences of a more restrictive rating can be formidable. The "PG" rating is usually the sought-after prize, since it involves no box office restriction and, at the same time, avoids the sexless "Disney" stigma many believe associated with a "G" rating. Economically, an "X" is particularly restrictive, less because the under-seventeen audience is excluded than because many theaters and some of the circuits do not book "X" films at all. With the rare exception of *Midnight Cowboy*, which had the advantage of being a major critical success, even a film with a medium-sized budget bearing an "X" is unlikely to turn a profit. With these prospects, many proprietors are willing to alter a film in order to acquire the less restrictive "R" on bookings is substantially less than that of the "X." A large-budget film with an "R" rating may have difficulty as well, because of the relatively smaller audience from which it may draw and because of a smaller number of bookings, though the effect of an "R" on bookings is substantially less than that of the "X."Probably the most severe challenge the rating system has faced in its short history arose over an individual rating when James Aubrey, the president of MGM, threatened to release *Ryan's Daughter*, a film that had a reputed $14 million budget, without any rating if its designated rating were not changed from "R" to "GP" (the former designation for "PG"). On appeal to the Code and Rating Appeal Board, the rating was changed, a decision that may have headed off MGM's threatened withdrawal from the MPAA, which would have removed a major organizational support for the rating system.

Any proprietor who is not satisfied with the rating of the Code and Rating Office may take an appeal to the Code and Rating Appeal Board, a body of twenty-five members representing the three major segments of the industry—production, distribution, and exhibition. However, since twelve of its seats are filled by executives of member companies through appointment by the MPAA president, who is, himself, a mem-

Jon Voight and Dustin Hoffman in *Midnight Cowboy,* directed by John Schlesinger (United Artists, 1969)

ber, the board tends to be dominated by MPAA interests. In about two-thirds of the cases it has heard, the board has sustained the original rating. In a few of these, the film in question did eventually receive a less restrictive rating after its proprietors agreed to make changes in it. Intraindustry charges of a "double standard" at the appeal or at the rating level are difficult to evaluate since overt evidence on the point is slim. However, the very structure of the rating system, with ratings administered by an agency responsible to a trade association representing the largest production interests, at least raises an organizational possibility that the raters could be more sensitive to the pleas of the large companies with big-budget productions than to others.

Another source of complaint, mainly from small producers and importers, is that the rating fee schedule discriminates against the small proprietor. However, the MPAA has, in fact, graduated the fee schedule for feature films, from $300 to $3,000, depending on the proprietor's aggregate domestic rentals during the previous year and on the cost of producing the negative of the film.

Credibility with the public at large has always been a major problem for a self-regulatory system. The Production Code was criticized by some who viewed it as a kind of sieve largely ineffective in keeping erotica and other sensationalism off the screen. At the same time, it was regarded by others, including many artists, critics, civil libertarians, and some film proprietors, as oppressive and a bar to honesty and maturity in the Hollywood film. The rating system runs the same hazards. Yet since the degree of freedom in the medium is much greater today than at any time in the past, the more frequently heard criticism tends to come from those who see it as not performing the function it is officially held to do—informing parents of the content of films that may be harmful to youthful viewers. Specifically, the rating criteria are said to be too much concerned with sex, too little with violence, and related less to the psychological realities of child and adolescent development than to the legalistic aspects of obscenity. Language and visual elements are said to be weighed more heavily than general treatment or theme. In this view, many films should receive a more restrictive rating than they have, and a few, a less restrictive one. Further criticism alleges that the rating criteria frequently shift, possibly for reasons of expediency, and have become much more permissive since the system began. Reflecting these charges, two influential religious organizations, the United States Catholic Conference (formerly the Legion of Decency) and the Broadcasting and Film Commission of the Protestant Council of Churches, withdrew their support for the rating system in 1971. For its part, the MPAA has claimed, on the basis of studies it has periodically conducted, that the system is increasingly effective, in terms of both its general public acceptance and the advisory service it performs for parents.

Credibility within the industry and with the general public will probably remain a problem as long as the rating system is totally dependent on certain powers within the industry. The possibility of "double standards" and rulings of expediency could be minimized by some restructuring of the system so that it had greater independence from the MPAA and from the industry generally. Inclusion of outsiders both in the Code and Rating Office and on the appeal board and the creation of a largely public "blue ribbon" appeal board are two suggestions frequently made.

Other Censorships

Censorship of the movies cannot be fully comprehended unless the role of informal pressures and control is recognized. Unlike the relatively structured controls of governmental boards, obscenity prosecutions, and the industry's rating system, informal censorship ranges over a wide field of individual and collective behavior. Though these pressures are almost always brought to bear on local exhibitors, they can and often do affect production when they are "passed along" economically and psychologically. Local pressure, which is as old as the medium itself, involves attempts by authorities or private parties, or both, to influence exhibition through tactics ranging from friendly persuasion to outright coercion. In many cases, these pressures may be anticipated by the exhibitor who then, in effect, becomes the censor himself. This kind of self-regulation often leaves little or no public trace. In its more overt manifestations, however, informal censorship appears to have increased steadily and markedly since the days of the *Miracle* decision.

Much low-level informal pressure takes place by a simple visit to the theater or a telephone call by police or representatives of community groups. If these tactics are unsuccessful, the conflict may escalate and eventually precipitate other official action, including occasionally a formal obscenity prosecution. However, where there is little likelihood that the objectionable film could be proven obscene in court, which is often the case, escalation may take other forms and run in other directions. As a local entrepreneur and often a local resident as well, an exhibitor is vulnerable to threats of or actual attempts at interference with his property, reputation, convenience, and safety, as well as those of his customers and employees.

Since theaters in most communities are licensed for business like other commercial enterprises, an exhibitor may be refused a renewal of license, sometimes on a technicality, or be forced to agree to conditions' being placed upon renewal, such as not playing "X" films. New "inspections" of the theater may be made by fire marshals or representatives of the board of health, who may discover violations under highly detailed and often antiquated fire and health codes. Obsolete curfew ordinances and Sunday blue laws may be capriciously enforced against a theater.

In many communities, movies and theaters have been the object of new restrictive legislation or threats of such legislation. Drive-ins in many rural and suburban areas have been required to construct high fences so that the screen is not visible from the surrounding highways, houses, or trees. Zoning laws have been changed to the disadvantage of theaters or to prevent the construction or the opening of new theaters. Many local and some state tax laws have been passed or proposed which place a large levy on tickets to "X" films or which adopt a sliding-scale levy coinciding with MPAA ratings. City and town councils have attempted to embarrass an exhibitor who is a local resident by passing resolutions of "censure." And, in a few communities, officials have made available municipal facilities for the showing of films in competition with an uncooperative exhibitor.

Other pressures have involved the harassment of theater patrons. At one Texas drive-in, police succeeded in getting a film removed by telling the manager they would otherwise begin arresting patrons for fornication. Elsewhere, police have threatened to arrest patrons of four-wall theaters showing allegedly obscene films, on charges of frequenting a disorderly house. In some communities, patrons have been photographed leaving the theater.

Where arrests and seizures have been made, police overkill is not uncommon. In such cases, not only the film but also the "instruments" or "fruits" of the alleged illegal activity may be confiscated, including the projectors, box office receipts, and, in at least one reported case, a number of seats. Arrests may include various theater employees as well as the manager. A tactic used by New York City police in a periodic Times Square cleanup was arrest of the projectionist, not for the purpose of bringing charges against him—as a nonproprietor, his conviction would be difficult to obtain even if the film were proven obscene—but to force him to spend a night in jail among a collection of prostitutes, vagrants, and addicts picked up in an average night's roundup. This "experience" was calculated to provoke the militant projectionists' local to pressure theater owners either to discontinue hard-core films or face the threat of a walkout.

Many of the pressures on exhibitors, at least in the first instance, are the work of private groups of citizens rather than public authorities. In Milwaukee, a neighborhood organization waged a three-month fight against a local theater showing *Deep Throat* that included daily picketing of the theater and such tactics as infiltrating the admission line to purchase the three-dollar ticket with pennies or with hundred-dollar bills and painstakingly counting the change, or asking the ticket seller repeated questions—all designed to slow up or disrupt the admission of patrons. A tactic used with some success in New York City as well as in smaller towns was that of pressuring landlords of the theaters in question to find ways to break the exhibitor's lease or, where landlords were reluctant to do that, embarrassing them by publishing their names,

as those of persons—often including members of the local establishment—leasing premises for exhibition of allegedly pornographic films.

Where local authorities have been reluctant to undertake an obscenity prosecution they might not be able to win, private citizens or
groups have sometimes filed civil suits against exhibitors for maintaining common law "public nuisances." Even when such suits are
unsuccessful, they force the exhibitor to undertake a legal defense and
bear its cost. Exhibitors have also been subject to personal abuse of
various sorts, such as being expelled from a local church congregation
or receiving anonymous notes and, paradoxically, obscene telephone
calls. Though actual violence and physical harassment are rare, instances of planted bombs have been reported, as well as at least one
case of theater arson.

A special kind of informal censorship is that exercised by newspapers
and occasionally other media on movie advertising. Many papers regularly alter ads and, in some cases, may refuse to accept them altogether. Provocative titles may be changed, descriptive phrases eliminated, and pictorial matter cut out or literally toned down. In one case,
the country's largest newspaper, the *New York Daily News*, actually
changed the name of the theater itself, from Tomcat to Thom. Since
newspaper advertising is the chief means by which exhibition is publicized, refusal to accept an ad or a class of ads, such as for films with
"X" ratings, can have severe economic consequences for the theater
and the film in question.

Not all informal action and pressure against exhibitors is aimed at
the banning or removal of a film. Some complaints have to do with
classification, that is, with the admission of children or adolescents.
The drive-in fencing requirements, for example, are aimed mainly at
avoiding exposure to juveniles outside the theater, as well as preventing
highway accidents. In some cases, the censorship interest has been
satisfied by modification of an exhibition policy so that "X" films were
shown only during certain weeks or days of the week. Other complaints
have had to do with the "mixing" of films, especially of an "X" or
"R" with a "PG" or "G" on a double bill, or the inclusion of an "X"
trailer with a "PG" or "G" feature. In other cases, the pressure appears
to have been focused on, or at least generated by, sensationalist ads
or outer lobby displays, the discontinuance of which sometimes re-
lieved the pressure. On the other hand, where actual removal of a film
was the object of the censorship, pressures have occasionally intensified
and have been directed against an entire hard-core exhibition policy,
particularly where the theater was a suburban or neighborhood house.
Such campaigns are apt to be marked by considerable hostility, since

they often involve large segments of the community and actual closing of the theater may be among the censorship aims.

Exhibitors have responded to informal pressure in various ways. Limited resistance resulting in compromise with the censorship interest or in capitulation to it is common. Overt resistance, which may include bringing counter legal action, is not common but appears to have increased, particularly as profits from soft-core and especially hard-core films increase. Exhibitors who play many types of films or who have large theaters may "pass along" the pressure through exhibitor organizations and call for a modification of content at the production level or for some other accommodation of censorship pressures. It was such pipelining of local pressure that helped to bring about the rating system.

The relationship of the rating system to informal censorship is complex and difficult to assess with any precision, especially with the latter censorship being as varied, diffuse, and often obscured from public view as it is. It does seem clear that the mere existence of the system, with its someone-minding-the-store appearance, has probably allayed some censorship interest. Though a few towns have tried to enact the rating system into law by making enforcement at "R" and "X" levels mandatory upon exhibitors, the system has probably been a major reason that neither Congress nor any state legislature has enacted official age classification of movies. Thus, the system tends to bear out the view of the MPAA and of many others in the industry who see ratings as a kind of preventive censorship and, therefore, the "least of the evils." Yet, it is also clear that the system, with its "X" category and label, does itself draw additional censorial attention to particular films. Since many persons and local authorities incorrectly assume an "X" rating indicates pornography, a film so labeled may become the object of pressure from those who know little about it except its rating. This, of course, is also one of the reasons that "X" films can expect fewer bookings than other-rated films. In those localities that have tried to make "X" and "R" films unprofitable by levying higher admission taxes on their bookings, the system, in effect, becomes an instrument of further censorship. Newspaper ad restriction is another instance where an "X" rating alone may place a film at a disadvantage, its particular content notwithstanding.

The chief difficulty in assessing the impact of the rating system on informal censorship is that the two types of control tend to address different types of films and to have different goals. A film submitted for rating is usually one aimed at a fairly large audience and wide distribution. Even one that receives an "X" rating is unlikely to be of the soft-core or hard-core type that is the object of most censorship pressure today. Films of the latter sort, though occasionally bearing the self-applied "X," are almost never submitted for rating, since it is obvious which rating they would obtain. While the rating system aims at classification rather than prohibition, the pressures and goals of informal censorship, more often than not, seek to remove or ban the film. Finally, there seems to be little doubt that some of the censorship energy aroused by soft-core and hard-core unrated films spills over in its reactive force to both "X" and "R" films and, in some cases, may be so undiscriminating as to cast its net of condemnation over the entire medium.

Conclusion

The censorship interest in movies seeks to keep certain content and depiction from being seen by some or all persons in the belief that harm may result to those exposed and, indirectly at least, to the community or society at large. Whether this assumption is valid is a factual question about which available evidence is inconclusive. Whether the censorship goal is desirable given these factual uncertainties, is essentially a moral or philosophical question which tends to be answered differently by different persons.

Because censorship is an interest that is both strongly and widely held, it is also a source of considerable political energy and, like other activated political interests, tends to make public demands, including demands upon lawmakers. As such, it is a political and social force that cannot be realistically ignored or repressed by officials acting in a representative capacity. It should not be surprising, then, to see officials responsive to this interest and, at least to some degree, seeking to accommodate it, especially where it may appear to represent the will of the majority. Where *anti*-censorship policies have been made by government, they have invariably originated in the Supreme Court, a nonelected body, and have been applied by the lower judiciary, much of which is also nonelected and, in any case, bound by decisions of the highest court. We see, then, the phenomenon of elected and nonelected officials often being on different sides of the censorship question.

Although the censorship interest is a social and political force to be reckoned with, it would be incorrect to think of it as static or even necessarily permanent (though, to date at least, it is as old as the movies themselves). Levels of tolerance and popular acceptability change just as the content of movies does. Much cinematic depiction objectionable a few years ago is generally accepted today, and the sort that is now the object of censorship would have been considered altogether unthinkable for the commercial medium a few years ago. The trend of the past twenty years in all media of communication has clearly been in the direction of increasing acceptance of frankness and detail in both erotic and violent representation and greater ease with sexual themes. The desirability of this development may be debated, but it seems clear that some change of attitude in the general population has taken place. If not exactly glacial in pace, this change has at least been fairly gradual and has taken perhaps a generation to advance. As such, it is in marked contrast to the change in movies, which has been precipitated largely, though not entirely, by philosophical decisions about freedom of speech and by economic ones dictated by intermedia competition and the marketplace generally. The fact that the one change has run by a far different clock than the other is at the heart of much of the censorship tension surrounding the medium today.

It should also be understood that the operating (as opposed to the legal) degree of freedom in any medium of communication depends, to a large extent, on the nature of the audience for the particular medium. For years movies were a genuine mass medium, in the company of newspapers, mass circulation magazines, and radio. As such, their audience included the entire family and tended to cut across class, ethnic, educational, and social boundaries. Thus, the movies were very different from the "elite" media of hardcover books or the theater, the audience for which has always tended to be highly select, conspicuously adult, above average in education, and able to pay a relatively high "admission" price. The degree of functional freedom has always been greater in the elite than in the mass media, and the movies in the past were no exception to this rule.[14]

Today, however, movies present a special problem. Having been replaced by television as the chief medium of family entertainment and having been freed of many of their previous controls, the movies have developed, in terms of media sociology, a kind of split person-

14. It is true, of course, that some mass media— movies and magazines, for example— have had "underground" or, more accurately, under-the-counter segments that had illegal and limited distribution but also great freedom of content with regard to erotica. The old "stag" film was the segment in the movies. However, such freedom of content was possible, that is, tolerated, only to the extent that distribution of the product was clandestine and in numbers that were small. In effect, freedom of content was inversely related to freedom of dissemination. And it is not insignificant that the cost of access to or purchase of such clandestine communication was usually considerably higher than that of legitimate, above-ground expression in a medium.

ality. In their content they have come to resemble closely the elite media; yet, continuing to address a large and still fairly heterogeneous audience, they remain in other respects a mass medium. For example, most major productions with their sizable budgets cannot hope even to recover costs without playing to a large audience. Most films are still advertised to the public at large, usually in the same space in the same newspapers as were the old family films. Their physical outlet often remains the same neighborhood theater or drive-in, and the price of admission is still modest compared with that of the older elite media. Though the moviegoing audience is much less the family one today than in the past, and though some audiences, such as those for certain foreign films, have always been small and select, it is still true that the larger audience for movies remains a fairly general and undifferentiated one.

Given this disequilibrium, it is not surprising that the movies should generate considerable censorial tension today and come under attack more frequently than any other medium of communication. The breakdown of the traditional division of labor among the media in the case of the movies makes clear why there is much concern about classification, on the one hand, and why, on the other, some hard-core films can be shown with little or no censorial attention beyond that of classification. The occasional tolerance of hard-core occurs where exhibition is unobtrusive—usually low-key advertising or no advertising at all in the mass media and modest out-front displays at the theater—where the theater itself is located in a downtown restricted area, such as the "combat zone" in Boston, and where admission prices are fairly high. The concern with classification is, in effect, an attempt to restore the traditional audience-content balance. The "immune" exhibition of some hard-core films becomes possible where presentation is restricted in much the same way that it is in the elite media. Thus here, too, there is an attempt to restore, at least for the moment, the appearance of the traditional equilibrium.

It is where classification breaks down or seems ineffective, or where hard-core fare breaks out of its cinematic closet and is marketed like other films, that censorial tensions are apt to rise to a peak and also manifest far-reaching backlash potential. Because the film medium is no longer strictly a mass medium and yet is not fully or completely an elite medium, it will have a continuing censorship problem that may or may not be eased by further change in popular attitudes.

MICHAEL CONANT

The Paramount Decrees Reconsidered

Introduction

The Supreme Court's decision in the *Paramount* case[1] brought to an end decades of control of the motion picture industry in violation of the antitrust laws. The subsequent decrees enjoining restrictive trade practices and ordering divorcement of theaters brought radical changes to the marketing of motion pictures.[2] The question treated in this study is the extent to which these decrees brought competition to the industry. The economic framework of the inquiry, like all studies of industrial organization, concerns the smallest size of firm which can achieve the economies of scale that exist at its level of production or marketing. In motion pictures, the three levels are production (making of pictures), distribution (marketing of pictures to exhibitors), and exhibition (operation of theaters).

In the thirty years since the *Paramount* decision, other major factors have had great impact on the motion picture industry. The most significant of these is television. Some classes of features, such as musicals, have been virtually replaced by television programs. The sale of

From *Law and Contemporary Problems,* 44 (Autumn 1981): 79–107.

1. *United States v. Paramount Pictures, Inc.,* 344 U.S. 131 (1948).

2. See M. Conant, *Antitrust in the Motion Picture Industry* (Berkeley and Los Angeles: University of California Press, 1960) for a review of the early impacts of the decrees. The most recent economic survey of the industry is B. Compaigne, ed., *Who Owns the Media? Concentration of Ownership in the Mass Communications Industry* (1979), chap. 5.

Mirisch Corporation's *West Side Story,* directed by Robert Wise and Jerome Robbins (United Artists, 1960)

theatrical motion pictures to television within a few years after the first run has made television a continuous competitor for feature film customers. It has also wiped out most of the theater market for reruns of classic features. As the quality of films produced specifically for television has increased over the years, competition has provoked motion picture producers to concentrate efforts and assets on fewer, more expensive films. These and other competitive factors have had profound effects on the economic structure and output of the industry which one must attempt to distinguish from the impact of the antitrust decrees.

One result of the rivalry of television and increased public interest in other forms of recreational activities was a sharp decline in motion picture attendance for about fifteen years. Estimated attendance of indoor theaters dropped from 3,352 million in 1948[3] to 1,011 million in 1958[4] and to 553 million in 1967[5]. Thereafter, attendance began to recover. In 1972 indoor theater attendance was estimated at 942 million,[6] and in 1979 the estimate was 1,120 million.[7] Domestic theater admission revenues dropped from $1,245 million in 1948[8] to about $900 million in 1958[9] and then recovered to $1,082 million in 1967.[10] Thereafter, revenues increased, especially in the late 1970s. Admission revenues reached $1,570 million in 1972[11] and an estimated $2,165 million in 1977.[12]

The Paramount Decrees

The *Paramount* case was a civil antitrust action against the eight major motion picture distibutors. Before the *Paramount* decision, the motion picture industry was effectively controlled by five major pro-

3. U.S. Bureau of the Census, *Census of Business, Selected Service Industries, Summary Statistics* (1948), 9.08.

4. U.S. Bureau of the Census, *Census of Business, Selected Service Industries, Summary Statistics* (1958), pp. 8–16.

5. U.S. Bureau of the Census, *1967 Census of Selected Services, Motion Pictures* (1970), pp. 4–15.

6. U.S. Bureau of the Census, *1972 Census of Selected Service Industries*, pp. 3–14.

7. U.S. Dep't of Commerce, *1981 U.S. Industrial Outlook*, p. 530.

8. U.S. Bureau of the Census, *Census of Business, Selected Service Industries, Summary Statistics* (1948), 9.08.

9. U.S. Bureau of the Census, *Census of Business, Selected Service Industries, Summary Statistics* (1958), pp. 8–12.

10. U.S. Bureau of the Census, *1967 Census of Selected Services, Motion Pictures* (1970), pp. 4–9.

11. U.S. Bureau of the Census, *1972 Census of Selected Service Industries*, pp. 3–11.

12. U.S. Bureau of the Census, *1977 Census of Selected Service Industries, Motion Picture Industry*, pp. 4–15.

ducer-distributors who were also exhibitors. These were Loew's (MGM), Paramount, R.K.O., Twentieth Century-Fox and Warner Brothers. These five companies owned chains of first-run theaters, each of them concentrated primarily in one section of the country. Through a broad policy of reciprocity, each of the five, as distributor, agreed to give first-run status to the theaters of the other four. In effect, their control of exhibition was a bottleneck on the final market. It enabled the five majors to control distribution, production, and the key personnel who were inputs to production.

Of the three minor distributors, Columbia and Universal were producer-distributors, and United Artists was only a distributor for independent producers. Since the three owned no theaters, they had much less bargaining power than the five majors in securing exhibition in the first-run theaters of the latter.[13]

The combination fixed admission prices, clearances between runs of films, and other marketing practices. Since the details of the conspiracy are reported elsewhere,[14] only the elements of the resultant decrees will be summarized here. The decree of December 1946 prohibited the defendants as distributors from engaging in the following practices: (1) fixing admission prices in film licenses; (2) maintaining systems of clearances; (3) maintaining clearances between theaters not in substantial competition; (4) continuing clearance in excess of what was "reasonably necessary" to protect the licensee in the run granted; (5) franchising; (6) engaging in formula deals and master agreements; and (7) conditional block booking.[15] Where an exhibitor chose to license films in groups, he was to be given the right to reject 20 percent of such films. All pooling agreements and joint interests in theaters of two defendants or a defendant and independents were ordered terminated.[16]

The district court had denied the government's plea that the five majors be required to divorce their theaters. Instead it had ordered competitive bidding for licensing of each film in each run to be open to all theaters.[17] On appeal, the Supreme Court ordered divorcement

13. See Conant, *Antitrust in the Motion Picture Industry*, pp. 204–7, concluding that the three minor distributors were mostly victims of the illegal monopoly of the five majors and that the three minor distributors should not have been made defendants in the *Paramount* case.

14. Ibid., chap. 5.

15. Ibid., pp. 98–99.

16. Ibid., pp. 99–100.

17. *United States v. Paramount Pictures*, 66 F. Supp. 323, 358 (S.D.N.Y. 1946); 70 F. Supp. 53, 74 (S.D.N.Y. 1947).

but not competitive bidding.[18] This was followed by consent decrees in which each of the five firms divorced its theater circuit and disposed of individual theaters in towns where the majors had a monopoly on exhibition.[19] The five divorced circuits were prohibited from acquiring additional theaters unless they established to the satisfaction of the district court that such acquisitions would not unreasonably restrain trade.[20]

One significant effect of the *Paramount* decison was that hundreds of private treble-damage actions were filed by exhibitors against the eight Paramount defendants. Since others have reported on these cases[21] they will not be reviewed here.

Production

Economic Factors

The key characteristic of motion pictures is that each one is unique. Imperfect competition in motion picture marketing begins with this underlying fact. It is not accurate to think of all pictures on release at the same time as significant rival services. If any picture gains good reviews and positive initial acceptance, large segments of the public will allocate income for tickets. Instead of thinking of two films which have received positive initial sales as rivals, the moviegoing public will allocate recreational funds to attend both. The most important factor in public acceptance of new films in an era when television constantly offers reruns of the old films is novelty. The limited supply of creative writing that will appeal to substantial segments of the viewing public is a primary factor in the declining supply of new films.

The great uncertainties that make motion picture production more of a gamble than a rational endeavor are clearly illustrated by Columbia Pictures Industries, Inc. In fiscal 1970 Columbia had income

18. *United States v. Paramount Pictures*, 334 U.S. 131, 161–66 (1948).
19. *United States v. Paramount Pictures, Inc.*, 1948–49 Trade Cas. ¶ 62,335 (S.D.N.Y. 1948) (RKO Consent Decree); *United States v. Paramount Pictures, Inc.*, 1948–49 Trade Cas. ¶ 62,377 (S.D.N.Y. 1949) (Paramount Consent Decree); *United States v. Loew's, Inc.*, 1950–51 Trade Cas. ¶ 62,765 (S.D.N.Y. 1951) (Warner Consent Decree); *United States v. Loew's, Inc.*, (1950–51 Trade Cas. ¶ 62,861 (S.D.N.Y. 1951) (Twentieth Century-Fox Consent Decree); *United States v. Loew's, Inc.*, 1952–53 Trade Cas. ¶ 67,228 (S.D.N.Y. 1952) (Loew's Consent Decree). Subsequent references to these decrees will be made without reporter citation.
20. *United States v. Loew's, Inc.*, 1950–51 Trade Cas. ¶ 62,573, at 63,679 (S.D.N.Y. 1950).
21. See R. Cassady & R. Cassady, *The Private Antitrust Suit in American Business Competition: A Motion-Picture Industry Case Analysis* (1964).

before taxes of $10.9 million[22] and management was lauded. In 1971 it lost $140.7 million.[23] In 1972 the pretax loss was only $665,000, while in 1973 it was $65 million.[24] Its net worth declined to $8 million[25] and its loans payable reached $183 million.[26] Columbia chairman Abe Schneider and production head Mike Frankovich, Jr., were discharged.[27] As *Forbes* reported, Columbia wrote off about $75 million in inventory losses on such forgettable Frankovich films as *Castle Keep, Lost Horizon*, and *Oklahoma Crude*.[28] Allen Hirschfield was hired as Columbia's new chief executive, but before his decisions could have impact, fortunes changed and Columbia had three successes, *Funny Lady, Shampoo*, and *Tommy*. Columbia reported profits from filmed entertainment of $24.9 million in 1974, $33.2 million in 1975, $28.3 million in 1976, $30.8 million in 1977[29] and $80.1 million in 1978.[30] *Close Encounters of the Third Kind* had total worldwide box office gross of $182 million in fiscal 1978.[31] If film rentals on this picture approximated the industry average of 45 percent of box office gross,[32] this one film earned 30 percent of Columbia's 1978 total theatrical film rentals of $269 million.[33] The 1978 net income of $68.8 million was 101.5 percent of shareholders' equity as of the beginning of the fiscal year.[34]

More than half the pictures that are produced fail to earn rentals sufficient to recover their production and marketing costs. In 1967 it was estimated that 75 percent failed to recover their costs.[35] Although *Zorba the Greek* cost $700,000 and earned $10 million profits,[36] few low-budget films succeed. Producers, with great uncertainty about

22. Columbia Pictures Industries, Inc., 1971 Annual Report, p. 5.

23. Ibid.

24. Columbia Pictures Industries, Inc., 1973 Annual Report, p. 9.

25. Ibid., p. 11.

26. Ibid., p. 17.

27. "Only in Hollywood," *Forbes*, Nov. 1, 1977, p. 77.

28. Ibid.

29. Columbia Pictures Industries, Inc., 1978 Annual Report, p. 51, reporting earnings by operating divisions for years 1974 to 1978.

30. Ibid.

31. Ibid., pp. 12, 51.

32. See "Coming Attractions: Cable TV and Videocassettes Portend Bleak Future for Theaters that Show Movies," *Wall Street Journal*, Aug. 19, 1981, p. 19.

33. Columbia Pictures Industries, Inc., 1978 Annual Report, p. 51.

34. Ibid., pp. 38, 41.

35. "How a New Film Maker Made It in Hollywood," *Business Week*, Sept. 16, 1967, pp. 189, 192. See "MGM Film Gives Small Investors a Chance to Share in Rising Cost of Making Movies," *Wall Street Journal*, Aug. 13, 1981, p. 21.

36. "How a New Film Maker Made It in Hollywood."

whether the story behind the film will succeed, feel they greatly reduce uncertainty by employing the best known and therefore the most expensive actors. But scarcity of stars means fewer total films. The movement to fewer, more expensive films has increased the uncertainties in film production. In 1977 it was reported that about twelve of the most expensive pictures would have to earn $400 million in film rentals to recover their production and marketing costs.[37] This was equal to the film rentals of all nine leading distributors in 1971.[38] The investment is made in the hope of large returns such as the $100 million in film rentals Warner Communications received from *The Exorcist* in 1974[39] or the $200 million in rentals that Universal earned from *Jaws* in 1975.[40] The effect of concentrated investment in a few pictures per year is to aggravate the fluctuations in income.

One result from the concentration of production in fewer big-budget pictures is that some pictures have been co-produced by two major companies. Columbia Pictures Industries, for example, co-produced *1941* with Universal and *All That Jazz* with Twentieth Century-Fox.[41] In both cases the picture was distributed by the co-producer rather than Columbia. A number of other such co-productions have been reported.[42] These joint ventures are analogous to two major oil companies joining in a venture in oil drilling. No single firm wishes to risk such large amounts of capital in a single uncertain venture. Joint ventures are a risk-sharing device. Although they might result in antitrust prosecution, they are presumptively legal.[43]

Another result of the decline in feature film output, which was only partially offset by productions for television, was idle studio space. Paramount's Marathon Studio in Hollywood, for example, is 52 acres of urban land with 32 stages and 1,200 employees.[44] Metro-Goldwyn-Mayer's studio in Culver City, California, have 24 sound stages[45] on 44 acres[46] while Twentieth Century-Fox has 63 acres in Los Angeles.[47]

37. "Is It Worth Making Blockbuster Films?" *Business Week*, July 11, 1977, p. 36.
38. Ibid.
39. Ibid.
40. Ibid.
41. Columbia Pictures Industries, Inc., 1979 Annual Report, pp. 14–15.
42. Compaigne, *Who Owns The Media?* p. 224.
43. See *United States v. Penn-Olin Chemical Co.*, 378 U.S. 158 (1964), decision on remand, 246 f. Supp. 917 (D. Del. 1965), aff'd per curiam, 389 U.S. 308 (1967).
44. Gulf & Western Industries, Inc., Form 10K Report to the SEC (1977), p. 29.
45. Metro-Goldwyn-Mayer, Inc., 1978 Annual Report, p. 6.
46. Ibid., p. 16.
47. *Moody's Industrial Manual* (1979), pp. 2655, 3210.

Universal has the largest production facilities in the world with 420 acres and 33 sound stages.[48].

In order to meet the issue of too many studios and rising urban land values, some studios have been dismantled. Twentieth Century-Fox sold a major part of its studio property for urban development.[49] It also negotiated unsuccessfully to merge its remaining production facilities with MGM.[50] Columbia and Warner agreed in 1972 to combine studio properties, and Columbia production was moved to Warner's Burbank studio.[51] Parts of the former Columbia studios were leased to independent producers and the rest sold for alternate uses. Warner executives estimated that each firm would save two to three million dollars per year from joint use of the Burbank studios, the largest part being labor savings.[52]

The most significant impact of the Paramount Decrees on motion picture production was the great increase in the number of independent producers.[53] Although exact figures are not available, industry sources state that a substantial majority of films are independently produced. Since major distributors could no longer control the channels of distribution, they lost control of their input markets. Successful producers, directors, and actors chose to form their own production companies. First Artists Production Co., Ltd., for example, was organized mainly by such actors as Paul Newman, Sidney Poitier, and Barbra Streisand.[54] In 1975 First Artists had film rentals of $1.8 million,[55] and in 1980 rentals were $10 million.[56] With output declining, the leading producer-distributors competed to lease space to independent producers. In most cases, the distributors contributed part of the financing for the independent producers and secured distribution rights to their pictures.

Remedies Available to Independent Producers

Since independent producers were the group most obviously injured by the conspiracy of the five majors to control the entire industry through the exhibition markets before the *Paramount* decision, one would expect many treble-damage actions by them. In one of the few

48. Ibid., p. 3948.
49. *Moody's Industrial Manual* (1973), p. 2818.
50. "Fox-MGM Merger Is Put on Ice," *Broadcasting*, Feb. 1, 1971, p. 47.
51. Columbia Pictures Industries, Inc., Form 10K Report to the SEC (1979), p. 10.
52. "Economics v. Egos: Film Firms Mull Merging Studio Facilities, Seeking to Cut Costs, Revive Industry," *Wall Street Journal*, July 13, 1971, p. 34.
53. See Conant, *Antitrust in the Motion Picture Industry*, pp. 112–18.
54. See "Barbra & Paul & Steven & Sidney," *Forbes*, Jan. 15, 1972, p. 14.
55. First Artists Production Co., 1979 Annual Report, p. 3.
56. Standard & Poors, *Standard Corporation Descriptions* (Feb. 1981), p. 9088.

reported cases, the complaint was dismissed.[57] Other actions may have been filed and settled and are therefore unreported. There are only two reported decisions of actions by independents against one or more of the five major defendants that went to trial, and one precedent-setting suit was lost.

In *Eagle Lion Studios, Inc., v. Loew's, Inc.,*[58] the plaintiffs charged Loew's and RKO Theaters, the two large affiliated circuits in the New York metropolitan area, with conspiracy to exclude the majority of plaintiffs' films from first subsequent run between 1946 and 1951. Although the original *Paramount* judgment was entered in 1945, the plaintiffs argued correctly that the same pattern of control persisted until the final order in the case in 1950.[59] The court of appeals, by a 2-1 vote, affirmed a trial court judgment for the defendants.[60] The most important issue was the breadth assigned to section 5 of the Clayton Act,[61] which makes a final judgment or decree in an antitrust action by the government prima facie evidence against defendants in subsequent actions by injured parties. A finding of fact in the *Paramount* case had been that, in New York City, Loew's and RKO had divided neighborhood prior runs so that there would be no competition between them in obtaining films from the other defendants.[62] One conclusion of law was that Loew's and RKO had conspired to monopolize and had monopolized first neighborhood runs in New York City.[63] The trial court had held that the findings and conclusion were not evidence that there was no competition between Loew's and RKO to obtain films from independent producers.[64] The majority of the appeals court held that other evidence was not sufficient to justify reversal of the trial court.[65] Judge Clark, dissenting, said the trial court had given the *Paramount* judgment not only a niggardly construction, but one quite opposite to its intended meaning.[66]

57. *Independent Prod. Corp. v. Loew's, Inc.,* 24 F.R.D. 360 (S.D.N.Y. 1959). See also Conant, *Antitrust in the Motion Picture Industry,* pp. 36–38.
58. 248 F.2d 438 (2d Cir. 1957), aff'd by equally divided court, 358 U.S. 100 (1958).
59. *United States v. Paramount Pictures, Inc.,* 85 F. Supp. 881 (S.D.N.Y. 1949), aff'd, 339 U.S. 974 (1950).
60. 248 F.2d at 449.
61. 38 Stat. 731 (1914) (current version at 15 U.S.C. § 16 [1979 Supp.]).
62. *United States v. Loew's Inc.,* No. 87-273, Finding of Fact No. 154(d) (S.D.N.Y. 1950).
63. *United States v. Loew's Inc.,* No. 87-273, Conclusion of Law No. 16 (S.D.N.Y. 1950).
64. *Eagle Lion Studios, Inc., v. Loew's Inc.,* 141 F. Supp. 658, 667 (S.D.N.Y. 1956).
65. 248 F.2d at 444–45.
66. 248 F.2d at 449.

In *Twentieth Century-Fox Film Corp. v. Goldwyn*,[67] Samuel Goldwyn and associated independent producers recovered $300,000 treble damages against Fox and its National Theatres and Fox West Coast Theatres subsidiaries. The circuit buying power of the defendants had enabled them to set fixed runs and clearances so that a producer of outstanding pictures could not bargain for more first-run time. It had enabled the defendants to bargain to pay significantly lower film rentals than the market would have otherwise provided. The fact that Goldwyn pictures were distributed by RKO, one of the *Paramount* defendants, was not relevant when the case centered on circuit buying power of National and Fox in the western United States, where they were dominant. This ruling recognized that the bottleneck on first-run exhibition of the five majors was their key source of monopoly power. Although the trial judge had ruled that the *Paramount* findings could not be admitted as prima facie evidence under section 5 of the Clayton Act, the plaintiff established the liability of all defendants for the years 1947 to 1950.[68] The court of appeals held that the exclusion of the *Paramount* findings had been in error, as was the exclusion of the claims regarding the years 1935 to 1947.[69] Under section 5 of the Clayton Act, the statute of limitations was suspended from 1938 to 1950 during the litigation of the *Paramount* case. The case was remanded for further proceedings on the claims for the earlier period.[70]

Industry Self-Censorship

In the period before the Paramount Decrees, the Motion Picture Production Code was also used by the major companies to reinforce their illegal cartel.[71] No potential entrant to motion picture production could treat controversial subjects and expect to find a national distributor. Following the Paramount Decrees, the code was greatly liberalized in 1956. In 1968 the Motion Picture Association of America adopted a system of rating films according to their suitability for various age groups.[72] Most persons in the industry felt there was no longer

67. 328 F.2d 190 (9th Cir. 1964), cert. denied, 379 U.S. 880 (1964).

68. *Samuel Goldwyn Prods., Inc., v. Fox West Coast Theatres Corp.*, 194 F. Supp. 507, 512–13 (N.D. Cal. 1961) (citing Conant, *Antitrust in the Motion Picture Industry*).

69. 328 F.2d at 220–21.

70. Ibid., p. 226.

71. See Conant, *Antitrust in the Motion Picture Industry*, p. 113.

72. See *International Motion Picture Almanac* (1981), p. 36A. See generally Ayer, Bates & Herman, "Self-Censorship in the Movie Industry: An Historical Perspective on Law and Social Change," *Wisconsin Law Review* (1970), p. 791; Friedman, "Motion Picture Rating System of 1968: A Constitutional Analysis of Self-Regulation by the Film Industry," *Columbia Law Review* 73 (1973): 185. Note, "Antitrust Challenge to the GGPRX Movie Rating System," *Harvard Civil Rights Law Review* (1971), p. 545.

any barrier to entry. The view of industry executives was that this limited control by the industry would prevent more serious attempts at censorship by the states.[73] The American Civil Liberties Union charged that the rating code was unevenly enforced,[74] but a congressional investigation found no evidence of any discrimination against independent productions by the rating system.[75]

One legal action was brought alleging that an "X," adults only, rating of a film was a barrier to the market, and hence a group boycott. In *Tropic Film Corp. v. Paramount Pictures Corp.*,[76] a preliminary injunction to eliminate the rating "X" for the film *Tropic of Cancer* was denied. The court found that submission of a picture for rating by the Rating Program of the Motion Picture Association of America was purely voluntary even though all unsubmitted pictures were rated "X." At least at the preliminary hearing, there was no evidence that any exhibitor had agreed not to show the picture. It was impossible to determine if the "X" rating would hurt or help the film's marketing.[77]

Feature Production by Television Networks

Television networks had been licensees of older motion picture features from their earliest days of operation. Feature films eventually became a significant portion of prime-time television. In 1967 both CBS and ABC announced plans to enter feature motion picture production.[78] Even before this, NBC had established a program for the financing of feature pictures for its television network, but Universal Pictures had been employed to do the production. CBS, which had leased the former Republic Pictures Corp. studio facilities since 1963, purchased the seventy-acre property in 1967 for $9.5 million.[79] ABC established its production jointly with a subsidiary of Cinerama, Inc., which announced an intention to open ten branch offices in the United States.[80]

An immediate result of the beginning of feature film production by CBS and ABC was a complaint to the Justice Department by the Motion Picture Association of America on behalf of the leading motion

73. Randall, "Censorship: From The Miracle to Deep Throat," in this volume.

74. See Gumpert, "Movie Industry Code Is Unevenly Enforced and Causing Protest," *Wall Street Journal*, Oct. 10, 1969, p. 13.

75. House Comm. on Small Business, *Movie Ratings and the Independent Producer*, H.R. Rep. No. 996, 95th Cong., 2d Sess. 77 (1978).

76. 319 F. Supp. 1247 (S.D.N.Y. 1970).

77. Ibid., 1255.

78. See "CBS Moves into Moviemaking," *Broadcasting*, Mar. 20, 1967, pg. 70; "ABC Leaps into Motion Picutres," *Broadcasting*, Aug. 21, 1967, p. 52.

79. *Moody's Industrial Manual*, (1968), p. 313; (1971), p. 1974.

80. "ABC Leaps into Motion Pictures," p. 52.

picture distributors.[81] Vertical integration by television broadcasters to the feature production function was alleged to violate the antitrust laws. The former *Paramount* defendants, who were barred from integrating forward into exhibition, opposed the backward integration of certain of their best customers.[82] In 1970 the leading distributors filed an antitrust action against CBS and ABC which charged monopolizing and attempting to monopolize feature film production and distribution for television.[83] The plaintiffs also charged that the entry of defendants into production would reverse the divorcement of exhibition for two of the firms. ABC operated the 418 theaters of the former Paramount Theater circuit, and its distributor, Cinerama, Inc., had ties to the 115-unit Pacific Theatres Corp. CBS had contracted with National Theatres Corp., the divorced Twentieth Century-Fox circuit, to distribute its features. National had about 250 theaters at that time.

ABC responded to the lawsuit by the motion picture distributors with a $100 million counterclaim.[84] ABC charged the plaintiffs and the Motion Picture Association of America with conspiring to monopolize feature film production and distribution. It also alleged that the plaintiffs had block-booked features in licensing to television broadcasters. CBS followed with a similar counterclaim.[85]

By 1972 ABC had produced thirty-nine feature films and stopped production. Its annual reports noted that motion picture production was not profitable.[86] CBS produced twenty-seven feature films by the end of 1971 and also announced it was considering termination of production.[87]

In 1972 ABC released one of the feature films it had produced over its own network, and the plaintiffs filed an objection with the district court where the litigation was pending.[88] The judge warned ABC that it was proceeding on its own responsibility.[89] In 1973 ABC announced

81. Penn, "Movie Producers Complain to Justice Unit of Network, National General Film Plans," *Wall Street Journal*, Oct. 5, 1967, p. 32.

82. Ibid.

83. Penn, "Movie Concerns Sue CBS, ABC on Making Films," *Wall Street Journal*, Sept. 30, 1970, p. 2.

84. See "ABC Asks Damages Totalling $100 Million Against Movie Group," *Wall Street Journal*, Apr. 14, 1971, p. 5.

85. *Columbia Pictures Indus., Inc., v. American Broadcasting Cos.*, 501 F.2d 894, 895 (2d Cir. 1974).

86. American Broadcasting Cos., 1969 Annual Report, p. 19; 1970 Annual Report, p. 13; 1971 Annual Report, p. 14.

87. Columbia Broadcasting System, 1971 Annual Report, p. 9.

88. *Columbia Pictures, Indus., Inc., v. American Broadcasting Cos.*, 1974-1 Trade Cas. ¶ 74,912, at 96,094 (S.D.N.Y. 1974).

89. Ibid.

it would exhibit four of its own films on television, and the plaintiffs moved for an injunction. They asked that ABC be prohibited from exhibiting on television any theatrical films it had produced or financed during the pendency of the litigation. The injunction was denied.[90] The plaintiffs were unable to demonstrate probable success on the merits and possible irreparable injury. ABC contended that it was merely integrating vertically by internal expansion. It cited the *Paramount* decison for the proposition that vertical integration was not illegal per se.[91] This follows accepted economic analysis that vertical integration cannot by itself create economic power. The court found the television networks to be in vigorous competition with each other. It noted the shortage of available feature films and the uncertainties attendant on successful television programming. Its preliminary conclusions were that the defendants had acted without apparent intent to injure the plaintiffs, and that their primary concern was to increase the supply of motion pictures available for television exhibition.

The action of Columbia and the other producers against ABC and CBS has not gone to trial. In April 1975 all parties agreed to suspend the action pending disposition of subsequent lawsuits brought by the Antitrust Division of the Justice Department against the television networks.[92] In December 1974 the United States filed complaints against ABC, CBS, and NBC charging violation of sections 1 and 2 of the Sherman Act in producing, procuring, and distributing prime-time television programs.[93] Only two to the five classes of acts allegedly used to monopolize the market for prime-time television programming pertained to motion pictures. These included: (1) controlling the prices paid by the networks for motion picture feature films; and (2) obtaining a competitive advantage over other producers and distributors of television programs and motion pictures.[94] The remedy sought was a prohibition on television networks' showing any program, including

90. *Columbia Pictures Indus., Inc., v. American Broadcasting Cos.*, 1974-1 Trade Cas. ¶ 74,912 (S.D.N.Y. 1974), aff'd, 501 F.2d 894 (2d Cir. 1974).

91. *United States v. Paramount Pictures*, 334 U.S. 131, 174 (1948).

92. Warner Communications Inc., Form 10K Report to the SEC (1978), pp. 22–23.

93. *United States v. American Broadcasting Cos.*, No. 74-3600HP; *United States v. Columbia Broadcasting Sys., Inc.*, No. 74-3599DWW; *United States v. National Broadcasting Co.*, 449 F. Supp. 1127 (C.D. Cal. 1978). These suits were similar to 1972 suits against the three major networks which were dismissed without prejudice when the government refused to turn over an investigation by the Watergate Special Prosecution Force as to any "improper motivation" underlying the filing of these suits. *See United States v. National Broadcasting Co.*, 65 F.R.D. 415 (C.D. Cal. 1974).

94. *United States v. National Broadcasting Co.*, 449 F. Supp. 1127, 1130 (C.D. Cal. 1978).

feature films, produced by a television network. In essence, the remedy would end vertical integration in television.

The television networks moved to dismiss the complaint, primarily on the ground of implied immunity from antitrust law because of the pervasive regulation of television by the Federal Communications Commission.[95] Following the holding of *United States v. RCA*,[96] implied immunity was not recognized by the court. Although the FCC may consider antitrust policy in its regulatory decisions, the Communications Act did not expressly authorize or direct the FCC to resolve antitrust questions bearing on matters within its jurisdiction.[97]

In 1978 NBC reached a settlement of the issues with the antitrust division and a consent decree was approved by the district court.[98] Section 5 of the consent decree was the most controversial since it set for ten years the hours NBC could exhibit programs that it had produced internally. The restriction was two and one-half hours per week during prime time, eight hours per week during daytime hours, and eleven hours per week during fringe hours. The provision did not take effect until similar relief was obtained against CBS and ABC in 1980.[99] Among the other restrictions were those precluding reciprocal dealing between NBC, CBS, and ABC and a prohibition on the exclusive licensing of feature films from other distributors.[100]

Pursuant to the Antitrust Procedures and Penalties Act,[101] the leading motion picture distributors and leading independent television producers had filed comments in opposition to the NBC consent decree. These nonnetwork suppliers of programming for television had objected that NBC was permittted to produce internally two and one-half hours of prime-time programs per week while, at the time, NBC was producing only one hour of such programs per week.[102] The commentators had urged a total ban on NBC internal production.[103] Motion picture distributors argued that NBC would increase internal productions to drive down the price of features bought from them. Notwithstanding these objections, the court approved the consent de-

95. *United States v. CBS, Inc.*, 1977-1 Trade Cas. ¶ 61,327 (C.D. Cal. 1977).

96. 358 U.S. 334 (1959).

97. *United States v. CBS, Inc.*, 1977-1 Trade Cas. ¶ 61,327 (C.D. Cal. 1977).

98. 449 F. Supp. at 1127.

99. *United States v. CBS, Inc.*, 1980–81 Trade Cas. ¶ 63,594 (Consent decree, July 3, 1980); *United States v. American Broadcasting Cos.* [1981-1 Transfer Binder] Trade Reg. Rep. (CCH) ¶ 64,150 (Consent decree, Nov. 14, 1980).

100. 449 F. Supp. at 1132–33.

101. 15 U.S.C. § 16 (1979 Supp.).

102. 449 F. Supp. at 1135.

103. Ibid., pp. 1135–36.

cree as being in the public interest.[104] As an incident of this litigation, the court held that CBS could not intervene formally as a party to the proposed consent decree of NBC.[105]

In January 1977 the FCC began an inquiry into the television industry that covers almost every issue treated in the antitrust case.[106] This inquiry continues. Meanwhile, in July 1979 ABC announced plans to resume feature film production after a hiatus of seven years.[107] The plan is to produce three or four theatrical films per year. Management felt that uncertainties of the industry were less than in the past as theater admissions have increased.

Distribution

Market Structure

The structure of motion picture distribution in the United States is determined primarily by the number of pictures produced for the U.S. market and the optimum size of firm for efficient national distribution. The Motion Picture Association of America reported the number of new pictures released by national distributors as follows: 425 films by 15 firms in 1950, 233 films by 12 firms in 1960, 267 films by 22 firms in 1970, and 154 films by 16 firms in 1977.[108] These figures aggregate domestic and foreign productions, including foreign language films. In fact, only 11 firms had effective national distribution systems in 1970.[109] The leading 7 were the remaining *Paramount* defendants. (RKO had closed its exchanges and left motion picture distribution in 1957.)[110] The other 4 national distributors of significance were Allied Artists, Avco Embassy, Buena Vista (Disney), and American International. The 11 leaders together released 198 films in 1970 and 114 in 1977, the share being 74 percent of total national releases in each year.[111]

104. 449 F. Supp. at 1145.

105. CBS and five of the nonnetwork producers had petitioned to intervene as parties in order to be able to appeal the NBC decree. The court held that the movants had failed to make a strong showing that the United States inadequately represented their interests. Denial of these petitions was affirmed by the court of appeals. *United States v. National Broadcasting Co.*, Nos. 77-381, 78-1068 (C.D. Cal. June 4, 1979), aff'd mem., 603 F.2d 227 (9th Cir. 1979), cert. denied sub. nom., *Columbia Pictures Indus., Inc., v. United States*, 444 U.S. 991 (1979). See "Justices Reject CBS Intervention in an NBC Suit," *Wall Street Journal*, Dec. 11, 1979, p. 8.

106. 449 F. Supp at 1139.

107. See "ABC Plans to Produce 3 or 4 Theatrical Films a Year for $25 Million," *Wall Street Journal*, July 13, 1979, p. 6.

108. Compaigne, *Who Owns the Media?* pp. 214–15.

109. Ibid., pp. 222–23.

110. Conant, *Antitrust in the Motion Picture Industry*, p. 132.

111. Compaigne, *Who Owns the Media?* p. 222.

The charge is made that motion picture distribution is still controlled by the seven former *Paramount* defendants. In 1970 they released 76 percent of the films that earned $1 million or more in rentals, and in 1978 they released 89 percent of these successful films.[112] Given the declining film production, however, entry of new national distributors or growth of the smaller ones was unlikely. Efficient marketing required screening rooms for exhibitors or their booking agents in each major metropolitan area.[113] Paramount, for example, operated twenty branch offices in the United States, one in Puerto Rico, and six in Canada for licensing and distribution of motion pictures.[114] To compete, other national distributors needed similar marketing organizations. With the great increase in independent productions, a distribution system could operate efficiently only by securing distribution contracts with a significant number of independent producers. In fiscal 1973, for example, Paramount produced ten of the twenty-two pictures it distributed, and in 1974 it produced fourteen of the twenty-five pictures it distributed.[115] In 1975, however, Paramount produced only four of the twenty pictures it distributed.[116] In 1976 it distributed seventeen pictures and ceased releasing information on how many it produced.[117]

Metro-Goldwyn-Mayer, Inc., terminated its distribution activities entirely. It had adopted a policy of reduced production and was not prepared to finance independent producers to secure their distribution contracts in order to have the critical minimum films necessary to cover the costs of an efficient national distribution system of about twenty branches.[118] In 1973 MGM sold its seven domestic branches and its thirty-seven overseas branches.[119] It announced it would reduce its production from approximately nineteen pictures per year to approximately seven.[120] The decision in part resulted from net losses on a number of pictures in 1973,[121] which indicated to management that only "special," high-cost films should be produced. MGM signed a

112. Ibid., p. 223.

113. See Conant, *Antitrust in the Motion Picture Industry*, pp. 118–20.

114. Gulf & Western Industries, Inc., Form 10K Report to the SEC, p. 6.

115. Gulf & Western Industries, Inc., 1974 Annual Report, p. 19.

116. Gulf & Western Industries, Inc., 1975 Annual Report, p. 34.

117. Gulf & Western Industries, Inc., 1972 Annual Report, p. 15.

118. See Gottschalk, "MGM to Sell Studio, Give Up Film Distribution," *Wall Street Journal*, Sept. 18, 1973, p. 40.

119. "MGM, United Artists Sign Distribution Pact," *Wall Street Journal*, Oct. 19, 1973, p. 2; "MGM to Sell Theaters Abroad for $17.5 Million to MCA, G&W Group," *Wall Street Journal*, Oct. 31, 1973, p. 6.

120. Gottschalk, "MGM to Sell Studio."

121. Ibid.

ten-year contract with United Artists Corp. to distribute its productions in the United States and Canada.[122] It contracted with Cinema
International Corporation to distribute its films in foreign countries
and sold its interest in thirty-five foreign theaters to that firm.[123] Cinema International is joint venture of Paramount and Universal for
foreign distribution with eighty-eight branch offices in the free world.[124]
Thus, one sees cost structures dictating joint marketing ventures of
leading distributors, both domestically and overseas.

In 1980 MGM decided to increase production substantially and determined to reenter film distribution via acquisition.[125] In 1981 MGM
purchased United Artists Corp. from its parent, Transamerica Corp.
for about $380 million.[126] The Antitrust Division of the Department
of Justice was expected to investigate the merger.

The Paramount Decrees had one significant effect on the relative
importance of the leading distributors. Before the decrees, MGM
(Loew's, Inc.), as one of the five majors that controlled the industry,
was the industry leader. It had long-term contracts with more leading
actors than any other producer-distributor. This enabled it to earn
larger film rentals than any other distributor.[127] In 1946, for example,
MGM had $61 million in domestic film rentals while the three minor
distributors, Columbia, Universal, and United Artists, had domestic
film rentals of $23 million to $27 million.[128] By 1978 MGM ranked
seventh in film rentals among the seven surviving *Paramount* defendants.[129] It had worldwide film rentals of $97 million in 1978, $68

122. "MGM, United Artists Sign Distribution Pact."

123. "MGM to Sell Theaters Abroad for $17.5 Million."

124. Gulf & Western Industries, Inc., Form 10K Report to SEC 6 (1979). In 1977,
Cinema International accounted for one-third of foreign rentals of all U.S. films with
revenues of about $133 million. See Compaigne, *Who Owns the Media?* p. 221.

125. "MGM Film Bid to Buy United Artists Marks Push for Fast Success," *Wall
Street Journal*, May 18, 1981, p. 1; "MGM Film Offers to Buy United Artists," ibid.,
May 18, 1981, p. 23; "MGM Film Signs Accord to Acquire United Artists Corp.," ibid.,
May 22, 1981, p. 14; "MGM Film Discloses Plans for Purchase of United Artists,
Financing of Movies," ibid., July 7, 1981, p. 8; "Holders of MGM Film Approve Moves
to Aid United Artists Bid," ibid., July 28, 1981, p. 34.

126. "MGM Filing Discloses Transamerica Dispute over United Artists," *Wall Street
Journal*, July 30, 1981, p. 36.

127. Cf. "Loew's, Inc.," in this volume (noting that MGM had "more stars than there
are in heaven").

128. Conant, *Antitrust in the Motion Picture Industry*.

129. Annual reports to stockholders of the seven companies show the ranking in
worldwide theatrical film rentals in 1978 to be as follows: Twentieth Century-Fox Film
Corp. $309.9 million (Twentieth Century-Fox Film Corp., 1978 Annual Report p. 3);
MCA, Inc. (Universal) $318.7 million (MCA, Inc., 1978 Annual Report, p. 16); Gulf &

million of which were domestic,[130] and, therefore, also part of United Artists' $294 million worldwide rentals.[131] In 1978, Universal had worldwide rentals of $318.7 million[132] and Columbia had $269 million.[133] Thus, in a freer market, the minor distributors, who had never been part of the illegal exhibition cartel that dictated first-run theater priorities, became equal competitors with the four surviving majors. Their much larger film rentals indicate that they were able to succeed.

Control by Conglomerates

The highly fluctuating income of motion picture distributors, due to the uncertainty of public reception of each film, and the distributors' need for sources of risk capital make film distributing corporations likely targets for control by conglomerate corporations. Paramount Pictures Corp. is owned by Gulf & Western Industries, Inc. Paramount's 1979 aggregate revenues of $664 million from motion pictures, television films, and foreign theaters[134] were only 10.2 percent of Gulf & Western's 1979 revenues.[135] Universal is owned by MCA, Inc. Universal's $724 million revenues from filmed entertainment in 1978 were 64.6 percent of MCA's revenues.[136] United Artists Corp. was owned by Transamerica Corp. United Artists' revenues of $462.3 million were 11.4 percent of Transamerica's revenues.[137] Warner Communications, Inc. had 1978 revenues from filmed entertainment of $393 million, which was 30 percent of Warner's revenues.[138] Another 47 percent was from recorded music and music publishing.[139]

Other leading motion picture distributors have also diversified. Metro-Goldwyn-Mayer, Inc., reduced investment in highly uncertain motion picture distribution and made large investments in two major hotels and gambling casinos.[140] In 1980, however, motion picture pro-

---

Western Industries, Inc. (Paramount) $287.0 million (Gulf & Western Industries, Inc., 1978 Annual Report, p. 8); Columbia Pictures Industries, Inc. $269.0 million (Columbia Pictures Industries, Inc., 1978 Annual Report, p. 51); Warner Communications, Inc. $261.3 million (Warner Communications, Inc., 1978 Annual Report, p. 17).

130. *Moody's Industrial Manual* (1979), p. 2655.
131. Transamerica Corp., 1979 Annual Report, p. 35.
132. MCA, Inc., 1978 Annual Report, p. 16.
133. Columbia Pictures Industries, Inc., 1979 Annual Report, p. 51.
134. Gulf & Western Industries, Inc., 1979 Annual Report, p. 20.
135. Ibid., p. 54.
136. See MCA, Inc., 1978 Annual Report, p. 16.
137. See Transamerica Corp., 1979 Annual Report, p. 30.
138. See Warner Communications Inc., 1978 Annual Report, pp. 17, 78.
139. Ibid., p. 78.
140. Metro-Goldwyn-Mayer Inc., 1979 Annual Report, p. 1, noting MGM revenue from filmed entertainment was $193 million or 39.3 percent of its total revenue.

duction was transferred to a separate corporation, Metro-Goldwyn-Mayer Film Co.[141] Twentieth Century-Fox diversified into soft drink bottling, television broadcasting, film processing and record and music publishing.[142] Its 1978 revenue from filmed entertainment of $408 million was 66.8 percent of its total revenue.[143] Columbia Pictures Industries, Inc., was the least diversified of the former *Paramount* defendants. Its 1979 revenues from filmed entertainment were $458 million or 74.7 percent of its total revenues.[144]

Decline of Smaller Distributors

The smaller national distributors have felt the impact of declining domestic motion picture production the most. The new, extravagant pictures usually can be secured for distribution only if the distributor supplies millions of dollars in financing. Marketing costs will also require millions of dollars. A small firm, with fewer branch offices than the larger distributors and distributing only a few pictures a year, risks a much larger percentage of its assets and credit on any single picture. Avco-Embassy pictures is an example. Embassy Pictures Corp. was acquired by Avco Corp., a large financial institution, in 1968, and in 1977 it supplied only 1.2 percent of Avco's revenues.[145] In spite of the fact that Avco Corp. can suppy it with financing, it has not been successful. In 1977 Avco-Embassy released six pictures,[146] down from fifteen in 1975.[147] Its 1977 film rentals were $19 million and its net loss was $4.3 million.[148] In fact, its annual revenues had declined from $34 million in 1974 and it had five straight years of net losses.[149] This was in spite of the fact that in both 1977 and 1978 it had two new pictures with over $2 million in film rentals.[150]

American International Pictures, Inc., was founded in 1956 as a distributor and expanded into production after 1960. It has offices in twenty-six cities in the United States.[151] In each of the three years 1976

141. See Metro-Goldwyn-Mayer Film Co., 1980 Annual Report, p. 2; "MGM Film Co.'s First Holders Meeting Focuses on Roles of Kerkorian, Begelman," *Wall Street Journal*, Jan. 12, 1981, p. 12.

142. Twentieth Century-Fox Film Corp., 1978 Annual Report, p. 32.

143. Ibid.

144. See Columbia Pictures Industries, Inc., 1979 Annual Report, p. 47.

145. Motion picture revenues were $19 million and total revenues were $153.8 million. Avco Corp., 1977 Annual Report, pp. 2–3.

146. Ibid., p. 12.

147. Compaigne, *Who Owns the Media?* p. 222.

148. Avco Corp., 1977 Annual Report, pp. 2–3.

149. Ibid. See Avco Corp., 1976 Annual Report, p. 12.

150. Compaigne, *Who Owns the Media?* p. 220.

151. *Moody's Industrial Manual* (1979), p. 1392.

to 1978, it had $51 million in revenues,[152] about 96 percent of which was film rentals from theaters and television.[153] Its 1978 net profits before taxes were $2.34 million on total assets of $50.9 million, and in 1979 its net loss before tax credits was $4.3 million.[154] American International released eighteen pictures in 1977, down from twenty-eight in 1972.[155] In 1977 it distributed eight of the seventy-eight total U.S. films released with rentals of over $2 million, but in 1978 it distributed only one of the eighty-two new films with over $2 million rentals.[156] While American International seems to survive the great uncertainties of the industry, its return on investment is much lower than the uncertainties warrant. This may have made it a takeover candidate. Filmways, Inc., merged with American International on July 12, 1979.[157] Filmways, with $153.4 million in revenues in 1979, received only $28.1 million from its entertainment division, primarily television films.[158] The division also includes motion picture production, recording studios, music publishing, and other activities. Its studio in New York with two sound stages will complement the American International distribution system.

Allied Artists Pictures Corp. was formerly Monogram Pictures, a producer of "B" grade films before the Paramount Decrees. After the decrees it was able to enter the market to distribute "A" grade films.[159] In 1976 it was merged with Kalvex, Inc., and became Allied Artists Industries, Inc.[160] Of its 1977 revenues of $53.2 million, only $12.5 million was in filmed entertainment.[161] Excluding tax credits for loss carryover, it had net losses in all four years—1975 to 1978.[162] In the eight years 1970 to 1977, it distributed a total of forty-four pictures,[163] an average of five and one-half per year. In April 1979 Allied Artists Industries filed petitions under Chapter 11 of the Federal Bankruptcy

152. Ibid.

153. Ibid.

154. Ibid.

155. Compaigne, *Who Owns the Media?* p. 222.

156. Ibid., p. 220.

157. *Moody's Industrial Manual* (1980), p. 2155.

158. Filmways Inc., 1979 Annual Report, p. 34. See "Filmways Gets Buyer for Unit, Loan Extension," *Wall Street Journal*, Mar. 6, 1981, p. 7.

159. See Conant, *Antitrust in the Motion Picture Industry*, pp. 128–29.

160. *Moody's Industrial Manual* (1979), p. 1371. See Penn, "Film Fade-out: How 'Little Guy' Allied Artists Tumbled from Moviemaking Role into Chapter 11," *Wall Street Journal*, May 4, 1979, p. 38.

161. Compaigne, *Who Owns the Media?*, p. 203.

162. *Moody's Industrial Manual* (1979), p. 1371.

163. Compaigne, *Who Owns the Media?*, p. 222.

Act to operate under protection of the federal court against creditor lawsuits while it tried to work out a plan to pay its debts.[164] In February 1980 the federal judge approved the sale of Allied Artists Pictures Corp. and its television corporations to Lorimar Productions, Inc.[165] Allied maintained that its relatively small size and the 1976 change in the federal income tax laws wiping out motion picture tax shelters limited its sources of funds and spelled its doom.[166] Outsiders attributed part of Allied's trouble to lack of competent management.[167] It is clear that Allied was below the critical minimum size for national distribution. In 1973, for example, 86 percent of its gross revenues were rentals on one picture, *Cabaret*, and in 1974, 80 percent of gross revenues were from *Papillon* and 13 percent from *Cabaret*.[168] In such circumstances, one or two net-loss films could cause insolvency.

Distribution by Divorced Circuits

Under the Paramount Decrees, the corporations succeeding to the theater circuits of the five major producer-distributors were barred from engaging in production or distribution of pictures without special permission of the district court. Few such applications were filed since the theater corporations did not have the systems of distribution centers necessary to execute successful marketing. A few applications were made for distribution by the circuits as they strove to find, and even finance, additional film production, The first significant case was the permission granted Stanley Warner Corp. to produce and distribute the experimental Cinerama pictures.[169] In 1963, as picture output declined, National General Corp., the theater successor of Twentieth Century-Fox, was granted permission to produce and distribute films for six years.[170] Between 1963 and 1969 National distributed six pictures, two of which it produced itself.[171] In 1969 the permission was extended for three years on the condition that National continue to

164. See Penn, "Film Fade-out."

165. *Moody's Industrial News Reports*, Feb. 26, 1980, p. 2801. In 1979, Lorimar Productions entered a three-year contract for United Artists to distribute thirteen motion pictures which it was producing. Transamerica Corp., 1979 Annual Report, p. 22; "Lorimar Finds Its Success in Television Doesn't Carry Over into Moviemaking," *Wall Street Journal*, Aug. 4, 1981, p. 38.

166. Penn, "Film Fade-out," p. 40.

167. Ibid.

168. Allied Artists Picture Corp., Notice of Meeting, Jan. 20, 1976, p. 85.

169. *United States v. Loew's, Inc.*, 1969 Trade Cas. ¶ 72,767 (S.D.N.Y. 1969), at 86,761 (not reported offically, but noted by Judge Palmieri).

170. Ibid.

171. Ibid., p. 86,762.

refrain from giving exhibition preferences to its own theaters.[172] Later in 1969 the court approved a distribution agreement between National General and First Artists Production Company, Ltd.[173] National was allowed to distribute nine pictures, three each featuring Paul Newman, Sidney Poitier, and Barbra Streisand. This permit also was strictly conditioned to prevent preferences to National theaters in its operating areas.

Loew's Corp. was granted permission by the district court in 1980 to engage in motion picture production and distribution.[174] This permit to resume production after a hiatus of twenty-eight years was strictly conditional. Loew's was prohibited from distributing its productions to its own theaters.

Marketing Policies

Marketing policies of distributors have changed radically as population has moved to the suburbs and the number of films has declined. In the period before 1960 most distributors followed the pre-1940 pattern of first run in one theater in the central business district of cities followed by a period of clearance before multiple second runs in other neighborhoods and the suburbs. As long as each distributor made the decision individually to continue this pattern (i.e., without agreement with other distributors, or without agreement with one exhibitor to refrain from licensing to another), the practice was legal.[175] Mere conscious parallelism of action, without agreement, does not violate the language of section 1 of the Sherman Act.[176] But where the owner of a drive-in theater demonstrated that exactly the same pattern of runs and clearances as existed in a metropolitan area before 1945 still prevailed after the Paramount Decrees, this was sufficient additional evidence to find conspiracy.[177] Since conspiracy usually must be found from circumstantial evidence, different triers of fact in two separate cases can reach opposite results upon considering substantially similar evidence from the same market area.[178]

172. *United States v. Loews, Inc.,* 1969 Trade Cas. ¶ 72,767 (S.D.N.Y. 1969).

173. *United States v. Loew's, Inc.,* 1970 Trade Cas. ¶ 72,992 (S.D.N.Y. 1969).

174. *United States v. Loew's, Inc.,* 1980–81 Trade Cas. ¶ 63,662 (S.D.N.Y. 1980). See "Loew's Intends to Sell Warwick Hotel, Wins Right to Make Movies," *Wall Street Journal,* Feb. 29, 1980, p. 5.

175. *Theatre Enterprises v. Paramount Film Distrib. Corp.,* 346 U.S. 537, 540–42 (1954).

176. *Naumkeag Theatres Co. v. New England Theatres,* 345 F.2d 910,911 (1st Cir. 1965), cert. denied, 382 U.S. 906 (1965).

177. *Basle Theatres, Inc., v. Warner Bros. Pictures Distrib. Corp.,* 168 F. Supp. 553 (W.D. Pa. 1958). See Conant, "Consciously Parallel Action in Restraint of Trade," *Minnesota Law Review* 38 (1954): 797.

178. See *Fox West Coast Theatres Corp. v. Paradise Theatre Building Corp.,* 264 F.2d 602, 605 (9th Cir. 1958).

As central cities declined and many persons refused to enter these areas at night, new, smaller theaters were being built in new shopping centers in the suburbs. Since many of these suburbs were on opposite sides of cities and many miles apart, it made sense for distributors to modify their release patterns to multiple first runs. This increased the complexity of negotiating rentals since many theater owners could argue that there was some rivalry between theaters in adjacent suburbs.

One charge of violation of its 1951 consent decree was made against Warner Bros., Inc., to stop the practice of four-walling.[179] Under this method, a distributor leased the theater for the period of screening a particular feature film. The theater owner received a fixed rental payment. The distributor operated the theater and set admission prices. In 1976 Warner entered a consent decree to discontinue the practice for a period of ten years.[180] While this enforces the plain language of the decree, its effect may be unfortunate. A lease of one theater for exhibiting one picture is not reentry into exhibition by Warner in any more than a trivial sense. A vertical agreement with one customer cannot create monopoly power, since market power must be measured horizontally. If Warner had a higher evaluation of the earnings probabilities of a picture than did the exhibitor, leasing the theater was a method by which the distributor could bear the uncertainties of exhibition in the theater and reap the profits if the picture was successful.

One of the key issues was competitive bidding by exhibitors for the first run of pictures. In *Paramount* the district court mandate of competitive bidding had been reversed by the Supreme Court when it ordered the alternative remedy of divorcement of the five affiliated circuits. While one would expect distributors to adopt competitive bidding between exhibitors in order to maximize film rentals, only a small proportion of film licensing is subject to bidding.[181] One problem is that bids may not be comparable. A dollar bid, a percentage bid, a percentage bid on admission revenues above a stated weekly theater expense, or a percentage bid with a guaranteed minimum rental are some of the various possibilities. There can be comparable bids only if a distributor sets strict limits on the method of bidding. The more important reason that few film licenses are subject to competitive bidding is that the exhibitors dislike it. Film rentals are raised to their true competitive price. Competition in film licensing in any city, town,

179. *United States v. Warner Bros. Pictures, Inc.*, 1979-1 Trade Cas. ¶ 62,504 (S.D.N.Y. 1976). See "Warner Bros. Inc. Theater Rentals Spur U.S. Action," *Wall Street Journal*, Apr. 5, 1976, p. 5.

180. Ibid.

181. See Cassady, "Impact of the Paramount Decision on Motion Picture Distribution and Price Making," *Southern California Law Review* 31 (1958): 150, 160–65.

or section is highly imperfect because so many theaters are owned by local circuits. Either individually or in concert with other exhibitors in their area, they refuse to engage in competitive bidding. Collusion of exhibitors to allocate or to split distributors' pictures is discussed below in the section concerning exhibition.

In those cases where competitive bidding was used and all theaters in a market were allowed to bid, it was unlikely that any single exhibitor could show antitrust violations by distributors. As one court noted, bidding was the truly competitive method of motion picture distribution as long as it was open to all rivals.[182] If each distributor, acting independently, set his own bidding zones for theaters in a city, no single exhibitor could legally complain that the zone system made him bid in a run against theaters against which he would prefer not to bid.[183] No firm can legally demand isolation from competition. This does not mean the volume of antitrust litigation in the industry subsided. As reviewed in detail below, issues relating to circuit buying power and to exhibitors' splits of the available pictures led to large series of lawsuits.

Block Booking

The prohibitions in the Paramount Decrees against block booking effectively required the defendant distributors to license each film in each theater individually. There have been few charges of violation of this section of the decrees, but one major action was brought under section 1 of the Sherman Act for block booking of pre-1948 pictures for television exhibition. In *United States v. Loew's, Inc.*,[184] six distributors were charged with block booking successful films with inferior films in licenses to television stations. The distributors were not charged with conspiring with each other. Following the rationale of the *Paramount* case, the court held that tying two or more copyrighted films in a single license was a per se violation of the Sherman Act.[185] The one reported contempt citation for block booking took place in 1978. Twentieth Century-Fox was cited as a result of a New York grand jury investigation in which twenty-five New England theater owners provided evidence.[186] The charge was block booking *The Other Side of*

182. *Royster Drive-in Theatres, Inc., v. American Broadcasting-Paramount Theatres, Inc.*, 268 F.2d 246, 250 (2d Cir. 1959).

183. See *A.L.B. Theatre Corp. v. Loew's, Inc.*, 355 F.2d 495, 500 (7th Cir. 1966).

184. 371 U.S. 38 (1962). See Stigler, "United States v. Loew's Inc.: A Note on Block-Booking," in Philip Kurland, ed., *Supreme Court Review* (1963), p. 152.

185. 371 U.S. 45–47.

186. See "Fox Films Says It Faces Possible Indictments from Booking Probe," *Wall Street Journal*, Mar. 8, 1978, p. 10.

Midnight with *Star Wars*. Twentieth Century-Fox pleaded *nolo contendere* to the charge of criminal contempt and was fined $25,000.[187] The block booking occurred in only two of the company's twenty-six film exchange areas. The company asserted that certain employees had violated a longstanding policy of strict compliance with the 1951 decree. Its license agreements clearly state the policy.

One reported exception to the prohibition of block booking was permitted by a district court in 1972.[188] Columbia Pictures petitioned the court for permission to block release a series of eight to twelve pictures. The "Repertory Cinema" plan was to produce and distribute a set of pictures based on literary works or stage productions that had received critical acclaim. Each theater would set aside two days per month to show these films and theaters would take public subscriptions in advance. The project was not economically feasible unless Columbia could license the package to individual theaters in advance. Since the concept was new and had not been considered at the time of the Paramount Decrees, the court permitted the experimentation for one year.

Exhibition

Market Changes

Motion picture exhibition in theaters has changed radically in the past thirty years. This is due mostly to demographic changes, but is in part also a result of television competition and costs of theater operation. The great demographic change has been the movement of population to the suburbs and the resultant construction of suburban shopping centers with new theaters. The 1972 census reported 12,699 theaters.[189] There were 11,670 theaters with payrolls, of which 8,328 were indoor and 3,342 were drive-ins.[190] Of these, 37.7 percent of the indoor theaters and 44.5 percent of the drive-ins were constructed after 1954.[191] Essentially all of these are in the suburbs. In 1979 the Department of Commerce estimated there were 9,021 indoor theaters with 13,331 screens and 3,197 drive-ins with 3,570 screens.[192]

187. "Fox Film Is fined $25,000 on a Charge of Forcing Block-Booking on Theaters," *Wall Street Journal*, Sept. 13, 1978, p. 8.
188. *United States v. Loew's, Inc.*, 1972 Trade Cas. ¶ 74,017 (S.D.N.Y. 1972).
189. U.S. Bureau of the Census, *1972 Census of Selected Service Industries* (1972), pp. 3–17.
190. Ibid.
191. Ibid.
192. U.S. Dep't of Commerce, *1981 U.S. Industrial Outlook* (1981), p. 530.

The average indoor theater declined in size from 750 seats in 1950 to 500 seats in 1977.[193] The movement to smaller theaters and multi-screens was related to the decline in paid admissions resulting from the competition of television and other recreational activities and to the costs of operation. In 1970 United Artists Theatre Circuit reported it could operate a new small theater with two employees, a manager-projectionist and a cashier-candy seller.[194] A small theater, showing films on first or second run in the suburbs, can avoid booking those films that have failed on prior first runs in other areas of the state or nation and thereby reduce uncertainty. Likewise, the shift to multi-screen theaters enables owners to offset low revenues from a failing film in one auditorium with larger revenues of a successful film in an adjacent auditorium. Since one projectionist serves all the screens of a multiscreen theater, there is no extra labor cost.[195]

General Cinema Corp., with the largest chain of theaters in the country, is illustrative of the dramatic changes in exhibition. It was incorporated in 1950 as a developer of drive-in theaters. It has become the leading builder of multiscreen indoor theaters in suburban shopping centers. By 1970 General Cinema had 203 theaters with 256 screens.[196] In October 1979 it had 337 theaters with 843 screens in thirty-seven states and the District of Columbia.[197] Its theater revenues in 1979 were $266.5 million. General Cinema illustrates the trend away from drive-ins as suburban land values increase and alternative indoor theaters are built in shopping centers. Its number of drive-ins declined from 36 in 1966[198] to 10 in 1978.[199] Little of General Cinema's growth is due to purchase of existing theaters. In 1970 it acquired the 15

193. *International Motion Picture Almanac* (1981), p. 30A. See Conant, *Antitrust in the Motion Picture Industry*, p. 48.

194. "Movie Theater Gets Cut to Size," *Business Week*, Mar. 14, 1970, p. 29.

195. See Edmands, "Twin, Quad, and Six-Plex," *Barrons*, June 28, 1971, p. 11; Gottschalk, "Film Exhibitors Face a Financial Crisis as Hollywood Studios Slash Production," *Wall Street Journal*, Feb. 8, 1977, p. 46.

196. *Moody's Industrial Manual* (1971), p. 421.

197. General Cinema Corp., 1979 Annual Report, p. 8. The ranking of U.S. theater chains in 1977–78, according to number of screens, is as follows: General Cinema, 791; United Artists Theatre Circuits, 712; American Multi-Cinema, 462; Plitt Theatres, 412; Commonwealth, 347; Mann Theatres, 310; Fuqua (Martin Theatres), 283; Kerasotes, 180; Cinemette, 160; Stewart and Everett, 138; Loew's, 127; Cablecom-General, 125; Pacific Theatres, 125; Cobb, 125; Gulf States, 120; Cooperative Theatres of Michigan, 105. See Compaigne, *Who Owns the Media?* p. 226.

198. "Movies, Soda Pop Enable General Cinema to Grow," *Barrons*, Oct. 14, 1974, p. 39.

199. "Movie Theaters, Soft Drinks Prove Profitable Combo for General Cinema," *Barrons*, July 10, 1978, pp. 32, 33.

theaters of Mann Theatre Circuit in Minneapolis.[200] This acquisition resulted in a divorcement action by the Justice Deparment, charging violation of section 7 of the Clayton Act. In 1973 a consent decree ordered sale of 10 of General's 21 theaters in Minneapolis.[201] In 1972 General Cinema purchased 48 indoor theaters from Loew's Corp.,[202] 21 of which were sold in 1973.[203]

United Artists Theatre Circuit, Inc., (unrelated to United Artists Corp.), the second largest chain, had 835 screens and theater revenues of $223.5 million in 1980.[204] It, too, has been a leader in the trend to build multiscreen theaters in suburban shopping centers. But its one major acquisition of existing theaters had antitrust consequences. In 1968 United Artists Theatre Circuit acquired Prudential Theatres Co., Inc., which had 85 theaters in New York, New Jersey, Connecticut and Wisconsin.[205] In 1971 the Justice Department brought a civil action charging United with violation of section 7 of the Clayton Act.[206] In 1976 the case was settled by a consent decree requiring United to divest 23 theaters in the New York metropolitan area within five years and barring it from acquiring any other theaters in those counties for ten years unless it obtained prior consent of the Justice Department or approval of the court.[207]

Another striking change in exhibition has been the growing importance of refreshment sales. Census reports indicate such sales at 13 to 15 percent of total theater revenues.[208] At drive-in theaters, food and drink sales are even more important. Commonwealth Theatres, with 252 conventional theaters and 106 drive-ins in 1979, reported 23 percent of revenues from refreshments and miscellaneous sales.[209] Since these sales are in an isolated market, being made after tickets are collected, the markups are higher than in food stores. For many ex-

200. *Moody's Industrial Manual* (1979), p. 748.

201. *United States v. General Cinema Corp.*, 1973-1 Trade Cas. ¶ 74,569 (S.D.N.Y. 1973).

202. "General Cinema: King of the Flicks," *Business Week*, May 20, 1972, p. 31.

203. *Moody's Industrial Manual*, (1979), p. 748.

204. Standard & Poor, *Standard Corporation Descriptions* (Mar. 1981), p. 2463.

205. *Moody's OTC Industrial Manual* (1980), p. 1522.

206. *United States v. United Artists Theatre Circuit, Inc.*, 1971 Trade Cas. ¶ 73,751 (E.D.N.Y. 1971).

207. *United States v. United Artists Theatre Circuit, Inc.*, 1977–1 Trade Cas. ¶ 61,389 (E.D.N.Y. 1976). Modification of this decree was denied in 1980. *United States v. United Artists Theatre Circuit*, 1980–2 Trade Cas. ¶ 63,549 (E.D.N.Y. 1980).

208. See U.S. Bureau of the Census, *1972 Census of Selected Service Industries*, pp. 3–11.

209. *Standard OTC Stock Reports*, May 9, 1980, p. 3586.

hibitors, refreshment profits are a major part of net earnings and theaters would close without such sales. As a consequence, an exhibitor can bid for a popular film 90 percent of box office receipts above a house allowance for expenses. The large attendance will enable him to make his main profit on refreshments.

Divorced Theater Circuits

The five successor corporations that had acquired the theater chains of the five major *Paramount* defendants met the dynamic changes in exhibition under the disadvantages of the severe restrictions of the decrees. They could acquire theaters to replace those sold but could acquire no new theaters unless they could convince the district court that the acquisition would not unduly restrain competition.

Each petition of one of the successor theater companies to acquire one or more theaters required a hearing before the district court and probable opposition by attorneys from the Department of Justice. An exceptions clause in the decrees for acquiring substantially equivalent replacements for theaters closed by one of the five circuits was narrowly construed. Closing an old downtown theater and purchasing a new one in a suburban shopping center were held not to be substantially equivalent. The court treated this in the same way as a net addition to the circuit and required proof that it would not unduly restrain competition.[210] It was not until 1974 that the district court agreed to an exception to this rule for theaters newly constructed by one of the five circuits.[211] And this exception did not apply to theaters constructed by others, such as developers of shopping centers, and then leased or sold to one of the circuits.

The series of decisions by the district court on petitions of the divorced circuits to acquire theaters show no clear standards.[212] Amer-

210. *United States v. Paramount Pictures, Inc.,* 1963 Trade Cas. ¶ 70,760 (S.D.N.Y. 1963).

211. *United States v. Paramount Pictures, Inc.,* 1974-2 Trade Cas. ¶ 75,378 (S.D.N.Y. 1974).

212. See Note, "Experiment in Preventive Anti-Trust: Judicial Regulation of the Motion Picture Exhibition Market under the Paramount Decrees," *Yale Law Journal* 74 (1965): 1041. The number of petitions of the divorced circuits to acquire new theaters was as follows:

1960: 10	1964: 27	1968: 50	1972: 12	1976: 2
1961: 15	1965: 47	1969: 55	1973: 32	1977: 1
1962: 13	1966: 74	1970: 30	1974: 26	1978: 2
1963: 11	1967: 50	1971: 25	1975: 3	1979: 1

United States v. Paramount Pictures, 1980-2 Trade Cas. ¶ 63,553, at 76,953 (S.D.N.Y. 1980).

ican Broadcasting Companies, owner of the former Paramount Theatres, was allowed to acquire four drive-ins in Knoxville, Tennessee, even though it would substantially increase its market share, because the former owners had died and ABC had made the highest bid for the theaters.[213] Conversely, ABC owned only two of the twenty-two theaters in the Wilkes-Barre, Pennsylvania, area when it was denied permission to acquire a drive-in there.[214] Stanley Warner Corp. and National General Corp. were permitted to buy whole circuits of thirty-seven[215] and thirty-one theaters,[216] respectively. The court, in both instances, held that circuit buying power was effectively curtailed by other provisions of the Paramount Decrees requiring licensing of each film to each theater separately.

In a leading decision, the district court permitted National General Corp., whose theaters were mainly in the West, to acquire a small chain of eight theaters in New York and Rhode Island.[217] The government argued that the acquisition would not only violate the standards of the decrees but also the potential competition doctrine the Surpeme Court had adopted in interpreting section 7 of the Clayton Act. The court rejected the argument. National General was not shown to be a potential competitor in the East as a possible builder of new theaters. Hence, its acquisition of an existing small circuit did not eliminate it as a potential competitor. Since National had declined to one-half the number of theaters permitted by the consent decree,[218] it was allowed this expansion in large markets with large populations marked by active competition in the exhibition field. In an analogous case, ABC, whose Paramount Theatres group had never operated in Sacramento, California, was permitted to acquire two dual theaters in two shopping centers.[219] As in many earlier cases, a rival circuit sought to intervene as a party to oppose the acquisition here. Following prior precedents the court denied intervention, holding that the attorney general adequately represented the public in preserving a competitive system.[220]

213. *United States v. Paramount Pictures, Inc.,* 1969 Trade Cas. ¶ 72,720 (S.D.N.Y. 1968).
214. *United States v. Paramount Pictures, Inc.,* 1962 Trade Cas. ¶ 70,519 (S.D.N.Y. 1962).
215. *United States v. Warner Bros. Pictures, Inc.,* 1962 Trade Cas. ¶ 70,512 (S.D.N.Y. 1962)
216. *United States v. Loews, Inc.,* 1967 Trade Cas. ¶ 72,243 (S.D.N.Y. 1967).
217. *United States v. Loew's, Inc.,* 251 F. Supp. 201 (S.D.N.Y. 1966).
218. Ibid., p. 209.
219. *United States v. Paramount Pictures, Inc.,* 333 F. Supp. 1100 (S.D.N.Y. 1971).
220. Ibid., pp. 1102–3.

The cases demonstrate that a costly litigation process was added to any plans of the five divorced circuits to follow the demographic trend and expand into the suburban shopping centers. The result was that the five circuits declined as the major central cities where most of their theaters were located decayed. By 1979 only one of the five former circuits was still operated by its original successor corporation.

Loew's, Inc., which controlled 129 theaters in 1952[221] when the consent decree separated it from MGM, was still operating theaters in 1980. In 1959, after divesting 17 theaters pursuant to the decree and closing unprofitable ones, it operated 111 theaters.[222] By 1978 Loew's had only 61 theaters with 127 screens.[223] Its primary business was operating hotels. Its 1978 theater revenues of $47.3 million were only 1.4 percent of its total revenues.[224]

American Broadcasting Companies, Inc. resulted from the 1953 merger of the former ABC into United Paramount Theatres, Inc., the successor company that acquired the theaters of Paramount Pictures. In 1949, the year of its consent decree, this largest of the five major circuits had 1,424 theaters.[225] After the specific theater divestitures ordered in the decree, it had only 534 theaters in 1957.[226] By the end of 1970 ABC operated only 411 theaters.[227] In 1974 the northern group of 123 ABC theaters was sold to a newly formed firm, Plitt Theaters, Inc., for $25 million.[228] H. G. Plitt, organizer of the new firm, had been a theater executive of ABC's northern group. In 1978 ABC left the theater business as it sold the rest of its theaters to Plitt Theaters, Inc. for about $50 million.[229] The 173 theaters operated by ABC at the end of 1977 had included 91 single screens, 79 twin screens, and 3 triple screens.[230] By 1977 theater revenues of $81.2 million had constituted only 5 percent of ABC's total revenues.[231] As noted, ABC has entered

221. Conant, *Antitrust in the Motion Picture Industry*, p. 108.

222. *Moody's Industrial Manual* (1960), p. 2750.

223. See Loew's, Inc., 1978 Annual Report, p. 14.

224. Ibid.

225. Conant, *Antitrust in the Motion Picture Industry*, p. 108.

226. Ibid.

227. 333 F. Supp. at 1104.

228. See "ABC Plans to Sell Northern Theaters to Plitt for Cash," *Wall Street Journal*, Oct. 18, 1973, p. 14; *Moody's Industrial Manual* (1973), p. 83.

229. *Moody's Industrial Manual* (1980), p. 585; See *Broadcasting*, Nov. 13, 1978, p. 45; "American Broadcasting Cos. Complete the Sale of Unit," *Wall Street Journal*, Nov. 30, 1978, p. 4.

230. "ABC is Negotiating $50 Million Sale of Its Theater Unit," *Wall Street Journal*, March 31, 1978, p. 4.

231. *Moody's Industrial Manual* (1978), p. 90.

motion picture production and was sued on this account by major distributors and by the Department of Justice. Sale of its theaters eliminates one possible basis for a holding that its entry into feature production was anticompetitive.

National General Corp., successor to the theaters of Twentieth Century-Fox, controlled 549 theaters at the time of the 1951 consent decree.[232] After specific divestitures, it controlled 321 theaters in 1957.[233] By 1970 it had closed and disposed of unprofitable theaters and reduced its total to 301.[234] In June 1973 National General had only 240 theaters and sold all the assets of its theater business to Mann Theatre Corp. of California for an estimated $67.5 million.[235]

RKO Theatres Corp., exhibition successor to RKO Corp., controlled 124 theaters at the time of its consent decree in 1948.[236] Pursuant to the decree, Howard Hughes sold his controlling interest in RKO theaters in 1953 to Albert A. List[237] and the company was renamed List Industries Corp. In 1959 List Industries Corp. was merged into Glen Alden Corp.[238] By 1967 the RKO divison of Glen Alden operated only 32 theaters.[239]

Stanley Warner Corp., successor to Warner Bros. theater divison, controlled 436 theaters at the time of the 1951 consent decree.[240] After divestitures pursuant to the decree, it had 297 theaters in 1957.[241] By 1960 it had only 225 theaters in 17 states and the District of Columbia.[242] In August 1967 Stanley Warner had 162 theaters in 97 cities, of which 139 were indoor and 19 were drive-ins.[243] Theater and television revenues declined from $40.4 million in 1960 to $38.4 million in 1967.[244] In 1967 Stanley Warner Corp. was merged into Glen Alden

232. Conant, *Antitrust in the Motion Picture Industry*, p. 108.

233. Ibid.

234. *Moody's Industrial Manual* (1971), p. 2190.

235. See "National General To Sell Theaters To Mann Theatre," *Wall Street Journal*, March 30, 1973, p. 16.

236. Conant, *Antitrust in the Motion Picture Industry*, p. 108.

237. Ibid., p. 109.

238. See "Glen Alden Holders Approve List Merger," *Wall Street Journal*, April 22, 1959, p. 18.

239. Glen Alden Corp., Notice of Special Meeting of Stockholders, Nov. 20, 1967, p. 39.

240. Conant, *Antitrust in the Motion Picture Industry*, p. 108.

241. Ibid.

242. *Moody's Industrial Manual* (1961), p. 1391.

243. Glen Alden Corp., Notice of Special Meeting of Stockholders, Nov. 20, 1967, p. 49.

244. Stanley Warner Corp., 1964 Annual Report, p. 2; 1967 Annual Report, p. 2.

Corp.[245] Under the RKO consent decree of 1948, Glen Alden, as successor to RKO Theatres, was required to secure permission of the district court to acquire Stanley Warner.[246] However, there is no reported decision that such permission was secured. Glen Alden combined its two theater groups into RKO-Stanley Warner Theatres, Inc., and in 1971 sold this subsidiary to Cinerama, Inc., for $21.5 million.[247] In 1977 Cinerama, Inc., reported that its RKO-Stanley Warner circuit had only 54 theaters.[248] These and another 28 theaters held by its Cinerama Theaters subsidiary had combined 1977 admission revenues of $34.7 million.[249]

Prices and Price Policies

Theater admission prices have risen with the general inflation. Average admission prices for 1978 were $2.34 for all theaters including drive-ins[250] and $2.40 for indoor theaters only.[251] Based on a 1967 price index of 100, the 1978 estimates have index numbers for indoor admission prices at 194, and for drive-ins it was 203.[252] While more recent data are not available for motion pictures alone, the index for all admissions to entertainment showed prices to have risen 25.1 percent between the end of 1977 and May 1981.[253]

The highly imperfect competition between pictures and the geographical distance set by distributors between theaters showing the same feature greatly limit competition between exhibitors. Consequently, interfirm price rivalry between exhibitors is very limited. Even without the distributor control of admission prices which existed before the Paramount Decrees, admission prices for films that are not hits and that leave theaters largely empty do not result in admission price cutting. The exhibitors generally consider demand to be relatively inelastic. The question is whether they have tested this hypothesis with price changes for films of different quality.

245. See "Glen Alden Corp., Stanley Warner Agree to Merge," *Wall Street Journal*, Aug. 7, 1967, p. 24; "Stanley Warner Corp., Glen Alden Corp. Boards Approve Merger Plan," *Wall Street Journal*, Aug. 21, 1967, p. 2.

246. Glen Alden Corp., Notice of Meeting, Nov. 21, 1967, p. 40.

247. *Moody's Industrial Manual* (1978), p. 1497.

248. Cinerama, Inc., 1977 Annual Report, p. 22.

249. Ibid., p. 23.

250. U.S. Dep't of Commerce, *1980 U.S. Industrial Outlook* (1980), p. 493.

251. Estimated from data in U.S. Dep't of Commerce, *1979 U.S. Industrial Outlook* (1979), p. 503.

252. Ibid.

253. U.S. Bureau of Labor Statistics, *CPI Detailed Report* (May 1981), p. 27.

Collusion of Exhibitors

As has been noted, the freer market for the distribution of motion pictures after the Paramount Decrees led to the adoption of competitive bidding by distributors in some markets. The negative reactions of exhibitors, who would assume a large part of the market uncertainties if required to bid with guaranteed minimum rentals, led to the discontinuance of most bidding. One must conclude that circuit bargaining power was sufficient to enable exhibitors to force negotiated licensing rather than competitive bidding.

In many markets exhibitors went further and actually colluded to divide the product of the various distributors among them. This was called a split.[254] Under the antitrust laws one would expect division of product to be treated the same way as division of territories. It should be illegal per se under the rule of the *Addyston* case.[255] The courts held otherwise.[256] This type of combination was ruled to be legal provided the distributors did not participate in the split and deny any exhibitor the opportunity to bid for films. The early approach of the antitrust division was to acquiesce in this view.[257] The leading case upholding the legality of exhibitor splits of product was the *Viking* case,[258] which was affirmed by an equally divided Supreme Court. Plaintiff theater owner sued the two local exhibitor circuits in Philadelphia and the six major distributors, maintaining that the division of product denied him access to a market. The district court directed a verdict for defendants, and this was affirmed on appeal. The plaintiff did not argue that all split systems were illegal, but that failure to include all exhibitors made them illegal. Thus, his argument was that failure to include all rivals in an anticompetitive scheme was the factor which made it illegal. The Court found against the plaintiff on this limited claim and, in the absence of evidence convincing the Court that the split unreasonably restricted the competitive market, the claim failed. The Court noted that the plaintiff had been able to license some pictures of each distributor in spite of the split.

The *Viking* precedent has caused later courts to rule for defendants

254. See Conant, *Antitrust in the Motion Picture Industry*, pp. 61–65.
255. *United States v. Addyston Pipe & Steel Co.*, 85 F. 271 (6th Cir. 1898), aff'd, 175 U.S. 211 (1899).
256. *Wilder Enterprises, Inc., v. Allied Artists Pictures Corp.*, 632 F.2d 1135, 1140 (4th Cir. 1980).
257. Gordon, "Horizontal and Vertical Restraints of Trade: The Legality of Motion Picture Splits under the Antitrust Laws," *Yale Law Journal* 75 (1965): 239, 240.
258. *Viking Theatre Corp. v. Paramount Film Distrib. Corp.*, 320 F.2d 285 (3d Cir. 1963), aff'd per curiam, 378 U.S. 123 (1964).

in other cases challenging splits. In *Seago v. North Carolina Theatres, Inc.*,[259] a summary judgment against the plaintiff exhibitor was granted. Even assuming the existence of the split and its effect of limiting competition among exhibitors, the court held it would not have damaged the plaintiff. The admitted fact was that the plaintiff was able to bid against any of the exhibitors in the split. The split merely reduced the number of rivals against whom the plaintiff would have to bid. Hence, there was no evidence in the depositions that the plaintiff was foreclosed from a competitive market.

A similar ruling occurred in the grant of summary judgment in *Dahl, Inc., v. Roy Cooper Co.*[260] The plaintiff had converted stores to establish an art theater. When he subsequently bid for first-run pictures, he found that most had been allocated to conventional theaters in a split. The evidence on discovery showed Dahl was allowed to bid against exhibitors in the split and did obtain a few first-run films. The court of appeals concluded, "There is no evidence that the agreement, although anticompetitive in character and as such subject to complaint by the distributors, served to exclude Dahl from the market or give it any antitrust claim."[261] The court referred to the *Goldwyn*[262] case, where a split of exhibitors without consent of the distributors had been held illegal.

In the *Cinema-Tex*[263] case of 1975, a district court held that a split agreement of all exhibitors in an area was illegal per se. The plaintiff had been dissatisfied with the films he got from the split and, when his financial position became untenable, he had sold out to one of the defendants. The court distinguished the *Viking* case, because the distributors were not a party to the split in this case and their solicitations of bids were ignored by exhibitors.[264] The plaintiff claimed he did not respond to the solicitations because he was afraid of reprisals by the members of the split. Despite the finding that the split was illegal per se, the defendants' motion for directed verdict was granted because the plaintiff failed to show that harm was proximately caused by the violation. The court of appeals upheld the ruling that the plaintiff had

---

259. 42 F.R.D. 267 (N.C. 1967), aff'd per curiam, 388 F. 2d 987 (4th Cir. 1967), cert. denied, 390 U.S. 959 (1968).
260. 448 F.2d 17 (9th Cir. 1971).
261. Ibid., p. 20.
262. *Twentieth Century-Fox Film Corp. v. Goldwyn*, 328 F.2d 190, 204 (9th Cir. 1964), cert. denied, 379 U.S. 880 (1964).
263. *Cinema-Tex Enterprises, Inc., v. Santikos Theaters, Inc.*, 414 F. Supp. 640 (W.D. Tex. 1975).
264. 414 F. Supp. at 643.

failed to show damage, but it reversed the conclusion that the split was illegal per se.[265] It held that conclusion was unnecessary in deciding the case.[266]

In *Admiral Theatre Corp. v. Douglas Theatre Co.*,[267] another directed verdict for defendants was affirmed on appeal. The plaintiff, operator of three theaters in Omaha, was never a member of the split adopted by the defendant exhibitors in operating fifteen theaters in the area. The plaintiff contended that the split had caused it to be successful in licensing only the lower-quality first-run films. The evidence showed it was able to obtain 60 percent of the pictures on which it made specific offers. The court found that in no case was a bid by plaintiff demonstrably superior to that of the competitor who successfully licensed a picture.[268] It also found that the distributor defendants did not acquiesce in the split and therefore did not make the bidding process a sham.[269]

The court rejected the argument that the split agreement of exhibitor defendants was illegal per se, although it held it did not have to make a final decision on the issue because plaintiffs failed to show legal injury, proximate cause, and damages sufficient to get to the jury. After an extensive review of the many indirect methods of price fixing discussed in the *Socony-Vacuum*[270] case, the court rejected its application here. "Thus while it appears that price fixing may not necessarily require a 'fixed price' or a 'fixed price range,' it is unclear whether an agreement to reduce competitive bidding in private business activities is sufficient to be categorized as price fixing and thus per se illegal."[271] This narrow view of *Socony-Vacuum* was followed by a ruling that, even if price effects were not the central issue, splits were not illegal per se. This was the rule of the *Viking* case.

Wilder Enterprises, Inc., v. Allied Artists Pictures Corp.[272] was one of the most recent in the series of cases attacking splits. The facts were similar to the *Admiral* case, and the trial court granted defendants' motion for a directed verdict.[273] The three defendant exhibitors in the Norfolk-Virginia Beach area admitted the existence of the split. The

---

265. *Cinema-Tex Enterprises, Inc., v. Santikos Theaters, Inc.*, 535 F.2d 932 (5th Cir. 1976).

266. Ibid., p. 933.

267. 585 F.2d 877 (8th Cir. 1978).

268. Ibid., p. 885.

269. Ibid., pp. 887–88.

270. *United States v. Socony-Vacuum Oil Co.*, 310 U.S. 150 (1940).

271. 585 F.2d at 887–88.

272. *Wilder Enterprises, Inc., v. Allied Artists Pictures Corp.*, 632 F.2d 1135 (4th Cir. 1980).

273. 1979-2 Trade Cas. ¶ 62,886 (E.D. Va. 1979).

court of appeals followed the standing law that an exhibitor does not have a claim against other film exhibitors who, without distributor involvement, split the films they will bid on. In this case, however, there was material evidence that six major distributors were participants in the split. Consequently, the court of appeals vacated the directed verdict, holding there was sufficient proof against defendants to warrant submission of the case to a jury. It also found sufficient proof of injury to be considered by a jury. Furthermore, evidence that the plaintiff was denied first-run films by the split was a sufficient basis for a futility theory of damages.

Critics of the decisions validating splits of available films by exhibitors have continued to argue that division of product, like division of territories, should be held illegal per se under section 1 of the Sherman Act.[274] The avowed purpose of splits is to end bidding in the free market for licensing of pictures. In April 1977 the antitrust divison finally announced that it was reversing its earlier view and now considered all splits illegal.[275] Notice to the exhibitors to cease the practice pointed out that splits were virtually indistinguishable from bid-rigging practices, which clearly violate the antitrust laws. The Justice Department indicated that if splits continued, it would bring prosecutions to stop the practice. The immediate response of large exhibitors was negative. General Cinema Corp., the largest circuit in the country, said it viewed the warning with regret but would abide by the ban.[276]

While most exhibitors terminated splits in response to the warning of the antitrust division, some did not. In August 1977 a Virginia theater company filed suit to challenge the government's new position on splits. The suit went to trial on May 6, 1980.[277] On that same day the Justice Department filed a civil suit against United Artists Theatre Circuit and three other exhibitors in Milwaukee charging illegal allocation of feature films between them.[278] While the defendants are confident that long usage will be important in sustaining their anticompetitive practice, few disinterested observers believe there can be a successful defense.

274. See Gordon, "Horizontal and Vertical Restraints of Trade."

275. "Movie Industry's Distribution Practices May Spark Antitrust Action, U.S. Warns," *Wall Street Journal*, April 4, 1977, p. 4.

276. "General Cinema Critical of U.S. Proposal to End 'Split' Exhibition Pacts", *Wall Street Journal*, April 5, 1977, p. 7.

277. "Justice Agency Sues to Block Allocating of Feature Films by Theater Companies," *Wall Street Journal*, May 6, 1980, p. 21. This action by Greenbrier Cinemas, Inc., on behalf of the National Associaton of Theater Owners, is unreported.

278. *United States v. Capitol Services, Inc.,* 1981-1 Trade Cas. ¶ 63,972 (E.D. Wis. 1981). See "Justice Agency Sues to Block Allocating of Feature Films by Theater Companies."

Conclusions

The unique character of each unit of input and output makes the motion picture industry one of highly imperfect competition. Within the constraints of these product and market structures, the Paramount Decrees had profound effects on the industry. Before the decrees, the five major firms controlled the industry by virtue of their control on first-run theaters and the system of reciprocity in access to each other's theaters administered by their illegal cartel. After the decrees, a much freer market was created. The *Paramount* defendants lost control of motion picture production. In the freer market, the independent producer, not the studio owners, proved to be the optimum production unit. The six remaining *Paramount* defendants which owned studios became primarily lessors of studio space and financiers of independent producers. On the distribution level, the Paramount Decrees did not promote the entry of significant new rivals. The concurrent rise of television and increased public interest in other recreational activities created great competititon for motion pictures. Mediocre pictures no longer had a market, and the output of motion pictures dropped sharply. Since the optimum domestic marketing firm structure required approximately twenty branch offices with screening rooms and sales forces, entry of new distributors in a declining total market was unlikely. In fact, MGM left motion picture distribution, and minor distributors have been merging in an effort to reach optimum size. The decrees have provoked greater competition in marketing by barring block booking and requiring that each picture be licensed to each theater separately.

On the exhibition level, the Paramount Decrees have had significant effects. Independent exhibitors, that majority not formerly part of the illegal cartel, have found themselves bidding for smaller supply of films in a more competitive market. They have sought ways to reduce the intensity of competition. One of these is the horizontal divison of product in their local markets, which is now under attack by the antitrust division. The five theater circuits of the major *Paramount* defendants have been especially impaired by the decrees. As population moved to the suburbs, they were prohibited from acquiring new theaters there without costly legal proceedings. All five circuits contracted in size, and four have been sold to new owners. While the input side of exhibition, the licensing of films, is now an open market, the output side does not seem highly competitive. Unique product and geographical separation of theaters in any metropolitan area results in little admission price rivalry between theaters.

21

ROBERT GUSTAFSON

"What's Happening to Our Pix Biz?" From Warner Bros. to Warner Communications Inc.

The common criticism of today's motion picture conglomerate organizations is that the film industry has become bland, and that it is run by outsiders who lack any traditional Hollywood respect for its history, institutions, and products. It is said that the old familiar studios are being turned into office buildings and parking lots by giant money-hungry corporations, in a sort of grim final chapter to Hollywood's reigning years as worldwide entertainment king. These ideas were shared by many film industry personnel who saw their formerly secure positions evaporate during the sixties and seventies when conglomerate and merger activity was at its height. It is certainly true that a new breed of entrepreneur now runs these organizations, but these executives and managers are no different from their predecessors the movie moguls in their interest in profits. The criticisms of the new organizations tend to ignore the business conditions that led to the creation of these entertainment-based conglomerates and disregard the operations of the motion picture industry.

As an example of a modern Hollywood film company and its role within a conglomerate, Warner Bros. and its operation as part of the world's largest leisure-time corporation, Warner Communications Inc. (WCI), will be examined. The significance of WCI is not that it represents the new American motion picture industry. No corporation

574

can portray the variety of organizational configurations that the Hollywood companies have taken on. Instead, WCI exemplifies the major trends in the motion picture business for the careful way in which it has constructed a broad yet synergistically connected set of entertainment-related subsidiaries. The examination of WCI will show that the evolution of Warner Bros. into WCI was in response to the serious financial risks facing Hollywood in the late 1960s. As a weak subsidiary, Warner Bros. was supported by WCI's recorded music and television operations. Although it continues to be supported by the other subsidiaries, Warner Bros. has simultaneously expanded its position to support mutually the other subsidiaries by becoming the producer of "software" for the music, television, publishing, and electronic games companies allied with it in WCI. Its role as a distributor has also changed, as the perennially risky theatrical distribution of films has become secondary to the more stable broadcast television sales of films and the lucrative new technologies of cable television and satellite transmission which also support the film industry. Warner Bros. has therefore found itself to be protected rather than devoured by its new conglomerate structure.

It was during the early sixties that Warner Bros. like many of the other major Hollywood studios appeared to be in its death throes. Jack L. Warner, president of the company and last of the founding brothers, found it expedient to sell off the television rights of 110 of its post-1948 films to Seven Arts Productions, Ltd., of Toronto which distributed them to American and Canadian television networks and stations.[1] While Warner's financial health grew worse as its theatrical income declined, Seven Arts grew more and more powerful as its television rental income expanded. The major factor in Seven Arts' financial success was that by 1966, the three American television networks had discovered that the presentation of feature films during prime time could very often attract a larger percentage of the viewing public than could regular television programs. The networks found that even if a film were a disaster at the box office, it could attract a substantial number of television viewers. If the film had been a hit, it could easily win the Nielsen ratings.[2]

Because of this great interest in films by the networks, there was a dramatic increase in the amount of money they were willing to pay for leasing motion pictures. As a result, the book value of the film libraries of most motion picture companies increased to two or three

1. *Variety*, July 2, 1960, p. 4.
2. *Wall Street Journal*, January 5, 1966, p. 25; July 26, 1966, p. 10.

times the market price of their stock. This unequal relationship was widely recognized as a strong lure for attempted takeovers by other organizations. Furthermore, the attraction of this lure was intensified by the belief that these new television-related profits would be stable, independent of the whims of the public at the box office.[3]

At the same time, it was rumored that Jack L. Warner was retiring and as the largest stockholder in Warner Bros. was considering selling his holdings. Fears that "outsiders" would buy the studio were widely published, but when Jack Warner announced in November 1966 that he had indeed chosen to retire and sell his shares to Seven Arts, an "outsider" that had no glamorous traditions and was just a "conduit for material to the tiny screen," these fears grew shrill. When Seven Arts bought out the rest of the Warner Bros. stockholders and took complete possession of the company, *Variety's* headline worried, "What's Happening to Our Pix Biz?"[4]

Within a year after its creation, the new organization Warner Bros.-Seven Arts, Ltd., expanded its film library to include 122 Warner, 486 Twentieth Century-Fox, 400 Allied Artists, and 215 Universal films for distribution to television in the United States, Canada, and Mexico. It also acquired the Atlantic Recording Corporation to augment its Warner and Reprise record labels.[5] Yet during this same period, the *Wall Street Journal* already considered "Warner Bros.-Seven Arts to be a prime candidate for takeover."[6] Such prophecies about another buyout so soon after the initial takeover were well founded. The attraction of Warner Bros.-Seven Arts' solid position in the distribution of motion pictures to television, plus its motion picture, television, and musical recording production facilities, was so strong that many corporations seriously bid for it.

Kinney National Services, Inc., a New York-based conglomerate engaged primarily in car rental, parking lots, construction, and funeral homes made the most serious bid. Murmurs about "outsiders" taking over Warner became positive shrieks as a funeral home and parking lot operator absorbed this glamorous institution on July 9, 1969. The acquisition was the brainchild of Steven Ross who, as an executive trainee in his father-in-law's Riverside Memorial Chapel funeral home in Manhattan, had expanded the business into Kinney National, which included such other diverse operations as publishing, merchandizing tie-ins, and creative talent management. The acquisition of Warner Bros.-Seven Arts was the direct result of Ross' purchase of the Ashley

3. *Barrons*, October 24, 1966, p. 9.
4. *Variety*, November 16, 1966, p. 3; November 23, 1966, p. 5.
5. *Wall Street Journal*, October 19, 1967, p. 22.
6. *Wall Street Journal*, November 27, 1968, p. 11.

Famous Agency, when Ted Ashley, the agency's head, let it be known that he was seeking an arrangement with a much larger organization through which he could "get financial support for new entertainment ventures." After the buyout of the talent agency, Ross explained that the acquisition was made to "use Ashley's show business expertise, but it isn't clear just where. But we feel confident about the leisure field's future."[7]

Before buying Warner Bros.-Seven Arts, Ross made four other leisure industry acquisitions to utilize Ashley's experience. These included National Periodical Publications, the publishers of more than fifty comic magazines including *Superman, Batman,* and *Mad Magazine*; Independent News, the distributor of dozens of publications ranging from *Playboy* to *Family Circle*; the Licensing Corporation of America, a merchandizing tie-in and personality-licensing agency whose clients include all the teams of major league baseball and the Players Associations of the National Football League and National Hockey League; and Panavision, the manufacturer of professional motion picture cameras and lenses. It was this synergistic combination of talent management, entertainment licensing, and entertainment-related manufacturing that led to Ross' interest in purchasing Warner Bros.-Seven Arts.

With the takeover of the company in 1969, Ted Ashley was named the new chairman and chief executive officer of Warner Bros. After five months of study, Ashley released the results of his studio-restructuring plan. To reduce the operating costs of the Burbank studio, personnel reductions were made in the executive, production, technical, and clerical departments. For example, six of the seven members of Warner's story department were let go. Furthermore, most employees of Warner's New York headquarters were either moved to California or dismissed. The Ashley management team did remain "totally committed to the reactivation of all studio facilities" and announced that, with Columbia Pictures, they would form a company to operate jointly the twenty-three sound stages at Burbank and use Columbia's fifty-acre ranch. Columbia and Warner would not only share studio space, but also rent their space and facilities from the new consolidated company, the Burbank Studios, to third-party motion picture and television production companies. The profits from this leasing would be shared by both, but each company would operate and conduct its activities completely independently of the other as in the past.[8]

While Ashley reshaped the motion picture and television production

7. *Fortune*, April 1974, p. 124.
8. *Variety*, June 9, 1971, p. 3.

and distribution divisions, Ross added more companies to Kinney's leisure-time branch. For example, in 1970, Sterling Publications, the publisher of nineteen movie and television fan magazines was acquired; Coronet Communications, the publisher of paperback books, was bought out and later renamed Warner Books; the Elektra Corporation, manufacturer and packager of popular musical recordings, became a subsidiary; and to strengthen the Warner, Elektra, and Atlantic record labels, the WEA Corporation (Warner/Elektra/Atlantic) was created to distribute records to wholesale and retail outlets, coordinate orders, supervise all shipping and bill collecting, and devise national advertising strategies and in-store promotions for its records and prerecorded tapes.

The next year, Kinney's entertainment branch grew to include three large cable television operations which made Kinney the owner of one of the largest cable systems in the United States; and Goldmark Communications whose chairman, Dr. Peter Goldmark, the inventor of the long-playing record, was assigned the task of "develop[ing] electronic video recording for the home, cable television applications, and electronic publishing."[9]

As Kinney's entertainment subsidiaries grew more and more independent of the original divisions of funeral homes, construction, and maintenance, financial analysts on Wall Street declared that this was a mature case of "the strain of the conglomerate" and warned of possible problems, especially as Kinney's top executives grew farther and farther apart in their interests and as investors began to conceive of Kinney's diversity in similarly negative terms. To put an end to these tensions, Kinney was eventually split into two entirely separate corporations: National Kinney, the construction and maintenance firm, and Warner Communications Inc. (WCI), the entertainment group. Ross was elected to head the leisure organization; now both he and the other executives of the film, music, television, and publishing divisions were able to devote their full attention and financial resources to their plans of operating and acquiring entertainment-related companies within an interlocking system of research, production, promotion, and distribution.[10]

During the late 1970s, Warner Communications continued to acquire and expand its leisure industry companies. For instance, it set up a London-based television production company, WB-TV, Ltd., that would arrange co-productions throughout Britain and Europe; it ac-

9. *Broadcasting*, June 10, 1972, p. 55.
10. *New York Times*, July 1, 1972, p. 24.

quired Atari, Inc., the manufacturer and distributor of video games; and in Columbus, Ohio, Warner Cable Communications presented QUBE, the most sophisticated cable television system in the world, which offered ten channels for motion pictures, ten for television programs, and ten two-way interactive channels which allowed viewers to register their reactions with broadcasters over commercial content, to participate in talk shows and political debates, and to buy displayed products. Warner Cable later took on the American Express Company as a full partner in the renamed Warner Amex Cable Communications Company, because of its considerable experience with computer technology and consumer credit—the fundamental skills for selling products via television. Warner Communications bought the New York Cosmos Soccer Club, Warner Bros. acquired David Wolper Productions, the producer of theatrical and television documentaries, docudramas, and entertainment programs. Warner Communications bought the Knickerbocker Toy Company, the manufacturer and owner of the soft toy rights to Raggedy Ann, Holly Hobbie, "Sesame Street" characters, Warner cartoon characters, and all Walt Disney characters.[11]

From these acquisitions and expansions, WCI has become a conglomerate which is organized according to the principle of multiple profit centers which reinforce each other in an interlocking and financially conservative pattern that is designed not only to generate revenues and profits, but to keep such monies within the corporation. In order to understand how such a system works, it is helpful to refer to the following chart which shows the divisional arrangement of Warner Communications today.

The structure of WCI should not be viewed as favoring motion pictures as the primary source of revenues. No division is specifically designed to hold that rank. In the 1970s, the music subsidiaries received the most income, but in the early 1980s, it was the electronic game and home computer company Atari that held that role, with cable television poised for that position in the second half of the 1980s. All subsidiaries within WCI are structured so that an increase in one area can aid the others. A hit film can certainly lead to a television program, as was the case when Warner's *Alice Doesn't Live Here Anymore* inspired the even more successful "Alice" series for Warner Television. Warner books can lead to films. For example, the publication of *All the President's Men* led to the eminently successful Warner film, while the Warner's publication *Scruples* led to a Warner miniseries. Warner comic book characters have made many motion pictures, the

11. *Moody's Industrial Manual*, 1978, p. 4329.

WARNER COMMUNICATIONS INC. (WCI)

Recorded Music & Music Publishing
  Warner Bros. Records
  Atlantic Records
  Elektra/Asylum/Nonesuch Records
  WEA Corporation
  WEA International
  WEA Manufacturing
  Warner Bros. Music Publishing

Filmed Entertainment
  Warner Bros.
  Warner Bros. Television
  Licensing Corporation of America
  Panavision
  Warner Bros. Distributing Corporation
  David Wolper Productions
  Warner Home Video

Publishing & Related Distribution
  Warner Books
  Warner Publisher Service
  Mad Magazine
  DC Comics

Cable Communications (50% owned)
  Warner Amex Cable Communications
  Warner Amex Satellite Entertainment Company

Consumer Electronics & Toys
  Atari
  Malibu Grand Prix
  Knickerbocker Toys

Other Operations
  New York Cosmos Soccer Club
  Warner Cosmetics
  Warner Theatre Productions
  Franklin Mint

most popular being the triple *Superman* films, which in turn have resulted in even more Superman products, including an Atari game, Knickerbocker dolls, and greater licensing of the Superman logo which is controlled by Warner's Licensing Corporation of America. Strong sales of a record under the Warner label, for instance a Rolling Stones album, can easily lead to Warner-produced television specials and video productions for Warner Amex Cable's music television channel (MTV), to Warner books, Warner-distributed magazines, or Warner films featuring the musicians. An increase in the number of Warner Amex cable television systems strengthens the other WCI divisions through a gain in the number of outlets for motion picture and television presentations and, in the long run, leads to potentially more production for Warner Bros. rental of the studios, and sales for Panavision.

Unlike many other conglomerates, WCI does shift after-tax earnings and profits from one area of the organization to another. This is not done in many diversified firms simply because it involves taking money from a well-run division and putting it into one that is losing. However, with the high degree of compatability between Warner's products, the shifting of funds between them functions to support the interlocking arrangement of subsidiaries.[12]

This arrangement, especially regarding motion pictures, was very much a product of the late sixties when the music business was expanding exponentially, while many believed the motion picture business was dying. To make certain that Warner Bros. would remain a producer of motion pictures and not just a film library for television distribution, Ted Ashley purchased the rights to film the rock festival Woodstock as one of the first motion pictures made after Kinney's takeover of the company. When their subsidiary Atlantic Records released a double-album set of the music performed at Woodstock, Warner released the film. The enormous success of both the record and the motion picture proved the value of the interlocking arrangement as a potentially great risk reducer.

Ever since the experience of Woodstock, Warner's theatrical films have been regularly protected and supported by other divisions within WCI. It is often as if the film company were the most frail of the subsidiaries. This kind of protection extends to include the financing arrangements for motion picture production. Many films released by Warner Bros. are financed internally by WCI, which makes loans to its film company for an eighteen-month period during which Warner can use these funds as it sees fit. The minimum monthly payments to WCI are pegged at 10 percent of the film company's share of each picture, or are set according to flexible schedules created for special circumstances. Thus, the financing of Warner Bros. productions by WCI tends to seal capital within the corporate divisions and gives the film company the advantages of on-the-spot repayment flexibility.[13]

12. Warner Communications, Inc. , 1977 Annual Report, pp. 24–25.
13. *Variety*, January 21, 1970, p. 7; Warner Communications, Inc., 1977 Annual Report, pp. 54–55.

However, most films released by Warner Bros. are only partially financed by WCI. Private investors, individual filmmakers, and banks, for instance, often finance productions that the Warner Bros. Distributing Corporation handles for a fee of about 30 percent of the box office gross. These motion pictures are also often produced at the Burbank Studios or at Warner's newest facilities, the former Goldwyn Studios, now renamed the Warner Hollywood Studios. All of these facilities lease Panavision optical equipment, further adding to WCI's income. Many individuals and organizations who choose to use the Warner production studios, back lot, and distribution network are increasingly attracted to Warner because of the ease of access to ancillary markets through WCI's other subsidiaries, rather than as in the past to just its theatrical distribution chain.

Although it is the theatrical market that generally sets the asset value of each film for the posttheatrical markets, it is the television rights that remain the single most important factor in the revenues generated by a motion picture. After all, it was the television rights to films that had originally attracted Seven Arts to purchase Warner Bros., and later led to Kinney's acquisition of them both. Since then, the various configurations of television distribution continue to affect profoundly motion picture production and distribution.

For example, the promotion of a Warner film is no longer based on traditional patterns. Instead, each film receives individualized treatment. WCI's experience with television ratings, record promotion, and advertisements for consumer products has been instrumental in diversifying promotional techniques. The appeal of the film is tested in sample markets according to demographic studies. QUBE's two-way interactive cable television channels have already been used for just such experiments. From these studies, each motion picture is assigned a specific advertising strategy involving the press and radio and/or television, while it is likewise assigned to specific theaters classified according to size and location.

With the three *Superman* films, for instance, the decision was made to go broad, that is, to mount a massive television, radio, magazine, and newspaper advertising campaign during the opening playdates of many theaters. This enabled each of the films to receive substantial box office revenues almost immediately. The full-scale advertising campaigns were feasible because the films' characters were familiar and because major box office stars were featured cast members.

There is a second approach to marketing a film for motion pictures whose stories are generally unfamiliar to the public. For example, with

Dog Day Afternoon, Warner Distributing relied on selected preview screenings to test carefully the audience's interest, then presented a limited number of television advertisements in only the largest American cities where the film was first released. Only after the initial reaction to *Dog Day Afternoon* had been judged as positive was the film released nationally. This very cautious delayed release allowed Warner Distributing to receive revenues from theaters that otherwise would not have originally accepted the film.

Another technique is designed for those films whose initial box office reception is very mediocre. In the case of *Blade Runner*, Warner quickly pulled the film from theatrical distribution, and then released it on pay television through its Warner Amex Satellite Entertainment Network on the Movie Channel, and on videocassette for rental or purchase through its Warner Home Video outlets.

These three approaches of saturation booking, guarded release, and rapid pullback reveal clearly the change from the old first-, second-, and third-run release schedules of the past. It is in part because of the greater revenues being paid for the television rights to films that these new forms of theatrical distribution have arisen. With higher and higher sums being paid by the television networks for motion pictures, plus the growth of pay television with its demand for recent films, many new organizations have entered the motion picture industry. With this increased competition, more money has been spent to advertise and promote films. Simultaneously, the television networks have received higher and higher sums for advertising time a fact that has brought about further expense and greater risk for theatrical distribution.

Many of the new film companies and independent filmmakers have reversed the traditional sales pattern with respect to the rights to their motion pictures by selling off the television rights first and then later contracting with a major organization to distribute them theatrically. Those independents who distribute through Warner Bros., for example the Ladd Company with *Body Heat*, have found that the order of the sale of rights has to some extent become a moot question. The structure of WCI is designed to keep the rewards from a film's ancillary rights within the organization, whether the film was independently produced, jointly produced, or internally produced. Theatrical, pay cable, network television, and domestic or international television syndication are merely variations rather than competitors within the distribution chains of the Warner subsidiaries. Music rights, book rights, serial rights, and toy and game rights can likewise be put into action by still more Warner subsidiaries. In fact, the production of motion pictures at Warner Bros. is now often referred to within the company as "the creation of software," to supply the Warner television, musical recording, publishing, and electronic games divisions.[14]

To some extent, WCI has relegated the theatrical market to a subordinate position in its operations. Warner Bros. now sees its primary responsibility as "bring[ing] movies conveniently and economically into the home, [which] will allow the industry to reach the enormous market that rarely, if ever, attends movie theatres."[15] The transition from a theatrical market to new nontheatrical markets has also been the result of new technologies such as home video equipment, subscription pay networks, advertiser-supported cable systems, and two-way cable television with its ability to offer films on a pay-per-view basis. The organization of WCI is such that this transition has already occurred, with WCI maintaining control over the material. Warner Home Video, Warner Amex Cable's development of the Movie Channel, and QUBE are just three examples.

As in the past, the key to the longevity and strength of the motion picture industry has been its distribution branch. In the case of Warner Bros., this branch has now combined with its powerful recorded music distribution organization, WEA Incorporated, which also distributes Atari games and home computers. In particular, WEA distributes feature films from the Warner Bros. film library as Warner Home Video VHS and Beta format videocassettes to record stores, electronics stores, home appliance centers, and other outlets including the Fotomat kiosks

The Movie Channel distributes via satellite uninterrupted, unedited feature films to its subscribers twenty-four hours per day. Because the volume of material is so large, the motion pictures presented include films acquired from other companies besides those from the Warner library.

QUBE possesses the ability to present motion pictures on a pay-per-view basis, making it the virtual in-home mate of theatrical distribution. But in this case the distributor does not have to share the box office gross with any exhibitor, a situation that delights Warner and terrifies theater owners. Even though QUBE's role as a direct rival to the motion picture theater is still in its infancy, its potential has aroused a great deal of speculation about the fate of theatrical distribution. However, QUBE as developed by Warner Amex is much more than just another new form of film distribution. It is the promotional and technological tool that directly aids the entire WCI organization. It

14. Warner Communications, Inc., 1981 Annual Report, p. 25.
15. Ibid.

helps the Warner Amex Cable companies in the franchising process with local communities by generating public interest. In turn, expansion of cable television leads to increased demand for films, television programs, specials, and children's shows to present to subscribers, which helps to increase production and distribution for Warner Bros. as well as give business opportunities to WCI's licensing, manufacturing, and publishing subsidiaries. Again, a pattern of reinforcement and internal promotion/protection emerges since this arrangement works even without Warner Amex's owning the cable systems. Any increase in the number of multiple-channel systems can aid Warner Bros. More options for the subscribers means greater revenues for cable system operators and program suppliers. WCI is both.

Because of these interconnecting distribution chains between WCI subsidiaries, an unsuccessful film can cause serious repercussions along a wide section of the entire conglomerate. It is no wonder then that Warner is increasingly careful in selecting which films to undertake based on this risk—and potential. All Warner films generate revenues for Warner Distributing, the Movie Channel, Warner Home Video, Warner Amex Cable, and Warner Television Distribution. The films can spawn all kinds of new products for Warner Television, Atari, Warner Records, and Warner Books. The various forms of risk reduction are geared to gaining revenues in conjunction with the success of the film, but the availability of associated products is not necessarily based on the success of the film because many are created and marketed simultaneously with it. For instance, the common notice on a newspaper advertisement for a Warner-distributed film often says, "Read the Warner Paperback," or "Sound Track Available on Warner Bros. Records." Therefore, all the more care is taken in selecting the "software." The notion that the roller coaster financial cycles of the motion picture industry could be smoothed out by employing additional subsidiaries to produce and market related products may often be viable, but it nevertheless contains the potential for broad failures and the crashing of fads.

From past failures, WCI like the other major entertainment organizations is becoming less bold in promoting a property simultaneously across subsidiaries, but rather is allowing it to grow across subsidiaries once success has been initially proven. Probably the most familiar item of evidence for this is the banner on a bestselling book, "Now a Major Motion Picture."

Another corporate maneuver aimed at risk reduction through property growth is WCI's creation of a subsidiary to finance Broadway plays. Warner Theatre Productions assists the Warner motion picture division by testing the economic potential of properties much earlier than would be otherwise possible. Even more important, as the producer of a play, Warner Theatre Productions possesses the film rights to that play and thereby grants Warner Bros. a route of easy access to the acquisition of successful Broadway properties as source material for motion pictures. Warner Theatre Productions also, and no less importantly, retains the musical recording rights, pay television rights, broadcasting rights, and home video rights to each of its productions and transfers these rights to the other appropriate WCI subsidiaries once the play has proven itself worthy of expansion across allied markets.

The threat of widespread failure is precisely why the motion picture business at Warner today is so different from that of the past. Those who feared that the conglomerate takeover of Warner would forever change the traditional Hollywood studio were correct. Independent and joint financing ventures are welcomed; the studio facilities are rented out; the films are produced according to a wide variety of formats, including feature-length motion pictures, television series, and television miniseries; video production is promoted and also includes television series as well as special products such as the video versions of contemporary music for Music Television; the ancillary rights are fully utilized within the organization; and most important, the distribution chains cover a wide variety of methods that embrace television and the new technologies while downplaying theatrical distribution. Those who feared these changes did not foresee that the new conglomerate structure would result in a new flexibility, more complex than the old vertically integrated studio system, but one that nevertheless protects its motion picture industry.

Supplement:
Warner Communications'
International Operations

In 1982, Warner Communications had a banner year: revenues hit just under $4 billion, netting an income of $258 million or $3.96 a share for each of the 65 million shares outstanding. It was an all-time earnings record for the company.

The following essay, reprinted from WCI's *Annual Report 1982,* highlights the company's international operations. Overseas sales came to nearly $1 billion, with the prospect for the future looking even brighter. As WCI Chairman Steven J. Ross confidently announced, "Consumers around the world will continue to devote a substantial, and in many cases a growing, portion of their income to 'entertainment.' "

In celebrating WCI's accomplishments, the essay is aimed at stockholders and prospective investors. It proudly proclaims that Warner Communications is among the top American corporations in terms of world-wide business and has penetrated 166 markets, touching the lives of countless people in countries as varied as Thailand, Kenya, New Guinea, and Japan.

This essay is important because it documents the corporate philosophy guiding WCI's operations. The widespread distribution of Warner motion pictures, TV programs, and computer games; the synergy created by WCI's organizational structure; and the flow of talent between foreign and domestic markets are presented in a positive light, and indeed have a profound effect on the profitability of Warner Communications. But the student of film may also want to know how these operations influence the nature of entertainment and its impact on cultures, including our own, issues that the essay steadfastly avoids.

Warner Communications Annual Report 1982

The geography of the world has been recast with every era in history. Today, we are said to reside in one "global village," and in a sense this is true: words and pictures, people and ideas, raw materials and finished goods flow essentially uninterruptedly between countries and across oceans. Warner Communications plays an active part in this exchange; but the world is not so easily reduced to a single homogeneous entity. To speak of the "international marketplace," in fact, is to oversimplify what is actually a rich diversity of individual markets.

The impact of Warner Communications' activities around the world illustrates both the diversity of the international markets and the unity of the global village. There is a natural demand for entertainment the world over, and WCI's products have become an integral part of many different cultures in a variety of ways. A Clint Eastwood movie in the form of a videocassette might be rented and enjoyed at home by a family in Munich, while on a tributary of the Amazon River, viewing the same movie becomes an inherently tribal experience that borders on magic. A new Donna Summer recording might provide the beat in a Tokyo nightclub, while in Kenya it becomes an exotic sound heard by local villagers on a battery-powered record player.

The rapid growth of Warner Communications domestically has been mirrored by the growth of its international operations over the past five years. Taken by itself, WCI's international revenues in 1982, including exports, approximate those for the entire company as little as five years ago. WCI's international sales are more than three times the comparable figure for 1977. The relatively untapped potential of many foreign markets indicates substantial growth in the years ahead.

Warner Communications, Inc. *Annual Report 1982,* pp. 41–70.

In a small village in England, a local resident decides to purchase an Atari home computer to keep track of his finances and to challenge him in chess. He might notice that Atari is "a Warner Communications Company," but he doesn't realize the extent to which WCI touches his life. His favorite sport is football, or what Americans call soccer; he once saw the Cosmos in London, little realizing that this famous

In Castle Coombe, west of London, a resident makes his way home with a new Atari 400 computer. Atari 400's and 800's are among the best-selling home computers in England.

team was part of WCI. His eight-year-old grandson just asked to see *Superman III*, a Warner Bros. film, as soon as it arrives at the cinema in Reading, while his son and daughter-in-law drove to Wembley Stadium the previous weekend to see Warner Bros. artists Fleetwood Mac in concert. His wife's collection of porcelain plates commemorating the Chelsea Flower Show and his prized collection of "Greatest Big Band" records came from the Franklin Mint Ltd. And, a year earlier, all the generations of his family joined together to watch the Warner Bros. Television mini-series *Roots II* on the telly.

There is a continuous flow of products and ideas between WCI's domestic and foreign operations. A hit video game, record, film or television series in the US will eventually make its way to any number of countries. Sometimes this distribution is immediate—it is not unheard of for an album or single to be number one in as many as 15 different countries simultaneously. Conversely, it can often take two years or more for a film to appear in all of the major world markets. New releases must be dubbed or subtitled for each new language and advertising campaigns must often be developed to suit individual countries, employing measures ranging from placards on a double-decker bus in London to hand-painted posters on a "ballyhoo truck" in rural Thailand.

Near Ayutthaya, the ancient Thai capital north of Bangkok, a "ballyhoo truck" decorated with hand-painted posters and equipped with a loudspeaker is used to advertise the recent arrival of Clint Eastwood's *Every Which Way But Loose*.

WCI's international activities are not confined to marketing domestic products to a worldwide audience; the creative output of artists from all over the world is also brought to eager audiences in the US and abroad. While the music charts in America have long reflected the importance of British rock and pop artists, such international artists as Jamaican reggae star Bob Marley and the Swedish supergroup Abba have also had significant impact in the US. The 1982 Academy Award-winning film *Chariots of Fire* was an English production, distributed in the US by Warner Bros. People all over the world have submitted original computer programs to the Atari Program Exchange, and one of Atari's most popular coin-operated video games, *Pole Position*, was licensed from the Japanese company Namco, Ltd., also the creators of the phenomenally successful *Pac-Man*. *Cats*, the Broadway hit for co-producer The Geffen Company, first came to life on the London stage. This creative exchange is the lifeblood of WCI, and underscores the company's global scope.

Although Warner Communications has long been a leader in the US in almost all of its businesses—from comic books to home computers— its presence abroad is in most cases much more recent. The video game business, which Atari pioneered in America, is proving very popular in a foreign market which contains nearly twice as many television households as the US. The international potential for cable television, which is just now beginning to be introduced on a worldwide scale, is significant, and Warner Bros. possesses the extensive software library to become a beneficiary of this industry's development. Panavision, through the efforts of its worldwide network of representatives, has become an increasingly frequent part of film productions around the world in the past few years; its state-of-the-art cameras were used recently to film an American television series on location in China.

Because music is a universal language, the same recording from a WEA International–distributed artist can be heard in an apartment in Paris, on a ranch in Australia, and in a Massi village at the foot of Mt. Kilimanjaro. New technological advances have important implications for worldwide music sales, especially if piracy and unauthorized taping can be controlled. The recent widespread availability of relatively inexpensive personal cassette players makes the playback of recorded music suddenly accessible to people around the world for whom it was once prohibitively expensive. This continuing increase in the size of the international audience for music should stimulate the sales of prerecorded music in a wide variety of foreign markets.

Over the centuries, games—from the physical competition of the

A sign in front of the offices of Atari's Hong Kong distributor contributes to the neon landscape of Granville Road, in the Kowloon section of the city.

Greek Olympics to the cerebral combat of chess—have always been an important part of daily life. It is perhaps not surprising, then, that when semiconductor technology finally turned its attention to games, a game-playing phenomenon unprecedented in history was created.

Atari—the name itself was borrowed from the ancient Japanese strategy game GO—introduced its first electronic video game in 1972, and set in motion a series of events that has redefined our concept of play. The fascination with arcade and home video games that swept the US has similarly occurred in many countries around the world in which video games have been introduced. Although the development of international markets is several years behind that of the domestic market, Atari believes that a significant percentage of the 150 million television households outside of the US will someday own a video game. In order to fulfill growing worldwide demand, Atari opened a manufacturing facility in Taiwan in 1982 and is currently renting facilities in Ireland in advance of opening its own operations in 1983. And as for the games themselves, they have a universal appeal that transcends cultural barriers; thousands of participants from more than 20 countries competed in an international Atari *Pac-Man* contest this year which culminated in a playoff in Paris, where victory was achieved by a 16-year-old boy from England.

A simple electrical outlet in a corner bistro in Paris or an airport in Auckland enables it instantly to become home to a state-of-the-art video game machine, and it is in such locations that most people experience for the first time the unique thrill of playing a video game. Despite restrictive legislation in some countries, the foreign market continues to be an important source of coin-operated game sales as well as a significant origin of game designs themselves. Atari, which has achieved an enviable record of success developing its coin-operated and home video games internally, also has long-term relationships with Japanese game developers which have resulted in such hit US arcade game licenses as *Pole Position* and *Dig Dug* from Namco; such popular home games as *Pac-Man* and *Galaxian* from Namco and *Space Invaders* from Taito; and for Atari home computers, the license to the successful *Donkey Kong* and *Donkey Kong Jr.* from Nintendo. As a result of the proven skill of its own research and design staff and its international licensing agreements, Atari will remain a leader in the coin-operated game industry. This is significant not only because of the importance of the coin-operated industry itself, but also because popular coin-operated video games continue to become the most successful home cartridges around the world.

In Hong Kong—where children have learned to add and subtract with the abacus for thousands of years—students in more than 500 secondary schools will soon have access to a new learning tool which promises to make even the abacus obsolete. Atari's local distributor in Hong Kong was recently awarded a contract to supply the city's school system with home computers, thanks in part to the company's extensive catalog of educational software. When the program is complete, as many as 5,000 Atari computers will be in use in the school system.

By the end of 1982, France's Club Med had established computer workshops exclusively using Atari home computers in eight locations—from Spain, Guadeloupe and the Bahamas to Malaysia, New Caledonia and Senegal. Although the idea that anyone would prefer the intricacies of computer programming to a Club Med beach was initially greeted with skepticism by Club counselors, the program has become of the most popular activities among Club Med vacationers, and workshops are rapidly being established in new locations around the world. Ultimately, visitors will be able to purchase Atari hardware and software at Clubs around the world.

Whether they first discover computers in a classroom or on a Club

Atari was recently awarded a contract to provide 500 Hong Kong schools with computers.

Med vacation, people all over the world are exploring a new universe opened up by the home computer. Idealists once dreamed of creating one universal language—Esperanto. That dream is today on its way to becoming a reality, but the global tongue will more likely be Basic, Pascal or Logo—the languages of the microcomputer.

As communication over vast distances has become simpler, so too has the ability of one culture to influence another. Nowhere is this more apparent than in music. The Rolling Stones derived much of their early inspiration from such great American rhythm and blues artists as Muddy Waters, Ray Charles and Chuck Berry. Reggae, a musical form which itself is a Jamaican hybrid of black American pop and Caribbean rhythms, has become popular throughout the world; the work of such artists as Bob Marley and Black Uhuru has influenced countless musicians. Today, African pop music is having increasing influence on such innovators as Talking Heads in the US and Peter Gabriel in England. Such cross-fertilization occurs largely as a result of the worldwide availability of records and prerecorded tapes. WEA International's global scope is revealed by its increasing activity in recording local artists from all over the world. This artist development opens up new opportunities for WEA International abroad, and inevitably becomes a source of world music for audiences in the US.

Unlike the classical virtuoso, whose technique and knowledge of the repertoire are achieved through years of formal training, the popular musician's classroom is often the street. The musical lessons are handed down informally and the style is honed through experience and intuition. When Simon and Garfunkel returned to Paris as part of their 1982 reunion tour, Paul Simon told an audience of 75,000 fans that the first time he was in Paris, he was chased out of the Metro by gendarmes for singing and passing the hat. Those few who graduate from the street to the concert stage often do so thanks to exceptional songwriting ability. The responsibility of protecting the fruit of the artist's creativity is the music publisher's and Warner Bros. Music has consistently demonstrated its ability to bring its composers to a wider audience, as well as discover new talent ready for success. Warner Bros. Music has achieved particularly significant results in Europe. In London, one of the creative centers of the music business, such important new artists as the Clash, Human League, Soft Cell and Madness have been signed by the company and have gone on to major success within the past several years.

One reason for the success of Warner Communications internationally is the fact that its products know no geographical boundaries. The motion picture is a powerful case in point: all over the world there

The première of *Superman II* at the Mt. Hagen Haus Piksa—"picture house" in pidgin English—is a special event, drawing crowds from all over the Highlands of Papua New Guinea.

is a fascination with the magic of the cinema. It is a magic that does not depend upon literal translation, only on the moviemaker's skill at conjuring illusions and making them appear real, for the moving image conveys its own message in a manner that has new resonance for every different audience. In Papua New Guinea, children and adults marvel at Superman's ability to fly and cheer the antics of Terence Hill and Bud Spencer, sometimes without understanding a word of dialogue. And the images are taken seriously: during the climatic battle in one particular film, a Goroka tribesman was quick to avenge the killing of an African warrior, hurling his six-foot hunting spear through the assailant's image on the screen.

Though motion pictures produced and distributed by the Hollywood studios continue to attract the largest worldwide audiences, there has been a substantial increase in foreign independent film production around the world in the past few years. Warner Bros. becomes involved in the production of foreign features—particularly those with an English language version—when there appears to be a significant international market for a specific project. One result of such activity was Warner Bros.' involvement in Australian director George Miller's two *Mad Max* films, which were originally acquired for foreign distribution only. Both films have been successful internationally, and *The Road Warrior*, the second of the *Mad Max* films, ultimately proved very popular in the US as well. Warner Bros.' international operation not only distributes domestic feature films on a worldwide basis, but also is on the lookout around the world for new sources of product for the US market.

Since the introduction of television 35 years ago, the TV screen has served as the portal to a changing world. It has brought the Apollo moon landing and *Roots* and Bugs Bunny into the living room, and its cable and computer-directed future stretches beyond the imagination. The development of television in the US has in essence been successfully duplicated throughout the world, and many of WCI's activities—from Atari games to home video—are predicated on the worldwide availability of television.

Television has also had an increasingly profound effect on the motion picture industry as a new outlet for existing films and original television productions. Warner Bros. Television is one of the most active producers of television series and specials, and its television distribution company provides the world with feature films, TV series and other TV material. The company's product appears in 104 countries in 24 languages, from Ecuador, Iceland and Qatar to the Ivory Coast, Barbados and Thailand. David Wolper and Stan Margulies'

A Buddhist monk watches the Warner Bros. television series *Kung Fu* as he maintains his nightly temple vigil guarding the interior courtyard of Bangkok's Wat Saket.

landmark production of *Roots* was sold in 73 countries alone, and such popular WB-TV series as *The Waltons, Kung Fu, Wonder Woman,* and the cartoons *Roadrunner* and *Bugs Bunny* have generated substantial revenues for WCI in numerous countries around the world.

An avid moviegoer in Munich missed the theatrical exhibition of Clint Eastwood's *Firefox*; as the evening manager of the local *Biergarten,* he is regularly frustrated by the fact that the television has stopped broadcasting when he gets home at three a.m.; and one of his favorite films is Alfred Hitchcock's *Dial M for Murder*, a picture he hasn't had the opportunity to see in years. Until recently, his schedule and interests had to correspond to the theatre program or the TV listings; today, a growing array of entertainment is available whenever he chooses.

In the general absence of cable TV abroad, the videocassette recorder has in most countries around the world become the primary method of viewing first-run feature films in the home. In Oslo, a couple enters a rental shop with a bag full of videocassettes; they leave 20 minutes later, loaded down with films they've rented for the following week.

In the Bavarian town of Bad Wiessee, south of Munich, the grand opening of a videocassette rental shop comes complete with brass band and beer.

In Glasgow, a group of Scottish schoolchildren stops every Friday at the neighborhood video store to choose the family's weekend entertainment. The convenience of the videocassette has created an international industry—in which Warner Home Video plays a leading role—that is already having a significant impact on the way the world spends its leisure time. This trend offers further proof that motion pictures continue to hold a place of great importance in people's lives.

Since its inception, television has entertained and frequently educated a worldwide audience. However, this audience's option to express a contrary opinion about what it was seeing was limited to changing the channel—usually to one of only three or four alternatives—or turning off the set. Today the second era of television is upon us, an era in which cable television is bringing into the home an electronic window on the world, carrying as many as 110 channels. This is an era in which a television of limited scope is becoming, in a memorable phrase, a "television of abundance," and it is developing with startling rapidity. New programming—the software of this technology—is already giving television audiences a remarkable array of choices that as little as five years ago would have been unthinkable.

Warner Amex and Warner Amex Satellite Entertainment Co. are helping define this future through the development of innovative cable technology and new forms of television programming. *MTV*'s combination of video imagery and musical performance is the first new means of enjoying music in the home at any hour of the day or night since the advent of the stereo phonograph record, while WASEC's cable sports channels in Houston, Pittsburgh and Dallas are pioneering a concept of total regional sports coverage, including both professional and collegiate competition. And Warner Amex's unique interactive QUBE system, which transforms the television set into a means of both receiving and sending information from the home, is perhaps the most revolutionary development in television history. As cable television begins to be introduced in foreign markets, media specialists and consultants from around the world will make the pilgrimage to Warner Amex's QUBE systems to observe and study the most advanced cable operations in the world.

In the early 1600's, a high quality clay was found near Arita, Japan, that has ever since been used by succeeding generations of a family of master porcelain artists. The head of the family today, Kakiemon XIII, has been declared a Living National Treasure, the country's greatest artistic honor, and is widely regarded as Japan's finest porcelain artist. He has agreed, in an unprecedented event, to create several limited edition vases for Franklin Mint.

In London, L.J. Pearce, one of the most respected marine artists in the world, has recaptured on canvas the images of 12 magnificent vessels from the clipper ship era; his paintings have been painstakingly transferred to fine porcelain plates and offered to a select number of Franklin Mint subscribers in countries around the globe.

And in Switzerland, Igor Carl Fabergé, the grandson of the Fabergé who served the Imperial Russian Court, has created an exquisite jeweled ring in the style of his forebearer. These stories illustrate the reasons for Franklin Mint's success: the company searches the globe for the most accomplished craftsmen and artists and makes limited, high quality series of their work available to subscribers in 21 countries.

In Mexico City, Alfred E. Neuman is heard to say *¿Que, preocupado yo?* while in Australia, *Mad* is as likely to be found lampooning life in Perth as it is life in Los Angeles. In Guadalajara, children avidly follow the adventures of Superman's sister, *Superchica,* while in Tokyo, the Warner Books license *The Complete Book of Sports Medicine* vies for shelf space with more traditional manuals on herbal remedies and acupuncture.

A newsstand in a Mexican town square prominently displays the Spanish-language version of *Mad* magazine and a wide assortment of DC Comics.

WCI's worldwide publishing comprises two basic activities: the international distribution of *Mad*, DC Comics, Warner Books, and Warner Publisher Services-distributed magazines in their US editions; and the licensing of many of those titles to foreign publishers for reprint in the local language.

As a company primarily involved in bringing entertainment to a worldwide market, Warner Communications depends on the talent of the artists who create its products and the skill of its approximately 8,000 people working in extraordinarily diverse capacities in 76 countries. Their stories are at the heart of WCI's international success.

Although tribal clashes occasionally make it unsafe to travel the road from Goroka to Mt. Hagen in the Highlands of Papua New Guinea, an employee of Warner Bros.' distribution company in Australia regularly visits a circuit of theatres that has been established in that remote part of the country.

The managing director of Warner-Pioneer, WEA International's Japanese affiliate, makes a longer though less adventurous trip every time he travels to America to keep in touch with the newest developments in the US music business.

In Africa, a WEA promotion manager spends his day taking the newest releases from village to village in a van equipped with loudspeakers; the recordings are played at each stop along the way and sold from the back of the vehicle.

There are other stories of accomplishment. WCI's current international cooordinator in Europe founded the Montreux International Jazz Festival in 1967; it has become one of the major music festivals in the world, and is an important means of presenting WEA artists— from Brazil's Gilberto Gil to Germany's Ideal to the US's Rickie Lee Jones—to audiences from around the globe.

For the first time in its history, the Centre Georges Pompidou in Paris has joined with a private corporate sponsor—Atari—to present an exhibition on the world's new technologies: "Au Temps de L'Espace." The cooperative venture, which will feature 30 Atari home computers, is expected to draw three million visitors this summer, and was arranged by the director of Atari's French operations.

One of the responsibilities of the Warner Cosmetics office in Puerto Rico is to regularly tour duty-free locations from the Caribbean island of St. Thomas to Caracas, Venezuela. The combined purchase of duty-free products in the worldwide market now totals over $2 billion; this market also accounts for the largest part of Warner Cosmetics' overseas revenues.

Finally, WCI's best-known worldwide ambassadors are most likely the Cosmos. One of the most popular sports teams in the world, the Cosmos and their international superstars—starting with Pelé and continuing through Beckenbauer and Chinaglia—have over the years played matches in 42 countries, delighting soccer fans and carrying Warner Communications' name to every part of the globe.

WCI has always managed its businesses in a way that recognizes their diversity and creativity while at the same time encouraging those cooperative activities that benefit the company as a whole. This philosophy of management—which is the essence of the company's international operations as well—exphazises the creative, entrepreneurial nature of each division while at the same time recognizing the unity of WCI's vision, the products it creates, and the markets it serves.

22

DAVID J. LONDONER

The Changing Economics of Entertainment

The Universal Puppet Show

One hundred years ago, the cultural contour of America was a series of islands.

Constrained by inadequate means of distribution, a cultural or entertainment creation in music, comedy, or drama languished within a regional or social class milieu, incapable of reaching large audiences. The theater existed for New Yorkers and Bostonians, upper classes only, if you please. Country music was still for country people. Books were published essentially for educational or special interest purposes, rarely attaining mass readership.

Perhaps the only national, wide ranging form of popular entertainment was the traveling circus. Even the puppet show, the other hardy survivor from the Middle Ages, remained essentially a local phenomenon.

Things have changed radically in the past hundred years, however. Technology has produced a bewildering variety of facilities for the mass dissemination of culture: recordings, radio, movies, paperbacks, and television. A single book is published in five million copies, and read by half again that many people. During an evening half-hour, fifteen million homes will view a typical prime-time TV show, and

Abridged by the editor from two Wertheim & Co. reports, "The Changing Economics of Entertainment" (April 1978) and "Like No Business We Know" (October 1979) written by David J. Londoner

twice that many—representing perhaps fifty million people—will watch a special event or a particularly popular movie.

Probably 90 percent of the adult population of this country has at one time or another heard Debby Boone sing "You Light Up My Life." We know that thirty million Americans watched *Star Wars* (at least once) in 1977 and, the telecast included, probably one hundred and thirty million have by now seen *Gone with the Wind*. For the first time in recorded history, it is possible for substantially all the people in the United States—and a vast portion of the world—to witness a particular cultural or entertainment creation.

This multidimensional burgeoning of the means of disseminating amusement is still far from complete; we have witnessed only the early stages in this broadening process of distribution. Still more advanced technology exists for the next stage and we are already entering it.

It is the objective of this paper to discuss the immediate and upcoming outlook for entertainment, America's most pervasive form of culture. We will review the changing patterns of entertainment distribution and will venture some speculation about additional changes that will evolve in the near future.

As befits our métier, the focus is economic, not philosophical. We admit to taking greater delight in the commercial opportunities inherent in a changing industry than in the social and cultural effects those changes may bring about.

1. The Shifting Locus of Profits

The theme of this report is that supply/demand relationships are changing within the entertainment industry, with implications for both the immediately upcoming years and the years beyond. The principal beneficiaries of the relationships which existed during the 1960s and early 1970s were the broadcasters, both networks and stations. By virtue of their control of the principal method of entertainment distribution they have been able to dam up a reservoir of profits, feeding out portions at their will to the program suppliers.

This oligopsony/oligopoly control over the major method of distribution is weakening, however. At present the cause is heightened competition among the networks; in future years the cause will be alternative means of distribution. Over the next several years, we envision a deterioration of the position of the networks vis-à-vis both the stations and the program suppliers. Longer range, we see a deterioration of the position of the stations themselves against the suppliers, as innovative developments and new technology break up the stations' oligopolies of directly reaching the home.

Furthermore, new methods of entertainment distribution will eventually come to the fore, such as satellite transmission, pay TV, videotape and videodisc, fragmenting the distribution process even more, to the ultimate benefit of the producers of entertainment. The technology for each of these developments already exists and emplacement has already begun with consumers.

Metaphorically, there are only three theaters in networkland—ABC, CBS, and NBC. As such, they have exercised great power over the producers of entertainment. This oligopsony position enjoyed by the networks has permitted them to dictate prices of the series programming that they buy, and to an extent to influence the price advertisers pay to exhibit that product along with their commercials.

The change taking place today in the network business stems from the emergence of ABC as a truly viable competitor to CBS and NBC, and from the intensified competition for program material and for station clearances which that represents.

Over the intermediate term, the networks are at a minor disadvantage. The next step in the changing distribution pattern is expected to be the rise of a quasi fourth network or, more properly, a limited direct syndication effort which will utilize local television stations to carry entertainment not broadcast by any of the existing networks. The implication is that local television outlets can increase revenues and, depending on the price they pay for this entertainment, increase their profitability. We suspect that this fourth alternative will develop a meaningful existence within the next five years, to the minor detriment of the generally good economics of networking.

Longer range, say over a twenty-year period, the networks will become only three of many channels of distribution, and, with less absolute control over the dissemination of programming, will have to bid more competitively for both programs and audiences.

The major threat to the program suppliers, the MCAs, Warners, and Paramounts of this world, was felt in 1969–71. The threat came from within via the escalation of film budgets to a level unsupportable by theatrical demand, and from without as new entrants into the production and distribution businesses increased the supply of films and bid aggressively for talent and properties. In the case of the film companies, the excesses quickly produced deficits, the new entrants disappeared, and the business returned to equilibrium. While such a threat could arise in the future, there are no signs of imminence. Repetition of the 1969 and 1971 problems does not appear likely.

Section 2 describes the 1969–71 experience, which is the necessary history for an understanding of the future projections made herein. Section 3 looks at television and its changing economics in the distribution process. With those as background, section 4 views the upcoming events insofar as the suppliers are concerned, and how theatrical film profitability is influenced by television. Finally, section 5 treats the longer range outlook for entertainment and offers some speculation on changes in the distribution patterns over the next five to twenty years.

Essentially, the immediate years should witness heightened competition from within the network business; later years should witness competition from outside. The ultimate beneficiaries of this competition are the motion picture companies and other program suppliers which, as owners of the product, will be able to command increasingly higher prices for it as the varying methods of distribution compete for their property. In effect, the networks should be swimming upstream and the program suppliers downstream.

2. Coming of Age in Hollywood

For the makers of motion pictures, the 1960s began in the doldrums. Attendance at theaters was declining as television drained off the vast bulk of film audiences, and the advent of color television portended even more damage. Despite this, the industry managed to stabilize itself, perhaps with the James Bond pictures or, later, with *The Sound of Music*, and audiences continued to attend theaters. Prices at the box office began to rise, and the film business entered a healthy period. Three developments arising from that profitability and the complacency it brought were to have dire consequences by the end of the decade.

First was the acceptance of the big-budget philosophy. *The Sound of Music* cost Twentieth Century-Fox a hefty $10 million to produce in 1965, but it grossed over $100 million in rentals during the ensuing two years. Fox and other studios quickly embraced the larger risks of high-cost films, and by 1968 six of the eight major studios were contentedly producing blockbuster movies.

Second was the expanding population of film companies, which altered the supply/demand relationships in the industry. Three "instant majors" sprang forth in the mid-1960s with ambitious production schedules, boosting the number of principal suppliers from eight to eleven.

The three newcomers—CBS, ABC, and National General—each produced around ten films per year in the late sixties, many with distressingly high budgets. In order to break into this market, they paid up for properties, stars, and directors, and they allowed theater owners a larger percentage of the box-office dollars in order to win broader exhibition.

Third was the appetite that television was developing for feature films and the rose-colored glasses through which the film industry viewed this market. In 1961, the average motion picture leased to a televison network received $150,000 for two airings during a three-year period. This figure was growing. A film released theatrically in that year would play off in theaters. The film company would amortize the typically two-million-dollar negative cost down to $150,000, which was left as a residual to be amortized against an expected network lease. When it was finally leased to the network three years later, the price had risen—it brought not $150,000 but $300,000. Profit was even larger than anticipated.

Prices continued to rise. By 1968, deals were being signed at $800,000, and it became obvious that historical residuals left to amortize against TV, even though raised, were still ridiculously low.

Everything seemed to come apart by late 1968. The three networks, which had bid aggressively for future rights to exhibit feature films during the 1969–72 period, suddenly stopped buying. An important market seemed lost. On the theatrical side, the marketplace became choked by the expanded and expensive product of the increased number of producer-distributors. But there were financial problems also. Theatrical production had typically been financed by short-term bank borrowing. As the big-budget pictures swelled inventories, short-term debt ballooned.

The inevitable happened. The big inventories worked their way through the distribution system at staggering losses. When the networks, by this time fully positioned with feature films, stopped buying, prices dropped to the $400,000 range. The three new entrants to the film business lost collectively over $80 million.

Hollywood nearly collapsed. Only Disney and MCA escaped without deficits, and even MCA's film arm lost money. The other majors absorbed losses of between $15 and $145 million, leaving both Fox and Columbia as potential candidates for receivership. The three "instant majors" dropped out of the business. Even MGM, at one time Hollywood's most glamorous studio, stopped distributing its own films and cut down sharply on its production activities.

In a way, it was probably fortunate that the industry had such high bank loans. If they had been only modest, the banks might possibly have protected their investments through the bankruptcy courts, leaving the debenture owners and stockholders to foot the bill. As it was, the banks could ill afford the huge loan losses this would have entailed, and decided instead to work for a restructuring of the industry.

Taking a more active part in management, the banks forced the film companies to reduce branch office overhead, combine studio facilities with competitors, distribute jointly in foreign areas and, most important, stop making blockbuster pictures.

The position of the broadcasting networks during this period is interesting, and had a profound influence on the economics of the entertainment industry in the early 1970s. When Hollywood was in trouble, film production was curtailed. In order to cover fixed studio overhead, the film companies anxiously solicited the production of television series, often at prices which would cover variable costs and make only a minor contribution toward defraying fixed costs.

Deficit financing—so called because the full cost of the TV program is not paid for by the network—became the accepted rule during this period, with suppliers having to go along in order to maintain staffs and keep studios occupied. If the series was successful, that is, lasted three years or longer, a profit would be made from syndication (selling the show to local TV stations for nonnetwork programming); if not, the supplier would lose the difference. This could amount to as much as 20–25 percent of the cost of the program.

To look back for a moment, this was the position of the entertainment industry by the end of 1972: the networks were in the dominant position, just beginning to recover from the loss of tobacco advertising; the local stations had fully recovered from tobacco's effects with a 38 percent profit increase; and the film studios were restructured, more efficient, and essentially rid of the flamboyant managers who had led them in the 1960s, but still constrained by the banks from aggressive feature development.

The next five years witnessed the strengthening of all parts of the entertainment business except theatrical exhibition. How this came about and what should happen afterward are discussed in the next two sections; the first about television, the second about theatrical motion pictures.

3. The Role of the Networks

The removal of tobacco advertising in 1971 altered the supply/demand relationship of advertisers and broadcasters. Tobacco had accounted for 12 percent of network advertising, and the sudden availability of that much commercial time weakened prices across the board.

The harsher realities of the marketplace forced the networks to tamp down on costs. One of the places where costs could be controlled was programming, and the networks used their considerable influence to keep program expenditures low. With Hollywood ill financed and largely out of work, this was not difficult. Talent was available at a low price; studio space was ample and film companies were willing to take network series business without full cost recoupment.

Even as the studios regained financial composure, as employment picked up, as activity strengthened, the networks were able to maintain program costs at reasonable levels—escalating at perhaps 6 or 7 percent annually. Part of the reason for this was the option contract, which is crucial to the cost structure of the networks.

The option contract is the standard arrangement between a network and a program supplier. If the network approves a series, it typically orders thirteen programs to play for as many weeks. It also takes an option on another nine to twelve programs for that season, plus options on that series at a 3–7 percent annual price escalation for seven years. The contract calls for a pass-through of union labor increases.

What the option clause does, in effect, is to concentrate most of the risk and all of the reward from network programming in the hands of the network. If a show is a failure, the network cancels it and absorbs the bulk of the program cost, normally more than offset by the advertising it has sold. Under deficit financing, the supplier has a loss—perhaps $1 million or so if the show runs thirteen weeks or less. On the other hand, if the show is a hit the lucrative incremental advertising dollars that it can command inure entirely to the network for as long as the show continues to play well. For the first two years of the contract—prior to producing sufficient episodes for syndication—the supplier continues to show a loss.

If the option clause were to vanish, it is obvious that a supplier would demand a higher price for shows in the second season. While some restraint would be put on prices by competing shows, a proprietary product, once well accepted by audiences, would command a higher price in a free market and be more profitable to its supplier.

The Emergence of ABC

For twenty years, the positions of the three networks were essentially fixed; CBS first, NBC second, ABC third. Undercapitalized, operating at losses until 1972 and with narrower affiliate coverage, the ABC network was less able to compete for programming than its rivals. With what can only be described as brilliant program strategy, both in creation and placement, ABC succeeded in 1976 at overtaking both competitors and catapulting itself into first place in prime time. In so doing, it has emerged highly profitable, has taken its parent company to a point where it is no longer financially leveraged, and has dramatically escalated the war for program ratings.

For the first time, there are now three well-capitalized networks jockeying for increasingly profitable rating points. As television prices and profits have increased, so has the incentive to come up with top-ranked shows. The best-capitalized networks are now on the bottom; that implies a more competitive market. There are two good examples of the aggressiveness with which the networks are bidding for programming—sports and movies.

Sports represent proprietary products for the "owner," the NFL for instance. The cost of NFL football to the networks (all three participate) under the four-year contract that recently expired was just over $300 million. Negotiations for the next four years have been completed, and the franchise rights have been sold for $624 million.

ABC recently made an interesting comment. For its sixteen Monday Night Football games (against fourteen under the old contract), ABC will increase advertising from twenty to twenty-two minutes per game, will raise the per minute price to advertisers 39 percent, and will also run a number of pregame "warm-up specials" the night before—and make less money from football in 1978 than in 1977. Presumably football earnings will rise over the following three years as the price to advertisers is increased further, but we suspect that in the aggregate, the networks will earn less money on NFL football in the next four years than they did in the past four.

Motion pictures are another area where competition is driving up prices. It was mentioned earlier that during the 1960s the cost of a typical movie to the networks for a three-year license rose from $150,000 to about $800,000, then dropped in half during 1970–71. By 1972, prices had recovered, and gradually worked up to about $1 million by 1975. In the past two years, film licenses have more than doubled, and the typical network quality film can now command close to $2.5 million. As will be discussed later, a number of spectacular examples exist at prices well above this range.

The point being made is that proprietary products can command prices that may not directly yield a profit to the networks, because they help the networks bolster affiliate relationships and show advertisers higher ratings. We do not imply that the networks will be willing to lose money on a broad range of their programming for these purposes, but it appears clear that they are becoming increasingly agreeable to buying ratings out of profit dollars. It is our view that this will continue.

The Affiliates, the Independents, and the Suppliers

Among local broadcasting stations as well, competition is becoming more intense. In a way, local competition is a microcosm of network economics, only in a telescoped time frame. Television stations operate in an environment not dissimilar to the networks, with one exception—there are often fourth alternatives for viewing in the form of independent stations free of network affiliation.

As with the networks, the affiliated stations have long been accustomed to relatively fixed positions within their markets, but they are not invariably positioned parallel to their respective affiliated networks. Afternoon programming, prime-time access, and local news are areas where an individual station can program competitively, and a station's prominence in its market is to some measure a function of its own programming.

Perhaps because of the heightened profitability of broadcasting stations during the past two years, or perhaps because of the upset in the traditional order of network ratings, local stations have accelerated their own competition. Technological developments have fostered some of the competition. For instance, electronic news gathering (ENG) has made possible on-the-spot reporting from remote locations where news is breaking, in contrast to filmed episodes which are broadcast hours after the event. ENG is expensive, but is achieving rapid acceptance in larger markets.

The real competition, however, is coming in syndicated programming, both series and motion pictures. Afternoon and access time are dominated by off-network series, normally "stripped"—that is, shown in the same time slot five times a week—usually over a two- or three-year period with many reruns.

The price of off-network series has roughly doubled in the past two years, in part owing to a shortage of family acceptable (i.e., nonviolent) product. Contracts entered into for *Welcome Back Kotter*, a half-hour series on ABC, will aggregate well over $300,000 per episode when Warner Communications is finished marketing it for 1981 release. A year ago, *Happy Days* broke the record for half-hour syndication prices with $275,000 per episode; *Happy Days* was a higher-rated show than *Kotter* and commanded nearly double the top prices paid only two years earlier.

Motion pictures are another example where prices have risen dramatically the past two years. Stations buy rights to view movies, normally for multiple runs over a period of three or four years after the films have completed their network runs. Like network movie license fees, syndication prices have also more than doubled in the past two years. In some markets, notably those with more than three stations, prices have advanced even more rapidly.

It is our view that this aggressive competition for programming will continue in the future, to the extent that margins in station broadcasting—currently near record highs—will return to more normal levels. In effect, much of the incremental revenues will be passed on to the suppliers gradually through more aggressive bidding for quality programming. In part, this will be funded by the networks in the form of increased station compensation, so the stations may not see as serious a margin erosion as might otherwise prevail.

The Fourth Network

Much discussion has taken place about a fourth network. Advertisers are anxious for one to develop, since it would increase the supply of network advertising minutes and presumably result in lower prices. Suppliers are anxious for one because it would increase the market for their programming and presumably strengthen the prices they would receive. Independent stations are excited over the prospects.

Networks and their affiliates, perhaps understandably, would prefer otherwise. We believe it will happen, but not the way most observers think. The implications are profound for the entire industry.

A full-fledged fourth network comparable to an existing network is probably a long way off. The economic effects of one are less remote, however, because even a partial fourth network should increase competition for programming. In the view of this observer, a fourth entertainment alternative will have an important impact on the economics of entertainment.

It is not feasible to launch a full network to compete with the existing three. It was attempted by the Overmyer Network in 1967, but this effort failed after eleven days on the air because program quality was poor and there was not enough advertiser money to support the AT&T line charges to its 127 stations.

There may or may not be enough advertising money today to launch a fourth network; a year ago in the frenzied advertising market there might have been. Today, the network market is soft, and a fourth network would no doubt have considerable difficulty. The major obstacle, however, is not lack of demand, but an important technical problem.

If all the independent stations in the country were joined together in a network, they would reach only about 60 percent of the country's TV homes. That is because many important markets have only three channels authorized, and a fourth cannot be authorized because its signal would interfere with an adjacent broadcasting area. A fourth network, if it tried to program a full day, would compete head-on with existing networks which, reaching 99 percent of the country, could command considerably more advertising dollars to acquire better programming.

CATV is not the answer, at least not for many years. CATV passes only twenty million homes now, or 27 percent of the country. To wire 80 percent of the United States into a programmable network could take thirty years and $25 billion; it will not happen at today's economics. It is unlikely that a full-scale, forty- or fifty-hour-per-week fourth network could produce enough acceptably popular programming; failing to do so, it would be unable to capture sufficient market share to be viable.

What may occur, though, is a *partial* fourth network using normal broadcasting facilities—a network which does not compete with local affiliated stations but one which uses them. A fourth network, or, more accurately, a large-scale syndication effort, can be put together by taking both independent stations and network affiliates and offering them programming as an alternative to the network feed. It could be successful if a sufficient number of network affiliates were to preempt a portion of their regular network programming in certain time periods to run the competing programs.

This fourth alternative will probably program only a few hours a week to compete against the lowest-rated network shows. Whether this is done by broadcasting from a central place to local stations via satellite, or by taping the show and delivering the tape by mail or courier, makes little difference. The important point is that in order to achieve a broad enough reach, the attempt would have to include affiliated as well as independent stations. Affiliates appear to be interested if it is possible to garner more revenues than from the network offering.

Such an arrangement was actually tried in May 1977. *Operation Prime Time* was a program source organized by an individual from Telerep, the Cox Broadcasting sales representative subsidiary. It consisted of a group of ninety-five stations, twenty-two independents, and seventy-three network affiliates, who put up the money for a five-hour special of Taylor Caldwell's *A Testimony of Two Men*. MCA produced the show and was paid almost enough to cover its out-of-pocket costs. OPT sold about half the time nationally, and the stations sold the remainder locally. Because it sold advertising nationally as well as locally, it was in effect a quasi network, although its economic impact was marginal. The show received high ratings.

The reason the fourth alternative possibility is so interesting is that it could diminish the existing networks' control over prices paid to the suppliers. A quasi network will probably be undercapitalized from the start and will in all probability need to rely on suppliers to fund its growth. Its financial backer, whether an advertiser, an unaffiliated corporation, or the participating stations themselves, might pay for only a portion of the up-front cost of the programs, with the program supplier funding the rest in exchange for a direct or indirect participation in the advertising revenues.

If a fourth alternative takes shape, it is logical for it to rely on this financial support from the program producers. It is to the advantage of the well-capitalized suppliers to fund the entertainment cost if in some way a portion of the benefits of a successful show can be passed on to them. If a supplier can finance half the cost of a show in exchange for a portion of the advertising revenues generated, it can obtain benefits from a successful series, something not possible under the present system because of the network option clause.

We believe that this is the ultimate meaning of a fourth network; not merely that there is another outlet for product, but that it will eventually weaken or break the network option clause.

The economically logical course of events is for such a quasi network to expand to several hours per week. It is to the supplier's advantage to offer its very best programming to the fourth network rather than to an existing one. That is where the profit leverage exists if the supplier can share in the results of the ratings garnered. Should a fourth alternative develop, the existing networks would be pressured to pay still higher prices for programming lest the best programming and the ratings fall into the hands of the junior competitor.

At stake is the option clause. It is our view that the economics of a fourth source of program distribution will eventually break the practice of long-term program options with fixed escalations or alternatively that prices for programming will rise significantly to allow the suppliers a more generous profit from network exhibition.

What we are saying is that the network oligopoly over the means of program distribution will fragment; that the profit reservoir in the stream of entertainment revenues will move further downstream to the suppliers.

4. Motion Picture Companies: Crosscurrents

The motion picture producer-distributors seem still to be the important beneficiaries of the marketplace changes in the entertainment industry, although there are signs that they are developing a few vulnerabilities. A number of influences are at work:

On the one hand,
- the relationship of the number of theaters to the supply of films—the supply/demand ratio—seems to be shifting from favorable to neutral as the major distributors increase the number of releases and new, well-financed production companies increase the supply of films;
- advertising and promotion costs are increasing especially rapidly, the industry having taken note of their value in attracting box office dollars, and
- talent, both acting and producing, is exerting leverage against the studios, and commanding still higher upfront money and profit participations.

On the other hand, though,
- box office dollars continue to rise, especially in foreign markets;
- secondary markets—most notably network television—are offering important offsets to higher production and advertising costs, and
- new ancillary markets which barely produce revenues today seem likely to emerge as important contributors over the next five to ten years.

The motion picture business has made a remarkable transformation over the past decade—from deficits and shaky capitalizations to prosperity and strong balance sheets. There is reason to believe that profits will continue to expand although not at the breakneck pace of the past five years.

Supply and Demand in the Film Industry

Profit growth has been exemplary. Operating profits of the film and television divisions (the two are inseparable because of joint costs and shared revenues) have risen 140 percent from 1974 to 1978 and show indications of another—albeit modest—advance in 1979.

The aggregate statistics still trend upward. A good year was seen in 1978, with domestic and foreign theatrical film rentals expanding a staggering 34 percent to just under $2 billion. The outlook for 1979 is for a more modest advance, but one which consolidates at these high levels. (See Table 1.)

If one compares domestic box office admissions dollars with domestic rentals an interesting fact emerges. Rentals grow a lot faster than box office dollars. Looked at another way, the percentage of the admissions money paid over by the theaters to distributors is escalating. Table 2 is not statistically accurate, because the rental figure (numerator) is for the nine companies above while box office admis-

TABLE 1
Film Rentals—Nine U.S. Companies

	U.S. & Canada	Foreign	Total
1979	$1,125,000	$775,000	$1,900,000
1978	1,216,000	750,000	1,966,000
1977	926,000	535,000	1,461,000
1976	698,000	547,000	1,245,000
1975	752,000	579,000	1,331,000
1974	649,000	470,000	1,119,000
1973	471,000	415,000	886,000
1972	500,000	389,000	889,000
1971	402,000	340,000	742,000
1970	443,000	355,000	798,000
1969	375,000	340,000	715,000
1968	431,000	323,000	754,000
1967	408,000	346,000	754,000
1966	378,000	355,000	733,000

Note: The nine companies are Allied Artists, Columbia, Disney, MGM, Paramount, Fox, United Artists, Universal, and Warner Bros.
Source: Warner Communications; 1979 Wertheim & Co.

TABLE 2
U.S.-Canada Film Rentals As Percentage of Boxoffice Gross

1970	1971	1972	1973	1974	1975	1976	1977	1978	1979 Est.
31.0%	29.8%	31.6%	30.9%	34.0%	35.6%	34.4%	39.0%	45.8%	44.5%

Note: Rentals are for nine distributors only; figures probably understate actual percentages somewhat because of omission of rentals paid to minor distributors.
Source: Rentals, Warner Communications; Boxoffice, MPAA; Estimates, Wertheim & Co.

sions (denominator) is total domestic gross from all companies' films including those of numerous minor distributors; however, the trend itself is altogether reflective of events.

What is happening in 1978 and 1979 is not so much that contractual terms between distributors and theater owners have stiffened, as was the case a few years ago, as that films are doing more business, and faster. It works this way.

Typical terms for the splitting of box office receipts call for a fixed dollar amount to be retained by the theater before any split, with a high percentage of the remainder turned over to the distributor as his share. The so-called "90–10 deal," the license format for important films, calls for house expenses to come out first, and then 90 percent of the remainder to be paid to the film company and 10 percent retained by the theater. Typically, these terms stand for the first one or two weeks of a run, then drop to 80–20, 70–30, etc. If the film plays poorly, the theater may not recoup its house expenses; if the film plays brilliantly, the theater can double or triple its house "nut," but the distributor may end up with as much as 80 or 85 percent of the total admissions money. Terms on the most important films often specify a "floor" of 70 percent even if the house nut is not fully earned.

In 1978, the blockbuster films *Grease, Saturday Night Fever, Jaws 2, Animal House,* and others showed large admissions throughout their runs, so that the residual percentage paid to distributors after house expenses was proportionately larger than usual. This is what accounted for the particularly large rise in the percentage flowing to distributors in 1978; it did not represent a further stiffening of contractual terms.

Informed observers judge that today's exhibition plant—currently seventeen thousand screens (see Table 3)—has an appetite for about 150–175 "quality" features a year, quality being defined as the type of release normally offered by a major studio. This would naturally include some consideration of reissues, of which there are normally somewhat more than a dozen.

Today's level would appear to be about a hundred thirty giving half weight to some twenty reissues and counting the five or six films of good quality from nonmajors (see Table 4). There have been almost

TABLE 3
Number of Screens in the United States

1979 Est.	17,100
1978	16,755
1977	16,554
1976	15,976
1975	15,969
1974	15,384
1973	14,650
1972	14,370
1971	14,070
1970	13,750

Source: National Assn. of Theatre Owners. 1979 Estimate Wertheim & Co.

TABLE 4
Number of Domestic Theatrical Releases (excludes reissues)

	1977	1978	1979
Columbia	10	14	19
Disney	5	4	4
Paramount	14	15	17
Twentieth Century-Fox	13	9	12
United Artists[a]	14	18	23
Universal (MCA)	16	19	19
Warner Bros.	12	18	20[b]
Total	84	97	114

[a]Includes MGM
[b]Includes Orion
Source: Exhibitor Relations Corp.

no meaningful foreign entries which were not distributed by a major except for *The Muppet Movie*, currently in distribution from Associated Film Distributors.

The supply of films is still not excessive, even not adequate if one listens to the pleadings of exhibitors and network executives. Oversupply will be reached, we suspect, when most of the six majors adopt the "tonnage thesis," now practiced by MCA, United Artists, and Warner. The tonnage thesis states that distribution overhead is essentially fixed and that incremental product put through above break-even carries a disproportionately high profit contribution. Remember that producers and other participants are paid only after deducting a 20 to 40 percent distribution charge which is deducted even before recoupment of out-of-pocket costs. Enough of this 20 to 40 percent and the distributor makes money even if all the pictures break even for the other participants.

Any practice that says "go for market share, and the earnings will take care of themselves" is a fine one until the competition emulates it. Obviously, if every one of the majors adopts it, there will be too much product, audiences will be spread too thin, and losses on the production side may be so great as to offset the profit contribution from distribution.

For the industry to remain healthy, it must not overproduce films. The 1968–69 experience was sobering. The majors released an abundance of product with high budgets; several other entities went into or expanded distribution; and two of the networks produced films. Called "instant majors" by virtue of their sudden accession to a full line of competitive films, the two networks and their distributors collectively released over 30 films a year at their peak. An estimated 225 films were released by the traditional and instant majors in 1969, a total simply too high to afford adequate exhibition for all.

It is our expectation that the domestic industry can accommodate one major distributor in addition to the current six (plus Disney) without altering its basically good economics. Two or three more might be difficult to digest, especially if release schedules from the existing majors are materially expanded.

The Cost Side

The risks to the industry can best be described as those of *hubris*—a term out of Greek literature whose meaning is somewhere between pride and *chutzpah*. Tendencies are noted inching toward the pitiable mistakes of the late 1960s: budgets are rising; promotional and advertising costs are burgeoning; and the number of films produced is increasing. Most recent evidence suggests that the problem is not yet critical, but there are tendencies toward excesses which bear scrutiny.

In terms of truly heavy budgets, the numbers are now beginning to change. The number of over-$20 million pictures released in a year is going from three to four, and the budgets now go into the $30–$40 million category. (See Table 5)

The heavier negative costs would be alarming, to say the least, were it not for one fact. In the case of *Superman* last Christmas, and in the case of *Apocalypse Now* this fall, the major risks were borne by the independent producer, not by the distribution company. In both cases, distributor outlays were smaller, either because it paid only for territorial distribution rights (*Superman*) or because personal assets of the producer were pledged to reduce expense (*Apocalypse*). *1941* is a joint venture between two studios, which of course does not reduce the risk but shares it between two companies. The negative cost of *Star Trek* does give rise to some concern.

One of the mistakes made in the late 1960s was for distributors to make deals whose profitability relied on huge box office volume. Columbia made good pictures and bad deals under its old management. National General gave away so much of its distribution fee to CBS that even the network's classy and well-received production failed to generate a profit for NGC's distribution arm.

History repeats itself, and there appears to be an uncomfortable tendency to make deals which require excessive grosses to come out. Marlon Brando is said to have negotiated $3 million in salary plus 10 percent of the *gross* rentals above $60 million for *Superman*. The

TABLE 5
Major Budget Films, 1977–1979

	Title	Distributor	Estimated Cost ($ mil.)
1979	Moonraker	United Artists	$35
	Apocalypse Now	United Artists	34
	1941	Columbia/MCA	31
	Star Trek	Paramount	41
1978	Jaws II	MCA	27
	The Wiz	MCA	25
	Superman	Warner	35
1977	Sorcerer	MCA/Paramount	21
	A Bridge Too Far	United Artists	22
	Close Encounters	Columbia	20

Note: Grouped by release date.

producers—not Warner—negotiated a deal under which he will earn close to $10 million for a performance which may have added credibility to the production but probably not much else.

Terms of contracts are difficult to come by for the investment community, but they are becoming increasingly important if one is to determine the profitability of key films.

New Markets

There are several new markets opening up for the film companies. The most prominent among these, pay TV, now represents an important auxiliary source of income. Others are less important today but show excellent promise—videocassettes and videodiscs. It is possible even at this early stage to make some judgments about the growth of these markets—tentative, of course—and some documentation is offered in the final section of this report.

The example in Table 6 approximates the revenue and expense breakdown for the average motion picture distributed by a major. It should be quickly apparent that this average is taken from a very wide variety of releases, low-budget pickup to $30 million heavyweight, turkey to blockbuster. The example represents an average that is not necessarily typical.

It is presented to demonstrate the importance of auxiliary markets:

TABLE 6
Economics of the Average Film

First-run revenues:	10.0	Domestic theatrical
	6.5	Foreign
	$16.5	Total theatrical first-run
Auxiliary revenues:	3.0	Network TV
	1.4	Off-network syndication
	.8	Pay TV
	.1	Videocassette/videodisc
	1.5	Theatrical reissue
	$6.8	Total auxiliary
Total revenues:	$23.3	
Costs:	$ 9.3	Negative ($6.0), prints ($0.8), national advertising ($2.5)
	4.0	Releasing costs
	2.7	Participants' shares
	2.5	Allocated share of fixed overhead
	$18.5	Total costs
Pretax profit:	$ 4.8	
Income taxes:	2.0	
Net income:	$ 2.8	

they can represent fully one-third of a picture's revenues, and an amount more than equal to its initial negative cost. (Theatrical reissue income is included in auxiliary markets to distinguish it from original first-run, a possibly controversial position but one which emphasizes the enduring value of feature films.)

Over the past three years, the growth of these auxiliary markets has been salutary. On a per-picture basis, revenues have risen approximately as shown in Table 7.

TABLE 7
Estimated Three-Year Increase in Sources of Revenues per Film

Domestic theatrical	+110%
Foreign theatrical	+ 65%
Network TV	+175%
Off-network syndication	+200%
Pay-TV	+500%
Videocassette/videodisc	N.M.
Theatrical reissue	+100%

N.M.=Not meaningful

The increase in pay TV videocassette/videodisc revenues are from low bases, which tend to distort their percentage gains. But these are precisely the areas which are expected to demonstrate the most rapid growth in the future.

In sum, then, we see new markets growing in the future for the creators of entertainment. If the field does not become overcrowded, either by too many new entrants or by dramatically expanded release schedules from the existing participants, the profitability of the film industry should continue to expand.

5. The Next Ten Years

Radio and television differ from other forms of entertainment in one vital respect: their costs are borne by advertisers, not by consumers. It is a fundamental difference that results in a limitation on the amount of money that can be paid for this entertainment.

Consider for a moment the six-tenths of a cent that an advertiser will pay to reach one television home—a rate of $6.00 per thousand homes for a typical one-minute prime-time network commercial. With twelve minutes in a typical two-hour show, the price paid by all advertisers to the network per home is only 7.2 cents plus another fraction of a cent for local time sold. The typical home has 2.9 viewers. If two of those persons watch the show, that is less than 4 cents per viewer. Four cents for two hours of entertainment.

We know that the value of that entertainment to the *viewer* is significantly greater. But to the advertiser, it may not be. Where the viewer pays directly for his entertainment, revenues are greater by orders of magnitude.

This is easily demonstrated. For two hours of motion picture entertainment, viewers readily pay $2.00 to $4.00, not to mention associated costs such as transportation, baby-sitting, and other outlays. Even for entertainment of television's mediocre quality, viewers will spend money if they have to—for cable TV, for instance. Standard cable costs are $7.00 per month or, using the above parameters, about four cents per two-hour show per viewer.

How valuable is entertainment? The Detroit *Free Press* performed an intriguing experiment last year. The newspaper approached 120 families and offered them each $500 if they would watch no television for a month. Amazingly, 93 families refused the offer entirely. Of the remaining 27, the *Free Press* selected 5 from diverse social and economic backgrounds, all avid television watchers, and disconnected their sets for a month. The results, well worth reading, included various forms of withdrawal symptoms: increased smoking, nervousness, insomnia, and even a lack of communication within one family. It also produced more radio listening, more motion picture attendance, and more sex. All the families were anxious for the month to end.

It is fascinating that fully 80 percent of the families approached turned down the offer. It is hard to conceive of many families *paying* $6,000 a year to watch television, if the choice were reversed, but strangely enough that is the implication of the experiment. It demonstrates that the value placed on convenient entertainment—i.e., entertainment in the home—is considerable.

The dilemma for the Hollywood studios, then, becomes this: how to shift more of their production from advertiser- to consumer-supported viewing, knowing that people are willing to pay more.

The problem is being solved. Technology is once again changing the means of distributing entertainment. This time it has produced convenient methods for distributing more or better video entertainment directly into the home. Pay cable, offering first-run movies, sports, and specialized viewing, is one means; videocassette, either tape or disc, is another. Over-the-air pay TV is a third, and two-way cable, such as Warner's QUBE, is the fourth. Satellite transmission of video product is another development worth watching. The next ten years will witness the blossoming of one or more of these distribution methods. It will again alter the economics of entertainment.

Before going further, it is necessary to treat a possible objection. Why, one might ask, would the public pay money for entertainment when it can receive other entertainment free? The answer takes two forms. It has to do with the quality—imagined or real—that more expensive entertainment offers, and it also has to do with convenience.

Pay TV, videotape, and videodisc offer greater quality—the quality of a first-run movie or a sports event which may not be carried on network TV, or other entertainment exclusive with the particular medium. They also offer convenience. The viewer can select his own entertainment, or choose a time to watch it.

How much will the consumer pay for this quality and convenience? Probably quite a bit. The radio-phonograph trade-off is an interesting example. All the popular contemporary music is heard on the radio. Yet in 1977, sales of phonograph records and tapes in this country totalled $2.7 billion at retail (not list) prices. That is equal to the total amount spent by advertisers on all radio, including news, sports, drama, other entertainment, *and* music.

We suspect that comparable economics await the video medium once the technological innovations have been put into place. This emplacement process is already under way, and should become meaningful during the early 1980s.

It is probably too early to determine which of the four means of distributing video for pay will predominate or, indeed, if other methods will supersede them. Of equal interest, however, is the effect they will have on the relationships between the producers of entertainment and their existing outlets, such as motion picture theaters and television networks and stations.

The most logical conclusion is that alternative means of distributing filmed products will again increase the competition for those products. It spells an even more difficult period than the present one for the theater chains, which will see some of their customers lured away by the prospect of seeing the same motion picture at home. The networks could fare badly as well. Advertiser supported, they would be less able to compete for the higher-quality programming that purchased cassettes or discs could offer, and could be forced either to use profit dollars to purchase more expensive programming or to suffer the loss of a portion of their viewers.

There should logically be two results. On the one hand, the pay viewer will preempt a certain portion of time from the networks to watch his paid-for show. This should be small, not more than a few hours per week, at most. There is obviously some limit to how much an individual will spend on entertainment, and he clearly will not wish to purchase enough programming to fill an entire prime-time week. He will probably preempt, wherever possible, the least popular network programs in order to watch the new media. Why turn off *Happy Days* if he can watch his new cassette when only unwanted shows are playing?

The second effect is more profound from the networks' viewpoint. The competition for good programming could intensify dramatically. Instead of competing for programming against other networks which have similar economics, an existing network could be competing with a means of distribution having entirely different and ultimately far more favorable economics.

In effect, if highly popular programming can be produced, the networks will get the second shot at it. The best talent will avoid appearing on free television, using much the same logic that keeps Paul Newman from starring in a network series. Left to carry less attractive programming, the networks could witness the gradual diminution of their audiences.

This section looks at the new means of entertainment distribution, attempts to assess their popularity and prospects, but sadly offers only a few clues regarding the ultimate outcome of these dynamic changes.

The simple fact is that we do not know which of the new delivery systems will predominate ten years from now, nor can we see if still other technologies may come forward and overshadow today's likely contenders.

There appear to be two genuses, with several species. Genus I is the videotape/videodisc format, in which the consumer specifically purchases the program he wishes to view from among a large catalogue of alternatives. Genus II is the pay TV system, wherein the viewer is offered a limited number of programming alternatives for which he pays either a one-time charge for a specific program or a monthly charge for a variety of programs. They and their principal species are considered in turn.

The Cassette/Disc Format

There are two species within the "genus *Cassettus*"—videotape and videodisc. Within those two, there are a number of variations, each having certain essential differences.

The principal differences between videotape and videodisc are that the videotape has recording capabilities as well as prerecorded playback features, whereas the videodisc, which has playback only, is less expensive and, in the optical configuration (Philips-MCA), has a freeze frame capability which gives it considerable value for educational and reference purposes.

There are two principal reasons why today's prerecorded tape is expensive. The cassette is costly, and replication must be done in real time. It is widely expected that the longitudinal video recorder will bring down prices significantly. The longitudinal cassette can be recorded at up to 220 times real time. We would place the probable introduction of the LVR in 1983 or 1984.

Our own information suggests that the LVR will not offer a material price advantage. The major cost of a cassette is tape, and the LVR uses more of it than Beta or VHS. While the player has fewer moving parts, the tape moves so much faster that the mechanics involved probably cost almost as much. We would not look for LVR to make much real difference in overall tape sales, but it may take market share from other systems. Our view has been that videodisc, not tape, will emerge as the preferred medium for delivering prerecorded software. Tape would be used principally as a time-shift device, mostly for rescheduling favorite television programs. This view is based on the relative price structures of the two systems coupled with the public's greater familiarity with the disc.

As mentioned, the crucial question about the eventual dominance of videodisc or videotape is one of price. If in fact the videodisc price remains near the current MCA price of $25, and tape becomes available at only a few dollars more, the advantages of tape's recording capability would appear to be so compelling that tape will probably become the preferred delivery system. The optical videodisc might then be relegated to the industrial market where it has clearly superior capability (freeze frame and slow motion), developing only a modest consumer presence.

If, as we anticipate, the price differential stays wide, with preprogrammed tape material selling at $45 or more versus disc's $25, or alternatively if disc software can become available below $20 against tape's $35, then we suspect that the videodisc will dominate.

For the owners of entertainment, the movie producers, which system wins is probably not material; what is vastly more important is the size of the market. Demand is a function of price. To the extent that technology permits lowering the price of hardware and software, the market could take on very sizable proportions.

It is our view that by the year 1990, one-third to one-half the homes in the United States will possess a videodisc or videocassette player. We believe that both devices will be owned in a substantial portion of video playback households. Most disc players today appear to be sold to owners of tape players. It is likely that ownership of one system will stimulate ownership of the other, being components of a whole video home system.

These projections would imply a sales growth rate of 40–60 percent annually from the present level of units—tape and disc combined—until 1986 or 1987, and then a stabilized rate of production and sales for the remainder of the decade. This would mean thirty to forty-five million homes containing video playback devices by the end of the coming decade. It is our opinion that the home video center, quite possibly including a projection screen, could be the major new prestige consumer durables item during the 1980s, a market comparable to but larger than that of high-fidelity audio equipment.

Speculating on the impact for the entertainment industry by 1990, one can derive rather attractive prospects. Will an average family purchase four cassettes or discs a year at $20 each—a retail market of $2.5–$3.5 billion a year? Is that too low? The early buyers of videodisc players appear to have purchased an average of ten discs in the first few *months*. While new products typically have high initial usage rates, and the early results of disc sales are no doubt obscured by purchases of collectors, souvenir hunters, and the like, four discs a year may turn out to be too low by a matter of magnitude.

Pay TV

Like the cassette/disc format, there are two species of pay TV—cable and over-the-air. Both offer movies and sports as their principal attractions. The larger by far is pay cable, currently with approximately 4.5 million subscribers, but over-the-air-now around three hundred thousand subscribers—is growing rapidly. The cable system is more flexible but as a higher capital cost; over-the-air is lower cost but presents a less-clear signal and has certain other disadvantages such as greater potential for signal theft.

Pay cable's advantages include an excellent signal and the availability of many channels. Its growth, slow for a number of years, has been dramatic recently as new services have been offered in addition to the Movie Channel. There is a body of opinion which suggests that pay cable has reached a "critical mass" of subscribers, bringing in enough income to enable the cable systems and their wholesalers such as Home Box Office (HBO) to offer still more services to attract still more viewers.

The attractiveness of pay cable is evidenced by the penetration of a few systems. San Diego, the nation's largest system, connects to 168,000 homes, 35 percent of which also take pay channels. Pensacola has an incredible 12,000 pay subscribers out of 13,000 connections. Right now, it is estimated that 4.5 million homes subscribe to pay cable, out of approximately 10.5 million basic cable subscribers offered it. Some 20 million homes are passed by those systems which offer pay, and another 8 million homes are passed by basic cable systems which do not yet offer pay services. Another 56 million homes are not served by cable at all, and there is a race now among the major cable companies to sign up the best parts of that market. It is generally agreed that the industry is destined for another round of rapid expansion.

Of particular note is Warner Communications' QUBE, an impressive experiment with two-way cable, which offers the viewer an opportunity to respond to questions on surveys asked on the screen, to select programs and pay for them on a per program basis, and eventually to offer a variety of protection and other services.

Over-the-air is a more recent innovation, although the technology is not new. Over-the-air seems to work best in urban areas, where the UHF signal reaches a large number of homes in close proximity, homes which probably would not subscribe to basic cable because their signal is good enough without it. Over-the-air's drawback is that it transmits only one channel and operates only during evening hours. Daytime broadcasts on the channel are reserved for commercial television and operate just like other independent UHFs.

It appears as though over-the-air pay TV has a difficult time competing with cable where both systems are offered to the same households. However, there are undoubtedly important markets specifically suited to each of the systems, and large portions of the country could be offered some form of pay TV within five years.

Communications Satellite Corp. recently announced that it intends to offer a third form of pay TV service, possibly as early as 1983. Comsat's entry would be a direct satellite-to-home system, requiring installation of small receiving dishes on rooftops. FCC clearance would be required, but presumably no local franchise.

The announcement from Comsat may be premature, since no arrangements have yet been made with either program suppliers or hardware manufacturers, but it reflects the prevalent attitude of the FCC to encourage proliferation of the means of delivering programming. Numerous obstacles exist, not the least of which is the lack of a service organization trained to sell and service satellite receivers and their related electronics.

There is quite apparently a race among the major cable participants to "wire America," evidenced by the $250 million program of Storer Broadcasting, the joint venture of Warner and American Express, and the rapid expansion of Time, Incorporated. Some estimate that pay cable will encompass 15 million homes by 1985, a number which strikes us as optimistic but not inconceivable. It would imply, perhaps, a penetration of 40–50 percent of 30–35 million homes attached to basic cable, a percentage which appears plausible if trends now in place continue unfettered. We have heard no judgments on the eventual size of over-the-air pay or satellite-to-home systems. The program suppliers will benefit handsomely from this growth.

Satellites and Superstations

Satellite transmission is a technological advance of significant dimensions which seems certain to alter the means of entertainment distribution. Rental of a transponder is surprisingly inexpensive—less than $200 an hour, or as little as $1 million a year for full 24-hour, 365-day coverage. With a transmitting station and studio costing a few million dollars, a company can beam a signal to any receiving dish tuned to it, even to hundreds of receivers at one time.

Local delivery of satellite-transmitted product to individual homes can be accomplished through cable systems or through broadcasting stations, even, as Comsat is proposing, directly. Satellite feed holds the potential to spawn dozens or even hundreds of part-time "networks," reaching audiences through cable systems, over the air, by rooftop receivers on apartments, or via inexpensive dishes on private homes. Real economic incentive for creating "ad hoc networks"—confederations of cable or other systems allied during specific time periods to carry specialized programming—will exist in three years.

The incentive will come when enough subscribers can receive program offerings from satellites. Right now, an estimated 6 million of the 14.5 million cable-connected homes are on CATV systems that have a satellite receiving dish at the head end. Even at the current low penetration, it is feasible to have syndicated specials—a Broadway play, for instance, or a Las Vegas nightclub act. With perhaps 4 million upscale homes as an audience, $1 million could be generated from advertising along to support the cost of live transmission of the show and throw off reasonable performer fees to the entertainment production company.

Developments with satellites appear to be taking a variety of directions, no one of which clues us to the ultimate outcome. There are twenty–two services currently being carried by satellite, including HBO, Showtime, Star Channel, Reuters and UPI News Services, Spanish International Network (to UHF stations), and three superstations.

Most controversial of all is the so-called superstation. It works this way. A company rents a transponder, then picks up the signal of an independent broadcast station and transmits it to cable systems outside the station's broadcast range. Subscribing cable systems pay this company $0.10 a month for each subscriber connected, none of which is remitted to the broadcaster or the copyright owners of the program material.

Some broadcasters favor this form of retransmission, on the assumption that they will be able to sell national advertising based on the number of homes reached by the CATV coverage as well as those in their own area of broadcast coverage. Others—Metromedia, for one—oppose retransmission as an unauthorized pirating of their signal.

The most vocal objections come from program suppliers, since their copyrighted material is being transmitted against their permission into areas where it has not been sold. If Oakland, California, cable subscribers can watch an off-network program licensed in Atlanta to WTBS but not yet to an Oakland station, the value of that program for eventual syndication in Oakland is severely diminished.

The battle is being fought in Congress, with rules proposed that require consent of either the broadcast station or copyright owner before retransmission can be effected. This would have the effect of forcing the cable companies to pay market prices for the program material, not the tiny copyright fees they now pay.

Within three years, virtually all television stations should be able to receive signals from satellites. This will enable local stations to subscribe easily to an ad hoc network, such as was just described for use by CATV stations. Again, opportunistic alliances of broadcasters and cable systems for periodic programming seem to be the wave of the future, offering part-time competition to the existing networks. We suspect that the significance of this development is largely unappreciated by the broadcasting community.

The Challenge to Hollywood

We said we could offer very few conclusions about the ultimate outcome of the various battles being or about to be fought in these areas. The battles today are videodisc versus tape; optical disc versus stylus; VHS against Beta and possibly soon against longitudinal recording; satellite-to-cable versus satellite-to-broadcast station versus broadcast station-to-satellite. We can offer one tentative conclusion, however.

The likely beneficiary of these battles is the copyright owner. To the extent that he can broaden the distribution channels of his product, his sunk or fixed cost of producing the program is spread over a larger paying audience.

Indeed, for Hollywood and the other producers of entertainment it is the challenge of the 1980s to convert a portion of the 2,300 hours per year that the average home watches television from 100 percent commercially sponsored broadcasting to consumer-paid-for viewing. This could be in various forms—cable, disc, cassette, or over-the-air.

The numbers are staggering. If every home were to watch one hundred hours a year of pay viewing (under 5 percent of its total viewing time), and pay for it at a rate of $1.00 an hour (less than $2.00 per week), it would inject another $9 billion into the stream of entertainment. That is an amount equal to the total retail sales of the record business, plus twice that of the movie business in 1978.

It is our view, one which dominates our investment thinking about the entertainment industry, that this expansion of expenditure will take place largely during the 1980s. We are about to witness another wave of industry growth comparable to the development of motion pictures and then of television. There will be many subindustries which will share in it—not only Hollywood, but other entertainment participants, no doubt including the networks and the record companies. Both hardware and software producers are alert to these developments, and one can logically expect numerous opportunities for investment within both industries.

The initial success of these new developments attests to the attractiveness of the products and services. Still far from universally available, their outlook is colored brightly by sizable capital commitments from large corporations anxious to enter the field. We note significant participation in these new areas by the likes of Time, Incorporated, American Express, IBM, RCA, and Philips, as well as the traditional entertainment producers. The 1980s should be an exciting decade.

Stay tuned.

Bibliography
Contributors
Indexes

Selected Bibliography

The following selected bibliography lists publications on the history of the American motion picture industry, its trade practices, and its leaders. A more comprehensive listing of the literature may be found in *Industrial Arts Index,* vols. 1–45, 1913–57; *Business Periodicals Index,* vols. 1—, 1958—; *International Index to Film Periodicals* (New York: FIAF, 1972—), *Film: A Reference Guide,* ed. Robert A. Armour (Westport, Conn: Greenwood Press, 1980); *The New Film Index: A Bibliography of Magazine Articles in English, 1930–1970,* ed. Richard Dyer MacCann and Edward S. Perry (New York: E. P. Dutton and Company, 1975); and *The Critical Index: A Bibliography of Articles on Film in English, 1946–1973,* ed. John C. Gerlach and Lana Gerlach (New York: Teachers College Press, 1974).

The standard references on all aspects of the industry are *Film Daily Year Book of Motion Pictures,* published annually from 1917 to 1969, and *Motion Picture Almanac* and its successor, *International Motion Picture Almanac,* published annually from 1929.

The standard trade publications are *Variety,* published from 1905, and *Moving Picture World* (1907–27), which merged with *Exhibitors' Herald* and later became known as *Motion Picture Herald.*

Special attention should be given to the *Journal of the Producers Guild of America* (known more familiarly as the *Journal of the Screen Producers Guild*), which since 1958 has analyzed contemporary conditions in the industry.

Allen, Robert C. *Vaudeville and Film, 1895–1915: A Study in Media Interaction.* New York: Arno, 1980.

Allvine, Glendon. *The Greatest Fox of Them All.* New York: Lyle Stuart, 1969.

Balaban, Carrie. *Continuous Performance.* New York: A. J. Balaban Foundation, 1964.

Balio, Tino. *United Artists: The Company Built by the Stars.* Madison: University of Wisconsin Press, 1975.

Balshofer, Fred J., and Miller, Arthur E. *One Reel a Week.* Berkeley and Los Angeles: University of California Press, 1967.

Barnouw, Erik. *Tube of Plenty: The Evolution of American Television.* New York: Oxford University Press, 1975.

Baumgarten, Paul A., and Farber, Donald C. *Producing, Financing, and Distributing Film.* New York: Drama Book Specialists, 1973.

Behlmer, Rudy, ed. *Memo from David O. Selznick.* New York: Viking, 1972.

Bernheim, Alfred L. *The Business of the Theater*. New York: Actors' Equity Association, 1932; rpt. ed., New York: Benjamin Blom, 1964.

Bertrand, Daniel; Evans, W. Duane; and Blanchard, E. L. *The Motion Picture Industry: A Pattern of Control*, TNEC Monograph 43. Washington, D.C.: U.S. Government Printing Office, 1941.

Bordwell, David; Staiger, Janet; and Thompson, Kristin. *The Classical Hollywood Cinema: Film Style and Mode of Production to 1960*. London: Routledge & Kegan Paul, 1985.

Brown, Les. *Television: The Business behind the Box*. New York: Harcourt Brace Jovanovich, 1971.

Brownlow, Kevin. *The Parade's Gone By*. New York: Alfred A. Knopf, 1968.

Campaigne, Benjamin M., ed. *Who Owns the Media?* White Plains, N.Y.: Knowledge Industry Publications, 1979.

Carmen, Ira H. *Movies, Censorship, and the Law*. Ann Arbor: University of Michigan Press, 1966.

Ceplair, Larry, and Englund, Steven. *The Inquisition in Hollywood: Politics in the Film Community, 1930–1960*. New York: Doubleday, 1980.

Ceram, C. W. *Archaeology of the Cinema*. New York: Harcourt, Brace, and World, 1955.

Chanan, Michael. *The Dream That Kicks: The Prehistory and Early Years of Cinema in Britain*. London: Routledge & Kegan Paul, 1980.

Cogley, John. *Report on Blacklisting I: The Movies*. Fund for the Republic, 1956.

Conant, Michael. *Antitrust in the Motion Picture Industry*. Berkeley and Los Angeles: University of California Press, 1960.

Crowther, Bosley. *The Lion's Share: The Story of an Entertainment Empire*. New York: E. P. Dutton, 1957.

_____. *Hollywood Rajah: The Life and Times of Louis B. Mayer*. New York: Holt, Rinehart and Winston, 1960.

Daly, David A. *A Comparison of Exhibition and Distribution Patterns in Three Recent Feature Motion Pictures*. New York: Arno, 1980.

Danielian, N. R. *AT & T: The Story of Industrial Conquest*. New York: Vanguard, 1939.

Dowdy, Andrew. *The Films of the Fifties: The American State of Mind*. New York: William Morrow, 1973.

Drinkwater, John. *The Life and Adventures of Carl Laemmle*. New York: G. P. Putnam's Sons, 1931.

Facey, Paul W. *The Legion of Decency: A Sociological Analysis of the Emergence and Development of a Pressure Group*. New York: Arno, 1974.

Farber, Stephen. *The Movie Rating Game*. Washington, D.C.: Public Affairs Press, 1972.

Fell, John L. *Film and the Narrative Tradition*. Norman: University of Oklahoma Press, 1974.

Fernett, Gene. *Poverty Row*. Satellite Beach, Fla.: Coral Reef Publications, 1973.

Fielding, Raymond. *A Technological History of Motion Pictures and Television.* Berkeley and Los Angeles: University of California Press, 1967.

———. *The American Newsreel, 1911–1967.* Norman: University of Oklahoma Press, 1972.

French, Philip. *The Movie Moguls: An Informal History of the Hollywood Tycoon.* Chicago: Henry Regnery, 1971.

Geduld, Harry. *The Birth of the Talkies: From Edison to Jolson.* Bloomington: Indiana University Press, 1975.

Grau, Robert. *The Theatre of Science: A Volume of Progress and Achievement in the Motion Picture Industry.* New York: Broadway Publishing Company, 1914.

Green, Abel, and Laurie, Joe, Jr. *Show Biz: From Vaudeville to Video.* New York: Henry Holt, 1951.

Green, Fitzhugh. *The Film Finds Its Tongue.* New York: G. P. Putnam's Sons, 1929.

Gregory, Mollie. *Making Films Your Business.* New York: Schocken, 1979.

Griffith, Richard. *Samuel Goldwyn: The Producer and His Films.* New York: Simon and Schuster, 1956.

———. *The Movie Stars.* Garden City, N.Y.: Doubleday, 1970.

Guback, Thomas H. *The International Film Industry.* Bloomington: Indiana University Press, 1969.

Hall, Ben M. *The Best Remaining Seats.* New York: C. N. Potter, 1961.

Hampton, Benjamin B. *A History of the Movies.* New York: Covici, Friede, 1931.

Handel, Leo A. *Hollywood Looks at Its Audience.* Urbana: University of Illinois Press, 1950.

Harley, John E. *World-Wide Influences of the Cinema.* Los Angeles: University of Southern California Press, 1940; rpt. ed., New York: Jerome S. Ozer, 1971.

Harmetz, Aljean. *The Making of "The Wizard of Oz."* New York: Alfred A. Knopf, 1977.

Hays, Will H. *The Memoirs of Will H. Hays.* Garden City, N.Y.: Doubleday, 1955.

Henderson, Robert M. *D. W. Griffith: His Life and His Work.* New York: Oxford University Press, 1972.

Hendricks, Gordon. *The Edison Motion Picture Myth.* Berkeley and Los Angeles: University of Calfornia Press, 1961.

———. *Beginnings of the Biograph.* New York: Beginnings of American Film, 1966.

———. *The Kinetoscope.* New York: Beginnings of American Film, 1966.

Huettig, Mae D. *Economic Control of the Motion Picture Industry.* Philadelphia: University of Pennsylvania Press, 1944; rpt. ed., New York: Jerome S. Ozer, 1971.

Inglis, Ruth. *Freedom of the Movies.* Chicago: University of Chicago Press, 1947.

Irwin, William Henry. *The House That Shadows Built*. Garden City, N.Y.: Doubleday, 1928.

Jacobs, Lewis. *The Rise of the American Film*. New York: Teachers College Press, 1939.

Jarvie, I. C. *Movies and Society*. New York: Basic Books, 1970.

Jowett, Garth. *Film: The Democratic Art*. Boston: Little, Brown, 1976.

———, and Linton, James M. *Movies as Mass Communication*. Beverly Hills: Sage Publications, 1980.

Kennedy, Joseph P., ed. *The Story of the Films*. Chicago: A. W. Shaw, 1927; rpt. ed., New York: Jerome S. Ozer, 1971.

Kindem, Gorham, ed. *The American Movie Industry*. Carbondale: Southern Illinois University Press, 1982.

Knox, Donald. *The Magic Factor: How MGM Made "An American in Paris"*. New York: Praeger, 1973.

Lahue, Kalton, C. *Dreams for Sale: The Rise and Fall of Triangle Film Corporation*. New York: A. S. Barnes, 1971.

———. *Motion Picture Pioneer: The Selig Polyscope Company*. New York: A. S. Barnes, 1973.

Lasky, Jesse L. *I Blow My Own Horn*. Garden City, N.Y.: Doubleday, 1957.

Lees, David, and Berkowitz, Stan. *The Movie Business*. New York: Vintage, 1981.

Lewis, Howard T. *The Motion Picture Industry*. New York: Van Nostrand, 1933.

Limbacher, James L. *Four Faces of the Film*. New York: Brussel and Brussel, 1968.

MacCann, Richard Dyer. *Hollywood in Transition*. Boston: Houghton Mifflin, 1962.

Macgowan, Kenneth. *Behind the Screen*. New York: Dell, 1965.

McCarthy, Todd, and Flynn, Charles, eds. *Kings of the B's*. New York: E. P. Dutton, 1975.

McClure, Arthur F., ed. *The Movies: An American Idiom*. Rutherford, N.J.: Fairleigh Dickinson University Press, 1971.

McLaughlin, R. G. *Broadway and Hollywood: A History of Economic Interaction*. New York: Arno, 1974.

McLean, Albert F. *American Vaudeville as Ritual*. Lexington: University of Kentucky Press, 1965.

Madsen, Axel, *The New Hollywood*. New York: Thomas Y. Crowell, 1975.

Martin, Olga G. *Hollywood's Movie Commandments*. New York: H. W. Wilson, 1975.

Marx, Samuel. *Mayer and Thalberg: The Make-Believe Saints*. New York: Random House, 1975.

Mayer, Arthur. *Merely Colossal*. New York: Simon and Schuster, 1953.

Mayer, Michael, *The Film Industries*. New York: Hastings House, 1978.

Moley, Raymond. *The Hays Office*. Indianapolis: Bobbs-Merrill, 1945; rpt. ed., New York: Jerome S. Ozer, 1971.

Momand, A. B. *The Hays Office and the NRA*. Shawnee, Okla.: Shawnee Printing Company, 1935.

Monaco, James. *American Film Now*. New York: Oxford University Press, 1979.

Nizer, Louis. *New Courts of Industry: Self-Regulation under the Motion Picture Code*. New York, Longacre Press, 1935; rpt. ed., New York: Jerome S. Ozer, 1971.

North, Joseph H. *The Early Development of the Motion Picture, 1887-1909*. New York: Arno, 1973.

O'Connor, John E. and Jackson, Martin A. *American History/American Film*. New York: Ungar, 1979.

Pirie, David, ed. *Anatomy of the Movies*. New York: Macmillan, 1981.

Poggi, Jack. *Theater in America: The Impact of Economic Forces, 1870-1967*. Ithaca, N.Y.: Cornell University Press, 1968.

Powdermaker, Hortense. *Hollywood: The Dream Factory*. Boston: Little, Brown, 1950.

Pratt, George, ed. *Spellbound in Darkness: A History of the Silent Film*. Rev. ed., Greenwich, Conn.: New York Graphic Society, 1973.

Pye, Michael, and Myles, Lynda. *The Movie Brats: How the Film Generation Took Over Hollywood*. New York: Holt, Rinehart and Winston, 1979.

Quigley, Martin. *Decency in Motion Pictures*. New York: Macmillan, 1937; rpt. ed., New York: Jerome S. Ozer, 1971.

Quigley, Martin, Jr. *Magic Shadows: The Story of the Origin of Motion Pictures*. Washington, D.C.: Georgetown University Press, 1948

Ramsaye, Terry. *A Million and One Nights*. New York: Simon and Schuster, 1926.

Randall, Richard S. *Censorship of the Movies*. Madison: University of Wisconsin Press, 1968.

Roddick, Nick. *A New Deal in Entertainment: Warner Brothers in the 1930s*. London: British Film Institute, 1983.

Ross, Murray. *Stars and Strikes: Unionization of Hollywood*. New York: Columbia University Press, 1941.

Rosten, Leo C. *Hollywood: The Movie Colony and the Movie Makers*. New York: Harcourt, Brace, 1941.

Sands, Pierre Norman. *A Historical Study of the Academy of Motion Picture Arts and Sciences, 1927-1947*. New York: Arno, 1973.

Schary, Dore. *Case History of a Movie*. New York: Random House, 1950.

Schickel, Richard. *The Disney Version*. New York: Avon, 1968.

———. *His Picture in the Papers*. New York: Charterhouse, 1973.

Schumach, Murray. *The Face on the Cutting Room Floor*. New York: William Morrow, 1964.

Seabury, William Marston. *The Public and the Motion Picture Industry*. New York: Macmillan, 1926; rpt. ed., New York: Jerome S. Ozer, 1971.

Seldes, Gilbert. *The Great Audience*. New York: Viking, 1950.

Sinclair, Upton. *Upton Sinclair Presents William Fox*. Los Angeles: Upton Sinclair Publishing Company, 1933; rpt. ed., Jerome S. Ozer, 1971.

Sklar, Robert. *Movie-Made America: A Social History of American Movies.* New York: Random House, 1975.

Smith, Albert E., and Koury, Phil. *Two Reels and a Crank.* Garden City, N.Y.: Doubleday, 1952.

Squire, Jason, ed. *The Movie Business Book.* Englewood Cliffs, N.J.: Prentice-Hall, 1983.

Stanley, Robert. *The Celluloid Empire: A History of the American Motion Picture Industry.* New York: Hastings House, 1978.

Thorp, Margaret. *America at the Movies.* New Haven: Yale University Press, 1939.

Turan, Kenneth, and Zito, Stephen F. *Sinema.* New York: Praeger, 1974.

Vardac, Nicholas, *From Stage to Screen.* Cambridge: Harvard University Press, 1949.

Vaughan, Floyd L. *Economics of Our Patent System.* New York: Macmillan, 1925.

Wagenknecht, Edward. *The Movies in the Age of Innocence.* Norman: University of Oklahoma Press, 1962.

Walker, Alexander. *Stardom: The Hollywood Phenomenon.* New York: Stein and Day, 1970.

Wallis, Hal B., and Higham, Charles. *Starmaker.* New York: Macmillan, 1980.

Wasko, Janet. *Movies and Money.* Norwood, N.J.: Ablex, 1982.

Wenden, D. J. *The Birth of the Movies.* New York: E. P. Dutton, 1974.

Zierold, Norman. *The Moguls.* New York: Avon, 1972.

Zukor, Adolph. *The Public Is Never Wrong.* New York: G. P. Putnam's Sons, 1953.

Articles

Allen, Jeanne Thomas. "Copyright and Early Theater, Vaudeville and Film Competition." *Journal of the University Film Association* 31 (Spring 1979): 5–11.

Allen, Robert C. "Vitascope/Cinematographe: Initial Patterns of American Film Industrial Practice." *Journal of the University Film Association* 31 (Spring 1979): 13–18.

———. "Motion Picture Exhibition in Manhattan, 1906–1912: Beyond the Nickelodeon." *Cinema Journal* 18 (Spring 1979): 2–15.

———. "Contra the Chaser Theory," *Wide Angle*, vol. 3, no. 1; pp. 4–11.

Anderson, Robert. "The Role of the Western Film Genre in Industry Competition, 1907–1911." *Journal of the University Film Association* 31 (Spring 1979): 19–27.

Andrew, Dudley. "The Postwar Struggle for Color." *Cinema Journal* 18 (Spring 1979): 41–52

Ayer, Douglas, et. al. "Self-Censorship in the Movie Industry: An Historical Perspective on Law and Social Change." *Wisconsin Law Review* 3 (1970): 791–838.

Balio, Tino. "Charles Chaplin, Entrepreneur: A United Artist." *Journal of the University Film Association* 31 (Winter 1979): 11–21.

Batman, Richard Dale. "The Founding of the Hollywood Motion Picture Industry." *Journal of the West* 10 (October 1971): 609–23.

Beach, E. R. "Double Features in Motion-Picture Exhibition." *Harvard Business Review* 10 (July 1932): 505–15.

Behlmer, Rudy. "Technicolor." *Films in Review* 15 (June-July 1964): 333–51.

Borneman, Ernest. "Rebellion in Hollywood: A Case Study in Motion Picture Finance." *Harper's* 193 (October 1946): 337–43.

———. "United States versus Hollywood: The Case Study of an Antitrust Suit." *Sight and Sound* 19 (February 1951): 418–20+; (March 1951): 448–50. [reprinted herein]

Brady, Robert A. "Monopoly and the First Freedom." *Hollywood Quarterly* 2 (April 1947): 225–41.

Brannigan, Edward. "Color and Cinema: Problems in the Writing of History." *Film Reader* 4 (1979): 16–34.

Brauer, Ralph A. "When the Lights Went Out: Hollywood, the Depression, and the Thirties." *Journal of Popular Film and Television* 7 (Winter 1981): 18–29.

Brown, Stanley, "That Old Villian TV Comes to the Rescue and Hollywood Rides Again." *Fortune* 74 (November 1966): 181–82+.

Buscombe, Edward. "Notes on Columbia Pictures Corporation, 1926–1941." *Screen* 16 (Autumn 1975): 65–82.

Cassady, Ralph, Jr. "Some Economic Aspects of Motion Picture Production and Marketing." *Journal of Business of the University of Chicago* 6 (April 1933): 113–31.

———. "Impact of the Paramount Decision on Motion Picture Distribution and Price Making." *Southern California Law Review* 31 (February 1958): 150–80.

———. "Monopoly in Motion Picture Production and Distribution; 1908–1915." *Southern California Law Review* 32 (Summer 1959): 325–90.

Chambers, R. "Double Features as a Sales Problem." *Harvard Business Review* 16 (Winter 1938): 226–36.

———. "Block Booking—Blind Selling." *Harvard Business Review* 19 (July 1941): 496–507.

Corliss, Richard. "The Legion of Decency." *Film Comment* 4 (Summer 1968): 25–61.

Crandall, Robert W. "Postwar Performance of the Motion Picture Industry." *Antitrust Bulletin* 20 (Spring 1975): 49–88.

Davis, John. "RKO: A Studio Chronology." *Velvet Light Trap*, no. 10 (Fall 1973); pp. 6–12.

Dawson, Anthony H. "Motion Picture Economics." *Hollywood Quarterly* 3 (Spring 1948): 217–40.

———. "Hollywood's Labor Troubles." *Industrial and Labor Relations Review* 1 (July 1948): 638–47.

_____. "Patterns of Production and Employment in Hollywood." *Hollywood Quarterly* 4 (Summer 1950): 338–53.

Eckert, Charles. "The Carole Lombard in Macy's Window." *Quarterly Review of Film Studies* 3 (Winter 1978): 1–21.

Fortune. "The Case of William Fox." 1 (May 1930): 48–49+.

_____. "Body and Soul Is (Here) Put Together." 4 (August 1931): 26–34+.

_____. "Metro-Goldwyn-Mayer." 6 (December 1932): 51–58+. [reprinted herein]

_____. "What? Color in Movies Again." 10 (October 1934): 92–97+.

_____. "The Big Bad Wolf." 10 (November 1934): 88–95+.

_____. "Twentieth Century-Fox." 12 (December 1935): 85–93+.

_____. "Paramount Pictures." 15 (March 1937): 87–96+.

_____. "Warner Brothers." 16 (December 1937): 110–13+.

_____. "Put Their Names in Lights." 18 (September 1938): 71–73+.

_____. "The Hays Office." 18 (December 1938): 69–72+.

_____. "Loew's, Inc." 20 (August 1939): 25–30+. [reprinted herein]

_____. "Deanna Durbin." 20 (October 1939): 66–69+.

_____. "United Artists: Final Shooting Script." 22 (December 1940): 95–102+.

_____. "Hollywood in Uniform." 25 (April 1942): 92–95+.

_____. "Hollywood's Magic Mountain." 31 (February 1945): 152–56+.

_____. "Movie Missionary." 32 (October 1945): 149–51+.

_____. "Paramount: Oscar for Profits." 35 (June 1947): 90–94+.

_____. "What's Playing at the Grove?" 38 (August 1948): 94–99+.

_____. "The Fortune Survey." 39 (March 1949): 39–40+.

_____. "Movies: End of an Era?" 39 (April 1949): 99–102+.

_____. "Cinerama: The Broad Picture." 47 (January 1953): 92–93+.

_____. "RKO: It's Only Money." 47 (May 1953): 122–27+.

_____. "The Derring-Doers of Movie Business." 57 (May 1958): 137–41+.

Gomery, Douglas. "Writing the History of the American Film Industry." *Screen* 17 (Spring 1976): 40–53.

_____. "Problems in Film History: How Fox Innovated Sound." *Quarterly Review of Film Studies* 2 (August 1976): 315–30.

_____. "The Warner-Vitaphone Peril: The American Film Industry Reacts to the Innovation of Sound." *Journal of the University Film Association* 28 (Winter 1976): 11–19.

_____. "Failure and Success: Vocafilm and RCA Innovate Sound." *Film Reader* 2 (January 1977): 213–21.

_____. "The Picture Palace: Economic Sense or Hollywood Nonsense?" *Quarterly Review of Film Studies* 3 (Winter 1978): 23–36.

_____. "The Movies Become Big Business: Publix Theatres and the Chain Store Strategy." *Cinema Journal* 18 (Spring 1979): 26–40.

_____. "Hollywood Converts to Sound: Chaos or Order?" in Evan W. Cameron, ed., *Sound and the Cinema* (Pleasantville, N.Y.: Redgrave, 1980), pp. 24–37.

_____. "Rethinking U.S. Film History: The Depression Decade and Monopoly Control." *Film and History* 10 (May 1980): 32–38.

_____. and Staiger, Janet. "The History of World Cinema: Models for Economic Analysis." *Film Reader* 4 (December 1979): 35–44.

Gordon, David. "Why the Movie Majors Are Major." *Sight and Sound* 42 (Autumn 1973): 194–96; *Journal of the Producers Guild of America* 16 (June 1974): 9–15, 24.

_____. "Mayer, Thalberg and MGM." *Sight and Sound* 45 (Summer 1976): 186–87.

Guback, Thomas H. "American Interests in the British Film Industry." *Quarterly Review of Economics and Business* 7 (1967): 7–21.

_____"Film as International Business." *Journal of Communication* 24, (Winter 1974): 90–101.

_____. and Dombkowski, Dennis J. "Television and Hollywood: Economic Relations in the 1970's." *Journal of Broadcasting* 20 (Fall 1976): 511–27.

Hellmuth, William F., Jr. "The Motion Picture Industry." In Walter Adams, ed., *The Structure of the American Industry: Some Case Studies*. New York: Macmillan, 1961, pp. 393–429.

Herzog, Charlotte. "The Movie Palace and the Theatrical Sources of Its Architectural Style." *Cinema Journal* 20 (Spring 1981): 15–37.

Houseman, John. "Hollywood Faces the Fifties." *Harper's* 200 (April 1950): 50–59; (May 1950): 51–59.

Hughes, E. J. "MGM: War among the Lion Tamers." *Fortune* 56 (August 1957): 98–103.

Jeter, Ida. "The Collapse of the Federated Motion Picture Crafts: A Case Study of Class Collaboration," *Journal of the University Film Association* 31 (Spring 1979): 37–45.

Jowett, Garth S. "The First Motion Picture Audiences." *Journal of Popular Film* 3 (Winter 1974): 39–54.

_____. "American Domination of the Motion Picture Industry: Canada as a Test Case." *Journal of the University Film Association* 27 (1975): 58–61, 72.

Kael, Pauline. "Why Are Movies So Bad? or, The Numbers." *New Yorker*, June 23, 1980, pp. 82–93.

Kehr, David. "A Star Is Made." *Film Comment* 15 (Jan–Feb. 1979): 7–12.

Kindem, Gorham, "The Demise of Kinemacolor: Technological, Legal, Economic, and Aesthetic Problems in Early Color Cinema History." *Cinema Journal* 29 (Spring 1981): 3–14.

Lincoln, Freeman. "The Comeback of the Movies." *Fortune* 51 (February 1955): 127–31+.

Luther, Rodney. "Television and the Future of Motion Picture Exhibition." *Hollywood Quarterly* 5 (Winter 1950): 164–77.

_____. "Drive-in Theaters: Rags to Riches in Five Years." *Hollywood Quarterly* 5 (Summer 1951): 401–11.

McDonald, Gerald D. "Origin of the Star System." *Films in Review* 4 (November 1953): 449–58.

Monaco, James. "Images and Sounds as Cultural Commodities." *Sight and Sound* 49 (Autumn 1980): 229–33.

Musser, Charles. "The Early Cinema of Edwin Porter." *Cinema Journal* 19 (Fall 1979): 1–38.

———. "American Vitagraph, 1897–1901." *Cinema Journal* 22 (Spring 1983): 4–46.

Nelson, Richard Alan. "Florida: The Forgotten Film Capital." *Journal of the University Film Association* 29 (Summer 1977): 9–21.

Norden, Martin F. "The Pathé Frères Company during the Trust Era." *Journal of the University Film Association* 3 (Summer 1981): 15–32.

Onosko, Tim. "Monogram: Its Rise and Fall in the Forties." *Velvet Light Trap*, no. 5 (Summer 1972), pp. 5–9.

Paletz, David, and Noonan, Michael. "The Exhibitors." *Film Quarterly* 19 (Winter 1965–66): 14–40.

Pratt, George. "No Magic, No Mystery, No Sleight of Hand." *Image* 8 (December 1959): 192–211.

Sanders, Terry B. "The Financing of Independent Feature Films." *Quarterly of Film, Radio and Television* 9 (Summer 1955): 380–89.

Schuyten, Peter. "How MCA Rediscovered Movieland's Golden Lode." *Fortune* 94 (November 1976): 122–27+.

———. "United Artists' Script Calls for Divorce." *Fortune* 97 (January 16, 1978): 130–33+.

Sherman, Stratford P. "The Empire Pays Off." *Fortune* 102 (October 6, 1980): 52–55.

Slide, Anthony. "The Evolution of the Film Star." *Films in Review* 25 (December 1974): 591–94.

Smith, Richard Austin. "RKO: A Crisis of Responsibility." In *Corporations in Crisis*. Garden City, N.Y.: Doubleday, 1963.

Smythe, Dallas W., et al. "Portrait of an Art-Theater Audience." *Quarterly of Film, Radio and Television* 8 (Fall 1953): 28–50.

———. "Portrait of a First-Run Audience." *Quarterly of Film, Radio and Television* 9 (Summer 1955): 390–409.

Staiger, Janet. "Dividing Labor for Production Control: Thomas Ince and the Rise of the Studio System." *Cinema Journal* 18 (Spring 1979): 16–25.

———. "Mass-Produced Photoplays: Economic and Signifying Practices in the First Years of Hollywood." *Wide Angle*, vol. 4, no. 3; pp. 12–27.

———. "Individualism versus Collectivism." *Screen* 24 (July–October, 1983): 68–79.

———, and Gomery, Douglas. "The History of World Cinema: Models for Economic Analysis." *Film Reader* 4 (December 1979): 35–44.

Stern, Seymour. "The Birth of a Nation." *Sight and Sound*, Index Series No. 4 (July 1945), pp. 2–16.

Strauss, W. V. "Foreign Distribution of American Films." *Harvard Business Review* 8 (April 1930): 307–15.

Swenson, Joel. "The Entrepreneur's Role in Introducing the Sound Motion Picture." *Political Science Quarterly* 63 (September 1948): 404–23.

Thomas, David O. "From Page to Screen in Smalltown America: Early Motion Picture Exhibition in Winona, Minnesota." *Journal of the University Film Association* 33 (Summer 1981): 3–13.

Twomey, John E. "Some Considerations on the Rise of the Art Film Theater." *Quarterly of Film, Radio and Television* 10 (1955–56): 239–47.

Watkins, G. S., ed. "The Motion Picture Industry." *Annals of the American Academy of Political and Social Science* 256 (November 1947): entire issue.

List of Contributors

ROBERT C. ALLEN

is Associate Professor in the Department of Radio, Television and Motion Pictures, University of North Carolina at Chapel Hill. He is co-author with Douglas Gomery of *Film History: Theory and Practice* and has completed a book on soap opera.

ROBERT ANDERSON

taught film as an Assistant Professor at Washington State University and is an independent filmmaker.

TINO BALIO

is Professor of Communication Arts, University of Wisconsin-Madison. He is the author of *United Artists: The Company Built by the Stars* and General Editor of the Wisconsin/Warner Bros. Screenplay Series.

ERNEST BORNEMAN

was Director of Distribution for the National Film Board of Canada.

JOHN COGLEY

was Executive Editor of *The Commonweal* and prepared the two-volume *Report on Blacklisting* for the Fund for the Republic.

MICHAEL CONANT

is Professor of Business Administration, University of California, Berkeley, and author of *Antitrust in the Motion Picture Industry*.

A.R. FULTON

taught film for many years in the Department of English at Purdue University. He now lives in Poughkeepsie, New York.

DOUGLAS GOMERY

is Associate Professor in the Department of Communication Arts and Theatre, University of Maryland, the author of *Hollywood Studio System*, and co-author with Robert C. Allen of *Film History: Theory and Practice*.

THOMAS H. GUBACK

is Research Professor, Institute of Communication Research, University of Illinois-Urbana, and author of *The International Film Industry: Western Europe America since 1945*.

ROBERT GUSTAFSON

is Assistant Professor, Department of Communication and Theatre, George Washington University.

GORDON HENDRICKS

has done pioneering research on the origins of the American film. His latest contribution is *Eadweard Maybridge: The Father of the Motion Picture*. He resides in New York City.

MAE HUETTIG

received her Ph.D. from the University of Pennsylvania and conducted her research for *Economic Control of the Motion Picture Industry* under a grant from the Rockefeller Foundation.

RUTH A. INGLIS

is the author of *Freedom of the Movies*.

CATHY ROOT KLAPRAT

is a graduate student at the University of Wisconsin-Madison and is currently completing a dissertation on Val Lawton's RKO Horror Films.

DAVID J. LONDONER

is a financial analyst for Wertheim & Co. Inc.

RUSSELL MERRITT

is Professor of Communication Arts and Director, Wisconsin Center for Film and Theatre Research, University of Wisconsin-Madison.

RICHARD S. RANDALL

is Associate Professor, Department of Politics, New York University and author of *Censorship of the Movies: the Social and Political Control of a Mass Medium.*

JANET STAIGER

is Assistant Professor in the Department of Cinema Studies, New York University and is co-author with David Bordwell and Kristin Thompson of *The Classical Hollywood Cinema: Film Style and Mode of Production to 1960.*

Index of Motion Picture Titles

General Index

653

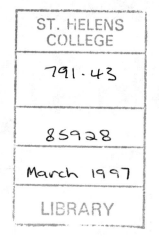
The University of Wisconsin Press
114 North Murray Street
Madison, Wisconsin 53715

3 Henrietta Street
London WC2E 8LU, England

10   9   8   7   6   5   4   3

Printed in the United States of America

Library of Congress Cataloging in Publication Data
Main entry under title:
The American film industry.
  Bibliography: pp. 633–643.
  Includes indexes.
  1. Moving-picture industry—United States—History—
Addresses, essays, lectures. I. Balio, Tino.
PN1993.5.U6A87   1985   384'.8'0973   84-40143
ISBN 0-299-09870-2
ISBN 0-299-09874-5 (pbk.)

The American
Film Industry

Revised Edition

edited by

Tino Balio

The University of Wisconsin Press

The American Film Industry